CAMBR  SSICS

P. E. EASTERLING
*Regius Professor Emeritus of Greek, University of Cambridge*

PHILIP HARDIE
*Senior Research Fellow, Trinity College, and Honorary Professor of Latin, University of Cambridge*

NEIL HOPKINSON
*Fellow, Trinity College, University of Cambridge*

RICHARD HUNTER
*Regius Professor of Greek, University of Cambridge*

E. J. KENNEY
*Kennedy Professor Emeritus of Latin, University of Cambridge*

S. P. OAKLEY
*Kennedy Professor of Latin, University of Cambridge*

# DEMOSTHENES

# SELECTED POLITICAL SPEECHES

EDITED BY
JUDSON HERRMAN
*Frank T. McClure Professor of Greek and Latin*
*Allegheny College, Pennsylvania*

## CAMBRIDGE
UNIVERSITY PRESS

University Printing House, Cambridge CB2 8BS, United Kingdom

One Liberty Plaza, 20th Floor, New York, NY 10006, USA

477 Williamstown Road, Port Melbourne, VIC 3207, Australia

314–321, 3rd Floor, Plot 3, Splendor Forum, Jasola District Centre, New Delhi – 110025, India

79 Anson Road, #06–04/06, Singapore 079906

Cambridge University Press is part of the University of Cambridge.

It furthers the University's mission by disseminating knowledge in the pursuit of education, learning, and research at the highest international levels of excellence.

www.cambridge.org
Information on this title: www.cambridge.org/9781107021334
DOI: 10.1017/9781139108799

© Cambridge University Press 2019

This publication is in copyright. Subject to statutory exception and to the provisions of relevant collective licensing agreements, no reproduction of any part may take place without the written permission of Cambridge University Press.

First published 2019

Printed in the United Kingdom by TJ International Ltd. Padstow Cornwall

*A catalogue record for this publication is available from the British Library.*

*Library of Congress Cataloging-in-Publication Data*
Names: Demosthenes, author. | Herrman, Judson, author of commentary.
Title: Selected political speeches / Demosthenes ; [introduction and commentary by] Judson Herrman.
Description: Cambridge : Cambridge University Press, 2019. | In Greek with introduction and commentary in English. | Includes bibliographical references and indexes.
Identifiers: LCCN 2019008713 | ISBN 9781107021334 (alk. paper)
Subjects: LCSH: Speeches, addresses, etc., Greek. | Athens (Greece) – Politics and government – Early works to 1800. | Demosthenes – Criticism and interpretation.
Classification: LCC PA3949 .A3 2019 | DDC 885./01–dc23
LC record available at https://lccn.loc.gov/2019008713

ISBN 978-1-107-02133-4 Hardback
ISBN 978-1-107-61084-2 Paperback

Cambridge University Press has no responsibility for the persistence or accuracy of URLs for external or third-party internet websites referred to in this publication and does not guarantee that any content on such websites is, or will remain, accurate or appropriate.

*To the memory of*
*Albert Henrichs*

# CONTENTS

| | |
|---|---|
| Preface | page ix |
| Abbreviations | xi |
| Map of Greece, Macedon, and the Aegean | xii |

| | |
|---|---|
| Introduction | 1 |
| 1 Historical Background | 1 |
| 2 Assembly Speeches | 9 |
| 3 Language and Style | 14 |
| 4 Publication | 20 |
| 5 The Afterlife of the Speeches | 26 |
| 6 The Text | 33 |

| | |
|---|---|
| 1 ΟΛΥΝΘΙΑΚΟΣ Α | 39 |
| 2 ΟΛΥΝΘΙΑΚΟΣ Β | 45 |
| 3 ΟΛΥΝΘΙΑΚΟΣ Γ | 51 |
| 4 ΚΑΤΑ ΦΙΛΙΠΠΟΥ Α | 57 |
| 9 ΚΑΤΑ ΦΙΛΙΠΠΟΥ Γ | 65 |

| | |
|---|---|
| Commentary | 77 |
| 1 First Olynthiac | 77 |
| 2 Second Olynthiac | 100 |
| 3 Third Olynthiac | 129 |
| 4 First Philippic | 161 |
| 9 Third Philippic | 203 |

| | |
|---|---|
| Works Cited | 267 |
| Indexes | 285 |
| Greek | 285 |
| English | 292 |

# PREFACE

Demosthenes, as an emerging political leader between 351 and 341 BC, delivered a series of fiery speeches to the collected citizenry of Athens in its democratic Assembly. In these speeches he attacked the Macedonian king Philip II as an aggressive imperialist bent on destroying Athens and its way of life. The surviving written texts are the only extant examples of actual Athenian Assembly speeches. This volume presents the Greek text of five of these speeches, with introduction and commentary. In them we can see how the foremost politician of the day presented his arguments to the people who made policy decisions in the Assembly, and how he eventually persuaded the voters to support his doomed militaristic position in preference to the more pragmatic stance of accommodation advocated by his political opponents. These speeches are not only invaluable sources for the ideology and political history of this crucial period; they are the best examples of persuasive rhetoric in action from democratic Athens. Demosthenes was an admired master of Greek prose style, and in these speeches he developed a deliberative mode that utilized striking sentence structures and dense metaphorical imagery to build and reinforce his arguments.

The primary audience for this book are advanced students who may have little experience with Demosthenic Greek. The notes are designed to elucidate this difficult text so that they can read and appreciate its distinctive style. Furthermore, since we lack recent commentaries intended for specialists, I have also endeavored to address some of the concerns of scholarly readers; my notes consider political, cultural, and literary history and aim to provide references to key discussions and sources.

The speeches are presented here in the traditional sequence, which places the first *Philippic* of 351 after the *Olynthiacs* of 349/8. I have decided to keep this order because the *Olynthiacs* are shorter, and students may find it more manageable to begin with them before reading the longer *Philippics*. As an accommodation, this volume's notes on the first *Olynthiac* are deliberately simpler and less specialized than the commentaries on the other speeches. Ample cross-references link the notes, and I hope those will forestall any chronological confusion arising from my decision to begin with the *Olynthiacs*.

It has taken me almost as long to write this book as it took Demosthenes to develop the series of speeches. Along the way I have received much help and support, and it is a pleasure to acknowledge friends, colleagues, and benefactors. In 2012 I received support from the Margo Tytus Visiting Scholars Program at the University of Cincinnati, and I wish to thank Getzel Cohen for his hospitality, and the staff of the John Miller Burnam Classics Library, who have welcomed my repeated and ongoing visits to

Cincinnati. I am also grateful for a 2012 fellowship award from the Loeb Classical Library Foundation. The book was finished in 2017 thanks to a visiting fellowship at University College Oxford, and I am especially grateful to William Allan for welcoming me in Oxford. Along the way I have received continued generous support from Allegheny College: I wish to thank the College's Academic Support Committee; the History Department for grants from the Jonathan E. and Nancy L. Helmreich History Research Fund and the Bruce Harrison Fund; and most of all, the Frank T. McClure endowment for a professorship in Greek and Latin. This support has given me regular time in research libraries, without which I could not have written the book. I am grateful to the staff of Widener Library at Harvard, the Institute of Classical Studies, and the Fondation Hardt.

Colleagues have given vital feedback on work in progress. The 2009 Classical Commentary Writers Workshop came at a formative moment, and I thank especially Douglas Olson, Alex Sens, and William Race. Ariana Traill sent speedy responses to library queries, and invited me in 2012 to present at the University of Illinois at Urbana-Champaign, where Kirk Sanders welcomed me in his seminar on Greek oratory. More recently, Nigel Wilson helpfully discussed Demosthenes' publication and afterlife; Antonis Kotsonas suggested bibliography; and Mirko Canevaro answered queries and shared work in progress. Edward Harris, too, sent forthcoming work, and gave quick and thorough comments on each section of the book. Thanks to Christopher Pelling for helpful suggestions. Carolin Hahnemann carefully read sections and helped shape my purpose and method. Above all, the series editors have been prompt and constructive critics; I am grateful to Neil Hopkinson and Richard Hunter for detailed comments, and especially to Pat Easterling for welcoming the proposal and support too along the way.

Thanks to all who have helped me improve this book. The remaining weaknesses are my responsibility. I am also responsible for its appearance; I have typeset it with open source software; thanks are due to the creators of X₃TEX, a unicode version of TEX, and of the EDMAC and Eplain extensions. I am also grateful to Michael Sharp and Mary Bongiovi at Cambridge University Press, and to John Jacobs for his careful copyediting.

My greatest personal debts are to Robin Orttung, who gave much to make it possible for me to complete this work, and to Albert Henrichs, with whom I first read these speeches, and who provided feedback and inspiration as the work progressed. We miss him very much.

# ABBREVIATIONS

| | |
|---|---|
| APF | J. K. Davies, *Athenian propertied families, 600–300 BC*. Oxford 1971. |
| CAH | D. M. Lewis, J. Boardman, S. Hornblower, and M. Ostwald (eds.), *Cambridge ancient history*. Vol. 6: The fourth century BC. 2nd ed. Cambridge 1994. |
| FGrHist | F. Jacoby, *Die Fragmente der griechischen Historiker*. 15 vols. Berlin 1923–1958. |
| GHI | P. J. Rhodes and R. Osborne, *Greek historical inscriptions 404–323 BC*. Oxford 2003. |
| GP | J. D. Denniston, *The Greek particles*. 2nd ed. Oxford 1954. |
| GPM | K. J. Dover, *Greek popular morality in the time of Plato and Aristotle*. Oxford 1974. |
| GPS | J. D. Denniston, *Greek prose style*. Oxford 1952. |
| Harris | E. M. Harris, *Aeschines and Athenian politics*. New York and Oxford 1995. |
| HM | N. G. L. Hammond and G. T. Griffith, *A history of Macedonia*. Vol. 2. Oxford 1979. |
| IG | *Inscriptiones Graecae*. Berlin 1873–. |
| K–A | R. Kassel and C. Austin, *Poetae comici Graeci*. 8 vols. Berlin 1983–2001. |
| LGPN | M. J. Osborne and S. G. Byrne, *A lexicon of Greek personal names*. Vol. 2: Attica. Oxford 1994. |
| LSJ | H. G. Liddell, R. Scott, and H. S. Jones, *A Greek–English lexicon*. 9th ed. with revised supplement. Oxford 1940 and 1996. References are to word entries and their sections. |
| OLD | P. G. W. Glare (ed.), *Oxford Latin dictionary*. Oxford 1982. |
| PAA | J. S. Traill, *Persons of ancient Athens*. 21 vols. Toronto 1994–2012. |
| P.Oxy. | *The Oxyrhynchus papyri*. London 1898–. References are to volume and item number. See www.papyrology.ox.ac.uk/POxy (accessed August 11, 2017). |
| Ronnet | G. Ronnet, *Étude sur le style de Démosthène dans les discours politiques*. Paris 1951. |
| Sealey | R. Sealey, *Demosthenes and his time: a study in defeat*. New York and Oxford 1993. |
| SEG | *Supplementum epigraphicum Graecum*. Leiden, Amsterdam 1923–. |
| Smyth | H. W. Smyth, *Greek grammar*. Cambridge, MA. 1920. |
| Wooten | C. Wooten, *A commentary on Demosthenes' Philippic I: with rhetorical analyses of Philippics II and III*. New York and Oxford 2008. |
| Yunis | H. Yunis, *Demosthenes. On the crown*. Cambridge 2001. |

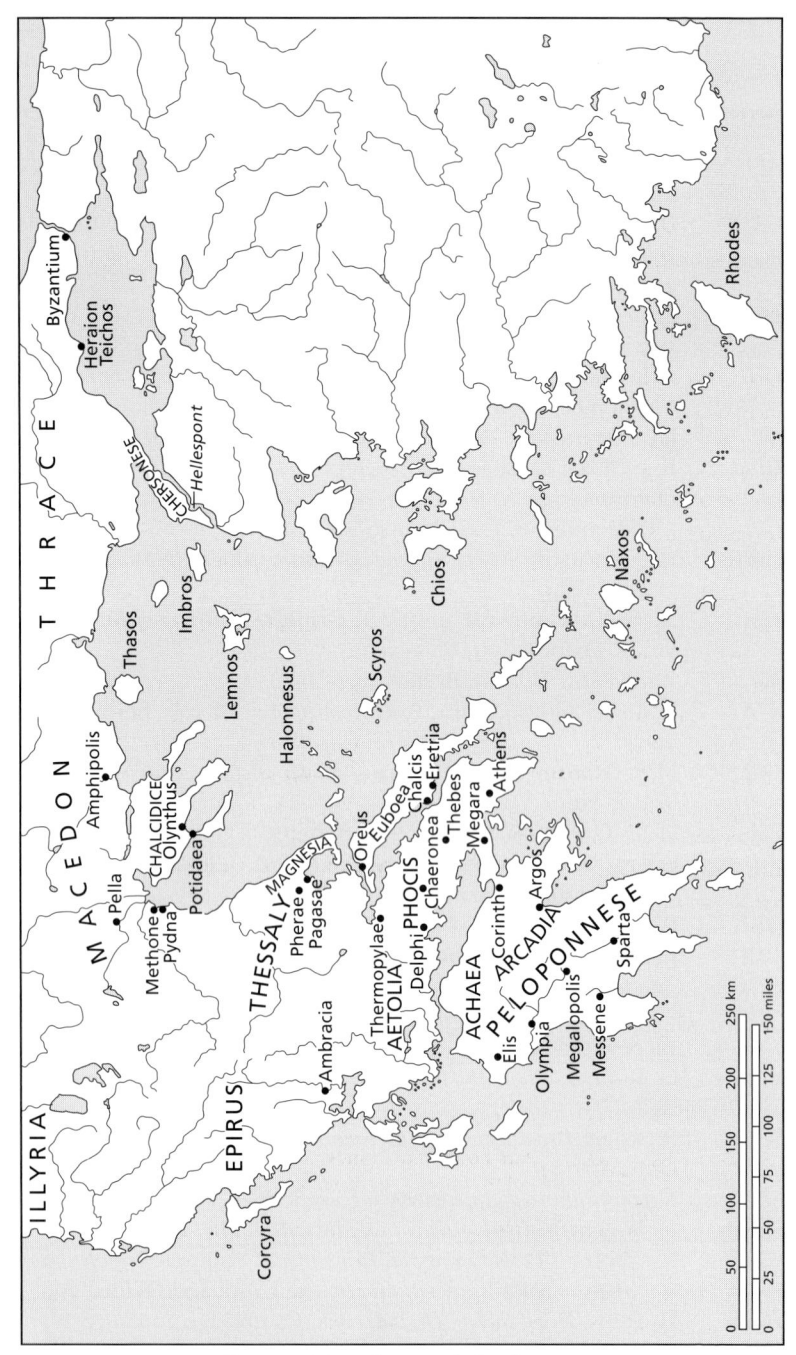

Greece, Macedon, and the Aegean

# INTRODUCTION

## 1 HISTORICAL BACKGROUND

### 1.1 The Early Career of Demosthenes

Demosthenes (D.) was born in 384 to a prominent and wealthy family.[1] His father died when he was a child, in 376, and his earliest speeches were prosecutions of his appointed guardians for financial mismanagement of the estate, delivered in the late 360s, after he had reached the age of majority in 366.[2] Although the suits appear to have been successful, much of the money and property could not be recovered, and D. apparently published his early speeches against his guardians as a vehicle to launch his career as a speechwriter (a λογογράφος) for hire.[3] This work was lucrative; D. acquired the means to make substantial tax contributions to the city, both by paying special war levies for several years (the εἰσφορά), and by funding a ship in the Athenian navy as a voluntary trierarch in 357.[4] A few items in the Demosthenic corpus are perhaps speeches of this sort from early in his career; their content provides no reason to believe that D. (if he wrote them) had any ulterior personal or political motive beyond earning his fee.[5]

D. continued to write speeches for others in private court cases in the 340s, while at the same time cultivating a public role as a politician.[6] He composed speeches for several prosecutions in public cases of γραφὴ παρανόμων, in which he charged that other politicians had passed improper measures (3.12n. παθεῖν).[7] Cases of this sort, concerned with the general laws of Athens, were high-profile; D.'s involvement in them signals a move toward a political career. Three of these orations were written for others to deliver in court, but they differ from the private court

---

[1] D. was son of Demosthenes of the deme Paiania: *LGPN* s.v. 37, *PAA* 318625; also *APF* no. 3597. For a general discussion see MacDowell 2009: 14–58. Details of D.'s early life can be gathered from Plutarch's biography (Lintott 2013: 47–81), the anonymous life preserved in [Plut.] *Mor.* 844a–8d (see Roisman et al. 2015: 211–46) and from the Demosthenic speeches against his guardians (or. 27–31, MacDowell 2004: 9–11, 19–83).

[2] Or. 27–8: 364/3; or. 29–31: 362/1.   [3] Carey and Reid 1985: 18–19.

[4] D. 21.157, 161. D. had borrowed money to serve as trierarch in 364/3 (D. 28.17). For these types of service see 1.6n. χρήματα, 2.30n. τριηραρχεῖν.

[5] Usher 1999: 184–9 discusses 41 and 55 as speeches that D. wrote as a λογογράφος prior to his trierarchy in 357. There are, however, stylistic reasons for doubting D.'s authorship of both: McCabe 1981: 170.

[6] Surviving speeches written by D. for the court cases of others in the 340s: or. 39 (348/7) and 38 (346 or later). Other speeches unlikely to have been written by D.: 40 (347), 43 (late 340s), 48 (343/2 or 342/1).

[7] Or. 20 and 24 were written for a different, but related, legal procedure, the γραφὴ νόμον μὴ ἐπιτήδειον θεῖναι. See Canevaro 2016b.

cases in that D. is able to discuss issues of public import, such as the public finances, the rule of law, and foreign policy.[8] During this period D. began to address the δῆμος directly on political matters, first in a public prosecution, and in the following years in speeches to the Assembly.[9] These speeches cover a variety of topics, and what links them is D.'s effort as a budding political advisor with the best interests of the city at heart; as in his recent public prosecution speeches, he continues to focus on public finance and foreign policy. In *Against Leptines* (or. 20) he argued against a proposal to curtail honorary exemptions from taxation; he maintained that the financial benefits accruing from the objectionable proposal were small, and that the measure would discourage benefactors and harm the city. In *On the Symmories* (or. 14) D. proposed reforms to the system for taxes and military funding as a response to the threat of Persian interference with Athenian allies.[10] And in *For the Megalopolitans* (or. 16) he argued that it was in the interests of the Athenians to prevent Sparta from dominating neighboring states in the Peloponnese.

At the end of the 350s D. commenced a series of Assembly speeches against Philip, which will be discussed below (Introd. §1.3), after a consideration of Philip's activity during the period leading up to the debates regarding him in Athens (Introd. §1.2). To conclude this account of D.'s activity prior to his focus on Philip, it should be observed that D. continued to address other topics in the Assembly even after taking notice of Philip. Indeed, in *For the Freedom of the Rhodians* (or. 15), delivered in 351/0, the year after the first *Philippic*, he advocated support for exiled Rhodian democrats opposed to the newly established government in Rhodes that was backed by the Persian king. In one brief aside he even suggested that Philip posed little threat to Athens.[11]

In summary, the first decade of D.'s career as an orator finds him engaged with various topics, private and public, both working as a speechwriter for hire and speaking in his own voice on key political issues, including, but not limited to, the question as to how Athens should respond to Philip of Macedon. Although D.'s positions in these early political speeches evince a real effort to serve the city, it is clear that he was not a prominent

---

[8] Public prosecutions written for others: 22 (355/4), 24 (353/2), 23 (352/1); for an overview see Canevaro 2015: 326–8. Dion. Hal. *Amm.* 1.4 presents the chronology for D.'s early public prosecutions and Assembly speeches; for a full discussion see Sealey 1955.

[9] Or. 20 (355/4) is a prosecution. D.'s earliest Assembly speeches are or. 14 (354/3) and 16 (353/2). Or. 13 is Demosthenic in style (McCabe 1981: 170); if it is authentic, it may have been delivered in 353/2. Or it may be a third-century pastiche of Demosthenic material: Sing 2017.

[10] For the symmories see 2.29n. πρότερον.

[11] D. 15.24. Dion. Hal. *Amm.* 1.4 provides the date, which has been doubted (Trevett 2011: 257–8) but is supported by historical detail in the speech (Badian 2000: 31–2).

# 1 HISTORICAL BACKGROUND

leader in Assembly debate, and the policies he advocated may not have been realistic or well conceived; his speech *Against Aristocrates* (or. 23) does not notice Philip as a threat to Athenian interests in the Chersonese, and *For the Megalopolitans* perhaps misjudged the political situation in the Peloponnese.[12] These strengths and weaknesses would be visible in his later speeches too, after he focused his attention on Philip.

## 1.2 Macedon and the Rise of Philip

Macedon was a Greek kingdom extending northwest from the Thermaic Gulf, bordered by Thessaly to the south, Illyria to the west, Paeonia to the north, and Chalcidice and Thrace to the east.[13] It stood apart from other Greek states in various ways: it was ruled by a king, who held sway among a group of lesser tribal kings and leaders; the basis of the status of these men was their ability on the battlefield and in the hunt; settled cities were fewer in number, smaller in size, and established later than elsewhere in Greece. Macedon during the classical period is reminiscent of Homeric Greece, where local warrior kings banded together to fight for the cause of a powerful leader. Athenian critics focus on these distinctive aspects and ignore the Hellenic heritage of the Macedonian royal house; D. characterizes Philip as a violent tyrant opposed to Greek values (1.3n. τὰ δ', 2.18n. τήν, 9.16n. τό).

Philip II was born in 383 or 382, the third son of the Macedonian king Amyntas III.[14] After his father's peaceful death in 369, his two elder brothers ruled in succession. The eldest, Alexander II, was assassinated by a rival for the throne, just a year or two after his father's death. The next son, Perdiccas III, eventually consolidated his rule in 365 after a period of strife, only to die in battle against the Illyrians in 359. Philip inherited a kingdom that was politically unstable and threatened by its neighbors.

The situation was pressing, and from the start of his rule Philip devoted himself to training and leading a capable military force; his position depended entirely on its support. Its effectiveness was demonstrated quickly, as Philip defeated a royal pretender, Argaeus, close to home in 360 or 359, and then led campaigns against the Paeonians and Illyrians in order to secure the state's mountainous borders to the north and west.[15] These regions were the source of the most immediate and urgent threats, and once they had been stabilized, he was able to direct his attention to the east and south. From these quarters there was less fear of imminent

---

[12] Cawkwell 1978: 79–80.
[13] Macedon is the political state, Macedonia the geographic region. On the Greek ethnicity, see 3.16n. βάρβαρος.
[14] For a succinct biography see Heckel 2008: s.v. Philip [1].
[15] *HM* 210–14, Cawkwell 1978: 29–30.

invasion; rather Philip stood to gain material resources along with further stability on his borders.

To the east, the city of Amphipolis was strategically located not far from the mouth of the river Strymon; it was one of the few places where armies could cross, and the river provided access to valuable mines and timber. The Athenians had founded a military colony there in 437/6, only to lose it in battle with the Spartan general Brasidas in 424; they aspired to reestablish their presence in the years leading up to 357 (2.2n. πόλεων). To this end, they had supported the pretender Argaeus, and their fleet had gained control of the important northern port of Methone.[16] Philip was eager to reduce their influence in the region, and, according to D., he took advantage of their interest in Amphipolis by offering control of the city to them if they did not interfere with his assault on it, and if they would refrain from aiding their ally Pydna when Philip proceeded to march on it (1.5n. Ἀμφιπολιτῶν, 2.6n. τῶι). If there was such an agreement, Philip declined to keep it.[17] After his capture of Amphipolis his position was stronger, and the Athenians became tied down with the Social War.[18]

Philip took the opportunity to subdue and detach three key maritime positions from the Athenian alliance. Between late 357 and early 354 he gained control of Pydna and Methone, which were in the heart of Macedonian territory, just south of the royal cities, while also moving against Potidaea, on the Chalcidice (1.9nn.). He formed an alliance with the Chalcidian League, and by offering the League control of Potidaea he sought to reduce the prospect of Athenian influence in the Thermaic Gulf (2.1n. τάς).

In the late 350s Philip extended Macedonian control further south. Several considerations may have motivated him: he may have worried that conflicts between Thessaly and Pherae could destabilize his southern frontier; or he may have been drawn by the military capability of the large and skilled corps of Thessalian cavalry; perhaps he saw the potential advantages that the port of Pagasae offered. His support of the Thessalians in the third Sacred War against Pherae and Phocis prolonged that conflict and enabled him to pursue his goals in the north without worrying about interference from the south.[19] As part of this effort on behalf of Thessaly, he suffered his first military setbacks with a pair of losses to the Phocian general Onomarchus in 353. But after regrouping over the winter he gained a decisive victory at the battle of the Crocus Field in 352, which extended his sphere of influence into Thessaly and allowed him to gain and keep control of Pagasae (2.7n. Θετταλούς, 2.14n. νυνί).

---

[16] Heskel 1996.
[17] On the alleged pact see de Ste Croix 1963. D. consistently refers to Philip's seizure of Amphipolis as the beginning of war with Athens: 4.25n. Φιλίππωι.
[18] Cf. 3.28n. οὕς.    [19] On the third Sacred War see Introd. §1.3.

1 HISTORICAL BACKGROUND 5

These conflicts brought Philip into direct contact with central Greece, and that narrative will be continued in the next section. In conclusion to this account of Philip's activity over the years leading up to the first *Philippic*, we should add that Philip was considering expansion to the east too already in the 350s. In 356, after the capture of Amphipolis, Philip had established a settlement at Philippi in Thrace; later, in 352, after the victory at the Crocus Field, he initiated a siege of Heraion Teichos, on the shore of the approach to the Hellespont, but is reported by D. to have abandoned the mission due to illness (1.13nn. τούς and ἠσθένησεν). Philip's activity in central Greece and Thrace anticipates his direction in the 340s.

*1.3 D., Athens, and Philip*

Following Philip's victory over Onomarchus in 352, before his attempt on Heraion Teichos, he marched on the pass at Thermopylae, where he was met by Athenian forces and rebuffed without an engagement (1.13n. πάνθ᾽, 1.26n. ἐάν). Philip also provoked the Athenians in late 352 with raids on their territories in the northern Aegean, at the islands Lemnos and Imbros, and on the coast of Attica itself at Marathon (4.34nn. εἰς Λῆμνον and εἰς Μαραθῶνα). His support of the Thessalians in battle against Pherae and Phocis involved him closely in the affairs of central Greece; these states had been opponents in the third Sacred War since 355 (3.8n. ἀπειρηκότων). Philip's role in ending that war in 346 will be considered below in this section as a defining moment in his relations with Athens, and in the career of D.

These provocations and, more generally, the future threat that Philip posed to Athenian interests, were the context for the debate in Athens at which D. delivered his first *Philippic* in 352/1.[20] At the start of the speech D. describes it as his first foray into the question of policy regarding Philip, and there is no clear indication of a precise point in time for the debate. Philip had not yet attacked Olynthus, but the Chalcidian League was increasingly wary of his intentions after he failed to keep his promise regarding Potidaea (D. 4.4, 2.1n. τάς), and they provoked him by harboring his step-brothers, rivals for the throne.[21] D.'s proposal to locate a permanent fleet in the north was unrealistic and unfeasible, due to the lingering financial pressure in the aftermath of the Social War. Instead, the Athenians decided to dispatch a small fleet with Charidemus at this time, though its departure was seriously delayed (D. 3.5).

Such a small force was unable to prevent Philip's operation against the cities of the Chalcidian League, and during the year leading up to his

---

[20] For the date and context see Badian 2000: 33–4, Cawkwell 2011: 370–7.
[21] *HM* 315, Harris 46.

siege of Olynthus in 349/8 he conducted an offensive campaign against the smaller cities of the League (2.1n. δύναμιν, 9.26n. δύο). After these cities were reduced, Olynthus was in a very weak position. D. presents their appeals for an alliance with Athens as an opportunity to stop Philip in the north and prevent him from renewing his attempts on central and southern Greece (D. 1.2–9, 25). The Athenians made a formal alliance with the Chalcidian League, and approved three separate forces to come to the aid of Olynthus that year (3.6n. παντί). D.'s three *Olynthiac* speeches address the question of aid for the Chalcidian League during the siege of Olynthus.[22] The Athenians' first two forces appear to have achieved little, and the third fleet arrived too late.[23] Philip destroyed the city and enslaved its inhabitants.[24]

After destroying Olynthus, Philip was in firm control of neighboring regions. He had already shown interest in extending his reach into Thrace, a territory with abundant natural resources and access to the Hellespont. The Athenians had long laid claim to the Chersonese, which was vital for the security of the grain trade from the Black Sea on which the city depended, and Athens had recently made an alliance with various kings in the region.[25] Philip saw that diplomacy could smooth his path in Thrace, but the Athenians were slow to respond to his overtures. However, in 346 the Athenian politician Philocrates passed a decree in the Athenian Assembly to initiate the peace process; after a period of protracted negotiations, Philip and the Athenians agreed to peace and an alliance.[26] D. was one of the ambassadors who negotiated the terms, and for a brief period he put aside his hostility to Philip and supported the peace.[27]

At the same time, Philip took a role in the Sacred War. His previous support for Thessaly aligned him with Thebes in opposition to Phocis. When in mid-346 the Phocian leader Phalaecus was forced to flee central Greece after being abandoned by his Athenian allies, Philip granted him safe passage. The Phocians had no choice but to surrender and agree

---

[22] It is tempting to take D.'s three *Olynthiacs* as documents from the three debates in which the Assembly decreed to send forces to support Olynthus. However, the speeches are too vague about their precise context and specific proposals to permit such an assumption. Discussions of the chronology have pointed to changes in tone and focus among the three speeches, but none of these differences amount to compelling evidence for a particular sequence; they could be placed in any order. See Tuplin 1998: 276–80.
[23] Sealey 138–43, Cawkwell 2011: 381–7.
[24] On current excavations at Olynthus see sites.lsa.umich.edu/olynthos-project (accessed August 11, 2017). Cf. 9.26n. Ὄλυνθον.
[25] *IG* II$^2$ 127 = *GHI* no. 53. Cf. 9.16n. βασιλεύς.
[26] For the detailed terms see 9.1n. τήν.
[27] In late 346, in *On the Peace* (or. 5), he advises the Athenians to abide by the arrangement they have made with Philip and to wait for the right moment to go to war (5.17 ὁ μέλλων πόλεμος).

to the harsh terms set by the Amphictyonic Council. Philip probably welcomed the advantages granted to the Thebans, while the Athenians saw their hopes and expectations thwarted (9.11nn. εἰς and ἤριζον). In addition to this tension, the Athenians were frustrated by Philip's renewed activity in Thrace beginning earlier that year (9.15nn. Σέρριον and τούς). The peace had become an embarrassment to Athens, and in later years, D., among others, denied his own culpability during the peace process and accused his fellow ambassadors of corruption. The year 346 marked an important development in D.'s policy: he began to blame his political opponents in Athens for Philip's success (9.53n. μισῆσαι).

To Philip, the resolution of the Sacred War offered a new basis for power in central Greece. He assumed the seat of Phocis on the Amphictyonic Council, and at the Phocians' behest he sent a deputy to preside at the Pythian Games in 346 (9.32n. τίθησι). He was given special privileges in consulting the oracle at Delphi, which was a mark of his new standing in Greece (9.32n. τήν). More significantly, he now had control of Thermopylae, which made it possible for him to intervene readily in Greek affairs (9.32n. Πυλῶν). He demonstrated his power in central Greece by reorganizing the political system and installing military garrisons in Thessaly by 344 (9.26nn. οὐχί and τετραρχίας). He took an interest in the Peloponnese, where he sought to diminish the power of Sparta by supporting Argos and Messene (9.17n. τά). Outside of Athens, Philip came to be seen as a powerful ally, who could guarantee the independence and autonomy of smaller cities.[28]

D. presents these activities as evidence of Philip's disregard for the peace, but his perspective did not win approval in the Assembly until later. In 344 he went on a diplomatic mission that seems only to have prompted Argos, Messene, and Philip himself to complain to the Assembly about Athenian meddling and collusion with Sparta.[29] On that occasion D. delivered the second *Philippic* (or. 6), in which he decried Philip's plans to isolate Athens, and complained that the peace had helped Philip and was a hindrance to Athens (e.g., D. 6.7, 28–36). In the aftermath of this debate disagreement about the Athenian commitment to the peace grew. Philip proposed modifications that were rejected in Athens; furthermore, there were new efforts to undermine public confidence in the peace: Philocrates was prosecuted as a traitor in 343, and in the same year D. accused his political opponent Aeschines of corruption during the negotiation of the peace.[30] Philocrates fled Athens, and Aeschines was narrowly acquitted; this is an indication of how closely divided the city was over the issue.

Athenian dissatisfaction did not hinder Philip's efforts in Greece. According to D., in 343 Philip installed his partisans in the Peloponnesian

[28] Cawkwell 1963: 203. Cf. Plb. 18.14 on the Peloponnesians and Philip.
[29] Harris 110–12.   [30] Harris 112–15.

city of Elis and, closer to Athens, at Megara (9.17nn. τά and Μεγάρων), and he was behind political revolutions in Euboea that began at this time (9.33n. τούς μέν, 9.58n. Ἱππόνικον, 9.59n. Φιλιστίδης). In early 342 Philip descended from Epirus toward the Ambracian Gulf on what was likely an exploratory mission; the Macedonians did not try to hold the position after the Athenians displayed their readiness to resist the incursion into western Greece (9.27n. πρότερον). Philip instead turned his attention to Thrace, and that brought him into direct conflict with the Athenians, who had sent their general Diopeithes to protect a military colony in the Chersonese in 343 (9.15n. οὔπω).

Philip's campaigning in Thrace from 342 added greatly to the tension with Athens arising from the recent political revolutions in various Greek cities. This tension is the background to the two speeches that D. delivered in the first part of 341. In *On the Chersonese* (or. 8), he defends Athenian activity in the region (9.2n. τούς), and then, not much later, in the third *Philippic*, he insists that the Athenians should regard Philip's activities as open warfare, and that they should send diplomats around Greece and mobilize a sizable force to join Diopeithes and fight Philip. Unlike in his earliest speeches against Philip, with the third *Philippic* D. succeeded in convincing the Athenians to follow his advice. At the end of 341, by D.'s proposal, embassies were dispatched, and an alliance was made with Callias of Chalcis that removed the tyrants in Euboea (9.71n. εἰς, 9.59n. οἵπερ).

Direct engagement with Philip was soon to follow. The third *Philippic* marked a turning point in D.'s career. The δῆμος followed his call to abandon the peace and commit to war with Philip. The king himself adopted a more aggressive stance too, first in 340 by attacking Athenian allies along the grain route at the Hellespont and impounding an Athenian transport ship, and then in 339 by invading central Greece and threatening Athens.[31] D.'s most glorious political act, in his own view at least, was brokering the alliance between Thebes, Athens, and other Greeks who fought Philip at Chaeronea in 338 (D. 18.153, 211–26). The result was a disaster for Athens, but the city stood by D.; he received honorary crowns and was chosen to give the funeral oration over the many who had died in battle.[32] The defeat ended Athens' role as a leading power in Greece. Yet, for the rest of his career, D. defended the policy of military resistance that he had

[31] Harris 124–33, Sealey 187–98, *HM* 566–81, 585–603.
[32] *On the Crown* (or. 18) is spoken in defense of a proposal to crown D. made by Ctesiphon after the battle. In that speech he refers to a similar decree before the battle, sponsored by Demomeles and Hyperides (D. 18.223–4). An extensive fragment of Hyperides' speech regarding that crown has been recovered from the Archimedes Palimpsest (Carey et al. 2008). D. was proud of his selection as orator over the war dead (18.285), and the funeral oration preserved in the Demosthenic corpus (or. 60) is likely to be authentic; see Herrman 2008.

long espoused in the *Olynthiacs* and *Philippics* by arguing that the Athenians had no alternative but to fight for the liberty of Greece, just as they had done in the Persian Wars.[33]

## 2 ASSEMBLY SPEECHES

Aristotle's *Rhetoric*, a handbook on persuasive discourse, distinguishes three types of oratory, which differ according to the speaker's purpose and institutional context: forensic (or dicanic) speeches present accusations or defenses regarding past actions in a courtroom context; display (or epideictic) speeches praise or blame the present condition of their subject in the context of a formal ceremony or a rhetorical performance; deliberative (or symbouleutic) speeches advocate policy regarding future events at a political meeting such as the Athenian Assembly (Arist. *Rh.* 1.3.1–2 [1358a–b]).

The Assembly (ἡ ἐκκλησία) met in the open air at the Pnyx, a hill near the Agora and Acropolis in central Athens. Meetings were held at least 40 times per year, and the Assembly was the main democratic body in Athens, making policy decisions on a wide range of topics, including war and peace, public finances, and foreign diplomacy.[34] The agenda for each meeting was set in advance by the Council (ἡ βουλή), a group of 500 annually appointed representatives of the citizenry, and a rotating subset of the Council officiated at the Assembly meetings (9.60n. πρυτανευόμενοι); any citizen could debate or propose motions to be decided upon by the collective body of citizens in attendance (ὁ δῆμος), who typically numbered at least 6000 (cf. 2.29n. ῥήτωρ). Decisions were determined by majority vote, as demonstrated by a show of hands, but extensive debate and other institutional measures were designed to achieve a large degree of consensus among voters.[35] Meetings began with a public sacrifice (2.1n. τήν), and then speakers were invited to address the points on the agenda, with priority given to older speakers; in practice, there seems to have been a small number of 10 or 20 frequent contributors at any particular time, and a large number of men who spoke more rarely (4.1n. οἱ).

The surviving texts of the Attic orators preserve examples of the three types of speeches distinguished by Aristotle, but deliberative oratory is the least well represented.[36] The Demosthenic corpus includes 15 speeches addressed to the Athenian Assembly, and those works are the

---

[33] Yunis 2000.
[34] General background: Hansen 1991: 125–60, 1987. Frequency and schedule of meetings: E. M. Harris 2006: 81–120.
[35] Canevaro 2018, 2019. See also 3.4n. θορύβου, 9.38n. τὴν πρὸς ἀλλήλους.
[36] The bulk of these texts are forensic speeches; surviving display speeches include the Athenian state funeral orations and most of the writings of Isocrates.

best sources for the nature of Assembly speeches, though there are serious limitations to their value as evidence: most speeches were written by a single politician; they concern a narrow range of topics; and they are chronologically concentrated, covering a relatively brief span of time. Let us consider these difficulties, and then look at other sources of information on oratory in the Assembly, before concluding with a brief assessment of what we can learn from these speeches.

13 of the 15 Assembly speeches in the Demosthenic corpus were composed by D.[37] The two remaining speeches must have been included in the corpus by an early scribe or editor because they concern war with Philip (or. 7) or his son Alexander (or. 17), or simply because they are Assembly speeches. They are similar in policy and outlook to the other speeches by D., though they differ in style and tone. Or. 7 addresses the same points as does the second *Philippic*, and it adopts an even more aggressive stance toward Philip in 344 (cf. 9.72n. Ἡγήσιππος). Or. 17 is later, probably from 331, and it too calls for the Athenians to abandon the terms of their alliance with Alexander and go to war.[38] Thus all these Assembly speeches reflect the perspective of D. and his political allies in opposition to Macedon. Or. 17 is the only surviving speech that was delivered after the period from 354 to 340.

No earlier Assembly speeches survive among the works of the Attic orators,[39] and it is likely that D. was innovative in his decision to circulate written versions of the speeches he made in the Assembly.[40] The surviving speeches must have been selected deliberately: they are thematically linked and represent two important phases of D.'s career. Or. 13–16 were designed to establish a place for D. among the politicians of Athens; older speakers spoke first at Assembly meetings, and in these written speeches the young D. takes an opportunity to show how he handles key questions of finance and international relations. Or. 1–6 and 8–10 all focus on Athenian policy regarding Philip, spanning the period from D.'s first speech on the topic to the outbreak of war in 340, during which he emerges as the leading politician opposed to Philip. We do not have later Assembly speeches by D., from the period after the

---

[37] D.'s Assembly speeches leading up to the third *Philippic* were surveyed above; on or. 13–16 see Introd. §1.1, and for or. 1–6 and 8–9 see Introd. §1.3. The fourth *Philippic* (or. 10) is also by D., and was delivered not long after the third *Philippic* in 341. For the authenticity of these see McCabe 1981: 170–1, 196–7.

[38] Herrman 2009a: 180–2.

[39] Andoc. 3 purports to be an address to the Assembly regarding peace with Sparta in 392/1 (or possibly 387/6). However, the speech uses anachronistic terminology, and its extensive historical account is based on Aesch. 2; it should be regarded as a rhetorical fabrication written after 343, probably after the fourth century. See E. M. Harris 2000.

[40] See further Introd. §4.

## 2 ASSEMBLY SPEECHES     11

defeat at Chaeronea in 338, nor is there any reason to suppose that D. ever published more Assembly speeches than those that survive today.[41] D. passed many motions in the Assembly for various sorts of proposals that are not addressed or attested in the surviving speeches, e.g., decrees of honors and citizenship, alliances, embassies, and infrastructure repair.[42] Beyond these, he must have contributed to debate regularly. The surviving speeches are packaged to present a vivid picture of D.'s position on a few key questions regarding finance, foreign policy, and Philip; they do not provide a representative or comprehensive view of his political career.

Nor do later Assembly speeches survive from other orators, though there are some paltry testimonia for later fourth-century items, whose authors presumably followed D.'s model in circulating their works.[43] Beyond the texts of the Attic orators, there are additional works that are relevant to Assembly speeches: the historians Thucydides and Xenophon recreate Assembly debates of the late fifth and early fourth centuries, and the rhetorical works of Aristotle and Anaximenes provide contemporary practical guides for the preparation of deliberative speeches.

Thucydides, writing at the end of the fifth century, explains his method for reporting speeches in his account of the Peloponnesian War: they are historical reconstructions intended to reflect the actual content of speeches as delivered when possible, while also including material that the historian imagines would have suited the occasion.[44] He does not provide clear indications of what is reported and what is created, and it is impossible for a critic to know how closely this material reflects actual practice in the Assembly. The Assembly speeches in Thucydides are carefully crafted instruments designed to express and epitomize the qualities that define the characters in the narrative. In this regard they are comparable to the speeches in Homer or Athenian tragedy; although speakers have their own individual styles, these appear to be a literary creation of Thucydides rather than a representation of speeches as actually delivered.[45] Further, the Assembly speeches in Thucydides are consistently shorter than surviving deliberative speeches; this is evidence that they

---

[41] Hansen 1989: 286–9.
[42] Hansen 1989: 41–2 provides the evidence for 39 decrees; a supporting speech exists for only one of these, the first *Philippic*.
[43] Hansen 1989: 286–94 collects the evidence for at most six speeches from the last half of the fourth century.
[44] Thuc. 1.22.1 ὡς δ' ἂν ἐδόκουν ἐμοὶ ἕκαστοι περὶ τῶν αἰεὶ παρόντων τὰ δέοντα μάλιστ' εἰπεῖν, ἐχομένωι ὅτι ἐγγύτατα τῆς ξυμπάσης γνώμης τῶν ἀληθῶς λεχθέντων, οὕτως εἴρηται ("[speeches] are presented in accordance with what I think each speaker would have been likely to say about his respective affairs. I have kept as close as possible to the overall intention of what was really said").
[45] Tompkins 2013: 457–60, 1993: 111, 1972: 214.

have been reworked by the historian. He employs a selection of speeches delivered over a number of years to create a specific narrative arc, and the knowledge that comes with hindsight motivates him to stress connections that must have been less clear or developed in the immediate debates.[46] For example, Thucydides uses speeches to draw a contrast between the generalships of Pericles and Cleon, and his omission of other Assembly speeches during the period between their commands distorts the record and creates an anachronistic link between these two; similarly, his presentation of the Assembly debate regarding the punishment of Mytilene in 427 is written so as to provide a deliberate contrast with the discussion of Melos in 416.[47] The speeches of D. provide a single viewpoint from a wider debate, and in a similar way Thucydides chooses not to present a range of different opinions, but instead tends to give polarized speeches that represent extreme positions.[48]

The argumentation of Thucydides' Assembly speeches is frequently similar to D.'s approach. Both authors suggest that speakers in the Assembly were more likely to rely on arguments of expediency or advantage than on ethical considerations.[49] For example, in Thucydides' Mytilenian debate both Cleon and Diodotus address the question of justice and expediency in their speeches, but Cleon wins the day with his analysis of the advantage for Athens in punishing the revolutionary allies.[50] Similarly D. stresses the benefits that his proposals will bring to Athens in preference to appeals to justice or other ethical considerations.[51] It is true that D. often reminds the Athenians of their duty to act, but this obligation is presented as the means to preserve the city and bring advantage to it, not as a moral imperative (2.3n. προτρέπειν). D.'s speeches present a wider array of argumentation than one finds in the more streamlined Assembly speeches in Thucydides. In particular, D. often employs extended accounts of historical precedents and examples to make his point (e.g., D. 2.14, 3.24–6, 4.24, 9.36–46), whereas the Assembly speeches in Thucydides generally lack historical examples.[52]

Aristotle and Anaximenes each composed rhetorical handbooks that are contemporary with the speeches of D. These do not preserve evidence

---

[46] Marincola 2007: 121–2, S. Hornblower 1987: 55–66.
[47] For a catalogue of speeches in Thucydides see W. C. West 1973: 7–15.
[48] Cf. Thuc. 3.36.6: there were many speeches about Mytilene, but only two are presented.
[49] Speakers may stress τὸ συμφέρον more than τὸ δίκαιον, but the concepts are interrelated rather than antithetical: Low 2007: 160–73.
[50] On justice (τὸ δίκαιον and related terms), cf. 3.39.3, 40.3, 44.4, 47.5; on expediency (τὸ ξυμφέρον and related terms), cf. 38.1, 39.3, 40.4, 44.2–3, 47.5.
[51] Heath 1990: 391–6; cf. 1.1n. τό, 9.16n. τό.
[52] References to the Persian Wars come in addresses to audiences outside Athens: e.g., Thuc. 1.73.2, 3.10.2–6, 5.89, 6.83.1; Connor 1984: 93 n. 32.

for particular deliberative speeches; rather they are guides for prospective orators studying persuasive discourse in the Assembly, informed more by theory than by experience of actual speeches.[53] Although they give much specific advice for budding orators, they provide an extremely vague and abstract view of debate in the Assembly. Still, these guides are helpful for situating the speeches of D. within a broad context of deliberative speech. For example, Anaximenes outlines a variety of topics for speeches to the Assembly: public religion, law and institutions, international alliances, peace and war, and public finance ([Arist.] *Rh.Al.* 2.2 [1423a]; cf. Arist. *Rh.* 1.4.7 [1359b]). This comprehensive list confirms that the preserved speeches of D., in which war is the dominant theme and finance and alliances appear to a lesser extent, are a focused and select group.

The rhetorical handbooks recommend certain themes for arguments: persuasive speakers ought to address questions of justice, law, and advantage, and consider whether actions are noble, satisfying, and manageable.[54] Whereas the deliberative speeches in Thucydides are concerned primarily with justice and expediency, Xenophon's *Hellenica* illustrates a wider interest in other approaches, with attention to the feasibility and opportunity for particular policy proposals.[55] Xenophon's Assembly speeches are like Thucydides' in that they are crafted to fit a historical narrative,[56] but in this regard they are more varied and align with D.'s approach. For example, D. highlights the theme of καιρός in the *Olynthiacs*, and the first *Philippic* presents an extended argument for the means of achieving D.'s proposed goals (1.2n. καιρός, D. 4.28–30).

The Demosthenic Assembly speeches are our best sources for the nature of democratic debate in fourth-century Athens. They create a vivid picture of one politician's position regarding a few key policy areas, and they illustrate its development over a number of years. But the background to the picture is in many respects quite blurred. The specific historical moment for each of the surviving speeches is hard to pinpoint, and it is unclear how they fit into a particular debate and how they respond to other participants. Only the first *Philippic* puts forward a proposal for the approval of the δῆμος (4.16–22), and that was unsuccessful. Other evidence for Assembly debate in the historians and rhetoricians confirms that D.'s speeches address typical topics with suitable arguments, but it is very

---

[53] Cf. Trevett 1996b. At least the disengagement from actual Assembly speeches means that the evidence in the rhetorical handbooks is not likely to be based on the surviving texts of D. and the historians.
[54] [Arist.] *Rh.Al.* 1.4 (1421b) τὸν μὲν προτρέποντα χρὴ δεικνύειν ταῦτα ἐφ' ἃ παρακαλεῖ δίκαια ὄντα καὶ νόμιμα καὶ συμφέροντα καὶ καλὰ καὶ ἡδέα καὶ ῥᾴδια πραχθῆναι ("the advisor must show that his recommendations are just, advantageous, noble, pleasant, and easy to accomplish"). Aristotle's discussion is more diffuse but includes similar themes; cf. Usher 2008: 1–2, Heath 1990: 395–6.
[55] Usher 2008: 11–13.    [56] Gray 1989: 137–40.

14 INTRODUCTION

difficult to judge how the audience responded. Early in his career D.'s proposals appear to have had little effect on Athenian policy, but by the late 340s his opposition to Philip won wide assent. These speeches played an important part in bringing about this change in direction, but new military and political realities must have influenced the δῆμος too.

## 3 LANGUAGE AND STYLE

In his Assembly speeches D.'s distinctive deliberative mode is characterized by the periodic structure of his sentences, rhythm and sound, rhetorical figures, metaphorical imagery, and variation in word choice and tone.

### 3.1 Sentence Structure and Word Order

D. constructs his periods in a variety of styles. The most elaborate are built on a frame of complex subordination (hypotaxis, or λέξις κατεστραμμένη); an initial main clause introduces a dependent clause that leads to further levels of subordination in a series (2.5n., 4.17n. δεῖ, 9.2n.);[57] these sentences stress the contingencies in D.'s political analysis, and they carry along the audience by "rising to a crescendo, and sinking again gradually to a quiet close."[58] At other times D. avoids subordination and instead uses a pair of syntactically parallel clauses or cola,[59] often linked by sound, sometimes to draw connections (4.33n. τῶν, 2.13n. τά), or alternatively to emphasize a point of contrast (2.3n. ὁ, 4.3n. παραδείγμασι), or again to encompass a range of possibilities (1.18n. εἴτε γάρ, 2.9n. ὅταν). This sort of parallelism stands out as D. frequently varies his constructions to avoid monotony (1.10n. εὐεργέτημ', 3.25n. ἐπί, 9.7n. μήποτε). A third common sentence structure is the tricolon, in which a sequence of three elements creates an effect of abundance: a period may comprise three main clauses (4.28n. τάλαντα); subordinate clauses may have three linked verbs (1.15n. δέδοικα); genitives absolute are placed in groups of three (3.8n. οὐδέ, 9.6n. πόλεις); a clause may contain three objects (1.6n. καί, 1.28n. τοὺς δὲ λέγοντας, 2.13n. εἰσφέροντας). Often the third item is a capping phrase, a broadly general term following two specific items, creating an effect of comprehensiveness (1.24n. πρεσβευομένους, 2.13n. εἰσφέροντας, 9.21n. πάνθ'). In general, D.'s complex structures may serve a larger goal: some of his most elaborate sentences are crafted so that the syntax reflects the content of what is described (4.17n. δεῖ, 9.14n. ἐκλύσας).

[57] Here and throughout this section references to D.'s speeches are not comprehensive, but rather *exempli gratia*.
[58] *GPS* 7 on Hdt. 1.1.1.
[59] Here and in the notes "colon" is used to designate a grammatically complete segment of a sentence, an element that is punctuated with a raised dot; a clause may be main or subordinate, and is defined as a unit built around a finite verb.

## 3 LANGUAGE AND STYLE

D. mitigates the risk of overwhelming or tiring his audience by varying the pace. He follows long, difficult periods with shorter and simpler constructions (2.7n. ὅλως, 4.43n. ἀλλά, 9.27n. καί). He is particularly fond of brief rhetorical questions that engage the audience and take the place of more ponderous arguments (2.3n. διά, 4.2n. τί). Sometimes he imagines an audience member addressing such questions to him, so that his own presentation depicts the audience's involvement (1.14n. τί). He also strings together items in a manner that is easier to follow (parataxis, or λέξις εἰρομένη); the effect of this style is an accumulation of detail, or an impression of either the rapidity, or alternatively of the delay, involved in a sequence of actions or events (1.12n. τὸ πρῶτον, 4.8n. ἀλλά, 4.17n. εἰς). These series are often marked out with an abundance of connectives that contribute to this effect (polysyndeton; 4.4n. Πύδναν, 4.36n. ἅμα). Conversely, at other points D. accelerates his pace and adopts a more jarring tone by omitting connectives (asyndeton; 2.25n. μελλόντων, 4.29n. ἐγώ, 9.65n. καλήν).

Within his sentences D. employs several techniques of syntax and word order for varied effect. Extended articular infinitive phrases function as highly flexible substantive noun units that can incorporate their own subjects, objects, and adverbial modifiers. D. can pack significant content into these long infinitival phrases, which may then function as the subjects of much simpler main clauses (1.4n. τό, 2.1n. τό), or be incorporated in prepositional phrases (3.26n. ἐκ, 4.43n. τήν). A pair of infinitives at the start of successive clauses can highlight antithetical ideas (1.10n. τὸ μὲν ... ἄν, 2.5n.). A series of infinitives in apposition may provide an emphatic answer to a simple question or allusive assertion (2.5n. τοῦ, 9.18n. τίσιν, 9.22n. τό), or serve as a means for the presentation of sequential points in a list of parallel examples or arguments (2.6–7n.). Articular infinitive phrases are a prominent and characteristic feature of D.'s Greek; these speeches are the culmination of a trend toward increased use of infinitives throughout the classical period.[60]

D. uses word order to convey emphasis and help the audience follow his presentation. We have just observed that he may put antithetical infinitives at the start of clauses, and similar placement of other items achieves the same contrasting effect (2.3n. ὁ). More generally, initial position may stress a particular word (2.8n. καιροῦ, 2.16n. κοπτόμενοι, 4.1n. τότ'), or introduce a major theme or specific example (4.11n. Ὀλυνθίοις, 4.28n. χρήματα). The initial position can spotlight a key point (4.44n. εὑρήσει), or outline a difficult sentence by marking important items that are to be understood in a series of subsequent clauses (9.3n. ὑμεῖς, 9.4n. εἶθ'). Conversely, D. frequently delays material until the end of a sentence for the

---

[60] Cf. Dover 1997: 34–6.

opposite effect, to leave it hanging in the air as a closing comment (1.16n. συμβούλου, 1.19n. στρατιωτικά, 3.7n. ὁπωσδήποτε, 3.9n. δήπου, 3.18n. ἑλέσθαι). Artful word order also occurs between the initial and final positions of periods. D. links clauses and stresses key terms by pulling them from a subordinate into a main clause (prolepsis; 1.21n. τὰ πράγματα). He frequently separates adjectival modifiers from their nouns in order to hold the audience's attention as they wait for the delivery of the delayed material (hyperbaton; 1.8n. τήν, 2.1n. δαιμονίαι, 3.24n. πολλά).[61] At other times he fuses different elements of a clause into a single expression by means of an interlocked word order (synchysis; 2.8n. συμφέρον, 3.2n. τοῦθ', 4.51n. ἐπὶ τῶι). Short phrases are juxtaposed within or between sentences to express succinct pointed criticism or to make subtle suggestions to the audience (1.16n. συμβούλου, 2.6n. θρυλούμενον, 3.12n. μή, 4.37n. οἱ), and similar ordered placement of a series of items in a chiastic sequence helps the audience follow the structure of extended trains of thought (2.26n. ὥστε, 3.1n. εἰς, 9.13n. τούτους).

## 3.2 Rhythm and Sound

Fourth-century prose stylists employed certain sound effects to catch the ear of a listening audience. Isocrates was famous among critics for avoiding hiatus, the pause that resulted from ending one word with a vowel immediately before another that started with a vowel, and in his rhetorical writings he explicitly acknowledges this tendency.[62] D. occasionally imitates Isocrates (4.15n. ἤ, 9.47n. ἁπάντων), and some of his choices regarding word order can be explained by the desire to avoid hiatus (1.1n. προθύμως, 2.7n. τὴν γάρ, 2.8n. συμφέρον, 4.34n. τοῦ). Isocrates prioritized euphony and relied on various devices to achieve this goal, and many of these are employed, though more sparingly, by D.: isocolon balances clauses of equal length (2.29n. ὑμεῖς, 4.5n. οὐδέν, 4.33n. τῶν, 9.6n. πόλεις); homoioarchon marks a series of clauses or list items with the same sound at the start (1.1n. προθύμως, 4.5n. οὐδέν, 9.73n. συγκαλεῖν), often in conjunction with homoioteleuton, or rhyming endings (2.13n. πολλήν, 3.26n. ἐκ).

Other elements of sound and rhythm were not explicitly discussed by D.'s contemporaries, but they contribute to the distinctive style of D.'s Greek. Alliteration, the repetition of consonants, stresses key points (2.23n. πολεμοῦσι, 3.36n. καὶ ... κατέλιπον, 9.38n. ποιεῖν). Clausulae, or rhythmic patterns at the ends of sentences, do not appear as recurring

---

[61] Cf. Vickers 1988: 298–9.
[62] McCabe 1981: 17–22, Kennedy 1963: 73, 209. See below (Introd. §6.3) on elision and *scriptio plena* in the MSS of D.

features in D.'s speeches (as they do in Cicero's), though he does have distinctive tendencies.[63] D.'s prose sometimes slips for a moment into a metrical mode, with an extended sequence or cluster of poetic rhythm, but in this regard it is not unusual, and most examples should be regarded as unintentional, without a deliberate effect.[64] That is not to say that D. is unaware of all such effects; he changes his pace and avoids monotony by varying his rhythm, and these changes can reinforce the sense and imagery (2.3n. διά, 2.13n. πολλήν). One metrical tendency is so pronounced that it serves as a criterion to distinguish authentic from inauthentic works in the Demosthenic corpus: D. avoids sequences of three or more short syllables to a much greater extent than do other contemporary prose writers ("Blass's Law").[65]

## 3.3 Rhetorical Figures

Rhetorical figures (σχήματα) include the techniques of verbal arrangement already discussed, such as antithesis, asyndeton, hyperbaton, and isocolon; metaphor, a defining aspect of D.'s thought, will be discussed below (Introd. §3.4). This section considers a miscellany of other devices, pertaining both to D.'s wording and to his thought; all of these are linked in that they follow schematic verbal and logical patterns in order to convey meaning and feeling.[66] They are the elements of rhetorical eloquence.

D. employs various sorts of phrasing, in addition to word order, to underscore his message: combined negatives stress a positive point (litotes; 1.27n. οὐδεμιᾶς, 4.36n. οὐδέν, 9.11n. ἤριζον), result clauses emphasize the extremeness of a quality or action (hypostasis; 3.1n. τά, 4.37n. ὁ). Verbal paraphrases frequently stress the Athenians' obligation to do their duty (2.3n. προτρέπειν). D. expresses vehemence through repetition of the verb εἰμί (epanadiplosis; 1.19n. ἔστιν, 2.10n. οὐ, 4.18n. εἰσί), marks key themes by repeating them in close sequence (1.19n. ἔστιν, 2.23n. οὐ), and links successive clauses by repeating an initial key word (anaphora; 9.68n. πόλλ'). On a larger scale, he often marks the close of an extended argument or section of a speech by echoing or repeating the opening words (ring composition; 1.11n. τι, 3.26n. εὐδαιμονίαν, 4.42n. ἄ).

---

[63] McCabe 1981: 138 observes that D. closes periods with the rhythm long-short-short-anceps more than do other authors. However, this clausula is not stressed in such a way that the audience would have taken special note of it, and D. himself may not have been conscious of this tendency.
[64] See Dover 1997: 160–82, 9.20n. ἐάν. Sandys' commentaries frequently observe such instances; e.g., on 4.10, 8.31, 9.20.
[65] McCabe 1981: 1–4; his study demonstrates that the difference between D. and others is statistically significant. See also Yunis 25.
[66] Vickers 1988: 305–22 argues for the perennial expressive vitality of rhetorical figures. Lausberg 1998 is a voluminous guide.

There is a continuum connecting specific rhetorical devices with larger methods of presentation, and on a structural level D. organizes his thoughts and arguments themselves according to rhetorical patterns. He frequently addresses his audience and uses the vocative emphatically to emphasize particular items or mark segments of the argument (apostrophe; 1.14n. ἵνα, 2.4n. μεγάλα, 4.1n.).[67] He engages the audience by imagining exchanges between them and himself (hypophora; 1.14n. τί, 1.26n., 3.16n. τίνα). He poses riddles and presents paradoxes to hold their attention and demonstrate his ability to apprehend the political situation (1.4n. τοῦθ', 1.11n. γάρ, 4.2n. ὅ, 9.5n. παράδοξον); he similarly points to the absurdity of existing Athenian policies by combining opposite terms (oxymoron; 2.6n. θρυλούμενον, 9.55n. καί). He makes telling assertions with quick references to material he is unwilling or unable to argue more carefully (paraleipsis; 1.13n. παραλείπω, 2.4n. ταῦτα, 3.27n. οἷς, 9.21n.). He creates an air of spontaneity by correcting himself (epidiorthosis; 2.2n. μᾶλλον, 3.14n. οὔτ' ἄν, 9.24n. μᾶλλον), breaking off his thought mid-sentence (aposiopesis; 3.27n. οἷς, 9.54n. οὐκ), changing the syntactical construction (anacolouthon; 1.24n. πῶς, 4.28n. χρήματα), or inserting parenthetical asides (1.3n. ἀξιόπιστος, 4.17–18n., 9.35n. ἐῶ) or exclamations (9.31n. Ἡράκλεις, 9.65n. καλήν).

## 3.4 Metaphorical Imagery

Among the most striking characteristics of D.'s language in these speeches is his use of personification, simile, and metaphor. This type of imagery is a distinctive feature of D.'s Assembly speeches; the expression in these speeches is more bold than that of his forensic speeches.

D. breathes life into his arguments by personifying abstract concepts such as opportunity, fortune, the political circumstances, or the Athenian δῆμος, and by invoking them in support of his proposals (1.2n. καιρός, 3.1n. τά, 3.30n. πράττειν) or as divine agents responsible for Athenian successes and failures (2.2n. τῶν, 9.38n. ἡ). Similes make an explicit comparison for the purpose of explanation or illustration, and D. often frames his policy discussion in everyday terms that the audience can easily understand: his comparisons look to the marketplace (9.39), sports (4.40n. οὐδέν), public religious festivals (18.122), or household finance (1.15n. τόν, 9.30n. ἄξιον), material familiar to his Athenian listeners.[68] He is particularly fond of medical similes, which emphasize his role as a knowledgeable advisor (2.21n., 3.33n. τοῖς, 9.29n. ὥσπερ). Rarely he presents a vivid comparison with the natural world, a type of simile more common in Homer than in Assembly speeches (9.33n. ὥσπερ).

[67] On the use of the vocative for emphasis, see Fraenkel 1965: 30–49.
[68] Ronnet 176–82.

# 3 LANGUAGE AND STYLE

Metaphors are implicit comparisons that arise from the use of unexpected language to put a point in terms that properly refer to another realm. Such expressions surprise the audience and add compelling vividness to a speaker's arguments.[69] Like similes, metaphorical expressions can facilitate understanding by putting technical material in a more familiar light; D. frequently uses language pertaining to hunting, sailing, or athletics to describe the political situation and his proposals (1.16n. ὑποστείλασθαι, 3.7n. ἐφορμεῖν, 4.5n. ἆθλα, 4.9n. κύκλωι, 9.64n. ἕως). It can be difficult to assess the effect of such expressions: language is full of "dead" metaphors that have lost their effect through time and use, and we are in a poor position to judge classical Greek usage since we have so much less exposure to the language than D.'s audience had.[70] Two methods help us judge the novelty of D.'s expressions. First, we can consider whether D.'s imagery is widely paralleled in contemporary and earlier writers; these comparanda may suggest that some of D.'s metaphors are widespread and unlikely to make a distinctive impression on the audience (3.3n. τὰ πλείω, 3.22n. προπέποται, 4.37n. τόν, 9.47n. οὐκ, 9.60n. ὑβρίζετο), while others stand out for their originality (9.28n. διορωρύγμεθα, 9.36n. τοῦ), or are consistent with the sort of unique stylistic quirks identified and mocked by D.'s political opponents (3.31n. ἐκνενευρισμένοι).[71] The second method is to examine the context for the metaphor; often there is a cluster of related language that shows that the usage was deliberate, that the speaker was attuned to the precise sense of the terms being used (2.9n. ἅπαντα, 2.10n. φωρᾶται, 2.14n. νοσοῦσι, 3.11n. τήν, 9.12n. τοῖς).

## 3.5 Word Choice and Tone

Many of the devices and techniques described above impart distinctive tones to D.'s presentation. For example, the use of imaginary dialogues often expresses indignation at the behavior of the Athenian δῆμος, or antithesis may highlight the absurdity of their decisions (Introd. §3.3, 3.29n. καί, 3.9n. ἰδεῖν). The most frequent means that D. uses to vary the tone is word choice.

In D., as in all Greek authors, particles often set the mood.[72] D. also adopts different registers of phrasing to achieve similar effects and variety.

---
[69] Vickers 1988: 320–2.
[70] For example, in modern English the verb "inspire" is unlikely to make many listeners think of the physical act of inhalation, and a computer mouse probably does not evoke images of a rodent. On the difficulty of distinguishing a striking "live" metaphor from standard everyday usage ("dead" metaphor) see Rutherford 2012: 127–8, Dover 1997: 122–30, Silk 1974: 27–56.
[71] Ps.-Longin. (32.1–4) similarly focuses on the strikingly unique aspect of metaphor in D.'s speeches; cf. Silk 1974: 221.
[72] See Index (Greek) s.vv. ἄρα, γάρ, γε, δή, μέν, μέντοι, μήν, οὖν, τοι, etc.

At times his diction appears to be colloquial or conversational (1.26n. μή, 2.20n. ἄν, 4.24n. παρακύψαντα, 9.44n. τί, 9.72n. οὐδ'), and his frequent use of oaths contributes to this impression (1.23n. μά, 3.32n. μά, 4.10n. νή, 4.49n. οὐ). At other times he adopts a more severe or elevated mode, reflected in a preference for expressions from tragedy (1.19n. ἔστιν, 3.33n. ἐάν, 4.36n. ἄτακτα, 9.69n. ἕως) or usages possibly inspired by Homer (2.22n. μεγάλη, 4.8n. ἀλλά, 4.42n. τήν, 9.33n. ὥσπερ). He has a fondness for unusual compound verbs (2.5n. ὑπερεκπεπληγμένους, 4.7n. τά, 4.41n. συμπαραθεῖτε), which align with other analytical expressions to put him in the role of a specialist advisor (2.15n. ἐπισφαλεστέραν, 3.33n. τοῖς). This impression of expertise is reinforced by D.'s regular habit of doubling verbs; often the verbs are nearly synonymous and the pairing adds gravity and emphasis (1.14n. ἵνα, 4.3n. ἴδητε, 4.13n. ὡς), while in other instances he combines a term that is broad in sense with one that is more technical (9.31n. ἀπώλλυε, 9.39n. ἀπόλωλε).

## 4 PUBLICATION

We cannot know how closely the surviving texts of the Assembly speeches correspond to actual oral presentations; it seems highly improbable that D. memorized written scripts for Assembly debate, and the unpredictable nature of such discussions undoubtedly necessitated extemporaneous responses to others' speeches. Our texts may have been written as advance preparation for oral delivery, or they may have been composed afterward to preserve a written record of the debate. (In the case of the third *Philippic* we may have material of both types; see Introd. §6.2.) Some regard the surviving written speeches as polished pieces intended for circulation by D., while others believe that what survives is a more or less finished assortment of materials gathered by others after D.'s death.[73] Above (Introd. §2) it was argued that D.'s Assembly speeches are a select group. This section extends that argument to suggest that D. himself was responsible for the selection and circulation of the surviving speeches. Three types of evidence are relevant to the question: a possible fourth-century testimonium for the speeches, the physical evidence preserved in ancient and medieval manuscripts, and internal indicators of deliberate refinement within the speeches themselves.

---

[73] Polished pieces published by D.: Usher 2007: 228, Tuplin 1998: 300, Yunis 1996: 246–7, Sealey 229, Hansen 1989: 286–9. Unfinished material gathered by others at a later time: Canevaro 2013a: 325 n. 25, MacDowell 2009: 8, Trevett 1996b, Goldstein 1968: 24–5.

## 4.1 A Fourth-Century Testimonium?

There is a reference to written texts of D.'s speeches in Plutarch's *Life of Demosthenes* that perhaps attests to their existence in the fourth century: "Hermippus says that Aesion, when asked about the orators of long ago and those of his own time, said that someone who heard those [earlier orators] would have been in awe of their orderly and grand addresses to the people, while the speeches of D., when read, stand out for their preparation and power."[74] Plutarch continues by focusing on the difference between scripted and unrehearsed presentations; the larger context for this anecdote from Aesion is not a chronological contrast, but rather one between unstudied extemporaneous speech and polished written material. The central juxtaposition of διαλεγομένους and ἀναγινωσκόμενοι highlights the key point. However, there are difficulties: who is this Aesion, and did he refer to written versions of the speeches, or did that reference arise later as part of the reporting by Hermippus, who wrote anecdotal biographies some time in the third century, or by Plutarch, active four centuries after that?

This testimonium seems to refer to a contemporary of D. who was able to read his speeches and recall earlier speakers. The name Aesion was rare in Attica: there is a handful of references from the fourth century, and a single reference from the third.[75] The information from the fourth century refers to an Aesion who was a trierarch in the 350s (*IG* II² 1612.293), probably the same person as a rhetorician who studied with D. (Arist. *Rh.* 3.10.7 [1411a], *Suda* δ 454); the third-century Aesion is known only from an inscribed list of men who were probably members of the Council (*IG* II² 2441.3). This interest in oratory seems to confirm that Plutarch's Aesion is the fourth-century figure.[76]

Moreover, the testimonium appears to refer specifically to the reading of written texts of D.'s Assembly speeches. Plutarch's overall argument and specific phrasing point in this direction: elsewhere the phrase τῶι δήμωι διαλέγεσθαι refers to deliberative oratory (D. 24.48, Aesch. 2.12); Dionysius of Halicarnassus uses the same phrase οἱ Δημοσθένους λόγοι to

---

[74] Plut. *Dem.* 11.4 = Hermipp.Hist. *FGrHist* 1026 F 52 Αἰσίωνα δέ φησιν Ἕρμιππος ἐπερωτηθέντα περὶ τῶν πάλαι ῥητόρων καὶ τῶν καθ' αὑτὸν εἰπεῖν ὡς ἀκούων μὲν ἄν τις ἐθαύμασεν ἐκείνους εὐκόσμως καὶ μεγαλοπρεπῶς τῶι δήμωι διαλεγομένους, ἀναγινωσκόμενοι δ' οἱ Δημοσθένους λόγοι πολὺ τῆι κατασκευῆι καὶ δυνάμει διαφέρουσιν.

[75] *LGPN* s.v. Αἰσίων. Cf. also *APF* no. 315, *PAA* 114530, 114535, 114540, 114545.

[76] Westwood 2017b suggests that Plutarch's Aesion may belong to the third century, if the fourth-century Aesion was dead by the time his son was a trierarch in 348 (D. 21.165), before the delivery of many of D.'s Assembly speeches. However, sons could be trierarchs before their fathers died (see MacDowell 1990: 384), and Aesion may have lived beyond 348.

describe the collected addresses to the Assembly (Dion. Hal. *Amm.* 1.3); and the verb ἀναγιγνώσκω is a technical term for reading aloud a written text (LSJ II).

Skeptics have maintained that the attention to written style and extemporaneous speech reflects the interests of Hermippus or Plutarch, who may have paraphrased Aesion in their own words. However, the characterization of D. as a careful writer who was not naturally gifted at speaking, although it was memorably developed in Plutarch and Quintilian, appears quite early on: according to Dionysius of Halicarnassus this theme was prominent in the account of Demetrius of Phalerum at the turn of the third century, and the brief life in the Plutarchean *Moralia* quotes fourth-century Athenian comedians who mocked D.'s affected style.[77] Similarly, Aeschines ridicules D.'s dependence on written notes and his failed oral presentation during the embassy to Philip in 346 (Aesch. 2.34–5). Although we cannot fully discount the paraphrasing role of Plutarch or Hermippus, the testimonium is consistent with fourth-century interests in D.[78]

The fourth century was a time of transition. Written speeches were coming into vogue, and a lively debate on oral and written media is illustrated by, among other works, Alcidamas' treatise on the superiority of extempore speech to written preparations, by Plato's *Phaedrus*, and by the sophistic works of Isocrates. In the *Philippus*, for example, Isocrates blends the genres of epistle and oratory. This sprawling letter is addressed to Philip, but it is also designed to convince Athenians to endorse Philip's panhellenic mission. Written versions of D.'s speeches may have been read by the same audience that read Isocrates, and they take the other side of the debate.[79] Considering that there was no precedent for the publication of Assembly speeches, perhaps it is easier to imagine D. himself taking the innovative step, rather than some later compiler. Written versions of D.'s Assembly speeches clearly came into circulation at some point, and the hypothesis that they were published by their author is at least as plausible as the alternatives. Abundant witnesses to this fact are lacking, but that is the case for much other fourth-century prose. It is widely assumed that written versions of forensic speeches and most works by Plato and Isocrates circulated in the fourth century, despite the lack of explicit testimonia.

---

[77] Dion. Hal. *Dem.* 53.3 = Dem. Phal. *FGrHist* 228 F 17b; [Plut.] *Mor.* 845b = Antiph. fr. 288 and Timocl. fr. 41 (K–A).

[78] On Hermippus as a compiler of earlier material, see Bollansée 1999: 118–41, who demonstrates that he preserves accurate historical material while rearranging and inventing detail for the sake of storytelling.

[79] Cf. [Plut.] *Mor.* 845c, where Philip is said to have compared the deliberative speeches of D. with the works of Isocrates.

## 4.2 Evidence from Papyri and MSS

The ancient and medieval manuscripts show that D.'s Assembly speeches against Philip were among the most widely read of his works and that they were gathered as a collection, probably in Athens before the third century. Although this material does not confirm or refute the hypothesis that D. published his speeches, an account of our understanding of the earliest written texts informs the inquiry. The medieval manuscripts provide a fuller view of the nature of the corpus, and thus it is easier to begin with them, before turning back chronologically to consider the papyri.

Some early medieval manuscripts of D. preserve marginal line counts and tallies (stichometry) measuring the length of individual works. These line counts originate from the practice of ancient scribes in Athens,[80] and they do not measure the actual written lineation of surviving manuscripts, but rather they count notional lines of a standard length based on the number of syllables in a line of hexameter poetry; they were transmitted in place from one manuscript to the next.[81] Furthermore, in accordance with the variation in the number of syllables in a hexameter, the stichometry varies among the works of D.: for some speeches a στίχος is 12 syllables, for others 15 or 16. D.'s works can thus be sorted into sub-groups; one group includes all the speeches about Philip, along with or. 13, 18–24, the *Prooemia*, and *Letters* 1–4.[82] These are D.'s most famous speeches, the Assembly speeches concerning Philip, the public trial speeches, including those in which D. defends his career, and the authentic biographical letters. The fact that these speeches were all counted by the same sized στίχος, together with the fact that they are D.'s best known and arguably most widely interesting works, suggests that they were packaged together as a collection in early book rolls. This group must have been gathered before the entire corpus had coalesced in Alexandria in the third century; for the full corpus includes works that lack stichometry, and it includes stichometric works based on differently sized line units. On the other hand, D. himself cannot have been responsible for the compilation of this sub-group, since it includes or. 7, which he did not write.

The papyri from Egypt attest to the ancient popularity of this sub-group.[83] Although none of the papyri for the Assembly speeches are

---

[80] The use of Athenian acrophonic numbers attests to the Athenian origins of the practice. See further Canevaro 2013a: 325–6. Despite its presence in the medieval manuscripts, stichometry is rarely found in the Egyptian papyri of Attic prose works; for an example see *P.Oxy.* 78.5151 (2nd cent. AD, D. 27.39).

[81] See further Canevaro 2013a: 10–11, 320–1, Obbink 1996: 62–3 n. 1.

[82] Goldstein 1968: 13–15.

[83] The preface in Dilts 2002 gives an inventory of published papyri: of the 160 unique papyri listed, only 23 contain fragments from works other than those belonging to this selection. The trend is maintained in more recently published

Hellenistic or earlier, they confirm that by the first or second century AD the speeches against Philip were regularly grouped together in collected bookrolls.[84] Similarly, in first-century BC Rome Cicero regarded D.'s speeches against Philip as a collected body of works, a σῶμα (*Att.* 2.1.3; cf. Introd. §5). Although the evidence is not compelling, these data perhaps corroborate, or are at least consistent with, the early circulation of a subgroup of D.'s works including the Assembly speeches, perhaps during D.'s lifetime and certainly before the middle of the third century.

## 4.3 *Indicators within the Speeches*

The best argument that the speeches were intended by D. for a reading public is to be found in the content of the speeches themselves. We have observed that they were chosen to reflect certain themes and periods of D.'s career (Introd. §2). Their style and content, too, point to deliberate preparation for an audience of readers.

All literary Greek prose from the late fifth and the fourth century contains elements of oral and written style; the distinction is difficult because the written texts to a greater or lesser extent contain performative elements and episodes, or strive to represent oral performances or conversations.[85] If we may posit, for the sake of analysis, a continuum from oral to written style, while acknowledging that all texts include an admixture of both, we may put the history of Thucydides and the tetralogies of Antiphon far on the "written" side of the line, as being among the clearest examples of texts that eschew orality and embrace a style meant for reading. Thucydides asserts that his work rejects entertaining performative elements (1.21.1), and we have seen that the consistently distinct style of his speeches reflects his own voice more than that of his speakers. Antiphon presents imaginary sets of four speeches representing both sides of legal cases specially concocted to illustrate a variety of argumentative approaches; the scenarios are extremely vague and they epitomize the difficulty of determining justice. (E.g., who is responsible if a coach instructs a thrower to hurl a javelin and a bystander who had strayed into the field is accidentally killed?)

The style of these texts presupposes an analytical reader: they are marked by complex sentences that often feature extended participial constructions or difficult variation in syntax, by bold usage of abstract expres-

---

papyri, such as the new items in *P.Oxy.* vol. 62; cf. Hernández Muñoz 2007.
  [84] Johnson 2004: 143–4 and Grusková 2009: 43–5, 51–2 consider *P.Oxy.* 15.1810 (2nd cent. AD), with fragments of or. 1–5, and *P.Oxy.* 62.4314 + *P.Oxy.* 70.4764 (1st/2nd cent. AD), with fragments of or. 1–4. The subscript at the end of or. 7 in MS S (see Introd. §6.1) attests to an ancient bookroll containing or. 1–4, 8, 7.
  [85] See further Thomas 2003.

sions, paraphrasing, and personification, and by unexpected and potentially confusing word order.[86] In contrast, epideictic display speeches crafted for performance are texts that could be considered more oral in nature; for example, Gorgias' live prose presentations were famous, and his style was "lively, clear, argumentative, demonstrative, syntactically uncomplicated, possibly even rhyming, with a strong first-person presence."[87]

D.'s Assembly speeches move between these broad stylistic categories. Like Gorgias, he mixes elevated diction with a conversational style (Introd. §3.5), often speaks in the first-person, and directly engages his audience with apostrophe and lively rhetorical questions (Introd. §3.3), and sometimes he cannot resist stylized sound effects (Introd. §3.2). On the other hand, some passages evince the sort of written style found in Thucydides and Antiphon; we have considered his use of complex subordination, syntactical variation, extreme hyperbaton, use of abstract expressions and extended paraphrases, and personification (Introd. §§3.1, 3.3, 3.4). These characteristics of his Assembly speeches, even if they are not as pervasive as in Thucydides or Antiphon's tetralogies, seem to show that he crafted them with an analytical reader in mind. And in fact the ancient critic Dionysius of Halicarnassus treats D. as a follower of Thucydides, while noting that D. includes an admixture of a simpler style (Dion. Hal. *Dem.* 9–10). Dionysius goes on to describe how D.'s written text impels a reader to reenact a live performance (21–2).[88]

Those who believe that the surviving Assembly speeches were not meant by their author to be read often point to further difficulties: the lengthy repetitions between *On the Chersonese* and the fourth *Philippic*,[89] the different versions of the third *Philippic*,[90] and the collection of sample speech beginnings, the *Prooemia* (1.1n.). But just as the difficulty in identifying contemporary testimonia for the circulation of written texts is not unusual, so too these aspects of the corpus have parallels among polished literary works. Orators did not avoid repeating themselves verbatim,[91] and they even borrowed wording from their peers and predecessors,[92] a practice that probably attests to the circulation of written versions of speeches. In other respects the Demosthenic corpus has affinities with the sophists,

---

[86] Gagarin 1997: 24–35, Rusten 1989: 21–8.
[87] Thomas 2003: 174. Cf. Gagarin 1998: 168–73, *GPS* 10–13.
[88] 3.23n. Cf. Hunter 2003: 215–18.    [89] D. 8.38–67 = 10.11–27, 55–70.
[90] This issue is discussed below (Introd. §6.2).
[91] E.g., Ant. 5.87–9 = 6.5–6. Cf. Dyck 2013: 93, who argues that repetitions in Cicero's *Pro Caelio* are not to be taken as evidence that it was unfinished and published posthumously.
[92] Cf. D. 27.2–3 and Is. 8.5; Hyp. *Against Diondas* 137v/136r 3 and D. 2.10; D. 18.177 and Hyp. *Against Diondas* 137r/136v 1; Lycurg. 1.48–50 and Dem. 60 with Maas 1928.

who embraced the emerging medium of the book. Plato's *Phaedrus* begins with a bookroll of Lysias' speech on love, an *Eroticus* (228b), and we find a similar speech in D.'s corpus (or. 61), quite possibly by D. himself.[93] Similarly, the *Prooemia* appear to follow an established sophistic tradition.[94]

We have observed that the three *Olynthiac* speeches are vague about their setting (Introd. §1.3); they do not illustrate the development of historical events, but instead experiment with different approaches to their circumstances. In the first *Olynthiac* D. stresses Philip's strength and develops the theme of opportunity, καιρός (see Introd. §2). In the second speech he completely dismisses Philip's strength and focuses on the theme of possibility, τὸ δυνατόν, for the Athenians. The third speech focuses on the political tradition in Athens, with a contrast between fifth- and fourth-century attitudes to war. The three speeches are complementary, and the interconnected themes and differences in emphasis bind them as a unit and create a varied and comprehensive appeal to a reader; this would be less effective for listeners who heard a single speech on one occasion.

## 5 THE AFTERLIFE OF THE SPEECHES

From antiquity to modern times, D.'s speeches, particularly the *Olynthiacs* and *Philippics*, have held a prominent and influential place in the history of rhetoric, and have been a core element in the educational curriculum. Although D. is best known as an orator and his speeches are usually read as rhetoric, at times, especially in the early Hellenistic period and much more recently, in the early twentieth century, D.'s political stance has attracted readers. D.'s popularity and influence can be seen in the sheer number of ancient papyri and medieval manuscripts,[95] in the frequent discussions of his works through the ages, and in the continued production of editions and translations from the Renaissance onward.

In the years after D.'s death in 322, he became a symbol for democratic independence and resistance to the Macedonian-backed rule of Demetrius of Phalerum (*LGPN* s.v. 448, *PAA* 312150) in Athens from 317 to 307. D.'s nephew Demochares (*LGPN* s.v. 31, *PAA* 321970) was a leading politician and opponent of Demetrius, and in 280/79 he passed a motion for an honorary statue of D. in the Agora in recognition of his role as a

---

[93] Cf. MacDowell 2009: 29.
[94] Yunis 1996: 288 n. 4 collects the evidence for similar collections made by Antiphon, Critias, and Thrasymachus.
[95] The *Leuven Database of Ancient Books* (www.trismegistos.org/ldab, accessed August 11, 2017) provides data on published papyri; more papyri of D. survive than of any other author save Homer and Euripides. Similarly, Homer and D. are the best attested classical authors in the medieval period; for a catalogue of 279 manuscripts of D., see Canfora 1968: 31–71.

## 5 THE AFTERLIFE OF THE SPEECHES

political leader for the cause of freedom and democracy.[96] D.'s role as a democratic model put him at odds with Demetrius, who fashioned himself as a Peripatetic philosopher. We have seen how D. was criticized for his reliance on study and preparation (Introd. §4.1), and that characterization of him developed in philosophical circles during the Hellenistic period, when he came to represent the paradigm of a speaker of inferior natural talent succeeding through diligence.[97]

At the same time, D.'s attention to detail came to be admired by critics of rhetoric and students of history, who looked back to the classical Athenian democracy as an ideal setting for political oratory, the type of political venue that had disappeared under the Hellenistic kings. Different aspects of this tradition are represented now by the works of Didymus of Alexandria and Dionysius of Halicarnassus (both active late first cent. BC). Didymus gives a sample of ancient scholarship on D. He is reported to have written some 4000 bookrolls of critical studies.[98] A copy of one of these rolls survives, containing extensive fragments of a commentary on D.'s Assembly speeches.[99] Didymus is especially interested in historical material contained in the speeches, but he also discusses vocabulary and questions of authenticity and classification.[100] He refers to earlier studies of D. and cites numerous other sources, most of which do not survive: historians, poets, biographers, political theorists, collectors of proverbs.[101] He confirms that D. was widely read and studied during the Hellenistic period.

Dionysius represents a different strand of interest in D. His essays focus on D.'s language and style. He refers to D. often in several of his critical essays, and devotes one of his longest treatises to him. In *On Demosthenes* he presents D. as a master stylist and shows how he is distinct from other authors in his ability to move among, and combine elements from, a variety of styles, ranging between the polar extremes of simple style (represented by Lysias) and grand style (exemplified by Thucydides).[102] He is interested in the language and the speeches for their own sake, and does not dwell on the type of historical or scholarly questions that Didymus addresses. He offers close readings of passages from D.'s Assembly speeches (3.23n., 4.30n.), showing sensitivity to argument, imagery, and rhythm. He demonstrates D.'s central position in the study of literature, and his focus on D. as the premier Attic orator is echoed in a host of

---

[96] [Plut.] *Mor.* 851c ἄλλων πολλῶν καὶ καλῶν τῶι δήμωι συμβούλωι γεγονότι καὶ πεπολιτευμένωι τῶν καθ' ἑαυτὸν πρὸς ἐλευθερίαν καὶ δημοκρατίαν ἄριστα. See MacDowell 2009: 424–6 and Habicht 1997: 139.
[97] Cooper 2000: 225–9, 2009.
[98] Montana 2015: 172, Reynolds and Wilson 2013: 17–18.
[99] The papyrus preserves notes on or. 9–11 and 13.
[100] Harding 2006: 9–13 provides a helpful overview.
[101] Gibson 2002: 35–8 surveys his sources.   [102] Wooten 1989: 576–81.

rhetorical works from the first century BC onward, which take many of their quotations from D., and especially from the Assembly speeches.[103] Cicero provides the fullest illustration of D.'s emerging reputation as the leading Greek orator in mid-first-century BC Rome. Early in his career, Cicero identified the collected Assembly speeches as a document of D.'s political leadership and as a generic model for written versions of his own speeches (Cic. *Att.* 2.1.3). Later, as the political situation in Rome became more fraught after Caesar's victory in the Civil War, Cicero presented himself in his works on rhetorical theory and oratory as a new D., standing up for democratic principles in the face of tyrannical aggression.[104] He pointed to the likeness by titling his speeches against the triumvir Marcus Antonius as *Philippics*, and beyond the political parallels, in his later rhetorical works he identifies D. as the orator *par excellence*.[105] Both men were further linked by the political changes that their states saw in the aftermath of their deaths – Athens became subordinate to Macedon in foreign and military matters, and the Roman Republic was transformed into an imperial state – and the tradition connecting them developed as those changes in Rome became more apparent during the first century AD.[106]

By the end of the first century D. is firmly established as foremost of the Attic orators, a master of rhetoric whose career fortunately coincided with a historical period that allowed his brilliance to shine, and from this perspective he is regularly paired with Cicero. Quintilian takes it for granted that D. is the most perfect of the Greek orators (10.1.76, 10.2.24) and treats Cicero as his Roman counterpart (2.5.16, 10.1.105). Similarly, the speakers in Tacitus' *Dialogus* assume D.'s primacy (25.3, 32.5) and observe that he and Cicero rose to the greatest heights because of the political turmoil all around them (37.6). Quintilian quotes the Assembly speeches (6.5.7, 9.4.63; cf. 3.8.65), and Tacitus' stress on political circumstances implies that the characters in his dialogue recall D. primarily in his role as political advisor to the Assembly. This tradition culminates in direct comparisons of D. and Cicero: ps.-Longinus distinguishes different elements in the sublime effect of their styles (12.4); Plutarch pairs extensive biographies of the two orators, who are linked not only by their stature as speakers and by the political setting of their careers, but also by biographical details such as the loss of a daughter and political exile, and

---

[103] E.g., Hermogenes of Tarsus (2nd cent. AD) cites D. more often than any other author; cf. 3.22n. προπέποται, 3.30n. τότε. For abundant examples of quotations of D. among Greek rhetorical critics, lexicographers, and grammarians, see the apparatus of testimonia in Dilts 2002.
[104] Bishop 2016.
[105] Ramsey 2003: 17–18. For the development of Cicero's turn to D. as a model, see Wooten 1983: 46–57.
[106] Bishop 2015: 284–94.

## 5 THE AFTERLIFE OF THE SPEECHES

by fundamental aspects of their temperaments (Plut. *Dem.* 3.2–4).[107] For Plutarch, it is the boldness of D.'s Assembly speeches that is the basis for his rhetorical eminence (*Dem.* 12.3–4).

D.'s speeches continued to be read and studied in the centuries after Plutarch. Harpocration's *Lexicon of the ten orators* confirms that there was an interested readership in the second century.[108] Later, the hypotheses, or short summaries, of the speeches produced by Libanius in fourth-century Antioch are evidence of a continued interest in the individual speeches, arising from a growing movement toward classical rhetorical models, and Themistius records that D. was on the standard syllabus in fourth-century Byzantium.[109] D. and the material he addressed appear as topics in declamations from this period, fictional speeches composed as part of rhetorical education; students would compose accounts of the pitiful fate of the citizens of Olynthus after the city fell to Philip.[110] In fact, D.'s central place in schools reaches from the Hellenistic period through to the modern era. In the Greek east he is regularly cited in scholia as "the orator", the prose counterpart to Homer "the poet", and his status is confirmed in written accounts of what was read and by the existence of multiple manuscripts of carefully produced full editions of the corpus already by the tenth century.[111] His Assembly speeches appear prominently in accounts throughout the Byzantine period; the texts were read as examples of deliberative rhetoric and Attic dialect.[112]

In the west, knowledge of Greek was increasingly rare in the era following the move of the capital to Byzantium in the fourth century.[113] At the end of the fourteenth century, the eastern diplomat Manuel Chrysoloras began teaching Greek to Italian humanists, and the fifteenth century saw a rebirth of attention and awareness of Greek texts in Italy.[114] This interest in Greek authors developed as a corollary of the study of better-known Latin writers, and Italian intellectuals turned quickly to D., following the direction of Cicero, who had translated *On the Crown*. The early humanists focused especially on D.'s two speeches against Aeschines; new

---

[107] Plutarch structures the lives around these parallels: Lintott 2013: 11–15.
[108] For Harpocration's date see Gibson 2002: 137, Keaney 1991: ix–xi. For his references to the Assembly speeches, see 4.34n. τήν, 4.40n. προβάλλεσθαι, 4.46n. ὅταν, 9.20n. ἐάν, 9.44n. ἀλλ', 9.59n. Εὐφραῖος.
[109] On Libanius' frequent mentions of D., see Cribiore 2013: 108–9; cf. Reynolds and Wilson 2013: 51–2, Wilson 1996: 28, 1.19n. στρατιωτικά, 2.19n. Καλλίαν, 3.11n. τούς. On Themistius see Wilson 1996: 50.
[110] D. A. Russell 1983: 118–19.
[111] Reynolds and Wilson 2013: 67, Wilson 1996: 24, 138.
[112] Wilson 1996: 72, 141–2, 168–71, 185, 188–9.
[113] On the rare instances in which specific Greek texts, mainly philosophic and scientific, were known in the west, see Reynolds and Wilson 2013: 120–2.
[114] Reynolds and Wilson 2013: 148–9.

translations appeared and lectures were given in fifteenth-century Florence and Rome, and the foundation was laid for a Greek curriculum focused on Homer and D., a core that remained central until the twentieth century.[115] The Assembly speeches make an appearance too, when the Greek cardinal Bessarion, living in Rome, translated the first *Olynthiac* and made an explicit analogy between fourth-century Athens and current circumstances as part of an appeal to westerners to join a crusade against the Ottomans.[116] This turn from the speeches against Aeschines to the Assembly orations anticipates the culminating moment of the new western revival of interest in D., the publication of the first printed edition by Aldus Manutius in 1504 in Venice, which included all the texts now preserved, accompanied by the synopses of Libanius and Plutarch's biography.[117] Aldus' preface recognized the contemporary political currency of the Assembly speeches; he quotes three passages from the first *Olynthiac* and second *Philippic* as he presents D.'s campaign against the tyranny of Philip as a model for his addressee, who was influential in resisting the Ottomans in Greece.[118]

In the sixteenth century D. continued to be read widely as a Greek stylist, and occasionally invoked as a political model. Most notably, the first English translation of any of D.'s speeches, by Thomas Wilson in 1570, prefaced the *Olynthiacs* with an explicit comparison of Elizabethan England and fourth-century Athens and a call for English unity both against internal dangers and the threat posed by Philip II of Spain.[119] Wilson was a student of the first Regius Professor of Greek at Cambridge, John Cheke, who produced Latin translations of D.'s Assembly speeches, as did his successor in that chair, Nicholas Carr; they were part of a wider circle of intellectuals closely linked with the cause of the Reformation and the court of Elizabeth I, and in D.'s works they focused especially on the ideal of patriotic political policy in an environment of treachery.[120] This circle illustrates the close link between academic study of oratory and public careers in politics that flourished under parliamentary democracy. The trend developed together with the British empire; new translations by and for an elite political class continued to appear in the eighteenth century and in Victorian England, and speeches in Parliament conspicuously referred to and emulated classical oratory, D. in particular.[121] More broadly, British liberalism of the nineteenth century idealized classical

[115] Wilson 2017: 40; cf. 19, 56, 79–80, 90–1.
[116] Wilson 2017: 67, who quotes Bessarion's paraphrase of D. 2.23 as part of this appeal.
[117] Wilson 2017: 150–1.   [118] D. 1.5, 6.21, and 6.24–5; Wilson 2016: 186–91.
[119] Blanshard and Sowerby 2005: 55–8, Harding 1979: 52–7.
[120] Blanshard and Sowerby 2005: 68–72, Harding 2000: 252–4, 1979: 58–61.
[121] Harding 2000: 254–5, Jenkyns 1980: 62; for a catalogue of translations, see Schindel 1963: 223–4. For a similar trend in the US, cf. Adams 1927: 164–72. And

## 5 THE AFTERLIFE OF THE SPEECHES

Athenian democracy, and this attitude is best reflected in the *History of Greece* written by the English banker George Grote, published in eight volumes between 1846 and 1856.[122] For Grote, D. is a prescient democratic hero who foresaw the danger posed to Athens by Philip, and whose Assembly proposals were wise and practicable. Grote follows D. in viewing the δῆμος as lazy and negligent, and he blames them for their losses to Philip.[123]

Interest in D. in the German states of the early modern period began with a similar trajectory, but then went in a different direction. In 1495 Johannes Reuchlin translated the first *Olynthiac* as part of an effort to inspire a united position among German leaders against Charles VIII of France, and later he translated the first and second *Philippics*.[124] This aspirational admiration for D. continued into the nineteenth century, when it became tempered by a nationalistic perspective that saw Philip as a model who unified weak states into a powerful single nation. This paradoxical approval of both D. and Philip is most clearly seen in Barthold Georg Niebuhr, who translated the first *Philippic* in 1805 and presented the speech as a call for opposition to Napoleon, while praising Philip in his academic lectures as an antecedent for Frederick II of Prussia.[125] Later in the nineteenth century the first comprehensive modern academic accounts appeared. Arnold Schaefer's *Demosthenes und seine Zeit* was published in three volumes between 1856 and 1858.[126] It is a monumental account of D.'s role in fourth-century political and military history, and its detailed attention to difficult particulars remains invaluable; its perspective is the idealization of D. as a heroic leader, and the narrative is sometimes distorted by the focus on D. as a central figure, whose moral compass guides him through the vicissitudes of the fourth century.[127] Not long after, Friedrich Blass's massive *Die attische Beredsamkeit* included a volume first published in 1877 with more than 600 pages devoted to literary analysis of D., giving detailed attention to rhetorical technique, rhythm, and prose style and featuring full discussions of every speech.[128]

While in England at the start of the twentieth century there was admiration for Athenian democracy and eloquent individual orators, a

---

for a wider range of attitudes toward D. in eighteenth-century France, see Carlier 1990: 289–91 and the catalogue of editions and translations in Schindel 1963: 219.
[122] On Grote and Athenian democracy, see Nippel 2015: 251–9, Liddel 2014: 235–43, Roberts 1994: 238–46.
[123] For Grote's reliance on D.'s speeches to the Assembly as an exclusive source, see his 1821 essay on Athenian government (Buckler et al. 1996).
[124] Harding 2000: 258, 1979: 54–5, Adams 1927: 135–6.
[125] Briant 2017: 264–8, Nippel 2015: 190, Lehmann 2004: 222.
[126] Schaefer 1885–7.
[127] Cf. Harding 2000: 257, Jaeger 1938: 4, 57.
[128] Blass 1893.

contemporary German intellectual trend expressed antipathy to ancient and modern democracies and vilified D. as a corrupt demagogue who led Athens to ruin and stood in the way of the rise of a Hellenic nation under the leadership of Philip and Alexander. This hostile perspective is exemplified especially in Engelbert Drerup's *Aus einer alten Advokatenrepublik*, an aggressive attack published during the First World War that developed positions earlier articulated in the late nineteenth-century histories of Eduard Meyer and Karl Julius Beloch.[129] Drerup introduces his account with an impassioned denunciation of politicians in France and England, whom he sees as modern-day counterparts to D.[130] On the other side, the first extended historical study of D. in English was published by A. W. Pickard-Cambridge in 1914, who celebrated D. as the last defender of freedom in Greece; he presents his hero almost "as if he had been formally elected Prime Minister," and he is frequently critical of Beloch's narrative.[131] After the war, the former French Prime Minister Georges Clemenceau wrote an exuberant eulogy of D. couched in terms of the recent conflict: "[The *Philippics* are] formidable bursts of oratorical artillery fire, the object of which was to dislodge the enemy from all his positions at the beginning of battle."[132]

Interest in D. and his Assembly speeches declined in the years following the First World War, but D. still served as a political touchstone during the rise of fascism in Germany and Italy. Piero Treves revived Pickard-Cambridge's perspective and published *Demostene e la libertà greca* in 1933, before leaving Italy as a political exile. Werner Jaeger's 1934 Sather lectures illustrate changing attitudes toward D., as he begins with an apology for choosing to discuss a failed politician whose policy and reputation have fallen from favor.[133] Jaeger himself was caught between two sides. He had chosen his topic and drafted his manuscript in Germany in the early 1930s, and he did not make substantial changes after he moved to the US, where he published his *Demosthenes* in English in 1938, prior to a German version that appeared in Berlin in 1939; the work itself blends perspectives by rejecting Drerup's criticism of D.'s political influence while playing fast and loose with the historical background to present D. as an idealistic, even heroic, figure, to be viewed against the backdrop of an emerging world culture.[134] Despite their differences, both Jaeger and Treves were attacked and mocked by reviewers in Germany and Italy.[135]

[129] Nippel 2015: 308–9, Brun 2015: 52–4, Lehmann 2004: 223–4.
[130] Drerup 1916: 1–2; cf. Pernot 2006: 116–21.
[131] Pickard-Cambridge 1914: 298 (quotation); 169, 207, 356, 405, 421.
[132] Clemenceau 1926: 74. See further Pernot 2006: 122–7, Carlier 1990: 296–8.
[133] Jaeger 1938: 1.
[134] On Jaeger's chronology, the different directions of the two versions, and the historical distortions, see Badian 1992.
[135] For comparisons of the two and the reception of their work on D., see Canfora

More recently, D.'s Assembly speeches have received close attention from historians who recognize their importance for the understanding of political and military developments, and who at the same time urge caution against the biases and distortions represented in them.[136] Whereas previous eras focused on D.'s Assembly oratory, the last generation has been more interested in forensic speeches; these have been mined as sources for Athenian morality and social history, and they form the core of primary source material for much recent work on Athenian law.[137] D.'s Assembly speeches no longer hold a central place in the curriculum, as can be seen from the fact that the last detailed philological commentary on them as a group was composed before the First World War.[138] Still, very recently there has been a resurgence of interest in D. (and other orators). The last decade has seen biographies of D. for the general reader in English, French, and German, the first English translations of the deliberative orations in more than a generation, and the first comprehensive literary study of D.'s oratory since Blass.[139]

## 6 THE TEXT

### *6.1 Witnesses to the Text*

Whether D. himself was responsible for publishing his speeches, or someone else put them into circulation after his death, a full corpus resembling our modern collection was compiled in the third century in Alexandria.[140] This did not, however, establish a definitive text, to judge from the variations in phrasing and sequence of speeches in the surviving witnesses. These comprise three distinct types: (1) papyrus and parchment manuscript fragments surviving from ancient Egypt, ranging in date from the 1st cent. BC to the 6th cent. AD, (2) quotations in ancient authors, and (3) MSS from medieval Europe, dating from the 9th to the 15th cent. AD.

The medieval MSS provide the fullest view of the variations in the text and corpus. The 279 witnesses divide into four families; each family is represented by an early medieval MS, and these are abbreviated as SAFY in standard critical editions: S = Paris, *Bibliothèque nationale de France* ms.

2009: 174–7 and cf. Brun 2015: 60–2.
[136] E.g., Cawkwell 2011: 369–96, *HM*, Harris, Sealey.
[137] *GPM* xi–xii, 5–6, Todd 1990, E. M. Harris 2013b: 381–6.
[138] Sandys 1897 and Sandys 1913. More recent commentaries are selective and specialized: McQueen 1986 focuses on grammatical explanation in the *Olynthiacs*, Wooten on the rhetorical tradition of the *Philippics*.
[139] MacDowell 2009. Translations: Trevett 2011, Waterfield 2014: 3–67. Biographies: Worthington 2013, Brun 2015, Will 2013.
[140] See further Introd. §4. Callimachus, the compiler of the Alexandrian edition, included two non-Demosthenic speeches that remain in the corpus as it survives today, and he also included at least two speeches that do not survive: Dilts 2002: v.

34 INTRODUCTION

gr. 2934 (9th/10th cent.); A = Munich, *Bayerische Staatsbibliothek* cod. gr. 485 (10th cent.); F = Venice, *Biblioteca Nazionale Marciana* Marc. gr. 416 (10th cent.); Y = Paris, *Bibliothèque nationale de France* ms. gr. 2935 (10th cent.).[141] These four MSS present the speeches in different sequences (our modern numeration is based on F), and they sometimes offer a range of wordings that are all plausibly Demosthenic. Thus at 2.3 S and Y read ἔχειν φιλοτιμίαν, F ἔχειν φιλοτιμίαν τινά and A τινα ἔχειν φιλοτιμίαν; many of the variations reported in this volume's apparatus are of this sort, where there is not a single authoritative reading to be distinguished from obvious corruptions. Earlier witnesses are not decisive, in that ancient papyri and quotations display the same sort of variations and inconsistently agree now with one, now with another family.[142] So at 3.31 SFY read χρήματα συμμάχους and A reads χρήματα καὶ συμμάχους; one ancient quotation (by Hermogenes) agrees with SFY, others (Aristides and an anonymous critic) with A. And at 4.4 the A and Y families read ἡμῖν, as does an ancient quotation and a papyrus, while S and F and another papyrus read ὑμῖν.

The textual evidence thus indicates that there were different versions in circulation from an early date. Most of the differences are quite small. The most significant textual variants, in terms of length and content, occur in the third *Philippic*, and in this case, and perhaps elsewhere too, these alternative versions appear to originate from D. himself, who may have preserved various written versions of speeches, intended for different audiences of listeners and readers.

## 6.2 *Two Versions of the Third* Philippic

In 17 places the oldest medieval MS (S) presents a shorter version of the text of the third *Philippic* than do other early MSS; in 15 of these cases, the longer version appears in a later hand in the margin.[143] In the present edition these 15 passages are printed in the main text in smaller type, with a note in the apparatus ("om. d"); the two passages not preserved in S at all (in §§20, 65) are noted in the apparatus. The following table lists all 17 passages and the MSS in which they appear (S[mg] = marginalia in S):[144]

§2 οὐκοῦν ... ἔχειν                    S[mg]AFY
§§6–7 εἰ μὲν οὖν ἅπαντες ... πολεμεῖν δεῖ   S[mg]AFY
§20 καὶ τοῖς ... ἀποστεῖλαι              AFY

---

[141] Dilts 2002: ix–xii, MacDowell 1990: 48–57, Canfora 1968: 45, 48–50, 64.
[142] For details see Muñoz Flórez 2012, 2007, Hatzilambrou in *P.Oxy.* 70 (p. 30), Pasquali 1962: 281–8.
[143] The marginal additions range in date from "early" to the 15th cent.; see Sandys 1913: lix–lx.
[144] Manuscript readings for SAFY only, as reported by Fuhr 1914; the reports in Dilts 2002 and Butcher 1903 are less full and sometimes contradictory.

## 6 THE TEXT 35

§26 καὶ τοῦτ᾽ ... δεῖξαι     S^mgAFY
§32 κύριος ... μέτεστι     S^mgAFY
§37 οὐδὲν ... ἀλλ᾽ ὅτι     S^mgAF
§37 καὶ παραίτησις ... συγγνώμη     S^mgAF
§38 καὶ τοῖς μηδὲν ἐθέλουσι ... πραττόντων     S^mgAF
§39 συγγνώμη τοῖς ἐλεγχομένοις     S^mgAFY
§§41–2 οὐχ ἵνα ... τὰ γράμματα     S^mgAFY
§44 ἀλλ᾽ οὐ τοῦτο λέγει     S^mgAFY
§44 ἀλλ᾽ εὐαγὲς ᾖι τὸ ἀποκτεῖναι     S^mgAF
§46 ἴστ᾽ αὐτοί ... τίνος     S^mgAFY
§58 τότε μὲν πέμψας ... Παρμενίωνος     S^mgAFY
§65 καὶ τοὺς ... τὴν πόλιν     S^mgA
§65 καὶ προέσθαι ... τινάς     AFY
§71 πανταχοῖ ... καταστρέψασθαι     S^mgAFY

Each of the two versions has strong MS authority, and each was in circulation from an early date. The shorter version was used to calculate the stichometric line counts in S, attesting to its currency before the third century BC,[145] and one papyrus, like S, writes the short text and adds the long text in the margin.[146] The longer version appears in other ancient papyri.[147] Harpocration's *Lexicon* shows awareness of both versions.[148] The content of both versions appears to be Demosthenic. The prose rhythm of the added passages is entirely consistent with D.'s normal practice.[149] One addition makes a well-informed and subtle point about Athenian law, and others present accurate historical detail.[150] There is no reason to doubt Demosthenic authorship of both versions.[151]

It is not clear that one version precedes the other (in this section "addition" refers to the placement of the longer passages in the margins of S, regardless of whether they were originally additions to the short version or whether the short version was the result of "subtraction" from an original longer version), but one attractive hypothesis suggests that the longer version is a script for delivery in the Assembly, the shorter an abridged

---

[145] Sandys 1913: lxiii–lxiv; cf. Introd. §4.2.    [146] *P.Fay.* 8 (2nd cent. AD; D. 9.39).
[147] *P.Oxy.* 62.4333 (3rd cent. AD; D. 9.32), *P.Mich.* 918 (4th cent. AD; D. 9.65).
[148] Harp. Δ 85 and Υ 5, s.vv. δυσωποῦμαι and ὑπάγουσιν, refer to the longer version of D. 9.65. For the shorter version, see 9.44n. ἀλλ᾽.
[149] McCabe 1981: 170.
[150] 9.37n. καί; 9.58, 71 with Sealey 234 (who discusses an additional passage in 9.72 that should be regarded as a scribal note, rather than a Demosthenic variant, since it does not appear in the main text of any early manuscript; see the apparatus in Fuhr 1914).
[151] The Demosthenic prose rhythm and technical content outweigh rhetorical and stylistic arguments against D.'s authorship of the additions (most fully expressed in Bühler 1978).

version for readership outside Athens.[152] In many cases the longer version presents brief parenthetic assertions that do not change the argument (§§2, 26, 37, 38, 39, 44, 65); at other points further examples are adduced (§§32, 58, 71). However, if in fact the shorter version is a revision, it does not appear to have been completed carefully; in a few places its argument is abrupt or difficult to follow:

- Some critics regard the material in §§6–7 as an alternative for §8. This suggestion arises from textual difficulties in §7 and similarities in phrasing and argument between §§6–7 and §8. But §9 does not flow well from §7 (cf. Wooten 168–9), and perhaps in this instance, the longest variant passage in the speech, the omission is an accident of transmission (see Dilts 2002: xvi n. 29).
- The material in §§41–2 seems necessary to introduce the direct quotation in §42.
- In §46 the argument of the shorter version is unclear; with the sequence ἀλλὰ πῶς; εἴπω κελεύετε; καὶ οὐκ ὀργιεῖσθε; D. seems about to discuss examples of the Athenians' current tolerance of corruption, but instead the speech moves in a different direction beginning in §47. The longer version provides a smoother flow; D. explains that the Athenians know how things now stand, and that he does not need to discuss this topic further. Critics have suggested that the revision of the shorter version is unfinished here (Sandys 1913: lxvi, cf. Wooten 172).

The third *Philippic* provides a rare instance of multiple versions of a text by an ancient author. The speech was a major success for D. (cf. Introd. §1.3), and it is easy to imagine why he may have devoted special effort to its circulation. The MSS appear to attest to his continued work on the speech after its delivery.[153]

### 6.3 *The Text and Apparatus in This Volume*

The text here is based on the most recent critical edition (Dilts 2002). That edition relied on the primary MSS surveyed above (and later secondary MSS as needed to supplement and reconstruct lacunae or damage in the primary MSS); it also considers the numerous papyrus fragments published prior to 2002.[154] Various other critical editions provide additional reports on MS readings.[155]

---

[152] Wooten 167–8, with references to earlier discussions.
[153] Cf. Heslin 2016: 505–9, who questions the modern expectation of an authoritative single version of an ancient text composed in an era of handwritten books.
[154] Several relevant papyri were published in 1995 in *P.Oxy.* 62 (nos. 4310–33). Since 2002, nine more papyri for these speeches have appeared in *P.Oxy.* 70 (nos. 4763–71); this volume reports readings from these at 2.30.
[155] Hernández Muñoz 2014 (or. 9), 2012 (or. 4), Fuhr 1914, Butcher 1903.

# 6 THE TEXT

The text aims to represent the version (or versions) that circulated as written works (cf. Introd. §4). Those written versions must have differed considerably from the speeches presented to the Athenian Assembly. Whatever D. may have said there is lost, but a rich tradition preserves the written text of these works. Until recently, editors conflated these two strands, and adjusted the text of these speeches to fit their expectations for oral delivery. For example, Blass and later editors frequently insert a nu ἐφελκυστικόν (Smyth §134) or adopt elision in order to avoid a sequence of short syllables; more drastically, they change word order or adopt conjectures for similar reasons. Often these changes disregarded a consensus in the MSS (usually in cases of *scriptio plena*, i.e., a juxtaposition of final- and initial-vowels between two words, as opposed to hiatus), and usually that reading was not reported. As a result, it has been impossible to learn from modern editions what text the MSS actually transmit when it comes to matters of rhythm. The edition of Dilts follows the practice of MacDowell, who collated many MSS and prints their readings when there is consensus.[156] The resulting text, which is adopted here too, differs from earlier editions very frequently.

The textual apparatus is highly selective; for further information and details see Dilts 2002 and Fuhr 1914.[157] Because the papyri align with the family-divisions of the medieval MSS, both types of witnesses are grouped together in the apparatus. In the apparatus the following abbreviations are employed:

D      A reading found in all medieval MSS and fragments of ancient papyri that are direct witnesses to the text.

d      A reading found in one or more ancient and/or medieval manuscripts, but which is not the unanimous reading of all direct witnesses to the text.

i      Indirect tradition by quotation in antiquity.

c      Modern editorial conjecture.

---

[156] Dilts 2002: xvii–xviii, MacDowell 1990: 80–2.
[157] Dilts gives recent reports for papyri, and he offers abundant references to the indirect traditions. Fuhr gives the fullest report of the primary MSS.

# 1 ΟΛΥΝΘΙΑΚΟΣ Α

(1) ἀντὶ πολλῶν ἄν, ὦ ἄνδρες Ἀθηναῖοι, χρημάτων ὑμᾶς ἑλέσθαι νομίζω, εἰ φανερὸν γένοιτο τὸ μέλλον συνοίσειν τῆι πόλει περὶ ὧν νυνὶ σκοπεῖτε. ὅτε τοίνυν τοῦθ' οὕτως ἔχει, προσήκει προθύμως ἐθέλειν ἀκούειν τῶν βουλομένων συμβουλεύειν· οὐ γὰρ μόνον εἴ τι χρήσιμον ἐσκεμμένος ἥκει τις, τοῦτο ἂν ἀκούσαντες λάβοιτε, ἀλλὰ καὶ τῆς ὑμετέρας τύχης ὑπολαμβάνω πολλὰ τῶν δεόντων ἐκ τοῦ παραχρῆμα ἐνίοις ἂν ἐπελθεῖν εἰπεῖν, ὥστ' ἐξ ἁπάντων ῥαιδίαν τὴν τοῦ συμφέροντος ὑμῖν αἵρεσιν γενέσθαι.

(2) ὁ μὲν οὖν παρὼν καιρός, ὦ ἄνδρες Ἀθηναῖοι, μόνον οὐχὶ λέγει φωνὴν ἀφιεὶς ὅτι τῶν πραγμάτων ὑμῖν ἐκείνων αὐτοῖς ἀντιληπτέον ἐστίν, εἴπερ ὑπὲρ σωτηρίας αὐτῶν φροντίζετε· ἡμεῖς δ' οὐκ οἶδ' ὅντινά μοι δοκοῦμεν ἔχειν τρόπον πρὸς αὐτά. ἔστι δὴ τά γ' ἐμοὶ δοκοῦντα, ψηφίσασθαι μὲν ἤδη τὴν βοήθειαν καὶ παρασκευάσασθαι τὴν ταχίστην ὅπως ἐνθένδε βοηθήσετε (καὶ μὴ πάθητε ταὐτὸν ὅπερ καὶ πρότερον), πρεσβείαν δὲ πέμπειν, ἥτις ταῦτ' ἐρεῖ καὶ παρέσται τοῖς πράγμασιν· (3) ὡς ἔστι μάλιστα τοῦτο δέος, μὴ πανοῦργος ὢν καὶ δεινὸς ἄνθρωπος πράγμασι χρῆσθαι, τὰ μὲν εἴκων, ἡνίκα ἂν τύχηι, τὰ δ' ἀπειλῶν (ἀξιόπιστος δ' ἂν εἰκότως φαίνοιτο), τὰ δ' ἡμᾶς διαβάλλων καὶ τὴν ἀπουσίαν τὴν ἡμετέραν, τρέψηται καὶ παρασπάσηταί τι τῶν ὅλων πραγμάτων. (4) οὐ μὴν ἀλλ' ἐπιεικῶς, ὦ ἄνδρες Ἀθηναῖοι, τοῦθ' ὃ δυσμαχώτατόν ἐστι τῶν Φιλίππου πραγμάτων, καὶ βέλτιστον ὑμῖν· τὸ γὰρ εἶναι πάντων ἐκεῖνον ἕνα ὄντα κύριον καὶ ῥητῶν καὶ ἀπορρήτων καὶ ἅμα στρατηγὸν καὶ δεσπότην καὶ ταμίαν, καὶ πανταχοῦ αὐτὸν παρεῖναι τῶι στρατεύματι, πρὸς μὲν τὸ τὰ τοῦ πολέμου ταχὺ καὶ κατὰ καιρὸν πράττεσθαι πολλῶι προέχει, πρὸς δὲ τὰς καταλλαγάς, ἃς ἂν ἐκεῖνος ποιήσαιτο ἄσμενος πρὸς Ὀλυνθίους, ἐναντίως ἔχει. (5) δῆλον γάρ ἐστι τοῖς Ὀλυνθίοις ὅτι νῦν οὐ περὶ δόξης οὐδ' ὑπὲρ μέρους χώρας πολεμοῦσιν, ἀλλ' ἀναστάσεως καὶ ἀνδραποδισμοῦ τῆς πατρίδος, καὶ ἴσασιν ἅ τ' Ἀμφιπολιτῶν ἐποίησε τοὺς παραδόντας αὐτῶι τὴν πόλιν καὶ Πυδναίων τοὺς ὑποδεξαμένους· καὶ ὅλως ἄπιστον, οἶμαι, ταῖς πολιτείαις ἡ τυραννίς, ἄλλως τε κἂν ὅμορον χώραν ἔχωσι. (6) ταῦτ' οὖν ἐγνωκότας ὑμᾶς, ὦ ἄνδρες Ἀθηναῖοι, καὶ τἆλλ' ἃ προσήκει πάντα ἐνθυμουμένους φημὶ δεῖν ἐθελῆσαι καὶ παροξυνθῆναι καὶ τῶι πολέμωι προσέχειν εἴπερ ποτὲ καὶ νῦν, χρήματα εἰσφέροντας προθύμως καὶ αὐτοὺς ἐξιόντας καὶ μηδὲν ἐλλείποντας. οὐδὲ γὰρ λόγος οὐδὲ σκῆψις ἔθ' ὑμῖν τοῦ μὴ τὰ δέοντα ποιεῖν ἐθέλειν ὑπολείπεται. (7) νυνὶ γάρ, ὃ πάντες ἐθρύλουν τέως, Ὀλυνθίους ἐκπολεμῶσαι δεῖ Φιλίππωι, γέγονεν αὐτόματον, καὶ ταῦτα ὡς ἂν ὑμῖν μάλιστα συμφέροι. εἰ μὲν γὰρ ὑφ' ὑμῶν πεισθέντες ἀνείλοντο τὸν

---

2 βοηθήσετε d: βοηθήσητε d    3 ἄνθρωπος c: ἄνθρωπος D    τρέψηται D: καταστρέψηται c: ἀνατρέψηι te c: κλέψηι te c: alii alia    5 πολεμοῦσιν D: κινδυνεύουσιν i    7 ἐθρύλουν τέως d: ἐθρυλεῖτε ὡς d: ἐθρύλλουν τε d: ἐθρύλλουν ὡς i

39

πόλεμον, σφαλεροί σύμμαχοι καί μέχρι του ταΰτ' ἂν ἐγνωκότες ἦσαν ἴσως· ἐπειδή δὲ ἐκ τῶν πρὸς αὑτοὺς ἐγκλημάτων μισοῦσι, βεβαίαν εἰκὸς τὴν ἔχθραν αὐτοὺς ὑπὲρ ὧν φοβοῦνται καὶ πεπόνθασιν ἔχειν. (8) οὐ δεῖ δὴ τοιοῦτον, ὦ ἄνδρες Ἀθηναῖοι, παραπεπτωκότα καιρὸν ἀφεῖναι, οὐδὲ παθεῖν ταὐτὸ ὅπερ ἤδη πολλάκις πρότερον πεπόνθατε. εἰ γάρ, ὅθ' ἥκομεν Εὐβοεῦσιν βεβοηθηκότες καὶ παρῆσαν Ἀμφιπολιτῶν Ἱέραξ καὶ Στρατοκλῆς ἐπὶ τουτὶ τὸ βῆμα, κελεύοντες ἡμᾶς πλεῖν καὶ παραλαμβάνειν τὴν πόλιν, τὴν αὐτὴν παρειχόμεθ' ἡμεῖς ὑπὲρ ἡμῶν αὐτῶν προθυμίαν ἥνπερ ὑπὲρ τῆς Εὐβοέων σωτηρίας, εἴχετ' ἂν Ἀμφίπολιν τότε καὶ πάντων τῶν μετὰ ταῦτα ἂν ἦτε ἀπηλλαγμένοι πραγμάτων. (9) καὶ πάλιν ἡνίκα Πύδνα, Ποτείδαια, Μεθώνη, Παγασαί, τἄλλα, ἵνα μὴ καθ' ἕκαστα λέγων διατρίβω, πολιορκούμενα ἀπηγγέλλετο, εἰ τότε τούτων ἑνὶ τῶι πρώτωι προθύμως καὶ ὡς προσῆκεν ἐβοηθήσαμεν αὐτοί, ῥάιονι καὶ πολὺ ταπεινοτέρωι νῦν ἂν ἐχρώμεθα τῶι Φιλίππωι. νῦν δὲ τὸ μὲν παρὸν ἀεὶ προϊέμενοι, τὰ δὲ μέλλοντα αὐτόματα οἰόμενοι σχήσειν καλῶς, ηὐξήσαμεν, ὦ ἄνδρες Ἀθηναῖοι, Φίλιππον ἡμεῖς καὶ κατεστήσαμεν τηλικοῦτον ἡλίκος οὐδείς πω βασιλεὺς γέγονεν Μακεδονίας. νυνὶ δὴ καιρὸς ἥκει τις, οὗτος ὁ τῶν Ὀλυνθίων, αὐτόματος τῆι πόλει, ὃς οὐδενός ἐστιν ἐλάττων τῶν προτέρων ἐκείνων.

(10) καὶ ἔμοιγε δοκεῖ τις ἄν, ὦ ἄνδρες Ἀθηναῖοι, δίκαιος λογιστὴς τῶν παρὰ τῶν θεῶν ἡμῖν ὑπηργμένων καταστάς, καίπερ οὐκ ἐχόντων ὡς δεῖ πολλῶν, ὅμως μεγάλην ἂν ἔχειν αὐτοῖς χάριν, εἰκότως· τὸ μὲν γὰρ πολλὰ ἀπολωλεκέναι κατὰ τὸν πόλεμον τῆς ἡμετέρας ἀμελείας ἄν τις θείη δικαίως, τὸ δὲ μήτε πάλαι τοῦτο πεπονθέναι πεφηνέναι τέ τινα ἡμῖν συμμαχίαν τούτων ἀντίρροπον, ἂν βουλώμεθα χρῆσθαι, τῆς παρ' ἐκείνων εὐνοίας εὐεργέτημ' ἂν ἔγωγε θείην. (11) ἀλλ', οἶμαι, παρόμοιόν ἐστιν ὅπερ καὶ περὶ τῆς τῶν χρημάτων κτήσεως· ἂν μὲν γάρ, ὅσα ἄν τις λάβηι, καὶ σώισηι, μεγάλην ἔχει τῆι τύχηι τὴν χάριν, ἂν δ' ἀναλώσας λάθηι, συνανήλωσε καὶ τὸ μεμνῆσθαι τὴν χάριν. καὶ περὶ τῶν πραγμάτων οὕτως οἱ μὴ χρησάμενοι τοῖς καιροῖς ὀρθῶς, οὐδ' εἰ συνέβη τι παρὰ τῶν θεῶν χρηστὸν μνημονεύουσι· πρὸς γὰρ τὸ τελευταῖον ἐκβὰν ἕκαστον τῶν προϋπαρξάντων κρίνεται. διὸ καὶ σφόδρα δεῖ τῶν λοιπῶν ὑμᾶς, ὦ ἄνδρες Ἀθηναῖοι, φροντίσαι, ἵνα ταῦτ' ἐπανορθωσάμενοι τὴν ἐπὶ τοῖς πεπραγμένοις ἀδοξίαν ἀποτριψώμεθα. (12) εἰ δὲ προησόμεθα, ὦ ἄνδρες Ἀθηναῖοι, καὶ τούτους τοὺς ἀνθρώπους, εἶτ' Ὄλυνθον ἐκεῖνος καταστρέψεται, φρασάτω τις ἐμοὶ τί τὸ κωλῦον ἔτ' αὐτὸν ἔσται βαδίζειν ὅποι βούλεται. ἆρα λογίζεταί τις ὑμῶν, ὦ ἄνδρες Ἀθηναῖοι, καὶ θεωρεῖ τὸν τρόπον δι' ὃν μέγας γέγονεν ἀσθενὴς ὢν τὸ κατ' ἀρχὰς Φίλιππος; τὸ πρῶτον Ἀμφίπολιν λαβών, μετὰ ταῦτα Πύδναν, πάλιν Ποτείδαιαν, Μεθώνην αὖθις, εἶτα Θετταλίας ἐπέβη· (13) μετὰ ταῦτα Φεράς, Παγασάς, Μαγνησίαν, πάνθ' ὃν ἐβούλετ' εὐτρετίσας τρόπον ὤιχετ' εἰς Θράικην· εἶτ'

---

8 παρῆσαν D: παρῆσαν c    11 τὸ μεμνῆσθαι τὴν χάριν d: τὸ μεμνῆσθαι τῆι τύχηι τὴν χάριν d, i: τὸ μεμνῆσθαι Dobree    προϋπαρξάντων d: πρὶν ὑπαρξάντων i

ἐκεῖ τοὺς μὲν ἐκβαλὼν τοὺς δὲ καταστήσας τῶν βασιλέων ἠσθένησεν· πάλιν ῥάισας οὐκ ἐπὶ τὸ ῥαθυμεῖν ἀπέκλινεν, ἀλλ' εὐθὺς Ὀλυνθίοις ἐπεχείρησεν. τὰς δ' ἐπ' Ἰλλυριοὺς καὶ Παίονας αὐτοῦ καὶ πρὸς Ἀρύββαν καὶ ὅποι τις ἂν εἴποι παραλείπω στρατείας.

(14) τί οὖν, τις ἂν εἴποι, ταῦτα λέγεις ἡμῖν νῦν; ἵνα γνῶτε, ὦ ἄνδρες Ἀθηναῖοι, καὶ αἴσθησθε ἀμφότερα, καὶ τὸ προΐεσθαι καθ' ἕκαστον ἀεί τι τῶν πραγμάτων ὡς ἀλυσιτελές, καὶ τὴν φιλοπραγμοσύνην ἧι χρῆται καὶ συζῆι Φίλιππος, ὑφ' ἧς οὐκ ἔστιν ὅπως ἀγαπήσας τοῖς πεπραγμένοις ἡσυχίαν σχήσει. εἰ δ' ὁ μὲν ὡς ἀεί τι μεῖζον τῶν ὑπαρχόντων δεῖ πράττειν ἐγνωκὼς ἔσται, ἡμεῖς δὲ ὡς οὐδενὸς ἀντιληπτέον ἐρρωμένως τῶν πραγμάτων, σκοπεῖσθε εἰς τί ποτε ἐλπὶς ταῦτα τελευτῆσαι. (15) πρὸς θεῶν, τίς οὕτως εὐήθης ἐστὶν ὑμῶν ὅστις ἀγνοεῖ τὸν ἐκεῖθεν πόλεμον δεῦρο ἥξοντα, ἂν ἀμελήσωμεν; ἀλλὰ μήν, εἰ τοῦτο γενήσεται, δέδοικα, ὦ ἄνδρες Ἀθηναῖοι, μὴ τὸν αὐτὸν τρόπον ὥσπερ οἱ δανειζόμενοι ῥαιδίως ἐπὶ τοῖς μεγάλοις τόκοις μικρὸν εὐπορήσαντες χρόνον ὕστερον καὶ τῶν ἀρχαίων ἀπέστησαν, οὕτω καὶ ἡμεῖς {ἂν} ἐπὶ πολλῶι φανῶμεν ἐρραθυμηκότες, καὶ ἅπαντα πρὸς ἡδονὴν ζητοῦντες πολλὰ καὶ χαλεπὰ ὧν οὐκ ἐβουλόμεθα ὕστερον εἰς ἀνάγκην ἔλθωμεν ποιεῖν, καὶ κινδυνεύσωμεν περὶ τῶν ἐν αὐτῆι τῆι χώραι.

(16) τὸ μὲν οὖν ἐπιτιμᾶν ἴσως φήσαι τις ἂν ῥάιδιον καὶ παντὸς εἶναι, τὸ δ' ὑπὲρ τῶν παρόντων ὅ τι δεῖ πράττειν ἀποφαίνεσθαι, τοῦτ' εἶναι συμβούλου. ἐγὼ δ' οὐκ ἀγνοῶ μέν, ὦ ἄνδρες Ἀθηναῖοι, τοῦθ' ὅτι πολλάκις ὑμεῖς οὐ τοὺς αἰτίους, ἀλλὰ τοὺς ὑστάτους περὶ τῶν πραγμάτων εἰπόντας ἐν ὀργῆι ποιεῖσθε, ἄν τι μὴ κατὰ γνώμην ἐκβῆι· οὐ μὴν οἶμαι δεῖν τὴν ἰδίαν ἀσφάλειαν σκοποῦνθ' ὑποστείλασθαι περὶ ὧν ὑμῖν συμφέρειν ἡγοῦμαι. (17) φημὶ δὴ διχῆι βοηθητέον εἶναι τοῖς πράγμασιν ὑμῖν, τῶι τε τὰς πόλεις τοῖς Ὀλυνθίοις σώιζειν καὶ τοὺς τοῦτο ποιήσοντας στρατιώτας ἐκπέμπειν, καὶ τῶι τὴν ἐκείνου χώραν κακῶς ποιεῖν καὶ τριήρεσι καὶ στρατιώταις ἑτέροις· εἰ δὲ θατέρου τούτων ὀλιγωρήσετε, ὀκνῶ μὴ μάταιος ἡμῖν ἡ στρατεία γένηται. (18) εἴτε γὰρ ὑμῶν τὴν ἐκείνου κακῶς ποιούντων, ὑπομείνας τοῦτο Ὄλυνθον παραστήσεται, ῥαιδίως ἐπὶ τὴν οἰκείαν ἐλθὼν ἀμυνεῖται· εἴτε βοηθησάντων μόνον ὑμῶν εἰς Ὄλυνθον, ἀκινδύνως ὁρῶν ἔχοντα τὰ οἴκοι προσκαθεδεῖται καὶ προσεδρεύσει τοῖς πράγμασι, περιέσται τῶι χρόνωι τῶν πολιορκουμένων. δεῖ δὴ πολλὴν καὶ διχῆι τὴν βοήθειαν εἶναι.

(19) καὶ περὶ μὲν τῆς βοηθείας ταῦτα γιγνώσκω· περὶ δὲ χρημάτων πόρου, ἔστιν, ὦ ἄνδρες Ἀθηναῖοι, χρήματα ὑμῖν, ἔστιν ὅσα οὐδενὶ τῶν ἄλλων ἀνθρώπων στρατιωτικά· ταῦτα δὲ ὑμεῖς οὕτως ὡς βούλεσθε λαμβάνετε. εἰ μὲν οὖν ταῦτα τοῖς στρατευομένοις ἀποδώσετε, οὐδενὸς ὑμῖν προσδεῖ πόρου, εἰ δὲ μή, προσδεῖ, μᾶλλον δ' ἅπαντος ἐνδεῖ τοῦ πόρου. "τί οὖν;" ἄν τις εἴποι, "σὺ γράφεις ταῦτ' εἶναι στρατιωτικά;" μὰ Δί' οὐκ

14 τις ἂν εἴποι d: ἄν τις εἴποι d: om. d    15 τοῖς μεγάλοις τόκοις D: τοῖς μεγάλοις i    ἄν om. d    19 ἀνθρώπων στρατιωτικά D: ἀνθρώπων Bake

ἔγωγε. **(20)** ἐγὼ μὲν γὰρ ἡγοῦμαι στρατιώτας δεῖν κατασκευασθῆναι καὶ ταῦτ' εἶναι στρατιωτικὰ καὶ μίαν σύνταξιν εἶναι τὴν αὐτὴν τοῦ τε λαμβάνειν καὶ τοῦ ποιεῖν τὰ δέοντα, ὑμεῖς δὲ οὕτω πως ἄνευ πραγμάτων λαμβάνειν εἰς τὰς ἑορτάς. ἔστι δὴ λοιπόν, οἶμαι, πάντας εἰσφέρειν, ἂν πολλῶν δέηι, πολλά, ἂν ὀλίγων, ὀλίγα. δεῖ δὲ χρημάτων, καὶ ἄνευ τούτων οὐδὲν ἔστι γενέσθαι τῶν δεόντων. λέγουσι δὲ καὶ ἄλλους τινὰς ἄλλοι πόρους, ὧν ἕλεσθε ὅστις ὑμῖν συμφέρειν δοκεῖ· καὶ ἕως ἐστὶ καιρός, ἀντιλάβεσθε τῶν πραγμάτων. **(21)** ἄξιον δ' ἐνθυμηθῆναι καὶ λογίσασθαι τὰ πράγματα ἐν ὧι καθέστηκε νυνὶ τὰ Φιλίππου. οὔτε γάρ, ὡς δοκεῖ καὶ φήσειέ τις ἂν μὴ σκοπῶν ἀκριβῶς, εὐτρεπῶς οὐδ' ὡς ἂν κάλλιστ' αὐτῶι τὰ παρόντα ἔχει, οὔτ' ἂν ἐξήνεγκε τὸν πόλεμόν ποτε τοῦτον ἐκεῖνος, εἰ πολεμεῖν ὠιήθη δεήσειν αὐτόν, ἀλλ' ὡς ἐπιὼν ἅπαντα τότε ἤλπιζε τὰ πράγματα ἀναιρήσεσθαι, κἆιτα διέψευσται. τοῦτο δὴ πρῶτον αὐτὸν ταράττει παρὰ γνώμην γεγονὸς καὶ πολλὴν ἀθυμίαν αὐτῶι παρέχει, εἶτα τὰ τῶν Θετταλῶν. **(22)** ταῦτα γὰρ ἄπιστα μὲν ἦν δήπου φύσει καὶ ἀεὶ πᾶσιν ἀνθρώποις, κομιδῆι δ' ὥσπερ ἦν, καὶ ἔστι νῦν τούτωι. καὶ γὰρ Παγασὰς ἀπαιτεῖν αὐτόν εἰσιν ἐψηφισμένοι, καὶ Μαγνησίαν κεκωλύκασι τειχίζειν. ἤκουον δ' ἔγωγέ τινων, ὡς οὐδὲ τοὺς λιμένας καὶ τὰς ἀγορὰς ἔτι δώσοιεν αὐτῶι καρποῦσθαι· τὰ γὰρ κοινὰ τὰ Θετταλῶν ἀπὸ τούτων δέοι διοικεῖν, οὐ Φίλιππον λαμβάνειν. εἰ δὲ τούτων ἀποστερήσεται τῶν χρημάτων, εἰς στενὸν κομιδῆι τὰ τῆς τροφῆς τοῖς ξένοις αὐτῶι καταστήσεται. **(23)** ἀλλὰ μὴν τόν γε Παίονα καὶ τὸν Ἰλλυριὸν καὶ ἁπλῶς τούτους ἅπαντας ἡγεῖσθαι χρὴ αὐτονόμους ἥδιον ἂν καὶ ἐλευθέρους ἢ δούλους εἶναι· καὶ γὰρ ἀήθεις τοῦ κατακούειν τινός εἰσιν, καὶ ἄνθρωπος ὑβριστής, ὥς φασιν. καὶ μὰ Δί' οὐδὲν ἄπιστον ἴσως· τὸ γὰρ εὖ πράττειν παρὰ τὴν ἀξίαν ἀφορμὴ τοῦ κακῶς φρονεῖν τοῖς ἀνοήτοις γίγνεται· διόπερ πολλάκις δοκεῖ τὸ φυλάξαι τἀγαθὰ τοῦ κτήσασθαι χαλεπώτερον εἶναι. **(24)** δεῖ τοίνυν ὑμᾶς, ὦ ἄνδρες Ἀθηναῖοι, τὴν ἀκαιρίαν τὴν ἐκείνου καιρὸν ὑμέτερον νομίσαντας ἑτοίμως συνάρασθαι τὰ πράγματα, καὶ πρεσβευομένους ἐφ' ἃ δεῖ καὶ στρατευομένους αὐτοὺς καὶ παροξύνοντας τοὺς ἄλλους ἅπαντας, λογιζομένους, εἰ Φίλιππος λάβοι καθ' ἡμῶν τοιοῦτον καιρὸν καὶ πόλεμος γένοιτο πρὸς τῆι χώραι, πῶς ἂν αὐτὸν οἴεσθε ἑτοίμως ἐφ' ὑμᾶς ἐλθεῖν; εἶτ' οὐκ αἰσχύνεσθε, εἰ μηδ' ἃ πάθοιτ' ἂν, εἰ δύναιτ' ἐκεῖνος, ταῦτα ποιῆσαι καιρὸν ἔχοντες οὐ τολμήσετε;

**(25)** ἔτι τοίνυν, ὦ ἄνδρες Ἀθηναῖοι, μηδὲ τοῦθ' ὑμᾶς λανθανέτω, ὅτι νῦν αἵρεσίς ἐστιν ὑμῖν πότερ' ὑμᾶς ἐκεῖ χρὴ πολεμεῖν ἢ παρ' ὑμῖν ἐκεῖνον. ἐὰν μὲν γὰρ ἀντέχηι τὰ τῶν Ὀλυνθίων, ὑμεῖς ἐκεῖ πολεμήσετε καὶ τὴν ἐκείνου κακῶς ποιήσετε, τὴν ὑπάρχουσαν καὶ τὴν οἰκείαν ταύτην ἀδεῶς καρπούμενοι· ἂν δ' ἐκεῖνα Φίλιππος λάβηι, τίς αὐτὸν κωλύσει δεῦρο βαδίζειν; Θηβαῖοι; **(26)** μὴ λίαν πικρὸν εἰπεῖν ἦι — καὶ συνεισβαλοῦσιν

20 καὶ ταῦτ' εἶναι στρατιωτικὰ D: del. Dobree    21 ὡς ἐπιὼν D: ἁπλῶς ἐπιὼν c: εὐθέως ἐπιὼν c    25 τίς αὐτὸν D: εἰπέ μοι τίς αὐτὸν κωλύσει i βαδίζειν D: βαδίζοντα i

ἑτοίμως. ἀλλὰ Φωκεῖς; οἱ τὴν οἰκείαν οὐχ οἷοί τε ὄντες φυλάττειν, ἐὰν μὴ βοηθήσητε ὑμεῖς. ἢ ἄλλος τις; "ἀλλ', ὦ τᾶν, οὐχὶ βουλήσεται." τῶν ἀτοπωτάτων μεντἄν εἴη, εἰ ἃ νῦν ἄνοιαν ὀφλισκάνων ὅμως ἐκλαλεῖ, ταῦτα δυνηθεὶς μὴ πράξει. **(27)** ἀλλὰ μὴν ἡλίκα γ' ἐστὶν τὰ διάφορα ἐνθάδε ἢ 'κεῖ πολεμεῖν, οὐδὲ λόγου προσδεῖν ἡγοῦμαι. εἰ γὰρ ὑμᾶς δεήσειεν αὐτοὺς τριάκοντα ἡμέρας μόνας ἔξω γενέσθαι, καὶ ὅσα ἀνάγκη στρατοπέδωι χρωμένους τῶν ἐκ τῆς χώρας λαμβάνειν, μηδενὸς ὄντος ἐν αὐτῆι πολεμίου λέγω, πλείον' ἂν οἶμαι ζημιωθῆναι τοὺς γεωργοῦντας ὑμῶν ἢ ὅσα εἰς ἅπαντα τὸν πρὸ τοῦ πόλεμον δεδαπάνησθε. εἰ δὲ δὴ πόλεμός τις ἥξει, πόσα χρὴ νομίσαι ζημιώσεσθαι; καὶ πρόσεσθ' ἡ ὕβρις καὶ ἔτι ἡ τῶν πραγμάτων αἰσχύνη, οὐδεμιᾶς ἐλάττων ζημία τοῖς γε σώφροσιν.

**(28)** πάντα δὴ ταῦτα δεῖ συνιδόντας ἅπαντας βοηθεῖν καὶ ἀπωθεῖν ἐκεῖσε τὸν πόλεμον, τοὺς μὲν εὐπόρους, ἵν' ὑπὲρ τῶν πολλῶν ὧν καλῶς ποιοῦντες ἔχουσι μικρὰ ἀναλίσκοντες τὰ λοιπὰ καρπῶνται ἀδεῶς, τοὺς δ' ἐν ἡλικίαι, ἵνα τὴν τοῦ πολεμεῖν ἐμπειρίαν ἐν τῆι Φιλίππου χώραι κτησάμενοι φοβεροὶ φύλακες τῆς οἰκείας ἀκεραίου γένωνται, τοὺς δὲ λέγοντας, ἵν' αἱ τῶν πεπολιτευμένων αὐτοῖς εὔθυναι ῥάιδιαι γένωνται, ὡς ὁποῖ' ἄττ' ἂν ὑμᾶς περιστῆι τὰ πράγματα, τοιοῦτοι κριταὶ καὶ τῶν πεπραγμένων αὐτοῖς ἔσεσθε. χρηστὰ δὲ εἴη παντὸς εἵνεκα.

# 2 ΟΛΥΝΘΙΑΚΟΣ Β

(1) ἐπὶ πολλῶν μὲν ἄν τις ἰδεῖν, ὦ ἄνδρες Ἀθηναῖοι, δοκεῖ μοι τὴν παρὰ τῶν θεῶν εὔνοιαν φανερὰν γιγνομένην τῆι πόλει, οὐχ ἥκιστα δὲ ἐν τοῖς παροῦσι πράγμασιν· τὸ γὰρ τοὺς πολεμήσοντας Φιλίππωι γεγενῆσθαι καὶ χώραν ὅμορον καὶ δύναμίν τινα κεκτημένους, καὶ τὸ μέγιστον ἁπάντων, τὴν ὑπὲρ τοῦ πολέμου γνώμην τοιαύτην ἔχοντας, ὥστε τὰς πρὸς ἐκεῖνον διαλλαγὰς πρῶτον μὲν ἀπίστους, εἶτα τῆς ἑαυτῶν πατρίδος νομίζειν ἀνάστασιν, δαιμονίαι τινὶ καὶ θείαι παντάπασιν ἔοικεν εὐεργεσίαι. (2) δεῖ τοίνυν, ὦ ἄνδρες Ἀθηναῖοι, τοῦτ' ἤδη σκοπεῖν αὐτούς, ὅπως μὴ χείρους περὶ ἡμᾶς αὐτοὺς εἶναι δόξομεν τῶν ὑπαρχόντων, ὡς ἔστι τῶν αἰσχρῶν, μᾶλλον δὲ τῶν αἰσχίστων, μὴ μόνον πόλεων καὶ τόπων, ὧν ἦμέν ποτε κύριοι, φαίνεσθαι προϊεμένους, ἀλλὰ καὶ τῶν ὑπὸ τῆς τύχης παρασκευασθέντων συμμάχων καὶ καιρῶν.

(3) τὸ μὲν οὖν, ὦ ἄνδρες Ἀθηναῖοι, τὴν Φιλίππου ῥώμην διεξιέναι καὶ διὰ τούτων τῶν λόγων προτρέπειν τὰ δέοντα ποιεῖν ὑμᾶς, οὐχὶ καλῶς ἔχειν ἡγοῦμαι. διὰ τί; ὅτι μοι δοκεῖ πάνθ' ὅσ' ἂν εἴποι τις ὑπὲρ τούτων, ἐκείνωι μὲν ἔχειν φιλοτιμίαν, ἡμῖν δ' οὐχὶ καλῶς πεπρᾶχθαι. ὁ μὲν γὰρ ὅσωι πλείονα ὑπὲρ τὴν ἀξίαν πεποίηκε τὴν αὑτοῦ, τοσούτωι θαυμαστότερος παρὰ πᾶσι νομίζεται· ὑμεῖς δὲ ὅσωι χεῖρον ἢ προσῆκε κέχρησθε τοῖς πράγμασι, τοσούτωι πλείονα αἰσχύνην ὠφλήκατε. (4) ταῦτα μὲν οὖν παραλείψω. καὶ γὰρ εἰ μετ' ἀληθείας τις, ὦ ἄνδρες Ἀθηναῖοι, σκοποῖτο, ἐνθένδ' ἂν αὐτὸν ἴδοι μέγαν γεγενημένον, οὐχὶ παρ' αὑτοῦ. ὧν οὖν ἐκεῖνος μὲν ὀφείλει τοῖς ὑπὲρ αὐτοῦ πεπολιτευμένοις χάριν, ὑμῖν δὲ δίκην προσήκει λαβεῖν, οὐχὶ νῦν ὁρῶ τὸν καιρὸν τοῦ λέγειν· ἃ δὲ καὶ χωρὶς τούτων ἔνι καὶ βέλτιόν ἐστιν ἀκηκοέναι πάντας ὑμᾶς καὶ μεγάλα, ὦ ἄνδρες Ἀθηναῖοι, κατ' ἐκείνου φαίνοιτ' ἂν ὀνείδη βουλομένοις ὀρθῶς δοκιμάζειν, ταῦτ' εἰπεῖν πειράσομαι.

(5) τὸ μὲν οὖν ἐπίορκον καὶ ἄπιστον καλεῖν ἄνευ τοῦ τὰ πεπραγμένα δεικνύναι λοιδορίαν εἶναί τις ἂν φήσειε κενὴν δικαίως· τὸ δὲ πάνθ' ὅσα πώποτ' ἔπραξε διεξιόντα ἐφ' ἅπασι τούτοις ἐλέγχειν, καὶ βραχέος λόγου συμβαίνει δεῖσθαι, καὶ δυοῖν ἕνεχ' ἡγοῦμαι συμφέρειν εἰρῆσθαι, τοῦ τ' ἐκεῖνον, ὅπερ καὶ ἀληθὲς ὑπάρχει, φαῦλον φαίνεσθαι, καὶ τοὺς ὑπερεκπεπληγμένους ὡς ἄμαχόν τινα τὸν Φίλιππον ἰδεῖν ὅτι πάντα διεξελήλυθεν οἷς πρότερον παρακρουόμενος μέγας ηὐξήθη, καὶ πρὸς αὐτὴν ἥκει τὴν τελευτὴν τὰ πράγματα αὐτοῦ. (6) ἐγὼ γάρ, ὦ ἄνδρες Ἀθηναῖοι, σφόδρα ἂν ἡγούμην καὶ αὐτὸς φοβερὸν τὸν Φίλιππον καὶ θαυμαστόν, εἰ τὰ δίκαια πράττοντα ἑώρων ηὐξημένον· νῦν δὲ θεωρῶν καὶ σκοπῶν εὑρίσκω τὴν μὲν ἡμετέραν εὐήθειαν τὸ κατ' ἀρχάς, ὅτε Ὀλυνθίους

---

2 δόξομεν d: δόξωμεν d    3 ἔχειν φιλοτιμίαν d: ἔχειν φιλοτιμίαν τινὰ d: τινα ἔχειν φιλοτιμίαν d    4 οὐχὶ νῦν d: τούτων οὐχὶ νῦν d, i: ὑπὲρ τούτων οὐχὶ νῦν d
5 αὑτοῦ: αὑτῶι d    6 φοβερὸν τὸν Φίλιππον ... ἑώρων ηὐξημένον: φοβερὸν εἶναι τὸν Φίλιππον ... ἑώρων αὐτὸν ηὐξημένον d

ἀπήλαυνόν τινες ἐνθένδε βουλομένους ὑμῖν διαλεχθῆναι, τῶι τὴν Ἀμφίπολιν φάσκειν παραδώσειν καὶ τὸ θρυλούμενόν ποτε ἀπόρρητον ἐκεῖνο κατασκευάσαι, τούτωι προσαγαγόμενον, (7) τὴν δὲ Ὀλυνθίων φιλίαν μετὰ ταῦτα τῶι Ποτείδαιαν οὖσαν ὑμετέραν ἐξελεῖν καὶ τοὺς μὲν πρότερον συμμάχους {ὑμᾶς} ἀδικῆσαι, παραδοῦναι δὲ ἐκείνοις, Θετταλοὺς δὲ νῦν τὰ τελευταῖα τῶι Μαγνησίαν παραδώσειν ὑποσχέσθαι καὶ τὸν Φωκικὸν πόλεμον πολεμήσειν ὑπὲρ αὐτῶν ἀναδέξασθαι. ὅλως δ' οὐδεὶς ἔστιν ὅντινα οὐ πεφενάκικεν ἐκεῖνος τῶν αὐτῶι χρησαμένων· τὴν γὰρ ἑκάστων ἄνοιαν ἀεὶ τῶν ἀγνοούντων αὐτὸν ἐξαπατῶν καὶ προσλαμβάνων οὕτως ηὐξήθη. (8) ὥσπερ οὖν διὰ τούτων ἤρθη μέγας, ἡνίκα ἕκαστοι συμφέρον αὐτὸν ἑαυτοῖς ὤιοντό τι πράξειν, οὕτως ὀφείλει διὰ τῶν αὐτῶν τούτων καὶ καθαιρεθῆναι πάλιν, ἐπειδὴ πάνθ' ἕνεκα ἑαυτοῦ ποιῶν ἐξελήλεγκται. καιροῦ μὲν δή, ὦ ἄνδρες Ἀθηναῖοι, πρὸς τοῦτο πάρεστι Φιλίππωι τὰ πράγματα· ἢ παρελθών τις ἐμοί, μᾶλλον δ' ὑμῖν δειξάτω ὡς οὐκ ἀληθῆ ταῦτ' ἐγὼ λέγω, ἢ ὡς οἱ τὰ πρῶτα ἐξηπατημένοι τὰ λοιπὰ πιστεύσουσιν, ἢ ὡς οἱ παρὰ τὴν αὐτῶν ἀξίαν δεδουλωμένοι {Θετταλοὶ} νῦν οὐκ ἂν ἐλεύθεροι γένοιντο ἄσμενοι.

(9) καὶ μὴν εἴ τις ὑμῶν ταῦτα μὲν οὕτως ἔχειν ἡγεῖται, οἴεται δὲ βίαι καθέξειν αὐτὸν τὰ πράγματα, τῶι τὰ χωρία καὶ λιμένας καὶ τὰ τοιαῦτα προειληφέναι, οὐκ ὀρθῶς οἴεται. ὅταν μὲν γὰρ ὑπ' εὐνοίας τὰ πράγματα συστῆι καὶ πᾶσι ταὐτὰ συμφέρηι τοῖς μετέχουσι τοῦ πολέμου, καὶ συμπονεῖν καὶ φέρειν τὰς συμφορὰς καὶ μένειν ἐθέλουσιν ἄνθρωποι· ὅταν δ' ἐκ πλεονεξίας καὶ πονηρίας τις, ὥσπερ οὗτος, ἰσχύσηι, ἡ πρώτη πρόφασις καὶ μικρὸν πταῖσμα ἅπαντα ἀνεχαίτισεν καὶ διέλυσεν. (10) οὐ γὰρ ἔστιν, οὐκ ἔστιν, ὦ ἄνδρες Ἀθηναῖοι, ἀδικοῦντα καὶ ἐπιορκοῦντα καὶ ψευδόμενον δύναμιν βεβαίαν κτήσασθαι, ἀλλὰ τὰ τοιαῦτα εἰς μὲν ἅπαξ καὶ βραχὺν χρόνον ἀντέχει, καὶ σφόδρα γε ἤνθησεν ἐπὶ ταῖς ἐλπίσιν, ἂν τύχηι, τῶι χρόνωι δὲ φωρᾶται καὶ περὶ αὑτὰ καταρρεῖ. ὥσπερ γὰρ οἰκίας, οἶμαι, καὶ πλοίου καὶ τῶν ἄλλων τῶν τοιούτων τὰ κάτωθεν ἰσχυρότατα εἶναι δεῖ, οὕτω καὶ τῶν πράξεων τὰς ἀρχὰς καὶ τὰς ὑποθέσεις ἀληθεῖς καὶ δικαίας εἶναι προσήκει. τοῦτο δὲ οὐκ ἔνι νῦν ἐν τοῖς πεπραγμένοις Φιλίππωι.

(11) φημὶ δὴ δεῖν ἡμᾶς τοῖς μὲν Ὀλυνθίοις βοηθεῖν, καὶ ὅπως τις λέγει κάλλιστα καὶ τάχιστα, οὕτως ἀρέσκει μοι· πρὸς δὲ Θετταλοὺς πρεσβείαν πέμπειν, ἢ τοὺς μὲν διδάξει ταῦτα, τοὺς δὲ παροξυνεῖ· καὶ γὰρ νῦν εἰσιν ἐψηφισμένοι Παγασὰς ἀπαιτεῖν καὶ περὶ Μαγνησίας λόγους ποιεῖσθαι. (12) σκοπεῖσθε μέντοι τοῦτο, ὦ ἄνδρες Ἀθηναῖοι, ὅπως μὴ λόγους ἐροῦσιν μόνον οἱ παρ' ἡμῶν πρέσβεις, ἀλλὰ καὶ ἔργον τι δεικνύειν ἕξουσιν, ἐξεληλυθότων ὑμῶν ἀξίως τῆς πόλεως καὶ ὄντων ἐπὶ τοῖς πράγμασιν, ὡς ἅπας μὲν λόγος, ἂν ἀπῆι τὰ πράγματα, μάταιόν τι φαίνεται καὶ

---

7 ὑμᾶς D: del. Blass    8 δειξάτω ὡς d: δειξάτω ἢ ὡς d, i    Θετταλοὶ D: del. Rosenberg    9 ἄνθρωποι c: οἱ ἄνθρωποι d: ἄνθρωποι d    10 ἰσχυρότατα d: ἰσχυρότερα d    12 τὰ πράγματα d: τὰ ἔργα d, i

κενόν, μάλιστα δὲ ὁ παρὰ τῆς ἡμετέρας πόλεως· ὅσωι γὰρ ἑτοιμότατ᾽ αὑτῶι δοκοῦμεν χρῆσθαι, τοσούτωι μᾶλλον ἀπιστοῦσι πάντες αὐτῶι. (13) πολλὴν δὴ τὴν μετάστασιν καὶ μεγάλην δεικτέον τὴν μεταβολήν, εἰσφέροντας, ἐξιόντας, ἅπαντα ποιοῦντας ἑτοίμως, εἴπερ τις ὑμῖν προσέξει τὸν νοῦν. κἂν ταῦτα ἐθελήσητε ὡς προσήκει καὶ δὴ περαίνειν, οὐ μόνον, ὦ ἄνδρες Ἀθηναῖοι, τὰ συμμαχικὰ ἀσθενῶς καὶ ἀπίστως ἔχοντα φανήσεται Φιλίππωι, ἀλλὰ καὶ τὰ τῆς οἰκείας ἀρχῆς καὶ δυνάμεως κακῶς ἔχοντα ἐξελεγχθήσεται.

(14) ὅλως μὲν γὰρ ἡ Μακεδονικὴ δύναμις καὶ ἀρχὴ ἐν μὲν προσθήκηι μερίς ἐστί τις οὐ μικρά, οἷον ὑπῆρξέ ποθ᾽ ὑμῖν ἐπὶ Τιμοθέου πρὸς Ὀλυνθίους· πάλιν αὖ πρὸς Ποτείδαιαν Ὀλυνθίοις ἐφάνη τι τοῦτο συναμφότερον· νυνὶ δὲ Θετταλοῖς νοσοῦσι καὶ τεταραγμένοις ἐπὶ τὴν τυραννικὴν οἰκίαν ἐβοήθησεν· ὅποι τις ἄν, οἶμαι, προσθῆι κἂν μικρὰν δύναμιν, πάντ᾽ ὠφελεῖ· αὐτὴ δὲ καθ᾽ αὑτὴν ἀσθενὴς καὶ πολλῶν κακῶν ἐστι μεστή. (15) καὶ γὰρ οὗτος ἅπασι τούτοις, οἷς ἄν τις μέγαν αὐτὸν ἡγήσαιτο, τοῖς πολέμοις καὶ ταῖς στρατείαις, ἔτ᾽ ἐπισφαλεστέραν ἢ ὑπῆρχε φύσει κατεσκεύακεν αὐτῶι. μὴ γὰρ οἴεσθε, ὦ ἄνδρες Ἀθηναῖοι, τοῖς αὐτοῖς Φίλιππόν τε χαίρειν καὶ τοὺς ἀρχομένους, ἀλλ᾽ ὁ μὲν δόξης ἐπιθυμεῖ καὶ τοῦτο ἐζήλωκε, καὶ προήιρηται πράττων καὶ κινδυνεύων, ἂν συμβῆι τι, παθεῖν, τὴν τοῦ διαπράξασθαι ταῦτα ἃ μηδεὶς πώποτε ἄλλος Μακεδόνων βασιλεὺς δόξαν ἀντὶ τοῦ ζῆν ἀσφαλῶς ἡιρημένος· (16) τοῖς δὲ τῆς μὲν φιλοτιμίας τῆς ἀπὸ τούτων οὐ μέτεστιν, κοπτόμενοι δὲ ἀεὶ ταῖς στρατείαις ταύταις ταῖς ἄνω κάτω λυποῦνται καὶ συνεχῶς ταλαιπωροῦσιν, οὔτ᾽ ἐπὶ τοῖς ἔργοις οὔτ᾽ ἐπὶ τοῖς αὑτῶν ἰδίοις ἐώμενοι διατρίβειν, οὔτε ὅσ᾽ ἂν ποιήσωσιν οὕτως ὅπως ἂν δύνωνται, ταῦτ᾽ ἔχοντες διαθέσθαι κεκλειμένων τῶν ἐμπορίων τῶν ἐν τῆι χώραι διὰ τὸν πόλεμον. (17) οἱ μὲν οὖν πολλοὶ Μακεδόνων πῶς ἔχουσι Φιλίππωι, ἐκ τούτων ἄν τις σκέψαιτο οὐ χαλεπῶς· οἱ δὲ δὴ περὶ αὐτὸν ὄντες ξένοι καὶ πεζέταιροι δόξαν μὲν ἔχουσιν ὡς εἰσὶ θαυμαστοὶ καὶ συγκεκροτημένοι τὰ τοῦ πολέμου, ὡς δ᾽ ἐγὼ τῶν ἐν αὐτῆι τῆι χώραι γεγενημένων τινὸς ἤκουον, ἀνδρὸς οὐδαμῶς οἵου τε ψεύδεσθαι, οὐδένων εἰσὶν βελτίους. (18) εἰ μὲν γάρ τις ἀνήρ ἐστιν ἐν αὐτοῖς οἷος ἔμπειρος πολέμου καὶ ἀγώνων, τούτους μὲν φιλοτιμίαι πάντας ἀπωθεῖν αὐτὸν ἔφη, βουλόμενον πάντα αὑτοῦ δοκεῖν εἶναι τἄργα — πρὸς γὰρ αὖ τοῖς ἄλλοις καὶ τὴν φιλοτιμίαν ἀνυπέρβλητον εἶναι· εἰ δέ τις σώφρων ἢ δίκαιος ἄλλως, τὴν καθ᾽ ἡμέραν ἀκρασίαν τοῦ βίου καὶ μέθην καὶ κορδακισμοὺς οὐ δυνάμενος φέρειν, παρεῶσθαι καὶ ἐν οὐδενὸς εἶναι μέρει τὸν τοιοῦτον. (19) λοιποὺς δὴ περὶ αὐτὸν εἶναι ληιστὰς καὶ κόλακας καὶ τοιούτους ἀνθρώπους οἵους μεθυσθέντας ὀρχεῖσθαι τοιαῦτα οἷα ἐγὼ νῦν ὀκνῶ πρὸς ὑμᾶς ὀνομάσαι. δῆλον δ᾽ ὅτι ταῦτ᾽ ἐστὶν ἀληθῆ· καὶ γὰρ οὓς ἐνθένδε πάντες ἀπήλαυνον ὡς πολὺ τῶν θαυματοποιῶν ἀσελγεστέρους ὄντας, Καλλίαν ἐκεῖνον τὸν δημόσιον καὶ τοιούτους ἀνθρώπους, μίμους γελοίων καὶ ποιητὰς αἰσχρῶν ἀισμάτων, ὧν εἰς τοὺς συνόντας

13 κἂν ταῦτα d: κἀνταῦθα d    14 νοσοῦσι Cobet: νοσοῦσι καὶ στασιάζουσι d: στασιάζουσι d

ποιοῦσιν εἵνεκα τοῦ γελασθῆναι, τούτους ἀγαπᾶι καὶ περὶ αὑτὸν ἔχει. (20) καίτοι ταῦτα, καὶ εἰ μικρά τις ἡγεῖται, μεγάλα, ὦ ἄνδρες Ἀθηναῖοι, δείγματα τῆς ἐκείνου γνώμης καὶ κακοδαιμονίας ἐστὶ τοῖς εὖ φρονοῦσιν. ἀλλ᾽, οἶμαι, νῦν μὲν ἐπισκοτεῖ τούτοις τὸ κατορθοῦν· αἱ γὰρ εὐπραξίαι δειναὶ συγκρύψαι τὰ τοιαῦτα ὀνείδη· εἰ δέ τι πταίσει, τότε ἀκριβῶς αὐτοῦ ταῦτα ἐξετασθήσεται. δοκεῖ δ᾽ ἔμοιγε, ὦ ἄνδρες Ἀθηναῖοι, δείξειν οὐκ εἰς μακράν, ἂν οἵ τε θεοὶ θέλωσι καὶ ὑμεῖς βούλησθε. (21) ὥσπερ γὰρ ἐν τοῖς σώμασιν, τέως μὲν ἂν ἐρρωμένος ᾖ τις, οὐδὲν ἐπαισθάνεται, ἐπὰν δ᾽ ἀρρώστημά τι συμβῇ, πάντα κινεῖται, κἂν ῥῆγμα κἂν στρέμμα κἂν ἄλλο τι τῶν ὑπαρχόντων σαθρὸν ᾖ, οὕτω καὶ τῶν πόλεων καὶ τῶν τυράννων, ἕως μὲν ἂν ἔξω πολεμῶσιν, ἀφανῆ τὰ κακὰ τοῖς πολλοῖς ἐστιν, ἐπειδὰν δὲ ὅμορος πόλεμος συμπλακῇ, πάντα ἐποίησεν ἔκδηλα.

(22) εἰ δέ τις ὑμῶν, ὦ ἄνδρες Ἀθηναῖοι, τὸν Φίλιππον εὐτυχοῦντα ὁρῶν ταύτηι φοβερὸν προσπολεμῆσαι νομίζει, σώφρονος μὲν ἀνθρώπου λογισμῶι χρῆται· μεγάλη γὰρ ῥοπή, μᾶλλον δὲ τὸ ὅλον ἡ τύχη παρὰ πάντ᾽ ἐστὶ τὰ τῶν ἀνθρώπων πράγματα· οὐ μὴν ἀλλ᾽ ἔγωγε, εἴ τις αἵρεσίν μοι δοίη, τὴν τῆς ἡμετέρας πόλεως τύχην ἂν ἑλοίμην, ἐθελόντων ἃ προσήκει ποιεῖν ὑμῶν αὐτῶν καὶ κατὰ μικρόν, ἢ τὴν ἐκείνου· πολὺ γὰρ πλείους ἀφορμὰς εἰς τὸ τὴν παρὰ τῶν θεῶν εὔνοιαν ἔχειν ὁρῶ ὑμῖν ἐνούσας ἢ ἐκείνωι. (23) ἀλλ᾽, οἶμαι, καθήμεθα οὐδὲν ποιοῦντες· οὐκ ἔνι δ᾽ αὐτὸν ἀργοῦντ᾽ οὐδὲ τοῖς φίλοις ἐπιτάττειν ὑπὲρ αὑτοῦ τι ποιεῖν, μή τί γε δὴ τοῖς θεοῖς. οὐ δὴ θαυμαστόν ἐστιν, εἰ στρατευόμενος καὶ πονῶν ἐκεῖνος αὐτὸς καὶ παρὼν ἐφ᾽ ἅπασι καὶ μήτε καιρὸν μήθ᾽ ὥραν παραλείπων ἡμῶν μελλόντων καὶ ψηφιζομένων καὶ πυνθανομένων περιγίγνεται. οὐδὲ θαυμάζω τοῦτ᾽ ἐγώ· τοὐναντίον γὰρ ἂν ἦν θαυμαστόν, εἰ μηδὲν ποιοῦντες ἡμεῖς ὧν τοῖς πολεμοῦσι προσήκει τοῦ πάντα ποιοῦντος περιῆμεν. (24) ἀλλ᾽ ἐκεῖνο θαυμάζω, εἰ Λακεδαιμονίοις μέν ποτε, ὦ ἄνδρες Ἀθηναῖοι, ὑπὲρ τῶν Ἑλληνικῶν δικαίων ἀντήρατε, καὶ πόλλ᾽ ἰδίαι πλεονεκτῆσαι πολλάκις ὑμῖν ἐξὸν οὐκ ἠθελήσατε, ἀλλ᾽ ἵνα οἱ ἄλλοι τύχωσι τῶν δικαίων, τὰ ὑμέτερα αὐτῶν ἀνηλίσκετε εἰσφέροντες καὶ προὐκινδυνεύετε στρατευόμενοι, νυνὶ δ᾽ ὀκνεῖτε ἐξιέναι καὶ μέλλετε εἰσφέρειν ὑπὲρ τῶν ὑμετέρων αὐτῶν κτημάτων, καὶ τοὺς μὲν ἄλλους σεσώκατε πολλάκις πάντας καὶ καθ᾽ ἕνα αὐτῶν ἕκαστον ἐν μέρει, τὰ δ᾽ ὑμέτερ᾽ αὐτῶν ἀπολωλεκότες κάθησθε. (25) ταῦτα θαυμάζω, κἄτι πρὸς τούτοις, εἰ μηδεὶς ὑμῶν, ὦ ἄνδρες Ἀθηναῖοι, δύναται λογίσασθαι πόσον πολεμεῖτε χρόνον Φιλίππωι, καὶ τί ποιούντων ὑμῶν ὁ χρόνος διελήλυθεν οὗτος. ἴστε γὰρ δήπου τοῦθ᾽, ὅτι μελλόντων αὐτῶν, ἑτέρους τινὰς ἐλπιζόντων πράξειν, αἰτιωμένων ἀλλήλους, κρινόντων, πάλιν ἐλπιζόντων, σχεδὸν ταῦθ᾽ ἅπερ νυνὶ ποιούντων, ἅπας ὁ χρόνος διελήλυθεν. (26) εἶθ᾽ οὕτως ἀγνωμόνως ἔχετε, ὦ ἄνδρες Ἀθηναῖοι, ὥστε δι᾽ ὧν ἐκ χρηστῶν

20 συγκρύψαι d: συγκρύψαι καὶ συσκιάσαι d, i: συσκιάσαι i  21 ἐπαισθάνεται d: ἐπαισθάνεται τῶν καθ᾽ ἕκαστα σαθρῶν d, i   23 μήτε ... μήθ᾽ c: μηδὲ ... μηδ᾽ d: μηδένα ... μηδ᾽ d   ποιοῦντος d: ποιοῦντος ἃ δεῖ d, i   24 αὐτῶν ἕκαστον c, d: αὐτῶν d   25 αὐτῶν d: ὑμῶν d: ἡμῶν d

φαῦλα τὰ πράγματα τῆς πόλεως γέγονεν, διὰ τούτων ἐλπίζετε τῶν αὐτῶν πράξεων ἐκ φαύλων αὐτὰ χρηστὰ γενήσεσθαι; ἀλλ' οὔτ' εὔλογον οὔτ' ἔχον ἐστὶ φύσιν τοῦτό γε· πολὺ γὰρ ῥᾶιον ἔχοντας φυλάττειν ἢ κτήσασθαι πάντα πέφυκεν. νῦν δ' ὅ τι μὲν φυλάξομεν, οὐδέν ἐστιν ὑπὸ τοῦ πολέμου λοιπὸν τῶν πρότερον, κτήσασθαι δὲ δεῖ. αὐτῶν οὖν ἡμῶν ἔργον τοῦτ' ἤδη.

(27) φημὶ δὴ δεῖν εἰσφέρειν χρήματα, αὐτοὺς ἐξιέναι προθύμως, μηδέν' αἰτιᾶσθαι πρὶν ἂν τῶν πραγμάτων κρατήσητε, τηνικαῦτα δ' ἀπ' αὐτῶν τῶν ἔργων κρίναντας τοὺς μὲν ἀξίους ἐπαίνου τιμᾶν, τοὺς δ' ἀδικοῦντας κολάζειν, τὰς προφάσεις δ' ἀφελεῖν καὶ τὰ καθ' ὑμᾶς ἐλλείμματα· οὐ γὰρ ἔστι πικρῶς ἐξετάσαι τί πέπρακται τοῖς ἄλλοις, ἂν μὴ παρ' ὑμῶν αὐτῶν πρῶτον ὑπάρξηι τὰ δέοντα. (28) τίνος γὰρ ἕνεκα, ὦ ἄνδρες Ἀθηναῖοι, νομίζετε τοῦτον μὲν φεύγειν τὸν πόλεμον πάντας ὅσους ἂν ἐκπέμψητε στρατηγούς, ἰδίους δ' εὑρίσκειν πολέμους, εἰ δεῖ τι τῶν ὄντων καὶ περὶ τῶν στρατηγῶν εἰπεῖν; ὅτι ἐνταῦθα μέν ἐστι τἆθλ' ὑπὲρ ὧν ἐστιν ὁ πόλεμος ὑμέτερα· Ἀμφίπολίς γ' ἂν ληφθῆι, παραχρῆμ' ὑμεῖς κομιεῖσθε· οἱ δὲ κίνδυνοι τῶν ἐφεστηκότων ἴδιοι, μισθὸς δ' οὐκ ἔστιν· ἐκεῖ δὲ κίνδυνοι μὲν ἐλάττους, τὰ δὲ λήμματα τῶν ἐφεστηκότων καὶ τῶν στρατιωτῶν, Λάμψακος, Σίγειον, τὰ πλοῖα ἃ συλῶσιν. ἐπ' οὖν τὸ λυσιτελοῦν αὑτοῖς ἕκαστοι χωροῦσιν. (29) ὑμεῖς δ', ὅταν μὲν εἰς τὰ πράγματα ἀποβλέψητε φαύλως ἔχοντα, τοὺς ἐφεστηκότας κρίνετε, ὅταν δὲ δόντες λόγον τὰς ἀνάγκας ἀκούσητε ταύτας, ἀφίετε. περίεστι τοίνυν ὑμῖν ἀλλήλοις ἐρίζειν καὶ διεστάναι, τοῖς μὲν ταῦτα πεπεισμένοις, τοῖς δὲ ταῦτα, τὰ κοινὰ δ' ἔχειν φαύλως. πρότερον μὲν γάρ, ὦ ἄνδρες Ἀθηναῖοι, εἰσεφέρετε κατὰ συμμορίας, νυνὶ δὲ πολιτεύεσθε κατὰ συμμορίας. ῥήτωρ ἡγεμὼν ἑκατέρων, καὶ στρατηγὸς ὑπὸ τούτωι καὶ οἱ βοησόμενοι τριακόσιοι· οἱ δὲ ἄλλοι προσνενέμησθε οἱ μὲν ὡς τούτους, οἱ δ' ὡς ἐκείνους. (30) δεῖ δὴ ταῦτα ἐπανέντας καὶ ὑμῶν αὐτῶν ἔτι καὶ νῦν γενομένους κοινὸν καὶ τὸ βουλεύεσθαι καὶ τὸ λέγειν καὶ τὸ πράττειν ποιῆσαι. εἰ δὲ τοῖς μέν, ὥσπερ ἐκ τυραννίδος, ὑμῶν ἐπιτάττειν ἀποδώσετε, τοῖς δ' ἀναγκάζεσθαι τριηραρχεῖν, εἰσφέρειν, στρατεύεσθαι, τοῖς δὲ ψηφίζεσθαι κατὰ τούτων μόνον, ἄλλο δὲ μηδ' ὁτιοῦν συμπονεῖν, οὐχὶ γενήσεται τῶν δεόντων ὑμῖν οὐδὲν ἐν καιρῶι· τὸ γὰρ ἠδικημένον ἀεὶ μέρος ἐλλείψει, εἶθ' ὑμῖν τούτους κολάζειν ἀντὶ τῶν ἐχθρῶν ἐξέσται. (31) λέγω δὴ κεφάλαιον, πάντας εἰσφέρειν ἀφ' ὅσων ἕκαστος ἔχει τὸ ἴσον· πάντας ἐξιέναι κατὰ μέρος, ἕως ἂν ἅπαντες στρατεύσησθε· πᾶσι τοῖς παριοῦσι λόγον διδόναι, καὶ τὰ βέλτιστα ὧν ἂν ἀκούσητε αἱρεῖσθαι, μὴ ἃ ἂν ὁ δεῖνα ἢ ὁ δεῖνα εἴπηι. κἂν ταῦτα ποιῆτε, οὐ τὸν εἰπόντα μόνον παραχρῆμ' ἐπαινέσεσθε, ἀλλὰ καὶ ὑμᾶς αὐτοὺς ὕστερον, βέλτιον τῶν ὅλων πραγμάτων ὑμῖν ἐχόντων.

28 γ' ἂν c: κἂν D   30 τὸ γὰρ ἠδικημένον d: τὸ γὰρ ἄδικον μὲν d   ἐξέσται d: περιέσται d

# 3 ΟΛΥΝΘΙΑΚΟΣ Γ

(1) οὐχὶ ταὐτὰ παρίσταταί μοι γιγνώσκειν, ὦ ἄνδρες Ἀθηναῖοι, ὅταν τε εἰς τὰ πράγματ' ἀποβλέψω καὶ ὅταν πρὸς τοὺς λόγους οὓς ἀκούω· τοὺς μὲν γὰρ λόγους περὶ τοῦ τιμωρήσασθαι Φίλιππον ὁρῶ γιγνομένους, τὰ δὲ πράγματα εἰς τοῦτο προήκοντα, ὥσθ' ὅπως μὴ πεισόμεθα αὐτοὶ πρότερον κακῶς σκέψασθαι δέον. οὐδὲν οὖν ἄλλο μοι δοκοῦσιν οἱ τὰ τοιαῦτα λέγοντες ἢ τὴν ὑπόθεσιν, περὶ ἧς βουλεύεσθε, οὐχὶ τὴν οὖσαν παριστάντες ὑμῖν ἁμαρτάνειν. (2) ἐγὼ δέ, ὅτι μέν ποτε ἐξῆν τῆι πόλει καὶ τὰ αὑτῆς ἔχειν ἀσφαλῶς καὶ Φίλιππον τιμωρήσασθαι, καὶ μάλα ἀκριβῶς οἶδα· ἐπ' ἐμοῦ γάρ, οὐ πάλαι γέγονεν ταῦτα ἀμφότερα· νῦν μέντοι πέπεισμαι τοῦθ' ἱκανὸν προλαβεῖν ἡμῖν εἶναι τὴν πρώτην, ὅπως τοὺς συμμάχους σώσομεν. ἐὰν γὰρ τοῦτο βεβαίως ὑπάρξηι, τότε καὶ περὶ τοῦ τίνα τιμωρήσεταί τις καὶ ὃν τρόπον ἐξέσται σκοπεῖν· πρὶν δὲ τὴν ἀρχὴν ὀρθῶς ὑποθέσθαι, μάταιον ἡγοῦμαι περὶ τῆς τελευτῆς ὁντινοῦν ποιεῖσθαι λόγον.

(3) ὁ μὲν οὖν παρὼν καιρός, εἴπερ ποτέ, πολλῆς φροντίδος καὶ βουλῆς δεῖται· ἐγὼ δὲ οὐχ ὅ τι χρὴ περὶ τῶν παρόντων συμβουλεῦσαι χαλεπώτατον ἡγοῦμαι, ἀλλ' ἐκεῖν' ἀπορῶ, τίνα χρὴ τρόπον, ὦ ἄνδρες Ἀθηναῖοι, πρὸς ὑμᾶς περὶ αὐτῶν εἰπεῖν. πέπεισμαι γὰρ ἐξ ὧν παρὼν καὶ ἀκούων σύνοιδα, τὰ πλείω τῶν πραγμάτων ἡμᾶς ἐκπεφευγέναι τῶι μὴ βούλεσθαι τὰ δέοντα ποιεῖν ἢ τῶι μὴ συνιέναι. ἀξιῶ δὲ ὑμᾶς, ἂν μετὰ παρρησίας ποιῶμαι τοὺς λόγους, ὑπομένειν, τοῦτο θεωροῦντας, εἰ τἀληθῆ λέγω, καὶ διὰ τοῦτο, ἵνα τὰ λοιπὰ βελτίω γένηται· ὁρᾶτε γὰρ ὡς ἐκ τοῦ πρὸς χάριν δημηγορεῖν ἐνίους εἰς πᾶν προελήλυθε μοχθηρίας τὰ παρόντα.

(4) ἀναγκαῖον δ' ὑπολαμβάνω μικρὰ τῶν γεγενημένων πρῶτον ὑμᾶς ὑπομνῆσαι. μέμνησθε, ὦ ἄνδρες Ἀθηναῖοι, ὅτ' ἀπηγγέλθη Φίλιππος ὑμῖν ἐν Θράικηι τρίτον ἢ τέταρτον ἔτος τουτὶ Ἡραῖον τεῖχος πολιορκῶν. τότε τοίνυν μὴν μὲν ἦν μαιμακτηριών· πολλῶν δὲ λόγων καὶ θορύβου γιγνομένου παρ' ὑμῖν ἐψηφίσασθε τετταράκοντα τριήρεις καθέλκειν καὶ τοὺς μέχρι πέντε καὶ τετταράκοντα ἐτῶν αὐτοὺς ἐμβαίνειν καὶ τάλαντα ἑξήκοντα εἰσφέρειν. (5) καὶ μετὰ ταῦτα διελθόντος τοῦ ἐνιαυτοῦ τούτου ἑκατομβαιών, μεταγειτνιών, βοηδρομιών· τούτου τοῦ μηνὸς μόγις μετὰ τὰ μυστήρια δέκα ναῦς ἀπεστείλατε ἔχοντα κενὰς Χαρίδημον καὶ πέντε τάλαντα ἀργυρίου. ὡς γὰρ ἠγγέλθη Φίλιππος ἀσθενῶν ἢ τεθνεώς (ἦλθε γὰρ ἀμφότερα), οὐκέτι καιρὸν οὐδένα τοῦ βοηθεῖν νομίσαντες ἀφεῖτε, ὦ ἄνδρες Ἀθηναῖοι, τὸν ἀπόστολον. ἦν δ' οὗτος ὁ καιρὸς αὐτός· εἰ γὰρ τότ' ἐκεῖσε ἐβοηθήσαμεν, ὥσπερ ἐψηφισάμεθα, προθύμως, οὐκ ἂν ἠνώχλει νῦν ἡμῖν ὁ Φίλιππος σωθείς.

(6) τὰ μὲν δὴ τότε πραχθέντα οὐκ ἂν ἄλλως ἔχοι· νῦν δ' ἑτέρου πολέμου καιρὸς ἥκει τις, δι' ὃν καὶ περὶ τούτων ἐμνήσθην, ἵνα μὴ ταὐτὰ

πάθητε. τί δὴ χρησόμεθα, ὦ ἄνδρες Ἀθηναῖοι, τούτωι; εἰ γὰρ μὴ βοηθήσετε "παντὶ σθένει κατὰ τὸ δυνατόν," θεάσασθε ὃν τρόπον ὑμεῖς ἐστρατηγηκότες πάντα ἔσεσθε ὑπὲρ Φιλίππου. (7) ὑπῆρχον Ὀλύνθιοι δύναμίν τινα κεκτημένοι, καὶ διέκειθ᾽ οὕτω τὰ πράγματα· οὔτε Φίλιππος ἐθάρρει τούτους οὔθ᾽ οὗτοι Φίλιππον. ἐπράξαμεν ἡμεῖς κἀκεῖνοι πρὸς ἡμᾶς εἰρήνην· ἦν τοῦτο ὥσπερ ἐμπόδισμά τι τῶι Φιλίππωι καὶ δυσχερές, πόλιν μεγάλην ἐφορμεῖν τοῖς ἑαυτοῦ καιροῖς διηλλαγμένην πρὸς ἡμᾶς. ἐκπολεμῶσαι δεῖν ὠιόμεθα τοὺς ἀνθρώπους ἐκ παντὸς τρόπου, καὶ ὃ πάντες ἐθρύλουν, πέπρακται νυνὶ τοῦθ᾽ ὁπωσδήποτε. (8) τί οὖν ὑπόλοιπον, ὦ ἄνδρες Ἀθηναῖοι, πλὴν βοηθεῖν ἐρρωμένως καὶ προθύμως; ἐγὼ μὲν οὐχ ὁρῶ· χωρὶς γὰρ τῆς περιστάσης ἂν ἡμᾶς αἰσχύνης, εἰ καθυφείμεθά τι τῶν πραγμάτων, οὐδὲ τὸν φόβον, ὦ ἄνδρες Ἀθηναῖοι, μικρὸν ὁρῶ τὸν τῶν μετὰ ταῦτα, ἐχόντων μὲν ὡς ἔχουσι Θηβαίων ἡμῖν, ἀπειρηκότων δὲ χρήμασι Φωκέων, μηδενὸς δὲ ἐμποδὼν ὄντος Φιλίππωι τὰ παρόντα καταστρεψαμένωι πρὸς ταῦτα ἐπικλῖναι τὰ πράγματα. (9) ἀλλὰ μὴν εἴ τις ὑμῶν εἰς τοῦτ᾽ ἀναβάλλεται ποιήσειν τὰ δέοντα, ἰδεῖν ἐγγύθεν βούλεται τὰ δεινά, ἐξὸν ἀκούειν ἄλλοθι γιγνόμενα, καὶ βοηθοὺς ἑαυτῶι ζητεῖν, ἐξὸν νῦν ἑτέροις αὐτὸν βοηθεῖν· ὅτι γὰρ εἰς τοῦτο περιστήσεται τὰ πράγματα, ἐὰν τὰ παρόντα προώμεθα, σχεδὸν ἴσμεν ἅπαντες δήπου. (10) ἀλλ᾽ ὅτι μὲν δὴ δεῖ βοηθεῖν, εἴποι τις ἄν, πάντες ἐγνώκαμεν, καὶ βοηθήσομεν· τὸ δὲ ὅπως, τοῦτο λέγε. μὴ τοίνυν, ὦ ἄνδρες Ἀθηναῖοι, θαυμάσητε, ἂν παράδοξον εἴπω τι τοῖς πολλοῖς. νομοθέτας καθίσατε. ἐν δὲ τούτοις τοῖς νομοθέταις μὴ θῆσθε νόμον μηδένα (εἰσὶ γὰρ ὑμῖν ἱκανοί), ἀλλὰ τοὺς εἰς τὸ παρὸν βλάπτοντας ὑμᾶς λύσατε. (11) λέγω τοὺς περὶ τῶν θεωρικῶν, σαφῶς οὑτωσί, καὶ τοὺς περὶ τῶν στρατευομένων ἐνίους, ὧν οἱ μὲν τὰ στρατιωτικὰ τοῖς οἴκοι μένουσι διανέμουσι θεωρικά, οἱ δὲ τοὺς ἀτακτοῦντας ἀθώιους καθιστᾶσιν, εἶτα καὶ τοὺς τὰ δέοντα ποιεῖν βουλομένους ἀθυμοτέρους ποιοῦσιν. ἐπειδὰν δὲ ταῦτα λύσητε καὶ τὴν τοῦ τὰ βέλτιστα λέγειν ὁδὸν παράσχητε ἀσφαλῆ, τηνικαῦτα τὸν γράψοντα ἃ πάντες ἴσθ᾽ ὅτι συμφέρει ζητεῖτε. (12) πρὶν δὲ ταῦτα πρᾶξαι, μὴ σκοπεῖτε τίς εἰπὼν τὰ βέλτιστα ὑπὲρ ὑμῶν ὑφ᾽ ὑμῶν ἀπολέσθαι βουλήσεται· οὐ γὰρ εὑρήσετε, ἄλλως τε καὶ τούτου μόνου περιγίγνεσθαι μέλλοντος, παθεῖν ἀδίκως τι κακὸν τὸν ταῦτ᾽ εἰπόντα καὶ γράψαντα, μηδὲν δὲ ὠφελῆσαι τὰ πράγματα, ἀλλὰ καὶ εἰς τὸ λοιπὸν μᾶλλον ἔτι ἢ νῦν τὸ τὰ βέλτιστα λέγειν φοβερώτερον ποιῆσαι. καὶ λύειν γε, ὦ ἄνδρες Ἀθηναῖοι, τοὺς νόμους δεῖ τούτους τοὺς αὐτοὺς ἀξιοῦν οἵπερ καὶ τεθήκασιν· (13) οὐ γάρ ἐστι δίκαιον, τὴν μὲν χάριν, ἢ πᾶσαν ἔβλαπτε τὴν πόλιν, τοῖς τότε θεῖσιν ὑπάρχειν, τὴν δ᾽ ἀπέχθειαν, δι᾽ ἧς ἂν ἅπαντες ἄμεινον πράξαιμεν, τῶι νῦν τὰ βέλτιστα εἰπόντι ζημίαν γενέσθαι. πρὶν δὲ ταῦτα εὐτρεπίσαι, μηδαμῶς, ὦ ἄνδρες Ἀθηναῖοι, μηδένα ἀξιοῦτε τηλικοῦτον εἶναι παρ᾽ ὑμῖν ὥστε τοὺς νόμους τούτους παραβάντα μὴ δοῦναι δίκην, μηδ᾽ οὕτως ἀνόητον ὥστ᾽ εἰς προῦπτον κακὸν αὑτὸν ἐμβαλεῖν.

11 θεωρικά D: del. Cobet

## 3 ΟΛΥΝΘΙΑΚΟΣ Γ 53

(14) οὐ μὴν οὐδ' ἐκεῖνό γ' ὑμᾶς ἀγνοεῖν δεῖ, ὦ ἄνδρες Ἀθηναῖοι, ὅτι ψήφισμα οὐδενὸς ἄξιόν ἐστιν, ἂν μὴ προσγένηται τὸ ποιεῖν ἐθέλειν τὰ δόξαντα προθύμως ὑμᾶς. εἰ γὰρ αὐτάρκη τὰ ψηφίσματα ἦν ἢ ὑμᾶς ἀναγκάζειν ἃ προσήκει πράττειν ἢ περὶ ὧν γραφείη διαπράξασθαι, οὔτ' ἂν ὑμεῖς πολλὰ ψηφιζόμενοι μικρά, μᾶλλον δ' οὐδέν, ἐπράττετε τούτων, οὔτε Φίλιππος τοσοῦτον ὑβρίκει χρόνον· πάλαι γὰρ ἂν εἵνεκά γε ψηφισμάτων ἐδεδώκει δίκην. (15) ἀλλ' οὐχ οὕτω ταῦτ' ἔχει· τὸ γὰρ πράττειν τοῦ λέγειν καὶ χειροτονεῖν ὕστερον ὂν τῆι τάξει, πρότερον τῆι δυνάμει καὶ κρεῖττόν ἐστιν. τοῦτ' οὖν δεῖ προσεῖναι, τὰ δ' ἄλλα ὑπάρχει· καὶ γὰρ εἰπεῖν τὰ δέοντα παρ' ὑμῖν εἰσιν, ὦ ἄνδρες Ἀθηναῖοι, δυνάμενοι, καὶ γνῶναι πάντων ὑμεῖς ὀξύτατοι τὰ ῥηθέντα, καὶ πρᾶξαι δὲ δυνήσεσθε νῦν, ἐὰν ὀρθῶς ποιῆτε. (16) τίνα γὰρ χρόνον ἢ τίνα καιρόν, ὦ ἄνδρες Ἀθηναῖοι, τοῦ παρόντος βελτίω ζητεῖτε; ἢ πότε ἃ δεῖ πράξετε, εἰ μὴ νῦν; οὐχ ἅπαντα μὲν ἡμῶν προείληφε τὰ χωρία ἄνθρωπος, εἰ δὲ καὶ ταύτης κύριος τῆς χώρας γενήσεται, πάντων αἴσχιστα πεισόμεθα; οὐχ οὕς, εἰ πολεμήσαιεν, ἑτοίμως σώσειν ὑπισχνούμεθα, οὗτοι νῦν πολεμοῦσιν; οὐκ ἐχθρός; οὐκ ἔχων τὰ ἡμέτερα; οὐ βάρβαρος; οὐχ ὅ τι ἂν εἴποι τις; (17) ἀλλὰ πρὸς θεῶν πάντ' ἐάσαντες καὶ μόνον οὐχὶ συγκατασκευάσαντες αὐτῶι, τότε τοὺς αἰτίους οἵτινες τούτων ζητήσομεν; οὐ γὰρ αὐτοί γ' αἴτιοι φήσομεν εἶναι, σαφῶς οἶδα τοῦτ' ἐγώ. οὐδὲ γὰρ ἐν τοῖς τοῦ πολέμου κινδύνοις τῶν φυγόντων οὐδεὶς ἑαυτοῦ κατηγορεῖ, ἀλλὰ τοῦ στρατηγοῦ καὶ τῶν πλησίον καὶ πάντων μᾶλλον, ἥττηνται δ' ὅμως διὰ πάντας τοὺς φυγόντας δήπου· μένειν γὰρ ἐξῆν τῶι κατηγοροῦντι τῶν ἄλλων, εἰ δὲ τοῦτ' ἐποίει ἕκαστος, ἐνίκων ἄν. (18) καὶ νῦν, οὐ λέγει τις τὰ βέλτιστα· ἀναστὰς ἄλλος εἰπάτω, μὴ τοῦτον αἰτιάσθω. ἕτερος λέγει τις βελτίω· ταῦτα ποιεῖτε ἀγαθῆι τύχηι. ἀλλ' οὐχ ἡδέα ταῦτα· οὐκέτι τοῦθ' ὁ λέγων ἀδικεῖ, πλὴν εἰ δέον εὔξασθαι παραλείπει. εὔξασθαι μὲν γάρ, ὦ ἄνδρες Ἀθηναῖοι, ῥάιδιον, εἰς ταὐτὸ πάνθ' ὅσα βούλεταί τις ἀθροίσαντα ἐν ὀλίγωι· ἑλέσθαι δέ, ὅταν περὶ πραγμάτων προτεθῆι σκοπεῖν, οὐκέθ' ὁμοίως εὔπορον, ἀλλὰ δεῖ τὰ βέλτιστα ἀντὶ τῶν ἡδέων, ἂν μὴ συναμφότερ' ἐξῆι, λαμβάνειν.
(19) εἰ δέ τις ἡμῖν ἔχει καὶ τὰ θεωρικὰ ἐᾶν καὶ πόρους ἑτέρους λέγειν στρατιωτικούς, οὐχ οὗτος κρείττων; εἴποι τις ἄν. φήμ' ἔγωγε, εἴπερ ἔστιν, ὦ ἄνδρες Ἀθηναῖοι· ἀλλὰ θαυμάζω εἴ τῳ πώποτε ἀνθρώπων ἢ γέγονεν ἢ γενήσεται, ἂν τὰ παρόντα ἀναλώσηι πρὸς ἃ μὴ δεῖ, τῶν ἀπόντων εὐπορῆσαι πρὸς ἃ δεῖ. ἀλλ', οἶμαι, μέγα τοῖς τοιούτοις ὑπάρχει λόγοις ἡ παρ' ἑκάστου βούλησις, διόπερ ῥᾶιστον ἁπάντων ἐστὶν αὑτὸν ἐξαπατῆσαι· ὃ γὰρ βούλεται, τοῦθ' ἕκαστος καὶ οἴεται, τὰ δὲ πράγματα πολλάκις οὐχ οὕτω πέφυκε. (20) ὁρᾶτε οὖν, ὦ ἄνδρες Ἀθηναῖοι, ταῦθ' οὕτως, ὅπως καὶ τὰ πράγματα ἐνδέχεται καὶ δυνήσεσθε ἐξιέναι καὶ μισθὸν ἕξετε. οὔ τοι σωφρόνων οὐδὲ γενναίων ἐστὶν ἀνθρώπων, ἐλλείποντάς τι δι' ἔνδειαν χρημάτων τῶν τοῦ πολέμου εὐχερῶς τὰ τοιαῦτα

14 τὰ δόξαντα d: τά γε δόξαντα d    προθύμως ὑμᾶς D: προθύμως Cobet

ὀνείδη φέρειν, οὐδ' ἐπὶ μὲν Κορινθίους καὶ Μεγαρέας ἁρπάσαντας τὰ ὅπλα πορεύεσθαι, Φίλιππον δ' ἐᾶν πόλεις Ἑλληνίδας ἀνδραποδίζεσθαι δι' ἀπορίαν ἐφοδίων τοῖς στρατευομένοις.

(21) καὶ ταῦτ' οὐχ ἵν' ἀπέχθωμαί τισιν ὑμῶν τὴν ἄλλως προῄρημαι λέγειν· οὐ γὰρ οὕτως ἄφρων οὐδὲ ἀτυχής εἰμι ἐγώ ὥστ' ἀπεχθάνεσθαι βούλεσθαι μηδὲν ὠφελεῖν νομίζων· ἀλλὰ δικαίου πολίτου κρίνω τὴν τῶν πραγμάτων σωτηρίαν ἀντὶ τῆς ἐν τῶι λέγειν χάριτος αἱρεῖσθαι. καὶ γὰρ τοὺς ἐπὶ τῶν προγόνων ἡμῶν λέγοντας ἀκούω, ὥσπερ ἴσως καὶ ὑμεῖς, οὓς ἐπαινοῦσι μὲν οἱ παριόντες ἅπαντες, μιμοῦνται δ' οὐ πάνυ, τούτωι τῶι ἔθει καὶ τῶι τρόπωι τῆς πολιτείας χρῆσθαι, τὸν Ἀριστείδην ἐκεῖνον, τὸν Νικίαν, τὸν ὁμώνυμον ἐμαυτῶι, τὸν Περικλέα. (22) ἐξ οὗ δ' οἱ διερωτῶντες ὑμᾶς οὗτοι πεφήνασι ῥήτορες "τί βούλεσθε; τί γράψω; τί ὑμῖν χαρίσωμαι;" προπέποται τῆς παραυτίκα χάριτος τὰ τῆς πόλεως πράγματα, καὶ τοιαυτὶ συμβαίνει, καὶ τὰ μὲν τούτων πάντα καλῶς ἔχει, τὰ δ' ὑμέτερα αἰσχρῶς. (23) καίτοι σκέψασθε, ὦ ἄνδρες Ἀθηναῖοι, ἅ τις ἂν κεφάλαια εἰπεῖν ἔχοι τῶν τ' ἐπὶ τῶν προγόνων ἔργων καὶ τῶν ἐφ' ὑμῶν. ἔσται δὲ βραχὺς καὶ γνώριμος ὑμῖν ὁ λόγος· οὐ γὰρ ἀλλοτρίοις ὑμῖν χρωμένοις παραδείγμασιν, ἀλλ' οἰκείοις, ὦ ἄνδρες Ἀθηναῖοι, εὐδαίμοσιν ἔξεστι γενέσθαι. (24) ἐκεῖνοι τοίνυν, οἷς οὐκ ἐχαρίζονθ' οἱ λέγοντες οὐδ' ἐφίλουν αὐτοὺς ὥσπερ ὑμᾶς οὗτοι νῦν, πέντε μὲν καὶ τετταράκοντα ἔτη τῶν Ἑλλήνων ἦρξαν ἑκόντων, πλείω δ' ἢ μύρια τάλαντ' εἰς τὴν ἀκρόπολιν ἀνήγαγον, ὑπήκουε δὲ ὁ ταύτην τὴν χώραν ἔχων αὐτοῖς βασιλεύς, ὥσπερ ἐστὶ προσῆκον βάρβαρον Ἕλλησι, πολλὰ δὲ καὶ καλὰ καὶ πεζῆι καὶ ναυμαχοῦντες ἔστησαν τρόπαια αὐτοὶ στρατευόμενοι, μόνοι δὲ ἀνθρώπων κρείττω τὴν ἐπὶ τοῖς ἔργοις δόξαν τῶν φθονούντων κατέλιπον. (25) ἐπὶ μὲν δὴ τῶν Ἑλληνικῶν ἦσαν τοιοῦτοι· ἐν δὲ τοῖς κατὰ τὴν πόλιν αὐτὴν θεάσασθε ὁποῖοι, ἔν τε τοῖς κοινοῖς κἀν τοῖς ἰδίοις. δημοσίαι μὲν τοίνυν οἰκοδομήματα καὶ κάλλη τοιαῦτα καὶ τοσαῦτα κατεσκεύασαν ἡμῖν ἱερῶν καὶ τῶν ἐν τούτοις ἀναθημάτων, ὥστε μηδενὶ τῶν ἐπιγιγνομένων ὑπερβολὴν λελεῖφθαι· ἰδίαι δ' οὕτω σώφρονες ἦσαν καὶ σφόδρα ἐν τῶι τῆς πολιτείας ἤθει μένοντες, (26) ὥστε τὴν Ἀριστείδου καὶ τὴν Μιλτιάδου καὶ τῶν τότε λαμπρῶν οἰκίαν εἴ τις ἄρα οἶδεν ὑμῶν ὁποία ποτ' ἐστίν, ὁρᾶι τῆς τοῦ γείτονος οὐδὲν σεμνοτέραν οὖσαν· οὐ γὰρ εἰς περιουσίαν ἐπράττετ' αὐτοῖς τὰ τῆς πόλεως, ἀλλὰ τὸ κοινὸν αὔξειν ἕκαστος ὤιετο δεῖν. ἐκ δὲ τοῦ τὰ μὲν Ἑλληνικὰ πιστῶς, τὰ δὲ πρὸς τοὺς θεοὺς εὐσεβῶς, τὰ δ' ἐν αὑτοῖς ἴσως διοικεῖν μεγάλην εἰκότως ἐκτήσαντο εὐδαιμονίαν.

(27) τότε μὲν δὴ τοῦτον τὸν τρόπον εἶχε τὰ πράγματα ἐκείνοις, χρωμένοις οἷς εἶπον προστάταις· νυνὶ δὲ πῶς ἡμῖν ὑπὸ τῶν χρηστῶν τούτων τὰ πράγματα ἔχει; ἆρά γε ὁμοίως ἢ παραπλησίως; οἷς — τὰ μὲν ἄλλα σιωπῶ, πόλλ' ἂν ἔχων εἰπεῖν· ἀλλ' ὅσης ἅπαντες ὁρᾶτ' ἐρη-

**22** τῆς παραυτίκα χάριτος d: τῆς παραυτίκα ἡδονῆς καὶ χάριτος d    **27** ὁμοίως ἢ d: ὁμοίως καὶ d, i    οἷς D: del. i: καί i

μίας ἐπειλημμένοι, {καὶ} Λακεδαιμονίων μὲν ἀπολωλότων, Θηβαίων δ' ἀσχόλων ὄντων, τῶν δ' ἄλλων οὐδενὸς ὄντος ἀξιόχρεω περὶ τῶν πρωτείων ἡμῖν ἀντιτάξασθαι· ἐξὸν δ' ἡμῖν καὶ τὰ ἡμέτερ' αὐτῶν ἀσφαλῶς ἔχειν καὶ τὰ τῶν ἄλλων δίκαια βραβεύειν, (28) ἀπεστερήμεθα μὲν χώρας οἰκείας, πλείω δ' ἢ χίλια καὶ πεντακόσια τάλαντα ἀνηλώκαμεν εἰς οὐδὲν δέον, οὓς δ' ἐν τῶι πολέμωι συμμάχους ἐκτησάμεθα, εἰρήνης οὔσης ἀπολωλέκασιν οὗτοι, ἐχθρὸν δ' ἐφ' ἡμᾶς αὐτοὺς τηλικοῦτον ἠσκήκαμεν. ἢ φρασάτω τις ἐμοὶ παρελθών, πόθεν ἄλλοθεν ἰσχυρὸς γέγονεν ἢ παρ' ἡμῶν αὐτῶν Φίλιππος. (29) "ἀλλ', ὦ τᾶν, εἰ ταῦτα φαύλως, τά γ' ἐν αὐτῆι τῆι πόλει νῦν ἄμεινον ἔχει." καὶ τί ἂν εἰπεῖν τις ἔχοι; τὰς ἐπάλξεις ἃς κονιῶμεν, καὶ τὰς ὁδοὺς ἃς ἐπισκευάζομεν, καὶ κρήνας, καὶ λήρους; ἀποβλέψατε δὴ πρὸς τοὺς ταῦτα πολιτευομένους, ὧν οἱ μὲν ἐκ πτωχῶν πλούσιοι γεγόνασιν, οἱ δ' ἐξ ἀδόξων ἔντιμοι, ἔνιοι δὲ τὰς ἰδίας οἰκίας τῶν δημοσίων οἰκοδομημάτων σεμνοτέρας εἰσὶ κατεσκευασμένοι, ὅσωι δὲ τὰ τῆς πόλεως ἐλάττω γέγονεν, τοσούτωι τὰ τούτων ηὔξηται.

(30) τί δὴ τὸ πάντων αἴτιον τούτων, καὶ τί δή ποθ' ἅπαντ' εἶχε καλῶς τότε, καὶ νῦν οὐκ ὀρθῶς; ὅτι τότε μὲν πράττειν καὶ στρατεύεσθαι τολμῶν αὐτὸς ὁ δῆμος δεσπότης τῶν πολιτευομένων ἦν καὶ κύριος αὐτὸς ἁπάντων τῶν ἀγαθῶν, καὶ ἀγαπητὸν ἦν παρὰ τοῦ δήμου τῶν ἄλλων ἑκάστωι καὶ τιμῆς καὶ ἀρχῆς καὶ ἀγαθοῦ τινος μεταλαβεῖν· (31) νῦν δὲ τοὐναντίον κύριοι μὲν οἱ πολιτευόμενοι τῶν ἀγαθῶν, καὶ διὰ τούτων ἅπαντα πράττεται, ὑμεῖς δ' ὁ δῆμος, ἐκνενευρισμένοι καὶ περιηιρημένοι χρήματα, συμμάχους, ἐν ὑπηρέτου καὶ προσθήκης μέρει γεγένησθε, ἀγαπῶντες ἐὰν μεταδιδῶσι θεωρικῶν ὑμῖν ἢ βοίδια πέμψωσιν οὗτοι, καὶ τὸ πάντων ἀνδρειότατον, τῶν ὑμετέρων αὐτῶν χάριν προσοφείλετε. οἱ δ' ἐν αὐτῆι τῆι πόλει καθείρξαντες ὑμᾶς ἐπάγουσιν ἐπὶ ταῦτα καὶ τιθασεύουσι χειροήθεις αὑτοῖς ποιοῦντες. (32) ἔστι δ' οὐδέποτ', οἶμαι, μέγα καὶ νεανικὸν φρόνημα λαβεῖν μικρὰ καὶ φαῦλα πράττοντας· ὁποῖ' ἄττα γὰρ ἂν τἀπιτηδεύματα τῶν ἀνθρώπων ἦι, τοιοῦτον ἀνάγκη καὶ τὸ φρόνημα ἔχειν. ταῦτα μὰ τὴν Δήμητρα οὐκ ἂν θαυμάσαιμι εἰ μείζων εἰπόντι ἐμοὶ γένοιτο παρ' ὑμῶν βλάβη τῶν πεποιηκότων αὐτὰ γενέσθαι· οὐδὲ γὰρ παρρησία περὶ πάντων ἀεὶ παρ' ὑμῖν ἐστιν, ἀλλ' ἔγωγε ὅτι καὶ νῦν γέγονεν θαυμάζω.

(33) ἐὰν οὖν ἀλλὰ νῦν γ' ἔτι ἀπαλλαγέντες τούτων τῶν ἐθῶν ἐθελήσητε στρατεύεσθαί τε καὶ πράττειν ἀξίως ὑμῶν αὐτῶν, καὶ ταῖς περιουσίαις ταῖς οἴκοι ταύταις ἀφορμαῖς ἐπὶ τὰ ἔξω τῶν ἀγαθῶν χρῆσθαι, ἴσως ἄν, ἴσως, ὦ ἄνδρες Ἀθηναῖοι, τέλειόν τι καὶ μέγα κτήσαισθε ἀγαθὸν καὶ τῶν τοιούτων λημμάτων ἀπαλλαγείητε, ἃ τοῖς ἀσθενοῦσι παρὰ τῶν ἰατρῶν σιτίοις διδομένοις ἔοικε. καὶ γὰρ ἐκεῖνα οὔτ' ἰσχὺν ἐντίθησιν οὔτ'

---

27 καὶ D: del. Dobree   30 τότε μὲν i: τὸ μὲν D, i   πράττειν c; cf. §33: πρῶτον D, i   31 χρήματα συμμάχους d, i: χρήματα καὶ συμμάχους d, i βοίδια d, i: βοηδρόμια d   ἀνδρειότατον d: ἀνανδρότατον d, i   32 τῶν πεποιηκότων d: ἢ τῶν πεποιηκότων d, i   γενέσθαι D: ἑκάστωι i   33 ἀσθενοῦσι D: del. Wolf   διδομένοις D: del. Cobet

ἀποθνήισκειν ἐᾶι· καὶ ταῦτα ἃ νέμεσθε νῦν ὑμεῖς, οὔτε τοσαῦτα ἐστὶν ὥστε ὠφέλειαν ἔχειν τινὰ διαρκῆ, οὔτ' ἀπογνόντας ἄλλο τι πράττειν ἐᾶι, ἀλλ' ἔστι ταῦτα τὴν ἑκάστου ῥαθυμίαν ὑμῶν ἐπαυξάνοντα. (34) "οὐκοῦν σὺ μισθοφορὰν λέγεις;" φήσει τις. καὶ παραχρῆμά γε τὴν αὐτὴν σύνταξιν ἁπάντων, ὦ ἄνδρες Ἀθηναῖοι, ἵνα τῶν κοινῶν ἕκαστος τὸ μέρος λαμβάνων, ὅτου δέοιτο ἡ πόλις, τοῦθ' ὑπάρχοι. ἔξεστιν ἄγειν ἡσυχίαν· οἴκοι μένων βελτίων, τοῦ δι' ἔνδειαν ἀνάγκηι τι ποιεῖν αἰσχρὸν ἀπηλλαγμένος. συμβαίνει τι τοιοῦτον οἷον καὶ τὰ νῦν· στρατιώτης αὐτὸς ὑπάρχων ἀπὸ τῶν αὐτῶν τούτων λημμάτων, ὥσπερ ἐστὶ δίκαιον ὑπὲρ τῆς πατρίδος. ἔστι τις ἔξω τῆς ἡλικίας ὑμῶν· ὅσα οὗτος ἀτάκτως νῦν λαμβάνων οὐκ ὠφελεῖ, ταῦτ' ἐν ἴσηι τάξει λαμβάνων πάντ' ἐφορῶν καὶ διοικῶν ἃ χρὴ πράττεσθαι. (35) ὅλως δ' οὔτ' ἀφελὼν οὔτε προσθείς, πλὴν μικρῶν, τὴν ἀταξίαν ἀνελὼν εἰς τάξιν ἤγαγον τὴν πόλιν, τὴν αὐτὴν τοῦ λαβεῖν, τοῦ στρατεύεσθαι, τοῦ δικάζειν, τοῦ ποιεῖν τοῦθ' ὅ τι καθ' ἡλικίαν ἕκαστος ἔχοι καὶ ὅτου καιρὸς εἴη, τάξιν ποιήσας. οὐκ ἔστιν ὅπου μηδὲν ἐγὼ ποιοῦσι τὰ τῶν ποιούντων εἶπον ὡς δεῖ νέμειν, οὐδ' αὐτοὺς μὲν ἀργεῖν καὶ σχολάζειν καὶ ἀπορεῖν, ὅτι δὲ οἱ τοῦ δεῖνος νικῶσι ξένοι, ταῦτα πυνθάνεσθαι· ταῦτα γὰρ νυνὶ γίγνεται. (36) καὶ οὐχὶ μέμφομαι τὸν ποιοῦντά τι τῶν δεόντων ὑπὲρ ὑμῶν, ἀλλὰ καὶ ὑμᾶς ὑπὲρ ὑμῶν αὐτῶν ἀξιῶ πράττειν ταῦτα ἐφ' οἷς ἑτέρους τιμᾶτε, καὶ μὴ παραχωρεῖν, ὦ ἄνδρες Ἀθηναῖοι, τῆς τάξεως, ἣν ὑμῖν οἱ πρόγονοι τῆς ἀρετῆς μετὰ πολλῶν καὶ καλῶν κινδύνων κτησάμενοι κατέλιπον.

σχεδὸν εἴρηκα ἃ νομίζω συμφέρειν· ὑμεῖς δ' ἔλοισθ' ὅ τι καὶ τῆι πόλει καὶ ἅπασι συνοίσειν ὑμῖν μέλλει.

# 4 ΚΑΤΑ ΦΙΛΙΠΠΟΥ Α

(1) εἰ μὲν περὶ καινοῦ τινος πράγματος προὐτίθετο, ὦ ἄνδρες Ἀθηναῖοι, λέγειν, ἐπισχὼν ἂν ἕως οἱ πλεῖστοι τῶν εἰωθότων γνώμην ἀπεφήναντο, εἰ μὲν ἤρεσκέ τί μοι τῶν ὑπὸ τούτων ῥηθέντων, ἡσυχίαν ἂν ἦγον, εἰ δὲ μή, τότ' ἂν καὶ αὐτὸς ἐπειρώμην ἃ γιγνώσκω λέγειν· ἐπειδὴ δ' ὑπὲρ ὧν πολλάκις εἰρήκασιν οὗτοι πρότερον συμβαίνει καὶ νυνὶ σκοπεῖν, ἡγοῦμαι καὶ πρῶτος ἀναστὰς εἰκότως ἂν συγγνώμης τυγχάνειν. εἰ γὰρ ἐκ τοῦ παρεληλυθότος χρόνου τὰ δέοντα οὗτοι συνεβούλευσαν, οὐδὲν ἂν ὑμᾶς νῦν ἔδει βουλεύεσθαι. (2) πρῶτον μὲν οὖν οὐκ ἀθυμητέον, ὦ ἄνδρες Ἀθηναῖοι, τοῖς παροῦσι πράγμασιν, οὐδ' εἰ πάνυ φαύλως ἔχειν δοκεῖ. ὃ γάρ ἐστι χείριστον αὐτῶν ἐκ τοῦ παρεληλυθότος χρόνου, τοῦτο πρὸς τὰ μέλλοντα βέλτιστον ὑπάρχει. τί οὖν ἐστι τοῦτο; ὅτι οὐδέν, ὦ ἄνδρες Ἀθηναῖοι, τῶν δεόντων ποιούντων ὑμῶν κακῶς τὰ πράγματα ἔχει· ἐπεί τοι, εἰ πάνθ' ἃ προσῆκε πραττόντων οὕτως εἶχεν, οὐδ' ἂν ἐλπὶς ἦν αὐτὰ βελτίω γενέσθαι. (3) ἔπειτα ἐνθυμητέον καὶ παρ' ἄλλων ἀκούουσι καὶ τοῖς εἰδόσιν αὐτοῖς ἀναμιμνησκομένοις, ἡλίκην ποτ' ἐχόντων δύναμιν Λακεδαιμονίων, ἐξ οὗ χρόνος οὐ πολύς, ὡς καλῶς καὶ προσηκόντως οὐδὲν ἀνάξιον ὑμεῖς ἐπράξατε τῆς πόλεως, ἀλλ' ὑπεμείνατε ὑπὲρ τῶν δικαίων τὸν πρὸς ἐκείνους πόλεμον. τίνος οὖν εἵνεκα ταῦτα λέγω; ἵν' ἴδητε, ὦ ἄνδρες Ἀθηναῖοι, καὶ θεάσησθε, ὅτι οὐδὲν οὔτε φυλαττομένοις ὑμῖν ἐστιν φοβερόν, οὔτ', ἂν ὀλιγωρῆτε, τοιοῦτον οἷον ἂν ὑμεῖς βούλοισθε, παραδείγμασι χρώμενοι τῆι τότε ῥώμηι τῶν Λακεδαιμονίων, ἧς ἐκρατεῖτε ἐκ τοῦ προσέχειν τοῖς πράγμασι τὸν νοῦν, καὶ τῆι νῦν ὕβρει τούτου, δι' ἣν ταραττόμεθ' ἐκ τοῦ μηδὲν φροντίζειν ὧν ἐχρῆν. (4) εἰ δέ τις ὑμῶν, ὦ ἄνδρες Ἀθηναῖοι, δυσπολέμητον οἴεται τὸν Φίλιππον εἶναι, σκοπῶν τό τε πλῆθος τῆς ὑπαρχούσης αὐτῶι δυνάμεως καὶ τὸ τὰ χωρία πάντ' ἀπολωλέναι τῆι πόλει, ὀρθῶς μὲν οἴεται, λογισάσθω μέντοι τοῦτο, ὅτι εἴχομέν ποθ' ἡμεῖς, ὦ ἄνδρες Ἀθηναῖοι, Πύδναν καὶ Ποτείδαιαν καὶ Μεθώνην καὶ πάντα τὸν τόπον τοῦτον οἰκεῖον κύκλωι, καὶ πολλὰ τῶν μετ' ἐκείνου νῦν ὄντων ἐθνῶν αὐτονομούμενα καὶ ἐλεύθερ' ὑπῆρχε, καὶ μᾶλλον ἡμῖν ἐβούλετ' ἔχειν οἰκείως ἢ 'κείνωι. (5) εἰ τοίνυν ὁ Φίλιππος τότε ταύτην ἔσχε τὴν γνώμην, ὡς χαλεπὸν πολεμεῖν ἐστιν Ἀθηναίοις ἔχουσι τοσαῦτα ἐπιτειχίσματα τῆς αὑτοῦ χώρας ἔρημον ὄντα συμμάχων, οὐδὲν ἂν ὧν νυνὶ πεποίηκεν ἔπραξεν οὐδὲ τοσαύτην ἐκτήσατο δύναμιν. ἀλλ' εἶδεν, ὦ ἄνδρες Ἀθηναῖοι, τοῦτο καλῶς ἐκεῖνος, ὅτι ταῦτα μέν ἐστιν ἅπαντα τὰ χωρία ἆθλα τοῦ πολέμου κείμενα ἐν μέσωι, φύσει δ' ὑπάρχει τοῖς παροῦσι τὰ τῶν ἀπόντων, καὶ τοῖς ἐθέλουσι πονεῖν καὶ κινδυνεύειν τὰ τῶν ἀμελούντων. (6) καὶ γάρ τοι ταύτηι χρησάμενος τῆι γνώμηι

---

1 λέγειν D, i: σκοπεῖν i   καὶ αὐτὸς d: αὐτὸς d   4 ἡμῖν d, i: ὑμῖν d   5 ἐκτήσατο d: ἐκτήσατ' ἂν d

πάντα κατέστραπται καὶ ἔχει, τὰ μὲν ὡς ἂν ἑλών τις ἔχοι πολέμωι, τὰ δὲ σύμμαχα καὶ φίλα ποιησάμενος· καὶ γὰρ συμμαχεῖν καὶ προσέχειν τὸν νοῦν τούτοις ἐθέλουσιν ἅπαντες, οὓς ἂν ὁρῶσι παρεσκευασμένους καὶ πράττειν ἐθέλοντας ἃ χρή. (7) ἂν τοίνυν, ὦ ἄνδρες Ἀθηναῖοι, καὶ ὑμεῖς ἐπὶ τῆς τοιαύτης ἐθελήσητε γενέσθαι γνώμης νῦν, ἐπειδήπερ οὐ πρότερον, καὶ ἕκαστος ὑμῶν, οὗ δεῖ καὶ δύναιτ᾿ ἂν παρασχεῖν αὑτὸν χρήσιμον τῆι πόλει, πᾶσαν ἀφεὶς τὴν εἰρωνείαν ἕτοιμος πράττειν ὑπάρξηι, ὁ μὲν χρήματα ἔχων εἰσφέρειν, ὁ δ᾿ ἐν ἡλικίαι στρατεύεσθαι, — συνελόντι δ᾿ ἁπλῶς ἂν ὑμῶν αὐτῶν ἐθελήσητε γενέσθαι, καὶ παύσησθε αὐτὸς μὲν οὐδὲν ἕκαστος ποιήσειν ἐλπίζων, τὸν δὲ πλησίον πάνθ᾿ ὑπὲρ αὑτοῦ πράξειν, καὶ τὰ ὑμέτερα αὐτῶν κομιεῖσθε, ἂν θεὸς θέληι, καὶ τὰ κατερραθυμημένα πάλιν ἀναλήψεσθε, κἀκεῖνον τιμωρήσεσθε. (8) μὴ γὰρ ὡς θεῶι νομίζετ᾿ ἐκείνωι τὰ παρόντα πεπηγέναι πράγματα ἀθάνατα, ἀλλὰ καὶ μισεῖ τις ἐκεῖνον καὶ δέδιεν, ὦ ἄνδρες Ἀθηναῖοι, καὶ φθονεῖ, καὶ τῶν πάνυ νῦν δοκούντων οἰκείως ἔχειν· καὶ ἅπανθ᾿ ὅσα περ κἂν ἄλλοις τισὶν ἀνθρώποις ἔνι, ταῦτα κἀν τοῖς μετ᾿ ἐκείνου χρὴ νομίζειν ἐνεῖναι. κατέπτηχε μέντοι πάντα ταῦτα νῦν, οὐκ ἔχοντα ἀποστροφὴν διὰ τὴν ὑμετέραν βραδυτῆτα καὶ ῥαθυμίαν· ἣν ἀποθέσθαι φημὶ δεῖν ἤδη. (9) ὁρᾶτε γάρ, ὦ ἄνδρες Ἀθηναῖοι, τὸ πρᾶγμα, οἷ προελήλυθεν ἀσελγείας ἅνθρωπος, ὃς οὐδ᾿ αἵρεσιν ὑμῖν δίδωσι τοῦ πράττειν ἢ ἄγειν ἡσυχίαν, ἀλλ᾿ ἀπειλεῖ καὶ λόγους ὑπερηφάνους, ὥς φασι, λέγει, καὶ οὐχ οἷός ἐστιν ἔχων ἃ κατέστραπται μένειν ἐπὶ τούτων, ἀλλ᾿ ἀεί τι προσπεριβάλλεται καὶ κύκλωι πανταχῆι μέλλοντας ἡμᾶς καὶ καθημένους περιστοιχίζεται. (10) πότ᾿ οὖν, ὦ ἄνδρες Ἀθηναῖοι, πότε ἃ χρὴ πράξετε; ἐπειδὰν τί γένηται; "ἐπειδὰν νὴ Δία ἀνάγκη τις ἦι." νῦν δὲ τί χρὴ τὰ γιγνόμενα ἡγεῖσθαι; ἐγὼ μὲν γὰρ οἴομαι τοῖς ἐλευθέροις μεγίστην ἀνάγκην τὴν ὑπὲρ τῶν πραγμάτων αἰσχύνην εἶναι. ἢ βούλεσθε, εἰπέ μοι, περιιόντες αὑτῶν πυνθάνεσθαι, "λέγεταί τι καινόν;" γένοιτο γὰρ ἄν τι καινότερον ἢ Μακεδὼν ἀνὴρ Ἀθηναίους καταπολεμῶν καὶ τὰ τῶν Ἑλλήνων διοικῶν; (11) "τέθνηκε Φίλιππος;" "οὐ μὰ Δία, ἀλλ᾿ ἀσθενεῖ." τί δ᾿ ὑμῖν διαφέρει; καὶ γὰρ ἂν οὗτός τι πάθηι, ταχέως ὑμεῖς ἕτερον Φίλιππον ποιήσετε, ἄνπερ οὕτω προσέχητε τοῖς πράγμασι τὸν νοῦν· οὐδὲ γὰρ οὗτος παρὰ τὴν αὑτοῦ ῥώμην τοσοῦτον ἐπηύξηται ὅσον παρὰ τὴν ἡμετέραν ἀμέλειαν. (12) καίτοι καὶ τοῦτο· εἴ τι πάθοι καὶ τὰ τῆς τύχης ἡμῖν, ἥπερ ἀεὶ βέλτιον ἢ ἡμεῖς ἡμῶν αὐτῶν ἐπιμελούμεθα, καὶ τοῦτο ἐξεργάσαιτο, ἴσθ᾿ ὅτι πλησίον μὲν ὄντες, ἅπασιν ἂν τοῖς πράγμασι τεταραγμένοις ἐπιστάντες ὅπως βούλεσθε διοικήσαισθε, ὡς δὲ νῦν ἔχετε, οὐδὲ διδόντων τῶν καιρῶν Ἀμφίπολιν δέξασθαι δύναισθ᾿ ἄν, ἀπηρτημένοι καὶ ταῖς παρασκευαῖς καὶ ταῖς γνώμαις.

(13) ὡς μὲν οὖν δεῖ τὰ προσήκοντα ποιεῖν ἐθέλοντας ὑπάρχειν ἅπαντας ἑτοίμως, ὡς ἐγνωκότων ὑμῶν καὶ πεπεισμένων, παύομαι λέγων· τὸν δὲ τρόπον τῆς παρασκευῆς ἣν ἀπαλλάξαι ἂν τῶν τοιούτων πραγμάτων

12 τὰ τῆς τύχης d: τὸ τῆς τύχης d

ὑμᾶς οἴομαι, καὶ τὸ πλῆθος ὅσον, καὶ πόρους οὕστινας χρημάτων, καὶ τἄλλα ὡς ἄν μοι βέλτιστα καὶ τάχιστα δοκεῖ παρασκευασθῆναι, καὶ δὴ πειράσομαι λέγειν, δεηθεὶς ὑμῶν, ὦ ἄνδρες Ἀθηναῖοι, τοσοῦτον. (14) ἐπειδὰν ἅπαντα ἀκούσητε κρίνατε, μὴ πρότερον προλαμβάνετε· μηδ', ἄν ἐξ ἀρχῆς δοκῶ τινι καινὴν παρασκευὴν λέγειν, ἀναβάλλειν με τὰ πράγματα ἡγείσθω. οὐ γὰρ οἱ "ταχὺ" καὶ "τήμερον" εἰπόντες μάλιστα εἰς δέον λέγουσιν (οὐ γὰρ ἄν τά γ' ἤδη γεγενημένα τῆι νυνὶ βοηθείαι κωλῦσαι δυνηθεῖμεν), (15) ἀλλ' ὃς ἄν δείξηι τίς πορισθεῖσα παρασκευὴ καὶ πόση καὶ πόθεν διαμεῖναι δυνήσεται, ἕως ἄν ἢ διαλυσώμεθα πεισθέντες τὸν πόλεμον ἢ περιγενώμεθα τῶν ἐχθρῶν· οὕτω γὰρ οὐκέτι τοῦ λοιποῦ πάσχοιμεν ἄν κακῶς. οἶμαι τοίνυν ἐγὼ ταῦτα λέγειν ἔχειν, μὴ κωλύων εἴ τις ἄλλος ἐπαγγέλλεταί τι. ἡ μὲν οὖν ὑπόσχεσις οὕτω μεγάλη, τὸ δὲ πρᾶγμα ἤδη τὸν ἔλεγχον δώσει· κριταὶ δ' ὑμεῖς ἔσεσθε.

(16) πρῶτον μὲν τοίνυν, ὦ ἄνδρες Ἀθηναῖοι, τριήρεις πεντήκοντα παρασκευάσασθαι φημὶ δεῖν, εἶτ' αὐτοὺς οὕτω τὰς γνώμας ἔχειν ὡς, ἐάν τι δέηι, πλευστέον εἰς ταύτας αὐτοῖς ἐμβᾶσιν. πρὸς δὲ τούτοις τοῖς ἡμίσεσιν τῶν ἱππέων ἱππαγωγοὺς τριήρεις καὶ πλοῖα ἱκανὰ εὐτρεπίσαι κελεύω. (17) ταῦτα μὲν οἶμαι δεῖν ὑπάρχειν ἐπὶ τὰς ἐξαίφνης ταύτας ἀπὸ τῆς οἰκείας χώρας αὐτοῦ στρατείας εἰς Πύλας καὶ Χερρόνησον καὶ Ὄλυνθον καὶ ὅποι βούλεται· δεῖ γὰρ ἐκείνωι τοῦτο ἐν τῆι γνώμηι παραστῆσαι, ὡς ὑμεῖς ἐκ τῆς ἀμελείας ταύτης τῆς ἄγαν, ὥσπερ εἰς Εὔβοιαν καὶ πρότερόν ποτέ φασιν εἰς Ἁλίαρτον καὶ τὰ τελευταῖα πρώην εἰς Πύλας, ἴσως ἄν ὁρμήσαιτε — (18) οὔ τοι παντελῶς, οὐδ' εἰ μὴ ποιήσαιτ' ἄν τοῦτο, ὥς ἔγωγέ φημι δεῖν, εὐκαταφρόνητόν ἐστιν — ἵν' ἢ διὰ τὸν φόβον εἰδὼς εὐτρεπεῖς ὑμᾶς (εἴσεται γὰρ ἀκριβῶς· εἰσὶ γάρ, εἰσὶν οἱ πάντ' ἐξαγγέλλοντες ἐκείνωι παρ' ἡμῶν αὐτῶν πλείους τοῦ δέοντος) ἡσυχίαν ἔχηι, ἢ παριδὼν ταῦτα ἀφύλακτος ληφθῆι, μηδενὸς ὄντος ἐμποδὼν πλεῖν ἐπὶ τὴν ἐκείνου χώραν ὑμῖν, ἄν ἐνδῶι καιρόν. (19) ταῦτα μέν ἐστιν ἃ πᾶσι δεδόχθαι φημὶ δεῖν καὶ παρεσκευάσθαι προσήκειν οἴομαι· πρὸ δὲ τούτων δύναμίν τινα, ὦ ἄνδρες Ἀθηναῖοι, φημὶ προχειρίσασθαι δεῖν ὑμᾶς, ἢ συνεχῶς πολεμήσει καὶ κακῶς ἐκεῖνον ποιήσει. μή μοι μυρίους μηδὲ δισμυρίους ξένους, μηδὲ τὰς ἐπιστολιμαίους ταύτας δυνάμεις, ἀλλ' ἢ τῆς πόλεως ἔσται, κἄν ὑμεῖς ἕνα κἄν πλείους κἄν τὸν δεῖνα κἄν ὁντινοῦν χειροτονήσητε στρατηγόν, τούτωι πείσεται καὶ ἀκολουθήσει. καὶ τροφὴν ταύτηι πορίσαι κελεύω. (20) ἔσται δ' αὕτη τίς ἡ δύναμις καὶ πόση, καὶ πόθεν τὴν τροφὴν ἕξει, καὶ πῶς ταῦτ' ἐθελήσει ποιεῖν; ἐγὼ φράσω, καθ' ἕκαστον τούτων διεξιὼν χωρίς. ξένους μὲν λέγω — καὶ ὅπως μὴ ποιήσεθ' ὃ πολλάκις ὑμᾶς ἔβλαψεν· πάντ' ἐλάττω νομίζοντες εἶναι τοῦ δέοντος, καὶ τὰ μέγιστ' ἐν τοῖς ψηφίσμασιν αἱρούμενοι, ἐπὶ τῶι πράττειν οὐδὲ τὰ μικρὰ ποιεῖτε· ἀλλὰ τὰ μικρὰ ποιήσαντες καὶ πορίσαντες τούτοις προστίθετε, ἄν ἐλάττω φαίνηται. (21) λέγω δὴ τοὺς πάντας στρατιώτας δισχιλίους, τούτων δὲ Ἀθηναίους φημὶ δεῖν εἶναι πεντακοσίους, ἐξ ἧς ἄν

13 ὑμᾶς d: ἡμᾶς d    20 ποιήσεθ' c: ποιήσητε D

τινός ύμΐν ηλικίας καλώς έχειν δοκήι, χρόνον τακτόν στρατευομένους, μή μακρόν τούτον, άλλ' όσον άν δοκήι καλώς έχειν, έκ διαδοχής άλλήλοις· τούς δ' άλλους ξένους είναι κελεύω. καί μετά τούτων ιππέας διακοσίους, καί τούτων πεντήκοντα Άθηναίους τούλάχιστον, ώσπερ τούς πεζούς τόν αύτόν τρόπον στρατευομένους· καί ίππαγωγούς τούτοις. (22) είέν· τί πρός τούτοις έτι; ταχείας τριήρεις δέκα· δει γάρ, έχοντος έκείνου ναυτικόν, καί ταχειών τριήρων ήμίν, όπως άσφαλώς ή δύναμις πλέηι. πόθεν δή τούτοις ή τροφή γενήσεται; έγώ καί τούτο φράσω καί δείξω, έπειδάν, διότι τηλικαύτην άποχρήν οίμαι τήν δύναμιν καί πολίτας τούς στρατευομένους είναι κελεύω, διδάξω.

(23) τοσαύτην μέν, ώ άνδρες Άθηναίοι, διά ταύτα, ότι ούκ ένι νύν ήμίν πορίσασθαι δύναμιν τήν έκείνωι παραταξομένην, άλλά ληιστεύειν άνάγκη καί τούτωι τώι τρόπωι τού πολέμου χρήσθαι τήν πρώτην· ού τοίνυν ύπέρογκον αύτήν (ού γάρ έστι μισθός ούδέ τροφή), ούδέ παντελώς ταπεινήν είναι δεί. (24) πολίτας δέ παρείναι καί συμπλείν διά ταύτα κελεύω, ότι καί πρότερόν ποτ' άκούω ξενικόν τρέφειν έν Κορίνθωι τήν πόλιν, ού Πολύστρατος ήγείτο καί Ίφικράτης καί Χαβρίας καί άλλοι τινές, καί αύτούς ύμάς συστρατεύεσθαι· καί οίδα άκούων ότι Λακεδαιμονίους παραταττόμενοι μεθ' ύμών ένίκων ούτοι οί ξένοι καί ύμείς μετ' έκείνων. έξ ού δ' αύτά καθ' αύτά τά ξενικά ύμίν στρατεύεται, τούς φίλους νικά καί τούς συμμάχους, οί δ' έχθροί μείζους τού δέοντος γεγόνασιν. καί παρακύψαντα έπί τόν τής πόλεως πόλεμον, πρός Άρτάβαζον καί πανταχοί μάλλον οίχεται πλέοντα, ό δέ στρατηγός άκολουθεί, εικότως· ού γάρ έστιν άρχειν μή διδόντα μισθόν. (25) τί ούν κελεύω; τάς προφάσεις άφελείν καί τού στρατηγού καί τών στρατιωτών, μισθόν πορίσαντας καί στρατιώτας οικείους ώσπερ έπόπτας τών στρατηγουμένων παρακαταστήσαντας· έπεί νύν γε γέλως έσθ' ώς χρώμεθα τοίς πράγμασιν. εί γάρ έροιτό τις ύμάς, "ειρήνην άγετε, ώ άνδρες Άθηναίοι;" "μά Δί' ούχ ήμείς γε," είποιτ' άν, "άλλά Φιλίππωι πολεμούμεν." (26) ούκ έχειροτονείτε δ' έξ ύμών αύτών δέκα ταξιάρχους καί στρατηγούς καί φυλάρχους καί ίππάρχους δύο; τί ούν ούτοι ποιούσιν; πλήν ένός άνδρός, όν άν έκπέμψητε έπί τόν πόλεμον, οί λοιποί τάς πομπάς πέμπουσιν ύμίν μετά τών ίεροποιών· ώσπερ γάρ οί πλάττοντες τούς πηλίνους, είς τήν άγοράν χειροτονείτε τούς ταξιάρχους καί τούς φυλάρχους, ούκ έπί τόν πόλεμον. (27) ού γάρ έχρήν, ώ άνδρες Άθηναίοι, ταξιάρχους παρ' ύμών, ίππάρχους παρ' ύμών, άρχοντας οικείους είναι, ίν' ήν ώς άληθώς τής πόλεως ή δύναμις; άλλ' είς μέν Λήμνον τόν παρ' ύμών ίππαρχον δεί πλείν, τών δ' ύπέρ τών τής πόλεως κτημάτων άγωνιζομένων Μενέλαον ίππαρχείν. καί ού τόν άνδρα μεμφόμενος ταύτα λέγω, άλλ' ύφ' ύμών έδει κεχειροτονημένους είναι τούτον, όστις άν ήι.

(28) ίσως δέ ταύτα μέν όρθώς ήγείσθε λέγεσθαι· τό δέ τών χρημάτων, πόσα καί πόθεν έσται, μάλιστα ποθείτε άκούσαι. τούτο δή

27 ίππάρχους d: ίππαρχον d

καὶ περαίνω. χρήματα τοίνυν· ἔστι μὲν ἡ τροφή, σιτηρέσιον μόνον, τῆι δυνάμει ταύτηι τάλαντα ἐνενήκοντα καὶ μικρόν τι πρός, δέκα μὲν ναυσὶ ταχείαις τετταράκοντα τάλαντα, εἴκοσιν εἰς τὴν ναῦν μναῖ τοῦ μηνὸς ἑκάστου, στρατιώταις δὲ δισχιλίοις τοσαῦθ' ἕτερα, ἵνα δέκα τοῦ μηνὸς ὁ στρατιώτης δραχμὰς σιτηρέσιον λαμβάνηι, τοῖς δ' ἱππεῦσι διακοσίοις οὖσιν, ἐὰν τριάκοντα δραχμὰς ἕκαστος λαμβάνηι τοῦ μηνός, δώδεκα τάλαντα. (29) εἰ δέ τις οἴεται μικρὰν ἀφορμὴν εἶναι, σιτηρέσιον τοῖς στρατευομένοις ὑπάρχειν, οὐκ ὀρθῶς ἔγνωκεν· ἐγὼ γὰρ οἶδα σαφῶς ὅτι, τοῦτ' ἂν γένηται, προσποριεῖ τὰ λοιπὰ αὐτὸ τὸ στράτευμα ἀπὸ τοῦ πολέμου, οὐδένα τῶν Ἑλλήνων ἀδικοῦν οὐδὲ τῶν συμμάχων, ὥστ' ἔχειν μισθὸν ἐντελῆ. ἐγὼ συμπλέων ἐθελοντὴς πάσχειν ὁτιοῦν ἕτοιμος, ἐὰν μὴ ταῦθ' οὕτως ἔχηι. πόθεν οὖν ὁ πόρος τῶν χρημάτων, ἃ παρ' ὑμῶν κελεύω γενέσθαι; τοῦτ' ἤδη λέξω.

## ΠΟΡΟΥ ΑΠΟΔΕΙΞΙΣ

(30) ἃ μὲν ἡμεῖς, ὦ ἄνδρες Ἀθηναῖοι, δεδυνήμεθ' εὑρεῖν ταῦτ' ἐστίν· ἐπειδὰν δ' ἐπιχειροτονῆτε τὰς γνώμας, {ἃ} ἂν ὑμῖν ἀρέσκηι, χειροτονήσετε, ἵνα μὴ μόνον ἐν τοῖς ψηφίσμασι καὶ ταῖς ἐπιστολαῖς πολεμῆτε Φιλίππωι, ἀλλὰ καὶ τοῖς ἔργοις.

(31) δοκεῖτε δέ μοι πολὺ βέλτιον ἂν περὶ τοῦ πολέμου καὶ ὅλης τῆς παρασκευῆς βουλεύσασθαι, εἰ τὸν τόπον, ὦ ἄνδρες Ἀθηναῖοι, τῆς χώρας, πρὸς ἣν πολεμεῖτε, ἐνθυμηθείητε, καὶ λογίσαισθε ὅτι τοῖς πνεύμασιν καὶ ταῖς ὥραις τοῦ ἔτους τὰ πολλὰ προλαμβάνων διαπράττεται Φίλιππος, καὶ φυλάξας τοὺς ἐτησίας ἢ τὸν χειμῶνα ἐπιχειρεῖ, ἡνίκ' ἂν ἡμεῖς μὴ δυναίμεθα ἐκεῖσ' ἀφικέσθαι. (32) δεῖ τοίνυν ταῦτ' ἐνθυμουμένους μὴ βοηθείαις πολεμεῖν (ὑστεριοῦμεν γὰρ ἁπάντων), ἀλλὰ παρασκευῆι συνεχεῖ καὶ δυνάμει. ὑπάρχει δ' ὑμῖν χειμαδίωι μὲν χρῆσθαι τῆι δυνάμει Λήμνωι καὶ Θάσωι καὶ Σκιάθωι καὶ ταῖς ἐν τούτωι τῶι τόπωι νήσοις, ἐν αἷς καὶ λιμένες καὶ σῖτος καὶ ἃ χρὴ στρατεύματι πάνθ' ὑπάρχει· τὴν δ' ὥραν τοῦ ἔτους, ὅτε καὶ πρὸς τῆι γῆι γενέσθαι ῥάιδιον καὶ τὸ τῶν πνευμάτων ἀσφαλές, πρὸς αὐτῆι τῆι χώραι καὶ πρὸς τοῖς τῶν ἐμπορίων στόμασι ῥαιδίως ἔσται.

(33) ἃ μὲν οὖν χρήσεται καὶ πότε τῆι δυνάμει, παρὰ τὸν καιρὸν ὁ τούτων κύριος καταστὰς ὑφ' ὑμῶν βουλεύσεται· ἃ δ' ὑπάρξαι δεῖ παρ' ὑμῶν, ταῦτ' ἐστὶν ἁγὼ γέγραφα. ἂν ταῦτ', ὦ ἄνδρες Ἀθηναῖοι, πορίσητε, τὰ χρήματα πρῶτον ἃ λέγω, εἶτα καὶ, τἆλλα παρασκευάσαντες (τοὺς στρατιώτας, τὰς τριήρεις, τοὺς ἱππέας, ἐντελῆ πᾶσαν τὴν δύναμιν), νόμωι κατακλείσητε ἐπὶ τῶι πολέμωι μένειν, τῶν μὲν χρημάτων αὐτοὶ ταμίαι καὶ πορισταὶ γιγνόμενοι, τῶν δὲ πράξεων παρὰ τοῦ στρατηγοῦ τὸν λόγον ζητοῦντες, παύσεσθε ἀεὶ περὶ τῶν αὐτῶν βουλευόμενοι καὶ πλέον οὐδὲν ποιοῦντες, (34) καὶ ἔτι πρὸς τούτωι πρῶτον μέν, ὦ ἄνδρες Ἀθηναῖοι, τὸν μέγιστον τῶν ἐκείνου πόρων ἀφαιρήσεσθε. ἔστι δ' οὗτος

29 προσποριεῖ d: προσποριεῖται d  30 ἃ D: del. Dobree

τίς; ἀπὸ τῶν ὑμετέρων ὑμῖν πολεμεῖ συμμάχων, ἄγων καὶ φέρων τοὺς πλέοντας τὴν θάλατταν. ἔπειτα τί πρὸς τούτωι; τοῦ πάσχειν αὐτοὶ κακῶς ἔξω γενήσεσθε, οὐχ ὥσπερ τὸν παρελθόντα χρόνον εἰς Λῆμνον καὶ Ἴμβρον ἐμβαλὼν αἰχμαλώτους πολίτας ὑμετέρους ὤιχετ' ἔχων, πρὸς τῶι Γεραιστῶι τὰ πλοῖα συλλαβὼν ἀμύθητα χρήματ' ἐξέλεξε, τὰ τελευταῖα εἰς Μαραθῶνα ἀπέβη καὶ τὴν ἱερὰν ἀπὸ τῆς χώρας ὤιχετ' ἔχων τριήρη, ὑμεῖς δ' οὔτε ταῦτα δύνασθε κωλύειν οὔτ' εἰς τοὺς χρόνους, οὓς ἂν προθῆσθε, βοηθεῖν. (35) καίτοι τί δή ποτε, ὦ ἄνδρες Ἀθηναῖοι, νομίζετε τὴν μὲν τῶν Παναθηναίων ἑορτὴν καὶ τὴν τῶν Διονυσίων ἀεὶ τοῦ καθήκοντος χρόνου γίγνεσθαι, ἄν τε δεινοὶ λάχωσιν ἄν τε ἰδιῶται οἱ τούτων ἑκατέρων ἐπιμελούμενοι, εἰς ἃ τοσαῦτα ἀναλίσκεται χρήματα, ὅσα οὐδ' εἰς ἕνα τῶν ἀποστόλων, καὶ τοσοῦτον ὄχλον καὶ παρασκευὴν ὅσην οὐκ οἶδ' εἴ τι τῶν ἁπάντων ἔχει, τοὺς δ' ἀποστόλους πάντας ὑμῖν ὑστερίζειν τῶν καιρῶν, τὸν εἰς Μεθώνην, τὸν εἰς Παγασάς, τὸν εἰς Ποτείδαιαν; (36) ὅτι ἐκεῖνα μὲν ἅπαντα νόμωι τέτακται, καὶ πρόοιδεν ἕκαστος ὑμῶν ἐκ πολλοῦ τίς χορηγὸς ἢ γυμνασίαρχος τῆς φυλῆς, πότε καὶ παρὰ τοῦ καὶ τί λαβόντα τί δεῖ ποιεῖν, οὐδὲν ἀνεξέταστον οὐδ' ἀόριστον ἐν τούτοις ἡμέληται· ἐν δὲ τοῖς περὶ τοῦ πολέμου καὶ τῆι τούτου παρασκευῆι ἄτακτα ἀδιόρθωτα ἀόριστα ἅπαντα. τοιγαροῦν ἅμα ἀκηκόαμέν τι καὶ τριηράρχους καθίσταμεν καὶ τούτοις ἀντιδόσεις ποιούμεθα καὶ περὶ χρημάτων πόρου σκοποῦμεν, καὶ μετὰ ταῦτα ἐμβαίνειν τοὺς μετοίκους ἔδοξε καὶ τοὺς χωρὶς οἰκοῦντας, εἶτ' αὐτοὺς πάλιν, εἶτ' ἀντεμβιβάζειν, (37) εἶτ' ἐν ὅσωι ταῦτα μέλλεται, προαπόλωλεν τὸ ἐφ' ὃ ἂν ἐκπλέωμεν· τὸν γὰρ τοῦ πράττειν χρόνον εἰς τὸ παρασκευάζεσθαι ἀναλίσκομεν, οἱ δὲ τῶν πραγμάτων οὐ μένουσι καιροὶ τὴν ἡμετέραν βραδυτῆτα καὶ εἰρωνείαν. ἃς δὲ τὸν μεταξὺ χρόνον δυνάμεις οἰόμεθ' ἡμῖν ὑπάρχειν, οὐδὲν οἷαί τ' οὖσαι ποιεῖν ἐπ' αὐτῶν τῶν καιρῶν ἐξελέγχονται. ὁ δ' εἰς τοῦθ' ὕβρεως ἐλήλυθεν ὥστ' ἐπιστέλλειν Εὐβοεῦσιν ἤδη τοιαύτας ἐπιστολάς.

ΕΠΙΣΤΟΛΗΣ ΑΝΑΓΝΩΣΙΣ

(38) τούτων, ὦ ἄνδρες Ἀθηναῖοι, τῶν ἀνεγνωσμένων ἀληθῆ μέν ἐστι τὰ πολλά (ὡς οὐκ ἔδει), οὐ μὴν ἀλλ' ἴσως οὐχ ἡδέα ἀκούειν. ἀλλ' εἰ μέν, ὅσα ἄν τις ὑπερβῆι τῶι λόγωι, ἵνα μὴ λυπήσηι, καὶ τὰ πράγματα ὑπερβήσεται, δεῖ πρὸς ἡδονὴν δημηγορεῖν· εἰ δ' ἡ τῶν λόγων χάρις, ἂν ἦι μὴ προσήκουσα, ἔργωι ζημία γίγνεται, αἰσχρόν ἐστι φενακίζειν ἑαυτούς, καὶ ἅπαντ' ἀναβαλλομένους ἃ ἂν ἦι δυσχερῆ πάντων ὑστερεῖν τῶν ἔργων, (39) καὶ μηδὲ τοῦτο δύνασθαι μαθεῖν, ὅτι δεῖ τοὺς ὀρθῶς πολέμωι χρωμένους οὐκ ἀκολουθεῖν τοῖς πράγμασιν, ἀλλ' αὐτοὺς ἔμπροσθεν εἶναι τῶν πραγμάτων, καὶ τὸν αὐτὸν τρόπον ὥσπερ τῶν στρατευμάτων ἀξιώσειέ τις ἂν τὸν στρατηγὸν ἡγεῖσθαι, οὕτω καὶ τῶν πραγμάτων τοὺς βουλευομένους, ἵν' ἃ ἂν ἐκείνοις δοκῆι, ταῦτα πράττηται καὶ μὴ

38 ἃ ἂν ἦι δυσχερῆ d: ὅσα ἂν ἦι δυσχερῆ d

τὰ συμβάντα ἀναγκάζωνται διώκειν. (40) ὑμεῖς δέ, ὦ ἄνδρες Ἀθηναῖοι, πλείστην δύναμιν ἁπάντων ἔχοντες, τριήρεις, ὁπλίτας, ἱππέας, χρημάτων πρόσοδον, τούτων μὲν μέχρι τῆς τήμερον ἡμέρας οὐδενὶ πώποτε εἰς δέον τι κέχρησθε, οὐδὲν δ' ἀπολείπετε, ὥσπερ οἱ βάρβαροι πυκτεύουσιν, οὕτω πολεμεῖν Φιλίππωι. καὶ γὰρ ἐκείνων ὁ πληγεὶς ἀεὶ τῆς πληγῆς ἔχεται, κἂν ἑτέρωσε πατάξηι τις, ἐκεῖσε εἰσὶν αἱ χεῖρες· προβάλλεσθαι δ' ἢ βλέπειν ἐναντίον οὔτ' οἶδεν οὔτ' ἐθέλει. (41) καὶ ὑμεῖς, ἂν ἐν Χερρονήσωι πύθησθε Φίλιππον, ἐκεῖσε βοηθεῖν ψηφίζεσθε, ἂν ἐν Πύλαις, ἐκεῖσε, ἂν ἄλλοθί που, συμπαραθεῖτε ἄνω κάτω, καὶ στρατηγεῖσθ' ὑπ' ἐκείνου, βεβούλευσθε δ' οὐδὲν αὐτοὶ συμφέρον περὶ τοῦ πολέμου, οὐδὲ πρὸ τῶν πραγμάτων προορᾶτε οὐδέν, πρὶν ἂν ἢ γεγενημένον ἢ γιγνόμενόν τι πύθησθε. ταῦτα δ' ἴσως πρότερον μὲν ἐνῆν· νῦν δ' ἐπ' αὐτὴν ἥκει τὴν ἀκμήν, ὥστ' οὐκέτ' ἐγχωρεῖ. (42) δοκεῖ δέ μοι θεῶν τις, ὦ ἄνδρες Ἀθηναῖοι, τοῖς γιγνομένοις ὑπὲρ τῆς πόλεως αἰσχυνόμενος τὴν φιλοπραγμοσύνην ταύτην ἐμβαλεῖν Φιλίππωι. εἰ γὰρ ἔχων ἃ κατέστραπται καὶ προείληφεν ἡσυχίαν ἔχειν ἤθελε καὶ μηδὲν ἔπραττεν ἔτι, ἀποχρῆν ἐνίοις ὑμῶν ἄν μοι δοκεῖ, ἐξ ὧν αἰσχύνην καὶ ἀνανδρίαν καὶ πάντα τὰ αἴσχιστα ὠφληκότες ἂν ἦμεν δημοσίαι· νῦν δ' ἐπιχειρῶν ἀεί τινι καὶ τοῦ πλείονος ὀρεγόμενος ἴσως ἂν ἐκκαλέσαιθ' ὑμᾶς, εἴπερ μὴ παντάπασιν ἀπεγνώκατε. (43) θαυμάζω δ' ἔγωγε, εἰ μηδεὶς ὑμῶν μήτ' ἐνθυμεῖται μήτε ὀργίζεται, ὁρῶν, ὦ ἄνδρες Ἀθηναῖοι, τὴν μὲν ἀρχὴν τοῦ πολέμου γεγενημένην περὶ τοῦ τιμωρήσασθαι Φίλιππον, τὴν δὲ τελευτὴν οὖσαν ἤδη ὑπὲρ τοῦ μὴ παθεῖν κακῶς ὑπὸ Φιλίππου. ἀλλὰ μὴν ὅτι γε οὐ στήσεται, δῆλον, εἰ μή τις κωλύσει. εἶτα τοῦτο ἀναμενοῦμεν; καὶ τριήρεις κενὰς καὶ τὰς παρὰ τοῦ δεῖνος ἐλπίδας ἂν ἀποστείλητε, πάντ' ἔχειν οἴεσθε καλῶς; (44) οὐκ ἐμβησόμεθα; οὐκ ἔξιμεν αὐτοὶ μέρει γέ τινι στρατιωτῶν οἰκείων νῦν, εἰ καὶ μὴ πρότερον; οὐκ ἐπὶ τὴν ἐκείνου πλευσόμεθα; "ποῖ οὖν προσορμιούμεθα;" ἤρετό τις. εὑρήσει τὰ σαθρά, ὦ ἄνδρες Ἀθηναῖοι, τῶν ἐκείνου πραγμάτων αὐτὸς ὁ πόλεμος, ἂν ἐπιχειρῶμεν· ἂν μέντοι καθώμεθα οἴκοι, λοιδορουμένων ἀκούοντες καὶ αἰτιωμένων ἀλλήλους τῶν λεγόντων, οὐδέποτ' οὐδὲν ἡμῖν μὴ γένηται τῶν δεόντων. (45) ὅποι μὲν γὰρ ἄν, οἶμαι, μέρος τι τῆς πόλεως συναποσταλῆι, κἂν μὴ πᾶσα, καὶ τὸ τῶν θεῶν εὐμενὲς καὶ τὸ τῆς τύχης συναγωνίζεται· ὅποι δ' ἂν στρατηγὸν καὶ ψήφισμα κενὸν καὶ τὰς ἀπὸ τοῦ βήματος ἐλπίδας ἐκπέμψητε, οὐδὲν ὑμῖν τῶν δεόντων γίγνεται, ἀλλ' οἱ μὲν ἐχθροὶ καταγελῶσιν, οἱ δὲ σύμμαχοι τεθνᾶσι τῶι δέει τοὺς τοιούτους ἀποστόλους. (46) οὐ γὰρ ἔστιν, οὐκ ἔστιν ἕνα ἄνδρα δυνηθῆναί ποτε ταῦθ' ὑμῖν πρᾶξαι πάντα ὅσα βούλεσθε· ὑποσχέσθαι μέντοι καὶ φῆσαι καὶ τὸν δεῖνα αἰτιάσασθαι καὶ τὸν δεῖνα ἔστι, τὰ δὲ πράγματα ἐκ τούτων ἀπόλωλεν· ὅταν γὰρ ἡγῆται μὲν ὁ στρατηγὸς ἀθλίων ἀπομίσθων ξένων, οἱ δ' ὑπὲρ ὧν ἂν ἐκεῖνος πράξηι πρὸς ὑμᾶς ψευδόμενοι ῥαιδίως ἐνθάδ' ὦσιν, ὑμεῖς δ' ἐξ ὧν ἂν ἀκούσητε ὅ τι ἂν τύχητε ψηφίζησθε, τί καὶ χρὴ προσδοκᾶν;

40 πατάξηι τις d: πατάξηις d    45 πᾶσα d: πᾶσα παρῆι d

(47) πῶς οὖν ταῦτα παύσεται; ὅταν ὑμεῖς, ὦ ἄνδρες Ἀθηναῖοι, τοὺς αὐτοὺς ἀποδείξητε στρατιώτας καὶ μάρτυρας τῶν στρατηγουμένων καὶ δικαστὰς οἴκαδ᾽ ἐλθόντας τῶν εὐθυνῶν, ὥστε μὴ ἀκούειν μόνον ὑμᾶς τὰ ὑμέτερ᾽ αὐτῶν, ἀλλὰ καὶ παρόντας ὁρᾶν. νῦν δ᾽ εἰς τοῦθ᾽ ἥκει τὰ πράγματ᾽ αἰσχύνης ὥστε τῶν στρατηγῶν ἕκαστος δὶς καὶ τρὶς κρίνεται παρ᾽ ὑμῖν περὶ θανάτου, πρὸς δὲ τοὺς ἐχθροὺς οὐδεὶς οὐδ᾽ ἅπαξ αὐτῶν ἀγωνίσασθαι περὶ θανάτου τολμᾶι, ἀλλὰ τὸν τῶν ἀνδραποδιστῶν καὶ λωποδυτῶν θάνατον μᾶλλον αἱροῦνται τοῦ προσήκοντος· κακούργου μὲν γάρ ἐστι κριθέντ᾽ ἀποθανεῖν, στρατηγοῦ δὲ μαχόμενον τοῖς πολεμίοις. (48) ἡμῶν δ᾽ οἱ μὲν περιιόντες μετὰ Λακεδαιμονίων φασὶ Φίλιππον πράττειν τὴν Θηβαίων κατάλυσιν καὶ τὰς πολιτείας διασπᾶν, οἱ δ᾽ ὡς πρέσβεις πέπομφεν ὡς βασιλέα, οἱ δ᾽ ἐν Ἰλλυριοῖς πόλεις τειχίζειν, οἱ δὲ — λόγους πλάττοντες ἕκαστος περιερχόμεθα. (49) ἐγὼ δὲ οἶμαι μέν, ὦ ἄνδρες Ἀθηναῖοι, νὴ τοὺς θεοὺς ἐκεῖνον μεθύειν τῶι μεγέθει τῶν πεπραγμένων καὶ πολλὰ τοιαῦτα ὀνειροπολεῖν ἐν τῆι γνώμηι, τήν τ᾽ ἐρημίαν τῶν κωλυσόντων ὁρῶντα καὶ τοῖς πεπραγμένοις ἐπηιρμένον, οὐ μέντοι γε μὰ Δί᾽ οὕτω προαιρεῖσθαι πράττειν ὥστε τοὺς ἀνοητοτάτους τῶν παρ᾽ ἡμῖν εἰδέναι τί μέλλει ποιεῖν ἐκεῖνος· ἀνοητότατοι γάρ εἰσιν οἱ λογοποιοῦντες. (50) ἀλλ᾽ ἂν ἀφέντες ταῦτ᾽ ἐκεῖνο εἰδῶμεν, ὅτι ἐχθρὸς ἄνθρωπος καὶ τὰ ἡμέτερα ἡμᾶς ἀποστερεῖ καὶ χρόνον πολὺν ὕβρικε, καὶ ἅπανθ᾽ ὅσα πώποτ᾽ ἠλπίσαμέν τινα πράξειν ὑπὲρ ἡμῶν καθ᾽ ἡμῶν εὕρηται, καὶ τὰ λοιπὰ ἐν αὑτοῖς ἡμῖν ἐστί, κἂν μὴ νῦν ἐθέλωμεν ἐκεῖ πολεμεῖν αὐτῶι, ἐνθάδ᾽ ἴσως ἀναγκασθησόμεθα τοῦτο ποιεῖν, ἂν ταῦτ᾽ εἰδῶμεν, καὶ τὰ δέοντ᾽ ἐσόμεθα ἐγνωκότες καὶ λόγων ματαίων ἀπηλλαγμένοι· οὐ γὰρ ἄττα ποτ᾽ ἔσται δεῖ σκοπεῖν, ἀλλ᾽ ὅτι φαῦλα, ἂν μὴ προσέχητε τὸν νοῦν καὶ τὰ προσήκοντα ποιεῖν ἐθέλητε, εὖ εἰδέναι.

(51) ἐγὼ μὲν οὖν οὔτ᾽ ἄλλοτε πώποτε πρὸς χάριν εἱλόμην λέγειν ὅ τι ἂν μὴ καὶ συνοίσειν πεπεισμένος ὦ, νῦν τε ἃ γιγνώσκω πάνθ᾽ ἁπλῶς, οὐδὲν ὑποστειλάμενος, πεπαρρησίασμαι. ἐβουλόμην δ᾽ ἄν, ὥσπερ ὅτι ὑμῖν συμφέρει τὰ βέλτιστα ἀκούειν οἶδα, οὕτως εἰδέναι συνοῖσον καὶ τῶι τὰ βέλτιστα εἰπόντι· πολλῶι γὰρ ἂν ἥδιον εἶχον. νῦν δ᾽ ἐπ᾽ ἀδήλοις οὖσι τοῖς ἀπὸ τούτων ἐμαυτῶι γενησομένοις, ὅμως ἐπὶ τῶι συνοίσειν ὑμῖν, ἂν πράξητε, ταῦτα πεπεῖσθαι λέγειν αἱροῦμαι. νικώιη δ᾽ ὅ τι πᾶσιν μέλλει συνοίσειν.

49 γε om. d

# 9 ΚΑΤΑ ΦΙΛΙΠΠΟΥ Γ

(1) πολλῶν, ὦ ἄνδρες Ἀθηναῖοι, λόγων γιγνομένων ὀλίγου δεῖν καθ' ἑκάστην ἐκκλησίαν περὶ ὧν Φίλιππος, ἀφ' οὗ τὴν εἰρήνην ἐποιήσατο, οὐ μόνον ὑμᾶς, ἀλλὰ καὶ τοὺς ἄλλους ἀδικεῖ, καὶ πάντων οἶδ' ὅτι φησάντων γ' ἄν, εἰ καὶ μὴ ποιοῦσι τοῦτο, καὶ λέγειν δεῖν καὶ πράττειν ὅπως ἐκεῖνος παύσεται τῆς ὕβρεως καὶ δίκην δώσει, εἰς τοῦθ' ὑπηγμένα πάντα τὰ πράγματα καὶ προειμένα ὁρῶ, ὥστε – δέδοικα μὴ βλάσφημον μὲν εἰπεῖν, ἀληθὲς δ' ἦι – εἰ καὶ λέγειν ἅπαντες ἐβούλοντο οἱ παριόντες καὶ χειροτονεῖν ὑμεῖς ἐξ ὧν ὡς φαυλότατα ἔμελλε τὰ πράγμαθ' ἕξειν, οὐκ ἂν ἡγοῦμαι δύνασθαι χεῖρον ἢ νῦν διατεθῆναι. (2) πολλὰ μὲν οὖν ἴσως ἐστὶν αἴτια τούτων, καὶ οὐ παρ' ἓν οὐδὲ δύο εἰς τοῦτο τὰ πράγματ' ἀφῖκται, μάλιστα δ', ἄνπερ ἐξετάζητε ὀρθῶς, εὑρήσετε διὰ τοὺς χαρίζεσθαι μᾶλλον ἢ τὰ βέλτιστα λέγειν προαιρουμένους, ὧν τινες μέν, ὦ ἄνδρες Ἀθηναῖοι, ἐν οἷς εὐδοκιμοῦσιν αὐτοὶ καὶ δύνανται, ταῦτα φυλάττοντες οὐδεμίαν περὶ τῶν μελλόντων πρόνοιαν ἔχουσιν, οὐκοῦν οὐδ' ὑμᾶς οἴονται δεῖν ἔχειν, ἕτεροι δὲ τοὺς ἐπὶ τοῖς πράγμασιν ὄντας αἰτιώμενοι καὶ διαβάλλοντες οὐδὲν ἄλλο ποιοῦσιν ἢ ὅπως ἡ μὲν πόλις αὐτὴ παρ' αὑτῆς δίκην λήψεται καὶ περὶ τοῦτ' ἔσται, Φιλίππωι δ' ἐξέσται καὶ λέγειν καὶ πράττειν ὅ τι βούλεται. (3) αἱ δὲ τοιαῦται πολιτεῖαι συνήθεις μέν εἰσιν ὑμῖν, αἴτιαι δὲ τῶν κακῶν. ἀξιῶ δέ, ὦ ἄνδρες Ἀθηναῖοι, ἄν τι τῶν ἀληθῶν μετὰ παρρησίας λέγω, μηδεμίαν μοι διὰ τοῦτο παρ' ὑμῶν ὀργὴν γενέσθαι. σκοπεῖτε γὰρ ὡδί. ὑμεῖς τὴν παρρησίαν ἐπὶ μὲν τῶν ἄλλων οὕτω κοινὴν οἴεσθε δεῖν εἶναι πᾶσι τοῖς ἐν τῆι πόλει, ὥστε καὶ τοῖς ξένοις καὶ τοῖς δούλοις αὐτῆς μεταδεδώκατε, καὶ πολλοὺς ἄν τις οἰκέτας ἴδοι παρ' ἡμῖν μετὰ πλείονος ἐξουσίας ὅ τι βούλονται λέγοντας ἢ πολίτας ἐν ἐνίαις τῶν ἄλλων πόλεων, ἐκ δὲ τοῦ συμβουλεύειν παντάπασιν ἐξεληλάκατε. (4) εἶθ' ὑμῖν συμβέβηκεν ἐκ τούτου ἐν μὲν ταῖς ἐκκλησίαις τρυφᾶν καὶ κολακεύεσθαι πάντα πρὸς ἡδονὴν ἀκούουσιν, ἐν δὲ τοῖς πράγμασι καὶ τοῖς γιγνομένοις περὶ τῶν ἐσχάτων ἤδη κινδυνεύειν. εἰ μὲν οὖν καὶ νῦν οὕτω διάκεισθε, οὐκ ἔχω τί λέγω· εἰ δ' ἃ συμφέρει χωρὶς κολακείας ἐθελήσετ' ἀκούειν, ἕτοιμος λέγειν. καὶ γὰρ εἰ πάνυ φαύλως τὰ πράγματ' ἔχει καὶ πολλὰ προεῖται, ὅμως ἔστιν, ἐὰν ὑμεῖς τὰ δέοντα ποιεῖν βούλησθε, ἔτι πάντα ταῦτα ἐπανορθώσασθαι. (5) καὶ παράδοξον μὲν ἴσως ἐστὶν ὃ μέλλω λέγειν, ἀληθὲς δέ· τὸ χείριστον ἐν τοῖς παρεληλυθόσι, τοῦτο πρὸς τὰ μέλλοντα βέλτιστον ὑπάρχει. τί οὖν ἐστι τοῦτο; ὅτι οὔτε μικρὸν οὔτε μέγα οὐδὲν τῶν δεόντων ποιούντων ὑμῶν κακῶς τὰ πράγματ' ἔχει, ἐπεί τοι, εἰ πάνθ' ἃ προσῆκε πραττόντων οὕτως διέκειτο, οὐδ' ἂν ἐλπὶς ἦν αὐτὰ γενέσθαι βελτίω. νῦν δὲ τῆς ῥαθυμίας τῆς ὑμετέρας καὶ

---

1 τοὺς ἄλλους d: τοὺς ἄλλους Ἕλληνας d    ἀληθὲς δ' ἦι d, i: ἀληθὲς δέ d
2 οὐκοῦν … ἔχειν om. d    3 τῶν κακῶν d: τῶν κακῶν καὶ τῶν ἁμαρτημάτων d: τῆς ταραχῆς καὶ τῶν ἁμαρτημάτων d

65

τῆς ἀμελίας κεκράτηκε Φίλιππος, τῆς πόλεως δ' οὐ κεκράτηκεν· οὐδ' ἥττησθ' ὑμεῖς, ἀλλ' οὐδὲ κεκίνησθε.

(6) εἰ μὲν οὖν ἅπαντες ὡμολογοῦμεν Φίλιππον τῆι πόλει πολεμεῖν καὶ τὴν εἰρήνην παραβαίνειν, οὐδὲν ἄλλ' ἔδει τὸν παριόντα λέγειν καὶ συμβουλεύειν ἢ ὅπως ἀσφαλέστατα καὶ ῥᾶιστα αὐτὸν ἀμυνούμεθα· ἐπειδὴ δ' οὕτως ἀτόπως ἔνιοι διάκεινται, ὥστε, πόλεις καταλαμβάνοντος ἐκείνου καὶ πολλὰ τῶν ὑμετέρων ἔχοντος καὶ πάντας ἀνθρώπους ἀδικοῦντος, ἀνέχεσθαί τινων ἐν ταῖς ἐκκλησίαις λεγόντων πολλάκις ὡς ἡμῶν τινές εἰσιν οἱ ποιοῦντες τὸν πόλεμον, ἀνάγκη φυλάττεσθαι καὶ διορθοῦσθαι περὶ τούτου· (7) ἔστι γὰρ δέος μήποτε ὡς ἀμυνούμεθα γράψας τις καὶ συμβουλεύσας εἰς τὴν αἰτίαν ἐμπέσηι τοῦ πεποιηκέναι τὸν πόλεμον. ἐγὼ δὴ τοῦτο πρῶτον ἁπάντων λέγω καὶ διορίζομαι εἰ ἐφ' ἡμῖν ἐστι τὸ βουλεύεσθαι περὶ τοῦ πότερον εἰρήνην ἄγειν ἢ πολεμεῖν δεῖ. (8) εἰ μὲν οὖν ἔξεστιν εἰρήνην ἄγειν τῆι πόλει καὶ ἐφ' ἡμῖν ἐστι τοῦτο, ἵν' ἐντεῦθεν ἄρξωμαι, φήμ' ἔγωγε ἄγειν ἡμᾶς δεῖν, καὶ τὸν ταῦτα λέγοντα γράφειν καὶ πράττειν καὶ μὴ φενακίζειν ἀξιῶ· εἰ δ' ἕτερος τὰ ὅπλα ἐν ταῖς χερσὶν ἔχων καὶ δύναμιν πολλὴν περὶ αὐτὸν τοὔνομα μὲν τὸ τῆς εἰρήνης ὑμῖν προβάλλει, τοῖς δ' ἔργοις αὐτὸς τοῖς τοῦ πολέμου χρῆται, τί λοιπὸν ἄλλο πλὴν ἀμύνεσθαι; φάσκειν δ' εἰρήνην ἄγειν εἰ βούλεσθε, ὥσπερ ἐκεῖνος, οὐ διαφέρομαι. (9) εἰ δέ τις ταύτην εἰρήνην ὑπολαμβάνει, ἐξ ἧς ἐκεῖνος πάντα τἆλλα λαβὼν ἐφ' ἡμᾶς ἥξει, πρῶτον μὲν μαίνεται, ἔπειτα ἐκείνωι παρ' ὑμῶν, οὐχ ὑμῖν παρ' ἐκείνου τὴν εἰρήνην λέγει· τοῦτο δ' ἐστὶν ὃ τῶν ἀναλισκομένων χρημάτων πάντων Φίλιππος ὠνεῖται, αὐτὸς μὲν πολεμεῖν ὑμῖν, ὑφ' ὑμῶν δὲ μὴ πολεμεῖσθαι.

(10) καὶ μὴν εἰ μέχρι τούτου περιμενοῦμεν, ἕως ἂν ἡμῖν ὁμολογήσηι πολεμεῖν, πάντων ἐσμὲν εὐηθέστατοι· οὐδὲ γὰρ ἂν ἐπὶ τὴν Ἀττικὴν αὐτὴν βαδίζηι καὶ τὸν Πειραιᾶ, τοῦτ' ἐρεῖ, εἴπερ οἷς πρὸς τοὺς ἄλλους πεποίηκε δεῖ τεκμαίρεσθαι. (11) τοῦτο μὲν γὰρ Ὀλυνθίοις, τετταράκοντ' ἀπέχων τῆς πόλεως στάδια, εἶπεν ὅτι δεῖ δυοῖν θάτερον, ἢ ἐκείνους ἐν Ὀλύνθωι μὴ οἰκεῖν ἢ αὑτὸν ἐν Μακεδονίαι, πάντα τὸν ἄλλον χρόνον, εἴ τις αὐτὸν αἰτιάσαιτό τι τοιοῦτον, ἀγανακτῶν καὶ πρέσβεις πέμπων τοὺς ἀπολογησομένους· τοῦτο δ' εἰς Φωκέας ὡς πρὸς συμμάχους ἐπορεύετο, καὶ πρέσβεις Φωκέων ἦσαν οἳ παρηκολούθουν αὐτῶι πορευομένωι, καὶ παρ' ἡμῖν ἤριζον οἱ πολλοὶ Θηβαίοις οὐ λυσιτελήσειν τὴν ἐκείνου πάροδον. (12) καὶ μὴν καὶ Φερὰς πρώην ὡς φίλος καὶ σύμμαχος εἰς Θετταλίαν ἐλθὼν ἔχει καταλαβών, καὶ τὰ τελευταῖα τοῖς ταλαιπώροις Ὠρείταις τουτοισὶ ἐπισκεψομένους ἔφη τοὺς στρατιώτας πεπομφέναι κατ' εὔνοιαν· πυνθάνεσθαι γὰρ αὐτοὺς ὡς νοσοῦσι καὶ στασιάζουσιν, συμμάχων δ' εἶναι καὶ φίλων ἀληθινῶν ἐν τοῖς τοιούτοις καιροῖς παρεῖναι. (13) εἶτ' οἴεσθ' αὐτόν, οἳ ἐποίησαν μὲν οὐδὲν ἂν κακόν, μὴ παθεῖν δ' ἐφυλάξαντ' ἂν ἴσως, τούτους μᾶλλον ἐξαπατᾶν αἱρεῖσθαι μᾶλλον ἢ προλέγοντα βιάζεσθαι, ὑμῖν δ' ἐκ προρρήσεως πολεμήσειν, καὶ ταῦθ' ἕως ἂν ἑκόντες

---

6–7 εἰ μὲν οὖν ἅπαντες ... πολεμεῖν δεῖ om. d    13 αὐτόν, οἳ ἐποίησαν μὲν οὐδὲν ἂν κακόν d: οἳ μὲν οὐδ' ἂν αὐτὸν ἐδυνήθησαν ποιῆσαι κακόν d, i

ἐξαπατᾶσθε; (14) οὐκ ἔστι ταῦτα· καὶ γὰρ ἂν ἀβελτερώτατος εἴη πάντων ἀνθρώπων, εἰ τῶν ἀδικουμένων ὑμῶν μηδὲν ἐγκαλούντων αὐτῶι, ἀλλ' ὑμῶν αὐτῶν τινὰς αἰτιωμένων, ἐκεῖνος ἐκλύσας τὴν πρὸς ἀλλήλους ἔριν ὑμῶν καὶ φιλονικίαν ἐφ' αὑτὸν προείποι τρέπεσθαι, καὶ τῶν παρ' ἑαυτοῦ μισθοφορούντων τοὺς λόγους ἀφέλοιτο, οἷς ἀναβάλλουσιν ὑμᾶς, λέγοντες ὡς ἐκεῖνός γε οὐ πολεμεῖ τῆι πόλει. (15) ἀλλ' ἔστιν, ὦ πρὸς τοῦ Διός, ὅστις εὖ φρονῶν ἐκ τῶν ὀνομάτων μᾶλλον ἢ τῶν πραγμάτων τὸν ἄγοντ' εἰρήνην ἢ πολεμοῦνθ' αὑτῶι σκέψαιτ' ἄν; οὐδεὶς δήπου. ὁ τοίνυν Φίλιππος ἐξ ἀρχῆς, ἄρτι τῆς εἰρήνης γεγονυίας, οὔπω Διοπείθους στρατηγοῦντος οὐδὲ τῶν ὄντων ἐν Χερρονήσωι νῦν ἀπεσταλμένων, Σέρριον καὶ Δορίσκον ἐλάμβανε καὶ τοὺς ἐκ Σερρείου τείχους καὶ Ἱεροῦ ὄρους στρατιώτας ἐξέβαλλεν, οὓς ὁ ὑμέτερος στρατηγὸς κατέστησεν. (16) καίτοι ταῦτα πράττων τί ἐποίει; εἰρήνην μὲν γὰρ ὠμωμόκει. καὶ μηδεὶς εἴπηι, "τί δὲ ταῦτ' ἐστίν, ἢ τί τούτων μέλει τῆι πόλει;" εἰ μὲν γὰρ μικρὰ ταῦτα, ἢ μηδὲν ὑμῖν αὐτῶν ἔμελεν, ἄλλος ἂν εἴη λόγος οὗτος· τὸ δ' εὐσεβὲς καὶ τὸ δίκαιον, ἄν τ' ἐπὶ μικροῦ τις ἄν τ' ἐπὶ μείζονος παραβαίνηι, τὴν αὐτὴν ἔχει δύναμιν. φέρε δὴ νῦν, ἡνίκ' εἰς Χερρόνησον, ἣν βασιλεὺς καὶ πάντες οἱ Ἕλληνες ὑμετέραν ἐγνώκασιν εἶναι, ξένους εἰσπέμπει καὶ βοηθεῖν ὁμολογεῖ καὶ ἐπιστέλλει ταῦτα, τί ποιεῖ; (17) φησὶ μὲν γὰρ οὐ πολεμεῖν, ἐγὼ δὲ τοσούτου δέω ταῦτα ποιοῦντα ἐκεῖνον ἄγειν ὁμολογεῖν τὴν πρὸς ὑμᾶς εἰρήνην, ὥστε καὶ Μεγάρων ἁπτόμενον κἂν Εὐβοίαι τυραννίδα κατασκευάζοντα καὶ νῦν ἐπὶ Θράικην παριόντα καὶ τὰ ἐν Πελοποννήσωι σκευωρούμενον καὶ πάνθ' ὅσα πράττει μετὰ τῆς δυνάμεως ποιοῦντα, λύειν φημὶ τὴν εἰρήνην καὶ πολεμεῖν ὑμῖν, εἰ μὴ καὶ τοὺς τὰ μηχανήματα ἐφιστάντας εἰρήνην ἄγειν φήσετε, ἕως ἂν αὐτὰ τοῖς τείχεσιν ἤδη προσαγάγωσιν. ἀλλ' οὐ φήσετε· ὁ γὰρ οἷς ἂν ἐγὼ ληφθείην, ταῦτα πράττων καὶ κατασκευαζόμενος, οὗτος ἐμοὶ πολεμεῖ, κἂν μήπω βάλληι μηδὲ τοξεύηι. (18) τίσιν οὖν ὑμεῖς κινδυνεύσαιτ' ἄν, εἴ τι γένοιτο; τῶι τὸν Ἑλλήσποντον ἀλλοτριωθῆναι, τῶι Μεγάρων καὶ τῆς Εὐβοίας τὸν πολεμοῦνθ' ὑμῖν γενέσθαι κύριον, τῶι Πελοποννησίους τἀκείνου φρονῆσαι. εἶτα τὸν τοῦτο τὸ μηχάνημα ἐπὶ τὴν πόλιν ἱστάντα, τοῦτον εἰρήνην ἄγειν ἐγὼ φῶ πρὸς ὑμᾶς; (19) πολλοῦ γε καὶ δεῖ, ἀλλ' ἀφ' ἧς ἡμέρας ἀνεῖλε Φωκέας, ἀπὸ ταύτης ἔγωγ' αὐτὸν πολεμεῖν ὁρίζομαι. ὑμᾶς δέ, ἐὰν ἀμύνησθε ἤδη, σωφρονήσειν φημί, ἐὰν δὲ ἐάσητε, οὐδὲ τοῦθ' ὅταν βούλησθε δυνήσεσθαι ποιῆσαι. καὶ τοσοῦτόν γε ἀφέστηκα τῶν ἄλλων, ὦ ἄνδρες Ἀθηναῖοι, τῶν συμβουλευόντων, ὥστ' οὐδὲ δοκεῖ μοι περὶ Χερρονήσου νῦν σκοπεῖν οὐδὲ Βυζαντίου, (20) ἀλλ' ἐπαμῦναι μὲν τούτοις, καὶ διατηρῆσαι μή τι πάθωσι, βουλεύεσθαι μέντοι περὶ πάντων τῶν Ἑλλήνων ὡς ἐν κινδύνωι μεγάλωι καθεστώτων. βούλομαι δ' εἰπεῖν πρὸς ὑμᾶς ἐξ ὧν ὑπὲρ τῶν πραγμάτων οὕτω φοβοῦμαι, ἵνα, ἂν μὲν ὀρθῶς λογίζομαι, μετάσχητε τῶν λογισμῶν

---

20 πάθωσι, καὶ τοῖς οὖσιν ἐκεῖ νῦν στρατιώταις πάνθ' ὅσων ἂν δέωνται ἀποστεῖλαι, βουλεύεσθαι d (cf. Introd. §6.2)

καὶ πρόνοιάν τινα ὑμῶν γ' αὐτῶν, εἰ μὴ καὶ τῶν ἄλλων ἄρα βούλεσθε, ποιήσησθε, ἐὰν δὲ ληρεῖν καὶ τετυφῶσθαι δοκῶ, μήτε νῦν μήτ' αὖθις ὡς ὑγιαίνοντί μοι προσέχητε.

(21) ὅτι μὲν δὴ μέγας ἐκ μικροῦ καὶ ταπεινοῦ τὸ κατ' ἀρχὰς Φίλιππος ηὔξηται, καὶ ἀπίστως καὶ στασιαστικῶς ἔχουσι πρὸς αὑτοὺς οἱ Ἕλληνες, καὶ ὅτι πολλῶι παραδοξότερον ἦν τοσοῦτον αὐτὸν ἐξ ἐκείνου γενέσθαι ἢ νῦν, ὅθ' οὕτω πολλὰ προείληφε, καὶ τὰ λοιπὰ ὑφ' αὑτῶι ποιήσασθαι, καὶ πάνθ' ὅσα τοιαῦτ' ἂν ἔχοιμι διεξελθεῖν, παραλείψω. (22) ἀλλ' ὁρῶ συγκεχωρηκότας ἅπαντας ἀνθρώπους, ἀφ' ὑμῶν ἀρξαμένους, αὐτῶι, ὑπὲρ οὗ τὸν ἄλλον ἅπαντα χρόνον πάντες οἱ πόλεμοι γεγόνασιν οἱ Ἑλληνικοί. τί οὖν ἐστι τοῦτο; τὸ ποιεῖν ὅ τι βούλεται, καὶ καθ' ἕνα οὑτωσὶ περικόπτειν καὶ λωποδυτεῖν τῶν Ἑλλήνων, καὶ καταδουλοῦσθαι τὰς πόλεις ἐπιόντα. (23) καίτοι προστάται μὲν ὑμεῖς ἑβδομήκοντα ἔτη καὶ τρία τῶν Ἑλλήνων ἐγένεσθε, προστάται δὲ τριάκοντα ἑνὸς δέοντα Λακεδαιμόνιοι· ἴσχυσαν δέ τι καὶ Θηβαῖοι τουτουσὶ τοὺς τελευταίους χρόνους μετὰ τὴν ἐν Λεύκτροις μάχην. ἀλλ' ὅμως οὔθ' ὑμῖν οὔτε Θηβαίοις οὔτε Λακεδαιμονίοις οὐδεπώποτε, ὦ ἄνδρες Ἀθηναῖοι, συνεχωρήθη τοῦθ' ὑπὸ τῶν Ἑλλήνων, ποιεῖν ὅ τι βούλοισθε, οὐδὲ πολλοῦ δεῖ· (24) ἀλλὰ τοῦτο μὲν ὑμῖν, μᾶλλον δὲ τοῖς τότ' οὖσιν Ἀθηναίοις, ἐπειδή τισιν οὐ μετρίως ἐδόκουν προσφέρεσθαι, πάντες ᾤοντο δεῖν, καὶ οἱ μηδὲν ἐγκαλεῖν ἔχοντες αὐτοῖς, μετὰ τῶν ἠδικημένων πολεμεῖν· καὶ πάλιν Λακεδαιμονίοις ἄρξασι καὶ παρελθοῦσιν εἰς τὴν αὐτὴν δυναστείαν ὑμῖν, ἐπειδὴ πλεονάζειν ἐπεχείρουν καὶ πέρα τοῦ μετρίου τὰ καθεστηκότα ἐκίνουν, πάντες εἰς πόλεμον κατέστησαν, καὶ οἱ μηδὲν ἐγκαλοῦντες αὐτοῖς. (25) καὶ τί δεῖ τοὺς ἄλλους λέγειν; ἀλλ' ἡμεῖς αὐτοὶ καὶ Λακεδαιμόνιοι, οὐδὲν ἂν εἰπεῖν ἔχοντες ἐξ ἀρχῆς ὅ τι ἠδικούμεθα ὑπ' ἀλλήλων, ὅμως ὑπὲρ ὧν τοὺς ἄλλους ἀδικουμένους ἑωρῶμεν, πολεμεῖν ᾠόμεθα δεῖν. καίτοι πάνθ' ὅσ' ἐξημάρτηται καὶ Λακεδαιμονίοις ἐν τοῖς τριάκοντα ἐκείνοις ἔτεσιν καὶ τοῖς ἡμετέροις προγόνοις ἐν τοῖς ἑβδομήκοντα, ἐλάττονα ἐστίν, ὦ ἄνδρες Ἀθηναῖοι, ὧν Φίλιππος ἐν τρισὶ καὶ δέκα οὐχ ὅλοις ἔτεσιν, οἷς ἐπιπολάζει, ἠδίκηκε τοὺς Ἕλληνας, μᾶλλον δὲ οὐδὲ μέρος τούτων ἐκεῖνα. (26) καὶ τοῦτ' ἐκ βραχέος λόγου ῥάιδιον δεῖξαι. Ὄλυνθον μὲν δὴ καὶ Μεθώνην καὶ Ἀπολλωνίαν καὶ δύο καὶ τριάκοντα πόλεις ἐπὶ Θράικης ἐῶ, ἃς ἁπάσας οὕτως ὠμῶς ἀνήιρηκεν ὥστε μηδ' εἰ πώποτ' ὠικήθησαν προσελθόντ' εἶναι ῥάιδιον εἰπεῖν· καὶ τὸ Φωκέων ἔθνος τοσοῦτον ἀνηιρημένον σιωπῶ. ἀλλὰ Θετταλία πῶς ἔχει; οὐχὶ τὰς πολιτείας καὶ τὰς πόλεις αὐτῶν παρήιρηται καὶ τετραρχίας κατέστησεν, ἵνα μὴ μόνον κατὰ πόλεις ἀλλὰ καὶ κατ' ἔθνη δουλεύωσιν; (27) αἱ δ' ἐν Εὐβοίαι πόλεις οὐκ ἤδη τυραννοῦνται, καὶ ταῦτα ἐν νήσωι πλησίον Θηβῶν καὶ Ἀθηνῶν; οὐ διαρρήδην εἰς τὰς ἐπιστολὰς γράφει "ἐμοὶ δ' ἐστὶν εἰρήνη πρὸς τοὺς ἀκούειν ἐμοῦ βουλομένους"; καὶ οὐ γράφει μὲν ταῦτα, τοῖς δ' ἔργοις οὐ ποιεῖ, ἀλλ' ἐφ' Ἑλλήσποντον οἴχεται, πρότε-

26 καὶ τοῦτ' ... δεῖξαι om. d

ρον ἧκεν ἐπ' Ἀμβρακίαν, Ἦλιν ἔχει τηλικαύτην πόλιν ἐν Πελοποννήσωι, Μεγάροις ἐπεβούλευσε πρώην, οὔθ' ἡ Ἑλλὰς οὔθ' ἡ βάρβαρος τὴν πλεονεξίαν χωρεῖ τἀνθρώπου. (28) καὶ ταῦθ' ὁρῶντες οἱ Ἕλληνες ἅπαντες καὶ ἀκούοντες οὐ πέμπομεν πρέσβεις περὶ τούτων πρὸς ἀλλήλους κἀγανακτοῦμεν, οὕτω δὲ κακῶς διακείμεθα καὶ διορωρύγμεθα κατὰ πόλεις ὥστ' ἄχρι τῆς τήμερον ἡμέρας οὐδὲν οὔτε τῶν συμφερόντων οὔτε τῶν δεόντων πρᾶξαι δυνάμεθα, οὐδὲ συστῆναι, οὐδὲ κοινωνίαν βοηθείας καὶ φιλίας οὐδεμίαν ποιήσασθαι, (29) ἀλλὰ μείζω γιγνόμενον τὸν ἄνθρωπον περιορῶμεν, τὸν χρόνον κερδᾶναι τοῦτον ὃν ἄλλος ἀπόλλυται ἕκαστος ἐγνωκώς, ὥς γ' ἐμοὶ δοκεῖ, οὐχ ὅπως σωθήσεται τὰ τῶν Ἑλλήνων σκοπῶν οὐδὲ πράττων, ἐπεί, ὅτι γε ὥσπερ περίοδος ἢ καταβολὴ πυρετοῦ ἢ ἄλλου τινὸς κακοῦ καὶ τῶι πάνυ πόρρω δοκοῦντι νῦν ἀφεστάναι προσέρχεται, οὐδεὶς ἀγνοεῖ. (30) καὶ μὴν κἀκεῖνό γε ἴστε, ὅτι ὅσα μὲν ὑπὸ Λακεδαιμονίων ἢ ὑφ' ἡμῶν ἔπασχον οἱ Ἕλληνες, ἀλλ' οὖν ὑπὸ γνησίων γ' ὄντων τῆς Ἑλλάδος ἠδικοῦντο, καὶ τὸν αὐτὸν τρόπον ἄν τις ὑπέλαβεν τοῦτο, ὥσπερ ἂν εἰ υἱὸς ἐν οὐσίαι πολλῆι γεγονὼς γνήσιος διώικει τι μὴ καλῶς μηδ' ὀρθῶς, κατ' αὐτὸ μὲν τοῦτο ἄξιον μέμψεως εἶναι καὶ κατηγορίας, ὡς δ' οὐ προσήκων ἢ ὡς οὐ κληρονόμος τούτων ὢν ταῦτα ἐποίει, οὐκ ἐνεῖναι λέγειν. (31) εἰ δέ γε δοῦλος ἢ ὑποβολιμαῖος τὰ μὴ προσήκοντα ἀπώλλυε καὶ ἐλυμαίνετο, Ἡράκλεις, ὅσωι μᾶλλον δεινὸν καὶ ὀργῆς ἄξιον πάντες ἂν ἔφησαν εἶναι. ἀλλ' οὐχ ὑπὲρ Φιλίππου καὶ ὧν ἐκεῖνος πράττει νῦν, οὐχ οὕτως ἔχουσιν, οὐ μόνον οὐχ Ἕλληνος ὄντος οὐδὲ προσήκοντος οὐδὲν τοῖς Ἕλλησιν, ἀλλ' οὐδὲ βαρβάρου ἐντεῦθεν ὅθεν καλὸν εἰπεῖν, ἀλλ' ὀλέθρου Μακεδόνος, ὅθεν οὐδ' ἀνδράποδον σπουδαῖον οὐδὲν ἦν πρότερον πρίασθαι.

(32) καίτοι τί τῆς ἐσχάτης ὕβρεως ἀπολείπει; οὐ πρὸς τῶι πόλεις ἀνηιρηκέναι τίθησι μὲν τὰ Πύθια, τὸν κοινὸν τῶν Ἑλλήνων ἀγῶνα, κἂν αὐτὸς μὴ παρῆι, τοὺς δούλους ἀγωνοθετήσοντας πέμπει; κύριος δὲ Πυλῶν καὶ τῶν ἐπὶ τοὺς Ἕλληνας παρόδων ἐστί, καὶ φρουραῖς καὶ ξένοις τοὺς τόπους τούτους κατέχει; ἔχει δὲ καὶ τὴν προμαντείαν τοῦ θεοῦ, παρώσας ἡμᾶς καὶ Θετταλοὺς καὶ Δωριέας καὶ τοὺς ἄλλους Ἀμφικτύονας, ἧς οὐδὲ τοῖς Ἕλλησιν ἅπασι μέτεστι; (33) γράφει δὲ Θετταλοῖς ὃν χρὴ τρόπον πολιτεύεσθαι; πέμπει δὲ ξένους τοὺς μὲν εἰς Πορθμόν, τὸν δῆμον ἐκβαλοῦντας τὸν Ἐρετριέων, τοὺς δ' ἐπ' Ὠρεόν, τύραννον Φιλιστίδην καταστήσοντας; ἀλλ' ὅμως ταῦθ' ὁρῶντες οἱ Ἕλληνες ἀνέχονται, καὶ τὸν αὐτὸν τρόπον, ὥσπερ τὴν χάλαζαν, ἔμοιγε δοκοῦσιν θεωρεῖν, εὐχόμενοι μὴ καθ' ἑαυτοὺς ἕκαστοι γενέσθαι, κωλύειν δ' οὐδεὶς ἐπιχειρῶν. (34) οὐ μόνον δ' ἐφ' οἷς ἡ Ἑλλὰς ὑβρίζεται ὑπ' αὐτοῦ, οὐδεὶς ἀμύνεται, ἀλλ' οὐδ' ὑπὲρ ὧν αὐτὸς ἕκαστος ἀδικεῖται· τοῦτο γὰρ ἤδη τοὔσχατόν ἐστιν. οὐ Κορινθίων ἐπ' Ἀμβρακίαν ἐλήλυθε καὶ Λευκάδα; οὐκ Ἀχαιῶν Ναύπακτον ὀμώμοκεν Αἰτωλοῖς παραδώσειν; οὐχὶ Θηβαίων Ἐχῖνον ἀφήιρηται, καὶ νῦν ἐπὶ Βυζαντίους πορεύεται συμμάχους ὄντας; (35) οὐχ ἡμῶν, ἑῶ τἆλλα, ἀλλὰ

30 ἄξιον c: ἄξιος D    32 κύριος ... μέτεστι om. d

Χερρονήσου τὴν μεγίστην ἔχει πόλιν Καρδίαν; ταῦτα τοίνυν πάσχοντες ἅπαντες μέλλομεν καὶ μαλακιζόμεθα καὶ πρὸς τοὺς πλησίον βλέπομεν, ἀπιστοῦντες ἀλλήλοις, οὐ τῶι πάντας ἡμᾶς ἀδικοῦντι. καίτοι τὸν ἅπασιν ἀσελγῶς οὕτω χρώμενον τί οἴεσθε, ἐπειδὰν καθ᾽ ἕν᾽ ἡμῶν ἑκάστου κύριος γένηται, τί ποιήσειν; (36) τί οὖν αἴτιον τουτωνί; οὐ γὰρ ἄνευ λόγου καὶ δικαίας αἰτίας οὔτε τόθ᾽ οὕτως εἶχον ἑτοίμως πρὸς ἐλευθερίαν οἱ Ἕλληνες οὔτε νῦν πρὸς τὸ δουλεύειν. ἦν τι τότ᾽, ἦν, ὦ ἄνδρες Ἀθηναῖοι, ἐν ταῖς τῶν πολλῶν διανοίαις, ὃ νῦν οὐκ ἔστιν, ὃ καὶ τοῦ Περσῶν ἐκράτησε πλούτου καὶ ἐλευθέραν ἦγε τὴν Ἑλλάδα καὶ οὔτε ναυμαχίας οὔτε πεζῆς μάχης οὐδεμιᾶς ἡττᾶτο, νῦν δ᾽ ἀπολωλὸς ἅπαντα λελύμανται, καὶ ἄνω καὶ κάτω πεποίηκε πάντα τὰ πράγματα. (37) τί οὖν ἦν τοῦτο; οὐδὲν ποικίλον οὐδὲ σοφόν, ἀλλ᾽ ὅτι τοὺς παρὰ τῶν ἄρχειν βουλομένων ἢ διαφθείρειν τὴν Ἑλλάδα χρήματα λαμβάνοντας ἅπαντες ἐμίσουν, καὶ χαλεπώτατον ἦν τὸ δωροδοκοῦντα ἐλεγχθῆναι, καὶ τιμωρίαι μεγίστηι τοῦτον ἐκόλαζον, καὶ παραίτησις οὐδεμία ἦν οὐδὲ συγγνώμη. (38) τὸν οὖν καιρὸν ἑκάστου τῶν πραγμάτων, ὃν ἡ τύχη καὶ τοῖς ἀμελοῦσι κατὰ τῶν προσεχόντων καὶ τοῖς μηδὲν ἐθέλουσι ποιεῖν κατὰ τῶν πάντα ἃ προσήκει πραττόντων πολλάκις παρασκευάζει, οὐκ ἦν πρίασθαι παρὰ τῶν λεγόντων οὐδὲ τῶν στρατηγούντων, οὐδὲ τὴν πρὸς ἀλλήλους ὁμόνοιαν, οὐδὲ τὴν πρὸς τοὺς τυράννους καὶ τοὺς βαρβάρους ἀπιστίαν, οὐδ᾽ ὅλως τοιοῦτον οὐδέν. (39) νῦν δ᾽ ἅπανθ᾽, ὥσπερ ἐξ ἀγορᾶς, ἐκπέπραται ταῦτα, ἀντεισῆκται δ᾽ ἀντὶ τούτων ὑφ᾽ ὧν ἀπόλωλε καὶ νενόσηκεν ἡ Ἑλλάς. ταῦτα δ᾽ ἐστὶ τί; ζῆλος, εἴ τις εἴληφέ τι· γέλως, ἂν ὁμολογῆι· συγγνώμη τοῖς ἐλεγχομένοις· μῖσος, ἂν τούτοις τις ἐπιτιμᾶι· τἆλλα πάντα ὅσα ἐκ τοῦ δωροδοκεῖν ἤρτηται. (40) ἐπεὶ τριήρεις γε καὶ σωμάτων πλῆθος καὶ χρημάτων καὶ τῆς ἄλλης κατασκευῆς ἀφθονία, καὶ τἆλλ᾽ οἷς ἄν τις ἰσχύειν τὰς πόλεις κρίνοι, νῦν ἅπασι καὶ πλείω καὶ μείζω ἐστὶ τῶν τότε πολλῶι· ἀλλὰ ταῦτα πάντα ἄχρηστα ἄπρακτα ἀνόνητα ὑπὸ τῶν πωλούντων γίγνεται.

(41) ὅτι δ᾽ οὕτω ταῦτ᾽ ἔχει, τὰ μὲν νῦν ὁρᾶτε δήπου καὶ οὐδὲν ἐμοῦ προσδεῖσθε μάρτυρος· τὰ δ᾽ ἐν τοῖς ἄνωθεν χρόνοις ὅτι τἀναντία εἶχεν ἐγὼ δηλώσω, οὐ λόγους ἐμαυτοῦ λέγων, ἀλλὰ γράμματα τῶν προγόνων τῶν ὑμετέρων ἀκεῖνοι κατέθεντο εἰς στήλην χαλκῆν γράψαντες εἰς ἀκρόπολιν, οὐχ ἵνα αὐτοῖς ἦι χρήσιμα (καὶ γὰρ ἄνευ τούτων τῶν γραμμάτων τὰ δέοντα ἐφρόνουν), ἀλλ᾽ ἵνα ὑμεῖς ἔχητε ὑπομνήματα καὶ παραδείγματα ὡς ὑπὲρ τῶν τοιούτων σπουδάζειν προσήκει. (42) τί οὖν λέγει τὰ γράμματα; "Ἄρθμιος" φησί "{ὁ} Πυθώνακτος Ζελείτης ἄτιμος καὶ πολέμιος τοῦ δήμου τοῦ Ἀθηναίων καὶ τῶν συμμάχων αὐτὸς καὶ γένος." εἶθ᾽

---

35 μαλακιζόμεθα d: μαλκίομεν i    36 πάντα τὰ d, i: πάντα τὰ τῶν Ἑλλήνων d: τὰ τῶν Ἑλλήνων d    37 οὐδὲν ... ἀλλ᾽ ὅτι om. d    καὶ παραίτησις ... συγγνώμη om. d    38 καὶ τοῖς μηδὲν ἐθέλουσι ... πραττόντων om. d    39 συγγνώμη τοῖς ἐλεγχομένοις om. d    40 χρημάτων d: χρημάτων πρόσοδοι d: χρημάτων πρόσοδος d    ταῦτα πάντα d: ταῦτα d: ἅπαντα ταῦτ᾽ d: ἅπαντα d    41 ὑμετέρων d: ὑμετέρων δεικνύων d    41–2 οὐχ ἵνα ... τὰ γράμματα om. d    42 ὁ D: del. Dindorf

ἡ αἰτία γέγραπται, δι' ἣν ταῦτ' ἐγένετο· "ὅτι τὸν χρυσὸν τὸν ἐκ Μήδων εἰς Πελοπόννησον ἤγαγεν." ταῦτ' ἐστὶ τὰ γράμματα. (43) λογίζεσθε δὴ πρὸς θεῶν, τίς ἦν ποθ' ἡ διάνοια τῶν Ἀθηναίων τῶν τότε ταῦτα ποιούντων, ἢ τί τὸ ἀξίωμα. ἐκεῖνοι Ζελείτην τινά, Ἄρθμιον, δοῦλον βασιλέως (ἡ γὰρ Ζέλειά ἐστι τῆς Ἀσίας), ὅτι τῶι δεσπότηι διακονῶν χρυσίον ἤγαγεν εἰς Πελοπόννησον, οὐκ Ἀθήναζε, ἐχθρὸν αὑτῶν ἀνέγραψαν καὶ τῶν συμμάχων αὐτὸν καὶ γένος, καὶ ἀτίμους. (44) τοῦτο δ' ἐστὶν οὐχ ἣν οὑτωσί τις ἂν φήσειεν ἀτιμίαν· τί γὰρ τῶι Ζελείτηι, τῶν Ἀθηναίων κοινῶν εἰ μὴ μεθέξειν ἔμελλεν; ἀλλ' οὐ τοῦτο λέγει· ἀλλ' ἐν τοῖς φονικοῖς γέγραπται νόμοις, ὑπὲρ ὧν ἂν μὴ διδῶι φόνου δικάσασθαι, ἀλλ' εὐαγὲς ἧι τὸ ἀποκτεῖναι, "καὶ ἄτιμος" φησὶ "τεθνάτω." τοῦτο δὴ λέγει, καθαρὸν τὸν τούτων τινὰ ἀποκτείναντα εἶναι. (45) οὐκοῦν ἐνόμιζον ἐκεῖνοι τῆς πάντων τῶν Ἑλλήνων σωτηρίας αὑτοῖς ἐπιμελητέον εἶναι· οὐ γὰρ ἂν αὐτοῖς ἔμελεν εἴ τις ἐν Πελοποννήσωι τινὰς ὠνεῖται καὶ διαφθείρει, μὴ τοῦθ' ὑπολαμβάνουσιν· ἐκόλαζον δ' οὕτω καὶ ἐτιμωροῦντο οὓς αἴσθοιντο, ὥστε καὶ στηλίτας ποιεῖν. ἐκ δὲ τούτων εἰκότως τὰ τῶν Ἑλλήνων ἦν τῶι βαρβάρωι φοβερά, οὐχ ὁ βάρβαρος τοῖς Ἕλλησιν. ἀλλ' οὐ νῦν· οὐ γὰρ οὕτως ἔχετε ὑμεῖς οὔτε πρὸς τὰ τοιαῦτα οὔτε πρὸς τἆλλα. ἀλλὰ πῶς; (46) ἴστ' αὐτοί· τί γὰρ δεῖ περὶ πάντων ὑμῶν κατηγορεῖν; παραπλησίως δὲ καὶ οὐδὲν βέλτιον ὑμῶν ἅπαντες οἱ λοιποὶ Ἕλληνες· διόπερ φήμ' ἔγωγε καὶ σπουδῆς πολλῆς καὶ βουλῆς ἀγαθῆς τὰ παρόντα πράγματα προσδεῖσθαι. τίνος; εἴπω κελεύετε; καὶ οὐκ ὀργιεῖσθε;

{ΕΚ ΤΟΥ ΓΡΑΜΜΑΤΕΙΟΥ ΑΝΑΓΙΓΝΩΣΚΕΙ}

(47) ἔστι τοίνυν τις εὐήθης λόγος παρὰ τῶν παραμυθεῖσθαι βουλομένων τὴν πόλιν, ὡς ἄρα οὔπω Φίλιππός ἐστιν οἷοί ποτ' ἦσαν Λακεδαιμόνιοι, οἳ θαλάττης μὲν ἦρχον καὶ γῆς ἁπάσης, βασιλέα δὲ σύμμαχον εἶχον, ὑφίστατο δ' οὐδὲν αὐτούς· ἀλλ' ὅμως ἠμύνατο κἀκείνους ἡ πόλις καὶ οὐκ ἀνηρπάσθη. ἐγὼ δὲ ἁπάντων ὡς ἔπος εἰπεῖν πολλὴν εἰληφότων ἐπίδοσιν, καὶ οὐδὲν ὁμοίων ὄντων τῶν νῦν τοῖς πρότερον, οὐδὲν ἡγοῦμαι πλέον ἢ τὰ τοῦ πολέμου κεκινῆσθαι κἀπιδεδωκέναι. (48) πρῶτον μὲν γὰρ ἀκούω Λακεδαιμονίους τότε καὶ πάντας τοὺς ἄλλους, τέτταρας μῆνας ἢ πέντε, τὴν ὡραίαν αὐτήν, ἐμβαλόντας ἂν καὶ κακώσαντας τὴν χώραν ὁπλίταις καὶ πολιτικοῖς στρατεύμασιν ἀναχωρεῖν ἐπ' οἴκου πάλιν· οὕτω δ' ἀρχαίως εἶχον, μᾶλλον δὲ πολιτικῶς, ὥστε οὐδὲ χρημάτων ὠνεῖσθαι παρ' οὐδενὸς οὐδέν, ἀλλ' εἶναι νόμιμόν τινα καὶ προφανῆ τὸν πόλεμον. (49) νυνὶ δ' ὁρᾶτε μὲν δήπου τὰ πλεῖστα τοὺς προδότας ἀπολωλεκότας, οὐδὲν δ' ἐκ παρατάξεως οὐδὲ μάχης γιγνόμενον· ἀκούετε δὲ Φίλιππον οὐχὶ τῶι φάλαγγα ὁπλιτῶν ἄγειν βαδίζονθ' ὅποι βούλεται, ἀλλὰ τῶι ψιλούς, ἱππέας, τοξότας, ξένους, τοιοῦτον ἐξηρτῆσθαι στρατόπεδον. (50) ἐπειδὰν δ' ἐπὶ τούτοις πρὸς νοσοῦντας ἐν αὑτοῖς

44 ἀλλ' οὐ τοῦτο λέγει om. d, i    ἀλλ' εὐαγὲς ἧι τὸ ἀποκτεῖναι om. d, i    46 ἴστ' αὐτοί ... τίνος om. d    ΕΚ ΤΟΥ ΓΡΑΜΜΑΤΕΙΟΥ ΑΝΑΓΙΓΝΩΣΚΕΙ d: del. Voemel

προσπέσηι καὶ μηδεὶς ὑπὲρ τῆς χώρας δι' ἀπιστίαν ἐξίηι, μηχανήματ' ἐπιστήσας πολιορκεῖ. καὶ σιωπῶ θέρος καὶ χειμῶνα, ὡς οὐδὲν διαφέρει, οὐδ' ἐστὶν ἐξαίρετος ὥρα τις ἣν διαλείπει. (51) ταῦτα μέντοι πάντας εἰδότας καὶ λογιζομένους οὐ δεῖ προσέσθαι τὸν πόλεμον εἰς τὴν χώραν, οὐδ' εἰς τὴν εὐήθειαν τὴν τοῦ τότε πρὸς Λακεδαιμονίους πολέμου βλέποντας ἐκτραχηλισθῆναι, ἀλλ' ὡς ἐκ πλείστου φυλάττεσθαι τοῖς πράγμασι καὶ ταῖς παρασκευαῖς, ὅπως οἴκοθεν μὴ κινήσεται σκοποῦντας, οὐχὶ συμπλακέντας διαγωνίζεσθαι. (52) πρὸς μὲν γὰρ πόλεμον πολλὰ φύσει πλεονεκτήμαθ' ἡμῖν ὑπάρχει, ἄν περ, ὦ ἄνδρες Ἀθηναῖοι, ποιεῖν ἐθέλωμεν ἃ δεῖ, ἡ φύσις τῆς ἐκείνου χώρας, ἧς ἄγειν καὶ φέρειν ἔστι πολλὴν καὶ κακῶς ποιεῖν, ἄλλα μυρία· εἰς δὲ ἀγῶνα ἄμεινον ἡμῶν ἐκεῖνος ἤσκηται.

(53) οὐ μόνον δὲ δεῖ ταῦτα γιγνώσκειν, οὐδὲ τοῖς ἔργοις ἐκεῖνον ἀμύνεσθαι τοῖς τοῦ πολέμου, ἀλλὰ καὶ τῶι λογισμῶι καὶ τῆι διανοίαι τοὺς παρ' ὑμῖν ὑπὲρ αὐτοῦ λέγοντας μισῆσαι, ἐνθυμουμένους ὅτι οὐκ ἔνεστι τῶν τῆς πόλεως ἐχθρῶν κρατῆσαι, πρὶν ἂν τοὺς ἐν αὐτῆι τῆι πόλει κολάσητε ὑπηρετοῦντας ἐκείνοις. (54) ὃ μὰ τὸν Δία καὶ τοὺς ἄλλους θεοὺς οὐ δυνήσεσθε ὑμεῖς ποιῆσαι, ἀλλ' εἰς τοῦτο ἀφῖχθε μωρίας ἢ παρανοίας ἢ — οὐκ ἔχω τί λέγω (πολλάκις γὰρ ἔμοιγ' ἐπελήλυθε καὶ τοῦτο φοβεῖσθαι, μή τι δαιμόνιον τὰ πράγματ' ἐλαύνηι) — ὥστε λοιδορίας, φθόνου, σκώμματος, ἧστινος ἂν τύχητε ἕνεκ' αἰτίας ἀνθρώπους μισθωτούς, ὧν οὐδ' ἂν ἀρνηθεῖεν ἔνιοι ὡς οὐκ εἰσὶ τοιοῦτοι, λέγειν κελεύετε, καὶ γελᾶτε, ἄν τισι λοιδορηθῶσιν. (55) καὶ οὐχί πω τοῦτο δεινόν, καίπερ ὂν δεινόν· ἀλλὰ καὶ μετὰ πλείονος ἀσφαλείας πολιτεύεσθαι δεδώκατε τούτοις ἢ τοῖς ὑπὲρ ὑμῶν λέγουσιν. καίτοι θεάσασθε ὅσας συμφορὰς παρασκευάζει τὸ τῶν τοιούτων ἐθέλειν ἀκροᾶσθαι. λέξω δὲ ἔργα ἃ πάντες εἴσεσθε. (56) ἦσαν ἐν Ὀλύνθωι τῶν ἐν τοῖς πράγμασι τινὲς μὲν Φιλίππου καὶ πάνθ' ὑπηρετοῦντες ἐκείνωι, τινὲς δὲ τοῦ βελτίστου καὶ ὅπως μὴ δουλεύσουσιν οἱ πολῖται πράττοντες. πότεροι δὴ τὴν πατρίδ' ἐξώλεσαν; ἢ πότεροι τοὺς ἱππέας προὔδοσαν, ὧν προδοθέντων Ὄλυνθος ἀπώλετο; οἱ μὲν Φιλίππου φρονοῦντες καί, ὅτ' ἦν ἡ πόλις, τοὺς τὰ βέλτιστα λέγοντας συκοφαντοῦντες καὶ διαβάλλοντες οὕτως, ὥστε τόν γε Ἀπολλωνίδην καὶ ἐκβαλεῖν ὁ δῆμος ὁ τῶν Ὀλυνθίων ἐπείσθη. (57) οὐ τοίνυν παρὰ τούτοις μόνον τὸ ἔθος τοῦτο πάντα κακὰ εἰργάσατο, ἄλλοθι δ' οὐδαμοῦ· ἀλλ' ἐν Ἐρετρίαι, ἐπειδὴ ἀπαλλαγέντος Πλουτάρχου καὶ τῶν ξένων ὁ δῆμος εἶχε τὴν πόλιν καὶ τὸν Πορθμόν, οἱ μὲν ἐφ' ὑμᾶς ἦγον τὰ πράγματα, οἱ δ' ἐπὶ Φίλιππον. ἀκούοντες δὲ τούτων τὰ πολλὰ μᾶλλον οἱ ταλαίπωροι καὶ δυστυχεῖς Ἐρετριεῖς, τελευτῶντες ἐπείσθησαν τοὺς ὑπὲρ αὑτῶν λέγοντας ἐκβαλεῖν. (58) καὶ γάρ τοι πέμψας Ἱππόνικον ὁ σύμμαχος αὐτοῖς Φίλιππος καὶ ξένους χιλίους, τὰ τείχη περιεῖλε τοῦ Πορθμοῦ καὶ τρεῖς κατέστησε τυράννους, Ἵππαρχον, Αὐτομέδοντα, Κλείταρχον· καὶ μετὰ ταῦτα ταῦτα ἐξελήλακεν ἐκ τῆς χώρας

**57** τὰ πολλὰ μᾶλλον d: τὰ πολλὰ μᾶλλον δὲ πάντα d: τὰ πολλὰ μᾶλλον δὲ πάντα d ἤδη βουλομένους σώιζεσθαι, τότε μὲν πέμψας τοὺς μετ' Εὐρυλόχου ξένους, πάλιν δὲ τοὺς μετὰ Παρμενίωνος.

(59) καὶ τί δεῖ τὰ πολλὰ λέγειν; ἀλλ' ἐν Ὠρεῶι Φιλιστίδης μὲν ἔπραττε Φιλίππωι καὶ Μένιππος καὶ Σωκράτης καὶ Θόας καὶ Ἀγαπαῖος, οἵπερ νῦν ἔχουσι τὴν πόλιν (καὶ ταῦτ' ἤιδεσαν ἅπαντες), Εὐφραῖος δέ τις ἄνθρωπος καὶ παρ' ἡμῖν ποτ' ἐνθάδ' οἰκήσας, ὅπως ἐλεύθεροι καὶ μηδενὸς δοῦλοι ἔσονται. (60) οὗτος τὰ μὲν ἄλλ' ὡς ὑβρίζετο καὶ προὐπηλακίζετο ὑπὸ τοῦ δήμου, πόλλ' ἂν εἴη λέγειν· ἐνιαυτῶι δὲ πρότερον τῆς ἁλώσεως ἐνέδειξεν ὡς προδότην τὸν Φιλιστίδην καὶ τοὺς μετ' αὐτοῦ, αἰσθόμενος ἃ πράττουσιν. συστραφέντες δ' ἄνθρωποι πολλοὶ καὶ χορηγὸν ἔχοντες Φίλιππον καὶ πρυτανευόμενοι ἀπάγουσι τὸν Εὐφραῖον εἰς τὸ δεσμωτήριον, ὡς συνταράττοντα τὴν πόλιν. (61) ὁρῶν δὲ ταῦθ' ὁ δῆμος ὁ τῶν Ὠρειτῶν, ἀντὶ τοῦ τῶι μὲν βοηθεῖν, τοὺς δ' ἀποτυμπανίσαι, τοῖς μὲν οὐκ ὠργίζετο, τὸν δ' ἐπιτήδειον ταῦτα παθεῖν ἔφη καὶ ἐπέχαιρεν. μετὰ ταῦθ' οἱ μὲν ἐπ' ἐξουσίας ὁπόσης ἐβούλοντ' ἔπραττον ὅπως ἡ πόλις ληφθήσεται, καὶ κατεσκευάζοντο τὴν πρᾶξιν· τῶν δὲ πολλῶν εἴ τις αἴσθοιτο, ἐσίγα καὶ κατεπέπληκτο, τὸν Εὐφραῖον οἷ' ἔπαθεν μεμνημένοι. οὕτω δ' ἀθλίως διέκειντο, ὥστε οὐ πρότερον ἐτόλμησεν οὐδεὶς τοιούτου κακοῦ προσιόντος ῥῆξαι φωνήν, πρὶν διασκευασάμενοι πρὸς τὰ τείχη προσῆισαν οἱ πολέμιοι· τηνικαῦτα δ' οἱ μὲν ἠμύνοντο, οἱ δὲ προὐδίδοσαν. (62) τῆς πόλεως δ' οὕτως ἁλούσης αἰσχρῶς καὶ κακῶς οἱ μὲν ἄρχουσι καὶ τυραννοῦσι, τοὺς τότε σώιζοντας ἑαυτοὺς καὶ τὸν Εὐφραῖον ἑτοίμους ὁτιοῦν ποιεῖν ὄντας τοὺς μὲν ἐκβαλόντες, τοὺς δ' ἀποκτείναντες· ὁ δ' Εὐφραῖος ἐκεῖνος ἀπέσφαξεν ἑαυτόν, ἔργωι μαρτυρήσας ὅτι καὶ δικαίως καὶ καθαρῶς ὑπὲρ τῶν πολιτῶν ἀνθειστήκει Φιλίππωι.

(63) τί οὖν ποτ' αἴτιον, θαυμάζετε ἴσως, τὸ καὶ τοὺς Ὀλυνθίους καὶ τοὺς Ἐρετριέας καὶ τοὺς Ὠρείτας ἥδιον πρὸς τοὺς ὑπὲρ Φιλίππου λέγοντας ἔχειν ἢ τοὺς ὑπὲρ αὑτῶν; ὅπερ καὶ παρ' ὑμῖν, ὅτι τοῖς μὲν ὑπὲρ τοῦ βελτίστου λέγουσιν οὐδὲ βουλομένοις ἔνεστιν ἐνίοτε πρὸς χάριν οὐδὲν εἰπεῖν· τὰ γὰρ πράγματα ἀνάγκη σκοπεῖν ὅπως σωθήσεται· οἱ δ' ἐν αὐτοῖς οἷς χαρίζονται Φιλίππωι συμπράττουσιν. (64) εἰσφέρειν ἐκέλευον, οἱ δ' οὐδὲν δεῖν ἔφασαν· πολεμεῖν καὶ μὴ πιστεύειν, οἱ δ' ἄγειν εἰρήνην, ἕως ἐγκατελήφθησαν. τἆλλα τὸν αὐτὸν τρόπον οἶμαι πάντα, ἵνα μὴ καθ' ἕκαστα λέγω· οἱ μὲν ἐφ' οἷς χαριοῦνται, ταῦτ' ἔλεγον, οἱ δ' ἐξ ὧν ἔμελλον σωθήσεσθαι. πολλὰ δὲ καὶ τὰ τελευταῖα οὐχ οὕτως οὔτε πρὸς χάριν οὔτε δι' ἄγνοιαν οἱ πολλοὶ προσίεντο, ἀλλ' ὑποκατακλινόμενοι, ἐπειδὴ τοῖς ὅλοις ἡττᾶσθαι ἐνόμιζον. (65) ὃ νὴ τὸν Δία καὶ τὸν Ἀπόλλω δέδοικ' ἐγὼ μὴ πάθηθ' ὑμεῖς, ἐπειδὰν εἰδῆτ' ἐκλογιζόμενοι μηδὲν ὑμῖν ἐνόν. καὶ τοὺς εἰς τοῦθ' ὑπάγοντας ὑμᾶς ὁρῶν οὐκ ὀρρωδῶ, ἀλλὰ δυσωποῦμαι· ἢ γὰρ ἐξεπίτηδες ἢ δι' ἄγνοιαν εἰς χαλεπὸν πρᾶγμα ὑπάγουσι τὴν πόλιν. καίτοι μὴ

58 τότε μὲν πέμψας ... Παρμενίωνος om. d        64 ἐγκατελήφθησαν d: ἐγκατελείφθησαν d        οὔτε πρὸς χάριν οὔτε d: οὐδὲ πρὸς χάριν οὐδὲ d: πρὸς χάριν οὐδὲ d        65 μηδὲν ὑμῖν d: μηδὲν ἐν ὑμῖν d        καὶ τοὺς ... τὴν πόλιν d, i: om. d

γένοιτο μέν, ὦ ἄνδρες Ἀθηναῖοι, τὰ πράγματα ἐν τούτωι· τεθνάναι δὲ μυριάκις κρεῖττον ἢ κολακείαι τι ποιῆσαι Φιλίππωι. καλήν γ' οἱ πολλοὶ νῦν ἀπειλήφασιν Ὠρειτῶν χάριν, ὅτι τοῖς Φιλίππου φίλοις ἐπέτρεψαν αὑτούς, τὸν δ' Εὐφραῖον ἐώθουν· **(66)** καλήν γ' ὁ δῆμος ὁ Ἐρετριέων, ὅτι τοὺς ὑμετέρους πρέσβεις ἀπήλασεν, Κλειτάρχωι δ' ἐνέδωκεν αὑτόν· δουλεύουσί γε μαστιγούμενοι καὶ σφαττόμενοι. καλῶς Ὀλυνθίων ἐφείσατο τῶν τὸν μὲν Λασθένην ἵππαρχον χειροτονησάντων, τὸν δ' Ἀπολλωνίδην ἐκβαλόντων. **(67)** μωρία καὶ κακία τὰ τοιαῦτα ἐλπίζειν, καὶ κακῶς βουλευομένους καὶ μηδὲν ὧν προσήκει ποιεῖν ἐθέλοντας, ἀλλὰ τῶν ὑπὲρ τῶν ἐχθρῶν λεγόντων ἀκροωμένους, τηλικαύτην ἡγεῖσθαι πόλιν οἰκεῖν τὸ μέγεθος ὥστε μηδ' ἂν ὁτιοῦν ἦι δεινὸν πείσεσθαι. **(68)** καὶ μὴν ἐκεῖνό γε αἰσχρόν, ὕστερόν ποτ' εἰπεῖν "τίς γὰρ ἂν ὠιήθη ταῦτα γενέσθαι; νὴ τὸν Δία, ἔδει γὰρ τὸ καὶ τὸ ποιῆσαι καὶ τὸ μὴ ποιῆσαι." πόλλ' ἂν εἰπεῖν ἔχοιεν Ὀλύνθιοι νῦν, ἃ τότ' εἰ προείδοντο, οὐκ ἂν ἀπώλοντο· πόλλ' ἂν Ὠρεῖται, πολλὰ Φωκεῖς, πολλὰ τῶν ἀπολωλότων ἕκαστοι. **(69)** ἀλλὰ τί τούτων ὄφελος αὐτοῖς; ἕως ἂν σώιζηται τὸ σκάφος, ἄν τε μεῖζον ἄν τ' ἔλαττον ἦι, τότε χρὴ καὶ ναύτην καὶ κυβερνήτην καὶ πάντα ἄνδρα ἑξῆς προθύμους εἶναι, καὶ ὅπως μήθ' ἑκὼν μήτ' ἄκων μηδεὶς ἀνατρέψει, τοῦτο σκοπεῖσθαι· ἐπειδὰν δὲ ἡ θάλαττα ὑπέρσχηι, μάταιος ἡ σπουδή.

**(70)** καὶ ἡμεῖς τοίνυν, ὦ ἄνδρες Ἀθηναῖοι, ἕως ἐσμὲν σῶιοι, πόλιν μεγίστην ἔχοντες, ἀφορμὰς πλείστας, ἀξίωμα κάλλιστον — τί ποιῶμεν; πάλαι τις ἡδέως ἂν ἴσως ἐρωτήσας κάθηται. ἐγὼ νὴ Δί' ἐρῶ, καὶ γράψω δέ, ὥστε, ἂν βούλησθε, χειροτονήσετε. αὐτοὶ πρῶτον ἀμυνόμενοι καὶ παρασκευαζόμενοι — τριήρεσι καὶ χρήμασι καὶ στρατιώταις λέγω· καὶ γὰρ ἂν ἅπαντες δήπου δουλεύειν συγχωρήσωσιν οἱ ἄλλοι, ἡμῖν γ' ὑπὲρ τῆς ἐλευθερίας ἀγωνιστέον — **(71)** ταῦτα δὴ πάντ' αὐτοὶ παρεσκευασμένοι καὶ ποιήσαντες φανερὰ τοὺς ἄλλους ἤδη παρακαλῶμεν, καὶ τοὺς ταῦτα διδάξοντας ἐκπέμπωμεν πρέσβεις πανταχοῖ, εἰς Πελοπόννησον, εἰς Ῥόδον, εἰς Χίον, ὡς βασιλέα λέγω (οὐδὲ γὰρ τῶν ἐκείνωι συμφερόντων ἀφέστηκε τὸ μὴ τοῦτον ἐᾶσαι πάντα καταστρέψασθαι), ἵν' ἐὰν μὲν πείσητε, κοινωνοὺς ἔχητε καὶ τῶν κινδύνων καὶ τῶν ἀναλωμάτων, ἄν τι δέηι, εἰ δὲ μή, χρόνους γ' ἐμποιῆτε τοῖς πράγμασιν. **(72)** ἐπειδὴ γάρ ἐστι πρὸς ἄνδρα καὶ οὐχὶ συνεστώσης πόλεως ἰσχὺν ὁ πόλεμος, οὐδὲ τοῦτ' ἄχρηστον, οὐδ' αἱ πέρυσιν πρεσβεῖαι περὶ τὴν Πελοπόννησον ἐκεῖναι καὶ κατηγορίαι, ἃς ἐγὼ καὶ Πολύευκτος ὁ βέλτιστος ἐκεινοσὶ καὶ Ἡγήσιππος καὶ οἱ ἄλλοι πρέσβεις περιήλθομεν, καὶ ἐποιήσαμεν ἐπισχεῖν ἐκεῖνον καὶ μήτ' ἐπ' Ἀμβρακίαν ἐλθεῖν μήτ' εἰς Πελοπόννησον ὁρμῆσαι. **(73)** οὐ μέντοι λέγω μηδὲ αὐτοὺς ὑπὲρ αὑτῶν ἀναγκαῖον ἐθέλοντας ποιεῖν, τοὺς ἄλλους παρακαλεῖν· καὶ γὰρ εὔηθες τὰ οἰκεῖα αὐτοὺς προϊεμένους τῶν ἀλλοτρίων φάσκειν κήδεσθαι, καὶ τὰ παρόντα περιορῶντας ὑπὲρ τῶν

---

**65** Φιλίππωι d, i: Φιλίππου d      Φιλίππωι καὶ προέσθαι τῶν ὑπὲρ ὑμῶν λεγόντων τινάς. καλήν d (cf. Introd. §6.2)      **66** σφαττόμενοι d: στρεβλούμενοι d: στρεβλούμενοι καὶ σφαττόμενοι d      **69** ἀνατρέψει i: ἀνατρέψηι d      **70** ἐρωτήσας d: ἐρωτήσων d      **71** πανταχοῖ ... καταστρέψασθαι om. d

μελλόντων τοὺς ἄλλους φοβεῖν. οὐ λέγω ταῦτα, ἀλλὰ τοῖς μὲν ἐν Χερρονήσωι χρήματ' ἀποστέλλειν φημὶ δεῖν καὶ τἄλλ' ὅσα ἀξιοῦσι ποιεῖν, αὐτοὺς δὲ παρασκευάζεσθαι, τοὺς δ' ἄλλους Ἕλληνας συγκαλεῖν, συνάγειν, διδάσκειν, νουθετεῖν· ταῦτ' ἐστὶν πόλεως ἀξίωμα ἐχούσης ἡλίκον ὑμῖν ὑπάρχει. (74) εἰ δ' οἴεσθε Χαλκιδέας τὴν Ἑλλάδα σώσειν ἢ Μεγαρέας, ὑμεῖς δ' ἀποδράσεσθαι τὰ πράγματα, οὐκ ὀρθῶς οἴεσθε· ἀγαπητὸν γὰρ ἐὰν αὐτοὶ σώιζωνται τούτων ἑκάστοις. ἀλλ' ὑμῖν τοῦτο πρακτέον· ὑμῖν οἱ πρόγονοι τοῦτο τὸ γέρας ἐκτήσαντο καὶ κατέλιπον μετὰ πολλῶν καὶ μεγάλων κινδύνων. (75) εἰ δὲ ὃ βούλεται ζητῶν ἕκαστος καθεδεῖται, καὶ ὅπως μηδὲν αὐτὸς ποιήσει σκοπῶν, πρῶτον μὲν οὐδὲ μήποθ' εὕρηι τοὺς ποιήσοντας, ἔπειτα δέδοιχα ὅπως μὴ πάνθ' ἅμα ὅσα οὐ βουλόμεθα ποιεῖν ἡμῖν ἀνάγκη γενήσεται. (76) ἐγὼ μὲν δὴ ταῦτα λέγω, ταῦτα γράφω· καὶ οἴομαι καὶ νῦν ἔτι ἐπανορθωθῆναι ἂν τὰ πράγματα τούτων γιγνομένων. εἰ δέ τις ἔχει τούτων τι βέλτιον, λεγέτω καὶ συμβουλευέτω. ὅ τι δ' ὑμῖν δόξει, τοῦτ', ὦ πάντες θεοί, συνενέγκοι.

**74** ἑκάστοις c: ἕκαστοι D   **75** γενήσεται d: γένηται d

# COMMENTARY

## 1 FIRST OLYNTHIAC

### 1 Prooemium
The city can profit if it chooses the best proposals in the Assembly.

**1** Rather than introduce the specific business under debate, D.'s preamble reminds the citizens in the Assembly that they may benefit from the advice of any speaker. The passage is closely echoed in the *Prooemia* (3), a Demosthenic collection of generic introductions for Assembly speeches. Many of the items in this collection similarly focus on the process of democratic deliberation in order to depict the orator as an experienced and authoritative advisor (Yunis 1996: 247–57; 3.1n., 4.1n.). This passage is parodied by Lucian (2nd cent. AD; *JTr* 15).   ἀντὶ πολλῶν ἄν ... χρημάτων ὑμᾶς ἑλέσθαι "you would pay much"; lit. "you would choose at great expense." ἄν modifies the infinitive (Smyth §1848); ἑλέσθαι is aor. mid. of αἱρέω. On χρημάτων cf. §15n. τὸν αὐτόν.   τὸ μέλλον συνοίσειν τῆι πόλει "what is likely to benefit the city." Rhetorical handbooks define the advantage of the city as the central theme of deliberative oratory; [Arist.] *Rh.Al.* 2.21 (1424b), Arist. *Rh.* 1.6.1 (1362a), and the openings and conclusions of D.'s Assembly speeches regularly make an explicit appeal to expediency (Hunt 2010: 157–8). Throughout the speeches, the argument often focuses on practical benefits as opposed to moral motivations (Christ 2012: 163–71, but for an exception to this tendency see §9.16n. τό). Cf. 4.5.1n. συμφέρει.   περὶ ὧν = περὶ τούτων ἅ; "in regard to those matters which." Cf. 9.1n. περί.   ὅτε τοίνυν τοῦθ' οὕτως ἔχει "so then, since this is the case." ὅτε is causal (Smyth §2240b); τοίνυν marks a logical inference here (*GP* 569; cf. D. 2.29 and 4.7).   προθύμως modifies ἀκούειν (cf. D. 23.4). The early placement adds emphasis, avoids hiatus, and creates a striking sound pattern with repeated word beginnings in προ- (homoioarchon) and endings in -ειν (homoioteleuton).   συμβουλεύειν: in an Athenian political context this verb and its cognate noun σύμβουλος refer specifically to speakers in the Assembly (Hansen 1989: 14 n. 39). Throughout his career D. characterizes himself as the ideal Athenian σύμβουλος, the politician who gives the state the best advice (cf. §16 and 18.189 with Yunis 212–13).   οὐ γὰρ μόνον ... ἀλλὰ καὶ ... εἰπεῖν "you should listen and take it in not only if someone comes forward having thought out something useful, but also I consider it [to be] your good fortune that it would occur to some to say much of what is needed without preparation." D. distinguishes between planned and extemporaneous Assembly speeches. Fourth-century rhetoricians debated the merits of precomposed Assembly speeches (e.g., Alc. *Soph.* 11; cf. Hansen 1987:

77

155 n. 367) and D.'s critics faulted his reliance on written preparations and lack of improvisational skill in the Assembly (Plut. *Dem.* 8, Introd. §4.1). But in this generic prooemium he is not expressing preference for one or the other method of speaking, but rather praising the variety of potentially valuable contributions to democratic debate. **τῆς ὑμετέρας τύχης:** the genitive is a predicate describing a qualitative characteristic of the Athenians (Smyth §1304). **ἐνίοις ἂν ἐπελθεῖν εἰπεῖν:** LSJ ἐπέρχομαι I 3; for the construction with the dative and infinitive cf. D. 9.54, 18.263. **τῶν δεόντων:** cf. 2.3n. προτρέπειν. **ἐξ ἁπάντων** "from all [the proposals]." Cf. 3.1n. οὐδέν.

**2–9 Opportunity in the north**
We must seize the opportunity and support Olynthus. Philip is powerful, but the Olynthians distrust him. Now is the chance to join them. Consider how we lost Amphipolis while protecting Euboea. We allowed him to take other cities and ports, but now we have a new opportunity.

**2 μὲν οὖν** signals the movement from the generic opening to the specific topic of the speech and is reinforced by the following vocative; cf. 2.3n. μέν. **παρών:** cf. 2.1 ἐν τοῖς παροῦσι πράγμασιν. **καιρός:** a recurrent theme in all three *Olynthiacs* (cf. 2.3on. ἐν) and especially in this speech (e.g., §§8, 9, 20). The personification of the abstract concept as the subject of λέγει is striking, but not uncommon (cf. D. 18.172 with Usher 1993: 232; *GPS* 32 collects other passages, including D. 4.12 and 3.6; cf. also Wankel 1976: 131). **μόνον οὐχὶ λέγει φωνὴν ἀφιείς** "almost speaks audibly" (LSJ μόνος B II). For φωνὴν ἀφιείς cf. D. 18.170 and 222, Aesch. 3.16. **τῶν πραγμάτων ὑμῖν ἐκείνων αὐτοῖς ἀντιληπτέον ἐστίν** "you yourselves must take control of those affairs" (LSJ ἀντιλαμβάνω II 3). The unexpected placement of ὑμῖν in the middle of the genitive phrase draws attention to the pronoun, and the delayed addition of αὐτοῖς reinforces that emphasis. **εἴπερ:** the clause is subordinate to the preceding ὅτι clause. The conjunction is optimistic in tone, suggesting "that the supposition agrees with the fact" (LSJ II; cf. *GP* 223 n. 1). **ὑπὲρ σωτηρίας αὐτῶν φροντίζετε** "you are anxious in regard to their safety." αὐτῶν refers to πραγμάτων. **ἡμεῖς δ᾽ οὐκ οἶδ᾽ ὅντινά ... τρόπον** "but we seem to me to have an unclear attitude." οὐκ οἶδ᾽ ὅντινα τρόπον is a common idiom in an adverbial sense ("somehow"; frequently in Plato, e.g. *Grg.* 513c, *Phdr.* 227c, *R.* 4.430e), but here τρόπον is the object of ἔχειν, and is placed next to it to help clarify the construction. **ἡμεῖς:** D. regularly uses the first-person to describe his role as a participant in the debate, alongside second-person forms referring to the Assembly decisions that are in the hands of his addressees (cf. also D. 2.6 and 12). He similarly juxtaposes first- and second-person pronouns to include himself in the long-term effects of policy decisions, while being careful to refer to the voters in the audience in the second-person (§18, 2.22, 30, 3.3). **δή** introduces specific proposals; cf. 2.11n. φημί. **γ' stresses ἐμοί** and adds a note of humility: "to me, at any rate." **ψηφίσασθαι μὲν ἤδη τὴν βοήθειαν ... πρεσβείαν δὲ πέμπειν**: D. proposes the same two actions in 2.11 (βοηθεῖν ... πρεσβείαν πέμπειν). **παρασκευάσασθαι ... ὅπως ἐνθένδε βοηθήσετε** "make preparations to send help from here." ὅπως + fut. indic. is regular in object clauses with παρασκευάζομαι (Smyth §2210). The fut. indic. is preferable to the subj. reading found in most MSS because it stresses the action to be accomplished. **τὴν ταχίστην**: adverbial: "right away." **μὴ πάθητε** "so that you may not suffer." The subjunctive here stresses the intention behind the proposal to prepare a relief force. According to this interpretation, βοηθήσετε and πάθητε are not fully parallel in sense (the former verb is in an object clause, the latter in a final clause), and for that reason the latter clause is presented here as a parenthesis; unlike a modern editor, D. could not rely on punctuation to mark the parenthesis, and so καί indicates that both verbs are to be construed with ὅπως. For the subj. with ὅπως rather than a fut. indic., cf. Smyth §2214 and D. 24.107 (also dependent on παρασκευάζομαι) and examples in Sandys 1897: 128. **ταὐτόν** = τὸ αὐτό (crasis; on the final ν see Smyth §328N). **ὅπερ καὶ πρότερον**: sc. ἐπάθετε. In §§8–9 D. provides details regarding earlier missed opportunities for the Athenians to protect their interests in the north from Philip. **ἥτις ... ἐρεῖ καὶ παρέσται**: the future tense with the relative expresses purpose (Smyth §2554); cf. 2.11. **παρέσται τοῖς πράγμασιν** "be present for the events."

**3 ὡς ἔστι μάλιστα τοῦτο δέος** "For this especially is [our] fear." For similar uses of ὡς alone (without a connective particle) to introduce a main verb cf., e.g., D. 13.11 and 15.25. **μὴ ... τρέψηται καὶ παρασπάσηται**: fear clause introduced by δέος. **πανοῦργος** refers to a man who has no morals. The adjective is sometimes paired with more positive descriptors such as σοφός or κομψός (LSJ II). Here the pairing with δεινός ... πράγμασι χρῆσθαι ("adept at managing situations"; on the construction see 2.2on. δεινοί) presents Philip as one who can, and will, do anything. For the tone of admiration cf. 2.15n. πράττων. **ἄνθρωπος** = ὁ ἄνθρωπος, "the fellow." The term is "a slightly contemptuous expression" (MacDowell 1990: 392) often given a pejorative sense, as here, by modifying adjectives (other examples are discussed by Lefort 2016: 164– 5). D. is especially fond of this usage and frequently refers to Philip in this way (e.g., §23, 4.9, 50, 9.27), and here the expression marks Philip's first appearance in the speech (cf. 4.3n. τῆι νῦν). **τὰ μὲν εἴκων** "sometimes making concessions." τὰ μέν and τὰ δέ (twice) are adverbial (Smyth §1111). **ἡνίκα ἂν τύχηι** "on occasion" (LSJ τυγχάνω A I 3; cf. 2.10n. ἄν, 9.54n. ἧστινος). The idiom here suggests that Philip offers concessions somewhat rarely in comparison with other tactics. **τὰ δ' ἀπειλῶν** "sometimes making threats." Threats and slander were typical traits of the tyrant; cf. Creon in S. *Ant*. 280–314 with the discussion of Creon as a tyrant in Bowra 1944: 72–8. On D.'s characterization of Philip as a tyrant, see §5n. ἄπιστον, §14n. ὑφ', §23n. ὑβριστής, 2.17n. ξένοι, 2.19nn., 4.9n. ἀπειλεῖ, 9.16n. τό; E. M. Harris 2018. **ἀξιόπιστος δ' ἂν εἰκότως φαίνοιτο**: a parenthetical aside, "and he would likely appear convincing." D. incorporates these short asides to create a lively and extemporaneous tone, as if the thought had just occurred to him (cf. Yunis 115 on D. 18.13). These asides often involve a change of subject, and they briefly explain some detail, regularly with an explanatory γάρ (e.g., D. 3.5, 10, 4.23, 32, 9.43, 59). Here δέ is equivalent to γάρ; see *GP* 169. For the adjective cf. D. 19.232 and 54.40. **τὰ δ' ἡμᾶς διαβάλλων** "at other times slandering us"; 9.2n. τούς. **τρέψηται**: the desired sense may be "turn toward oneself" or "put to one's own use"; though we lack parallels for this meaning, the usage is perhaps influenced by the sense of παρασπάσηται. Alternatively, perhaps "he may change the direction [of events]" (LSJ τρέπω II 3). Others prefer to emend the text (see apparatus). καταστρέψηται is perhaps the most attractive of the proposed corrections: it would be an easy scribal slip, it fits this context well, and D. and other contemporaries elsewhere use the verb to describe Philip's conquests (e.g., §12, 3.8; Isoc. 5.21). **παρασπάσηταί τι τῶν ὅλων πραγμάτων** "he may detach for himself some part of our vital interests." For this sense of τι τῶν ὅλων, cf. D. 18.278. For Athenian interests in the north, cf. 2.2n. πόλεων.

**4 οὐ μὴν ἀλλ'** "but even so"; a Demosthenic idiom (*GP* 28–30; cf. 2.22n. οὐ). **ἐπιεικῶς** "arguably"; the adverb modifies βέλτιστον and the early placement just before the vocative stresses the word and draws attention to the following paradox. **τοῦθ' ὃ δυσμαχώτατόν ἐστι ... βέλτιστον ὑμῖν** "the aspect of Philip's situation that is most difficult to fight against is also the best for you." D. uses enigmatic paradoxes such as this at the beginning of his deliberative speeches to encourage the audience to be optimistic about their prospects while at the same time stressing the urgency of the situation at hand; cf. 4.2n. ὅ, 9.5n. παράδοξον. This section is the first in the speech to identify Philip and Olynthus by name; the paradox here also serves as a transition. The speech began with broad generalizations (§1), and then specific details started to reveal the precise context (§2–3: e.g., ἐνθένδε βοηθήσετε and ἄνθρωπος). Now D. finally tells the reader (an Assembly audience would of course know the matter under debate) whom he is talking about. **τῶν Φιλίππου πραγμάτων** refers specifically to Philip's capabilities for war (cf. D. 4.44). **τὸ γὰρ εἶναι ... καὶ ... παρεῖναι**: the compound articular infinitive phrase is subject of προέχει and ἔχει. **πάντων ... καὶ ῥητῶν καὶ ἀπορρή-**

## 1 FIRST OLYNTHIAC 4–5 81

**τῶν:** the genitive modifies κύριον: "master of all business, both open and secret." D. echoes this passage in *On the Crown* (18.235 αὐτὸς δεσπότης, ἡγεμών, κύριος πάντων) and provides more detail, explaining that Philip had a standing army and ample treasury, and that his command was not restricted by any political processes. By contrast, Athenian commanders were subject to "complex rules and procedures designed to maintain the rule of law" (E. M. Harris 2010: 414–15 on this passage). Similarly, Darius praises the efficiency of monarchs who can act according to their own judgment and conceal their plans from enemies (Hdt. 3.82.2). Cf. 3.30n. πράττειν. **ἕνα ὄντα** "although he is one man"; i.e., "all by himself." **δεσπότην:** the noun refers to a slave master, and is commonly used by extension for autocratic rulers; cf. D. 18.235, where Philip is described as an αὐτοκράτωρ ruling over his followers, Brock 2013: 157–8, 9.32n. τούς, 9.43n. τῶι. For a full survey of the noun's usage in the orators, see E. M. Harris 2006: 278. **ταμίαν:** Philip has full control of the state's finances; see Faraguna 1998: 360–7. Cf. 4.33n. αὐτοί. **αὐτὸν παρεῖναι:** the pronoun is intensifying. D. uses the same phrase to describe Philip at 2.23. **πρὸς μὲν τὸ τὰ τοῦ πολέμου … πράττεσθαι** "for the purpose of conducting the business of war." **κατὰ καιρόν** "at exactly the right time." **πολλῶι προέχει** "is highly advantageous." **πρὸς δὲ τὰς καταλλαγάς** "but for the purpose of [making] agreements." D. considers the prospects of the Olynthians surrendering. See 2.1n. τάς for the background to diplomatic relations between Philip and Olynthus.

**5 πολεμοῦσιν:** the reading of all MSS. Some editors prefer κινδυνεύουσιν (as quoted by Maximus Planudes [13th cent. AD]) on the grounds that D. here describes the Olynthians' apprehensions about peace negotiations, which perhaps implies that they are not actually fighting with Philip at this point. But D.'s rhetorical goal is to present Philip as an enemy at war, whatever the current circumstances may be. Certainly D. and others would view Philip's attacks on Olynthian allies and territory prior to the siege of the city in summer 348 as acts of war, and so the reading of the MSS should be retained. **ἀναστάσεως:** D. uses similar language to describe the fears of the Olynthians in 2.1. **ἀνδραποδισμοῦ:** Philip did in fact enslave the Olynthians after the city fell in 348. See 9.26n. Ὄλυνθον; cf. Pritchett 1991: 223–45, Ducrey 1999: 134–5, 9.22n. καταδουλοῦσθαι. **Ἀμφιπολιτῶν:** partitive gen. modifying τοὺς παραδόντας, placed near the front of the clause for emphasis. On Philip's capture of Amphipolis, see 2.2n. πόλεων. A scholiast (40a Dilts) reports that when Philip entered Amphipolis, he first killed the men who had betrayed the city to him, citing their betrayal of their own countrymen as an indication that he could not trust them in the future. This anecdote is at odds with our only other source for the capture of Amphipolis, which briefly states that Philip exiled his enemies and was otherwise merciful (D. S. 16.8.2).

An inscribed decree of Amphipolis confirms that Philip's enemies were exiled in 357/6 (*GHI* no. 49). **Πυδναίων**: partitive genitive modifying τοὺς ὑποδεξαμένους. Philip captured Pydna, an Athenian ally in the north, in 357, shortly after taking control of Amphipolis (D. S. 16.8.3; *HM* 356–7; on its betrayal cf. D. 20.63). A scholiast (41a Dilts) states that the men who allowed him into the city fled in fear of Philip, and that he, after promising not to harm them, killed them. Thus D.'s account of Philip's treatment of both Amphipolis and Pydna stresses Philip's duplicity. **τοὺς ὑποδεξαμένους:** sc. αὐτὸν εἰς τὴν πόλιν. **καὶ ὅλως** rounds off this account of the Olynthians' concerns as D. switches the focus back to Athens. **ἄπιστον:** neut. predicate: lit. "[is] an untrustworthy thing." D. develops this categorical assertion in later speeches (cf. 6.24, 9.38n. τήν), building on a typical trope in negative characterizations of tyrants (Leopold 1981). **ταῖς πολιτείαις:** here in a specific sense referring to states with democratic rule of law (LSJ III 2). **τυραννίς:** the term describes a state controlled by an autocratic individual, and thus summarizes the description of Philip's command in §4. **ἄλλως τε κἂν** "especially if." **ὅμορον χώραν:** D. elaborates on this point in 2.21 (cf. 2.1), where he presents the Olynthians' proximity to Macedon as a great opportunity to hurt Philip and demonstrate his weaknesses to others. Furthermore, if the Athenians face Philip in the north, they may avoid fighting him at home, as D. explicitly explains at §25 and 4.50. Business concerning threats to the Athenian homeland was given priority in the Assembly's agenda (Rhodes 1972: 231–5), and orators regularly presented even distant threats in terms of danger to Attica; see Munn 1993: 194.

**6 ταῦτ' οὖν ἐγνωκότας ὑμᾶς** "since you know these things." ὑμᾶς is the subject of the three infinitives following δεῖν. **ἃ προσήκει:** sc. ὑμῖν ἐνθυμεῖσθαι. D. frequently uses such periphrases to stress that the Athenians are neglecting their interests; cf. 2.3n. προτρέπειν and e.g. 2.22, 3.14, 8.77. **φημὶ δεῖν:** D. uses this formula to introduce specific motions in the Assembly. Cf. 2.11n. φημί. **εἴπερ ποτὲ καὶ νῦν:** lit. "if ever, also now"; i.e., "now more than ever." For the phrase cf. Ar. *Knights* 594 and see 3.3n. εἴπερ. **χρήματα εἰσφέροντας:** Assembly decrees mobilizing forces also stipulated exceptional tax levies (the εἰσφορά) for the wealthiest 1000 to 1200 Athenians (citizens and metics). This group of wealthy taxpayers was probably the same as those required to perform liturgies. Not long after this speech (in 347/6) the tax became a regular annual property tax on the wealthy, and additional levies could be imposed. See Hansen 1991: 112–15 and cf. 2.29n. πρότερον. **αὐτοὺς ἐξιόντας** "by going on expedition yourselves" (LSJ ἔξειμι (A), (εἶμι *ibo*) 3). D. repeatedly links the εἰσφορά and the need for the Athenians to fight for themselves (e.g., 2.24, 27, 31). D. avoids explaining that only the wealthy paid taxes and he prefers to ascribe both the financial provisioning and the active service on the front to the entire citizen body. Thus he presents the campaign as a common Athenian cause. **καὶ μηδὲν ἐλλείποντας:** the three participles form a tricolon. The first two items are parallel in that they describe specific actions, but this third element caps them with a broad generic formulation. **οὐδὲ γὰρ λόγος οὐδὲ σκῆψις ἔθ᾽ ὑμῖν ... ὑπολείπεται** "for you do not have any reason left, nor any excuse." **τοῦ μὴ τὰ δέοντα ποιεῖν ἐθέλειν** "for refusing to do your duty." On τὰ δέοντα see 2.3n. προτρέπειν.

**7 ὃ ... τέως:** the antecedent to the relative clause is omitted (sc. τοῦτο), and the clause stands in its place as the subject of γέγονεν. **ἐθρύλουν:** D. frequently uses this verb to mock others for speeches that are tedious and annoying (MacDowell 2000: 268; cf. 2.6n. θρυλούμενον, 3.7). D. uses it here to reinforce his insistence that the Athenians should stop talking and take action. **Ὀλυνθίους ἐκπολεμῶσαι δεῖν Φιλίππωι** "that [we] must embroil the Olynthians in war with Philip"; cf. D. 3.7. The ἐκ- prefix stresses the completion of the action ("involve them in a war once and for all"). For the construction with the dative (πρός + accus. is more common with the verb), cf. Hdt. 3.66. **καὶ ταῦτα** "and that [it has happened]"; the idiom adds a new circumstance "heightening the force of what has been said" (LSJ οὗτος C VIII 2). **εἰ ... ἀνείλοντο τὸν πόλεμον, ... ἂν ... ἦσαν:** a mixed contrary-to-fact condition: "if they had undertaken the war, ... they would [now] be." **σφαλεροί** "precarious"; the opposite of βεβαίαν in the δέ colon that follows. **καὶ μέχρι του ... ἐγνωκότες** "and resolved upon these matters only up to a point." του = τινος. **ἐκ τῶν πρὸς αὑτοὺς ἐγκλημάτων** "because of complaints on their own behalf"; i.e., the Olynthians have their own causes for complaint. ἔγκλημα is a technical term for a legal complaint (E. M. Harris 2013a: 156–7). The sense of πρός must be inferred from the context (Smyth §1695.3c; cf. D. 18.36, where the phrase πρὸς τοὺς Θηβαίους occurs twice in opposite senses). **βεβαίαν ... τὴν ἔχθραν** "an enmity that is unfaltering." The position of βεβαίαν before the article puts stress on it as a predicate. For enmity as a product of hatred, cf. 9.53n. τῶν.

**8 οὐ δεῖ ... ἀφεῖναι** "[you] must not neglect." For οὐ instead of μή with the infinitive, see Smyth §2714b. **τοιοῦτον ... παραπεπτωκότα καιρόν** "such an opportunity when it has fallen into our lap" (LSJ παραπίπτω II). The παρα- prefix has the sense "alongside"; the verb describes something that falls across one's path unexpectedly. **εἰ γὰρ ... παρειχόμεθ᾽..., εἴχετ᾽ ἄν:** past contrary-to-fact condition: "if we had displayed ..., you would have gained." The imperfect verbs (rather than the more usual aorist) stress the duration of time in the actions (Smyth §2304). **ἥκομεν:** imperf.: "we had come home" (LSJ 3). **Εὐβοεῦσιν βεβοηθηκότες:** in 357 Athens and Thebes fought over an alliance with the Euboeans. Athenian forces expelled the Thebans from the island in 30 days (Aesch. 3.85) and "the expedition became a touchstone for quick effective action" (Yunis 166 on D. 18.99), frequently cited by D., who was himself a trierarch in the campaign (D. 21.161). See Sealey 102–3. An inscription documenting the alliance with the Euboean city of Carystus survives (*IG* II² 124 = *GHI* no. 48). παρῆσαν: D. and others use πάρειμι with prepositional phrases to describe motion (e.g., D. 2.8, 8.11; Sandys 1897: 133–4), and the MS reading does not require emendation. Still, Dobree's conjecture παρῇσαν (from πάρειμι) cannot be ruled out, since Aeschines (3.159) uses that verb with ἐπί to describe a speaker approaching the platform in the Assembly. Ἀμφιπολιτῶν Ἱέραξ καὶ Στρατοκλῆς: the ambassadors arrived in Athens when Philip was threatening Amphipolis in 357 (cf. 2.2n. πόλεων). Hierax is known as the host of ambassadors (a θεαροδόκος) from Epidaurus (*IG* IV² i.94.18). After Philip took Amphipolis, Stratocles was exiled; the city's decree survives (*GHI* no. 49). κελεύοντες ἡμᾶς ... τὴν πόλιν: the Athenians apparently recognized how difficult it would be to take Amphipolis after Philip had laid siege (cf. *HM* 238 n. 1), and they did not send out forces. Now eight years after the fact D. describes the episode as a missed opportunity in order to add urgency to his picture of the current καιρός offered to Athens. τὴν αὐτὴν ... προθυμίαν: in this section D. repeatedly introduces an adjectival phrase and then delays the agreeing noun; cf. τοιοῦτον ... καιρόν above and πάντων τῶν μετὰ ταῦτα ... πραγμάτων below. This elaborate word order stresses the delayed noun and holds the audience's attention as they wait for the noun; see Ronnet 43–4. ἡμεῖς ὑπὲρ ἡμῶν αὐτῶν: the repetition of the personal pronoun emphasizes D.'s call for the Athenians to act for themselves. ἂν ἦτε ἀπηλλαγμένοι "you would have been free of" (LSJ ἀπαλλάσσω B 1).

9 καὶ πάλιν "and again." The adverb emphasizes that Athens repeatedly failed to protect its northern allies from Philip's incursions in the 350s. Πύδνα: §5n. Πυδναίων. The cities are listed here in the order in which they were captured by Philip. The lack of conjunctions (asyndeton) creates a cumulative effect emphasizing the extent of Philip's activity; cf. 4.4n. Πύδναν. Ποτείδαια: Potidaea was an Athenian possession (a cleruchy) from 430 to 404 and then again after the campaigns of Timotheus in the 360s (2.14n. ἐπί) until 356, when Philip won it (cf. 2.1n. τάς). He allowed the Athenians there to return to Athens, and enslaved the Potidaeans (D. S. 16.8.5). Μεθώνη: captured for Athens by Timotheus in the 360s. By 355 it was the only remaining maritime ally of Athens in the north, but the city surrendered to Philip in 354 after a long siege (*HM* 255). Παγασαί: another northern port, captured by Philip in 352 (2.11n. Παγασάς). καθ' ἕκαστα λέγων διατρίβω "waste time by enumerating [them] individually." πολιορκούμενα ἀπηγγέλλετο "were

## 1 FIRST OLYNTHIAC 9–10

reported to be under siege." The finite verb emphasizes that the Athenians were inactive at home during these crises. Cf. 9.17n. εἰ. **τούτων ἑνὶ τῶι πρώτωι** "any of these in the first place" or "as the first" (LSJ εἷς 4), i.e., at the first moment when each of the cities was threatened. **ὡς προσῆκεν:** §6n. ἄ. **αὐτοί** again emphasizes that the Athenians must act themselves. **ῥάιονι ... ταπεινοτέρωι** "easier [to resist] ... weaker" (LSJ ῥάιδιος 1). **νῦν δέ** signals the switch to reality ("but as it is") and is picked up more forcefully below in νυνὶ δὴ καιρὸς ἥκει. **ἀεὶ προϊέμενοι** "repeatedly neglecting." On ἀεί see 2.7n. τὴν γάρ. προΐεσθαι is a favorite word of D.'s in the Assembly speeches to describe how the Athenians neglect their affairs; e.g., §12, 2.2, 9.1, Sandys 1897: 135, LSJ Β II 5. **σχήσειν:** fut. of ἔχω. **ηὐξήσαμεν:** cf. 2.6–7, where D. credits Philip's growth not to his own actions, but to the naiveté of the Athenians and the other Greeks. **τηλικοῦτον ἡλίκος** "as great as." The accusative modifies Φίλιππον in the main clause; the nominative agrees with βασιλεύς in the relative clause. **οὐδείς πω βασιλεὺς ... Μακεδονίας:** D. similarly distinguishes Philip from his royal ancestors at 2.15 and 6.20. βασιλεύς can be used as a synonym for τύραννος; cf. S. *Ant.* 1172 and *Tr.* 316. **αὐτόματος:** D. uses this adjective repeatedly in this passage (§§7–9) and not elsewhere in the Assembly speeches, thereby creating a distinctive characterization of the καιρός unique to this speech. **οὐδενός ... ἐλάττων τῶν προτέρων ἐκείνων** "inferior to none of those earlier [opportunities]."

### 10–13 Obligation to the gods

We should thank the gods for these opportunities. But those who miss a chance are like those who squander their fortune; they forget their gratitude to the gods. We must look to the future and reverse his successes, or he will march on us. Look at his successful conquests in the north.

**10 ἔμοιγε δοκεῖ τις ἄν ... ἂν ἔχειν αὐτοῖς χάριν** "and it seems to me that someone appointed to give a fair calculation of the favors granted to us by the gods, even if many things are not as they should be, nevertheless would have great gratitude toward them." ἄν comes early in the sentence to signal the construction; it modifies ἔχειν and is repeated for the sake of clarity (Smyth §§1765, 1848). Cf. 2.11n. ἄν. **τῶν παρὰ τῶν θεῶν ἡμῖν ὑπηργμένων:** cf. LSJ ὑπάρχω A 4. For examples of the gods' support of Athens, see Hdt. 8.13.2 (Artemisium), Xen. *Hell.* 2.4.14. **εἰκότως** "and rightly so." D. often adds this type of commentary at the end of a statement in order to create a sense of thoughtfulness and sincerity and draw attention to the explanation that follows; cf. D. 4.24, 18.204, 209, 288 with Yunis 227. **τὸ μὲν ... ἂν ἔγωγε θείην:** the colon splits into two halves, which are parallel in structure. Both halves begin with antithetical articular infinitive phrases (τὸ μὲν ... ἀπολωλεκέναι and τὸ δὲ ...

πεπονθέναι πεφηνέναι τέ) and end with related constructions of τίθημι. D. cautiously describes the city's misfortunes with an indefinite third-person construction (ἄν τις θείη) and then optimistically asserts the gods' support of the city in the first-person, with ἔγωγε adding extra emphasis. **τὸ μὲν γὰρ πολλὰ ἀπολωλεκέναι ... τῆς ἡμετέρας ἀμελείας ἄν τις θείη** "one might attribute the fact that [we] have lost much at war to our negligence." τίθημι governs an accusative object (τὸ ἀπολωλεκέναι) and partitive genitive (LSJ B II 4). For ἀμέλεια cf. 3.33n. ἔστι. **τὸ δὲ μήτε πάλαι τοῦτο πεπονθέναι ... τούτων ἀντίρροπον** "the fact that [we] have not experienced this long ago and that an alliance has appeared to us as a counterweight to these [losses]." The infinitive phrase is the object of θείην. **πεφηνέναι τέ τινα ἡμῖν συμμαχίαν:** D.'s wording stresses that the Athenians have not done anything to bring about the opportunity; cf. 2.1. **ἀντίρροπον:** for a similar use to describe benefits that arise from losses at war, see *IG* I[3] 1179.12–13 (on the dead from Plataea in 432) φσυχὰς δ' ἀντίρρο[π]α θέντες | ἐ[λλ]άχσαντ' ἀρετὲν καὶ πατρ[ίδ'] εὐκλ[έ]ϊσαν, with the discussion by Finglass 2007: 134. **τῆς παρ' ἐκείνων εὐνοίας:** ἐκείνων = τῶν θεῶν. D. describes the favors of the gods in human terms and in so doing provides a model for Athenians to emulate; see 2.1n. δαιμονίαι. **εὐεργέτημ':** predicate (sc. εἶναι) to the preceding infinitive phrase. The change in the construction of τίθημι adds variety and avoids strict parallelism. **ἔγωγε:** with the emphatic pronoun D. stresses that his assessment of the political situation is distinctive.

**11 παρόμοιόν ἐστιν ὅπερ καὶ περὶ τῆς τῶν χρημάτων κτήσεως** "it is similar [to] what also [happens] regarding the acquisition of wealth." **γάρ** introduces an explanation of the preceding enigmatic statement, which is divided into two halves (ἄν μέν ... ἄν δ' ...), with each half consisting of a general condition. **ἄν μὲν γάρ ... καὶ σώισηι** "if one also keeps however much [wealth] one gets" (ἄν = ἐάν). The aorist verbs here and in the following condition are all gnomic, expressing a generalization. **τῆι τύχηι:** a personified agent responsible for the opportunity to form an alliance with Olynthus; cf. 2.2n. τῶν, 9.37n. ἡ. **ἄν δ' ἀναλώσας λάθηι** "but if [someone] squanders [wealth] thoughtlessly" (LSJ λανθάνω A 2b). **τὸ μεμνῆσθαι τὴν χάριν** "[his] memory of the favor." Dobree proposes to delete τὴν χάριν, because of the repetition. But the second iteration adds clarity and binds the μέν and δέ clauses (cf. §4 προέχει ... ἔχει). **καὶ περὶ τῶν πραγμάτων οὕτως** "thus too in political affairs" (LSJ πρᾶγμα III 2). καί and οὕτως highlight the πράγματα as the point of the comparison in the simile. **οἱ μὴ χρησάμενοι:** here μή is generalizing (Smyth §2735). **οὐδ' ... μνημονεύουσι** "also do not remember [a favor]." **τι παρὰ τῶν θεῶν χρηστόν** echoes τῶν παρὰ τῶν θεῶν ἡμῖν ὑπηργμένων above (§10) and signals that this line of thought will now wrap up with the following short summary introduced by γάρ. D. reiterates the theme in the final sentence of the speech (§28). **πρὸς ... τὸ τελευταῖον ἐκβάν** "according to the final outcome." **ἕκαστον τῶν προϋπαρξάντων** "every past event." This MS variant is preferable to the reading πρὶν ὑπαρξόντων because πρίν is not elsewhere attested as an adverb in Greek prose (Sandys 1897: 137). The reading πρὶν ὑπαρξάντων probably arises from a scribe who substituted more common words for the compound verb. **τῶν λοιπῶν ... φροντίσαι** "give thought to the future." **ἀποτριψώμεθα** "wipe away." There are just a few fourth-century parallels for this vivid usage (Aesch. 1.179, Arist. *EN* 2.3.8 [1105a]); this non-literal sense of the verb is unattested earlier.

**12 εἰ δὲ προησόμεθα:** §9n. ἀεί. εἰ + fut. indic. expresses heightened emotion and a somewhat threatening tone (Smyth §2328). **καὶ τούτους τοὺς ἀνθρώπους** "these people too," in addition to the people in the cities named in §§8–9. **εἶτ᾽** "and then in consequence." The future tense of καταστρέψεται (see 4.6n. πάντα) indicates that it is parallel to προησόμεθα continuing the conditional protasis. **φρασάτω τις:** D. invites a response as a rhetorical means of stressing his conviction. Cf. 2.8, 3.28, 9.76. **τί τὸ κωλῦον ἔτ᾽ αὐτὸν ἔσται βαδίζειν:** lit. "what will be a hindrance to him any longer [to keep him] from going." Cf. 9.49n. βαδίζονθ᾽. **ἆρα λογίζεταί τις ὑμῶν ... καὶ θεωρεῖ;** "does any one of you take into account and observe?" The two verbs differ only slightly in sense; the combination of both is emphatic. Cf. 2.6n. θεωρῶν. **τὸν τρόπον δι᾽ ὃν μέγας γέγονεν** "the means by which he has become great." A frequent theme: see, e.g., 2.4–5 and 8, 9.21. **τὸ κατ᾽ ἀρχάς** "at first"; a common prose idiom (e.g., D. 2.6, 9.21, Pl. *Lg.* 3.696b, 4.705d; and very frequently without the article). **τὸ πρῶτον ... ἐπέβη:** the rapid string of place names and lack of expansion or subordination stresses the speed and extent of Philip's rise (cf. 9.59n. Μένιππος). The list is in chronological order, and marked with sequential adverbs, and thus serves as a succinct historical outline of Philip's early career. **Ἀμφίπολιν:** in 357; 2.2n. πόλεων. **Πύδναν:** also in 357; §5n. Πυδναίων. **Ποτείδαιαν:** in 356; §9n. Ποτείδαια. **Μεθώνην:** in 354; §9n. Μεθώνη. **Θετταλίας:** in 352; 2.7n. Θετταλούς. **ἐπέβη** "he stepped on." The physical sense of the verb reinforces βαδίζειν and suggests that Philip took these regions with no fight or effort.

**13 μετὰ ταῦτα:** the rapid chronological list continues. **Φεράς, Παγασάς:** Philip's campaigns against Onomarchus in 352 (2.7n. Θετταλούς) involved operations against the tyrants of Pherae (2.14n. νυνί). After the defeat of Onomarchus at the battle of the Crocus Field, Philip gained control both of the city Pherae and its seaport Pagasae (Sealey 121–2, *HM* 224, 2.11n. Παγασάς). **Μαγνησίαν:** also in 352; 2.7n. Θετταλούς.

πάνθ' ὃν ἐβούλετ' εὐτρεπίσας τρόπον "after preparing everything as he wished" (LSJ τρόπος II 2). πάντα refers to the entire region of Thessaly. D. often uses εὐτρεπίζω and its cognates to describe military arrangements (e.g., 4.18, 18.32, 23.182; Yunis 128). After making arrangements in Thessaly Philip approached the pass at Thermopylae, but was turned away by an Athenian force under the command of Nausicles (Sealey 124, *HM* 279–80). τοὺς μὲν ἐκβαλὼν τοὺς δὲ καταστήσας: Thracian territory was divided among various regional kings. In 356 Philip was called upon to intervene in a territorial war among them; he established a foothold in the region at Philippi, threatening the Athenians' imports from the Black Sea. See Harris 44–6. ἠσθένησεν: Philip laid siege to Heraion Teichos in Thrace in late 352. Concerned by the threat to their grain supply, Athens voted for a substantial expedition, which was then not sent out because of reports regarding Philip's health (D. 3.4–5). In that passage and elsewhere (4.11) D. describes Philip's change in health as a rumor, but here he reports it as fact. Philip did abandon the siege unexpectedly and the reported illness was probably real (*HM* 284). εὐθύς: Philip threatened Olynthian territory in the winter of 352/1 (D. 4.17, Sealey 137, *HM* 298–9). τὰς ... στρατείας: this wide separation between article and noun puts strong emphasis on the noun phrase, which comes as the final culmination of the long list of Philip's campaigns. D. is particularly fond of this type of hyperbaton (e.g., 2.15 and *GPS* 52–3). ἐπ' Ἰλλυριοὺς καὶ Παίονας ... καὶ πρὸς Ἀρύββαν: Illyria was a nation to the west of Macedon, and Paeonia was in the north. Arybbas was king of the Molossians in Epirus, to the southwest. Little is known of these campaigns, which must have taken place between the actions against Olynthus in 351 and 349. The Illyrian campaign comes up as a reported rumor in a speech of 351 (D. 4.48). Nothing beyond this passage is known about a campaign against the Paeonians at this time. Arybbas was the uncle of Olympias, Philip's wife, and thus a relative of Philip's by marriage. By 343 Philip had replaced him with Olympias' brother, Alexander (not to be confused with her son, Alexander the Great), and Arybbas was given refuge in Athens (*IG* II² 226 = *GHI* no. 70; *HM* 304–7). καὶ ὅποι τις ἂν εἴποι "and anywhere else one might mention." The generic indefinite contributes to the impression that Philip's conquests are never-ending. παραλείπω: the rhetorical device of paraleipsis calls attention to material by claiming not to discuss it. Orators regularly signal the technique by using the verb παραλείπω (e.g., D. 2.4, 10.10, 18.100; Usher 1999: index s.v. *paraleipsis*).

## 14–15 Future losses

Philip will not stop. We must act or we shall pay later.

**14 τί οὖν ... ταῦτα λέγεις;** elsewhere D. uses rhetorical questions to vary the tone and pace of his argument (2.3n. διά). Here he puts a com-

## 1 FIRST OLYNTHIAC 14

parable question into the mouth of an audience member and thus creates a "reverse apostrophe" (Usher 1999: 221–2): instead of addressing his audience in the second-person, he imagines that he himself is addressed by one of them. After the list of Philip's campaigns this rhetorical device livens up the speech and draws in the audience as D. makes a key point (e.g., §19, 3.34, 18.220). Cf. 9.70n. πάλαι. **ἵνα γνῶτε, ὦ ἄνδρες Ἀθηναῖοι, καὶ αἴσθησθε** "[I say these things] so that you may recognize and perceive." D. frequently pairs virtually synonymous verbs, especially those denoting knowledge and perception, for emphasis (e.g, 2.6, 21.143). Often he inserts a vocative in the middle of such expressions to add weight to the pairing (e.g., §12, 4.3, 18.252, 20.83). **ἀμφότερα:** the two points are spelled out in what follows and coordinated by the repetition of καί. The rest of the section contrasts Athenian negligence with Philip's restlessness. **καὶ τὸ προΐεσθαι ... ὡς ἀλυσιτελές** "both how unprofitable [it is] to neglect." For the construction with αἰσθάνομαι, cf. D. 23.114. On προΐεσθαι see §9n. ἀεί. **καθ' ἕκαστον ἀεί τι τῶν πραγμάτων** "any of your interests one by one on each occasion"; cf. §3n. παρασπάσηται and 2.7n. τὴν γάρ. **καὶ τὴν φιλοπραγμοσύνην:** the noun has a negative tone and describes the quality of "the man who is determined to keep the initiative in dominating those whose interests he regards as conflicting with his" (*GPM* 188); cf. D. 4.42. **ᾗ χρῆται καὶ συζῇ** "which is his habit and instinct" (LSJ χράω C II). συζῶ is literally "live with," but the sense here seems similar to συνοικεῖν with an abstract noun in the dative referring to "feelings, circumstances, etc." (LSJ συνοικέω 3; Sandys 1897: 140). **ὑφ' ἧς οὐκ ἔστιν ὅπως ... ἡσυχίαν σχήσει** "because of which he will be unable to rest in satisfaction with his achievements." On οὐκ ἔστιν ὅπως + fut. indic., see Smyth §2551. On ἀγαπάω with the dative, see LSJ III 3. This characteristic is typical of the tyrant (cf. §3n. τά; Pl. *Rep.* 9.573c–5a on the restlessness of the ἀνὴρ τυραννικός); the characterization is reinforced too by the allegation that Philip monopolized the credit for achievements (D. 2.18). **εἰ δ' ... ἐγνωκὼς ἔσται** "if he is going to decide." ἐγνωκὼς ἔσται is fut. perf. indic. (Smyth §600), and the corresponding first-person plural form should be understood with ἡμεῖς δέ. The perfect tense stresses "the enduring result" of Philip's decision (Smyth §1946); he is determined to surpass his earlier achievements again and again. **ὡς ἀεί τι μεῖζον τῶν ὑπαρχόντων δεῖ πράττειν** "that he must do something better than before on every occasion." **ὡς οὐδενὸς ἀντιληπτέον ἐρρωμένως τῶν πραγμάτων** "that we are to take control firmly of none of our interests." The phrase echoes the speech's beginning, where the main theme of καιρός is introduced (§2; cf. 15.35). **ἐρρωμένως:** for the sense cf. 3.8, where the adverb is paired with προθύμως. **εἰς τί ποτε ἐλπὶς ταῦτα τελευτῆσαι** "how we can expect these matters to end"; lit. "at what point [there is] expectation that these matters will come to an end." ποτε underscores the interrogative. ἐλπίς is subject of an understood ἐστίν; for the construction with the infinitive, cf. 4.2.

**15 τίς οὕτως εὐήθης ἐστὶν ὑμῶν ὅστις ἀγνοεῖ;** the relative clause expresses a result (Smyth §2556; cf. D. 8.44). D. frequently attributes bad policy decisions regarding Philip to Athenian εὐήθεια, or naiveté; cf. D. 2.6, 9.51, 19.103. **τὸν ἐκεῖθεν πόλεμον δεῦρο ἥξοντα** "the war there will come here" (Smyth §1661). **δέδοικα ... μὴ ... ἐν αὐτῆι τῆι χώραι:** the fear clause forms a tricolon, with three parallel verbs (φανῶμεν, ἔλθωμεν, κινδυνεύσωμεν) coordinated by καί (but cf. below on {ἄν}). **τὸν αὐτὸν τρόπον ὥσπερ ... οὕτω καί** "in the same way as ... so too." The comparison expressed in the simile applies to all three points that follow: Athenian security will be short-lived and expensive, and will lead to a catastrophic loss. Advisors, whether financial or political, must look to "the prudent, long-range calculation of interests"; D. anticipated this tie between financial and political advice already in the first words of the speech, ἀντὶ πολλῶν ... χρημάτων (Mader 2007b: 355–6, Hunt 2010: 168). On D.'s use of similes, see Introd. §3.4. This comparison between negligence in performing military obligations and the inability to pay off large debts is repeated in a briefer form in the year 343, when D. describes the damaging effects of putting off fighting Philip during the peace of Philocrates (19.96). **οἱ δανειζόμενοι ῥαιδίως ἐπὶ τοῖς μεγάλοις τόκοις** "those who borrow thoughtlessly at high interest." Loans at a rate of 12% interest per year were typical (see Arist. *Ath. Pol.* 52.2 with Rhodes 1993: 585), but some fourth-century sources report instances of much higher rates (e.g., 36% per year in Lys. fr. 1.1 [Carey]). **μικρὸν ... χρόνον** modifies εὐπορήσαντες. **καὶ τῶν ἀρχαίων ἀπέστησαν** "lose their principle too" (LSJ ἀρχαῖος v). The gnomic aorist expresses a general truth. **{ἄν}**: although the oldest MSS are consistent in reading ἄν, the word ought to be deleted; a scribe's eye may have strayed, leading to the erroneous insertion of the word (dittography). Alternatively, it could be understood as "if" (ἄν = ἐάν), governing the verb φανῶμεν, so that the fear clause contains two verbs coordinated by καί ... καί. The earliest surviving MS (*P.Oxy.* 62.4310, 2nd/3rd cent. AD) is unfortunately lacunose at this point. **ἐπὶ πολλῶι** "at great expense" (LSJ ἐπί B III 4; cf. D. 8.53 and 19.96). **φανῶμεν ἐρραθυμηκότες** "that we may appear to have been negligent." The phrasing highlights the contrast between Philip's energy (§13 ῥαθυμεῖν) and Athenian negligence (cf. also 4.7n. τά, 10.29). **πολλὰ καὶ χαλεπὰ ὧν οὐκ ἐβουλόμεθα** "many difficult things we did not want [to do]." ὧν is partitive with πολλά (lit.: "many ... of the things we did not want"). The imperfect ἐβουλόμεθα looks back from the moment when the Athenians will be compelled to suffer hardships, referring to repeated instances of bad policy decisions. **εἰς ἀνάγκην ἔλθωμεν**

"that we may be compelled," governing ποιεῖν (for the construction cf. D. 19.341). **κινδυνεύσωμεν περὶ τῶν ἐν αὐτῆι τῆι χώραι** "that we may jeopardize our [property] in this land." The risk of losses at home is analogous to the borrowers losing their capital. On the potential cost of war, cf. §27.

### 16–20 Proposal
At the risk of your displeasure, I say you must send out two forces. You have the money; you should use the military fund for military purposes.

**16 τὸ μὲν οὖν ἐπιτιμᾶν ... τὸ δ' ... ἀποφαίνεσθαι:** the two articular infinitive phrases receive emphasis from their initial placement. Each is the accusative subject of the following εἶναι. μὲν οὖν marks a new topic (2.3n. μέν) and δέ alone signals the contrast between the two infinitive phrases; cf. D. 2.5.   **ῥάιδιον καὶ παντὸς εἶναι** "is simple and everyone can do it." The genitive identifies the person who is capable of doing the action expressed in the infinitive τὸ ... ἐπιτιμᾶν (see §1n. τῆς). The construction is repeated below with συμβούλου.   **ὑπὲρ τῶν παρόντων** "concerning your current circumstances."   **ὅ τι δεῖ πράττειν ... συμβούλου:** §2.3n. προτρέπειν.   **τοῦτ':** the demonstrative emphatically underscores τὸ δ' ... ἀποφαίνεσθαι.   **συμβούλου:** the sentence's emphasis culminates in this final noun, which is suggestively juxtaposed with the following ἐγώ.   **ἐγὼ δ' οὐκ ἀγνοῶ** "I am well aware." After the preceding generalizing statement, the first-person pronoun and following vocative begin to narrow the focus in anticipation of the proposals in §17.   **πολλάκις ὑμεῖς ... ἐν ὀργῆι ποιεῖσθε** "often you are angry at." D. echoes a common complaint of Assembly speakers and critics of democracy, who charge that the Athenians never took responsibility for their political decisions but instead blamed individual politicians. Cf. 8.57, 9.3n. μηδεμίαν, Xen. *Ath.* 2.17, Thuc. 3.43.4–5 and 2.60.5–61.3 with Rusten 1989: 198–9, Pl. *Grg.* 519a–b with Dodds 1959: 364.   **ἄν τι μὴ κατὰ γνώμην ἐκβῆι** "if something does not turn out according to your wishes" (ἄν = ἐάν).   **μήν** responds to the preceding μέν: "and yet" (*GP* 335).   **τὴν ἰδίαν ἀσφάλειαν σκοποῦνθ':** the accusative is generic ("one") and picks up on the preceding generic account of the δῆμος blaming individual politicians for their bad decisions. Cf. 9.55n. μετά.   **ὑποστείλασθαι** "refrain from speaking" (LSJ ὑποστέλλω II 4), a metaphor from furling a sail.   **ὑμῖν συμφέρειν ἡγοῦμαι:** the second-person pronoun and first-person verb quickly switch the focus back to the present situation and D.'s proposals.

**17 φημὶ δή:** this formula is often used by D. to introduce a specific proposal to the Assembly; cf. 2.11n. φημί, 15.16.   **βοηθητέον εἶναι τοῖς πράγμασιν ὑμῖν** "you must aid the situation."   **τῶι τε ... σώιζειν καὶ ... ἐκπέμπειν:** these two infinitives, linked by τε and καί, describe a single defensive action, the first of the two proposals. τὰς πόλεις: the cities of the Chalcidian League, many of which were attacked by Philip in the months leading up to the siege of Olynthus; cf. 2.1n. δύναμιν. τοὺς τοῦτο ποιήσοντας στρατιώτας: the specific references to the soldiers and triremes here and below underscore D.'s insistence that the Athenians must themselves fight actively (cf. D. 2.27–31, 4.16). τῶι τὴν ἐκείνου χώραν κακῶς ποιεῖν: in addition to the defensive force to protect Olynthus, D. calls for an offensive force to harass Philip's territory. This proposal was unsuccessful; see Cawkwell 2011: 381–5. ἑτέροις: the final position of this adjective stresses the need for a second force. θατέρου = τοῦ ἑτέρου (crasis). μάταιος "useless" (fem. nom. sing. of a two-termination adjective).

18 εἴτε γάρ: the sentence splits into two parallel halves describing how Philip will seize the advantage if the Athenians pursue only one of D.'s two proposals. Each half begins with an extended εἴτε clause (Smyth §2853b) presenting the Athenians' policy alternatives as genitives absolute (ὑμῶν ... ποιούντων and βοηθησάντων ... εἰς Ὄλυνθον), which are followed by nominative participles (ὑπομείνας and ὁρῶν) and finite verbs (all fut. indic.) describing Philip's reaction. εἴτε ... ὑπομείνας τοῦτο Ὄλυνθον παραστήσεται "if he withstands this [your harassment of his territory] and gains control of Olynthus" (LSJ παρίστημι C II). ἐπὶ τὴν οἰκείαν: sc. γῆν. εἴτε ... προσκαθεδεῖται καὶ προσεδρεύσει τοῖς πράγμασι "if he watches carefully and is attentive to the situation." The verbs are synonymous, and the combination is emphatic. Both commonly describe sieges, and so they contribute to the characterization of Philip as an active aggressor and anticipate the specific reference to the besieged Olynthians in the next clause. ἀκινδύνως ὁρῶν ἔχοντα τὰ οἴκοι "seeing that the situation at home is not in jeopardy." περιέσται τῶι χρόνωι "in time he will overcome." δεῖ δὴ ... εἶναι: the repetition of δή from §17 signals the closing of this section of the speech, and the close verbal echo of the beginning emphasizes and summarizes the main point. D. uses this technique (ring composition) to mark out the sections of his speech for the listening audience; cf. Wooten 52.

19 ταῦτα points to the preceding discussion (Smyth §1245). περὶ δὲ χρημάτων πόρου "but as for the raising of the money" (LSJ πόρος II 3). D. introduces the next topic. ἔστιν ... ἔστιν: repetition (epanadiplosis) creates a vehement tone, which is here amplified by the vocative. The mannerism is more characteristic of tragedy than oratory, but common in D. (e.g., 4.46, 18.208, 21.46; see Bers 2009: 122–4). The gap between the repeated terms is wider than usual here (GPS 91–2), and the word order puts emphasis on χρήματα, as does the repetition of that noun from the preceding genitive (the rhetorical device of polyptoton). στρατιω-

1 FIRST OLYNTHIAC 19–20    93

τικά modifies χρήματα, and the final position puts stress on the adjective: "[you have money] ... in the war fund." στρατιωτικά is read in all MSS, but many editors delete it because the hypothesis to this speech by Libanius (4th cent. AD) states that D. is referring to the Theoric Fund (Lib. *Arg.D.* or. 1.5). However, Libanius misunderstands the passage and should not be followed. When D. refers to the Theoric Fund he names it specifically (e.g., 3.11, 19 and 10.36); E. M. Harris 2006: 123–9 defends the MS reading and discusses inscriptions from the middle of the fourth century showing that these funds were regularly used for non-military purposes. D.'s point here is to criticize such spending and call for this fund to be used exclusively for the war effort. This designated war fund had existed at least since the early fourth century (Agyrrhios' grain-tax law of 374/3, *SEG* 47.96 = *GHI* no. 26, 54–5, is now the earliest attestation for the fund); see Stroud 1998: 78, Brun 1983: 170–6, Rhodes 1972: 105–6.    **ταῦτα δὲ ὑμεῖς οὕτως ὡς βούλεσθε λαμβάνετε** "you draw on these [funds] just as you wish" (LSJ λαμβάνω A II 1h).    **εἰ μὲν οὖν ταῦτα τοῖς στρατευομένοις ἀποδώσετε** "if you return these funds to those who are fighting." The ἀπο- prefix indicates that the funds ought to be rerouted away from civic expenditures (see §20n. εἰς), and dedicated again to paying for the war effort.    **οὐδενὸς ὑμῖν προσδεῖ πόρου** "you need no source of revenue." D. stresses the importance of the war funding by repeating the compounds of δεῖ and with the repeated placement of πόρου at the conclusion of each of the main clauses.    **μᾶλλον δ'**: 2.2n. μᾶλλον.    **τί οὖν;** §14n. τί.    **σὺ γράφεις;** "are you moving a proposal?"; 9.7n. μήποτε. D. answers in the negative (cf. §23n. μά) because no formal motion is needed to require the Athenians to use the war fund for military purposes (E. M. Harris 2006: 128).

**20 ἐγώ:** the immediate repetition of the pronoun highlights the following short summary of D.'s proposals, which is presented as a tricolon crescendo, made up of the three infinitive phrases (δεῖν κατασκευασθῆναι, εἶναι twice). These three infinitive phrases are linked by repeated καί, and are dependent on ἡγοῦμαι; δεῖν should be understood with each.    **στρατιώτας δεῖν κατασκευασθῆναι** "soldiers must be equipped."    **ταῦτ' εἶναι στρατιωτικά** "these [funds ought] to be a war fund." In other words, the money in the war fund should not be used for non-military purposes, as D. spells out below in the ὑμεῖς δέ clause. Editors often delete this phrase, which appears in all the MSS, under the mistaken belief that D. is talking about the Theoric Fund; see §19n. στρατιωτικά.    **μίαν σύνταξιν εἶναι τὴν αὐτήν** "the system [ought] to be one and the same" (LSJ σύνταξις 2). In the following genitive articular infinitives D. explains that he wants pay from the war fund to be tied to military service. This is a major theme in the third *Olynthiac*; see 3.35n. τήν.    **τοῦ τε λαμβάνειν καὶ τοῦ ποιεῖν τὰ δέοντα** "for drawing on [the funds] and for doing one's duty." The latter phrase is a euphemism for military service; see 2.3n. προτρέπειν.    ὑμεῖς ... λαμβάνειν "you [believe you ought] to use [the funds] just as you wish without worries." The language and sense are nearly equivalent to ταῦτα δὲ ὑμεῖς οὕτως ὡς βούλεσθε λαμβάνετε above (§19; cf. Sandys 1897: 146). For the idiom ἄνευ πραγμάτων, cf. Xen. *An.* 6.3.6.    εἰς τὰς ἑορτάς: contemporary inscriptions documenting expenditures from the war fund record payments for crowns that were presented at religious festivals, and for statues and vessels to be dedicated to Athena; see E. M. Harris 2006: 124–5. Beginning in the 350s, increasing amounts of the state's revenues were applied to the Theoric Fund for public works (3.11n. τούς). But D. wildly exaggerates here with his suggestion that the Athenians prioritized festival spending; detailed comparison of festival and military expenditures shows that they allocated much more money to campaigns than to festivals throughout the late fifth and fourth centuries (Pritchard 2015: 114–20; cf. 4.25n. εἰς).    ἔστι δὴ λοιπόν "all that remains."    πάντας εἰσφέρειν "[is that] everyone pays the war tax." In fact only the wealthiest Athenians paid this tax (2.29n. πρότερον and 2.30n. τοῖς δ᾽ ... στρατεύεσθαι); but D. wishes to emphasize the need for a widespread effort, and also to warn the Athenians that they must pay for the war one way or another.    οὐδὲν ἔστι γενέσθαι τῶν δεόντων "none of what is needed can happen."    λέγουσι δὲ καὶ ἄλλους τινὰς ἄλλοι πόρους "others are speaking about some other revenue sources too." D. refers to the proposals of other speakers in the Assembly debate.    ὧν ἕλεσθε ὅστις ὑμῖν συμφέρειν δοκεῖ "choose [the one] of these which seems advantageous to you."    ἕως ἐστὶ καιρός, ἀντιλάβεσθε τῶν πραγμάτων: D. again reiterates the main theme of the speech, which is marked by the repetition of the phrase ἀντιλαμβάνειν τῶν πραγμάτων in combination with the noun καιρός; cf. §14n. ὡς and §2.

## 21–24 Philip's weaknesses

Thessalians do not trust him. Others would like to revolt. He is arrogant. You have an opportunity. What would he do if he were in your position?

**21** D. repeatedly caters to Athenian optimism by stressing that Philip, despite his record of successes, is in a precarious position. Cf. D. 2.4–10, 15–16, Hunt 2010: 65–6.    ἐνθυμηθῆναι καὶ λογίσασθαι "ponder and consider." The two verbs are often linked as D. appeals to his listeners; cf. 4.31, 21.208–9.    τὰ πράγματα ἐν ὧι καθέστηκε νυνὶ τὰ Φιλίππου "how Philip's situation now stands." τὰ πράγματα are emphasized by being pulled out of the subordinate and into the main clause (prolepsis, cf. 3.17, 4.13, 9.12, 50; Smyth §2182). τὰ Φιλίππου is delayed until the emphatic position at the end of the sentence, where it strongly marks a new topic.    οὔτε γάρ ... αὐτῶι τὰ παρόντα ἔχει "it is not the case, as it seems, and as someone might claim if he did not consider carefully, that his present circumstances are well arranged, and they are not as favorable as they could be." μή indicates that σκοπῶν is conditional (Smyth §2067). εὐτρεπῶς refers specifically to military preparedness; cf. §13n. πάνθ'. With οὐδ' ὡς ἂν κάλλιστ' understand ἔχοι; for the omission of the verb after ὡς ἄν cf. D. 18.291, 24.79, 54.7. **οὔτ' ἂν ἐξήνεγκε τὸν πόλεμον** "nor would he have begun the war" (LSJ ἐκφέρω II 7). **αὐτόν** refers back to ἐκεῖνος and is emphatic ("himself"). **ὡς ἐπιὼν ἅπαντα τότε ἤλπιζε τὰ πράγματα ἀναιρήσεσθαι** "he expected then that he would succeed in the whole situation because he was attacking." The MS reading ὡς ἐπιών is difficult and may be corrupt (see the apparatus). LSJ ἔπειμι I 1b translates the phrase here as "by assault" but offers no parallels. If it is retained, ὡς should be taken with the participle to indicate that Philip expected his mere approach to be enough to bring victory (Smyth §2086b). **κᾆτα διέψευσται** "and in the event he has been found wrong." εἶτα answers τότε in the preceding clause and denotes a sequence. This concise conclusion to the sentence stresses that Philip's initial expectations were unrealistic and not borne out by subsequent events. **τὰ τῶν Θετταλῶν**: 2.7n. Θετταλούς.

**22 ταῦτα γὰρ ἄπιστα**: ταῦτα = τὰ τῶν Θετταλῶν. The Thessalians were proverbially perfidious: cf. Eur. fr. 422 (Kannicht) with the scholion to Ar. *Wealth* 521 (521b Chantry), Strömberg 1954: 98. **φύσει καὶ ἀεί** "by [their] nature, and at all times." **κομιδῆι δ' ὥσπερ ἦν** "just as they were" (LSJ κομιδῆι 1). **τούτωι** = Philip. **Παγασὰς ἀπαιτεῖν αὐτόν** "to ask him to restore Pagasae." See §13n. Φεράς. **εἰσιν ἐψηφισμένοι**: sc. οἱ Θετταλοί. **Μαγνησίαν**: 2.7n. Θετταλούς. **κεκωλύκασι τειχίζειν**: sc. αὐτόν: "they have prevented him from fortifying." **ἤκουον δ' ἔγωγε**: two optative verbs of indirect statement follow ὡς. On D.'s informants see 2.17n. ὡς. **οὐδὲ τοὺς λιμένας καὶ τὰς ἀγορὰς ... καρποῦσθαι** "that they would not even assign to him any longer their harbors and markets for profit." Cf. *HM* 222–3. **τὰ γὰρ κοινὰ ... δέοι διοικεῖν, οὐ Φίλιππον λαμβάνειν** "[that they think they] should supply ... the public funds, not [that] Philip [should] receive [the funds]" (LSJ κοινός II 3). **εἰς στενὸν κομιδῆι ... καταστήσεται** "the sources of provisions for his mercenaries will be put into very dire straits"; 4.19n. τροφήν. στενός describes a narrow space; this figurative usage of the phrase εἰς στενόν is quite unusual in the classical period (e.g., Hdt. 9.34).

**23 ἀλλὰ μὴν ... γε**: introduces the next item in a series of arguments (*GP* 119, 344). **τόν γε Παίονα καὶ τὸν Ἰλλυριόν**: the singulars refer to a collective group, not to specific individuals (Smyth §996), as the final capping phrase ἁπλῶς τούτους ἅπαντας indicates. Philip had recently campaigned against Paeonia and Illyria (§13n. ἐπ'). **ἡγεῖσθαι χρὴ ...**

ἥδιον ἄν ... εἶναι "[we] must believe that [they] would more gladly be." αὐτονόμους ... καὶ ἐλευθέρους: these terms are often used to describe the rule of law in Athens. The former refers to a state's self-rule (Hansen 1995: 25-8) and independence to enter into alliances with other Greek states, while the latter begins to be used in the fourth century specifically to mean freedom from external rulers (Dmitriev 2011: 63-4). The terms are frequently paired in later Athenian complaints about Philip and Alexander (e.g., [D.] 17.8, Hyp. *Epit*. 25 with Herrman 2009b: 93; cf. 9.36n. οὕτως). In attributing these ideals to the Paeonians and Illyrians, D. suggests that all peoples, not just the Athenians, shared in universal objections to Philip's style of rule. ἀήθεις τοῦ κατακούειν τινός εἰσιν "they are unaccustomed to obeying anyone." Strictly speaking this is untrue, in that the Paeonians and Illyrians were tribes ruled by kings. But D. continues to ascribe Athenian attitudes to Philip's opponents. ἄνθρωπος: §3n. ἄνθρωπος. ὑβριστής: hybris refers to violent action accompanied by an attitude of arrogance and the intention to humiliate and cause shame (in general see Cairns 1996, who discusses the large bibliography); such acts were viewed as transgressions of the city's social code, and Athenian law allowed any citizen to prosecute acts of hybris in order to prevent individual victims from seeking retribution and continuing the violence (D. 21.45-6; on the inauthenticity of the law quoted at 21.47 see Harris in Canevaro 2013a: 224-31). Beyond Athens, hybris was particularly associated with tyrants (e.g., S. *OT* 872, Hdt. 3.80.3-4, Arist. *Pol*. 5.8.6 [1311a]) and barbarians (A. *Pers*. 808), and the hybristic behavior of foreign states was a common justification for war (Lendon 2000: 13-18). D.'s use of the term here thus implies that the Athenians are obliged to take action in order to protect their reputation and avoid being shamed. D. repeatedly describes Philip's aggressions against other states as hybris; see, e.g., the catalogue of offenses at 9.32-5, with the discussion by Fisher 1992: 141-2. μὰ Δί': the oath emphasizes a negative declaration (MacDowell 2009: 402-4). Cf. 3.32n. μά, 4.49, 9.54n. μά. οὐδὲν ἄπιστον "none [of this is] beyond belief." Litotes is the rhetorical device whereby the speaker emphasizes a point by negating its opposite. ἀφορμὴ τοῦ κακῶς φρονεῖν is predicate: "the means for madness"; cf. 2.20 and Mastronarde 2002: 213-14. τὸ φυλάξαι τἀγαθὰ τοῦ κτήσασθαι χαλεπώτερον εἶναι "protecting [one's] goods is more difficult than acquiring [them]." D. states the opposite below (2.26n. πολύ), as he warns the Athenians to protect their heritage. Here he has Philip in mind, and the difference reflects D.'s opposing characterizations of the Athenians as inactive and Philip as an aggressor.

**24 δεῖ τοίνυν ὑμᾶς:** the particle is transitional (*GP* 575-6), easing the change in focus from Philip back to the Athenians. τὴν ἀκαιρίαν τὴν ἐκείνου καιρὸν ὑμέτερον νομίσαντας "treating his misfortune as

your opportunity." The wordplay highlights the καιρός theme.     **συνάρασθαι τὰ πράγματα** "engage in the situation" (LSJ συναίρω ɪɪ 1).
**πρεσβευομένους … στρατευομένους … παροξύνοντας:** the three participial clauses are linked by the repetition of καί. The first two items are specific actions (diplomacy and fighting), and the link is reinforced by the homoioteleuton of the participles in -ευομένους. D. then adds a generic capping phrase in the third element, marked by ἅπαντας. Cf. 2.13n. εἰσφέροντας.     **ἐφ᾽ ἃ δεῖ:** lit. "for the purpose [of doing] what [you] must [do]."     **αὑτούς** "yourselves"; cf. §6n. αὑτούς.     **εἰ Φίλιππος λάβοι … καὶ πόλεμος γένοιτο πρὸς τῆι χώραι** "if Philip should get such an opportunity and war should break out near [our] territory." For this technique of contrast between Philip and the Athenians, see 2.15n. πράττων. **πῶς ἂν αὐτὸν οἴεσθε ἑτοίμως ἐφ᾽ ὑμᾶς ἐλθεῖν;** "how eagerly do you think he would proceed against you?" D. uses a new independent construction in place of an indirect statement dependent on λογιζομένους. This device (anacolouthon) imparts a lively tone (cf. Wooten 76).     **εἶτ᾽ οὐκ αἰσχύνεσθε εἰ;** "what then, are you not ashamed that …?" (4.43n. εἶτα). As in the previous sentence, the following grammatical construction shifts unexpectedly, creating a tone of spontaneity. After εἰ μηδ᾽ a subordinate verb is expected, but instead D. concludes with an abrupt independent indicative (οὐ τολμήσετε). The concept of shame links with the preceding description of Philip as an agent of ὕβρις (§23n. ὑβριστής) but now focuses attention on the responsibility of the Athenians. D. repeatedly characterizes their failure to defend themselves against Philip's aggressions as a source of shame (αἰσχύνη) for the city (e.g., §§27, 3.8, 4.10, 42; cf. 2.2), and in this sense that term approximates to the modern notion of "guilt"; it describes discreditable behavior that can be justifiably criticized by others (Cairns 1993: 296–303, Cairns and Fulkerson 2015: 14–15).     **μηδ᾽ … ταῦτα** "not even those things which you would experience if he should have the power." ταῦτα is the object of ποιῆσαι.

### 25–28 Fight here or there, now or later
No one will stop him from invading. A war here will be costly. Commit to fight there now, for the good of Athens.

**25 αἵρεσις:** the repetition from §1 signals that the speech is reaching its conclusion.     **ἐκεῖ χρὴ πολεμεῖν:** on this theme see §5n. ὅμορον. **παρ᾽ ὑμῖν ἐκεῖνον** "that man [must fight] in your territory."     **ἀντέχηι τὰ τῶν Ὀλυνθίων** "the situation at Olynthus continues" or "the Olynthians hold out" (LSJ ἀντέχω ɪɪ 3). For the neut. pl. cf. §21, 22, 4.10. **ὑμεῖς ἐκεῖ πολεμήσετε:** the repetition of the phrase from the previous sentence (and below in §27) is emphatic and reinforced by the pronoun. **τὴν ἐκείνου:** sc. γῆν or χώραν.     **τὴν ὑπάρχουσαν καὶ τὴν οἰκείαν ταύτην ἀδεῶς καρπούμενοι** "while securely enjoying this [land] that is here and ours." ἐκεῖνα = τὰ τῶν Ὀλυνθίων. τίς ... βαδίζειν; cf. §12. Again, the verbal repetition stresses a key theme. κωλύω with accus. and participle is generally rare (LSJ 1 b); Demosthenes regularly construes the verb with the accusative and infinitive (e.g., §§12, 22, 8.42). Θηβαῖοι: in the third Sacred War (355–346; see 3.8n. ἀπειρηκότων) the Thebans opposed Phocis, which was aided by Athens. In his Assembly speeches D. often refers to Thebes in negative terms; e.g., 5.18, 6.11, 9.11; cf. Harris 198–9 n. 15, Steinbock 2013: 147–53, Trevett 1999: 189–95.

26 D. continues the lively style with a series of rhetorical questions, which allow him to address possible objections (see Usher 1999: index s.v. hypophora). μὴ λίαν πικρὸν εἰπεῖν ἦι "may it not prove too painful to say"; πικρός has a threatening tone (LSJ III 1); it refers both to present anxiety and the prospect of disaster. μή and the independent subjunctive here make a hesitant statement; the construction is common in Plato, and may be colloquial in tone (Smyth §1801). For the rhetorical technique cf. 3.10n. μή.   καὶ συνεισβαλοῦσιν ἑτοίμως "they would also readily join the invasion." ἀλλά regularly introduces new questions in hypophora (*GP* 10–11).   ἐὰν μὴ βοηθήσητε ὑμεῖς: in 352 the Athenians sent infantry and cavalry to the pass of Thermopylae to oppose Philip en route to attack Phocis. There was no engagement, but Philip declined to enter central Greece (Cawkwell 2011: 393, Sealey 122).   ἀλλ᾽, ὦ τᾶν, οὐχὶ βουλήσεται "but, my friend, he [Philip] will not wish to [attack]." The colloquial phrase ὦ τᾶν appears regularly in Demosthenic hypophora and always marks a hypothetical address from the audience; cf. 3.29, 18.312 with Yunis 283. The term does not appear in the other orators, and its etymology and sense are obscure; its tone seems to have shades of politeness and condescension; see Dickey 1996: 158–60.   τῶν ἀτοπωτάτων μεντἄν εἴη "why, it would be utterly absurd." For the genitive see Smyth §1319 and cf. 2.2n. ὡς. μεντἄν = μέντοι ἄν; with the potential optative the particle expresses "lively surprise or indignation" (*GP* 402).   ἃ ... ταῦτα "those things that he now blabbers about even at the risk of appearing a fool"; the noun phrase is the object of πράξει. ἄνοιαν ὀφλισκάνων is lit. "although he is incurring a charge of foolishness" (LSJ ὀφλισκάνω II 2). D. is hinting at the possibility of an invasion of central Greece.

27 ἡλίκα ... πολεμεῖν "to what extent fighting there or here are different matters."   ᾽κεῖ πολεμεῖν: §25n. ὑμεῖς.   εἰ γὰρ ὑμᾶς ... ἔξω γενέσθαι "if you yourselves should have to be away [from the city]"; i.e., if the Athenians should have to take to the field abroad with provisions supplied by Athenian farmers.   ὅσα ἀνάγκη ... λαμβάνειν "and take from the countryside whatever men in camp must [take]."   μηδενὸς ὄντος ἐν αὐτῆι πολεμίου: genitive absolute. D. concedes that it will be difficult to provision an Athenian army for a campaign abroad, even if Attic

# 1 FIRST OLYNTHIAC 27–28

territory is secure.     λέγω "I mean" (LSJ III 9), introducing a point of clarification.     πλείον' ἄν ... ζημιωθῆναι "would suffer greater losses."     τοὺς γεωργοῦντας ὑμῶν: the farmers of Attica could suffer significant losses during invasions, and orators often appeal to concerns for them (cf. Ober 1985: 57–9).     εἰς ἅπαντα τὸν πρὸ τοῦ πόλεμον "for the entire war before this one." D. refers to campaigns to regain Amphipolis after Philip took it in 357 (cf. D. scholion 184 Dilts); the total expenditure for these was 1500 talents (D. 3.28, Aesch. 2.71).     εἰ δὲ δὴ πόλεμός τις ἥξει "but if a war comes here"; i.e., if Philip invades Attica. D. explains that the Athenians should shoulder the financial burden of dispatching their troops abroad because the alternative of facing a foreign invasion is even more damaging. Enemy occupiers of Attica would plunder for provisions; on this typical means for armies to find supplies, see Pritchett 1971: 38–41. καὶ πρόσεσθ᾿ "and there is also."     ὕβρις ... αἰσχύνη: Philip's hybristic offenses would result in shame for the Athenians; cf. §23n. ὑβριστής, §24n. εἶτ᾿, 4.10n. τοῖς.     οὐδεμιᾶς ἐλάττων ζημία "a loss inferior to none"; the litotes (§23n. οὐδέν) emphasizes the size of the potential damage.     τοῖς γε σώφροσιν "for sensible men, at least" (*GP* 141). Cf. D. 3.20, where D. similarly compliments his audience to win their assent.

**28 ἅπαντας:** cf. the similar speech ending at 2.31, where D. again stresses that all Athenians must contribute to the war effort. That passage follows an account of the different political roles played by the leaders in the Assembly and their supporters (2.29–30). Here D. does not focus on the political interactions of various groups of Athenians in the Assembly, but instead looks more specifically at how each group can contribute to the war effort.     ὑπὲρ τῶν πολλῶν ὧν ... ἔχουσι "for the protection of the many things they have."     καλῶς ποιοῦντες: an idiom that conveys parenthetic approval of the main idea in the clause: "[things they have] as they should"; cf. 18.231, 21.212 with MacDowell 1990: 415. τὰ λοιπὰ καρπῶνται ἀδεῶς "they may reap the benefits of the rest in security." For the phrasing cf. §25.     τοὺς δ᾿ ἐν ἡλικίαι: Athenian hoplites between the ages of 18 and 58 could be conscripted for service (Arist. *Ath. Pol.* 53.4, 7) and were usually called up by age groups (cf. 3.4n. τούς); see Christ 2001: 404, Liddel 2007: 185–6. For the phrase cf. D. 3.34, 4.7, 18.177, 19.65.     φοβεροὶ φύλακες τῆς οἰκείας: sc. χώρας. This alliterative phrase echoes the technical designation of certain Assembly decrees as being εἰς φυλακὴν τῆς χώρας. The protection of Attica was a set topic for the agenda in the Assembly at least once a month (at the κυρία ἐκκλησία meeting; see Hansen 1987: 22–3). Decrees assigned to this category were probably prioritized (although we do not know how exactly; see Rhodes 1972: 231–5).     ἀκεραίου: predicate adjective (Smyth §1040): "so that it may be inviolate." The adjective is striking: it occurs only here in authentic D.; elsewhere he uses σῶς in this sense (e.g., 5.17, 9.70).

The unusual word elevates the tone as the speech concludes. **τοὺς δὲ λέγοντας:** the third element in the tricolon is surprising, since D. often stresses tax-paying and fighting as paired imperatives for the Athenians (§6n. αὐτούς). The attention here to the orators in the Assembly closes the speech by recalling its initial concern with speakers in the Assembly (§1; ring composition). **αἱ τῶν πεπολιτευμένων αὐτοῖς εὔθυναι** "their accounts of what they have proposed." Athenian magistrates and others who did work for the state had to submit accounts, εὔθυναι, at the end of their term of office (Hansen 1991: 222–4). These accounts were audited by a board of λογισταί, and D. anticipated this language above when he characterized a good citizen in the Assembly as a δίκαιος λογιστής (§10). The term εὔθυνα could be used quite loosely to describe any sort of accountability for official acts (Efstathiou 2007: 124). ῥήτορες in the Assembly were not required to submit accounts, but they were subject to background checks (τῶν ῥητόρων δοκιμασία, Hansen 1991: 267), and prosecutions that could carry stiff penalties (3.12n. παθεῖν). See 9.2n. ἐξετάζητε. **ὡς** "since." **ὁποῖ᾽ ἄττ᾽ ... ἔσεσθε** "whatever type of situation confronts you, you will be suitable judges of their [the orators'] deeds too"; LSJ περιίστημι B I 2. ἄττ᾽ = τινα (Smyth §334a); it "adds a note of generality" (Rutherford 1992: 168 on H. *Od.* 19.218). **χρηστὰ δὲ εἴη παντὸς εἵνεκα** "I hope the situation is favorable for the sake of everyone." D. closes with an optimistic wish for the future; cf. 2.31n. βέλτιον. The theme was anticipated above (§11n. τι). After the attention to different groups of Athenians, it is preferable to take παντός as masculine (following the scholion, 195a Dilts), although parallels are lacking; at A. *Supp.* 188 παντός is neuter ("for every reason"), and that sense would be appropriate here.

# 2 SECOND OLYNTHIAC

## 1–4 Prooemium

The current crisis at Olynthus is like a blessing from the gods. The Athenians must not miss the opportunity to recover past losses. Philip's success owes more to Athenian negligence than to his own strength. D. will focus on Philip's weaknesses and Athenian failings.

**1 ἐπὶ πολλῶν:** sc. πραγμάτων (from ἐν τοῖς ... πράγμασιν immediately below): "in many situations" or "on many occasions." **ἄν τις ἰδεῖν ... δοκεῖ μοι** "it seems to me that one might see ..." ἄν modifies the infinitive (Smyth §1848). **τὴν παρὰ τῶν θεῶν εὔνοιαν:** it was a cliché of Athenian political discourse that the gods saved Athens despite the city's misguided policy; cf. Ar. *Clouds* 587–9, *Eccles.* 473–5, D. 19.256 with Sol. fr. 4.1–6 (West), 4.12n. ἥπερ; Martin 2009: 229. D. begins with the gods' goodwill toward the city, rather than its bad decisions, in order to strike a pious tone from the start (cf. D. 18.1–2). Later he repeats the phrase and adds that Athens has greater opportunities to gain the favor of the gods than does Philip (§22; cf. §9n. ὅταν). This introductory nod to the gods is particularly appropriate in an Assembly speech advocating a military expedition: the gods were thought to provide protection during war, and sacrifices and prayers for good outcomes were offered prior to each Assembly meeting (Aesch. 1.23, Din. 2.14, cf. the parody at Ar. *Thesmo.* 295–311, 331–51); see Parker 2005: 397–403 and 405–6. **τοῖς παροῦσι πράγμασιν** "the present opportunities" are the main theme of the speech, and D. presents the topic emphatically at the end of the first colon. He points to the theme with the adverb οὐχ ἥκιστα and by contrasting it with the reference to many previous occasions (πολλῶν) at the start of the sentence. Race 1982: 111–12 identifies several prose examples of this type of "summary priamel" (e.g., D. 18.5, 291), a device by which an author highlights the main topic by contrasting it with a vague reference to other material. **τὸ γάρ ... ἔχοντας** "the fact that there are men who are intent on fighting Philip, and who have acquired neighboring territory and considerable power, and who, above all, hold such an opinion concerning the war." This extended articular infinitive phrase is the subject of ἔοικεν; cf. *GPS* 37–8. **χώραν ὅμορον:** 1.5n. ὅμορον. **δύναμίν τινα:** D. provides no further details on their numbers because he will later urge the Athenians to act for themselves and not rely on others to fight their battle (§§27–31). According to D. (19.266) the Chalcidian League had 10,000 infantry and 1000 cavalry (see MacDowell 2000: 317); for Philip's army see 4.4n. **τό τε.** Philip gradually lessened the League's combined strength by fighting the allied cities one by one during the last half of 349 before attacking Olynthus in summer 348 (*HM* 316–17). **ὥστε ... νομίζειν** "that they regard their agreements with that man as untrustworthy in the first place, and further as the destruction of their own state." **τὰς πρὸς ἐκεῖνον διαλλαγὰς ... ἀπίστους:** Philip made an alliance with the Chalcidian League in 357/6 and, in order to drive a wedge between Olynthus and Athens, gave Olynthus control of Potidaea (cf. §§7, 14), which had previously been an Athenian holding. The terms of the alliance specified that neither party would make peace with Athens independently (*GHI* no. 50, *HM* 243–4). D. 23.107–9, delivered in 352, explains that the Olynthians eventually turned from Philip to Athens when they saw him growing "too powerful to trust." Philip responded in 351 with diplomatic overtures and military incursions (D. 1.13, 4.17, *HM* 298–9), and this further aggravated the Olynthians. **τῆς ἑαυτῶν πατρίδος ... ἀνάστασιν:** cf. D. 1.5, where D. adds more detail to the picture by linking the destruction of Olynthus with the enslavement of its inhabitants after the battle. **δαιμονίαι τινὶ ... εὐεργεσίαι** "seems entirely like some blessed and divine benefaction." εὐεργεσία and εὔνοια (§1) are standard labels applied to individual benefactions in Athenian honorary decrees (e.g., *IG* 11³ 352.24 [dated 330/29], 324.38 [322/1]; see Whitehead 1993: 52–5, Veligianni-Terzi 1997: 217–19, Low 2007: 138–9), and politicians describe their service to the city as εὔνοια (Sanders 2016: 173–5). By describing the gods' aid to Athens in these terms D. provides a paradigm for human action. For the emphatic hyperbaton, cf. 1.8n. τήν. **2 δεῖ ... σκοπεῖν:** τοίνυν and the repetition of the vocative mark a new stage in the thought; D. turns away from the external factors aiding the Athenians and urges them to help themselves (the particle and vocative signal that αὐτούς now refers to the Athenians). Transitional τοίνυν (*GP* 574–5) often reinforces exhortations to the audience and is much more common in D.'s Assembly speeches than in his forensic orations (Bers 2013: 36); here it adds force to the command δεῖ ... σκοπεῖν; cf. Pl. *Cr.* 51c (σκόπει τοίνυν), Lys. 13.51, D. 1.24, 21.204; see Wooten 42–3.   **ὅπως ... τῶν ὑπαρχόντων** "that we do not appear to be less good at [protecting] our own interests than the current circumstances [encourage us to be]." σκοπέω regularly takes ὅπως + fut. indic. (cf. §12n. σκοπεῖσθε; Smyth §2213).   **ὡς ... προϊεμένους** "since it is a shameful thing – in fact, one of the most shameful things – [for us] to be seen giving up ..." The genitives τῶν αἰσχρῶν and τῶν αἰσχίστων are predicates with ἔστι (Smyth §1319). προϊεμένους agrees with the understood subject (sc. ἡμᾶς) of the infinitive φαίνεσθαι. On shame see 1.24n. εἶτ'.   **μᾶλλον δέ:** the correction creates a tone of spontaneity (cf. Ronnet 133) and amplifies D.'s criticism.   **μὴ μόνον ... ἀλλὰ καί:** the use of μή, rather than οὐ, carries on the generalizing tone, but the first-person verb in the following relative clause (ἧμεν) makes it clear that D. has the Athenians specifically in mind.   **πόλεων καὶ τόπων** "cities and positions"; objects of προϊεμένους, attracted from the accusative to the genitive case by the following ὧν ("inverse attraction," Smyth §2533). The plurals here and below (συμμάχων καὶ καιρῶν) are generalizing. D.'s audience will think of Potidaea and Amphipolis. The former was taken by Philip in 356; see 1.9n. Ποτείδαια. In 357 Philip had captured Amphipolis, another fifth-century Athenian cleruchy (from 437/6 to 424), which the Athenians were eager to regain (see *HM* 231–3, Psoma 2001: 242). Potidaea, Amphipolis, and Olynthus could serve as strategic positions for operations against Philip (for this sense of τόπος cf. D. 14.9), and Amphipolis was particularly important for its location as a trading post along the coastal route of the northern Aegean.   **τῶν ... συμμάχων καὶ καιρῶν** "the allies and opportunities provided by chance." Here τύχη refers back to the gods' support for Athens (cf. §1n. τήν). Elsewhere D. alternates between the nouns δαίμων, θεός, and τύχη with little difference in meaning (18.192–4); see Mikalson 1983: 59–60, *GPM* 138–9. The pairing of συμμάχων and καιρῶν makes it clear that the opportunity at hand is the alliance with Olynthus. Cf. 1.11n. τῆι.               **3 τὸ μὲν οὖν … οὐχὶ καλῶς ἔχειν ἡγοῦμαι** "I do not believe it is right [for me] to give an account of Philip's strength … and thereby urge you to do your duty."       **μὲν οὖν** marks a transition. Here it introduces the first topic of the speech; cf. §§4 and 5, 1.2, 3.3, and 4.2.       **προτρέπειν τὰ δέοντα ποιεῖν ὑμᾶς:** in *On the Crown* D. asserts that an ideal orator is responsible "for creating the urge to perform one's duty" (D. 18.246 τοῦ τὰ δέοντα ποιεῖν ὁρμὴν προτρέψαι), and in his Assembly speeches he regularly uses the phrase τὰ δέοντα ποιεῖν to exhort the Athenian citizens to do their duty and fight for the state (e.g., D. 1.20, 8.50, 9.4; cf. Liddel 2007: 158–60). Athenian funeral orations echo this language to praise soldiers who died in the line of duty (Thuc. 2.43.1, D. 60.18).        **διὰ τί; ὅτι κτλ.** "Why? Because …" The brief rhetorical questions quicken the pace (cf. D. 6.7, 15.28, 18.26). Along with the omission of the verb (sc. ἡγοῦμαι), the change in rhythm, with a series of short syllables following the spondees that closed the previous sentence, contributes to the acceleration.       **ὑπὲρ τούτων** "concerning these matters."       **ἐκείνωι μὲν … πεπρᾶχθαι** "is to his credit, but has not turned out well for us." The parallel placement of the two datives before μέν and δέ stresses the contrast between Philip and the Athenians.       **ὁ μὲν γὰρ … ὑμεῖς δὲ κτλ.**: the structural parallelism continues. ὁ μέν and ὑμεῖς δέ are given extra emphasis by their initial placement before ὅσωι πλείονα and ὅσωι χεῖρον.     **ὅσωι πλείονα … τοσούτωι θαυμαστότερος** "however much more … the more worthy of admiration."      **ὑπὲρ τὴν ἀξίαν … τὴν αὑτοῦ** "beyond his deserts."      **ὑμεῖς:** elsewhere this sort of switch to the second-person marks a formal acknowledgment that the actual decision-making is in the hands of his listeners (cf. 1.2n. ἡμεῖς). Here he is sharply critical of past decisions; that tone is reflected in the judgmental words χεῖρον and αἰσχύνην.      **ὅσωι χεῖρον … τοσούτωι πλείονα** "however much worse … the more."     **τοῖς πράγμασι** "situations" or "occasions"; cf. §1n. τοῖς.

**4 ταῦτα μὲν οὖν παραλείψω:** ταῦτα points back to the points in the preceding section, namely the power (ῥώμη) of Philip and the shame (αἰσχύνη) of Athens. D. uses the device of paraleipsis to acknowledge this material briefly without offering a belabored analysis (1.13n. παραλείπω). He provides more details on Philip's successes elsewhere (e.g., D. 1.12–13).     **τις:** the indefinite third-person is used because D. himself does not intend to pursue this line of argument. Its usage suggests that anyone who considers the situation honestly (μετ' ἀληθείας, lit. "in accordance with the truth") would agree with D.'s assessment.      **ἐνθένδ' … οὐχὶ παρ' αὑτοῦ** "one would see that he has become great from here, not on his own part." ἐνθένδε refers to the decisions of the Athenian Assembly.

D. is thinking specifically of the role played by his political opponents in Athens, as the next sentence indicates (cf. also §6n. τινες). The assertion that Philip is not responsible for his own success anticipates the later point that his weakness will become apparent if the Athenians take action (§20). ὧν ... λαβεῖν "as for those matters for which he owes gratitude to those who have advocated on his behalf and for which you ought to punish [them]." τοῖς ὑπὲρ αὐτοῦ πεπολιτευμένοις: D.'s political opponents in Athens, those who would prefer to negotiate with Philip rather than fight. D. later uses similar phrasing to distinguish a leader such as himself, one who "acts sincerely for the [state's] best interests" from one "who speaks for profit and represents Philip" (D. 10.75 ἴστε ... τίς μισθοῦ λέγει καὶ τίς ὑπὲρ Φιλίππου πολιτεύεται, καὶ τίς ὡς ἀληθῶς ὑπὲρ τῶν βελτίστων). ἅ ... πειράσομαι "but as for the matters (ἅ) which it is possible [for me to address] apart from those other concerns (τούτων) and which it is better for all of you to have heard and which would appear as great ... reproaches against him if you are willing to judge correctly, these (ταῦτ') I will attempt to consider." ἔνι and ἐστιν and φαίνοιτ' are linked by the repetition of καί, and ἅ is to be understood with all three. ἔνι = ἔνεστι; sc. μοι λέγειν. μεγάλα modifies ὀνείδη; the placement before ὦ ἄνδρες Ἀθηναῖοι adds emphasis (cf. §20n. καίτοι) and signals the transition to the third element of the tricolon introduced by ἅ.

**5–10 Philip and his allies**
Philip has grown in strength by tricking his allies. Such an alliance is unsound and will be short-lived.

**5** The two cola of this sentence each begin with an extended articular infinitive phrase (τὸ ... καλεῖν and τὸ δὲ ... ἐλέγχειν); these phrases receive emphasis from their initial placement, and are opposed in meaning (δέ by itself signals the opposition; the preceding μὲν οὖν is repeated from above (§3n. μέν) in a transitional sense). In the first colon the infinitive phrase (underlined below) is the subject of the indirect statement that follows; translate in the following order: φήσειε τις ἂν δικαίως <u>τὸ ἐπίορκον καὶ ἄπιστον καλεῖν</u> ... εἶναι κενὴν λοιδορίαν. The second colon is much more complex. The infinitive phrase (also underlined) is the subject of the first main clause ("1."). The second main clause ("2.") introduces two articular infinitive phrases ("a." and "b.") in apposition to δυοῖν. Two indirect statements ("i." and "ii."), dependent on ἰδεῖν, then follow.

1. <u>τὸ δὲ ... ἐλέγχειν</u> καὶ βραχέος λόγου συμβαίνει δεῖσθαι
2. καὶ δυοῖν ἕνεχ' ἡγοῦμαι συμφέρειν εἰρῆσθαι
    a. <u>τοῦ τ' ἐκεῖνον ... φαῦλον φαίνεσθαι</u>
    b. <u>καὶ τοὺς ὑπερεκπεπληγμένους</u> ... ἰδεῖν
        i. ὅτι πάντα διεξελήλυθεν ...
        ii. καὶ πρὸς αὐτὴν ἥκει τὴν τελευτὴν τὰ πράγματα αὐτοῦ.

## 2 SECOND OLYNTHIAC 5–6

**τὸ ἐπίορκον καὶ ἄπιστον καλεῖν:** sc. Φίλιππον. See 1.5n. ἄπιστον, 9.16n. **τό.** **ἄνευ ... δεικνύναι** "without pointing out what he has done"; the phrase modifies καλεῖν. **λοιδορίαν ... κενήν** "baseless abuse." D. did not always refrain from attacks on his opponents (see Harding 1994: 212–16 on D. 22.47–59 and 18.126–31), and later in the speech he will consider Philip's lack of restraint and drunkenness (§18nn. τήν and μέθην), which are typical elements of invective. But first he stresses that he has proof (τὸ ... ἐλέγχειν) of Philip's perfidy. Cf. D. 22.21–2 for the same contrast between "baseless charges and insults" (αἰτίαι καὶ λοιδορίαι κεναί) and "proof" (ἔλεγχος). **τὸ ... ἐλέγχειν** "to go through all the things he ever did and convict [him] on all these points"; sc. Φίλιππον. **καὶ βραχέος λόγου συμβαίνει δεῖσθαι** "happens to require only a short speech." καί is adverbial with βραχέος (LSJ καί B 5). **ἡγοῦμαι συμφέρειν εἰρῆσθαι** "I believe that it is advantageous for it [the speech] to be said." **τοῦ ... ἰδεῖν** "so that man may be shown to be weak, which is indeed true, and so that those who are dumbfounded at Philip as if he were someone who cannot be beaten may see ..." The articular infinitives τοῦ τ᾽ ... φαίνεσθαι καὶ ... ἰδεῖν are in the genitive to agree with δυοῖν. After ἕνεχ᾽ they are equivalent in sense to purpose clauses. **ὑπερεκπεπληγμένους:** lit. "excessively amazed." The verb ἐκπλήσσω is common in Attic literature in this sense of "amaze, astound"; ὑπερ- adds the sense of excess and reinforces the critical tone. The compound is rarely attested in the classical period (only here and Xen. *Cyr*. 1.4.25). **ὡς ἄμαχόν τινα:** sc. ὄντα. With the understood participle ὡς indicates that this is not an objective truth (Smyth §2086). D. wants his listeners to realize that this is a false opinion held by some. **ὅτι πάντα ... ηὐξήθη** "that he has used up everything by means of which, with his deceptions, he previously grew great." Cf. 9.21. **παρακρουόμενος:** in the middle voice the verb routinely describes deception or cheating (LSJ 2), and D. often links it with φενακίζω (e.g., D. 20.88, 24.209, 29.36), which he uses below to sum up this account of Philip's deceptions (§7n. οὐδείς). **πρὸς αὐτὴν ... τὴν τελευτήν:** αὐτήν modifies τελευτήν; its position at the start of the clause prior to the verb adds emphasis to the phrase.

**6–7** The first colon of this long sentence consists of a pres. contrary-to-fact condition ("I would believe ... if I saw"). The second colon consists of three coordinated indirect statements introduced by εὑρίσκω. The participle προσαγαγόμενον ("winning over for himself," aorist middle) serves as the verb for each, and Philip is to be understood as the subject. The three statements are outlined below; each begins with an accusative object of προσαγαγόμενον that is followed by a compound articular infinitive phrase (underlined) functioning as a dative of means. The three clauses are put in sequence with the adverbial phrases τὸ κατ᾽ ἀρχάς ("in the first place"), μετὰ ταῦτα ("next"), and τὰ τελευταῖα ("finally").

νῦν δὲ θεωρῶν καὶ σκοπῶν εὑρίσκω

1. τὴν μὲν ἡμετέραν εὐήθειαν ... τῶι τὴν Ἀμφίπολιν φάσκειν παραδώσειν καὶ τὸ θρυλούμενόν ποτε ἀπόρρητον ἐκεῖνο κατασκευάσαι ... προσαγαγόμενον,
2. τὴν δὲ Ὀλυνθίων φιλίαν ... τῶι Ποτείδαιαν οὖσαν ὑμετέραν ἐξελεῖν καὶ τοὺς μὲν πρότερον συμμάχους ἀδικῆσαι, παραδοῦναι δὲ ἐκείνοις,
3. Θετταλοὺς δὲ ... τῶι Μαγνησίαν παραδώσειν ὑποσχέσθαι καὶ τὸν Φωκικὸν πόλεμον πολεμήσειν ὑπὲρ αὐτῶν ἀναδέξασθαι.

**6 ἐγώ ... καὶ αὐτός** "even I myself." The use of the pronoun at the start of the sentence is strongly assertive, and the confident tone is reinforced by adverbial καί and intensifying αὐτός after the main verb. **σφόδρα ἂν ἡγούμην** "I would firmly believe." **νῦν δέ** marks the switch to reality: "but as it is." **θεωρῶν καὶ σκοπῶν** "by observing and considering." Both verbs can refer to visual observation or mental contemplation, and the usage of both together is emphatic; cf. Pl. *Ph.* 99d, D. 38.11, Aesch. 3.176. **τὴν μὲν ἡμετέραν εὐήθειαν** "[Philip won over] our naiveté." Cf. 1.15n. τίς. **Ὀλυνθίους ... διαλεχθῆναι:** Olynthus, as the chief city of the Chalcidian League, must have been alarmed by Philip's siege of Amphipolis in 357, and it turned to Athens for support. The Athenians, however, hoped to obtain Amphipolis from Philip (cf. §6n. τῶι and [D.] 7.27) and declined to become involved; see *HM* 237–8. It is remarkable that this is the first mention by name of Olynthus in the speech. Up to this point D. has described the situation strictly as one concerning the Athenians and their enemy Philip, leaving the Olynthians aside. **τινες ἐνθένδε:** D.'s opponents in the Assembly; cf. §4n. ἐνθένδ'. **ὑμῖν διαλεχθῆναι** "to have a discussion with you." **τῶι τὴν Ἀμφίπολιν ... κατασκευάσαι** "by saying that he would hand over Amphipolis and by cooking up that much talked about, once secret, agreement." Philip is the subject of φάσκειν, παραδώσειν, and κατασκευάσαι. Theopompus (*FGrHist* 115 F 30) reports that Athenian ambassadors negotiated with Philip regarding a proposed agreement that he would turn Amphipolis over to the Athenians in exchange for Pydna, one of their northern allies. According to Theopompus, this proposal was discussed in secret with the Council. The negotiations must have taken place between 359 and 357, but no treaty could have been made without a public decision in the Assembly, and there is no evidence that this occurred; see *HM* 238–42, Badian 2000: 19–20. After 357 the Athenians were unable to recover Amphipolis because they were occupied with the Social War. **θρυλούμενον:** on the tone see 1.7n. ἐθρύλουν. Here the verb illustrates the Athenians' εὐήθεια. The juxtaposition with ἀπόρρητον creates a striking oxymoron. **κατασκευάσαι** has the pejorative sense of improvising something for a deceptive scheme (LSJ 4) and contributes to the characterization of Philip as a cheat. **τούτωι** refers to the articular infinitive phrase τῶι ... κατασκευάσαι.

**7 τὴν δὲ Ὀλυνθίων φιλίαν:** §1n. τάς. **τοὺς μὲν ... ἐκείνοις** "by wronging his former allies and giving it [Potidaea] to them [the Olynthians]." ἀδικῆσαι and παραδοῦναι describe different aspects of the same action. They are linked by μέν and δέ and by the chiastic word order. **τοὺς μὲν πρότερον συμμάχους:** the Athenian cleruchs resident in Potidaea, who reportedly made an alliance with Philip independently ([D.] 7.10; de Ste Croix 1963: 111 n. 1 defends the historical reliability of the passage). The Athenians themselves made no formal agreement with Philip before the peace of Philocrates in 346 (9.1n. τήν); ὑμᾶς should be deleted as a scribe's mistaken gloss. **Θετταλοὺς ... ἀναδέξασθαι** "finally, [he won over] the Thessalians recently by promising to hand over Magnesia and taking it upon himself to fight the Phocian war on their behalf." Philip supported allies in the Thessalian League in the campaign against the Phocian general Onomarchus in 352 (the widespread belief that he was an elected archon of Thessaly is incorrect: see Dmitriev 2011: 411–20, Harris 175–6), during the Sacred War between the Amphictyonic League and the Phocians (356–346). As part of an effort to consolidate the region, Philip seized Magnesia, on the Aegean coast east of Thessaly, which had been under the control of the tyrants of Pherae. According to D. (1.13, 22), the Thessalians were disturbed by Philip's decision to fortify the region rather than turn it over to them. See *HM* 221–2, 287–8; Buckler 1989: 79–80. The verb ὑποσχέσθαι, like φάσκειν above (§6), emphasizes that Philip's promises were unfulfilled. **ὅλως δ' ... οὕτως ηὔξήθη:** this pair of short cola summarizing the lengthy preceding sentence helps the audience digest what they have heard and allows D. to catch his breath. The first word, ὅλως ("in sum"), signals the change in pace. **οὐδείς ἔστιν ὄντινα οὐ πεφενάκικεν** "there is no one he has not tricked." φενακίζω refers to deception accomplished not by lying outright, but by making misleading statements that encourage false hopes; D. often uses it to describe Philip. See MacDowell 2000: 218–19 and cf. D. 6.29, 18.43, 19.42–3. **τῶν αὐτῶι χρησαμένων** "among those who have dealt with him" (LSJ χράω C III 4b); the genitive is partitive, modifying οὐδείς. **τὴν γὰρ ... προσλαμβάνων** "by exploiting and taking advantage of the foolishness of each party who misjudged him on each occasion." The plural ἑκάστων refers to repeated incidents such as those detailed in the preceding sentence. ἀεί modifies ἀγνοούντων and also refers to repeated incidents; cf. D. 4.40, 15.22 τοὺς ἀτυχοῦντας ἀεί ("those who were suffering at any time"), 21.223 οἱ ἀεὶ δικάζοντες ("the jurors on any occasion"). In this sense ἀεί usually comes between the article and the participle; the placement here avoids hiatus and forestalls misunderstanding (in the sense "perpetual ignorance").

**8 ὥσπερ οὖν ... οὕτως ... καὶ καθαιρεθῆναι πάλιν** "just as he rose to greatness by these means ... so too he is bound to be brought down again by these same means." **ἕκαστοι** and ἑαυτοῖς refer to the various states that were tricked by Philip in §§6–7. **συμφέρον αὐτὸν ἑαυτοῖς ᾤοντό τι πράξειν** "supposed he would do something useful for them." The word order is interlocked (ἑαυτοῖς depends on συμφέρον, which agrees with τι; αὐτόν is the subject of πράξειν), and the effect is to "bind the clause into a compact unity" (*GPS* 59). συμφέρον receives emphasis from its early placement in the clause, and its position between ἕκαστοι and αὐτόν avoids hiatus. **καιροῦ ... τὰ πράγματα** "Philip's affairs have come to this crucial moment of opportunity." καιροῦ depends on τοῦτο, and it receives emphasis from its initial position, μὲν δή, and the vocative. **ἢ παρελθών τις ... δειξάτω** "or else [if that is not the case], someone should come forward and show"; 3.28n. ἤ. The first ἤ is not parallel to those that come later in the sentence. **μᾶλλον δ' ὑμῖν:** the correction is deferential; cf. 9.20n. εἰ. **ὡς οὐκ ἀληθῆ ... λέγω:** cf. §28n. εἰ. The phrases ἢ ... πιστεύσουσιν and ἢ ... ἄσμενοι specify two absurd objections to D.'s account of the situation. **τὰ πρῶτα ... τὰ λοιπά** "in the beginning ... in the future." **Θετταλοί** is an explanatory gloss that has become incorporated into the text. οἱ ... δεδουλωμένοι has better rhetorical effect without any further specification, like the preceding οἱ ... ἐξηπατημένοι. **νῦν οὐκ ἂν ἐλεύθεροι γένοιντο ἄσμενοι** "would not now gladly be freed." ἄσμενος regularly has adverbial force (Smyth §1043). Cf. 9.36n. οὕτως.

**9 καὶ μὴν εἴ τις ὑμῶν ... οἴεται δέ** "and furthermore if any of you, while thinking these things are thus [as I have described], also supposes ..." The μέν and δέ clauses are both part of the conditional protasis; here μέν is concessive and the δέ clause bears more weight (*GP* 370). **βίαι ... προειληφέναι** "that he will maintain his position by force, because he has taken ..." βίαι is a dative of means and the articular infinitive τῶι ... προειληφέναι is in apposition to it. **τὰ χωρία ... τὰ τοιαῦτα:** the point is that these are strategic holdings (cf. [D.] 11.7, a close imitation of this passage probably written by the contemporary historian Anaximenes, in which the phrase χρήσιμα πρὸς πόλεμον is added as an explanation of τοιαῦτα). D. has in mind the territories of Potidaea and Magnesia, already mentioned above (§7), and the port of Pagasae, which he will identify below (§11n. Παγασάς). **ὅταν μὲν κτλ.:** this sentence presents a generalizing contrast between the strength that results from cooperative effort and power that is dependent on a single individual. Athenian prejudice against monarchy underlies both halves of the antithesis (for the development of this attitude in the Archaic period, see E. M. Harris 2006: 9–12). In the first colon (ὅταν μὲν ... ἄνθρωποι), D.'s word choices repeatedly stress the power of united groups: he uses four συν- compounds and μετέχω to underline that men at war must willingly work together for a common cause, as he hopes the Athenians and Olynthians will do (cf. 3.30n. ἀγαπητόν, 4.45n. μέρος), and his emphasis on εὔνοια recalls the initial description of Athens (§1; cf. de Romilly 1958: 94). By contrast, in the second colon (ὅταν δ' ... διέλυσεν), D. focuses on the commander rather than the soldiers, and the nouns πλεονεξίας and πονηρίας emphasize that in some cases, such as with Philip, the motivation for fighting is selfish. The verbs ἀναχαιτίζω and διαλύω stress the instability of such an arrangement. See 9.72n. πρός.    **πᾶσι** modifies τοῖς μετέχουσι and precedes the verb for emphasis. The juxtaposition with ταὐτά ("the same for all") stresses the democratic ideal of equality.    **μένειν** "stand firm [in battle]" (LSJ I 1).    **ἄνθρωποι** = οἱ ἄνθρωποι (crasis).    **πλεονεξίας** "greediness," a typical attribute of a tyrant, and often contrasted with democratic equality; cf. [And.] 4.13, Xen. *Hier.* 8.10, Rosivach 1988: 55–6, Balot 2001: 236–7, §16n. φιλοτιμίας.    **ἡ πρώτη πρόφασις καὶ μικρὸν πταῖσμα** "the first provocation, a tiny stumble." καί introduces the second item as an emphatic rephrasing of the first (Smyth §2870). **ἅπαντα ἀνεχαίτισεν** "upsets everything." The verb describes a horse that "throws back its mane" and "rears up"; as a secondary meaning it can refer to a thrown rider as its object, and so here lit. "throws off everything." The metaphorical usage is anticipated by πταῖσμα. The aorist tense is gnomic and equivalent in sense to the pres. ἐθέλουσιν in the previous colon (Smyth §1931a).    **διέλυσεν:** sc. ἅπαντα: "breaks apart [everything]." The verb describes the dissolution of a union.

**10 οὐ γὰρ ἔστιν, οὐκ ἔστιν:** 1.19n. ἔστιν.    **ἀδικοῦντα ... ψευδόμενον:** sc. τινα; D. continues to generalize until the final sentence of the section. The participles describe the sort of behavior that was attributed to Philip above (§7): ἀδικοῦντα repeats ἀδικῆσαι, ἐπιορκοῦντα points to the oath between Philip and the Athenian cleruchs at Potidaea (§7n. τοὺς μὲν πρότερον), and ψευδόμενον refers to the broken promises made to the Thessalians (§7n. Θετταλούς). On Philip's perjury see 9.16n. τό.    **τὰ τοιαῦτα:** the sort of power acquired by crime and deception, subject of the four following indicative verbs. μέν and δέ balance the verbs in two pairs: ἀντέχει and ἤνθησεν describe the success of a leader like Philip, while φωρᾶται and καταρρεῖ emphasize his eventual decline.    **εἰς μὲν ἅπαξ καὶ βραχὺν χρόνον ἀντέχει** "lasts for one brief moment"; Philip cannot keep getting away with the same tricks.    **καὶ ... γε:** the collocation of particles adds extra stress to this element (*GP* 157–8).    **ἤνθησεν ἐπὶ ταῖς ἐλπίσιν** "flourishes with [high] hopes"; a timeless gnomic aorist (see §9n. ἅπαντα).    **ἂν τύχηι** "perhaps" (LSJ τυγχάνω A I 3; cf. 1.3n. ἡνίκα, 9.54n. ἦστινος).    **τῶι χρόνωι δέ** "but in time."    **φωρᾶται ... καταρρεῖ** "is found out and falls down around itself." φωράω describes the pursuit of criminals, and in that sense builds on the participles at the start of the sentence. καταρρέω, elsewhere used for leaves falling from a withered flower (LSJ 3), continues the metaphor introduced by ἀνθέω, but it can also describe collapsed buildings (LSJ 4), and thus it anticipates the architectural detail in the following simile. τὰ κάτωθεν: lit. "the lower parts"; i.e., the foundation of a house or the keel of a boat. τὰς ἀρχὰς καὶ τὰς ὑποθέσεις "the basic principles"; or lit. "the foundations and supports." These nouns can refer to the physical base of a building (LSJ ἀρχή 1a) or statue (LSJ ὑπόθεσις VI 2) and thus reinforce the comparison with houses and boats, but they are usually more abstract in sense, as the adjectives ἀληθεῖς and δικαίας require. The pairing of the plural nouns is echoed in Hyp. *Against Diondas* 137v/136r 3 and in later critics (e.g., ps.-Longin. 5). τοῦτο ... ἐν τοῖς πεπραγμένοις Φιλίππωι "this is not currently present in the achievements of Philip." ἔνι = ἔνεστι.

**11–13 Athens and its allies**
The Athenians must commit to supporting their allies and making preparations for an expedition to demonstrate their commitment.

**11 φημὶ δή:** 1.17n. φημί. Below (§27) D. repeats the phrase with δεῖν and provides more detail. His recommendations are not spelled out as clearly in this speech as elsewhere (cf. 1.17–18, 4.16–22), and they do not provide enough information to date the speech precisely (see Introd. §1.3). ὅπως ... οὕτως "the best and swiftest plan that someone can propose is the plan I approve." πρὸς δὲ Θετταλοὺς πρεσβείαν: nothing suggests that the embassy was in fact sent. ἢ ... παροξυνεῖ "to inform some about these matters and to urge on others." D. describes two groups among the Thessalians: those who are opposed to Philip and concerned about the involvement of Athens, and those who are not yet ready to fight. ταῦτα must refer to the proposed dispatch of Athenian aid, since D. refers to Thessalian complaints about Philip elsewhere (1.22, cf. §7 above), and it is thus very unlikely that he would need to "teach" any of them about Philip (cf. 9.71n. τούς). The future verbs in the relative clause express purpose (Smyth §2554). Παγασὰς ἀπαιτεῖν ... λόγους ποιεῖσθαι "demand back Pagasae and hold discussions [with Philip] regarding Magnesia." Pagasae was a key port near southern Magnesia, important both as a potential base for a fleet and as a source of revenue from trade duty. Philip took control of the region from the tyrants of Pherae by defeating Phocis in 352; see 1.13n. Φεράς, §7n. Θετταλούς.

**12 σκοπεῖσθε ... ἔξουσιν** "see to it that our ambassadors not only make speeches, but also that they are able to point to some deed." ὅπως + fut. indic. marks an urgent command (Smyth §2213). ἐξεληλυθότων ὑμῶν ... καὶ ὄντων ἐπὶ τοῖς πράγμασιν "provided that you have set out ... and are engaged in the situation." For this sense of πράγματα cf. §1 above, and cf. 9.12 for the phrase.   ὡς ἅπας μὲν λόγος ... καὶ κενόν "since every speech, if the reality is lacking, appears useless and ineffectual" (LSJ πρᾶγμα II 2).   ὅσωι ... αὐτῶι "the more readily we are known to use it, the more all distrust it"; Smyth §2471 gives parallels for the combination of superlative and comparative adverbs. ἀπιστοῦσι: in §§6–7 D. explained why the Olynthians and Thessalians regarded Philip as duplicitous and untrustworthy. Here the verb ἀπιστέω emphasizes that the Athenians will appear similarly dishonest if they fail to send out a military force along with their diplomats. D.'s assertion echoes critics of Athenian policy, who charge the Athenians with lying to their allies: Theopompus observes that fifth-century Athenian imperialists euphemistically labeled mandatory tribute as "contributions" (*FGrHist* 115 F 98), and he accuses the Athenians of boasting about the battle of Marathon and "deceiving the Greeks" (F 153 ἡ Ἀθηναίων πόλις ... παρακρούεται τοὺς Ἕλληνας; the verb is commonly applied by D. to Philip: §5n. παρακρουόμενος). See Pownall 2003: 159, 163 and cf. also Thuc. 5.89.

**13 πολλὴν δὴ τὴν μετάστασιν καὶ μεγάλην ... τὴν μεταβολήν:** the sentence emphatically starts with four long syllables, and the initial main clause is interlinked by the repetition of -ην at word end (homoioteleuton) and με(τα)- at word beginnings (homoioarchon). The two noun phrases overlap in sense; the latter describes the process of change and the former the result of that process. The pleonasm underscores the insistent tone. **δεικτέον:** sc. ἐστι. D. reiterates δεικνύειν from the previous section. The verb is often used by prosecutors in court to describe their case, and in this sense it is frequently linked, as here, with ἐξελέγχω; cf. D. 19.8, 21.21, 29.1. The legal language (cf. §5 ἐλέγχειν) characterizes Philip as a criminal, and the Olynthians and Thessalians as judges.   **εἰσφέροντας ...** **ἑτοίμως** "by making war contributions, going out on the expedition, and doing everything eagerly." The three circumstantial participles (sc. ὑμᾶς) come quickly in asyndeton, forming an ascending tricolon, in which the third element is as long as the combination of the first two, which are themselves balanced in length. εἰσφέροντας and ἐξιόντας are balanced in sense, since each verb is used in a technical sense to describe specific action, while the generic capping phrase ἅπαντα ποιοῦντας ἑτοίμως broadly encompasses the preceding verbs.   **εἰσφέροντας:** 1.6n. χρήματα.   **ἐξιόντας:** 1.6n. αὐτούς.   **εἴπερ τις ὑμῖν προσέξει τὸν νοῦν** "if anyone is going to take you seriously."   **κἂν ταῦτα ἐθελήσητε ... περαίνειν** "if you are willing ... actually to accomplish these things." The switch to ἐάν + subj. adds a note of optimism (cf. Smyth §2328a).   **καὶ δὴ** "actually" or "at once," modifying περαίνειν and stressing that this result will follow immediately upon the decision implied in ἐθελήσητε (*GP* 253). **τὰ συμμαχικὰ ... ἐξελεγχθήσεται** "not only will Philip's alliance appear to be weak and mistrustful, but his rule and power at home will also be proven to be in trouble." The two apodoses are parallel both in word order and syntax. ἐξελεγχθήσεται: the sentence culminates with this striking compound verb, emphasizing Philip's criminality; cf. ἐξετασθήσεται in §20.

**14–21 Philip's weaknesses at home**
Philip has grown strong from constant campaigning that has exhausted his men. He and his companions alienate most Macedonians with their outrageous behavior. The state of the union is unhealthy.

**14 ἡ Μακεδονικὴ δύναμις καὶ ἀρχή** reiterates the theme from the previous sentence; the usage of the nominative noun after the substantive noun phrase (τὰ τῆς οἰκείας ἀρχῆς καὶ δυνάμεως) adds variety, and the reversed order produces a chiasmus. **ἐν μὲν προσθήκηι** "as an ally"; lit. "in supplement." After three examples μέν is answered by αὐτὴ δέ below. **μερίς ἐστί τις οὐ μικρά** "is no insignificant contributor." οὐ μικρά = μεγάλη (litotes). τις here has a strongly positive sense; on the idiom see LSJ A II 5a and cf. §1 δύναμίν τινα. **οἷον ὑπῆρξέ ποθ' ὑμῖν** "as it was for you then." οἷον introduces the first of three historical examples, which are put in chronological sequence by ποθ', πάλιν αὖ, and νυνὶ δέ. **ἐπὶ Τιμοθέου** "in the time of Timotheus." In late 364 or early 363 the Athenian general Timotheus (*LGPN* 32, *PAA* 886180) led a campaign against the Chalcidian League and captured Potidaea with the support of Macedonian forces (*HM* 186–7, Psoma 2001: 234). **πάλιν αὖ** "or again on another occasion." **πρὸς Ποτείδαιαν Ὀλυνθίοις:** on Philip's alliance with Olynthus in 357/6, see §1n. τάς. Although D. does not make the point explicitly, his examples illustrate Macedon's duplicity in switching from one ally to another. **ἐφάνη τι τοῦτο συναμφότερον** "this combination appeared to be something significant." τι is used in the same sense as τις earlier in the sentence. **νυνὶ δὲ Θετταλοῖς ... ἐπὶ τὴν τυραννικὴν οἰκίαν ἐβοήθησεν** "recently it was an aid to the Thessalians against their tyrant family, when they were plagued by factions and in a state of anarchy." Some Thessalians supported the tyrants of Pherae, while others wanted a popular government. As an ally of the Thessalian League during the war against Phocis in 352 (§7n. Θετταλούς), Philip took Pherae from the tyrants Lycophron and Peitholaus (*HM* 267–78); οἰκίαν refers to their family line. **νοσοῦσι:** the verb regularly describes physical illness, and is commonly applied to political unrest (e.g., Hdt. 5.28, S. *Ant.* 1015, LSJ 3; Brock 2013: 77 n. 7 and 180 n. 95). D. is particularly fond of using νοσέω and the cognate noun νόσημα in this political sense (e.g., 9.12, 39, 50, 19.259, 262), and it is clear that he intended to breathe life into this clichéd usage, since he continues the metaphor below with ἀσθενής and ταλαιπωρέω (§16). D. frequently uses much more specific medical terminology to describe the state of Greek politics (e.g., §21nn., 9.12n. τοῖς); see Wooten 1979, Ronnet 163–6, 177– 8. **ὅποι ... δύναμιν** "wherever someone, I suppose, contributes even a small force." **πάντ' ὠφελεῖ** "it helps with everything." **αὐτὴ δὲ καθ' αὑτήν** "but by itself"; sc. ἡ Μακεδονικὴ δύναμις καὶ ἀρχή. **15 οὗτος** = Philip. **ἅπασι τούτοις** "by all those means." The demonstrative is explained by the appositives τοῖς πολέμοις and ταῖς στρατείαις. **οἷς ἄν τις ... ἡγήσαιτο** "by which someone might suppose he [became] great." **ἐπισφαλεστέραν** "more unstable"; sc. τὴν δύναμιν. The adjective is not attested before the fourth century; it was used by Plato (*R.* 6.497d) and Aristotle (*Pol.* 2.2.15 [1264b]) to describe political systems. Here it lends an analytical tone to D.'s argument, which is reinforced by the comparison with the "natural status" (ὑπῆρχε φύσει) of Philip's rule. **μὴ γὰρ οἴεσθε κτλ.**: this extensive sentence begins with the main clause and then consists of two long limbs contrasting Philip and his subjects (τοὺς ἀρχομένους): the first (ἀλλ' ὁ μὲν ... ᾑρημένος) recognizes Philip's tireless pursuit of glory, while the second part, twice as long as the first (§16 τοῖς δὲ ... διὰ τὸν πόλεμον), puts even greater stress on the exhaustion of his men. **τοῦτο ἐζήλωκε** "he has set this as his goal." τοῦτο refers to the entire preceding phrase. **πράττων καὶ κινδυνεύων**: the phrase has a positive tone of admiration; cf. Isoc. *Ep.* 4.7, where the phrase is used in a letter of recommendation to describe the subject's past achievements. D. presents Philip's constant activity in these positive terms as a point of contrast for his criticism of Athenian apathy below (§§23–4); for a similarly positive description of Philip intended to highlight Athenian deficiencies, cf. D. 1.24, 4.5, 9.37 with Mader 2003: 58–9. **ἂν συμβῇ τι** "if anything [bad] happens" (ἄν = ἐάν; LSJ συμβαίνω III; cf. D. 21.112). Cf. 4.11n. καί, 9.17n. εἴ. **τὴν τοῦ διαπράξασθαι ... ᾑρημένος** "having preferred the glory of accomplishing what no other Macedonian king [ever did] instead of living safely." Philip's deliberate pursuit of glory is re-emphasized at the end of the colon by the repetition of δόξα and αἱροῦμαι (after the compound προῄρηται the simplex form ᾑρημένος assumes its force; see Watkins 1967 and Renehan 1969: 77–85).

**16 τοῖς δὲ τῆς μὲν φιλοτιμίας τῆς ἀπὸ τούτων οὐ μέτεστιν** "but they have no share in the glory that accrues from these [achievements]." τοῖς δέ refers back to τοὺς ἀρχομένους (§15n. μή). **φιλοτιμίας:** lit. "love of honor," commonly describing the behavior or attitude of an individual who strove for personal renown. This trait was sometimes viewed as antidemocratic (MacDowell 2000: 223–4): for example, Thucydides criticizes political leaders in Athens who made decisions "based on their personal glory" (2.65.7 κατὰ τὰς ἰδίας φιλοτιμίας; cf. 8.89.3), and in his description of civil strife in Corcyra he links the term with πλεονεξία ("greediness,"

3.82.8). Above D. asserted that leadership based on selfish greed is unstable (§9n). ὅταν), and this use of φιλοτιμία reinforces the characterization of Philip as such a leader. On the other hand, the noun is commonly used in a positive sense; in fourth-century Athenian honorary decrees φιλοτιμία is commonly specified as a basis for the city's praise, but in these instances the noun is usually linked with a synonym and qualified by a phrase such as πρὸς τὸν δῆμον τῶν Ἀθηναίων (e.g., repeatedly in *IG* II³ 367 [dated 325/4]; cf. Whitehead 1983: 63, Veligianni-Terzi 1997: 223, Henry 1983: 42–3). That positive sense of the term does not apply here, since Philip's φιλοτιμία does not serve the common good, as D. pointedly emphasizes (οὐ μέτεστιν). **κοπτόμενοι δὲ ... ταλαιπωροῦσιν:** the initial participle is emphatic and is to be taken with both finite verbs: "exhausted from these constant campaigns all over the place, they are worn out and continuously suffer." κόπτω is regularly "beat" or "strike," but it can also refer to one who is "beat" in the sense of physical exhaustion (LSJ I 13). **ἄνω κάτω** "all over the place"; lit. "up (and) down." The phrase suggests that the effort is futile; cf. Ar. *Birds* 3, D. 4.41, 9.36n. ἄνω. It also, together with ἀεί and συνεχῶς and the present-tense verbs, emphasizes that the men's continued exhaustion is a corollary of Philip's constant activity. **οὔτ' ἐπὶ τοῖς ἔργοις ... ἐώμενοι διατρίβειν** "allowed to spend their time neither on their livelihood nor on their private affairs." τὰ ἔργα refers to labor undertaken to obtain the necessities of life, whereas τὰ ἴδια are more generally the home life and individual concerns that the men must neglect for the sake of Philip's glory. **οὔτε ὅσ' ἂν ποιήσωσιν ... ταῦτ' ἔχοντες διαθέσθαι** "nor able to dispose of what they produce ..." The third οὔτε is not parallel to the preceding ones; it coordinates the participles ἐώμενοι and ἔχοντες. **οὕτως ὅπως ἂν δύνωνται** "in any way they can" or "one way or another"; for the idiom cf. D. 40.4. **κεκλειμένων τῶν ἐμπορίων:** the Macedonian ports were blockaded by pirates (D. 19.315) until Philip defeated them and took their base at Halonnesus in 345 or 344 ([D.] 12.13); see MacDowell 2000: 344.

**17 οἱ μὲν ... Φιλίππῳ** "how the majority of Macedonians are disposed toward Philip." D. stresses the contrast between the common Macedonians (οἱ μέν) and the specialist soldiers (οἱ δέ) by placing them at the front of the two halves of the sentence. **τούτων** refers to the preceding material in §16. **τις:** cf. §4n. τις. **δή** adds a slight hint of mockery (*GP* 236) as D. turns to the soldiers in Philip's immediate circle (περὶ αὐτόν). **ξένοι** "mercenaries." D.'s assertion that Philip relied on hired soldiers, of doubtful loyalty, is an element in the characterization of him as a tyrant; cf. 1.3n. τὰ δ' ἀπειλῶν. **πεζέταιροι:** at the time of this speech the πεζέταιροι were a chosen group of the largest and strongest men who protected the king (D. scholion 116b Dilts = Theopomp. *FGrHist* 115 F 348). After Chaeronea Philip seems to have increased the size of this corps as part of his plan to invade Asia, and so Anaximenes of Lampsacus (late 4th cent.), in contrast to this passage, describes the πεζέταιροι as a larger body, comprising the Macedonian component, either of the entire army, or within a particular squadron (*FGrHist* 72 F 4). On these institutional reforms see Anson 2009, *HM* 405–6 and 705–13, Erskine 1989. **συγκεκροτημένοι** "well trained." Lit. "knocked together," so that a group functions well as a team (LSJ συγκροτέω II 2d). **ὡς δ' … ἤκουον** "but, as I heard …" δέ introduces the second main verb εἰσίν, and the contrast is between the reputation (δόξα) of Philip's men and the reality as reported to D. The ὡς clause is parenthetical. D.'s frequent allusions to unnamed foreign informants (cf. D. 1.22, 4.9, 8.14) are intended to portray him as an expert who can give better political advice than his opponents in the Assembly. But at the same time, the Athenians were routinely skeptical of second-hand information, and its reporter could be characterized as a rumor-monger (Lewis 1996: 75–96). D. accuses his political opponents of rumor-mongering (λογοποιεῖν: 4.49, 6.14) about Philip, and is himself accused of the same by them (Din. 1.35). Here he tries to forestall such charges by stressing the credibility of his information. A likely source for this information may be the informal network of scouts who reported on Philip to the general Charidemus, since D. apparently received intelligence from them on a later occasion (Aesch. 3.77, cf. Plut. *Dem.* 22; F. S. Russell 1999: 139). **οὐδαμῶς οἵου τε ψεύδεσθαι** "incapable of lying." **οὐδένων εἰσὶν βελτίους** "they are better than no others"; i.e., "completely average."

**18 ἐν αὐτοῖς** = ἐν τοῖς περὶ Φίλιππον. **οἷος ἔμπειρος πολέμου καὶ ἀγώνων** "who is experienced in war and battles." οἷος refers to a generic category rather than a specific individual. D. frequently uses ἀγών to describe specific wartime engagements (9.52, 14.9, 60.25); for the development of this usage (beginning after the Persian Wars), see Krentz 2002: 37 and Pritchett 1974: 284 n. 28. **τούτους μὲν … ἔφη** "he [D.'s informant] said that he [Philip] drives them all away because of his desire for glory." Cf. D. 18.277 for the shift from sing. τις to pl. τούτους. μέν is repeated from the previous clause. **βουλόμενον … τἄργα** "because he wants all the achievements to seem to be his own." Cf. §1.14n. ὑφ'. **πρὸς γὰρ αὖ … ἀνυπέρβλητον εἶναι** "for in addition to his other [faults], his desire for glory too is unsurpassable." εἶναι continues the indirect statement introduced by ἔφη. The adjective ἀνυπέρβλητος is rarely attested before the fourth century, and is very frequently used to describe the collective valor of Athenian soldiers and their allies (Isoc. 4.71, D. 60.1, Lycurg. 101 and 105, Hyp. *Epit.* 7). D.'s tone is sarcastic; he highlights Philip's selfishness by employing terms that were commonly used to praise patriotic service for Athens (cf. §16n. φιλοτιμίας). **εἰ δέ τις:** sc. ἐστιν ἐν αὐτοῖς. **δίκαιος ἄλλως** "just in other ways"; for ἄλλως with an adjective, cf. D. 19.277 ἄλλως δημοτικός and 21.34 ἄλλως δίκαια.   **τὴν καθ' ἡμέραν ἀκρασίαν τοῦ βίου** "the day-to-day wildness of his life." The following description of Philip's court is closely paralleled in the fragments of Theopompus' *Philippica* (published after 324); for ἀκρασία cf. *FGrHist* 115 FF 40, 143, 210, 232. These points of correspondence probably reflect widespread characterizations of Philip that developed over the years as the king became a central subject of Athenian debates, rather than the direct influence of this speech. For Philip's private life and his reputation in Athens, see Flower 1994: 104–11.   **μέθην:** D. frequently presents drunkenness as a barbarian trait; cf. D. 4.49, 23.114, Todd 2007: 103. Archaeological evidence attests to a drinking culture among elite Macedonians generally; see Flower 1994: 107–8 and Carney 2007: 147–60.   **κορδακισμούς** "obscene dances," particularly associated with comedy. A scholion to Ar. *Clouds* 540 explains that the dance involves "shameful wiggling of the buttocks," and vase paintings depict dancers with their feet joined together, hunched over and pointing with their rear ends (see Lawler 1964: 69–71, 1965: 87, Prudhommeau 1965: 318–19). Theophrastus connects the dance with drunken behavior (*Char.* 6.3, with Diggle 2004: 252–3, Halliwell 2008: 148 n. 110), as does D. below (§19).   **παρεῶσθαι ... τὸν τοιοῦτον** "that sort of man has been swept aside and is considered worthless" (LSJ μέρος IV 3). The informant's report continues in indirect statement. The perf. pass. infin. of παρωθέω is used here in a gnomic sense. Theopompus similarly insists that "Philip rejected men of moderate character and those who took care of their lives; he honored and praised spendthrifts and those who lived for dice and drink" (*FGrHist* 115 F 225b). Cf. 9.32n. παρώσας.

**19 λοιπούς ... εἶναι** "those left surrounding him are ..." The indirect statement continues.   **λῃστάς** "bandits." D. characterizes Philip's associates, and later (10.34) Philip himself, as lawless thieves. Theopompus similarly reports that Philip's companions "live indecently and extravagantly just like bandits" (*FGrHist* 115 F 224 ζῆν μὴ κοσμίως ἀλλ' ἀσώτως καὶ τοῖς λῃσταῖς παραπλησίως). On the history and range of the term, see Pritchett 1991: 315–17, de Souza 1999: 2–12.   **κόλακας** "toadies" or "flatterers." Aristotle describes a κόλαξ as someone who behaves in an obsequious manner with hope for personal gain (*EN* 4.6.9 [1127a]), and he generally associates these "base friends" (οἱ ταπεινῶς ὁμιλοῦντες) with the courts of tyrants (*Pol.* 5.11.12 [1313b–14a]; cf. Pl. *Rep.* 9.575e, and Theopompus *FGrHist* 115 F 81 on Philip's court in particular); see Konstan 1997: 98–103. This sort of deferential submissiveness was antithetical to the ideal of democratic equality (Millett 1989: 25–37), and D. regularly refers to his political opponents in Athens, those who resisted war against Philip, as κόλακες (e.g., 8.34, 9.4n. κολακεύεσθαι, 18.46). κόλακες were stock characters in Athenian comedy of the fifth and fourth centuries, men who offered their companionship in exchange for a free meal (Olson 2007: 55, Damon 1997: 11–13, Nesselrath 1990: 309–17). D.'s use of the term here thus depicts Philip's associates as submissive and self-interested, and this characterization reinforces the argument that Philip's position is precarious. **μεθυσθέντας ὀρχεῖσθαι:** §18n. κορδακισμούς. **οἷα ἐγὼ ... ὀνομάσαι:** i.e., the lewd dances at Philip's court. D.'s emphatic use of ἐγώ stresses the contrast between himself and Philip's associates (cf. 21.79). His modesty creates a bond of decency between himself and his audience, and encourages his listeners to imagine the worst; cf. 18.103 and 54.9 with Carey and Reid 1985: 83–4. **δῆλον:** sc. ἐστί; D. introduces his own arguments in support of his informant's report. **οὓς ... τούτους:** the relative clause (οὓς ἐνθένδε πάντες ἀπήλαυνον ὡς ... ὄντας) stresses the contrast between the modesty of the Athenians and the indecency of Philip's friends. οὕς has τούτους as a delayed antecedent; the accusative noun phrases in-between (Καλλίαν ... ἀισμάτων) add specific details. **ἀπήλαυνον:** if in fact Callias or any other friends of Philip were legally exiled from Athens, we know nothing else of it. D. is probably exaggerating; his point here is simply to emphasize that Philip's associates are men whose presence is objectionable to all (πάντες) Athenians. As far as we know, the Athenians imposed exile as a legal penalty only for unintentional homicide and in certain types of treason cases (MacDowell 1978: 176–9, 255). **θαυματοποιῶν:** performers who put on "puppet-shows, juggling, circuses and other kinds of public entertainment" (Diggle 2004: 254). These θαύματα were common at symposia (e.g., Xen. *Smp*. 2.1, 8, 11 and cf. 7.2–5), and Aristotle criticizes tyrants in particular for their excessive devotion to such amusements (*EN* 10.6.3 [1176b]). Jesters were a stock feature in accounts of tyrants' courts (Halliwell 2008: 309 n. 116); e.g., the comparison of the outrageous behavior at the courts of Philip and Dionysius I of Syracuse at Ath. 6.260c–1b. **ἀσελγεστέρους** "more aggressive"; the adjective here refers to the mockery (cf. γελασθῆναι below) that characterized Philip's court entertainment. D. uses it in a similar sense to describe the boldness of Philip's aggressions against the Greeks (e.g., 4.9, 9.35, 19.342). See MacDowell 1990: 220. **Καλλίαν ἐκεῖνον τὸν δημόσιον** "that famous Callias the public slave" (*LGPN* s.v. 257, *PAA* 553587); in the absence of further detail he cannot be linked with any of his contemporary homonyms, and nothing further is known of him for certain. Athens employed public slaves in various clerical and administrative capacities (Hansen 1991: 123–4), including as bookkeepers on Athenian expeditions (Pritchett 1974: 38–9), and if Callias actually was tried for treason and exiled (but cf. §19n. ἀπήλαυνον), the charges may have arisen from such a role in a military or diplomatic expedition involving Philip. This passage may lie behind Plutarch's image of a corrupt royal court full of men like Callias (a generalizing plural), mercenaries, and low-class comedians (*Mor.* 1095d). It is certainly the source for the declamation by Libanius (4th cent. AD) in which Philip addresses D. and includes Callias in a list of Athenians resident in Macedon (*Decl.* 23.1.82; in that passage, *pace* Sandys 1897: 173, Callias and the son of Phrynon from Rhamnous must be distinct persons). **μίμους ... ἀισμάτων** "performers of farces and creators of sordid songs." Ancient mime was "popular, sub-literary entertainment" enacting scenes from daily life with dialogue, music, and dancing (Cunningham 1971: 3–11). As here, these performances are often attested in conjunction with other sorts of popular entertainment (Dickie 2001: 601–2), and so, for example, in Xenophon's *Symposium* the same dancer performs θαύματα (§19n. θαυματοποιῶν) and participates in a mime performance of the story of Dionysus and Ariadne (9.2–7). **γελοίων** "farces, jests, amusements" (neut. pl. substantive). Tactless hurtful humor (βωμολοχία, Arist. *EN* 4.8.3–4 [1128a]) was a characteristic of the courts of tyrants; see Hunter and Russell 2011: 102. **ὧν ... γελασθῆναι:** lit. "which they direct at their companions for the sake of a laugh being raised" (LSJ γελάω 1), i.e., to mock them. The relative pronoun is attracted to the case of its antecedent.

**20 καίτοι ταῦτα ... τοῖς εὖ φρονοῦσιν** "and yet, even if someone thinks these matters are small, they are great indicators ... of his disposition and doom, for those who are sensible" (9.15n. ὅστις). The placement of the concessive clause before μεγάλα heightens the antithesis between μικρά and μεγάλα, and the insertion of ὦ ἄνδρες Ἀθηναῖοι adds weight to μεγάλα δείγματα (cf. D. 1.1, 9.1). **γνώμης ... κακοδαιμονίας** "ill-fated intention." The former noun refers to Philip's internal motivations, the latter encompasses broader external forces; they express a single idea (hendiadys; Sansone 1984: 25). Cf. D. *Prooem.* 24.3 τὴν τούτων θρασύτητα καὶ κακοδαιμονίαν. **ἐπισκοτεῖ ... τὸ κατορθοῦν** "his success overshadows these." D. frequently accuses his Athenian audience of being "in the dark" regarding Philip's true nature. E.g., 18.159 πολύ τι σκότος ... ἐστὶν παρ' ὑμῖν πρὸ τῆς ἀληθείας; cf. 19.226, Ronnet 175. **αἱ ... εὐπραξίαι** "his accomplishments" (Smyth §1000 on plural of abstract nouns). **δειναὶ συγκρύψαι** "are marvelously apt to cover over." The predicate adjective δειναί (sc. εἰσι) governs the infinitive (LSJ III; cf. δεινὸς λέγειν "clever at speaking"). The adjective has a wide range of meaning; it can have a simple negative sense ("frightening" or "terrible"), but it can be used more positively to describe material that is "amazing" or "marvelous." Here it suggests that Philip's successes are "wondrous" beyond conventional achievements. **ἀκριβῶς ... ἐξετασθήσεται** "these [faults] of his will be shown clearly"; a striking sentence-end (§13n. ἐξελεγχθήσεται). D. frequently pairs this verb with ἀκριβῶς; e.g., 6.37, 20.18. **δοκεῖ ... δείξειν** "I think it will become clear." δείκνυμι is impersonal here; see LSJ 2 and cf. Ar. *Frogs* 1261. **οὐκ εἰς μακράν** "before too long." **ἂν οἵ τε θεοὶ θέλωσι** "if the gods are willing"; a colloquial Attic phrase, common in speeches (e.g., D. 4.7, Ar. *Wealth* 405, Xen. *Hell.* 2.4.17). The singular occurs with no difference in meaning (e.g., D. 4.7), and θέλω occurs only in this phrase in classical prose (LSJ ἐθέλω init.); see Olson 1998: 249–50. **καὶ ὑμεῖς βούλησθε**: this unexpected (although anticipated by τε) addition to the preceding conventional formulation emphasizes the necessity for Athenian action (cf. Martin 2009: 224–5).

**21  D.** concludes this section of the speech on Philip's weakness with an extended simile (cf. Introd. §3.4). By putting the situation in medical terms here D. assumes the role of a knowledgeable expert, with the ability to diagnose and heal the city's ills (cf. the close parallel at Hyp. *Phil.* fr. 10), and elsewhere he uses similar imagery to attack the advice of his opponents (3.33, 18.243). The halves of the simile have a parallel structure, outlined below. Each half begins with the main point of comparison ("1."), and then two main clauses ("3." and "5.") follow two generic temporal clauses ("2." and "4.") contrasted by μέν and δέ. Sound echoes (τέως μὲν ἄν/ἕως μὲν ἄν, ἐπὰν δ'/ἐπειδὰν δέ) and the emphatic repetition of πάντα further bind the two halves.

1. ὥσπερ γὰρ ἐν τοῖς σώμασιν,
2. τέως μὲν ἂν ἐρρωμένος ἦι τις,
3. οὐδὲν ἐπαισθάνεται,
4. ἐπὰν δ' ἀρρώστημά τι συμβῇ,
5. πάντα κινεῖται, κἂν ῥῆγμα ... ᾖ,
1. οὕτω καὶ τῶν πόλεων καὶ τῶν τυράννων,
2. ἕως μὲν ἂν ἔξω πολεμῶσιν,
3. ἀφανῆ τὰ κακὰ τοῖς πολλοῖς ἐστιν,
4. ἐπειδὰν δὲ ὅμορος πόλεμος συμπλακῇ,
5. πάντα ἐποίησεν ἔκδηλα.

**τέως** = ἕως, as often in D. (e.g., 14.36, 20.91).   **οὐδὲν ἐπαισθάνεται** "he perceives nothing," i.e., he feels no physical ailments. The addition of the phrase τῶν καθ' ἕκαστα σαθρῶν following οὐδέν in some MSS derives from the reworking of this passage at [D.] 11.14 and should be rejected: it entails an unnecessary repetition of the adjective σαθρός and disturbs the delicate balance between this clause and πάντα κινεῖται below.   **ἀρρώστημα** "illness." The term is non-technical and appears in other fourth-century material intended for a popular audience (e.g., Hyp. *Ath.* 15, Men. *Asp.* 337).   **πάντα κινεῖται** "everything erupts." The verb is middle and describes the sudden appearance of physical symptoms of illness; cf. D. 18.198 τὰ ῥήγματα καὶ τὰ σπάσματα ... κινεῖται ("ruptures and sprains erupt").   **κἂν ῥῆγμα ... σαθρὸν ᾖ** "whether it is a fracture or a sprain or some other element of his situation that is unsound." ῥῆγμα and στρέμμα are rarely found outside medical writers (but cf. D. 18.198, quoted above, with Goodwin 1901: 141). Here they add vivid detail to the image and contribute to D.'s persona as an expert. **τῶν πόλεων καὶ τῶν τυράννων:** the genitives modify τὰ κακά. The reference to different types of states reinforces the generalization in the simile and emphasizes that Philip's rule is unlike the governments of Greek πόλεις. **ἀφανῆ τὰ κακὰ ... ἐστιν:** the imagery was anticipated above; see §20n. ἐπισκοτεῖ. **συμπλακῆι** "gets a grip [on them]"; the passive of συμπλέκω describes the entanglement of wrestling combatants (LSJ συμπλέκω II) and here vividly reinforces the notion of proximity in ὅμορος. **ἐποίησεν:** gnomic aorist; see §9n. ἅπαντα. **ἔκδηλα** "completely clear"; a rarely attested term prior to D. (once in Homer, *Il.* 5.2). The ἐκ- prefix adds a sense of totality. The trisyllabic compound answers ἀφανῆ in the preceding indicative clause, and the two words frame the conclusion of the simile with the initial and final positions in the two main clauses.

### 22–26 The Athenian heritage

Up to now the Athenians have done nothing about recent losses and have failed to live up to past achievements. They must act to protect earlier gains.

**22 ταύτηι:** adverbial: "for this reason." **φοβερὸν προσπολεμῆσαι** "frightening to fight against"; the infinitive is explanatory and depends on the adjective. See 4.4n. εἰ. **σώφρονος** "judicious." This adjective often verges toward the sense of σοφός. Here it describes someone who "resists the temptations of wishful thinking" (*GPM* 121–2) and recognizes the reality of the situation. **μεγάλη ... ἡ τύχη** "luck is a great weight, or rather everything." ῥοπή is weight that tips the balance of a scale. The image of "weighing sides" is frequently used to compare the relative strength of opposed forces in battle (e.g., A. *Pers.* 437, Thuc. 1.105.5) and perhaps arises from Homeric depictions of Zeus weighing the fates of men to determine the outcome of battle (e.g., *Il.* 22.209–13 with de Jong 2012: 112–13). For the same imagery of weighing τύχη in battle, see A. *Pers.* 346 with Garvie 2009: 179, and cf. §2n. τῶν. **οὐ μὴν ἀλλ᾽** "but even so." D. often uses this idiom (cf. 1.4n. οὐ), as here, in place of δέ to introduce a point of contrast to a preceding μέν clause (e.g., 4.38, 19.201). The emphatic tone is reinforced by ἔγωγε (cf. also D. 34.4). **ἂν ἑλοίμην** "I would choose"; aor. mid. of αἱρέω. **ἐθελόντων ... ὑμῶν αὐτῶν** "if you yourselves are willing to do your duty" (1.6n. ἅ). **καὶ κατὰ μικρόν** "even just barely." The implication is that the Athenians are completely negligent, and that D.'s proposals are easily manageable. **ἢ τὴν ἐκείνου** "rather than his [luck]." ἤ introduces a comparison after αἱρέω (Smyth §2863b). **ἀφορμὰς εἰς τὸ ... ἔχειν** "means for acquiring." ἀφορμαί are most basically "starting points,"

## 2 SECOND OLYNTHIAC 22-24

and the noun developed various technical senses which D. employs frequently. Its sense here relates to its usage to denote property and wealth (e.g., 19.343, 21.137), or to indicate the basis for legal or rhetorical arguments (e.g., 61.22, *Ep.* 1.4). It also regularly describes military resources (e.g., 3.33, 4.29, 18.233). **τὴν παρὰ τῶν θεῶν εὔνοιαν** reiterates the initial theme of the speech; see §1n. τήν.

**23 ἀλλ' ... ποιοῦντες:** the concise statement encapsulates D.'s criticism; οἶμαι softens its bluntness (LSJ οἴομαι iv 2). **καθήμεθα:** D. frequently uses this verb to highlight the contrast between the Athenians' passivity and Philip's tireless activity; cf. §24, 4.9, 8.30. It has a pejorative sense, stressing that the Athenians are wasting time; on this usage see LSJ 7, Headlam 1922: 31-2, and Garvie 1994: 268. **ἔνι ... θεοῖς:** sc. τινά: "it is not possible [for someone] who is himself unoccupied to give orders, even to his friends, for some action on his behalf, to say nothing of [giving orders to] the gods." The statement is a generalization. ἔνι = ἔνεστι and οὐδέ is adverbial (Smyth §2931). **μή τί γε:** a common Demosthenic idiom; cf. D. 19.137 and 54.17 (strengthened by δή, as here), MacDowell 1990: 365. **οὐ δὴ θαυμαστόν ἐστιν:** D. now declares his theme for the next four sentences, each of which begins with a dramatically short main clause repeating the theme: οὐδὲ θαυμάζω τοῦτ' ἐγώ ... (§24) ἀλλ' ἐκεῖνο θαυμάζω ... (§25) ταῦτα θαυμάζω. On this use of repetition to emphasize a key theme, cf. D. 4.16-19 (δεῖ), 15.25 (δίκαιος) with Ronnet 63-4; see also *GPS* 80. **στρατευόμενος ... παραλείπων:** the string of four nominative participial phrases, each more grammatically complex than the last, gives abundant reasons for Philip's success, and also by contrast highlights the Athenians' failure to fight for themselves and capitalize on available opportunities. **αὐτός** is intensifying with ἐκεῖνος. Its usage echoes αὐτὸν ἀργοῦντ' above and underlines the semantic opposition between ἀργοῦντ' and πονῶν. The demonstrative ἐκεῖνος signals that D. is now talking about Philip specifically after the preceding generalization. **ἡμῶν ... πυνθανομένων περιγίγνεται** "is superior to us as we stall and hold elections and make inquiries." In contrast to Philip's activity in the field, these participles describe the Athenians as they sit in the Assembly (cf. 1.4n. πάντων). The absolute use of the participles, without any objects or modifiers, reflects the Athenians' failure to achieve any of their objectives. **μηδὲν ... ὧν ... προσήκει** "although we do nothing which those who are at war ought [to do]." ὧν = τούτων ἅ. **πολεμοῦσι ... περιῆμεν:** the alliteration of initial π links the notions of war, duty, energetic activity, and success. It could be accidental; but cf. 3.36n. καὶ ... κατέλιπον.

**24 ἐκεῖνο** anticipates the two main points in the lengthy indirect question: that the Athenians are currently hesitant to protect their possessions (νυνὶ δ' ... κτημάτων) and that they sit passively in the Assembly despite their losses (τὰ δ' ... κάθησθε). εἰ ... ἀντήρατε "that although you once rose up against the Spartans in defense of the Greeks' rights." This and the following μέν clause (καὶ τοὺς μὲν ... ἐν μέρει) are concessive (*GP* 370; cf. §9n. καί). The notion of physical movement in the verb contrasts with ὀκνεῖτε and κάθησθε below. D. refers to the Athenian alliance with Thebes in opposition to Sparta in the early 370s, when the Spartan king Agesilaus contended with Theban and Athenian forces in Boeotia (Buckler 2003: 231–7; see also 4.3n. ἡλίκην). This brief allusion to Athens as the selfless protector of Greece is indebted to the idealized histories of Athenian achievements that appeared regularly in state-sponsored funeral orations, where the Peloponnesian War could be presented as a victory; see Thomas 1989: 230 on Pl. *Menex.* 242c–e. **καὶ πόλλ' ... ἠθελήσατε** "and although you refused, when it was possible for you to gain many advantages individually on many occasions." **ἀλλ' ... στρατευόμενοι** "and instead you spent your own resources as contributors and took the foremost risk as fighters so that others might obtain justice." **εἰσφέροντες:** 1.6n. χρήματα. **προὐκινδυνεύετε:** the verb is used elsewhere to describe one of the Athenians' greatest victories, at the battle of Marathon (D. 18.208). **στρατευόμενοι:** the verb was just applied to Philip's current activity (§23); he acts more like the Athenians of old than they themselves do. **νυνὶ δ'** introduces the first main point after the preceding concessions. **ἐξιέναι ... εἰσφέρειν** forms a chiasmus with εἰσφέροντες and στρατευόμενοι. For the sense see 1.6nn. χρήματα and αὐτούς. **καὶ τοὺς μὲν ἄλλους ... πάντας** "and although you have often saved the others collectively." The idealized accounts in Athenian funeral orations highlight the Persian Wars, when Athens led the fight for the freedom of all the Greeks at Marathon and Salamis, and in mythical times the defense of Greece from the Amazons and Eumolpus; for discussion of this tradition, see Thomas 1989: 207–8 and 221–6. **καθ' ἕνα αὐτῶν ἕκαστον ἐν μέρει** "each of them individually in turn," as opposed to πάντας. D. is perhaps thinking of efforts by the Athenians during the first half of the fourth century on behalf of Thebes, Sparta, and Euboea, when Athens, according to D. (16.14–15), fought "to protect the victims of injustice" (τοὺς ἀδικουμένους σώιζειν). Some mss omit ἕκαστον as being redundant after καθ' ἕνα, but it helps clarify the construction and balances πάντας. For the phrase cf. D. 18.17 and 21.140. **ἀπολωλεκότες:** §2n. πόλεων. **κάθησθε:** §23n. καθήμεθα.

**25 εἰ** "that" (as in §24). **δύναται:** D.'s tone becomes more strident as he asserts that the Athenians are not just unwilling (§20 βούλησθε and §21 ἐθελόντων) but also incapable of considering the situation. **πόσον πολεμεῖτε χρόνον** "how long you have been at war." **τί ... οὗτος** "what you have been doing as this time has elapsed." D.

## 2 SECOND OLYNTHIAC 25-26

gives the emphasis to οὗτος by delaying it until the end of the period, and thus reinforces the urgency of the present opportunity. **ἴστε γὰρ δήπου** "since of course you know." **μελλόντων ... ποιούντων:** the string of short genitives absolute in asyndeton quickens the pace and expresses D.'s exasperation with the Athenians for doing all the wrong things. **αὐτῶν** = ὑμῶν αὐτῶν, juxtaposed with ἑτέρους τινάς for emphasis. **αἰτιωμένων** "making accusations." The pairing with κρινόντων lends the verb a specific legal sense here. **κρινόντων:** sc. ἀλλήλους: "condemning [each other]" (LSJ κρίνω III 3). Trials of generals were common in democratic Athens; cf. §29, 4.47n. τῶν and see Pritchett 1974: 5–10. A scholiast (175 Dilts) reports that D. refers to Chares (cf. §28n. ἰδίους), the leading Athenian general of the period, who commanded one of the forces eventually sent to relieve Olynthus in 349/8. Other sources (Aesch. 2.71, D. 19.332) suggest that Chares was repeatedly on trial, presumably during his εὔθυναι at the end of each of his annual appointments (Arist. *Rh.* 3.10.7 [1411a] refers to some controversy when Chares gave his accounts after the expedition to Olynthus). On the career of Chares see Pritchett 1974: 77–85, *LGPN* s.v. 17, *PAA* 979470. **πάλιν ἐλπιζόντων:** the repetition implies that the Athenians are going round in circles. **ἅπας ὁ χρόνος διελήλυθεν:** D. echoes the end of the previous sentence and creates a refrain stressing the urgency of the situation. After the long series of genitives absolute this short indirect statement (depending on ἴστε ... ὅτι) stands as a stark conclusion.

**26 εἶθ'** introduces an indignant question. **ἀγνωμόνως:** the tone becomes increasingly blunt; cf. §25n. δύναται. **ὥστε ... γενήσεσθαι** "that you expect the city's situation will turn from poor to prosperous because of those same practices, the ones which have caused the city's situation to go from prosperous to poor." The two clauses are integrated by the parallelism of δι' ὧν and διὰ τούτων at the beginning of each, by the repetition of γέγονεν/γενήσεσθαι at the end, and by the chiastic sequence χρηστῶν φαῦλα ... πράγματα ... πράξεων ... φαύλων ... χρηστά. **οὔτ' εὔλογον ... φύσιν** "is neither sensible nor natural." ἔχον φύσιν is to be construed as a single phrase, which receives emphasis from the inserted ἐστί; cf. D. 21.119 ἔχον ἐστὶν ὑπερβολήν with MacDowell 1990: 341. **τοῦτό γε:** D. frequently summarizes his points in short sentences ending in τοῦτό γε. Cf. 25.65 ἀλλ' ἄτοπον νὴ τὸν Δία καὶ θεοὺς τοῦτό γε, *GP* 146, Yunis 117. **πολὺ γὰρ ... πέφυκεν** "it is naturally much easier to protect everything while possessing it than to acquire it." D. made precisely the opposite assertion in the first *Olynthiac* (1.23n. τό), with reference to Philip. **νῦν δ' ... πρότερον** "but now there is nothing left of our previous [possessions] for us to protect because of the war." The placement of ὅ τι μὲν φυλάξομεν and τῶν πρότερον in emphatic positions near the start and at the end of the clause stress the contrast between past and future circumstances. **νῦν δ'** has a temporal sense anticipating ἤδη. **φυλάξομεν:** on the use of the future tense here, cf. §11n. ἤ. **αὐτῶν ... ἤδη:** the concision of this final statement reflects the urgency of the situation and concludes this series of arguments as D. segues into his proposals in the next section. The initial position of αὐτῶν ... ἡμῶν and ἤδη at the conclusion (cf. 4.8n. ἤδη) emphasize the key point of the argument, that the Athenians must act for themselves immediately.

## 27–31 The current situation

The Athenians must stop deliberating and relying on allies and mercenary armies. The Athenian leaders are powerless without the active support of the citizenry. The state must unite and take immediate action against Philip to ensure success in the future.

**27 φημὶ δὴ δεῖν:** §11n. φημί. The six infinitives that follow depend upon δεῖν. **εἰσφέρειν ... αἰτιᾶσθαι:** these three proposals are closely linked by asyndeton. See 1.6nn. χρήματα and αὐτούς and §25n. αἰτιωμένων. **πρὶν ... κρατήσητε** "until you master your affairs." This conditional clause modifies the preceding three infinitives. For the metaphorical usage, cf. 9.36n. τοῦ. **τηνικαῦτα ... κρίναντας** "then, after making judgment based on their actual accomplishments." D. uses the verb κρίνω above (§25n. κρινόντων) and below (§29) in a specialized legal sense, to describe judicial decisions against the leaders of military expeditions. Here that specialized sense predominates with the second of the following three infinitives (κολάζειν), but with the other two infinitives (τιμᾶν and ἀφελεῖν) κρίναντας is more generalized in sense, referring to broader deliberation. Cf. 4.14n. κρίνατε. **τοὺς μὲν ... ἐλλείμματα:** these three proposals are more long-range than the preceding set, and D. slows down the pace by using connective particles and longer phrases. The first two items (τοὺς μὲν ... τιμᾶν and τοὺς δ' ... κολάζειν) are two sides of the same coin, and the parallel structure of the phrases reflects that close link. The final infinitive phrase (τὰς προφάσεις ... ἐλλείμματα) caps all the others, and it is emphasized by its length, the variety in word order (infinitive in the middle of two objects rather than following a single object), its placement at the end of the sentence, and by the inclusion of the Athenians themselves (ὑμᾶς) in the final phrase. **τοὺς μὲν ἀξίους ἐπαίνου τιμᾶν:** sc. στρατηγούς. For examples of public honors for Athenian generals, see D. 18.114, where he lists four στρατηγοί who received honorary public crowns for their private donations to the war chest. Liddel 2007: 178–9 gives epigraphic examples. **τοὺς δ' ἀδικοῦντας κολάζειν:** §25n. κρινόντων. Below (§28) D. more specifically explains that generals were charged with profiteering. **τὰς προφάσεις δ' ἀφελεῖν:** the following section makes it clear that D. continues to refer to Athenian generals and the excuses they offered in court. Cf. D. 4.25 τὰς προφάσεις

## 2 SECOND OLYNTHIAC 27–28

ἀφελεῖν καὶ τοῦ στρατηγοῦ καὶ τῶν στρατιωτῶν. **τὰ καθ' ὑμᾶς ἐλλείμματα** "the weaknesses caused by you." This final phrase summarizes the initial items in D.'s list of proposals: the Athenians handicap their generals by failing to fight or make contributions, and with their prosecutions. **πικρῶς ἐξετάσαι** "to make strict inspections." The verb has a technical sense: Athenians sent out inspectors, ἐξετασταί, to audit the accounts of mercenary generals (for testimonia see Pritchett 1974: 39). For the phrase cf. D. 18.265 ἐξέτασον ... πράως, μὴ πικρῶς. **ἂν μὴ ... τὰ δέοντα** "if the necessary measures on your part are not in place first" (ἂν = ἐάν). On τὰ δέοντα see §3n. προτρέπειν.

**28 τοῦτον ... τὸν πόλεμον:** i.e., the war against Philip. **ἰδίους δ' εὑρίσκειν πολέμους** "invent their own wars" in order to secure sufficient resources to support their army (cf. §29n. τάς). The most famous commander of this sort was the general Chares (on whom see §25n. κρινόντων), and the following references to Lampsacus and Sigeum confirm that D. has him in mind here (as scholion 189 [Dilts] states). Several passages suggest that Chares was brutally effective at raising funds while on campaign (e.g., Aesch. 2.71; see also Pritchett 1974: 82–4), and other generals were accused of employing similar methods (Low 2011: 68–9). D. uses the plural στρατηγούς here, rather than naming Chares, to indicate that Athens has repeatedly failed to provide adequate support to its generals. D. perhaps exaggerates the extent of independence enjoyed by fourth-century generals; see Fröhlich 2008: 41–55. **εἰ δεῖ ... εἰπεῖν** "if I must tell you the truth about the generals too." D. often claims to present the truth to his audience and thus characterizes himself as a frank and well-informed advisor (e.g., 9.3, 10.53, 23.139; see Whitehead 2000: 400). **τι τῶν ὄντων:** lit. "something of the truth" (LSJ εἰμί III). **ἐνταῦθα μέν:** i.e., in the war against Philip, which is contrasted with the generals' private campaigns below (ἐκεῖ δέ). **Ἀμφίπολις** precedes ἄν for emphasis. D. mentions the city here because its seizure led to the war with Philip and the Athenians were especially eager to win it back (§2n. πόλεων). It also stands here as a point of contrast with Lampsacus and Sigeum below. **γ' ἂν ληφθῆι** "if indeed it is captured" (ἄν = ἐάν). Deuerling's conjecture γε softens the asyndeton (see *GP* 144–5 on this common usage) and adds a tone of doubt, which arises from D.'s assessment of past Athenian failures. **παραχρῆμ' ... κομιεῖσθε** "you will immediately take possession [of it] for yourselves." **οἱ δὲ κίνδυνοι τῶν ἐφεστηκότων ἴδιοι:** sc. εἰσι: "but the risks [are] the personal concern of the generals in command" (LSJ ἐφίστημι Β II). **μισθὸς δ' οὐκ ἔστιν** "and there is no reward." **ἐκεῖ δὲ κίνδυνοι μὲν ἐλάττους:** sc. εἰσι: "but there the risks [are] smaller." **τὰ δὲ λήμματα τῶν ἐφεστηκότων καὶ τῶν στρατιωτῶν** "while profits belong to the generals and soldiers." For the sense of λῆμμα, see 3.33n. τῶν. **Λάμψακος, Σίγειον,**

**τὰ πλοῖα**: nominatives in apposition to λήμματα. Lampsacus and Sigeum are both located on the Hellespont, and would thus serve as ideal bases from which to harass merchant ships. Chares attacked both cities while aiding the rebellion of the Persian satrap Artabazus in 356/5 (Pritchett 1974: 79) and maintained a residence in Sigeum (Theopomp. *FGrHist* 115 F 105, Arr. *An.* 1.1.12). **συλῶσιν** "plunder." In the fourth century the verb most commonly refers to theft from the gods' temples (e.g., Isoc. 4.96 and D. 22.74), but D. repeatedly uses it as a colorful verb to describe maritime seizures (also at 8.24–5, 18.139); see Pritchett 1991: 118–19. **ἐπ᾿ οὖν τὸ λυσιτελοῦν ... χωροῦσιν** "each group goes after what is profitable for them."

**29 ὑμεῖς δ᾿ κτλ.**: the initial ὑμεῖς signals D.'s change in focus from the commanders abroad to the Athenians at home. The two ὅταν clauses divide the sentences into contrasting halves, each of which ends emphatically with a main verb (κρίνετε and ἀφίετε). The parallelism is reinforced by the device of isocolon: the ὅταν clauses have a nearly identical number of syllables. **ὅταν μὲν εἰς τὰ πράγματα ἀποβλέψητε**: 3.1n. ὅταν. **κρίνετε** "you prosecute" (LSJ III 2). **δόντες λόγον** "after granting them a hearing" (LSJ λόγος VI 3 B). **τὰς ἀνάγκας ... ταύτας** "you hear [their pleas of] these daily necessities"; cf. §28n. ἰδίους. The demonstrative points back to the mention of the generals' fund-raising campaigns above. **περίεστι τοίνυν ὑμῖν** "so then, the net result for you is ..." The following three infinitives (ἐρίζειν, διεστάναι, and ἔχειν) depend on περίεστι. **τοῖς μὲν ... ταῦτα** "some of you convinced of this, others of that." μέν and δέ distinguish two different groups with the substantive articles, and that force colors the two instances of ταῦτα, which also refer to different things. **τὰ κοινὰ δ᾿ ἔχειν φαύλως** "and that the common good suffers." **πρότερον ... εἰσεφέρετε κατὰ συμμορίας** "in the past you made war contributions according to symmories." The symmories were groups of wealthy citizens and metics, first organized in 378/7 for the purpose of collecting the εἰσφορά (1.6n. χρήματα; after 358 the same system, or a related one, applied to the trierarchy). There were 100 symmories, each comprising about 15 men. The collective worth of each group was approximately equal, and the system was designed to balance the tax burden according to the worth of each individual. The three richest members of each group were required to pay taxed amounts in advance (the προεισφορά) and expected to recover payment themselves from the other members of the group. See Liddel 2007: 274–6, Christ 2007, Hansen 1991: 112–15, MacDowell 1990: 368–9, Wallace 1989. **πολιτεύεσθε κατὰ συμμορίας**: D.'s criticism has various points: the Athenians are not making financial contributions as they did in the past, and instead they waste time in the Assembly; their political debate is divisive; and the majority are not actively involved. **ῥήτωρ**

... τριακόσιοι: the three richest members of each of the symmories were known as "the ἡγεμόνες, the seconds and the thirds" (D. 18.103), or all together as "the Three Hundred" (D. 18.171, Is. 6.60). D. plays on that terminology here in order to criticize recent debate in the Assembly. He presents the speakers in the Assembly (the ῥήτορες) as the ἡγεμόνες, the mercenary generals as the seconds, and their vocal partisan supporters (cf. 3.4n. θόρυβου) as the remainder of the Three Hundred. Assembly meetings usually were attended by at least 6000 citizens (Hansen 1991: 130–2), and so the implication is that only 5% of them were actually involved in policy decisions. Whereas the tax system recognized differences in wealth and deliberately imposed an unequal burden on the elite for the costs of war, Athenian democratic ideology promoted the ideals of political equality and mass participation in government, and D. suggests here that those ideals have been abandoned. This sort of financial metaphor is typical of D.'s style; he puts his analysis in terms that were familiar to the Athenians (cf. Introd. §3.4). This is the only passage from classical Athens that refers to organized groups of political leaders and followers in the Assembly, but, considering D.'s critical tone here, his account should not be treated as unbiased descriptive evidence for any sort of party politics in the modern sense (cf. Hansen 2014: 397–9 and Ober 1989: 123). This image of party politics arises from the comparison with the tax system, in which there was an established hierarchy of leaders and followers, a hierarchy which had no institutional analog in the Assembly.  οἱ δὲ ἄλλοι ... ἐκείνους "the rest of you have been assigned, some to this group, others to that group." The verb's perfect tense suggests that the majority of Assembly-goers have fixed attitudes and are not responding to the current situation; the passive voice emphasizes their inactivity. The use of the substantives οἱ μέν and οἱ δ', repeated from above and continued below, reiterates the theme of discord.

**30 δεῖ δή:** D. summarizes his proposals in the final two sections of the speech. First in §30 he concludes his criticism of the divisiveness, and then in §31 he presents a positive vision of what needs to be achieved. For the use of δεῖ δή and λέγω δή, cf. §11n. φημί.  ταῦτα ... ποιῆσαι "that [you], after abandoning this practice and yet even now gaining control of yourselves, make deliberation and speech and action a shared concern." For the verbs see 9.1n. πάντων, 9.16n. ταῦτα.  ταῦτα refers to the practice of politics by symmories.  ὑμῶν αὐτῶν ... γενομένους: for γίγνομαι + genitive see LSJ II 3a.  εἰ ... ἀποδώσετε "but if you permit one group to give orders as if they were your rulers."  τοῖς μέν refers to the ῥήτορες and στρατηγοί of §29.  τοῖς δ' ... στρατεύεσθαι "and you permit another group to be compelled to be trierarchs, to pay war contributions, and to serve in the field." Few Athenians were required to be trierarchs or pay the εἰσφορά (cf. §29n. πρότερον). D. misleadingly suggests here that only this small group of Athenians served in the field because he wishes to make the point that the majority are not performing their duty. **τριηραρχεῖν:** the trierarchy was a liturgy, or obligatory public service, which required the richest citizens to pay for and administer the operation of a warship in the navy for one year, under the supervision of the elected στρατηγοί. Approximately 1200 men were eligible for this service, and after 358 a system of symmories was used to divide the burden among those who were eligible. For details see Gabrielsen 1994 and Hansen 1991: 110–15; cf. 4.36n. τίς. **εἰσφέρειν:** 1.6n. χρήματα. **στρατεύεσθαι:** service in the army was compulsory, but D. suggests that only a limited number of Athenians actually performed this duty. He may exaggerate the degree of draft-dodging, but accusations are frequent in oratory (e.g., D. 54.44) and comedy (e.g., Ar. *Wasps* 1117–19), and there was a legal procedure for failure to serve (ἀστρατεία). Citizens could simply decline to respond to call-ups, or obtain exemptions in various ways; for discussion of the phenomenon, see Christ 2006: 45–65. **τοῖς δὲ ψηφίζεσθαι … συμπονεῖν** "while you permit another group just to vote against these [leaders] and not even to contribute anything else at all." The third group is the 95% in attendance at the Assembly (cf. §29n. ῥήτωρ) who did not take an active role. **συμπονεῖν:** D. used the same verb above to describe the strength of governments based on collaborative participation (§9n. ὅταν). D. repeats the verb here to emphasize that Athenian cooperation is too limited, and to draw a contrast between the current situation and the ideal he presented earlier. **τῶν δεόντων:** §3n. προτρέπειν. **ἐν καιρῶι:** on the theme of καιρός, cf. §§2 and 8, where D. urges the Athenians not to miss the current opportunity. See further Trédé-Boulmer 2015: 236–40 and Usher 2004: 58–9. **τὸ γὰρ ἠδικημένον ἀεὶ μέρος ἐλλείψει** "the aggrieved party will constantly fall short in its share." D. refers to members of the symmories who are expected to underwrite the war. **εἶθ'** adds a sarcastic tone to the verb ἐξέσται. **κολάζειν:** D. has already suggested that the Athenians should wait to punish negligent generals until they have gained control of the military situation (§27). Now sarcastically suggests that they may as well punish Athenians at home too if the current situation continues.

**31 λέγω δὴ … τὸ ἴσον** "in summary, I propose that all should make war contributions equally, in accordance with the amount each possesses" (cf. 9.73n. οὐ). D. is summarizing the points made above in §§29–30, where it is clear that he expects all the elite members of the symmories to pay for the war, not the entire citizen body. The relative clause here clarifies D.'s meaning on this point. For the rhetorical effect see §1.6n. αὐτούς. **εἰσφέρειν … αἱρεῖσθαι:** these infinitives are commands in indirect discourse (Smyth §2633). D. is not stating a fact, but rather telling the Athenians what he thinks they should do. The repetition of πᾶς before each infinitive emphasizes the goal of cooperation (cf. 9.68n. πόλλ'). Asyndeton increases the pace of the sentence and adds a tone of urgency. κατὰ μέρος "in turn"; possibly referring to a specific system for calling up troops (cf. Aesch. 2.168 with Hamel 1998: 27 n. 75). ἅπαντες στρατεύσησθε responds directly to the complaint above that only a few are forced to serve (§30n. στρατεύεσθαι). πᾶσι τοῖς παριοῦσι λόγον διδόναι "that [you] give a hearing to all who come forward." Cf. §29n. δόντες. Above D. used a passive verb (§29 προσνενέμησθε) to describe the Athenians in Assembly; now he uses an active verb to insist that they take an active role in policy-making. ὧν = τούτων ἅ. μή is used, rather than οὐ, because the infinitives represent commands, not statements. ὁ δεῖνα ἢ ὁ δεῖνα "this one or that one" (LSJ δεῖνα I). D. rejects the leadership of this or that individual in order to emphasize that the Athenians need to work together collectively. "The expression ὁ δεῖνα is common in D. but rare in other Attic prose writers" (MacDowell 2009: 226 n. 61), and D. often employs this paired usage to criticize the "tediously repetitive routine" (Mader 2006: 379 n. 27) of ineffective debate in the Assembly or the courts (D. 4.46, 20.104, 22.18, *Prooem.* 55.2; cf. 19.168). κἂν ταῦτα ποιῆτε κτλ.: the final sentence ends the speech on an optimistic note; cf. 4.51n. ὅ. τὸν εἰπόντα: i.e., the ῥήτωρ with the best proposals (τὰ βέλτιστα). βέλτιον τῶν ὅλων πραγμάτων ὑμῖν ἐχόντων "when the whole situation is better for you." The speech began with attention to the past and present situation for the Athenians (§1 ἐπὶ πολλῶν and ἐν τοῖς παροῦσι πράγμασιν), and now D. looks to the future. βέλτιον, like βέλτιστα in the previous sentence, contributes to the upbeat tone.

## 3 THIRD OLYNTHIAC

### 1–3 Prooemium

The debate's focus on punishing Philip is out of touch with the reality of the situation. The Athenians must help their allies first. D. understands the situation, but the Athenians have suffered because they lack will, not understanding. D. asks that they allow him to speak frankly for their own good.

**1** The first sentence is echoed in *Prooemium* 2.1 (cf. 1.1n., 4.1n.); D. begins with the same phrase (οὐχὶ ταὐτὰ γιγνώσκειν ... παρίσταταί μοι) and similarly expands it with two ὅταν clauses that contrast the rhetoric that he hears in the Assembly with the reality of what he sees actually happening (the items contrasted there are different: democratic ideals versus oligarchic acts). This opening was well known to later authors: Sallust's version of Cato's speech in reply to Caesar in the *Conspiracy of Catiline* echoes it (52.2 *longe alia mihi mens est, patres conscripti, quom res atque pericula nostra considero, et quom sententias nonnullorum ipse mecum reputo*; the deliberate allusion is confirmed by other borrowings from Demosthenes in Sallust: cf. Sall. *Cat.* 51.1 and D. 8.1, Sall. *Cat.* 52.28 and D. 9.35, Sall. *Hist* fr. 77.12 [Reynolds] and D. 9.33). Lucian (29.26), in a mock trial between Hermes and Justice at Athens, has a personification of Rhetoric introduce a speech that patches together phrases from this sentence and D. 18.1. **οὐχὶ ταὐτὰ παρίσταταί μοι γιγνώσκειν** "it does not happen that I perceive the same things" (LSJ παρίστημι B IV). **εἰς τὰ πράγματ᾽ … πρὸς τοὺς λόγους … τοὺς μὲν γὰρ λόγους … τὰ δὲ πράγματα**: the chiastic structure of the sentence helps the audience follow; they expect D. to finish with τὰ πράγματα. **ὅταν τε εἰς τὰ πράγματ᾽ ἀποβλέψω**: cf. 2.29, where D. uses the same phrase in a similar contrast between the reality visible to the Athenians and the accounts they hear in speeches (cf. 9.4n. ἐν). There the use of μέν and δέ stresses the inconsistency of the Athenians; here the use of τε … καί links the two ὅταν clauses as a single thought (cf. *GP* 512). **περὶ τοῦ τιμωρήσασθαι Φίλιππον**: D. frames the situation in terms of a campaign against Philip, without mentioning the current situation at Olynthus. He deliberately delays those specific details (cf. §2 τοὺς συμμάχους) at the beginning of the speech. The effect is to stress Philip as a topic of general importance (cf. 1.4n. τοῦθ᾽) before D. turns to the urgency of the current situation at Olynthus beginning in §7. **τὰ δὲ πράγματα … σκέψασθαι δέον** "but our circumstances have come to the point that [we] must consider"; the key theme of the second *Olynthiac*, see 2.1n. τοῖς. D. is fond of personifying abstract πράγματα; *GPS* 33 collects examples, including D. 2.5 and 4.38, and cf. 1.2n. καιρός. The construction of a verb of motion (προήκοντα here) with the phrase εἰς τοῦτο (or εἰς τοσοῦτο) introducing a result clause is a common rhetorical device (hypostasis) that stresses the extreme degree of the described quality or situation. Cf. D. 21.12 with MacDowell 1990: 236, 22.65, 23.132, 24.172, 4.37n. ὁ and see Usher 1999: index s.v. *hypostasis*. **ὅπως μὴ πεισόμεθα αὐτοὶ πρότερον κακῶς** "how we ourselves may not first suffer badly" (Smyth §2211 on the ὅπως construction). The placement of the adverb at the end of the phrase gives it emphasis; cf. 4.43n. καλῶς. D. repeatedly uses the phrase πάσχειν κακῶς to describe the potential consequences if the Athenians ignore Philip (cf. 4.15, 4.43n. ὑπέρ on the same contrast with τιμωρήσασθαι Φίλιππον). **οὐδὲν οὖν ἄλλο μοι δοκοῦσιν οἱ τὰ τοιαῦτα λέγοντες ἤ** "those who speak thus seem to me [to do] nothing other than…" In his introductions D. often refers to a generic group of other speakers and speeches in order to stress the distinctiveness of his own viewpoint (e.g., 1.1, 4.1, 6.1, 8.1, 9.1); cf. §3n. ὁρᾶτε. **τὴν ὑπόθεσιν … οὐχὶ τὴν οὖσαν**: cf. S. *El.* 584 σκῆψιν οὐκ οὖσαν.

## 3 THIRD OLYNTHIAC 2–3

**2 τὰ αὐτῆς ἔχειν ἀσφαλῶς** "to protect its own [allies]"; D. refers to the period before Philip took Amphipolis and Potidaea from Athenian control in the 350s; cf. 2.2n. πόλεων. For this sense of ἀσφαλῶς, cf. §27, 4.22, 6.17. **καὶ μάλα ἀκριβῶς οἶδα** "I know very clearly" (*GP* 318). D. stresses his own knowledge by beginning the sentence with an emphatic ἐγώ and concluding it with this strong assertion. **ἐπ' ἐμοῦ** "in my own lifetime" (Smyth §1689b). **τοῦθ' ἱκανὸν προλαβεῖν ἡμῖν εἶναι τὴν πρώτην** "that it is sufficient for us to see to this right now" (LSJ προλαμβάνω I 2 and πρότερος B III 1). The interlocked word order binds together the phrase; cf. 2.8n. συμφέρον. The position of τὴν πρώτην at the end is emphatic. **τοὺς συμμάχους σώσομεν**: D. prefers to speak in generalities in the prooemium; cf. §1n. περί. On the alliance see §6n. παντί. **τοῦτο βεβαίως ὑπάρξηι** "this [the safety of the allies] is secure." **περὶ τοῦ τίνα τιμωρήσεταί τις καὶ ὃν τρόπον** "about whom we will punish and how [we will do that]." The article makes the phrase into a substantive (Smyth §1153g); τις is a generalizing indefinite ("one"; Smyth §1267). **σκοπεῖν** recalls the first sentence of the speech: after the Athenians have devised a policy for the safety of themselves and their allies, then (τότε) they can consider how to treat Philip. **πρὶν δὲ τὴν ἀρχὴν ὀρθῶς ὑποθέσθαι** "before [we] properly lay the foundation"; for this sense of ἀρχή, cf. 2.10n. τάς. **τῆς τελευτῆς** "the outcome." For a similar contrast, cf. 4.43.

**3 ὁ μὲν οὖν παρὼν καιρός**: repeated from 1.2. See notes there on μὲν οὖν and the theme of καιρός, and 2.30n. ἐν. Cf. §6 below, where the personification is continued. **εἴπερ ποτέ**: 1.6n. εἴπερ. The phrase reinforces exhortations: cf. Thuc. 4.20.1, 7.64.2, E. *Andr.* 553. **φροντίδος καὶ βουλῆς** "reflection and deliberation." Nearly synonymous, but perhaps referring to different stages of thought and discussion; cf. Isoc. *Ev.* 41 ἐν τῶι ζητεῖν καὶ φροντίζειν καὶ βουλεύεσθαι τὸν πλεῖστον τοῦ χρόνου διέτριβεν, "he would spend most of his time investigating and reflecting and deliberating." **ὅ τι χρὴ περὶ τῶν παρόντων συμβουλεῦσαι χαλεπώτατον** "that [it is] very difficult to recommend what [you] must [do] regarding the present circumstances." On D. as an ideal σύμβουλος, see 1.1n. συμβουλεύειν. This section contains a cluster of tropes on this topic, such as τὰ δέοντα, frankness, and truth-telling. **ἐξ ὧν παρὼν καὶ ἀκούων σύνοιδα** "from what I know as a witness and by hearsay" (LSJ ἀκούω I 2). The participles refer to different types of knowledge; the former refers to D.'s participation in Assembly debates, while the latter reinforces his self-characterization as an expert σύμβουλος who has access to reports from abroad unavailable to the other orators (see further 2.17n. ὥς). For this common polarization, see 4.47n. μή. **τὰ πλείω τῶν πραγμάτων ἡμᾶς ἐκπεφευγέναι**: D. frequently speaks of "situations that slip away" from the Athenians or Philip: e.g., 5.2, 18.33, 19.123. It is a

132    3 THIRD OLYNTHIAC 3–4

particularly Demosthenic phrase; τὰ πράγματα is not attested as a subject of ἐκφεύγω elsewhere in classical literature. The hunting metaphor (Sandys 1897: 187) is probably not felt; cf. 2.14n. νοσοῦσι.    **τὰ δέοντα ποιεῖν**: 2.3n. προτρέπειν.    **μετὰ παρρησίας**: παρρησία is the right of a citizen to speak frankly and openly about political issues, and is a central value in Athenian democratic ideology, complementing ἰσηγορία, the right of equality of speech, which permitted citizens of any background to speak. In the Assembly speeches D. frequently uses the noun specifically for his own political role (e.g., §32, 6.31, 8.21, 24, 32, 9.3, 10.53, 54, 76) in order to characterize himself as a frank speaker willing to give the best advice, however displeasing it may be. He thus distinguishes himself from the demagogues who pander to the δῆμος (Balot 2004: 238, Ober 1989: 321–2). The term first comes to prominence in the latter part of the fifth century, and Euripides especially uses it to describe the freedom enjoyed in a democracy: *Hipp.* 422, *Ion* 672–5, *Phoen.* 391; see Raaflaub 2004: 222–5.    **τἀληθῆ λέγω**: 2.28n. εἰ.    **διὰ τοῦτο**: sc. εἰ λέγω.    **ἵνα τὰ λοιπὰ βελτίω γένηται**: similarly the last sentence of the second *Olynthiac* (2.31) links the success of a speech with the prosperity of the city.    **ὁρᾶτε γὰρ ὡς ἐκ τοῦ πρὸς χάριν δημηγορεῖν ἐνίους ... τὰ παρόντα**: this conclusion to the prooemium, like the first sentence, is closely paralleled in the collection of Demosthenic speech introductions; cf. *Prooemium* 1.3. Here D. inserts a reference to other speakers as a foil to highlight the ideal advisor he has been describing. He presents those others as demagogues who pander to the pleasure of the δῆμος. The phrasing echoes famous accounts of demagogues and is continued below in §§21–2: cf. Thuc. 3.42.6, where Diodotus asserts that an ideal statesman does not speak παρὰ γνώμην ... καὶ πρὸς χάριν; similarly, Socrates in Pl. *Grg.* 521d. D. himself repeatedly uses similar language at the beginning and ends of his speeches to deny that he is a speaker of that sort: e.g., 4.53 and 8.1.    **εἰς πᾶν προελήλυθε μοχθηρίας τὰ παρόντα** "[our] present circumstances have reached the point of complete despair." μοχθηρία is a strong term (lit. "wickedness") not used elsewhere in the Assembly speeches; its delayed delivery adds emphasis.

## 4–5 An earlier opportunity missed

When Philip besieged Heraion Teichos the Athenians missed an opportunity by deciding upon an expedition and then delaying and sending out an insufficient force, and later disbanding it.

**4 μικρὰ τῶν γεγενημένων ... ὑμᾶς ὑπομνῆσαι** "to remind you about a few past events."    **μέμνησθε ... ὅτ' ἀπηγγέλθη Φίλιππος ... τρίτον ἢ τέταρτον ἔτος τουτὶ Ἡραῖον τεῖχος πολιορκῶν** "you remember when Philip was reported to be laying siege to Heraion Teichos, two or three years ago now." Lit.: "this is now the third or fourth year since"; the accusative denotes duration and the current year is included in the counting and marked with τουτί (Smyth §1585). D. refers to events of late 352; see 1.13n. ἠσθένησεν. Cf. 9.17n. εἰ. **τότε τοίνυν μήν** "so then, at that time." τοίνυν picks up the thread of the first sentence in the section, and μήν leads to D.'s point ("progressive," *GP* 336–8). **μαιμακτηριών:** the fifth of the 12 months in the Athenian year, which began in mid-summer; the debate took place about November 352. **θορύβου** "uproar." The δῆμος sitting in Assembly (and judges in courts) would regularly vocalize their opinion with shouts and clamor. D. himself describes his opponents shouting him down and interrupting him (19.23, 46), and the *Prooemia* refer to θόρυβος as a frequent occurrence (e.g., *Pr.* 4.1, 5.1, 21.4). See Tacon 2001, Wallace 2004: 223–7 (and Bers 1985 on the courts). The interaction was a vital part of the process of generating consensus during debate; see Canevaro 2018, 2019. **τετταράκοντα τριήρεις καθέλκειν** "to launch 40 triremes." This is a large force; "in the later 350s and early 340s a force of thirty ships seems to have been normal" (Cawkwell 1984: 334–5). **τοὺς μέχρι πέντε καὶ τετταράκοντα ἐτῶν αὐτοὺς ἐμβαίνειν** "those up to the age of 45 to man [the ships] themselves." Naval conscripts were called up according to age groups, like hoplites (cf. 1.28n. τοὺς δ' ἐν), ranging from age 20 to 59 (Arist. *Ath. Pol.* 53.4, 7). A few years later than this speech, Aesch. 2.133 (from the year 343) provides numbers for ships and age classes (cf. D. S. 18.10.2, for 323). He refers to conscripts up to age 40 to man 50 ships, which seems inconsistent with the number here; some suspect that one or the other figure in this passage is corrupt. On naval conscription see Rosivach 2001 and Gabrielsen 1994: 107–8 and 248–9. **αὐτούς:** 1.24n. αὐτούς. **τάλαντα ἑξήκοντα εἰσφέρειν** "to levy a tax of 60 talents." This total amount for the εἰσφορά (see 1.6n. χρήματα) would apply to the collective public expense of the campaign and would be supplemented by additional private donations. To put this cost in perspective: D. reckons that all the campaigns against Philip between 357 and 349 cost 1500 talents (1.27n. εἰς); he estimates that the combined public spending and private donations for the campaign at Thermopylae in 352 were more than 200 talents (19.84); he requests 92 talents per year to fund a standing defensive force of 10 ships and land forces in 351 (4.28). Public war expenditures have been estimated to be 1485 talents per annum during the Archidamian War (433–422) and 522 talents per annum in the 370s (Pritchard 2015: 92–111; cf. Pritchett 1991: 464–5, Gabrielsen 1994: 115).

**5 διελθόντος τοῦ ἐνιαυτοῦ τούτου** "when that year had gone by." The year 352/1 ended mid-summer 351. **ἑκατομβαιών, μεταγειτνιών, βοηδρομιών:** the first three months of the year 351/0, extending from July to October 351. Sc. διῆλθον. **τούτου τοῦ μηνὸς μόγις μετὰ**

τὰ μυστήρια "during that month, reluctantly, after the Mysteries." In other words, almost a year after the decree described in §4. By placing this sequence of adverbial phrases before the verb and object, and omitting a connective particle (asyndeton), D. creates suspense; the audience must wait for the action of the sentence, just as the Olynthians waited for an Athenian response. D. makes a similar point about the slowness of Athens at 4.35–7, when he complains about Athenian disorganization when it comes to managing expeditions. The Mysteries (the religious rites for Demeter at Eleusis) were celebrated from mid- to late Boedromion (i.e., late October; see Parke 1977: 55–72). **δέκα ναῦς ... κενὰς ... καὶ πέντε τάλαντα:** the adjectives highlight the inadequacy of the response, as compared to the details of the decree in §4. "Empty ships" is a technical term (cf. Thuc. 6.31.3, D. 4.43); the Athenians supplied equipment but did not man the ships themselves, though they had decreed to do so. The sum of five talents was provided for Charidemus to recruit mercenary crews; see Gabrielsen 1994: 108 and Pritchett 1974: 87. **Χαρίδημον:** Charidemus of Oreus was a mercenary general granted Athenian citizenship in 357 and thereafter frequently elected as στρατηγός in campaigns against Philip, until he fled to Persia in 335 under threat from Alexander. D. 23 provides much detail, biased against Charidemus; for an overview of his career, see Pritchett 1974: 85–9, Osborne and Byrne 1996: no. 7331. **ἠγγέλθη** = ἀπηγγέλθη; cf. 2.15n. τήν. **ἀσθενῶν ἢ τεθνεώς:** this rumor is reported as a fact by D. elsewhere, and the illness was probably real (see 1.13n. ἠσθένησεν). **ἦλθε:** Thucydides repeatedly uses the phrase (ἀγγελία) ἦλθε to describe messengers' reports to the Assembly on foreign affairs (Thuc. 1.61.1, 3.33.2, 8.96.1). The dispatch of the expedition may have been delayed because news from messengers was slow to arrive or unreliable (S. Lewis 1996: 94–5; cf. 2.17n. ὡς). **ἀφεῖτε ... τὸν ἀπόστολον** "you abandoned the expedition." This probably means that they withheld the funding to pay the mercenaries; cf. Demad. *Fr.* 10 (= Plut. *Mor.* 818e) [τῶν Ἀθηναίων] ἀφέντων τὸν ἀπόστολον, where the Athenians are convinced not to send out ships (in support of Agis' revolt) in order to have funds for festival distributions. **ἦν δ' οὗτος ὁ καιρὸς αὐτός** "that moment was the very one." **ἐβοηθήσαμεν:** for the switch to the first-person, see 1.2n. ἡμεῖς. **προθύμως** modifies ἐβοηθήσαμεν. The delayed delivery puts emphasis on this word (cf. 1.1n. προθύμως) and reminds the Athenians that their abandoned expedition was inadequate. **οὐκ ἂν ἠνώχλει νῦν ἡμῖν ὁ Φίλιππος σωθείς** "Philip would not now be a burden on us after his recovery." ἠνώχλει is imperf. of ἐνοχλέω.

### 6–9 Another opportunity to avoid danger

Now we have another chance. Our Olynthian allies need assistance against Philip. A war there is the only thing that can keep Philip away from Attica.

**6 τὰ ... πραχθέντα οὐκ ἄν ἄλλως ἔχοι** "what has been done could not be changed." This truism appears in much the same form in the *Prooemia* (30.2, 41.1); the thought appears already in H. *Il.* 18.112 (and cf. D. 18.192). **ἑτέρου πολέμου καιρός:** the phrase picks up on καιρός in §5; the Athenians missed one chance but now have another, and should act promptly. Cf. D. 24.95 (D. argues for swift dispatches of expeditions) δυναίμεθα καὶ τοῖς τοῦ πολέμου καιροῖς ἀκολουθεῖν καὶ μηδενὸς ὑστερίζειν. **περὶ τούτων:** i.e., the earlier missed opportunity described in §§4–5. **τί δὴ χρησόμεθα ... τούτωι;** "what use shall we make of this?" **παντὶ σθένει κατὰ τὸ δυνατόν:** this phrase appears regularly in inscribed treaties, e.g., *IG* II² 43.50–1 = *GHI* no. 22 (the charter for the second Athenian League, 378/7 BC), *IG* II² 116.16–17 and 26–7 = *GHI* no. 44 (alliance between Athens and Thessalians, 361/0); it must be a verbatim quotation from a treaty of alliance between Athens and the Chalcidians. In classical literary prose σθένος is rarely attested, and only in poetic contexts or in the phrase παντὶ σθένει (Sandys 1897: 191). This speech refers specifically to the Olynthians as allies (§2 τοὺς συμμάχους σώσομεν, §16 σώσειν ὑπισχνούμεθα), but it is not clear when this alliance would have been made and whether it was in existence when the first two *Olynthiacs* were delivered (Tuplin 1998: 277, cf. Psoma 2001: 244–5). Two badly preserved inscriptions from roughly this period attest to an Athenian alliance with the Chalcidians (*IG* II³ 388 and 489; see Lambert 2012: 185, 2010: 154). **ὃν τρόπον ὑμεῖς ἐστρατηγηκότες πάντα ἔσεσθε ὑπὲρ Φιλίππου** "how you will have conducted the war entirely to Philip's benefit."

**7** D. lists the recent events that have culminated in the present opportunity for action. The individual points are set out quickly and simply, without particles or connectives (asyndeton); each item in the list begins with a verb (ὑπῆρχον, ἐπράξαμεν, ἦν, ἐκπολεμῶσαι), and the effect is one of rapid accumulation (cf. Usher 1999: 224–5). **ὑπῆρχον Ὀλύνθιοι δύναμίν τινα κεκτημένοι** "the Olynthians were already in possession of a considerable force" (LSJ ὑπάρχω B I 5); 2.1n. δύναμιν. **διέκειθ' οὕτω τὰ πράγματα** "the situation was like this." **ἐθάρρει** "trust" or "have confidence in." For the background see 2.1n. τάς. **ἐπράξαμεν ἡμεῖς:** sc. πρὸς τούτους εἰρήνην; the phrasing emphasizes the reciprocity. In 352 D. referred to a recent peace treaty and a prospective alliance between Athens and the Olynthians (23.109 [οἱ Ὀλύνθιοι] ὑμᾶς ... φίλους πεποίηνται, φασὶ δὲ καὶ συμμάχους ποιήσεσθαι), and we know little else about this; see *HM* 298. **ὥσπερ ἐμπόδισμά τι** "some obstacle, as it were." **πόλιν μεγάλην ... διηλλαγμένην πρὸς ἡμᾶς** "that a powerful city on good terms with us was watching for opportunities from him." **ἐφορμεῖν:** a naval term for a fleet watching a position; for the metaphorical usage cf. S. *OC* 812. The infinitive explains τοῦτο. **ἐκπολεμῶσαι δεῖν**

ᾠόμεθα τοὺς ἀνθρώπους ἐκ παντὸς τρόπου "we thought [we] must embroil those people in war by any means," i.e., a war with Philip; cf. 1.7n. Ὀλυνθίους. ἐθρύλουν: 1.7n. ἐθρύλουν. ὁπωσδήποτε "somehow or another." The final position is emphatic and underlines D.'s point that the Athenians should have been involved in the war already. Cf. 1.7 γέγονεν αὐτόματον. **8 τί οὖν ὑπόλοιπον;** sc. ἐστί. The initial interrogative and οὖν and the vocative all mark the end of the asyndetic list of arguments in §7 and impart a sense of impatience. Cf. D. 21.99. **ἐρρωμένως καὶ προθύμως:** the former refers to physical strength, the latter to attitude. **ἐγὼ μὲν οὐχ ὁρῶ:** a favorite formulaic response to D.'s own rhetorical questions (8.37, 18.284, 20.28, 21.158, 23.137; not elsewhere in the orators). **χωρὶς γὰρ τῆς περιστάσης ἂν ἡμᾶς αἰσχύνης** "aside from the shame that would come upon us" (LSJ περιίστημι B I 2). Cf. the similar phrasing and argument, that neglect of allies is dangerous for the city, at 19.283 χωρὶς τῆς ἄλλης αἰσχύνης καὶ ἀδοξίας … καὶ μεγάλοι κίνδυνοι περιεστᾶσιν ἐκ τούτων τὴν πόλιν, and see Hunt 2010: 191, 1.24n. εἶτ'. **εἰ καθυφείμεθά τι τῶν πραγμάτων** "if we should betray any of our interests"; 1.14n. καθ'. καθυφίημι has a traitorous sense suggesting more than simple negligence (MacDowell 2000: 206). **οὐδὲ τὸν φόβον … μικρὸν ὁρῶ τὸν τῶν μετὰ ταῦτα** "I perceive that the fear for future repercussions [is] also considerable." Construe οὐδέ with μικρόν (for the litotes see 1.23n. οὐδέν). The three following conditional genitives absolute form a tricolon. **ἐχόντων μὲν ὡς ἔχουσι Θηβαίων ἡμῖν** "if the Thebans are inclined toward us as they are." Athens and Thebes were on hostile terms (see 1.26n. Θηβαῖοι) and D. suggests that Philip could take advantage of this. **ἀπειρηκότων δὲ χρήμασι Φωκέων** "and the Phocians have become bankrupt" (LSJ ἀπεῖπον IV 3c). The third Sacred War (355–346) began when Phocis appropriated the sacred funds of Delphi, but those funds ran out and there were allegations of mismanagement by the Phocian generals: see Aesch. 2.131, D. S. 16.56.3, *HM* 333. Athens had supported Phocis early in the war (1.26n. ἐάν). D.'s fears regarding Phocis were justified: in 346 the Phocians surrendered to Philip to end the Sacred War; the settlement provided Philip with a foothold in central Greece and a seat on the Amphictyonic Council (Harris 99–101). **μηδενὸς δὲ ἐμποδὼν ὄντος Φιλίππωι … πρὸς ταῦτα ἐπικλῖναι τὰ πράγματα** "and if there is nothing to stop Philip from turning toward these matters once he has control of his current situation." D. anticipates that Philip will now set his sights on central Greece after defeating Olynthus. Cf. 4.6n. πάντα. **9 ἀλλὰ μήν** signals the move from the specific details in §8 to a more general conclusion arising from them (*GP* 346–7). **εἰς τοῦτ' ἀνα-**

## 3 THIRD OLYNTHIAC 9–10

**βάλλεται ποιήσειν τὰ δέοντα** "postpones the performance of [his] duty until then." That is, until he turns toward southern Greece. The future infinitive emphasizes the notion of delay (Smyth §1865d). D. now picks up his point from §3, that the Athenians are aware of the situation but unwilling to act, and then concludes this section of the speech by reiterating the Athenians' knowledge. **ἰδεῖν ἐγγύθεν βούλεται τὰ δεινά** "he wants to witness atrocities from close by." βούλεται governs two infinitives (ἰδεῖν, ζητεῖν), each of which is in turn expanded by an accusative absolute (Smyth §2076) introduced by ἐξόν. Each pairing of accus. abs. and infin. features contrasted antithetical terms: ἰδεῖν/ἀκούειν; ἐγγύθεν/ἄλλοθι; βοηθοὺς ζητεῖν/βοηθεῖν; ἑαυτῶι/ἑτέροις; the antithesis highlights the absurdity of the Athenian policy. For the sense of τὰ δεινά, cf. Hyp. *Epit.* 17, where the sight of Macedonian atrocities (τὰ δεινά) in Thebes inspires the Athenians to fight. **ὅτι γὰρ εἰς τοῦτο περιστήσεται τὰ πράγματα** "that the situation will come to this point." **ἐὰν τὰ παρόντα προώμεθα:** 1.9n. ἀεί. **δήπου** "of course." The main clause is delayed for emphasis and the final word drives home the point. D. is fond of this particle at sentence-end: 14× in D. (e.g., §17, 9.15, 18.117) versus 3× in the other orators.

### 10–13 Change the laws

Appoint a board of lawmakers to repeal the laws regarding the financing of the military funds and the festival fund; remove the service exemptions. The existing laws harm the city because speakers who give sound advice are liable to be prosecuted.

**10 εἴποι τις ἄν:** for this rhetorical technique see 1.14n. τί. **τὸ δὲ ὅπως, τοῦτο λέγε** "how [we are to help], tell [us] that." The neuter article makes ὅπως a noun phrase (Smyth §1153g gives further examples from D.) and puts emphasis on that word: lit. "but the *how*." **μὴ ... θαυμάσητε, ἄν παράδοξον εἴπω τι:** ἄν = ἐάν. The rhetorical figure of prodiorthosis is an apology in advance for a provocative assertion and a request for patience from the audience (D. 1.26, 4.13, and 9.3 with Wooten 70 and 143). D. often uses θαυμάζω or θαυμαστός and παράδοξος in such contexts; cf. 18.199 (with Yunis 219), 24.122. **νομοθέτας καθίσατε** "appoint law-reviewers." The brief command without a connective particle is unparalleled in D. and very forceful in tone. The νομοθέται are a committee impaneled by the Assembly to review existing laws and consider replacing them with proposed alternatives; typically their activity was directed to enacting laws, and it would have been unusual (παράδοξον) for them to repeal laws. See Canevaro 2016b: 43, 2013b. **ἐν δὲ τούτοις τοῖς νομοθέταις μὴ θῆσθε νόμον μηδένα** "do not enact any law with these reviewers" (LSJ τίθημι A v and Smyth §1687c on ἐν). The law-review committees were formed from the annual panel of citizen judges (on whom see Hansen 1991: 155, 181–3); D. here addresses the δῆμος directly because the committee would be convened by the Assembly and composed of (selected) citizens. **εἰσὶ γὰρ ὑμῖν ἱκανοί:** elsewhere (in speeches for γραφὴ παρανόμων and related prosecutions arguing that new laws are inconsistent with those already on the books), D. frequently argues that there are too many laws in fourth-century Athens: 20.91, 23.87, 24.142; Thomas 1994: 128–31. **λύσατε** "repeal" (LSJ λύω II 4b).

**11 τοὺς περὶ τῶν θεωρικῶν ... καὶ τοὺς περὶ τῶν στρατευομένων ἐνίους** "the [laws] concerning the Theoric Fund and some of those concerning military service." The Theoric Fund distributed money to citizens to attend theater performances at festivals and financed significant public works such as the rebuilding of the Theater of Dionysus; its administrators had oversight of an increasingly large part of the Athenian budget beginning in the 350s, and they implemented far-reaching fiscal reforms that funneled revenues to the Theoric Fund (Csapo and Wilson 2014). This fund and the war fund (1.19n. στρατιωτικά) were financed in part by administrative surpluses, and available money from one could be diverted to the other. Thus, for instance, we have inscriptions reporting the use of war funds for festival expenses (1.20n. εἰς); and in the same year as this speech the Assembly approved a decree by Apollodorus to use available funds for military purposes ([D.] 59.4–6; D. 19.231 similarly suggests the possibility of converting Theoric Funds to the war fund). D.'s concern in this passage is with laws that allow war funds to be used for festival payments; Libanius' reference (Lib. *Arg.D.* or. 1.5) to a law preventing use of Theoric Funds for military purposes under penalty of death is erroneous and misleading (E. M. Harris 2006: 121–39). Scholars have devoted much energy to attempts to reconcile this passage with other evidence for the Theoric and war funds; cf. Sealey 256–8, Rhodes 1993: 514–15, Carey 1992: 152–6, Hansen 1976b, Rhodes 1972: 105–6. **σαφῶς οὑτωσί** "[to put it] very clearly"; cf. D. 23.35 and 53, 36.26. **οἱ μὲν τὰ στρατιωτικά ... διανέμουσι θεωρικά** "some distribute war funds to those who stay at home as festival funding." The lack of an article and the final position of θεωρικά indicate that it is a predicate (Smyth §1150). Cobet's proposal to delete it is attractive; it is unneeded for the sense and could have entered the text as a marginal note; without it the three final clauses of the sentence would be balanced by parallel verbs at the end of each. On the other hand, the construction and word order are paralleled below in ἀσφαλῆ. **οἱ δὲ τοὺς ἀτακτοῦντας ἀθῴους καθιστᾶσιν** "others make those not serving immune from prosecution." For this sense of ἀτακτέω, cf. §34 and Lycurg. 39. Festival chorus leaders, among others, were exempt from military service (Wilson 2000: 79). **εἶτα καὶ ... ποιοῦσιν** "and thus also make those who want to do their duty reluctant." This clause is parallel to the last; the same laws that exempt chorus leaders hinder political leaders who must fear prosecution (see §12n. παθεῖν) if they propose laws that curtail the prerogatives associated with festival productions and funding. The parallelism is stressed in the alliteration of ἀθῴους and ἀθυμοτέρους. τὴν τοῦ τὰ βέλτιστα λέγειν ὁδὸν ... ἀσφαλῆ "a path for giving the best advice that is safe." D. frequently describes principled political leadership in the Assembly with the phrase τὰ βέλτιστα λέγειν: e.g., 8.57 and 73, 9.2, 18.57, 19.185; see Wankel 1976: 361–3. This phrasing echoes the standard terminology of Athenian honorary decrees (e.g., IG II² 223.14 [dated 343/2] with Veligianni-Terzi 1997: 109, 283). The "path" of speech is a commonplace poetic metaphor (e.g., P. O. 1.110, A. Eu. 988–9, Ar. Knights 1015, Eur. Ph. 911), but the adjective ἀσφαλής suggests that it was still felt. τὸν γράψοντα ἃ πάντες ἴσθ' ὅτι συμφέρει ζητεῖτε "look for someone to propose what you all know to be beneficial" (9.7n. μήποτε). That is, that the war fund be used appropriately for campaign expenses and that festival appropriations be reduced.

**12 μὴ σκοπεῖτε τίς ... ὑπὲρ ὑμῶν ὑφ' ὑμῶν ἀπολέσθαι βουλήσεται** "do not look for someone who will want to be ruined by you for giving the best advice on your behalf." For the sense of ἀπολέσθαι, see below. The two prepositional phrases are juxtaposed to highlight the irrationality of the Athenians' inaction; cf. 14.31 ἐπὶ δὲ τὴν Ἑλλάδα "Ἕλλην" οὐδέν' ἂν ἐλθεῖν ἡγοῦμαι (Ronnet 50), 9.55n. μετά. **ἄλλως τε καὶ τούτου μόνου περιγίνεσθαι μέλλοντος** "in particular because there is likely to be this one result." The following three infinitives (παθεῖν, ὠφελῆσαι, ποιῆσαι) are in apposition to τούτου. **παθεῖν ἀδίκως τι κακὸν τὸν ταῦτ' εἰπόντα καὶ γράψαντα** "the one who advocates for and proposes such measures suffers some evil unjustly." τὸν ... γράψαντα is subject of παθεῖν, ὠφελῆσαι, and ποιῆσαι. D. refers obliquely here, and with ἀπολέσθαι above, to the fear of prosecution by political enemies for proposing illegal measures. A γραφὴ παρανόμων prosecution could claim that a new decree was either technically invalid for procedural reasons, or more generally not in accord with existing laws and potentially harmful or undesirable. A successful prosecution would invalidate the new proposal and impose fines, potentially very severe, on the proposer of the decree. Repeated judgments against a political leader could result in loss of citizenship, or political "destruction" (ἀπολέσθαι). See Hansen 1991: 205–12, and 1974 (in more detail). Such cases were frequent among the most active political leaders in fourth-century Athens; D.'s earliest political speeches are examples of prosecutions of this type (or. 22–23; or. 20 and 24 are closely related: Introd. §1.1, MacDowell 2009: 152–206), and his most famous court speech, On the Crown (or. 18), was presented at the peak of his career to support the defense in such a case (see Yunis 7–12). **μηδὲν δὲ ὠφελῆσαι τὰ πράγματα** "and does not help the situation." ἀλλὰ καὶ εἰς τὸ λοιπὸν μᾶλλον ἔτι ἢ νῦν "but also for the future even more than now." μᾶλλον ἔτι strengthens the comparative φοβερώτερον (Smyth §1084). τούτους τοὺς αὐτοὺς ἀξιοῦν οἵπερ καὶ τεθήκασιν "to ask those same men who proposed." D. calls for the νομοθέται (§10n. νομοθέτας) to repeal the two types of laws mentioned in §11. The scholion (Dilts 73) is mistaken in its suggestion that D. refers to a specific political opponent.

13 οὐ γάρ ἐστι δίκαιον: this main clause introduces the μέν and δέ clauses, which are parallel in structure and antithetical in sense. Contrasting opposite terms develop the antithesis: χάριν/ἀπέχθειαν, ἔβλαπτε/ἄμεινον πράξαιμεν, τότε/νῦν. τὴν μὲν χάριν, ἢ πᾶσαν ἔβλαπτε τὴν πόλιν, τοῖς τότε θεῖσιν ὑπάρχειν "that there be gratitude, [for policy] that was harmful to the whole city, toward those who proposed [the laws] then." D. refers to the laws allowing the war funds to be used for festivals and public works; cf. §11. ἥ: fem. sing. in agreement with χάριν, but referring widely to the policy or laws D. has been discussing. Similarly below δι' ἧς is in grammatical agreement with ἀπέχθειαν but refers to the policy proposals of those like D. who oppose the use of war funds for domestic purposes. τὴν δ' ἀπέχθειαν ... τῶι νῦν τὰ βέλτιστα εἰπόντι ζημίαν γενέσθαι "and that hostility is a punishment for the one who gives the best advice now." D. fears that new financial proposals regarding the war funds will be attacked as being inconsistent with existing laws regarding the Theoric Fund. He elsewhere refers to the δῆμος expressing χάρις toward his rivals and ἀπέχθεια toward himself (5.7). Similarly at 18.36 (at the end of the third Sacred War), Philip enjoys the Thebans' χάρις and Athens receives their ἀπέχθεια; cf. Pr. 38.2. πρὶν δὲ ταῦτα εὐτρεπίσαι "until you make right these matters." μηδαμῶς ... μηδένα ἀξιοῦτε τηλικοῦτον εἶναι ... μὴ δοῦναι δίκην "by no means expect anyone to be so mighty that he not pay the penalty after breaking those laws"; §12n. παθεῖν. εἰς προῦπτον κακὸν αὑτὸν ἐμβαλεῖν: προῦπτος (πρό-οπτος) describes "a calamity which one foresees as inevitable" (Barrett 1964: 404 on E. Hipp. 1366). The phrase has a proverbial ring. See Aristophon fr. 6.5 (K–A): a man marrying for the second time εἰς προῦπτον εἰδὼς αὑτὸν ἐνέβαλεν κακόν; Phoenicid. fr. 4.18 (K–A): a prostitute makes the mistake of getting involved with a philosopher, εἰς προῦπτον ... ἐμπεσοῦσα δὴ κακόν; Ath. 13.559f: men who marry younger women are εἰς προῦπτον κακὸν αὑτοὺς ἐμβάλλοντες.

### 14–20 Our duty to act

Decrees must be accompanied by action. Now we must save our allies from a barbarian aggressor. We support him by blaming each other, and we must choose the best policy even if it is difficult. The military funds should be reserved to finance the campaign. Inaction is shameful.

**14** οὐ μὴν οὐδ' ἐκεῖνό γ' ὑμᾶς ἀγνοεῖν δεῖ "nor should you fail to recognize this"; on οὐ μὴν οὐδέ see Smyth §2768 and *GP* 338–9. ψήφισμα: D. generalizes in this section about decrees for mobilization that the Athenians passed and then failed to act upon; cf. §§4–5. ἂν μὴ προσγένηται ... ὑμᾶς "if it is not supported by your willingness to do eagerly what was decreed" (ἂν = ἐάν). The articular infinitive phrase is the subject and the interlocked word-order binds it together as a unit; cf. 2.8n. συμφέρον. προθύμως is repeated from D.'s complaint in §5, and similarly delayed for emphasis. The MSS read τά γε δόξαντα, but the particle diminishes the force of the expression, and it is omitted in a papyrus (*P.Oxy.* 15.1810, 2nd cent. AD). εἰ γὰρ αὐτάρκη τὰ ψηφίσματα ἦν "if decrees were sufficient." ἀναγκάζειν and διαπράξασθαι depend upon αὐτάρκη. ἃ προσήκει: 1.6n. ἅ. περὶ ὧν γραφείη διαπράξασθαι "to achieve [those objectives] about which there were proposals." οὔτ' ἂν ὑμεῖς ... ἐπράττετε τούτων "neither would you be making many proposals and achieving few, or rather nothing, of these objectives." ἐπράττετε = διεπράττετε (2.15n. τήν). For the spontaneous effect of μᾶλλον δ' οὐδέν, see 2.2n. μᾶλλον. οὔτε Φίλιππος τοσοῦτον ὑβρίκει χρόνον "nor would Philip have abused [you] for such a long time." Sc. ἄν. The pluperfect verb stresses the continued effect of Philip's action; see Smyth §2306. On Philip's hybris see 1.23n. ὑβριστής. εἵνεκά γε ψηφισμάτων "as far as decrees are concerned" (LSJ ἕνεκα 2).

**15** τὸ γὰρ πράττειν ... τῆι τάξει "although action is later in sequence than speaking and voting." Ambitious Athenians would strive to excel in both τὸ πράττειν and τὸ λέγειν (see Denyer 2008: 95 and cf. D. 2.30, 18.57, 59, 21.190, 9.1n. πάντων); here D. repeats his main point that the Athenians' actions do not correspond to their rhetoric and decisions in the Assembly. τῆι δυνάμει "in importance" (LSJ δύναμις IV). τοῦτο = τὸ πράττειν. εἰπεῖν τὰ δέοντα παρ' ὑμῖν εἰσιν ... δυνάμενοι "there are [men] among you able to say what must be done." γνῶναι ... τὰ ῥηθέντα "judging the proposals." γνῶναι depends on ὀξύτατοι (cf. Thuc. 1.70.2, Chadwick 1996: 217). For τὰ ῥηθέντα as Assembly speeches, see D. 4.1, 5.4, *Pr.* 4.1, 9.2. καὶ πρᾶξαι δὲ δυνήσεσθε νῦν "what is more, you will be able to act now." καί ... δέ marks the final item in a series and puts stress on it (*GP* 202). ἐὰν ὀρθῶς ποιῆτε: a variation for ἐὰν τὰ δέοντα ποιῆτε.

**16** τίνα γὰρ χρόνον ἢ τίνα καιρόν; "what period of time, or what occasion?" The former noun is broad in scope, while the latter refers to a specific opportunity. D. 23.141 and 24.15 make the same distinction; on this sense of καιρός, see Race 1981: 211–12. The interrogatives begin a series of nine rhetorical questions that highlight D.'s key points and communicate a tone of urgency and exasperated impatience. For similar use of hypophora, see 1.26n. and 4.10–11 with Wooten 63–4. **οὐχ ἅπαντα μὲν ἡμῶν προείληφε τὰ χωρία ἄνθρωπος** "are not all the places ours, which that man has taken" (LSJ προλαμβάνω 2; cf. D. 18.26). For the Athenian possessions taken by Philip, see 2.2n. πόλεων. See 1.3n. ἄνθρωπος. **ταύτης ... τῆς χώρας** = Olynthus and Chalcidice. **πάντων αἴσχιστα πεισόμεθα;** "shall we [not] suffer the most shamefully of all?" αἴσχιστα is adverbial, πάντων is masc. That is, the Athenians will be the most humiliated of all those whom Philip has maltreated; cf. 1.24n. εἶτ'. **ἑτοίμως σώσειν ὑπισχνούμεθα** "we promised that we would be ready to come to their aid." See §6n. παντί. **ἐχθρός:** D. regularly uses this term to describe Philip as an object of personal hatred (e.g., 4.50, 8.3, 19.302), rather than the regular diplomatic term πολέμιος. The shortness of this and the following questions adds speed and emotional intensity. **οὐκ ἔχων τὰ ἡμέτερα;** "is he not occupying our [territories]?" **βάρβαρος:** in its simplest sense the term means "non-Greek," but by the fourth century it had acquired the further sense "rude" and "brutish" (LSJ βάρβαρος II). D. and others use it as a term of reproach for Philip (e.g., §24, 19.305 and 308 with MacDowell 2000: 339; cf. 9.31n. οὐδέ); there is no precedent for these allegations that the Macedonians are not Greek. This perception is convenient slander for D. and other opponents of Philip, who ignore the fact that the Macedonians are ethnically Greek in terms of their "ancestry, language, religion, customs" (Hatzopoulos 2011: 51; cf. J. M. Hall 2001, S. Hornblower 1996: 391–3). The label is rhetorically effective in that it assimilates Philip to the Persian kings and depicts him as a common enemy of all Greeks; see Herrman 2009b: 86–7 and Hunt 2010: 81–2. **οὐχ ὅ τι ἄν εἴποι τις;** "is he not whatever someone could say?"

**17 πάντ' ἐάσαντες ... αὐτῶι** "after permitting all that and practically supporting him in his campaign" (1.2n. μόνον). κατασκευάζω is "provide campaign equipment"; the συν- prefix sarcastically states that the Athenians are actually cooperating with Philip by refusing to take action despite his aggressions. **τότε τοὺς αἰτίους οἵτινες τούτων ζητήσομεν;** lit."then shall we look for the ones responsible for these acts, whoever [they are]?" τοὺς αἰτίους is placed at the start of the main clause for emphasis (prolepsis, cf. 1.21n. τὰ πράγματα). τότε stresses the temporal sense of the preceding participles (Smyth §2080). **αὐτοί γε** "we ourselves, at any rate." After the series of nine rhetorical questions γε "gives an air of liveliness, interest, or intensity to the opening of an answer" (*GP* 130). **σαφῶς οἶδα** "I am quite certain"; cf. D. 4.29, 22.4 and 6, 23.126. ἐγώ at the end of the period stresses D.'s individual position, in contrast with the repeated stress on ὑμεῖς in §§14–15 (6× in various cases). **ἐν τοῖς τοῦ πολέμου κινδύνοις:** cf. Lys. 2.70; the phrase may evoke the patriotic tone of the annual state funerals for the war dead and thus highlight the disgrace of cowardice. See further §36n. ἥν and notes on §24 on funeral orations and this speech. **τῶν φυγόντων οὐδεὶς ἑαυτοῦ κατηγορεῖ ... τῶν πλησίον καὶ πάντων μᾶλλον** "does any one of the deserters accuse himself? Instead [he accuses] the general and those alongside [him in battle] and everybody rather [than himself]." **ἥττηνται:** sc. πάντες, the whole army. **δήπου:** §9n. δήπου. **μένειν** "to stand firm" in battle (LSJ μένω I 1); the opposite of φεύγω. The verb may again echo Athenian funeral orations: cf. Thuc. 2.42.4 (φεύγω/ὑπομένω) with Rusten 1986: 67, D. 60.19, Hyp. *Epit.* 24. **εἰ δὲ τοῦτ' ἐποίει ἕκαστος, ἐνίκων ἄν** "if each had done this, they would have conquered." The imperfect verbs stress the "continued or habitual past act" (Smyth §2304), and the switch from the singular to the plural stresses the collective good that accrues from individual action (cf. Smyth §951).

**18 καὶ νῦν:** "so now too" (cf. D. 18.227) the Athenians should face their difficulties instead of casting blame. **οὐ λέγει τις τὰ βέλτιστα** "[suppose] someone does not offer the best advice." D. now introduces two short hypothetical suppositions that are linked by repetition of λέγει τις and βέλτιστα/βελτίω. Each is followed by brief commands (εἰπάτω, αἰτιάσθω, ποιεῖτε), and the series is delivered quickly without connectives or particles (asyndeton). D. frequently presents similar series, in which a supposition is juxtaposed with a recommendation or consequence, with multiple iterations of this structure listed in asyndeton. Cf. §34 and 21.101 with MacDowell 1990: 324, *GPS* 118–19. **αἰτιάσθω:** the verb (3rd sing. imperat.) has a legal sense and responds to κατηγορεῖ (§17). **ἕτερος λέγει τις βελτίω** "[suppose] someone else offers better advice." **ἀγαθῆι τύχηι** is a conventional phrase: "good luck" (LSJ τύχη III 4). It is a common introductory formula in Assembly decrees (e.g., Thuc. 4.118.11, *IG* II² 43.7 = *GHI* no. 22) and appears also, as here, in the context of speeches in the Assembly (e.g., D. *Pr.* 32.4, Ar. *Eccles.* 131) and as a more general wish for good auspices (e.g., Ar. *Birds* 435, *Thesmo.* 283, Pl. *Sym.* 177e). **ἀλλ' οὐχ ἡδέα ταῦτα** "but [suppose] these proposals are not agreeable." **οὐκέτι ... ἀδικεῖ** "still, [he] is not at fault." **πλὴν εἰ δέον εὔξασθαι παραλείπει:** lit. "unless he omits [a prayer] when one ought to pray." δέον is an accusative absolute. A great deal of the Assembly's time was spent on public religious business such as sacrifices and festivals, and arguments about religious matters may have been common in Assembly speeches; see Martin 2009: 222–4, Parker 1996: 123–4, cf. Connor 1988b: 171–7. D. mocks the Assembly for its punctilious observance of such matters, in contrast to the lackadaisical response to Philip. **εἰς ταὐτὸ πάνθ' ὅσα βούλεταί τις ἀθροίσαντα ἐν ὀλίγωι** "quickly mustering together as much as anyone wants." ἀθροίσαντα modifies the subject of εὔξασθαι. The phrase εἰς ταὐτὸ ἀθροίζειν describes a military muster (see Aen. Tact. 11.10 εἰς ταὐτὸ ἀθροισθέντες; cf. LSJ ἀθροίζω 1; for the κοινή psilosis see Colvin 2007: 27); the verb is only found here in D. ἐν ὀλίγωι refers to time (cf. Nic. Dam. *FGrHist* 127 F 90 §21 and Hdn. 1.10.1). D.'s use of technical military language here extends the criticism of the Athenians for their attention to prayers rather than to defense. The two prepositional phrases receive emphasis from their placement at the beginning and end of the clause: concerted (εἰς ταὐτό) quick (ἐν ὀλίγωι) action, not prayers, is exactly what D. is demanding. For prayers at the start of Assembly meetings, see 2.1n. τήν. **ἑλέσθαι** "to choose." The three infinitives in the sentence receive strong emphasis from their placement. εὔξασθαι and ἑλέσθαι begin each colon, contrasted by μέν and δέ, with the contrast further developed by their parallel syntactical function as explanations of the adjectives ῥάιδιον and εὔπορον (Smyth §2002). The third infinitive, λαμβάνειν, is here nearly synonymous with ἑλέσθαι; the pleonasm and final position of the word underscores it as D.'s main point. **ὅταν περὶ πραγμάτων προτεθῆι σκοπεῖν** "whenever there is a meeting to make a decision about [our] affairs." προτίθημι refers specifically to public debates in the Assembly (LSJ II 4; cf. D. 18.273, 4.1n. εἰ). **ἂν μὴ συναμφότερ' ἐξῆι** "if it is not possible [to obtain] both together."

**19 ἡμῖν:** the ethical dative (Smyth §1486) stresses the desirability of what follows. **καὶ τὰ θεωρικὰ ἐᾶν ... στρατιωτικούς** "both leave the Theoric Fund untouched and identify other funds for military use." D. reiterates his point that military funds should finance the campaign and not be applied to festival expenses; see §11n. τούς. **οὐχ οὗτος κρείττων;** lit. "isn't that man preferable?" D. means that the Athenians would reasonably choose this proposal from the options before them in the Assembly. **εἴποι τις ἄν:** 1.14n. τί. **φήμ' ἔγωγε, εἴπερ ἔστιν** "I agree, since in fact it is possible." For the emphatic tone of φήμ' ἔγωγε, cf. 9.8n. φήμ'. The present tense with εἴπερ communicates D.'s belief in this possibility (cf. D. 1.2; see LSJ εἴπερ II, Smyth §2246, *GP* 487–8, E. M. Harris 2006: 126–7). **ἀλλά** marks the switch from the possibility of using military funds for their designated purpose to the current reality that the Athenians misuse these funds for festival purposes. He expresses this complaint in vaguely generic terms. **εἴ τωι ποτε ἀνθρώπων ἢ γέγονεν ἢ γενήσεται** "if for any person ever it has happened or will happen." τῳ = τινι; its accent is caused by the following enclitic. **ἂν τὰ παρόντα ἀναλώσηι πρὸς ἃ μὴ δεῖ** "if he spends what is available on what is not necessary." μή has a generalizing force (cf. 1.11n. οἱ). D. regularly refers to the Athenians' military duty as τὰ δέοντα (2.3n. προτρέπειν), and here ἃ μὴ δεῖ refers to non-military expenses paid for with monies available in the war fund (for examples see 1.20n. εἰς). **τῶν ἀπόντων εὐπορῆσαι πρὸς ἃ δεῖ** "that he can draw on his losses to pay for necessities." τῶν ἀπόντων is the opposite of τὰ παρόντα and refers to money lost through frivolous spending. As above (§9n. ἰδεῖν), D. uses antithesis (also πρὸς ἃ μὴ δεῖ/πρὸς ἃ δεῖ) to point out the absurdity of the Athenians' behavior. **μέγα τοῖς τοιούτοις ὑπάρχει λόγοις ἡ παρ᾽ ἑκάστου βούλησις** "each man's desire greatly aids those sorts of speeches" (LSJ ὑπάρχω I B 4). Speeches proposing to use military funds for public festivals and the like were appealing (§18 ἡδέα). **ῥᾷστον ἁπάντων ἐστὶν αὑτὸν ἐξαπατῆσαι** "deceiving oneself is the easiest thing of all." At *Pr*. 9.1 D. similarly describes speakers in the Assembly who are not able to recognize what will truly benefit the city. Democratic ideology idealized the δῆμος for being resistant to deception (see Hesk 2001: 163–79); here D. suggests that the Assembly is failing in this role. **ὃ γὰρ βούλεται, τοῦθ᾽ ἕκαστος καὶ οἴεται** "whatever each wants, he also believes this [to be the case]." **τὰ δὲ πράγματα πολλάκις οὐχ οὕτω πέφυκεν** "but the reality is often not like that" (LSJ πρᾶγμα II 2). Cf. the similar use of πέφυκεν in D. 2.26.

**20 ὁρᾶτε ... ταῦθ᾽ οὕτως** "look at these matters in this way." **ὅπως καὶ τὰ πράγματα ἐνδέχεται** "what the circumstances allow [us to do]" (lit. "how the circumstances permit"). ὅπως introduces the three following finite verbs, each coordinated by καί. **καὶ δυνήσεσθε ἐξιέναι** "and how you will be able to go out on campaign" (1.6n. αὑτούς). **καὶ μισθὸν ἕξετε** "and receive pay." μισθός was daily pay, distinct (in the fourth century) from food allowances (σιτηρέσιον or τροφή); for amounts of payment for τροφή, see D. 4.23 and 28–29. Prolonged expeditions overseas required greater financial sacrifices from those on campaign, and the μισθός provided some compensation. See Pritchett 1971: 3–29. **οὔ τοι σωφρόνων οὐδὲ γενναίων ἐστὶν ἀνθρώπων** "it is not typical of reasonable and upstanding men." For the predicate genitive cf. D. 1.1, 16, 2.2. σώφρων describes someone with a realistic outlook (2.22n. σώφρονος); elsewhere D. uses γενναῖος to describe an ideal orator who rouses the city against dangerous enemies (18.278 ταῦτα γὰρ γενναίου καὶ ἀγαθοῦ πολίτου). τοι is extremely rare in D. (elsewhere only 4.18, [D.] 52.8, and in the combination καὶ γάρ τοι and ἐπεί τοι); here it marks the universality of the generalization in the first half of the sentence (*GP* 539 and 542; although Denniston treats it as οὔτοι here, 544). **ἐλλείποντάς τι ... τῶν τοῦ πολέμου** "after neglecting any of the war matters." ἐλλείποντας modifies the subjects of φέρειν. **εὐχερῶς τὰ τοιαῦτα ὀνείδη φέρειν** "to treat lightly the resulting disgraces." In *On the Crown* the traitor Aeschines is said to speak εὐχερῶς ("recklessly," D. 18.70) while D. himself refrains from ὀνείδη ... εὐχερῶς λέγειν ("casually reporting disgraces," 18.264). **ἐπὶ μὲν Κορινθίους καὶ Μεγαρέας ... πορεύεσθαι**: the point of the contrast (μέν and δέ) is that they are prepared to march against Greeks but not against Philip, a barbarian who is enslaving Greeks. D. must refer to recent Athenian campaigns. The Athenians and Megarians had a long-standing conflict regarding their borders, and in the late 350s the Athenians marched against Megara (Philoch. *FGrHist* 328 F 155 = Did. *in D.* 13.44–58 with Harding 2006: 246–7; cf. *IG* II³ 292 = *GHI* no. 58 and [D.] 13.32). Scholia report that Corinth aided the Megarians (100a Dilts), or that a separate dispute arose between Athens and Corinth over similar issues (100c Dilts), but we have no further information. **πόλεις Ἑλληνίδας ἀνδραποδίζεσθαι:** D. refers to the recent treatment of Amphipolis and Pydna by Philip, and the fear of similar treatment of Olynthus; see 9.22n. καταδουλοῦσθαι. **ἐφοδίων τοῖς στρατευομένοις** "[financial] provisions for those on campaign."

**21–32 Then and now**
In the past politicians considered the public good and were not demagogues, and the city flourished. Now we cannot manage our affairs even when we have no rivals among the Greeks. Our city has lost what it had, and now individual politicians flourish. The δῆμος used to control the state, but now it is content to be treated like the politicians' pet.

**21 ἵν' ἀπέχθωμαί τισιν ὑμῶν** "so that I may become an object of hatred to some of you." **τὴν ἄλλως:** sc. ὁδόν: "uselessly" (LSJ ἄλλως II 3), an Attic idiom. Cf. D. 19.181 and 336 with MacDowell 2000: 281, Pl. *Tht.* 172e. For similar adverbial accusatives cf. 1.2n. τήν and §2 τὴν πρώτην. **μηδὲν ὠφελεῖν νομίζων** "when I do not believe that I am helping at all." **δικαίου πολίτου κρίνω ... αἱρεῖσθαι** "I consider that it is the mark of a just citizen to choose security in political affairs instead of goodwill while he speaks." For the predicate genitive construction, cf. §20n. οὔ, and for the switch from προαιρέω to the simplex αἱρέομαι, see 2.15n. τήν. Elsewhere D. similarly asserts that a δίκαιος πολίτης considers only what benefits the state as a whole, not his private gain (8.52), and he used the same difference in outlook to characterize himself and his opponents in §3. This motif is common in accounts distinguishing good leaders from demagogues: Thucydides praises the γνώμη of Pericles (2.65.8), and Socrates seeks out the orator who says "what is best [for the citizens], whether it is pleasing or not" (Pl. *Grg.* 503a); see Yunis 1996: 263–8. On the theme of χάρις, see below §§22, 24, and §3n. ὁρᾶτε. **τοὺς ἐπὶ τῶν προγόνων ἡμῶν λέγοντας ἀκούω** "I hear that the orators in the time of our ancestors." τούς ... λέγοντας is the subject of χρῆσθαι in indirect statement. Cf. 4.24n. καί. **ὥσπερ ἴσως καὶ ὑμεῖς** "as, perhaps, you [have heard] too." **οἱ παριόντες ἅπαντες** "all those who come forward" to speak in the Assembly (LSJ πάρειμι [εἶμι *ibo*] III 2); cf. 2.31, 9.1. **μιμοῦνται δ' οὐ πάνυ** "although they do not at all imitate [them]." **τούτωι τῶι ἔθει καὶ τῶι τρόπωι τῆς πολιτείας χρῆσθαι** "[the orators then] used to employ this habitual mode of governing." For the hendiadys, cf. 2.20n. γνώμης. The infinitive has an imperfect sense (Smyth §1867b). Cf. 9.3n. αἱ. **τὸν Ἀριστείδην ἐκεῖνον** "that famous Aristides." Aristides son of Hipponicus, a prominent general at the time of the Persian Wars, commanded at Salamis and Plataea; see *LGPN* s.v. 32, *PAA* 165170, Rhodes 1993: 280–1, Bowie 2007: 169. He had a reputation for upstanding integrity in leadership, and was often contrasted with Themistocles, who was seen as being more concerned with personal connections and popular causes (Connor 1971: 55–6). He was known as Ἀριστείδης ὁ δίκαιος (e.g., Aesch. 3.181), and for that reason D. presents him as an example of a δίκαιος πολίτης. **τὸν Νικίαν:** Nicias son of Niceratus was a general during the Peloponnesian War, best known for the Peace of 421 named after him and for his command during the Sicilian Expedition from 415 to 413 (*LGPN* s.v. 95, *PAA* 712520). Thucydides presents him favorably, both as a commander and as an orator, the enemy of the demagogue Cleon and of the self-interested and short-sighted Alcibiades (Thuc. 4.27–8, 6.8–26, 7.86.5; Connor 1971: 140–9). For a fourth-century identification of Nicias as a good leader in contrast to corrupting demagogues, see Arist. *Ath. Pol.* 28.3 with Rhodes 1993: 351. **τὸν ὁμώνυμον ἐμαυτῶι** "my namesake." Demosthenes son of Alcisthenes was a general during the Peloponnesian War, the co-commander with Nicias of the Sicilian Expedition (*LGPN* s.v. 16, *PAA* 318425). He is not otherwise known as an orator, and D. mentions him here presumably in order "to give an impression that he himself was connected to the famous men of the past" (MacDowell 2009: 237 n. 93). **τὸν Περικλέα:** Pericles son of Xanthippus was the most important general and orator in the period leading up to the Peloponnesian War (*LGPN* s.v. 3, *PAA* 772645). Thucydides depicts him as a powerful speaker who put the good of the state before individual concerns or the immediate desires of the people (e.g., 2.60), and he famously contrasts Pericles with the leaders who came after him, because he had "foresight" (πρόνοια) and "judgment" (γνώμη), whereas they spoke "to please the people" (καθ' ἡδονὰς τῶι δήμωι, 2.65.6–10). D. names him here, like Aristides and Nicias, because of this reputation for far-seeing leadership, and other fourth-century authors similarly distinguished Pericles from the leaders who came after him; see Arist. *Ath. Pol.* 28.1 with other passages listed by Rhodes 1993: 344, E. M. Harris 2013b: 307–8 and 314–34, Connor 1971: 141–2. Cf. Pl. *Phdr.* 269a–70a and *Grg.* 502d–3d with Dodds 1959: 325–6.

**22 ἐξ οὗ δ' οἱ διερωτῶντες ὑμᾶς οὗτοι πεφήνασι ῥήτορες** "but since then these speakers have appeared who repeatedly ask you." **τί γράψω; τί ὑμῖν χαρίσωμαι;** "What should I propose? How may I please you?"; 9.7n. μήποτε. These short imaginary questions in asyndeton are lively in tone and more effective than would be another third-person statement maligning the selfish interests of contemporary orators. This rhetorical technique of parodic direct speech is rare in the Assembly speeches (Ronnet 130–1) but frequent in *On the False Embassy*; e.g., 19.320, where

Philip asks himself "how can I achieve all I want without openly lying or appearing to commit perjury?" (πῶς οὖν μήτε ψεύσωμαι φανερῶς, μήτ' ἐπιορκεῖν δόξας πάνθ' ἃ βούλομαι διαπράξωμαι;); cf. 19.22, 188– 9, 323–4, 335. **προπέποται ... τὰ τῆς πόλεως πράγματα** "the interests of the city have been handed off for momentary popularity." προπίνω is literally "drink a toast" to someone, and the verb comes to mean "give away" because after a toast the cup was handed to the honorand as a gift (LSJ προπίνω II 3; cf. Bowie 2013: 182). D. is fond of this idea (18.296, 19.139), and an ancient critic celebrates this passage as a notable metaphor ([Hermog.] *Inv.* 4.10.1–10, ps.-Longin. 32.2), but this sense is attested well before D., and the metaphor may not have been felt; see Dover 1997: 129–30. **τοιαυτὶ συμβαίνει** "these are the results"; i.e., that Philip occupies Athenian territories. The deictic iota (Smyth §333g) adds emphasis to τοιαυτί. **τούτων:** the other orators who consider their own profit and popularity instead of what is best for the city. **αἰσχρῶς:** 1.24n. εἶτ'.

**23** Dionysius of Halicarnassus (*Dem.* 21; 1st cent. BC/AD) quotes the entirety of §§23–32 to illustrate his argument for the superiority of D.'s style in comparison with Isocrates' treatment of a similar theme in *On the Peace* (8.41–50). He does not provide specific points of comparison, but singles out this passage's "energy, vehemence and feeling" (τὸ δραστήριον καὶ ἐναγώνιον καὶ ἐμπαθές, 21.4, trans. Usher 1974: 321) and goes on to describe the emotional experience of reading D.; in this passage "the reciter must feign now irony, now indignation, now rage, now fear, now solicitude, now admonition, now exhortation, everything, in fact, which the words require" (22.6 [τοὺς λόγους] ὑποκρίνεσθαι δεῖ νῦν μὲν εἰρωνευόμενον, νῦν δὲ ἀγανακτοῦντα, νῦν δὲ νεμεσῶντα, δεδιττόμενόν τε αὖ καὶ θεραπεύοντα καὶ νουθετοῦντα καὶ παρορμῶντα καὶ πάνθ', ἃ βούλεται ποιεῖν ἡ λέξις, trans. Usher 1974: 325). **καίτοι σκέψασθε** "so then, consider." καίτοι here indicates the continuation of the argument (*GP* 560). **ἅ τις ἂν κεφάλαια εἰπεῖν ἔχοι ... καὶ τῶν ἐφ' ὑμῶν:** lit. "what someone would be able to say as a summation of the accomplishments of your ancestors' time and of yours." **οὐ γὰρ ἀλλοτρίοις ὑμῖν χρωμένοις παραδείγμασιν ... ἔξεστι γενέσθαι** "it is possible for you, by following not foreign examples, but your own, ... to be prosperous." D. here recalls a standard motif in epideictic encomium, which advises its addressees to follow the example of their ancestors. Cf. Isoc. 9.77 (the Cyprian king Evagoras is presented as a model for the addressee Nicocles) οὐκ ἀλλοτρίοις παραδείγμασιν χρώμενος, ἀλλ' οἰκείοις, and Isoc. 5.113, where the author concludes his discussion of "your ancestors' [preferences] in their accomplishments" (ἐπὶ τῶν ἔργων οἱ πρόγονοι) by urging Philip to follow their example: μὴ δεῖν ἀλλοτρίοις χρῆσθαι παραδείγμασιν ἀλλ' οἰκεῖον ὑπάρχειν. See further Race 1987: 149–53.

**24** Orators in the Assembly frequently refer to a limited range of historical examples; their "picture of the Athenian empire is patriotic, nostalgic and exceedingly simple," and some of the details here connect with the idealized "official" version of Athenian history presented in the speeches each year at the state burial of the war dead (Thomas 1989: 196–237, quotation on 202). In the funeral orations those historical accounts are intended to glorify the state and assure the mourning audience that their loved ones died for a worthy cause. Those speeches stress the continuity of the Athenian tradition; here D. takes an opposite tack with the intent of shaming his audience for failing to live up to their ancestors (cf. *GPM* 108, Pritchard 2015: 100, 4.3n. ἀνάξιον, 9.41n. τῶν). **ἐκεῖνοι** = οἱ πρόγονοι. **ἐχαρίζονθ'** reiterates the theme of χάρις; see §21n. δικαίου and §3n. ὁρᾶτε. **αὐτούς** is used to avoid repetition of the relative pronoun in a new case (Smyth §2517; 9.47n. ὑφίστατο). **πέντε μὲν καὶ τετταράκοντα ἔτη ... ἑκόντων:** D. gives a round number for the period of the Delian League and Athenian empire (477–431), beginning after the Persian Wars and lasting until the start of the Peloponnesian War (cf. 9.23n. ἑβδομήκοντα). Strictly speaking, during this period the Athenians exercised more and more control over most of the Greek cities of the Aegean. What began as a voluntary defensive alliance became increasingly coercive, and this is the focus of Thucydides' famous account (1.89–117). D.'s phrasing underscores the strength of fifth-century Athens, and is consistent with other fourth-century rhetorical accounts. For the hyperbolic description of Athens "ruling the Greeks," cf. Andoc. 1.130, Lys. 34.9. The final position of ἑκόντων is emphatic; other orators similarly stress the willingness of the Greeks to follow Athens after the Persian Wars: Aesch. 3.58, Isoc. 8.30, Din. 4.37, Nouhaud 1982: 204. **πλείω δ' ἢ μύρια τάλαντ' εἰς τὴν ἀκρόπολιν ἀνήγαγον:** the treasury of the Delian League was kept on the Acropolis. "10,000 talents" is another standard detail in fourth-century accounts of Athenian resources at the start of the Peloponnesian War: cf. Isoc. 15.234, Lycurg. fr. 58 (Conomis), Nouhaud 1982: 208–9. πλείω ... ἢ could suggest a note of approximation, but it is also intended to stress the size of the sum; on such expressions see Rubincam 1979. Thuc. 2.13.3 reports a slightly lower number (or possibly much lower, depending on which textual variant one reads; see S. Hornblower 1991: 253–4). **ὑπήκουε δὲ ὁ ταύτην τὴν χώραν ἔχων αὐτοῖς βασιλεύς** "the king who occupied this land [Olynthus] obeyed them." There are no fifth-century sources to indicate that Macedonian kings paid tribute to Athens or were members of the Delian League. But neighboring states did pay tribute during the Peloponnesian War (see *IG* i[3] 61 = Meiggs and Lewis 1988: no. 65, 424/3 BC), and after the war the Macedonian king Amyntas may have joined the renewed Athenian alliance; see Harding 2006: 232. D.'s assertion is echoed in another fourth-century speech ([D.]

7.12), and the ancient commentator Didymus claims to have proved its veracity in a lost work (Did. *in D.* 12.35–7).   **βάρβαρον:** §16n. βάρβαρος.   **πολλὰ δὲ καὶ καλὰ ... στρατευόμενοι** "[fighting] both on land and at sea they raised many fine trophies, serving in the army themselves." The delayed placement of τρόπαια, with the intervening material between it and πολλὰ ... καὶ καλά, holds the attention of the audience and stresses the noun; see 1.8n. τήν and cf. §26 μεγάλην ... εὐδαιμονίαν, with Ronnet 44. αὐτοί stresses the point that the Athenians must take the field themselves; cf. 1.6n. αὐτούς and 1.9n. αὐτοί. Fourth-century orators, especially in funeral orations, frequently recall the battlefield trophies raised by fifth-century ancestors to commemorate victories over the Persian βάρβαροι; e.g., Lys. 2.20, 25, Pl. *Menex.* 240d, Isoc. 4.87, Lycurg. 73. On battlefield trophies see Pritchett 1974: 246–75.   **μόνοι δὲ ἀνθρώπων ... κατέλιπον** "they alone of mankind left behind a reputation for their accomplishment that is too great for people to envy." Athenian funeral orations often use μόνος to stress that the Athenians are unique: e.g., Thuc. 2.40.2, 40.5, 41.3, D. 60.4, Walters 1981. Fear of provoking φθόνος from the audience is another common trope in the funeral orations: e.g., Thuc. 2.35.2, Gorg. fr. B6 285.13 (Diels–Kranz), D. 60.23. On κατέλιπον cf. §36.

**25 ἐπὶ ... τῶν Ἑλληνικῶν ... ἐν δὲ τοῖς κατὰ τὴν πόλιν αὐτήν** "in Greek [affairs] ... in their [policies] within the city itself." Cf. D. 18.109 ταὐτὸ τοίνυν ἦθος ἔχων ἔν τε τοῖς κατὰ τὴν πόλιν πολιτεύμασι καὶ ἐν τοῖς Ἑλληνικοῖς φανήσομαι. On ἐπί and ἐν cf. 2.1.   **ἔν τε τοῖς κοινοῖς κἀν τοῖς ἰδίοις** "both in public and in private [policies]." The antithesis is developed below with δημοσίαι μέν and ἰδίαι δέ; for Attic prose examples of this common polar expression (a device that stresses totality by specifying two opposite extremes), see Kemmer 1903: 120–1, 170–3.   **οἰκοδομήματα καὶ κάλλη ... κατεσκεύασαν ἡμῖν** "they made for us buildings and beautiful objects, of such quality and so numerous." D. adapts an earlier version of this passage (D. 23.207) that uses closely similar phrasing but presents more detail, referring to the Propylaea and the Parthenon on the Acropolis (built during the era of Pericles in the 440s and 430s), the stoas (the most famous of which, the ποικίλη στοά, was built in the generation after the Persian Wars, before 450), and the docks and the port in Peiraeus (built during the period of the Persian Wars, in the 480s). In other earlier speeches (22.76, repeated in 24.184), D. makes a similar contrast between the "glory" (δόξα) of fifth-century Athenians that was manifest in public works and the private selfishness of fourth-century Athenians. For the same perspective cf. Pl. *Grg.* 517c and Isoc. 7.66.   **ἱερῶν καὶ τῶν ἐν τούτοις ἀναθημάτων:** here D. chooses to omit the specific examples of buildings and instead inserts this genitive phrase, somewhat awkwardly: "consisting of temples and the dedications within them." The material stored within the fifth-century temples included the treasury of the Delian League; D.'s focus here thus connects with the speech's attention to the military fund in his own day. **ὥστε μηδενὶ τῶν ἐπιγιγνομένων ὑπερβολὴν λελεῖφθαι** "such that [the possibility of] preeminence remains for none of their descendants." For the idiom see LSJ ὑπερβολή 3. **οὕτω σώφρονες ἦσαν καὶ ... μένοντες** "they were so unpretentious and completely in accord with the character of their constitution"; 2.22n. σώφρονος. For the coordination of the adjective and participle, cf. 2.26n. οὔτ'. D. used a similar phrase in §21 to praise the outlook of fifth-century orators; now he extends it to the whole δῆμος.

**26 ὥστε τὴν Ἀριστείδου καὶ τὴν Μιλτιάδου ... οὖσαν** "that one can see that the house of Aristides and that of Miltiades and those of the well-known men then are in no way more fancy than their neighbors' houses, if in fact any of you knows what [their houses] are like." In §21 D. singled out Aristides and others as examples of leaders who were more concerned about the welfare of the state than their own well-being. Now he brings in Miltiades son of Cimon (*LGPN* s.v. 13, *PAA* 653820), the Athenian general whose career culminated in the battle of Marathon (490), who was credited with leading the Athenians to victory. Like D.'s other examples in §21, Miltiades was sometimes classified as a politician who did not cater to popular whims, and in this regard he was contrasted with Themistocles (Arist. *Ath. Pol.* 28.2), whom D. included in the earlier version of this passage (23.207; cf. also Isoc. 8.75) but chooses to omit here. (For doubts about the historical accuracy of this contrast, see Rhodes 1993: 348 and Frost 1969: 110–12.) Regardless of whether Miltiades was the same type of leader as the others named in §21, already in 424 Aristophanes had paired Aristides and Miltiades as exemplary leaders to be contrasted with later demagogues (*Knights* 1325), and a decade or so later Eupolis has Solon, Miltiades, Aristides, and Pericles return to Athens from the underworld as the most esteemed leaders of Athens in its prime (*Demes* test. i K–A; Westwood 2017a: 66–70). In the Assembly speeches D. limits his selection of historical exempla to fifth-century figures, who are more relevant to the immediate democratic context (see Carey 2015: 117 on the exclusion of Solon here). **εἰ ... ἄρα:** in a conditional protasis the particle indicates that the possibility of this hypothesis has just occurred to the speaker (*GP* 35–6; e.g., D. 18.278, 317, 19.19, 21.138) and is perhaps to be doubted. In other words, since the houses are unremarkable, D. suddenly realizes his listeners may not know what they are like. The comment creates a note of extemporaneity. **τῆς τοῦ γείτονος οὐδὲν σεμνοτέραν οὖσαν:** archaeological evidence shows that houses in urban Athens were similar in size and plan; some had a specialized room for entertainment, the ἀνδρών, and that may be a sign of wealth. The Attic Stelae listing the property of Alcibiades and his associates confirm that the wealthiest Athenians in the late fifth century did not own extravagant furnishings (Pritchett 1956:

210–13; cf. 9.41n. ὑμεῖς). Although there are no remains of exceptionally large or extravagant urban dwellings in Athens, rural estates were often larger than urban homes (cf. Isoc. 7.52) and may have had more visible signs of wealth ([Xen.] *Ath. Pol.* 2.10). See Jameson 1990 (esp. 182–3) and Nevett 1999: 85–7. **οὐ γὰρ εἰς περιουσίαν ἐπράττετ᾽ αὐτοῖς τὰ τῆς πόλεως** "the affairs of the city were not conducted for them to profit"; cf. §33n. ταῖς. **τὸ κοινὸν αὔξειν** "to further the common good." The same phrase appears earlier in parallel contexts. Achilles contrasts his own interests with those of his fellow soldiers: οὐκ ἠρνούμεθ᾽ ἂν | τὸ κοινὸν αὔξειν ὧν μέτ᾽ ἐστρατευόμην (Eur. *IA* 966–7); and Alcibiades is distinguished from selfish leaders in Athens: ἐκείνου ἀεὶ τὸ κοινὸν αὔξοντος (Xen. *Hell.* 1.4.13). **ἐκ δὲ τοῦ ... διοικεῖν** "because they managed Greek affairs faithfully, and those pertaining to the gods piously, and those among themselves fairly." The extended articular infinitive has three objects. The parallelism is highlighted by the repetition τὰ μέν ... τὰ δέ ... τὰ δέ, each followed first by a topical specifier (Ἑλληνικά ... πρὸς τοὺς θεούς ... ἐν αὑτοῖς) and then by a rhyming adverb ending in -ως (homoioteleuton). On ἴσως see §34n. ἐν. **εὐδαιμονίαν:** the final word in this section of the speech receives emphasis from the delay after μεγάλην (see §24n. πολλά). It echoes the beginning of this passage in §23 and signals the conclusion of the discussion of this topic.

**27 τοῦτον τὸν τρόπον εἶχε τὰ πράγματα ἐκείνοις** "their situation was like that" (lit. "had that character"). **χρωμένοις οἷς εἶπον προστάταις** "[because they were] depending on the leaders I named." The relative pronoun is attracted to the case of προστάταις. προστάτης was a standard label for good political leaders in the fifth century (see Rhodes 1993: 97 and Connor 1971: 110–15). D. does not use the word elsewhere in this sense, but chooses it here because of its old-fashioned flavor. **ὑπὸ τῶν χρηστῶν τούτων** "thanks to these fine men." χρηστῶν is ironic; cf. D. 18.30, 89, 318. **ἆρά γε** imparts a lively tone to questions (*GP* 50). **ὁμοίως ἢ παραπλησίως;** ἤ is the preferable MS reading here (some MSS read καί instead); D. uses the same phrase in a rhetorical question with ἆρά γε at 19.63 and 307. Outside of these rhetorical questions καί is common in parallels (e.g., D. 19.196, Thuc. 1.140.1, Hdt. 3.101.3, Isoc. 7.78), and that may have led scribes and Dionysius of Halicarnassus to change the text here. **οἷς – τὰ μὲν ἄλλα σιωπῶ, πόλλ᾽ ἂν ἔχων εἰπεῖν** "as for them – I leave aside the rest, although there is much I would be able to say." After οἷς D. interrupts himself and breaks off the thought. This device (aposiopesis, see Wooten 79 on D. 4.20, Yunis 107–8 on D. 18.3) creates a sense of spontaneity. D.'s reticent and vague allusion allows him to imply that there are grounds for widespread complaint about the current situation without laboring the details (paraleipsis, 2.4n. ταῦτα). τὰ μὲν ἄλλα σιωπῶ is virtually formulaic in D. (e.g., 19.145, 175,

## 3 THIRD OLYNTHIAC 27–28

331, 20.33, 21.116, 132). ἂν ἔχων εἰπεῖν is likewise "common in D. both with and without ἄν" (MacDowell 1990: 285 on D. 21.65 discusses examples). Here ἄν gives a potential sense to the participle. **ὅσης ἅπαντες ὁρᾶτ' ἐρημίας ἐπειλημμένοι** "you all see how much room to maneuver we have gained"; sc. ἐσμέν. ἀλλ' introduces the contrast with the preceding μέν. ἐπιλαμβάνω governs the genitive ἐρημίας; ὅσης has been attracted to its case (Smyth §2522a). ἐρημία refers to an absence of competitors; cf. D. 4.49, Lys. 29.1, Lycurg. 117. The three genitives absolute that follow clarify the sense by providing details regarding the Athenians' rivals in the Greek world. **Λακεδαιμονίων μὲν ἀπολωλότων:** after the end of the Peloponnesian War in 404 the Spartans were the dominant state in Greece until they were defeated by the Thebans at Leuctra in 371 and at Mantinea in 362. **Θηβαίων δ' ἀσχόλων ὄντων** "and the Thebans are engaged" in the third Sacred War; see 1.26n. Θηβαῖοι. **τῶν δ' ἄλλων οὐδενὸς ... ἀντιτάξασθαι** "and none of the others is capable of opposing us for the top prizes." The phrase extends the imagery of a contest; cf. D. 18.66, 203, 209. **ἐξὸν δ':** the participle introduces an accusative absolute; the particle is a connective marking the transition (*GP* 162–4) to a new colon. **τὰ ἡμέτερ' αὐτῶν ἀσφαλῶς ἔχειν** "to protect our own allies." D. echoes the speech opening; see §2n. τά. **τὰ τῶν ἄλλων δίκαια βραβεύειν** "to adjudicate on the just claims of others" (LSJ δίκαιος B I 2); i.e., to serve as arbiter of justice for other Greek states.

**28 ἀπεστερήμεθα μὲν χώρας οἰκείας:** the four main clauses of the colon are delineated with μέν ... δέ ... δέ ... δέ. For the lost territories, cf. §16 and see 2.2n. πόλεων. **πλείω δ' ἢ χίλια καὶ πεντακόσια τάλαντα ἀνηλώκαμεν:** on the campaigns led by Chares to recover Amphipolis in the 350s, see 1.27n. εἰς. See also §24n. πλείω. **εἰς οὐδὲν δέον** "for no purpose." Cf. D. 4.14, 40 with Sandys 1897: 84, 115. D.'s point is that the campaign was mismanaged; Aeschines (2.71) provides more detail, referring to frivolous expenditures by Chares. On the failure of the campaign, see Cawkwell 2011: 341–3, 395–6. **οὓς δ' ἐν τῶι πολέμωι συμμάχους ... ἀπολωλέκασιν οὗτοι:** D. refers to the members of the second Athenian League founded by Athens in 378/7 in alliance with Thebes against Sparta; see 2.24n. εἰ, *IG* II$^2$ 43 = *GHI* no. 22. Many of these allies – most notably Byzantium, Cos, and Rhodes – became disaffected with the alliance and withdrew from it in the Social War in the 350s. D. exaggerates for rhetorical purposes when he describes this as a period of peace and Athenian supremacy (cf. 9.23n. ἴσχυσαν): there was no war with Sparta or Thebes, but Athens dispatched large naval forces in the Aegean and at the Hellespont (Cargill 1981: 182–4), and by the time of the Social War the League was a dead letter (Cawkwell 2011: 235–40). On the preference for recent historical examples, after the Peloponnesian War, see Grethlein 2010: 143–4. **οὗτοι** = οἱ χρηστοὶ οὗτοι

(§27). ἐχθρόν: §16n. ἐχθρός.    ἠσκήκαμεν "we have trained" (LSJ ἀσκέω II 1). The verb continues the imagery of games and contests from §27.    ἢ φρασάτω τις ἐμοὶ παρελθών "or else [if that is not the case] someone should come forward and explain for me"; 2.8n. ἤ. Speakers in court issue similar challenges to their opponents as a rhetorical display of confidence; cf. D. 19.117, Lys. 25.14.    πόθεν ἄλλοθεν ... ἢ παρ᾽ ἡμῶν αὐτῶν Φίλιππος "from what other source has Philip grown strong, other than from us ourselves"; 2.4n. ἐνθένδ᾽. The final position of Φίλιππος is emphatic and the juxtaposition with παρ᾽ ἡμῶν αὐτῶν reinforces the point that Philip's strength stems from the Athenians.

**29 ὦ τᾶν:** 1.26n. ἀλλ᾽.    εἰ ταῦτα φαύλως, τά γ᾽ ἐν αὐτῆι τῆι πόλει νῦν ἄμεινον ἔχει "perhaps these matters are in bad shape, but at least the situation in the city itself is now improving." Cf. 2.29.    καὶ τί ἂν εἰπεῖν τις ἔχοι; "what could someone name?" as examples of improvements. καί introduces an indignant question, often in response to imaginary dialogue (*GP* 309–11); e.g., 6.15, 18.282, 19.232.    τὰς ἐπάλξεις ἃς κονιῶμεν ... καὶ λήρους; "the city-walls that we plaster and the roads that we repair and the fountains and [all that] rubbish?" This list of public works paid for by the Theoric Fund echoes Plato's denunciation of politicians who ignore what is really important and pander to the immediate desires of the δῆμος: ἄνευ γὰρ σωφροσύνης καὶ δικαιοσύνης λιμένων καὶ νεωρίων καὶ τειχῶν καὶ φόρων καὶ τοιούτων φλυαριῶν ἐμπεπλήκασι τὴν πόλιν ("with no moderation or justice they have filled the city with harbors and docks and walls and tribute payments and [all] that sort of nonsense," Pl. *Grg.* 519a). See Yunis 1996: 266.    ἀποβλέψατε δή: the particle reinforces the imperative and indicates that the command arises as a logical consequence of the point just made (*GP* 216–7).    ἐκ πτωχῶν πλούσιοι γεγόνασιν "from [being] beggars have become wealthy." On ἐκ see Smyth §1688c. D. makes the same complaint about rival politicians at 8.66 (a reworking of this passage) and *Pr.* 53.3. The expression was a cliché (like "rags to riches"; cf. S. *OT* 455, Lys. 30.27, 32.17, D. 18.131) and is highlighted by the juxtaposition of the two opposites, a technique that is continued in the following clauses.    τὰς ἰδίας οἰκίας ... εἰσὶ κατεσκευασμένοι "some have built private homes that are fancier than the public buildings." D. points out the contrast between current leaders and those of the fifth century and signals the end of this section of the speech by repeating οἰκοδομήματα from §25 and σεμνότερος from §26.    ὅσωι δὲ τὰ τῆς πόλεως ... ηὔξηται "the worse the city's situation has become, the more theirs has improved." For the construction cf. 2.3n. ὅσωι. ηὔξηται is perf. of αὐξάνω.

**30 τί δή ποθ᾽**; "why ever?" (LSJ πότε III 3). For this technique of posing questions and providing an answer, cf. 2.3n. διά.    τότε μὲν πράτ-

## 3 THIRD OLYNTHIAC 30–31

τειν: the MSS read τὸ μὲν πρῶτον. Hermogenes (*Id.* 1.11.182) begins a condensed version of the sentence with τότε μέν, and the same reading appears in [D.] 13.31, a pastiche of this passage. τότε μέν makes good sense here with νῦν δέ below (§31); cf. 19.164 (also in answer to a rhetorical question). **πράττειν ... δεσπότης τῶν πολιτευομένων ἦν** "the δῆμος itself, daring to act and fight, was the master of its politicians." The striking personification of the δῆμος fighting in the field is underlined by αὐτός, which, together with στρατεύεσθαι, reiterates the point that the Athenians must not rely on mercenaries (see 1.6n. αὐτούς). D. typically uses the noun δῆμος in a narrow specific sense to describe business in the Assembly (e.g., 18.285, 19.35, 20.124), or in a broad generic sense to describe the Athenian state as a community (e.g., 15.22, 20.57), or to refer to democratic factions in Athens and elsewhere (e.g., 9.56, 20.48). This nostalgic image of the δῆμος as master of individual politicians is paralleled in other fourth-century accounts (e.g., D. 23.209–10 and Isoc. 7.26–7 with Seager 2001: 389; cf. Brock 2013: 158–9), and can be seen earlier in Aristophanes' *Knights* (e.g., 1111–14 and 1333, discussed by Kallet 2003: 137–9 and Henderson 2003: 167–8). D. stresses the inversion of this ideal when he characterizes Philip's tyranny; see 1.4nn. πάντων and δεσπότην. **κύριος αὐτὸς ἁπάντων τῶν ἀγαθῶν** "[was] itself in charge of all benefits." **ἀγαπητὸν ἦν ... μεταλαβεῖν** "each one of the other [politicians] was content to get a share of honor and administration and any benefit from the δῆμος." ἀγαπητόν is impersonal with a dative of reference; see LSJ ἀγαπητός 2 and for the dative cf. D. 45.36, 51.20. ἀρχαί are year-long political appointments (by lot or election) in the Athenian government. For the use of συν- and μετα- compounds to characterize Athenian democracy, see 2.9n. ὅταν.

**31 τοὐναντίον** "conversely"; adverbial accus. **διὰ τούτων** "by these men." **ὁ δῆμος:** in apposition to ὑμεῖς. **ἐκνενευρισμένοι** "hamstrung"; lit. "with the sinew out." Plato describes the debilitating effect of music as "cutting the sinew out of the soul" (*Rep.* 3.411b ἐκτέμηι ὥσπερ νεῦρα ἐκ τῆς ψυχῆς). In that passage ὥσπερ suggests that the metaphor "was not firmly established" (Dover 1993: 300 on Ar. *Frogs* 862; cf. ps.- Longin. 32.3) when Plato wrote the *Republic*, perhaps a generation before this speech. D.'s usage here would probably have appeared striking to his audience; his enemy Aeschines mocks D.'s portentous expressions, offering caricatures such as "the sinews of the situation have been cut away" (Aesch. 3.166 ὑποτέτμηται τὰ νεῦρα τῶν πραγμάτων). **περιηιρημένοι χρήματα, συμμάχους** "stripped of funds, allies." Paired items in asyndeton are generally unusual (*GPS* 105) but such pairings are a Demosthenic mannerism (MacDowell 1990: 301 collects examples, e.g., 18.67, 94, 100). MS A inserts καί here, but it has a tendency to insert connectives in other asyndetic pairs (e.g., 18.234 and 21.91). **ἐν ὑπηρέτου**

καὶ προσθήκης μέρει γεγένησθε "you have come to be considered as an underling and an appendage." See LSJ μέρος IV 3; cf. 2.18n. παρεῶσθαι. ἀγαπῶντες ἐὰν μεταδιδῶσι θεωρικῶν ὑμῖν "content if they give part of the Theoric Fund to you." The inversion of ἀγαπητὸν ἦν … μεταλαβεῖν (§30) draws out the absurdity of the current situation. ἀγαπάω is used similarly by Aristophanes (*Wasps* 684) and Plato (*Grg*. 483c) to characterize complaisance with corrupt leadership. βοίδια πέμψωσιν οὗτοι "they put cattle on parade." D. refers to sacrificial animals that would feed the Athenians at a festival. One scholion (146a Dilts) reports that in 356/5 the general Chares put on a parade for the Athenians that included 300 cattle for a public banquet (see Pritchett 1974: 79). Isocrates probably has this incident in mind when he complains about current religious practice (7.29 οὐδ᾿ ὁπότε μὲν δόξειεν αὐτοῖς, τριακοσίους βοῦς ἔπεμπον, "nor did they [our ancestors] put 300 cows on parade whenever it occurred to them"), and this confirms that it was a notorious event. An alternative reading is Βοηδρόμια ("they hold the Boedromion parade"), and another scholion (146b Dilts) suggests that the alternatives were ancient. If the latter reading is adopted, it is the only reference to such a procession in the classical period (Parker 2005: 463). For defense of βοίδια see MacDowell 2009: 237 n. 94 and cf. Trevett 2011: 66 n. 46. τὸ πάντων ἀνδρειότατον "most courageous of all" (lit. "manliest"); adverbial accus. The tone is sarcastic. τῶν ὑμετέρων αὐτῶν χάριν προσοφείλετε "you also offer thanks for what is your own [property]." The προσ- prefix means "in addition" (LSJ πρός E II). D. refers to public monies in the Theoric Fund. καθείρξαντες ὑμᾶς "confining you" like animals (LSJ καθείργνυμι 1). ἐπάγουσιν … χειροήθεις αὐτοῖς ποιοῦντες "they lead [you] to these [doles and parades] and tame [you], making [you] submissive to them." τιθασεύω and χειροήθης also refer to domesticated animals. For the imagery cf. Aristophanes' description of how demagogues manage the δῆμος: "they [the politicians] want you to be poor so that you may know your tamer" (Ar. *Wasps* 703–4 βούλονται γάρ σε πένητ᾿ εἶναι … ἵνα γιγνώσκῃς τὸν τιθασευτήν). Plato compares Pericles' job as a statesman to that of a herdsman (*Grg*. 516a–b).

**32 μέγα καὶ νεανικὸν φρόνημα** "a great and vigorous spirit." ὁποῖ᾿ ἄττα γὰρ ἂν τἀπιτηδεύματα … ἔχειν "whatever the daily habits of people are, that is the sort of spirit they must have too." Cf. 1.28n. ὁποῖ᾿. ταῦτα … παρ᾿ ὑμῶν βλάβη "I would not be surprised if the harm at your hands should be greater for me because I am saying these things." The asyndeton expresses emotion. On D.'s fear see §12n. παθεῖν. μὰ τὴν Δήμητρα: oaths are frequent in D. (cf. 1.23n. μά and see MacDowell 2009: 402–4, Torrance 2014: 348–9). In comedy men (never women) frequently swear by Demeter (e.g., Ar. *Acharn*. 708 and Men. *Dys*. 570), and the deity apparently has no special significance here. τῶν πεποι-

## 3 THIRD OLYNTHIAC 32-33

ἡκότων αὐτὰ γενέσθαι "than it is for those who have [actually] done them." D. refers to his political opponents. The genitive and the infinitive are introduced by the comparative (Smyth §2007), but the text may be corrupt (see apparatus). Instead of γενέσθαι, Dionysius of Halicarnassus reads ἤ ... ἑκάστωι ("than for each of those who have done"); this may be a paraphrase, but it clearly draws out the contrast between D. and the other politicians. οὐδὲ γὰρ παρρησία περὶ πάντων: D. characterizes himself as a leader who puts the interests of the state ahead of his own; see §3n. μετά. The limits on frank speech to which he alludes are the γραφὴ παρανόμων (§12n. παθεῖν) and interruptions in the Assembly (§4n. θορύβου); the latter seems most on his mind in the following sentence, with the perf. γέγονεν. D. similarly concludes the first *Philippic* by stressing the frankness of what he has said (πεπαρρησίασμαι) and voicing his worry about future repercussions for himself (4.51n. ἁπλῶς).

### 33-36 Not too late
There is still a chance for success if you apply yourselves abroad. We need a system for all to serve the city in some capacity.

**33 ἐὰν οὖν ἀλλὰ νῦν γ᾿ ἔτι ... ἐθελήσητε** "so then, if you are still willing, now at last." ἀλλὰ νῦν implies an elliptical "now [but not before]." The idiom is common in tragedy (e.g., S. *Ant.* 552, *El.* 411) but very rare in prose: see LSJ ἀλλά I 2b, *GP* 13, Smyth §2783. **ἀπαλλαγέντες τούτων τῶν ἐθῶν** "getting rid of these habits" of receiving theoric payments instead of paying for campaigns. Cf. 9.57n. τό. **στρατεύεσθαί τε καὶ πράττειν:** cf. §30n. πράττειν. **ταῖς περιουσίαις ταῖς οἴκοι ταύταις ... χρῆσθαι** "to employ these domestic surpluses as the means for benefits abroad." αἱ περιουσίαι (sc. χρημάτων) are the financial surpluses of the Athenian state (see D. 20.25 with Canevaro 2016a: 232, Kremmydas 2012: 233), which could be applied either to the military fund or the Theoric Fund (§11n. τούς). The call to use these surpluses for the public expense of war rather than as individual distributions is consistent with the description of fifth-century leaders in §26 εἰς περιουσίαν. **ἀφορμαῖς:** 2.22n. ἀφορμάς. **ἀγαθῶν** has a double sense here: it refers both to "favorable" results and to concrete assets, "wealth" abroad (LSJ ἀγαθός II 4). **ἴσως ... κτήσαισθε ἀγαθόν** "perhaps you would acquire some complete and substantial benefit." κτάομαι develops the sense of ἀγαθόν as tangible property, and its delayed position after the verb adds emphasis (cf. the similar technique in §24n. πολλά). For the repetition of ἴσως, cf. 1.19n. ἔστιν. **τῶν τοιούτων λημμάτων ἀπαλλαγείητε** "you would be rid of these [undeserved] gains." λῆμμα refers to theoric distributions and has a pejorative sense: cf. D. 5.12, where D. denies that his policies were motivated by λῆμμα, and 19.339, where a bad orator is described as one who is "corrupt and foul and predisposed to any profit" (δωροδόκου καὶ πονηροῦ καὶ παντὸς ἥττονος λήμματος). Cf. also 2.28n. τά. **τοῖς ἀσθενοῦσι παρὰ τῶν ἰατρῶν σιτίοις διδομένοις** "the foods prescribed by doctors for invalids." Frequently D. uses medical similes to assume the role of a specialized expert (2.21n.). Here he reinforces this self-characterization by describing his political opponents as ineffective doctors and the δῆμος as the victims of malpractice; see Wooten 1979: 157, 9.29n. ὥσπερ. **ἐκεῖνα οὔτ' ἰσχὺν ἐντίθησιν οὔτ' ἀποθνῄσκειν ἐᾷ** "these [foods] do not restore strength and do not aid dying." **ταῦτα ἃ νέμεσθε νῦν ὑμεῖς** "these [gains] that you share among yourselves." LSJ νέμω II 1; cf. D. 21.203 with MacDowell 1990: 408. **οὔτε τοσαῦτα ἐστὶν ὥστε ὠφέλειαν ἔχειν τινὰ διαρκῆ** "are neither sufficient to produce any lasting improvement," in contrast to the τέλειον ἀγαθόν anticipated above. **οὔτ' ἀπογνόντας ἄλλο τι πράττειν ἐᾷ** "nor do they allow [you] to do something else if you give [them] up." In other words, the distributed surplus funds are too meager to support any substantial project in and of themselves. **ἔστι ταῦτα τὴν ἑκάστου ῥᾳθυμίαν ὑμῶν ἐπαυξάνοντα** "these are the things that are amplifying the laziness of each of you." Laziness and negligence are a frequent theme in the Assembly speeches against Philip; cf. 1.10, 4.8, 9.5 and see Wooten 1979: 157 n. 5, Yunis 136. The combination of present participle and εἰμί emphasizes the adjectival nature of the participle (Smyth §1857).

**34 οὐκοῦν σὺ μισθοφορὰν λέγεις;** "are you referring to pay for military service?" οὐκοῦν introduces a question that expects a positive response and clarifies a point of detail (LSJ οὐκοῦν I, *GP* 434). D. now moves to specific aspects of his proposal for how to put surplus funds to the best use. On state military pay see §20n. καί. **φήσει τις:** 1.14n. τί; cf. §10. **καὶ παραχρῆμά γε τὴν αὐτὴν σύνταξιν ἁπάντων** "yes, and right away, [I propose] the same system for everything." For γε as "yes" see *GP* 130. For ἁπάντων as a neuter, cf. 1.20n. μίαν and §35 below, where D. outlines a system for different activities. Others take it as a masculine ("everyone"), since D. refers to different groups of Athenians here. **ἵνα ... τοῦθ' ὑπάρχοι:** lit. "so that each, getting a share of the public [funds], may be whatever the city should need." ὅτου δέοιτο is a future less vivid conditional relative protasis ("if the city should need anything," Smyth §2566), and ὑπάρχοι is assimilated to the optative (Smyth §2186c); a subjunctive would be more regular. **ἔξεστιν ἄγειν ἡσυχίαν** "[suppose] it is possible to be at peace." In this and the following two periods D. introduces an asyndetic series of three hypothetical suppositions, each of which is followed by an explanation of how his policy proposal would apply. For this rhetorical technique see §18n. οὐ. **οἴκοι μένων βελτίων** "[then each one is] better off staying at home." This personal construction is the equivalent of οἴκοι μένειν αὐτὸν βέλτιόν ἐστι (Smyth §2104). D.'s point here is that under his proposed system there would be opportunities for state payment for work in the city; below he gives the example of jury pay (§35 τοῦ δικάζειν). **τοῦ δι' ἔνδειαν ἀνάγκηι τι ποιεῖν αἰσχρὸν ἀπηλλαγμένος** "freed from [having] to do something shameful by compulsion because of poverty." D. appears to be promising more substantial payments in peace-time than the existing theoric distributions provide. **συμβαίνει τι τοιοῦτον οἷον καὶ τὰ νῦν** "[suppose] something happens such as the current events." καί reinforces οἷον (Smyth §1501a). **στρατιώτης ... ἀπὸ τῶν αὐτῶν τούτων λημμάτων** "[then each one is better off] being a soldier himself [paid] from those same distributions." D. again stresses the need for Athenian involvement in place of reliance on mercenaries; cf. §30 στρατεύεσθαι ... αὐτός. **ἔστι τις ἔξω τῆς ἡλικίας ὑμῶν** "[suppose] someone of you is not of age [to serve]." ἔξω τῆς ἡλικίας is the opposite of ἐν ἡλικίαι; see 1.28n. τούς. **ὅσα οὗτος ἀτάκτως νῦν λαμβάνων οὐκ ὠφελεῖ** "whatever amount that man gets now for not serving, he is not helping [the city]." ἀτάκτως is not being in position for battle; cf. §11n. οἱ δέ. **ταῦτ' ἐν ἴσηι τάξει ... ἃ χρὴ πράττεσθαι** "[he is better off if he is] overseeing and managing everything which must be done, getting those [payment amounts] as part of a fair system." D. refers to the opportunities for service to the state available to citizen men aged 59 and above, who were no longer liable for conscription. In their 59th year they served as public arbitrators (an administrative judicial panel; see Arist. *Ath. Pol.* 53.2–4 with Rhodes 1993: 589–91). After that they participated as before in the general institutions of the democracy, including the Assembly and the courts, for which they were paid (Hansen 1991: 150, 188–9). **ἐν ἴσηι τάξει:** the adjective would appeal to the democratic values of the audience. τὸ ἴσον ("equality") was a standard element in praises of Athens (e.g., Thuc. 2.37.1, Hyp. *Epit.* 5) and ἰσονομία ("equality before the law") was a value closely associated with the democratic rule of law; see E. M. Harris 2013b: 5–6, 136–7, S. Hornblower 1991: 455–6.

**35 οὔτ' ἀφελὼν οὔτε προσθείς, πλὴν μικρῶν** "while neither adding nor subtracting, except for small [amounts]." ἀφελών is aor. act. part. of ἀφαιρέω. D. proposes only to reallocate the budget surplus (§33), and not more substantial amounts, from the theoric distributions to the war funds. **τὴν ἀταξίαν ἀνελὼν εἰς τάξιν ἤγαγον τὴν πόλιν:** lit. "by ending the lack of service I led the city into order." The repetition of τάξις and related words in this section of the speech defines a specific theme that sets this speech apart from the other *Olynthiacs* (cf. only 1.20). The closing proposal is more specific than the conclusion of the other two speeches, which end with a general call to arms. Moreover, this specific proposal connects with that broader call to serve because D. presents it in military language: the phrase εἰς τάξιν ἤγαγον plays on a military term for drawing troops into order on the field; see Dunbar 1995: 290 on Ar.

*Birds* 400 ἄναγ' εἰς τάξιν. (Plato provides a close parallel too, similarly playing on military terminology to describe the process of creation: *Tim.* 30a εἰς τάξιν αὐτὸ ἤγαγεν ἐκ τῆς ἀταξίας, "he [the creator] put it [the world] into order from disorder.") The aorist ἤγαγον is puzzling; the past tense may refer to earlier material in the speech or to an earlier proposal in the Assembly; Sandys 1897: 222–3 points to εἶπον below and prefers the latter explanation. **τοῦ λαβεῖν** "for receiving [pay]." **τοῦ δικάζειν** "for serving as a judge"; cf. 34n. οἴκοι. **τοῦ ποιεῖν τοῦθ' ... ὅτου καιρὸς εἴη** "for doing whatever each should be capable of doing at their age, and whatever there may be opportunity for doing." The optatives are conditional ("if anyone should be capable ... if there should be some opportunity"); cf. §34n. ἵνα. **τάξιν ποιήσας**: redundantly summarizing the main point; the nominative modifies the first-person subject of ἤγαγον. **οὐκ ἔστιν ὅπου ... ὡς δεῖ νέμειν** "on no occasion did I propose that we must distribute [the pay] of those who are active to any [people] who do nothing" (LSJ ὅπου II 1). The participle ποιοῦσι without the article is indefinite (Smyth §2052a). For the interlocked word order, cf. §14n. ἄν. D. places ὡς δεῖ νέμειν at the end because the following infinitives are parallel to νέμειν. **αὐτοὺς μὲν ἀργεῖν ... καὶ ἀπορεῖν** "that [we] ourselves [must] be idle and at leisure and without means." μέν ... δέ contrasts the role of the Athenians with the mercenaries in the following clause. **ὅτι δὲ οἱ τοῦ δεῖνος νικῶσι ξένοι, ταῦτα πυνθάνεσθαι** "[that we must] be told that somebody or other's mercenaries are victorious." ταῦτα refers to the whole clause ὅτι ... ξένοι and adds emphasis. For the tone see 2.31n. ὁ, 4.10n. αὐτῶν.

**36 τὸν ποιοῦντά τι τῶν δεόντων** "the man who performs some part of your duty." D. refers to the mercenary forces. **ὑπὲρ ὑμῶν, ἀλλὰ καὶ ὑμᾶς ὑπὲρ ὑμῶν αὐτῶν ἀξιῶ**: the three instances of the pronoun (in a series of six words – there is no comparable concentration of the second-person pronoun elsewhere in surviving Greek literature) and the intensifying αὐτῶν hammer home the point that the Athenians must be self-reliant. Cf. 9.73n. ἀξίωμα. **πράττειν ταῦτα**: on πράττω and ποιέω see 9.16n. ταῦτα. **ἑτέρους τιμᾶτε**: 2.27n. τοὺς μὲν ἀξίους. **καὶ μὴ παραχωρεῖν ... τῆς τάξεως ... τῆς ἀρετῆς** "and not to abandon the post of virtue." τῆς ἀρετῆς modifies τῆς τάξεως; it is delayed for emphasis and to avoid piling up genitives. "The metaphor of the battle station" (Yunis 145) reminds the Athenians of their moral and legal obligation to do their duty for the state (see E. M. Harris 2013b: 217–22). D. frequently adds an abstract genitive qualifier to these expressions; e.g., 14.35 τὴν τάξιν τοῦ δικαίου, 15.32 τὴν τάξιν τῆς πολιτείας, 18.173 τὴν τῆς εὐνοίας τάξιν. **ἣν ὑμῖν οἱ πρόγονοι ... κατέλιπον**: lit. "that your ancestors bestowed on you after acquiring it in the course of many noble ventures." D. echoes the typical phrasing of praises of Athens at the annual state funeral orations. E.g., Lys. 2.61–2 (the war dead) καινοῖς κινδύνοις τὴν παλαιὰν ἀρετὴν τῶν προγόνων μιμησάμενοι; cf. Lys. 2.2–3 and see Todd 2007: 214 and Herrman 2004: 29, 96 on this usage of κίνδυνος. See 9.74n. οἱ. **καὶ ... κατέλιπον:** the alliteration perhaps emphasizes and binds key terms at the conclusion of the speech; for the technique, cf. Rutherford 2012: 113–18, Silk 1974: 173–87. There are very few instances in the Demosthenic corpus of comparable concentrations of consonants: cf. 2.23n. πολεμοῦσι and 9.37n. καί (the two passages are linked by content and phrasing), and 18.221, where D. summarizes his career as an advocate in the Assembly. (Other similarly dense clusters are probably unintentional: 10.5, 13.30, 24.85, 39.35, 50.6.) **σχεδὸν εἴρηκα** "I have more or less said." σχεδόν adds a tone of understatement at the end of a speech (cf. S. *Ant.* 470, *El.* 609), and the asyndeton brings the speech to a quick close after the forceful rhetoric of the preceding sentence. **ὑμεῖς δ' ἕλοισθ' ὅ τι καὶ τῆι πόλει καὶ ἅπασι συνοίσειν ὑμῖν μέλλει** "[I hope that] you may choose that which is likely to help both the city and yourselves." Without ἄν the independent optative expresses a wish (Smyth §1814). D. looks to the future with optimism, as at the end of the second *Olynthiac* (2.31n. βέλτιον; cf. 4.51n. ὅ τι πᾶσιν μέλλει συνοίσειν).

## 4 FIRST PHILIPPIC

### 1 A new perspective for debate

Our subject for deliberation is not new, and I may be forgiven for speaking first since others have not provided the best counsel in past debates.

**1** Like the first and third *Olynthiacs*, this speech, the earliest of D.'s speeches against Philip (Introd. §1.3), begins with a generic introduction that is paralleled in the collection of *Prooemia* (1.1n. and 3.1n.). The first *Prooemium*'s three sections align with §§1–3 here; at the start the correspondence is very close, but in §§2–3 here D. adapts the generic content to a live audience and specific circumstances by adding apostrophe (ὦ ἄνδρες Ἀθηναῖοι 3× in §§2–3), rhetorical questions, and historical detail. **εἰ μὲν ... προὐτίθετο ... λέγειν, ἐπισχὼν ἄν:** the participle is equivalent to an imperfect verb in a present contrary-to-fact condition ("if there were a proposal to debate concerning some new topic, I would wait"; LSJ ἐπέχω iv 2 a). The imperfect προὐτίθετο refers to the debate in progress; see 3.18n. ὅταν. **οἱ πλεῖστοι τῶν εἰωθότων** "the majority of those accustomed [to speak]" (cf. 3.1n. οὐδέν). At an earlier time, Assembly debates opened with a herald inviting anyone over the age of 50 to speak (Aesch. 1.23), but apparently this practice had ended by the time of this speech (Aesch. 3.4); see Hansen 1987: 91, 171 n. 581. D. was 33 years old when the speech was delivered in 351; his cautious opening here is a long-standing rhetorical trope of inexperienced speakers, parodied by Aristophanes a generation earlier (Ar. *Eccles.* 151–2). Any citizen was permitted to address the Assembly, but in practice a small group, perhaps some 10 or 20 politicians, were accustomed to speak often as regular participants in debate; many more spoke on rarer occasions, and here D. characterizes himself as a member of the latter group. See Hansen 1989: 123–4. **εἰ μὲν ἤρεσκέ τί μοι τῶν ὑπὸ τούτων ῥηθέντων** "if any of the proposals made by these [speakers] satisfied me." D. uses μέν and δέ to present two further present contrary-to-fact conditions. **τότ᾽ ἂν καὶ αὐτὸς ἐπειρώμην** "then I too would try." The initial adverb is emphatic, and the adverbial καί reinforces the intensifying αὐτός (similarly D. 2.6). **ἃ γιγνώσκω**: a variation for τὴν ἐμὴν γνώμην; cf. §30n. ἐπειδάν. **ἐπειδὴ δ᾽ … συμβαίνει καὶ νυνὶ σκοπεῖν** "since it happens that now too [we] are considering [topics] about which these men have often spoken before." **καὶ πρῶτος ἀναστάς** "although I am the first to rise"; LSJ καί в 9. **εἰ γὰρ ἐκ τοῦ παρεληλυθότος χρόνου … νῦν ἔδει βουλεύεσθαι** "if in the past those [orators] had advised you as they should, there would be no need now for you to deliberate." νῦν marks the switch in time in the mixed condition. ἐκ + perf. part. stresses the length of time squandered on inconclusive deliberation (LSJ II 1). Here the phrase τὰ δέοντα characterizes D. as a singular ideal political advisor (2.3n. προτρέπειν), and he draws attention to the need for good advice with a chiasmus (δέοντα … συνεβούλευσαν … ἔδει βουλεύεσθαι); contrast 1.1, where the plural ἐνίοις suggests that others too are capable of offering the best counsel (τὰ δέοντα).

## 2–12 The need for action

We should live up to our past successes. Philip has taken risks and controls our possessions in the north. If we change our approach we can recover them, because his allies and subordinates resent him. As long as we are negligent there will always be someone infringing on our interests.

**2** The generalizing opening continues; this section aligns itself closely with the stock speech-introduction in *Prooemium* 29.3. **πρῶτον μὲν οὖν οὐκ ἀθυμητέον**: this first point leads to a parallel second one in §3 ἔπειτα ἐνθυμητέον. On transitional μέν οὖν see 2.3n. **τοῖς παροῦσι πράγμασιν** "the present circumstances." This is an obvious place to begin an Assembly speech; cf. 2.1n. **πάνυ φαύλως ἔχειν** "to be in very bad shape"; cf. D. 2.29, 3.29, 9.1. **ὃ γάρ ἐστι χείριστον … βέλτιστον ὑπάρχει** "for the thing that is the worst of those [circumstances] in the past presents the best [prospect] for the future." The enigmatic paradox marks a transition to the first topic of the speech; see 1.4n. τοῦθ᾽, 9.5n. παράδοξον (9.5 repeats this passage almost verbatim). The chiastic arrangement of contrasting superlatives enclosing opposite time-phrases puts emphasis on the last items in the series, optimism for the future (Ronnet 59). **τί οὖν ἐστι τοῦτο;** D. highlights the riddle and varies his tone and pace with the rhetorical question and response (cf. 2.3n. διά); the specific phrasing is repeated often in the Assembly speeches (6.24, 8.7, 9.5, 22). **ὅτι οὐδέν … τὰ πράγματα ἔχει** "it is the fact that our situation is bad because you do none of your duties" (§36n. ὅτι). Above D. distinguished himself from the orators who do not provide the necessary advice; now he repeats τὰ δέοντα to associate his listeners with the bad policy of the other speakers. He characterizes himself as the only one who knows what must be done. **ἐπεί τοι, εἰ πάνθ᾽ ἃ προσῆκε πραττόντων οὕτως εἶχεν** "for indeed, if [our situation] were thus while [you] were doing all that you should." τοι adds emphasis to causal ἐπεί (cf. 3.20n. οὔ). For the tone see 1.6n. ἅ. **οὐδ᾽ ἂν ἐλπὶς ἦν** "there would not be any hope." οὐδέ is adverbial, emphatic for οὐ.

**3 ἔπειτα … ἀναμιμνηισκομένοις** "next, those [of you] who know, whether by hearing from others, or by remembering yourselves, must consider." The article makes εἰδόσιν a substantive, to be construed as the agent with ἐνθυμητέον. The repeated καί correlates two different subgroups (LSJ καί v); for these two distinct types of knowledge, cf. 3.3n. ἐξ. The verbal adj. then introduces two indirect questions; the first is a genitive absolute (ἡλίκην … Λακεδαιμονίων) and the second (ὡς … ἐπράξατε … ὑπεμείνατε) then follows without a coordinating conjunction. **ἡλίκην ποτ᾽ ἐχόντων δύναμιν Λακεδαιμονίων** "how much power the Spartans once had." The Athenians faced the Spartans when they invaded Boeotia in the early 370s; see 2.24n. εἰ. D. here refers more generally to their hegemony after the Peloponnesian War; see below on τῆι τότε ῥώμηι. **ὡς καλῶς καὶ προσηκόντως** "[and] how nobly and dutifully." The second adverb picks up προσῆκε above (§2) and contrasts the Athenians' current neglect of their own interests with their prior service on behalf of others. D. frequently pairs προσηκόντως with another strongly positive term (18.20 δικαίως, 69 εἰκότως, 19.245 ὀρθῶς). **ἀνάξιον … τῆς πόλεως:** politicians commonly use this phrase to appeal to the civic values of the audience in the Assembly or in court; e.g., Lys. 20.35, D. 18.109, 19.150, Lycurg. 40, Din. 4.41. Speakers in Athens regularly group together their contemporary audience with their more or less distant ancestors; they use the second-person pronoun in a timeless way to refer to historical events that those in attendance at the Assembly (or in the courts) could not possibly have taken part in; see Wolpert 2003: 545–9. Here D. uses this technique to highlight the failing of contemporary Athenians. On other occasions, he makes a similar criticism by pointing explicitly to the difference between Athenians past and present (e.g., 3.24n., 9.24, 36). **ἀλλ᾽ ὑπεμείνατε ὑπὲρ τῶν δικαίων τὸν πρὸς ἐκείνους πόλεμον:** ὑπὲρ τῶν δικαίων refers to the complaints of Athens and the other Greeks against the Spartans; for the phrasing and the boastful tone, see 2.24n. εἰ. The verb contributes to the patriotic tone; cf. Thuc. 2.42.4 and 3.17n. μένειν. ἴδητε … καὶ θεάσησθε: on emphatic paired synonyms see 1.14n. ἵνα. οὐδὲν οὔτε φυλαττομένοις ὑμῖν ἐστιν φοβερόν, οὔτ᾽, ἂν ὀλιγωρῆτε: οὐδέν is the subject of the two οὔτε clauses. τοιοῦτον (neuter) is parallel to φοβερόν (sc. ἐστιν again), and the conditional participle φυλαττομένοις (middle, "if you are on your guard") is syntactically parallel, though antithetical in sense, to ἂν [= ἐάν] ὀλιγωρῆτε. παραδείγμασι χρώμενοι: the pl. παραδείγμασι is predicate with the two following dative sing. nouns (ῥώμηι and ὕβρει), which are contrasted by τότε and νῦν. The pair of relative clauses develops the contrast through parallel antithetical terms: ἐκρατεῖτε/ταραττόμεθα, τοῦ προσέχειν … τὸν νοῦν/τοῦ μηδὲν φροντίζειν. The antithesis is marked by the strict parallel word order in the relative clauses. τῆι τότε ῥώμηι τῶν Λακεδαιμονίων: the Athenian activities in the early 370s occurred during the so-called Spartan hegemony, which began with the victory in the Peloponnesian War in 404 and was upheld by the King's Peace in 387, lasting until the Spartan defeat at Leuctra in 371 (cf. 9.47n. οἵ). The Athenian opposition to Sparta in 378 was closely followed by the formation of the second Athenian League (3.28n. οὕς), which, although it did not threaten Spartan supremacy on land, did eventually restore Athenian naval power in the Aegean (Sealey 55–9). τῆι νῦν ὕβρει τούτου: τούτου = Philip, who will be named in §4. This is the first reference in the speech to him or any contemporary detail; similarly at the start of the first *Olynthiac* he is contemptuously described as ἄνθρωπος before actually being named (1.3). On Philip's hybris see 1.23n. ὑβριστής. ἐκ τοῦ μηδὲν φροντίζειν ὧν ἐχρῆν "because [you] do not view any of these matters as you should"; μηδέν, not οὐδέν, because of the articular infin. (Smyth §2712). ὧν = τούτων ἅ.

**4 εἰ δέ τις ὑμῶν … οἴεται κτλ.**: D. frequently anticipates his audience's reactions in this manner (e.g., 2.22, §29, 20.25). Here he appears to recall Isoc. 4.138 (perhaps also in 2.22), a passage which similarly urges the reader not to regard the Persian king as δυσπολέμητον because of the extent of his power (Rauchenstein 1908: 10). Cf. 9.47n. οὐδέν. **τό τε πλῆθος τῆς ὑπαρχούσης αὐτῶι δυνάμεως**: Diodorus provides figures for Philip's forces for a few significant campaigns: in 358 he commanded more than 10,000 soldiers and 600 cavalry (Diod. 16.4.3, Sekunda 2010: 449, Hammond 1994: 26), and by 338 his army had grown to at least 30,000 infantry and 2000 cavalry (Diod. 16.85.5, Hammond 1994: 149), but it is impossible to determine how many of these troops were readily available as a standing force (*HM* 406–7); cf. 2.1n. δύναμιν. **τό τὰ χωρία πάντ᾽ ἀπολωλέναι τῆι πόλει**: for Philip's capture of Amphipolis, Pydna, Potidaea, and Methone, see 2.2n. πόλεων, 1.5n. Πυδναίων, 1.9n. Ποτείδαια, 1.9n. Μεθώνη, 1.12. For the rhetorical effect of the list, see

9.59n. **Μένιππος.** **τῆι πόλει:** the noun regularly refers to Athens, specifically as a political entity as opposed to an urban center or geographic territory (Hansen 2007: 193 classifies D.'s usages). **Πύδναν καὶ Ποτείδαιαν καὶ Μεθώνην:** the list of proper names and the polysyndeton (καί ... καί) highlight how much the Athenians have already lost to Philip (Ronnet 158, Wooten 53; cf. 1.9, 13). D. adds to the effect by piling on the following coordinated clauses (καὶ ... ὑπῆρχε, καὶ ... ἐβούλετο). **πάντα τὸν τόπον τοῦτον οἰκεῖον κύκλωι** "and [we held] that region all around as our own." κύκλωι modifies πάντα; for the idiom cf. Xen. *Hell.* 6.1.9 πάντα τὰ κύκλωι ἔθνη ὑπήκοα μέν ἐστιν ("the peoples all around are subject"). **αὐτονομούμενα καὶ ἐλεύθερ':** 1.23n. αὐτονόμους. Philip subdued Illyria and Paeonia in 358, just after taking the throne (*HM* 212–14). By 351 he controlled the territory of the Thracian kings Cetriporis and Amadocus (*HM* 251–3, 282–3). **μᾶλλον ἡμῖν ἐβούλετ' ἔχειν οἰκείως ἢ 'κείνωι** "[many of the peoples] preferred to be on our side rather than his."

**5 εἰ τοίνυν ὁ Φίλιππος τότε ταύτην ἔσχε τὴν γνώμην** "so then, if Philip had held this opinion then." **ἔχουσι τοσαῦτα ἐπιτειχίσματα τῆς αὑτοῦ χώρας** "because they have so many forts threatening his territory." ἔχουσι is pres. act. participle. D. imagines that Philip would view the cities listed in §4 as Athenian military outposts. D. will repeatedly employ the same metaphor to describe the threat to Athens from Philip's involvement with the tyrants of Euboea (8.37, 66, 10.68, 18.71, 87). Cf. 9.18n. τό. **ἔρημον ὄντα συμμάχων** "while he is without allies"; accus. subject of πολεμεῖν. **οὐδὲν ἂν ὧν νυνὶ πεποίηκεν ... δύναμιν:** Philip's accomplishments are stressed in two redundant apodoses (οὐδὲν ... ἔπραξεν and οὐδὲ τοσαύτην ἐκτήσατο δύναμιν) that are linked by their similar beginnings (οὐδέ, homoioarchon) and endings (-εν and -ιν, homoioteleuton) and isocolon (they differ by one syllable in length). On the sense of the verbs, see 9.16n. ταῦτα. For D.'s positive accounts of Philip, see 2.15n. πράττων. **ἆθλα τοῦ πολέμου κείμενα ἐν μέσωι** "prizes of war up for grabs." The phrase κείμενα ἐν μέσωι is used to describe prizes on offer to the winners of athletic contests; cf. H. *Il.* 18.507, Xen. *An.* 3.1.21, Arr. *An.* 2.26.7. For the metaphor of war as a contest, see 3.27nn. ὅσης and τῶν, Ronnet 169–70, Pritchard 2013: 165–6. **φύσει:** "naturally" (LSJ III). **ὑπάρχει τοῖς παροῦσι τὰ τῶν ἀπόντων** "the [property] of those who are absent belongs to those present." In this and the following clause D. highlights the contrast between Philip and the Athenians by juxtaposing opposite terms in parallel rhyming phrases; for this pair cf. 3.19, and for the technique see 3.29n. ἐκ.

**6 καὶ γάρ τοι** "in fact"; the combination introduces "a consequence or subsequent event which supports or explains what has just been said"

(MacDowell 2000: 231; cf. D. 8.66, 9.58, 18.99). **πάντα κατέστραπται**: καταστρέφομαι is a favorite verb to describe Philip (e.g., 1.12, 3.8, 18.44), repeated below in §§9, 42. **τὰ μὲν ὡς ἂν ἑλών τις ἔχοι πολέμωι**: sc. ἔχων (parallel to ποιησάμενος): "some [places] he holds as someone would do if he had taken them in war." Cf. 1.21n. οὔτε. **συμμαχεῖν καὶ προσέχειν τὸν νοῦν τούτοις**: τούτοις is to be taken with both verbs (for συμμαχεῖν with the dat., cf. S. *Ant.* 740). **οὓς ἂν ὁρῶσι**: ἄν (= ἐάν) + subj. mark an indefinite conditional relative clause (Smyth §2560). **παρεσκευασμένους καὶ πράττειν ἐθέλοντας ἃ χρή**: D. refers to Philip's preparedness and willingness to do what needs to be done. The phrasing draws out the contrast between his action and the Athenians' negligence. Already in this speech he has repeatedly pointed to the city's failure to do what is needed (§§1, 2, 3), and here and elsewhere he uses the verb παρασκευάζω in his proposals for the Athenians (e.g., 1.2, §§16, 19, 9.70). The simple contrast disregards the Athenians' inability to commit fully to campaigns in the north during and after the Social War (see Introd. §1.2).

**7 ἂν τοίνυν ... ἐπὶ τῆς τοιαύτης ἐθελήσητε γενέσθαι γνώμης** "and so, if you likewise agree to adopt this attitude." The protasis has four verbs, with ἄν [= ἐάν] repeated before the third: ἐθελήσητε ... καὶ ... ὑπάρξῃ ... ἄν ... ἐθελήσητε ... καὶ παύσησθε. γνώμη refers to the intellectual will of the speaker and the listeners, which is subject to change in accordance with reason and sound argumentation; for this concept see *GPM* 123–4. For the use of ἐπί, see MacDowell 1990: 222 (denoting "a person's internal state of mind"; cf. D. 21.213). **νῦν, ἐπειδήπερ οὐ πρότερον** "now, since you have not [done so] before." νῦν is delayed for emphasis (*GPS* 47). Cf. §44. **οὗ δεῖ καὶ δύναιτ' ἂν παρασχεῖν αὐτὸν χρήσιμον** "where he should and [where] he may be capable of making himself useful." **τὴν εἰρωνείαν** "evasiveness." εἰρωνεία refers to dissimulation, the pretense of not being sufficiently capable of serving the state (Diggle 2004: 166–7). D. anticipates that the citizens in the Assembly may seek to avoid service by claiming that they do not have the means to pay taxes or the experience to fight as well as professional soldiers. **ὁ μὲν ... εἰσφέρειν, ὁ δ' ... στρατεύεσθαι**: the ὁ μέν and ὁ δέ phrases are in apposition to ἕκαστος ὑμῶν, and the infinitives to πράττειν: "the one, if he has money, by paying taxes, and the other, if he is of age, by serving." For details as to these activities, see 1.6nn. χρήματα and αὑτούς, 1.28n. τούς. **συνελόντι δ' ἁπλῶς**: sc. εἰπεῖν: "to put it plainly" (LSJ συναιρέω 2 b). **ἂν ὑμῶν αὐτῶν ἐθελήσητε γενέσθαι** "if you resolve to gain control of yourselves" rather than rely on others; for the expression cf. 2.30. **παύσησθε αὐτὸς μὲν οὐδὲν ἕκαστος ποιήσειν ἐλπίζων** "each one of you stops hoping that he himself will do nothing." ἕκαστος often takes a plural verb (LSJ 1), and the effect here is a particular focus on the individual members of the audience in the Assembly. The placement of μέν after αὐτός marks a contrast between "he himself" and τὸν δὲ πλησίον in the next clause; πράξειν is parallel to ποιήσειν, depending upon ἐλπίζων.     **καὶ τὰ ὑμέτερα αὐτῶν κομιεῖσθε:** D. refers to the lost Athenian holdings and allies listed in §4. In contrast to the long and complex apodosis, the protasis contains three short main clauses, each beginning with καί and ending with a 2nd pl. fut. verb (καὶ ... κομιεῖσθε ... καὶ ... ἀναλήψεσθε, κ[αί] ... τιμωρήσεσθε). This change in syntactical complexity reflects D.'s larger message: if the Athenians will undertake the complicated reforms called for in the protasis, the result will be simple and direct. "Style reflects and reinforces thought" (Wooten 1977: 260, discussing this sentence).     **ἂν θεὸς θέληι:** 2.20n. ἄν.     **τὰ καταρραθυμημένα** "what you have lost through negligence." The compound verb creates a striking variation on D.'s regular terminology (Introd. §3.5): the κατα- prefix adds a pejorative note (cf. 2.6n. κατασκευάσαι), and the stem introduces the theme of Athenian laziness (§8n. διά).     **πάλιν ἀναλήψεσθε:** this redundant use of πάλιν with ἀναλαμβάνω is not uncommon; e.g., [D.] 11.21, Isoc. 8.6, Pl. *Plt.* 279a.     **κἀκεῖνον τιμωρήσεσθε:** cf. 3.1.

**8 μὴ γὰρ ... νομίζετε:** cf. 2.15, where D. employs a similar imperative (μὴ γὰρ οἴεσθε) to introduce the same point regarding the instability of Philip's internal support.     **τὰ παρόντα πεπηγέναι πράγματα ἀθάνατα:** lit. "his present circumstances are fixed so as to be immortal." The word-order and alliteration draw attention to the metaphorical use of πήγνυμι (LSJ IV).     **ἀλλὰ καὶ μισεῖ τις ἐκεῖνον** "no, many hate him." Philip's men regard him as a tyrant (cf. 1.3n. τὰ δ᾽ ἀπειλῶν). D. builds up an image of discontent by stringing together the verbs μισεῖ ... δέδιεν ... φθονεῖ in polysyndeton; all three have the same subject and object, and each adds further detail to D.'s allegation. τις is modified by τῶν ... δοκούντων, and the indefinite singular refers to a broad collective group (LSJ τις II 1); the idiom is akin to a Homeric technique that introduces anonymous speeches with τις in order to present views of the masses that differ from those of their leaders (Steiner 2010: 139–40, de Jong 1987: 82).     **καὶ τῶν πάνυ νῦν δοκούντων οἰκείως ἔχειν** "even from among those who now seem very close [to him]."     **ἅπανθ᾽ ὅσα περ κἂν ἄλλοις τισὶν ἀνθρώποις ἔνι:** lit. "all [the feelings] that are present in any other people too." ἔνι = ἔνεστι. The referent of the neuter plural is to be imagined on the basis of the preceding verbs (*GPS* 27). **κατέπτηχε** "have been in hiding." πτήσσω describes a hunted animal, birds especially, cowering in fear, and is sometimes used to characterize frightened men (Braswell 1988: 140). The extension here, from people to their feelings, is unusual and striking, and the metaphor is continued in §9. The κατα- prefix adds the sense "down" to the simplex verb.     **οὐκ**

ἔχοντα ἀποστροφήν "since they have no outlet." The noun suggests that Philip's men would act to vent their frustrations if only they had some opening to do so. The sense is similar to Hyp. *Dem.* 19, where the Greeks are said to send diplomats to Alexander only because they have no other recourse (ἀποστροφή: see LSJ II 2, Whitehead 2000: 417). διὰ τὴν ὑμετέραν βραδυτῆτα καὶ ῥαθυμίαν: the former noun refers to the delays that arise from the democratic process (cf. 3.4–5, 1.4n. πάντων); D. will propose that a standing force be maintained in the north in order to counteract these. The latter noun encapsulates D.'s recurrent complaint about the Athenians' complacency; see 3.33n. ἔστι. φημὶ δεῖν: the formula anticipates the specific proposal that will come later in the speech (§§16–22, 1.6n. φημί). ἤδη: the placement at sentence-end is strongly emphatic; cf. 2.26n. αὐτῶν, 6.33, 9.19. This short relative clause vehemently summarizes D.'s main point.

9 τὸ πρᾶγμα "the situation"; it is explained by the three following relative clauses (οἳ ... ὃς ... οἷός), the last two of which refer back to ἄνθρωπος. οἳ προελήλυθεν ἀσελγείας ἄνθρωπος "the extent of the aggression the man has reached." ἀσελγείας depends upon οἷ; see LSJ οἷ 1 and cf. D. 3.3; on the sense see 2.19n. ἀσελγεστέρους and 1.3n. ἄνθρωπος. ὃς οὐδ' αἵρεσιν ὑμῖν δίδωσι: this and the following relative clause describing Philip are parallel in structure. Each begins with a single negative statement (οὐδέ ... and οὐχ ...) that is then refuted in two clauses introduced by ἀλλά. Each pair of refutations builds in length; first ἀλλά introduces a relatively short point (ἀλλ' ἀπειλεῖ and ἀλλ' ... προσπεριβάλλεται) which is followed by a much longer one (καὶ λόγους ... λέγει and καὶ ... περιστοιχίζεται). This build-up is reinforced by the imagery: the first relative clause uses straightforward language, the second longer compounds and metaphor. ἀπειλεῖ: making threats and constantly striving to increase power (οὐχ οἷος ... μένειν) are typical characteristics of a tyrant; see 1.3n. τὰ δ' ἀπειλῶν. ὑπερηφάνους: an "arrogant, insulting, dismissive" attitude, ὑπερηφανία is often linked with ἀσέλγεια and ὕβρις (MacDowell 1990: 302–3, Diggle 2004: 445, Halliwell 2008: 33–4). ὥς φασι: 2.17n. ὥς. οὐχ οἷός ἐστιν ἔχων ἃ κατέστραπται μένειν ἐπὶ τούτων "he is not the sort to be content holding on to those [places] he has taken" (LSJ ἐπί A I 2; cf. §6n. πάντα). ἀεί τι προσπεριβάλλεται "he is constantly acquiring some new possession." περιβάλλεσθαι is "bring into one's power" (LSJ IV, D. 18.231 of Philip), and the προσ- prefix has the sense "in addition." κύκλωι πανταχῆι μέλλοντας ἡμᾶς καὶ καθημένους περιστοιχίζεται "he ensnares us on all sides as we hesitate and sit idle"; a continuation of the hunting metaphor above describing Philip's relations with his associates (§8n. κατέπτηχε). A στοῖχος is a line of poles to hold hunting-nets, and the περι- prefix reinforces the vivid image of Philip encircling the Athenians (D. reuses the imagery in 6.27, the only

other attested instance of the verb from the classical period). Cf. 2.23n. καθήμεθα, §4n. πάντα.

**10 πότ' οὖν** ... **πότε;** the particle and the questions add a sense of indignant exasperation to the vehemence expressed by the repetition; see 1.19n. ἔστιν, and for this use of οὖν, cf. D. 19.97, 267, Ronnet 70. **ἐπειδὰν τί γένηται;** "after what happens?" ἐπειδάν + subj. in an indefinite temporal clause referring to the future (Smyth §2399a). **νὴ Δία:** D. often uses νὴ Δία to mark imagined exchanges between himself and his audience (cf. D. 6.13–14, 8.7, 9, 9.68, MacDowell 2000: 269); here it designates this phrase as a possible response from his listeners. The omission of the article may add some informality to the oath (Sommerstein 2007: 128–9; cf. Dover 1997: 62–4). **νῦν** receives special stress at the start of the question; it answers πότε and flavors both the main verb and the participle: "what are we now to make of what is happening?" **τοῖς ἐλευθέροις** ... **αἰσχύνην εἶναι** "for free men shame concerning their affairs is the greatest compulsion," as compared to slaves, who are compelled by fear of physical blows (D. 8.51 expands on this passage). Athenian individuals were motivated by desire for public praise and fear of the shame of recrimination, and the Athenian state was often "addressed in the same terms as individuals" (*GPM* 227–8); cf. §42. For D.'s appeals to these values, cf. 1.24n. εἶτ'. **ἢ βούλεσθε:** this passage, down to ἕτερον Φίλιππον ποιήσετε, is quoted together with §44 by ps.-Longinus (18.1) to illustrate his discussion of the rhetorical technique of "interrogation and questions" (πεύσεις τε καὶ ἐρωτήσεις), which make speeches "more vigorous and forceful" (ἐμπρακτότερα καὶ σοβαρώτερα), and also spontaneous and convincing. **εἰπέ μοι:** a colloquialism, like ἄγε (e.g., Ar. *Wasps* 381), used regardless of the number of addressees (juxtaposed with plural also at D. 8.74, 24.57; Olson 2002: 161). **περιιόντες:** sc. κατὰ τὴν ἀγοράν (cf. D. 21.104, 25.85, Din. 4.32). The expression characterizes idle rumormongers (Wankel 1976: 823). **αὑτῶν πυνθάνεσθαι** "to ask of each other." Cf. 3.35, where the verb caps the description of the Athenians' laziness. **λέγεταί τι καινόν;** "is there any news?" For the idiom, which often has the comparative form in the same sense, see Diggle 2004: 281. **γένοιτο γὰρ ἄν τι καινότερον;** "come on, could any news be bigger?" γάρ expresses surprise at the ridiculousness of the preceding question (*GP* 79). **τὰ τῶν Ἑλλήνων διοικῶν** "managing the affairs of the Greeks," a reference to Philip's involvement in the third Sacred War. See 2.7n. Θετταλούς and 3.8n. ἀπειρηκότων.

**11 τέθνηκε Φίλιππος;** this and the next statement are sample items of gossip imagined by D. **ἀσθενεῖ:** 1.13n. ἠσθένησεν and 3.5n. ἀσθενῶν. **καὶ γὰρ ἄν οὗτός τι πάθηι** "even if something does happen to him" (ἄν = ἐάν), a euphemism for death or an accident (Chadwick 1996: 231–2);

e.g., D. 20.159, Ar. *Wasps* 385, *Peace* 169–70. Cf. 2.15n. ἄν, 9.17n. εἴ, 20. **ἄνπερ οὕτω προσέχητε τοῖς πράγμασι τὸν νοῦν** "at least if you [continue to] regard the situation thus [as you have done]." For ἄνπερ (limitative, *GP* 483) introducing similar warnings, cf. D. 19.241, 24.101. **οὐδὲ γὰρ οὗτος παρὰ τὴν αὑτοῦ ῥώμην τοσοῦτον ἐπηύξηται** "for indeed this man has become powerful not so much because of his own strength." For this use of ἐπαυξάνω to describe Philip, cf. 3.33. **ὅσον παρὰ τὴν ἡμετέραν ἀμέλειαν** "as because of our negligence" (LSJ παρά c III 7). Cf. 1.9n. ηὐξήσαμεν, 2.4n. ἐνθένδ'.

**12 καίτοι καὶ τοῦτο** "and there's this too." καίτοι καί adds a new point (*GP* 560–1); cf. D. 18.122, 45.23. **τὰ τῆς τύχης** "the matters of chance." Unlike the more abstract singular in §45, here "the plural suggests successive incidents" (Jebb on S. *OT* 977; cf. Thuc. 4.55.3, Eur. *Ph.* 1202, Smyth §1299). For the sense of τύχη, see 2.2n. τῶν. **ἥπερ ἀεὶ βέλτιον ἢ ἡμεῖς ἡμῶν αὐτῶν ἐπιμελούμεθα** "[chance] which always [cares for us] better than we care for ourselves." For this cliché see 2.2n. τήν. **ἴσθ':** imperat. of οἶδα, introducing the two dependent potential optatives (ὅτι ... ἂν ... διοικήσαισθε ... οὐδὲ ... δύναισθ' ἄν). **πλησίον μὲν ὄντες:** a conditional participle: "if you had a presence there." **ἅπασιν ἂν τοῖς πράγμασιν τεταραγμένοις ἐπιστάντες ... διοικήσαισθε** "you could be on top of the whole situation if trouble has arisen." ἄν comes early in the clause to signal that ἐπιστάντες (which is not coordinated with ὄντες) is to be taken as a potential, like διοικήσαισθε. They can be translated as a pair: "and you can manage [the whole situation] however you wish." **ὡς δὲ νῦν ἔχετε** "but, as you are now" (LSJ ἔχω B II 1). **διδόντων τῶν καιρῶν Ἀμφίπολιν:** gen. abs.: "if opportunity were to present Amphipolis [to us]." For the personification see 1.2n. καιρός; for Amphipolis see 2.2n. πόλεων. The plural continues from τὰ τῆς τύχης above. **ἀπηρτημένοι καὶ ταῖς παρασκευαῖς καὶ ταῖς γνώμαις** "since you are distant both with your forces and in your thoughts"; an example of syllepsis, the rhetorical device by which a single term is to be taken in two different senses: the Athenian forces are not on the scene, and their thoughts are elsewhere too. The pairing here prepares for the following proposal, since γνώμη also refers to specific speeches in the Assembly (§30n. ἐπειδάν). The simplex verb ἀρτάω is literally "to hang" and can describe physical connections; the ἀπο- prefix negates that sense, and this compound stresses the spatial distance of the Athenians.

### 13–15 A proposal
We need a standing force at the ready.

**13 ὡς μὲν οὖν δεῖ:** this clause depends upon the following genitive absolute (ὡς ... πεπεισμένων). **ἐθέλοντας ὑπάρχειν ἅπαντας ἑτοίμως** "that [you] all be resolved in readiness"; for the emphatic placement of ἑτοίμως, cf. D. 2.13, and for the participle with ὑπάρχειν cf. D. 14.10, 15.1, 18.95, 228. ὡς ἐγνωκότων ὑμῶν καὶ πεπεισμένων "since you are aware and convinced." On paired synonyms see 1.14n. ἵνα. τὸν δὲ τρόπον τῆς παρασκευῆς: the first of four objects (καὶ τὸ πλῆθος ... καὶ πόρους ... καὶ τἄλλα) of λέγειν. ἣν ἀπαλλάξαι ἂν τῶν τοιούτων πραγμάτων ὑμᾶς "that would deliver you from such difficulties"; ἄν with the infinitive (Smyth §1848; cf. D. 2.1). καὶ τὸ πλῆθος ὅσον "and the size [of the force] that [would deliver you ...]." Sc. ἀπαλλάξαι ἂν here and with πόρους οὕστινας χρημάτων. τἄλλα ὡς ἂν μοι βέλτιστα καὶ τάχιστα δοκεῖ παρασκευασθῆναι "the rest, how I think it could be equipped most effectively and expeditiously." D. maintains a parallel structure and clarity by pulling τἄλλα out of the indirect question and into the syntax of the main clause (prolepsis, see 1.21n. τὰ πράγματα.) καὶ δή: *GP* 252 and 2.13n. καί. δεηθεὶς ὑμῶν ... τοσοῦτον "after asking just this much from you."

**14 κρίνατε:** D. regularly labels the citizens in the Assembly as judges (§15 κριταί) who choose between the rhetors and decide the best policy; cf. 1.28 and see 2.27n. τηνικαῦτα. μὴ πρότερον προλαμβάνετε "do not prejudge [my proposal]." The lack of a conjunction (asyndeton) adds force to the brief command (cf. 3.10n. νομοθέτας). ἂν ἐξ ἀρχῆς δοκῶ τινι καινὴν παρασκευὴν λέγειν "if I seem to anyone to outline an entirely new type of force" (ἄν = ἐάν). For the idiom ἐξ ἀρχῆς καινός, lit. "new from the start" (cf. English "start from scratch"), cf. Pl. *Lg.* 5.738b, D. S. 1.10.4, 12.20.1. ἀναβάλλειν με τὰ πράγματα ἡγείσθω "let him not think that I am putting off the matter." ἡγείσθω is 3rd sing. pres. imperat. mid.; the subject is to be supplied from τινι, and it is modified by μηδ'. οὐ γὰρ ... εἰς δέον λέγουσιν "for those who say 'fast' and 'today' do not speak very fittingly." Cf. 3.28n. εἰς. τά γ' ἤδη γεγενημένα: γε stresses the following ἤδη (cf. 1.2n. γ'), to emphasize the contrast with νυνί in the following noun phrase.

**15 ὃς ἂν δείξῃ:** the main verb and subject are to be understood from the preceding material: "[the one who speaks fittingly is] whoever shows." τίς πορισθεῖσα παρασκευὴ καὶ πόση καὶ πόθεν "what [type] of supplied force, and how large and from what source." The three interrogatives correspond to the three topics introduced in §13. ἕως ἂν ἢ διαλυσώμεθα πεισθέντες τὸν πόλεμον "until we either are persuaded to stop the war." πεισθέντες acknowledges the decision-making role of citizens in the Assembly. For this use of the verb, cf. D. 6.6, 8.10, 43, 15.9. τῶν ἐχθρῶν: the plural is generalizing. For the word-choice see 3.16n. ἐχθρός. οὐκέτι τοῦ λοιποῦ "at no point in the future"; genitive of time (Smyth §1444). μὴ κωλύων εἴ τις ἄλλος ἐπαγγέλλεταί τι: the particle is to be taken closely with λέγειν and is thus negated with μή.

D.'s point continues his explanation for why he has chosen to speak first in the debate (§1). ἡ μὲν οὖν ὑπόσχεσις οὕτω μεγάλη "so then, the promise is very great." D. concludes this section of the speech with a succinct summary of why he has decided to speak. His expression here reflects a trope; cf. the preface of Isocrates' *Panegyricus*, where the author refers to the "great promises" of his work: οὕτω μεγάλας ποιοῦμαι τὰς ὑποσχέσεις (4.14). τὸ δὲ πρᾶγμα ἤδη τὸν ἔλεγχον δώσει "the outcome will soon provide the proof." The term ἔλεγχος anticipates the repeated reference to the members of the Assembly as judges; as here, it is often contrasted with oral statements (e.g., 2.5n. λοιδορίαν, Hyp. *Epit.* 25). κριταί: §14n. κρίνατε.

### 16–22 A standing force of citizens

We need triremes, transport for cavalry, and supply ships, and we must be prepared to man them ourselves. We must fight continuously and not rely exclusively on mercenaries.

**16 τριήρεις πεντήκοντα:** 50 triremes is a large number of ships to keep at the ready for a single expedition (cf. 3.4n. τετταράκοντα). The ships would require several thousand rowers if they were to be dispatched (at least 8,500; Cawkwell 2011: 413), and D. does not include pay for them in his figures in §28. An inscription from 353/2 indicates that the Athenians possessed 349 triremes in total that year, but were lacking necessary equipment for many (they were able to provide the oars for only 280–290 of the 349; *IG* II² 1613.284–310 with Cawkwell 1984: 341, Gabrielsen 1994: 127–9, 147). Ships required regular maintenance out of water; as they grew older, ships were used for infantry and cavalry transport (Morrison and Coates 1986: 151–8). D. refers to transport ships in this section and adds on ships for fighting below (§22n. δεῖ). **φημὶ δεῖν:** 1.6n. **αὐτοὺς οὕτω τὰς γνώμας ἔχειν ὡς** "[you] yourselves adopt mindsets"; i.e., they must be determined in their resolve (§7n. ἄν). οὕτω and ὡς are correlative; understand a participle (ὄν in an accus. abs.) with πλευστέον (for the construction cf. Ar. *Clouds* 520–1). Lit.: "[you must] adopt mindsets just as you must sail." **ἐάν τι δέῃ:** emphatic and redundant reinforcement of the obligation expressed in δεῖν and πλευστέον; cf. 9.71n. ἄν. **εἰς ταύτας αὐτοῖς ἐμβᾶσιν:** dat. of agent with πλευστέον. **τοῖς ἡμίσεσιν τῶν ἱππέων ἱππαγωγοὺς τριήρεις** "cavalry carriers for half of the cavalry." The Athenians tried to maintain 1000 men in the cavalry in the fourth century (D. 14.13, cf. Ar. *Knights* 225, Rhodes 1993: 303), but were not always able to reach that target (Bugh 1988: 154–6). They began to use refitted triremes as horse-transport for far-flung battles starting in the Peloponnesian War (Ar. *Knights* 599, Thuc. 2.56.2, Pritchett 1991: 198, Morrison and Coates 1986: 157), but the transport proposed here for half the cavalry is much larger than earlier missions (Bugh 1982: 31–

2). For the term, cf. τριήρεις ἱππηγοί on Attic naval inscriptions: *IG* II²  1627.241 (330/29) and 1629.722 (325/4). **πλοῖα** "supply ships" as distinct from transport ships and warships (LSJ πλοῖον). **εὐτρεπίσαι:** 1.13n. πάνθ'. **17 ὑπάρχειν** "to be available." **ἐπὶ τὰς … στρατείας** "for those sudden campaigns from his homeland." The long delay of στρατείας after the article holds attention and puts emphasis on the entire phrase; cf. 1.13n. τάς. **εἰς Πύλας καὶ Χερρόνησον καὶ Ὄλυνθον καὶ ὅποι βούλεται:** the string of names in polysyndeton with the generic capping phrase reinforces the sense of Philip's boundless ambitions; cf. §4n. Πύδναν, 1.13n. καί, 1.14n. ὑφ'. For the details of these three campaigns of 352/1 see 1.13nn. ἠσθένησεν and εὐθύς, 1.26n. ἐάν. **δεῖ … [§18] ἂν ἐνδῶι καιρόν:** this long sentence features a string of dependent clauses, each subordinate to the preceding, with additional inserted parentheses. The syntax models the semantics: the Athenians must undertake a sequence of actions that will eventually lead to a new outcome. The previous sentence ended with stress on Philip's offensive raids; now this sentence with its sequence of actions and results ends with the prospect of the Athenians sailing against Philip. The slow development of the sentence, with lengthy parenthetical asides, creates an effect of improvisation (Ronnet 132) and avoids a monotonous style. It begins with a main clause followed by an indirect statement (ὡς ὑμεῖς … ἴσως ἂν ὁρμήσαιτε) with two inserted parenthetical clauses (ὥσπερ εἰς Εὔβοιαν and οὔ τοι παντελῶς … εὐκαταφρόνητόν ἐστιν); that introduces a purpose clause (ἵν' … ληφθῆι) with another parenthesis (εἴσεται γὰρ … πλείους τοῦ δέοντος); the purpose clause introduces a genitive absolute (μηδενὸς ὄντος ἐμποδὼν … ὑμῖν) and conditional protasis (ἂν ἐνδῶι καιρόν). **ἐκείνωι τοῦτο ἐν τῆι γνώμηι παραστῆσαι:** lit. "put this into his mind" (LSJ παρίστημι A II; e.g., D. 18.1, 8, 21.15 with MacDowell 1990: 239). The following ὡς clause explains τοῦτο. **τῆς ἀμελείας ταύτης τῆς ἄγαν** "this extreme neglect"; for this theme see 3.33n. ἔστι, and for the rare use of ἄγαν to modify a noun (not found in other orators), cf. D. 19.272, 45.88. **ὥσπερ εἰς Εὔβοιαν καὶ … εἰς Πύλας:** sc. ὡρμήσατε with εἰς Εὔβοιαν and ὑμᾶς ὁρμῆσαι with φασιν. For the Athenian expedition to Euboea in 357, see 1.8n. Εὐβοεῦσιν. The mission to Haliartus was more than a generation earlier; φασιν stresses that it was beyond the immediate recollection of the audience. At the outbreak of the Corinthian War, in 395, Athens sent aid to the Theban allies who were fighting off a Spartan invasion at Haliartus in Boeotia (Xen. *Hell.* 3.5.16–20, Seager in *CAH* 100); the Spartan king Lysander died in this engagement, and D. cites it elsewhere as an example of Athenian valor despite adverse circumstances (D. 18.96). The final reference to Thermopylae repeats from the previous sentence the first item in the list of Philip's attacks and prepares the way for the transition in focus from the offensive campaigns of Philip to those of Athens. **ἴσως ἂν ὁρμήσαιτε** "you may possibly make a move [away from this extreme laziness]."

**18 οὔ τοι:** the particle adds a note of generality; it suggests that this parenthetical statement is true no matter what the Athenians do. Cf. 3.20n. οὔ. **οὐδ' εἰ μὴ ποιήσαιτ' ἂν τοῦτο:** the negative οὐδέ is redundant: "even if you would not do this" (Smyth §2353 on potential opt. with εἰ and ἄν). **εὐκαταφρόνητόν ἐστιν** "[putting this fear into his mind] is [not at all] to be disregarded." **διὰ τὸν φόβον** modifies ἡσυχίαν ἔχηι. **εἰδὼς εὐτρεπεῖς ὑμᾶς** "once he [Philip] has learned that you are well equipped." Elsewhere D. often uses εὐτρεπής to describe Philip's preparations (e.g., 1.13n. πάνθ', 1.21, 18.32); the usage here points to the shift in focus from Philip's threat to the Athenians' opportunity. **εἴσεται:** fut. of οἶδα. **εἰσί ... εἰσίν:** 1.19n. ἔστιν. **οἱ πάντ' ἐξαγγέλλοντες:** D. had scouts to report on Philip (2.17n. ὡς), and it was no doubt very easy for Philip to learn of democratic deliberations in Athens (see S. Lewis 1996: 116). D. elsewhere repeatedly suggests that the actor Neoptolemus reported to Philip from Athens (5.6–8, 19.12, MacDowell 2000: 210). **πλείους:** masc. pl. nom. of πλείων. **παριδὼν ταῦτα ἀφύλακτος ληφθῆι** "he may be caught off guard if he ignores these [developments]" (LSJ παροράω II 2). **μηδενὸς ὄντος ἐμποδὼν πλεῖν:** gen. abs.: "since there will be nothing to stop you from sailing." For the idiom cf. 3.8n. μηδενός (in an opposite sense, referring to the possibility of Philip moving against Athens), Pl. *Grg.* 492b. **ἂν ἐνδῶι καιρόν** "if he gives you the opportunity."

**19 ταῦτα μέν ... δεῖν:** the repetition from the start of §17 closes off the explanation of what Athens stands to gain; D. now turns to new details. **ἃ πᾶσι δεδόχθαι φημὶ δεῖν** "that I contend [you] must all agree upon." The perfect of δοκέω describes a state of resolution arising from a political decision (LSJ II 4 b). **πρὸ δὲ τούτων:** πρό may have either a temporal sense, indicating that this small force should be put in place before the larger standing force described above, or it may be spatial, suggesting that this small force will be the first guard against attacks. **ἢ συνεχῶς πολεμήσει:** for the sense of purpose, see 1.2n. ἥτις. This smaller force will not be kept in reserve, but will rather be stationed permanently in the north. **μή μοι μυρίους μηδὲ δισμυρίους ξένους** "Please [μοι] don't [suggest] 10,000 or 20,000 mercenaries" (LSJ ξένος IV). Such prohibitions idiomatically omit the verb (e.g. Ar. *Acharn.* 345 with Olson 2002: 166). In his insistence that the citizens must fight on their own behalf, D. exaggerates for rhetorical effect the extent of Athenian reliance on paid soldiers; it is true that Athenian expeditions in the fourth century did regularly incorporate large numbers of mercenaries, but citizens were also called upon to serve. Thus, for example, at the battle of Chaeronea in 338 the Athenians are said to have numbered 3000, their mercenary troops 5000. See Pritchett 1974: 104–9 (105 n. 252 on Chaeronea).    **τὰς ἐπιστολιμαίους ταύτας δυνάμεις:** troops that were approved by the Assembly but then not sent out; see, e.g., D. 3.4–5. ἐπιστολιμαίους refers to matters put in writing; here it indicates that these forces exist only in the written records of the Assembly meetings, and that they have not actually been mobilized (cf. Ceccarelli 2013: 276–7). This sense of the adj. derives from the use of ἐπιστέλλω to describe the sending of letters (e.g., §37).    **ἀλλ᾿ ἢ τῆς πόλεως ἔσται** "no, [I propose a force] that will be the city's"; i.e., directly accountable to the city, and not to a mercenary commander.    **κἂν ὑμεῖς ἕνα ... χειροτονήσητε στρατηγόν** "and whether you elect one or more or this one or that one as general." D. stresses the importance of an Athenian commander by stringing together this rising series of generalizing phrases, culminating in the key word στρατηγόν.    **πείσεται καὶ ἀκολουθήσει:** the redundant verbs further stress the key point, that the army will be led by an Athenian.    **τροφήν:** the τροφή, or σιτηρέσιον, was funding for food and supplies, as distinct from supplementary pay (3.20n. καί). This point connects with the stress on the commander in that Athenians often tasked a mercenary general with plundering to provide for his men (Pritchett 1991: 485–95). This led to the complaint that these generals prioritized their own campaigns over those of Athens (2.28n. ἰδίους).

**20 τίς ἡ δύναμις καὶ πόση, καὶ πόθεν;** these three questions recapitulate the topics introduced in §13, and now in this section they serve as an introduction to the detailed considerations that follow: §§21–2 on the nature of the force, §§23–7 on the size, and §§28–30 on the financing of it. **πῶς ταῦτ᾿ ἐθελήσει ποιεῖν;** "how will it resolve to do these [actions]," i.e., obey and follow the Athenian leader.    **καθ᾿ ἕκαστον τούτων διεξιὼν χωρίς** "going through each of these [questions] separately." Other instances of the phrase καθ᾿ ἕκαστον διεξιέναι in the orators are negated, introducing the device of paraleipsis (Isoc. 12.55, Hyp. *Epit.* 4; cf. 2.4n. ταῦτα). Here D. pointedly uses the phrase in a positive sense to anticipate and stress the importance of all the detail to follow.    **ξένους μὲν λέγω:** D. stresses that his proposal does include mercenary forces. After these words he breaks off the thought and does not present a balancing δέ clause. Following a parenthetical interruption (καὶ ὅπως ... ἂν ἐλάττω φαίνηται), this point resumes at §21 λέγω δή. The shift in construction imparts a tone of spontaneity; see 3.27n. οἷς.    **ὅπως μή** + fut. indic. expresses a negative command; cf. D. 19.46, 92, 21.216 (Wyse 1904: 682, Smyth §1920).    **πάντ᾿ ἐλάττω νομίζοντες εἶναι τοῦ δέοντος:** D. criticizes the Athenians for maintaining that nothing they could do would be sufficient. The neut. pl. here and below (τὰ μέγιστα, τὰ μικρά, τούτοις, ἐλάττω) is used to describe the general idea of mobilizing and supporting troops (Smyth §1003). **τὰ μέγιστ' ἐν τοῖς ψηφίσμασιν αἱρούμενοι** "although you vote for the most substantial [mobilizations] in your decrees." The point is strongly linked with the following clause in its chiastic word order and pairing of opposites: τὰ μικρά responds to τὰ μέγιστα, while ἐπὶ τῶι πράττειν is emphatically juxtaposed with αἱρούμενοι. **ἐπὶ τῶι πράττειν οὐδὲ τὰ μικρὰ ποιεῖτε** "when it comes to action you do not produce even the smallest [forces]." The repetition of τὰ μικρά draws the contrast between votes and action. For the complaint see §19n. τάς. **ἂν ἐλάττω φαίνηται** "if [the mobilization] seems insufficient." ἐλάττω is repeated from above and closes off this digression.

**21 λέγω δὴ τοὺς πάντας στρατιώτας δισχιλίους** "I call for 2000 soldiers in all" (cf. 9.73n. οὐ). πᾶς in the attributive position with numbers refers to a total sum (Smyth §1174N, LSJ C II). The στρατιῶται are the army forces, in addition to the men rowing the ships and in the cavalry (§16nn. τριήρεις and τοῖς). D. refers to the standing force to be at the ready in Athens, and in §22 turns to the smaller fleet to be stationed in the north. **ἐξ ἧς ἂν τινος ὑμῖν ἡλικίας καλῶς ἔχειν δοκῆι** "from whatever age-class you decide upon." ἧς ἄν τινος = ἧστινος ἄν. D.'s phrasing echoes the formal language of Assembly decrees, which included an "enactment formula" in the prescript, ἔδοξεν τῆι βουλῆι καὶ τῶι δήμωι (*GHI* xix, e.g., *IG* II² 43.5–6 = *GHI* no. 22). For age-classes see 1.28n. τούς. **χρόνον τακτόν** "for a prescribed length of time." **ὅσον ἂν δοκῆι καλῶς ἔχειν** "for as long as [you] decide is right"; D. again defers to the authority of the Assembly in an effort to make his proposal more appealing. **ἐκ διαδοχῆς ἀλλήλοις** "in succession to one another." With the plural ἀλλήλοις D. refers to successive groups of 500 Athenians. ἐκ διαδοχῆς may be specific terminology for a sequence of military deployments; cf. Aesch. 2.168 τὰς ἄλλας τὰς ἐκ διαδοχῆς ἐξόδους ... ἐξῆλθον. **τοὺς δ' ἄλλους ξένους:** D. devotes much less attention to the role of the mercenaries in order to stress the role of the citizens (Wooten 81). **ἱππέας διακοσίους:** sc. λέγω here and again with ἱππαγωγούς below. **τούτων πεντήκοντα Ἀθηναίους τοὐλάχιστον** "50 of these, at the least, Athenian [citizens]." **ὥσπερ τοὺς πεζοὺς τὸν αὐτὸν τρόπον στρατευομένους** "serving in the same manner as the infantry"; i.e., in successive deployments for fixed lengths of time. The πεζοί are the στρατιῶται above. For τὸν αὐτὸν τρόπον with ὥσπερ, cf. D. 1.15, §39, 9.33. **ἱππαγωγούς:** §16n. τοῖς.

**22 εἶέν** "well then." A conversational interjection found frequently in dialogue (drama and Plato) and occasionally in D. (e.g., 19.6, 20.23, 75) and other orators (Antiph. 4.2.3, 5.58). It often marks that "a speaker is ready to proceed to the next point" (Barrett 1964: 215). The spelling with internal aspiration follows the orthography of ancient grammarians' editions and scholarly Byzantine MSS of tragedians and other poets (Finglass 2011: 167). The usage here is the same as in poetry (cf. LSJ), but in prose texts Byzantine scribes and modern editors have tended to write εἶεν (as if 3rd pl. opt. of εἰμί; sc. ταῦτα: "be [all] that as it may"). **ταχείας τριήρεις δέκα:** sc. λέγω. The punchy short question and answer vary the pace and keep the audience engaged. **δεῖ γάρ ... καὶ ταχειῶν τριήρων ἡμῖν** "you see, since he has a fleet, we also need swift ships." D. now introduces the additional force to be kept in preparation in the north. "Swift ships" were those in best condition for fighting, not having been converted for transport (§16n. τοῖς); Thucydides makes a similar distinction: ναῦς ... ἑξήκοντα μὲν ταχείας, τεσσαράκοντα δὲ ὁπλιταγωγούς (6.31.3), and naval records also distinguished "new" and "old" ships (καιναί and παλαιαί, e.g., *IG* II² 1604.12–29, Morrison and Williams 1968: 248). **ἀσφαλῶς ἡ δύναμις πλέηι:** the larger fleet outlined in §16. See also 1.2n. τά. **ἡ τροφή:** §19n. τροφήν. **ἐγὼ καὶ τοῦτο φράσω καὶ δείξω:** with the personal pronoun and synonymous first-person future verbs (and also the aor. subj. διδάξω) D. asserts himself as a well-informed advisor. The sentence outlines the next section of the speech; D. will discuss provisions in §§28–30, after considering the number of troops and the role of citizens in §§23–7. **διότι τηλικαύτην ἀποχρῆν οἶμαι τὴν δύναμιν** "why I think a force of this size is sufficient." **πολίτας τοὺς στρατευομένους εἶναι:** as above (§21), D. focuses on the citizen contribution, and here completely omits the mercenary contingent.

### 23–27 The size of the force

The force should be of moderate size, so that we can provide adequate support. We ourselves must serve and supervise the mercenaries. As it is, our military commanders are figureheads who do not engage in war.

**23 τοσαύτην μέν ... διὰ ταῦτα:** sc. ἀποχρῆν οἶμαι τὴν δύναμιν. D. links the opening of this discussion to the preceding section by picking up the two key topics from the last sentence and expanding them in this and the next, linked by μέν and δέ and the parallel repetition of διὰ ταῦτα ... ὅτι. **ἔνι** = ἔνεστι. **δύναμιν τὴν ἐκείνωι παραταξομένην** "a force that will stand against his" in battle. ἐκείνωι = τῆι ἐκείνου δυνάμει (for this common type of compendious comparison, cf., e.g., H. *Il.* 17.51, *Od.* 2.121, 13.89). παρατάσσω describes the battle order of Greek armies, which consisted of long lines of hoplite soldiers, and increasingly in the fourth century other types of specialized forces too, fighting alongside one another. On recent approaches to hoplite warfare, see Krentz 2013. **ληιστεύειν** can refer to pirates or privateers, or be used as a term of invective (2.19n. ληιστάς). Here it refers to small raiding parties who would forage for supplies

(Xenophon uses similar terminology to describe guerrilla missions carried out by a portion of the Spartan or Athenian armies: *Hell.* 3.4.19, 4.8.35, Pritchett 1991: 316–17; cf. de Souza 1999: 36–7). This style of fighting is unorthodox for the Athenians; D. intends to shock the Athenians out of their complacency by insisting that they adopt new tactics; see in more detail D. 9.47–52.     **τὴν πρώτην** "right now"; LSJ πρότερος B III 1, cf. 3.2n. τοῦθ'.     **αὐτήν** = δύναμιν.     **τροφή:** §19n. τροφήν.

**24 καὶ πρότερόν ποτ' ἀκούω** "I hear that at some point in the past too." D. presents the historical example as something well known (cf. §17 φασιν); the diffident phrasing in ποτ' ἀκούω avoids an appearance of erudition. Cf. 3.21, 9.48.     **ξενικὸν τρέφειν ἐν Κορίνθωι τὴν πόλιν:** Athens maintained a mercenary force in Corinth during the Corinthian War (395–387) with the support of the Athenian naval general Conon and his access to Persian gold, beginning in 393. There was no real precedent for a large force being kept at the ready under Athenian control outside of Athens for such an extended period (Pritchett 1974: 117–23), and in that regard it is a good historical model for D.'s proposal to maintain a force in the north. It had some small successes in 391 and a major one with the defeat of a Spartan division of 600 men at Lechaeum in 390. See Xen. *Hell.* 4.5.7–18, Seager in *CAH* 105–11. This success is frequently recalled by orators; e.g., D. 23.198, Aesch. 3.243, Din. 1.75 (cf. Nouhaud 1982: 340–1).     **Πολύστρατος:** little else is known of this Polystratos (*PAA* 780970, no *LGPN* entry); D. 20.84 reports that he was given citizenship by Athens, presumably for his role as a mercenary commander.     **Ἰφικράτης:** famous as the commander responsible for defeating the Spartan division in 390 (*LGPN* s.v. 4, *PAA* 542925). He fought for the Athenians in Thrace and at the Hellespont in the 380s, and at Corcyra in 373/2, and received state honors in the form of a statue in the Agora and free meals at the Prytaneum (Dem. 23.130), although he fell out of favor with Athens in the 360s (E. M. Harris 1989); he was welcomed back to Athens during the Social War and died there before 352. For an overview of his career, see Kremmydas 2012: 335–7, Worthington 1992: 243–4.     **Χαβρίας:** a general (*LGPN* s.v. 2, *PAA* 970820) often linked with Iphicrates (D. 20.84–5, Aesch. 3.243, Din. 1.75), whom he replaced in command in Corinth (D. S. 14.92.2). He was famous for various Athenian naval successes between 390 and his death in 357/6. He was praised at length for these by D. (20.75–87) and received an honorary statue in Athens (Aesch. 3.243); see Kremmydas 2012: 320–1, Worthington 1992: 244–5, Pritchett 1974: 72–7.     **αὐτοὺς ὑμᾶς συστρατεύεσθαι:** Xenophon corroborates the Athenians' active role when he describes Athenian hoplites fighting alongside the troops of these mercenary commanders (*Hell.* 4.5.13). Here the συ(ν)- prefix stresses the collaboration.     **μεθ' ὑμῶν ἐνίκων οὗτοι οἱ ξένοι καὶ ὑμεῖς μετ' ἐκείνων:** the prepositional phrases are redundant, but they delimit the chiastic arrangement. The effect is to bind the two subjects together into a single phrase that reflects their cooperation. αὐτὰ καθ' αὑτὰ τὰ ξενικά "mercenary armies alone by themselves." D. switches to the plural (neut. pl. subjects with sing. verbs στρατεύεται, νικᾶι, and οἴχεται) to make a generalization. τοὺς φίλους νικᾶι: D. picks up on the concern that mercenary generals have their own priorities (2.28n. ἰδίους). μείζους τοῦ δέοντος "stronger than they should be." The phrase is similarly used to describe Sparta as a military rival (D. 16.31, Isoc. 7.7). παρακύψαντα ἐπὶ τὸν τῆς πόλεως πόλεμον "having cast a cursory glance at the city's war." The verb is literally "make a sideways glance" and has a colloquial or derogatory tone; it is not attested before the fifth century, and the other classical attestations are all Aristophanic descriptions of women "advertising their sexual availability" by peeking out of windows after men (Austin and Olson 2004: 266). Here it suggests a tentative and inconclusive engagement with the Athenian mission. πρὸς Ἀρτάβαζον καὶ πανταχοῖ μᾶλλον οἴχεται πλέοντα "they sail off to Artabazus or anywhere rather [than attend to our war]." Artabazus, a satrap in revolt against the Persian King Artaxerxes III, was aided by the Athenian general Chares (cf. 2.28n. Λάμψακος) in a plan to acquire funding for his force from outside Athens (D. S. 16.22.1) when the city was impoverished by the Social War in 356/5. Chares' army inflicted a significant defeat on the Persian king, who threatened to come to the aid of the enemies of the Athenians; this led Athens to recall Chares and settle the Social War. See Pritchett 1974: 78–80, S. Hornblower in *CAH* 89–90, Cawkwell 2005: 179. ὁ δὲ στρατηγὸς ἀκολουθεῖ: D. highlights the absurdity of relying on mercenary generals with insufficient funding by inverting the statement at the end of §19. εἰκότως: 1.10n. εἰκότως. οὐ γὰρ ἔστιν ἄρχειν μὴ διδόντα μισθόν "one cannot command unless one provides pay."

**25** τὰς προφάσεις ἀφελεῖν: sc. ὑμᾶς. Cf. 2.27n. τάς. στρατιώτας οἰκείους ... παρακαταστήσαντας "by appointing your own citizen soldiers as overseers, so to speak, of the campaign." ἐπόπτης usually refers to priests or gods (LSJ). On ὥσπερ see 3.31n. ἐκνενευρισμένοι. τῶν στρατηγουμένων is neuter; lit. "the things that have been done by the generals." ἐπεὶ νῦν γε γέλως ... τοῖς πράγμασιν "and yet, the way we manage the situation now is a joke" (9.40n. ἐπεί). D. frequently characterizes the policy of opponents as laughable in order to preempt serious debate; e.g., §45, 19.72, Spatharas 2006: 378. εἰ γὰρ ἔροιτό τις ὑμᾶς: for the imaginary dialogue see §10n. ἤ. D. "appeal[s] to the Athenians' confidence ... and their pride" and uses this short dialogue to show that "they have been deceiving themselves" (Pearson 1981: 126). D. continues to point to the absurdity of current policy, but he varies the tone by avoiding a string of confrontational assertions. οὐχ ἡμεῖς γε "no, we are not!" γε puts strong emphasis on both the preceding words. **Φιλίππωι πολεμοῦμεν:** D. presents the situation as an ongoing war, beginning with Philip's seizure of Amphipolis in 357 (and ending with the peace of Philocrates in 346; cf. §12, *HM* 312).

**26 ἐχειροτονεῖτε:** the imperfect is hard to explain. If the reading is correct, it must describe "customary action" in the past (Smyth §1893), and here the sense must extend to the present. Although most civic officials (archons) were chosen by lot, military commanders were elected by a show of hands (as the verb denotes) in the Assembly; see Hansen 1983: 103–21. **δέκα ταξιάρχους ... καὶ ἱππάρχους δύο:** the two numbers frame the polysyndetic list; δέκα applies to all but the last noun. Athenian citizens were classified into 10 tribes after the reforms of Cleisthenes, and these tribes were the basis for military organization. Each elected a hoplite division commander (ταξίαρχος) and cavalry division commander (φύλαρχος) for the tribe. They also elected a board of 10 generals (στρατηγοί) who were commanders in chief of the whole military, and two cavalry leaders (ἵππαρχοι). For details see Arist. *Ath. Pol.* 61.1–5 and Rhodes 1993: 684–6. **ὃν ἂν ἐκπέμψητε ἐπὶ τὸν πόλεμον:** see §6n. οὕς on the conditional relative clause. By the mid-fourth century the board of 10 generals had taken on specialized roles (details at Arist. *Ath. Pol.* 61.1); one of them was the στρατηγὸς ἐπὶ τὰ ὅπλα in charge of foreign wars (see Rhodes 1993: 677–9). **οἱ λοιποὶ τὰς πομπὰς πέμπουσιν:** although the Aristotelian description of the specialized roles for Athenian generals does not mention any responsibility for processions, all the commanders listed by D. are likely to have had a role in religious festivals; the Parthenon frieze depicts the cavalry members, and probably their commanders too (distinguished by their beards; see Bugh 1988: 78 n. 135), taking part in the Panathenaic procession (Parker 2005: 258–63, Shear 2001: 128–30, §35n. τήν). Above D. generalized about Athenian commanders "sailing off to Artabazus" (§24n. πρός), and now this generalization refers to the same incident. Chares sent spoils from his campaign of 356/5 to Athens and sponsored a lavish procession in the city that year; see 3.31n. βοίδια. For this common *figura etymologica* (πομπή and πέμπω are from the same root), see LSJ πέμπω III 2, Chadwick 1996: 239–40. This etymology reflects the religious purpose of these parades, to lead sacrificial offerings to the altar of a god at the start of a religious festival; see Parker 2005: 178–80. **τῶν ἱεροποιῶν:** archons chosen by lot to aid priests with religious processions, sacrifices, and the distribution of meat; see Naiden 2013: 206, Parker 2005: 98–9, Shear 2001: 451–5. **ὥσπερ γὰρ οἱ πλάττοντες τοὺς πηλίνους** "just like those who mold clay figurines." Literary evidence for the work of these κοροπλάσται is scant, but many fragments of miniature figures of men, women, children, and animals have been excavated from the Agora; see Burr 1933.

## 4 FIRST PHILIPPIC 27–28

**27 οὐ γὰρ ἐχρῆν ... ταξιάρχους παρ' ὑμῶν;** "should the hoplite commanders not [come] from you?" The imperfect refers to a current obligation that is not being met (Smyth §1774). The repetition of παρ' ὑμῶν is emphatic at the end of the two short clauses (*GPS* 88), and reiterated in οἰκείους. **ἄρχοντας οἰκείους εἶναι:** as often (e.g., §17n. εἶς), D. caps a list of specific items with a final generic term; the ἄρχοντες would include the specific types of commanders that D. indicates, as well as any other administrators involved in the campaign. D.'s point is that the campaign ought to be overseen by Athenians, not by hired mercenary leaders. **ἵν' ἦν ὡς ἀληθῶς τῆς πόλεως ἡ δύναμις** "so that the force may truly be the city's." The imperfect again denotes an unrealized situation (Smyth §2185c). D. marks the close of this section of the speech by repeating this key point from §19. **εἰς μὲν Λῆμνον τὸν παρ' ὑμῶν ἵππαρχον δεῖ πλεῖν:** Miltiades (3.26n. ὥστε) established Lemnos as an Athenian colony (for this and Lemnos in myth, see Schein 2013: 7–8), and the large island was an important Athenian stronghold (a cleruchy) from the fifth century on, vitally located along the main trade route for Athenian grain in the north Aegean, and itself a major producer (§32n. σῖτος). An Athenian hipparch (in addition to the two elected to oversee the entire force, mentioned above; see Whitehead 2000: 139) was specifically appointed to command cavalry stationed on the island (Arist. *Ath. Pol.* 61.6; Rhodes 1993: 686–7 collects other references to this appointment). **Μενέλαον:** Menelaus (*PAA* 644495, no *LGPN* entry) of Pelagon (a region in northwest Macedon) was a commander who in 363/2 was granted citizenship as a benefactor to the Athenians for his efforts in support of their northern campaigns (the decree is preserved: *IG* II² 110 = *GHI* no. 38). Apparently he subsequently continued to aid the Athenians. **ὑφ' ὑμῶν ἔδει κεχειροτονημένον εἶναι τοῦτον** "this man ought to have been elected by you." The same use of the imperfect as ἐχρῆν. **ὅστις ἂν ᾖ:** the indefinite conditional relative again echoes a key point from §19; D. argues for a general policy, not a specific individual.

### 28–30 A financial proposal

We now need maintenance funding. The force will take loot and spoils to supplement its pay.

**28 ἴσως δὲ ταῦτα μὲν ὀρθῶς ἡγεῖσθε λέγεσθαι** "perhaps you believe these [measures] are presented correctly"; i.e., "perhaps you will vote for these measures." Orators regularly use the phrase ὀρθῶς ... λέγειν to refer to the worthiness of their presentations as judged by the audience in the Assembly and the courts; e.g., And. 1.91, Lys. 10.15, D. 8.31, 15.6. **τὸ δὲ τῶν χρημάτων** "the matter of funds"; object of ἀκοῦσαι. D. succinctly summarizes his next point and introduces the subtopics of the amount of funding (πόσα) and its source (πόθεν). For the phrase see §12n. τά.   **τοῦτο δὴ καὶ περαίνω** "that is just what I am going to explain." δή καί strengthens τοῦτο ("precisely that"; *GP* 208–9, 307–8). περαίνω describes an oral account that moves from beginning to end (Garvie 2009: 281).   **χρήματα:** the initial nominative (or possibly accus.) reiterates the new topic. The construction is then abandoned; this technique (anacolouthon) adds an air of naturalness, and is typical of dialogue (Smyth §3007).   **ἔστι μὲν ἡ τροφή, σιτηρέσιον μόνον** "the amount for maintenance, just for provisions, comes to." See §19n. τροφήν.   **τάλαντα ἐνενήκοντα καὶ μικρόν τι πρός:** lit. "90 talents and a little bit more" (LSJ πρός D). The precise total comes to 92 talents. For perspective on this amount, see 3.4n. τάλαντα. Next D. breaks down this amount in a list of three neuter plural nominatives (underlined once in the outline below) in apposition to τάλαντα, which are itemized in a parallel tricolon ("1.", "2." and "3."), each following a dative specifying a subpart of the expedition (underlined twice). Each of the amounts receives a further explanatory clause.

1. <u>δέκα μὲν ναυσὶ ταχείαις</u> τεττᾰρᾰ́κοντα τάλαντα,
    εἴκοσιν εἰς τὴν ναῦν μναῖ τοῦ μηνὸς ἑκάστου,
2. <u>στρατιώταις δὲ δισχιλίοις</u> τοσαῦθ᾽ ἕτερα,
    ἵνα δέκα τοῦ μηνὸς ὁ στρατιώτης δραχμὰς σιτηρέσιον λαμβάνῃ,
3. <u>τοῖς δ᾽ ἱππεῦσι διακοσίοις οὖσιν,</u>
    ἐὰν τριάκοντα δραχμὰς ἕκαστος λαμβάνῃ τοῦ μηνός,
    <u>δώδεκα τάλαντα.</u>

D.'s figures are clear and precise. 1 talent = 60 mnai = 6000 drachmas = 36,000 obols (see further on currency and the calendar Carey 2012: 272–3, Sealey 268–9), and D.'s three different amounts break down as follows: (1.) for the 10 swift triremes, 20 mnai per ship per month = 2400 mnai = 40 talents per year. (2.) for the 2000 soldiers, monthly pay of 10 drachmas each = 240,000 drachmas = 40 talents per year. (3.) for the 200 cavalry, monthly pay of 30 drachmas each = 72,000 drachmas = 12 talents per year.   **εἴκοσιν εἰς τὴν ναῦν μναῖ** "20 mnai per ship." This sense of εἰς is unusual, and may arise from the idiom ἀναλίσκω εἴς τι, "to spend money on something" (LSJ ἀναλίσκω I 1). There were 200 crew members per ship (Morrison and Coates 1986: 107–8), and so each sailor would receive 2 obols per day. This is one third of the standard pay (total of μισθός and σιτηρέσιον) for soldiers and sailors since the time of the Peloponnesian War (Loomis 1998: 52–3), but as far as we can tell appears to be enough to pay for a sufficient amount of grain to keep the troops well nourished (calculations at Gabrielsen 1994: 120). At this period jurors were paid 3 obols per day, which did not cover lost wages, and Assembly pay was increased from 3 obols per day in the 390s to 6 or 9 obols per day before the 320s; a day's wages for a worker were 9 to 15 obols per day (Rhodes 1993: 691, Hansen 1991: 150, 188–9). **τοσαῦθ' ἕτερα** "the same amount again"; i.e., 40 talents. **δέκα τοῦ μηνὸς ... δραχμάς:** the infantry are paid the same as the sailors, 2 obols per day. **σιτηρέσιον:** D. reiterates that these amounts are a minimal maintenance pay, not a full μισθός (3.20n. καί). He wants his proposal to seem modest. **τριάκοντα δραχμὰς ... τοῦ μηνός:** the cavalry members are to be given 1 drachma per day for food, three times as much as the sailors and infantry; they must feed an attendant and their horses in addition to themselves, and so this figure is in line with those for soldiers and sailors (Loomis 1998: 52 n. 98).

**29 μικρὰν ἀφορμήν** "an insufficient provision." ἀφορμή has a wide range of meaning in D. and here refers to the material or means for war; see 2.22n. ἀφορμάς. **σιτηρέσιον ... ὑπάρχειν:** in apposition to ἀφορμή. **οὐκ ὀρθῶς ἔγνωκεν** "he has not come to a correct conclusion." The perfect describes the result of deliberation. **τοῦτ' ἂν γένηται:** ἂν = ἐάν. τοῦτο refers to the dispatching of the troops with pay only for provisions (σιτηρέσιον ... ὑπάρχειν). The pronoun is emphasized by its initial placement in the clause (*GPS* 49). **προσποριεῖ τὰ λοιπὰ αὐτὸ τὸ στράτευμα:** such a proposal is unparalleled; we are not aware of other politicians suggesting that soldiers should accept reduced pay with the encouragement to supplement it by looting, however often this may have actually happened. Thucydides reports that Athenian sailors received reduced pay of 3 obols per day instead of 1 drachma per day in the desperate period after the Sicilian Expedition (8.45.2; Loomis 1998: 44), and in the fourth century (and before) servicemen must often have been denied their allotted pay due to various circumstances in the field. Booty was a frequent means of funding ancient armies (see Pritchett 1971: 24–9, 69–75, Hamel 1998: 45 n. 13, Gabrielsen 1994: 117), and so, e.g., Isocrates reports (15.120) that when Athens failed to send funds to Timotheus as a commander of mercenaries in the 360s, he provided "full pay" (ἐντελεῖς ... τοὺς μισθούς) from his victories (see Pritchett 1991: 386 for other fourth-century examples). **ἀδικοῦν** "by wronging"; neut. pres. act. participle modifying στράτευμα. **ἐγὼ συμπλέων ἐθελοντὴς πάσχειν ὁτιοῦν ἕτοιμος:** lit. "I myself as a volunteer member of the fleet [am] ready to suffer anything at all." The asyndeton quickens the pace and reinforces the emotional tone of this vow. πάσχειν ὁτιοῦν is "a euphemism for risking death" (MacDowell 2000: 230). Cf. D. 8.24 for the phrase and rhetorical ploy. **πόθεν οὖν ὁ πόρος τῶν χρημάτων;** lit. "from where [will] the source of the funding come?" D. introduces his next topic. **ΠΟΡΟΥ ΑΠΟΔΕΙΞΙΣ:** a budget statement is read out to the Assembly. Its length and content are unknown. A "secretary of the people" was elected annually with the sole responsibility of reading documents to the Council and Assembly (Arist. *Ath. Pol.* 54.4–5 with Rhodes 1993: 604, Canevaro 2016a:

350). We have references to the reading of letters (Thuc. 7.10) and proposed laws (D. 20.94), but this is the only surviving Assembly speech containing documents to be read (also §37; see Hansen 1987: 170 n. 572); cf. 9.46n. EK.

**30** Dionysius of Halicarnassus (cf. 3.23n.) quotes the beginning of this section as the start of a new speech, subsequent to and separate from §§1–29 (*Amm.* 1.4, 10). Critics (as early as scholia 90a–b Dilts) have correctly concluded that Dionysius was somehow mistaken or misled, since D. has just stated that he will address a new topic (§29 λέξω), and that explanation here follows. See Badian 2000: 33–4.   **ἡμεῖς** includes allies or friends. The referent may have been clear either from the statement just read or from the larger context of the debate in the Assembly.   **ἐπειδὰν δ' ἐπιχειροτονῆτε τὰς γνώμας** "when you vote on the proposals." ἐπιχειροτονέω is simply "put the matter to a vote" with no suggestion of "approval" or "sanctioning" (LSJ, followed by Wooten 91, is incorrect); there is a thorough discussion of epigraphic and Demosthenic usage by Canevaro 2013a: 87–9. τὰς γνώμας refers to the various proposals under consideration by the Assembly at this and other debates (as at §§1, 12 above). Debate in the Assembly usually produced a large degree of consensus before proposals were approved; see Canevaro 2018, 2019.   **ἂν ὑμῖν ἀρέσκηι** "if [my proposal] satisfies you"; cf. D. 14.14.   **ἐν τοῖς ψηφίσμασι καὶ ταῖς ἐπιστολαῖς:** cf. §§19–20; D. repeats key points to close this part of the speech. The phrase must have appealed to Polybius, who was the source for Livy's reformulation describing relations between Athens and Philip v in 199 (33.44.9): *Athenienses quidem litteris verbisque, quibus solis valent, bellum adversus Philippum gerebant.*

### 31–32 Stationing the force
The force should be maintained in the north through the winter.

**31 τὸν τόπον** "the geographical position" (LSJ 1; Chadwick 1996: 280–1).   **ἐνθυμηθείητε … λογίσαισθε:** 1.21n. ἐνθυμηθῆναι.   **τοῖς πνεύμασιν καὶ ταῖς ὥραις τοῦ ἔτους:** D. first uses a broad generic description and then makes the same point more specifically in the following clause with τοὺς ἐτησίας ἢ τὸν χειμῶνα.   **τὰ πολλὰ προλαμβάνων διαπράττεται Φίλιππος** "by anticipating [us] Philip gains most of his successes." D. often uses both verbs to describe Philip's aggressions and success: e.g., προλαμβάνω, 2.9, 3.16, 18.26; διαπράττομαι, 2.15, 19.136, 320.   **φυλάξας τοὺς ἐτησίας ἢ τὸν χειμῶνα** "waiting for the Etesian winds or winter"; LSJ φυλάσσω B 2 b. The Etesian winds blow strongly from the northeast for some 40 days in late summer, preventing sea travel from Athens to the northern Aegean; cf. D. 8.14 and see Beresford 2013: 80–1, Loomis 1990: 489–90 n. 18. Traditionally the sailing season in the Aegean extended from late winter to mid-autumn (e.g.,

Hes. *Op*. 663–77), but as ship construction improved, it became increasingly possible for enterprising commanders to navigate during the winter months, and the nature of warfare changed in the fifth and fourth centuries (see further Beresford 2013: 10–22, 146–7, S. Hornblower 2011: 195–203). D. characterizes Philip as adapting better to these changes than did the Athenians; cf. 9.48–50, where D. contrasts the old style of war with that practiced by Philip, who uses new technology and fights summer and winter. **ἡνίκ᾽ ἂν ἡμεῖς μὴ δυναίμεθα** "when [he thinks] we would not be able." The temporal clause is modeled after a future less vivid condition imagining Philip's thoughts (Smyth §2406).

**32 βοηθείαις:** forces dispatched to meet a specific emergency; cf. 1.2, 19, 8.15. **ὑστεριοῦμεν:** D. will explain further below, §§34–5; cf. 3.4–5, 8.12. **παρασκευῆι συνεχεῖ καὶ δυνάμει:** D. reiterates the point from §19. **ὑπάρχει δ᾽ ὑμῖν χειμαδίωι ... Λήμνωι** "Lemnos is available for you to use as a winter harbor for the force." See §27n. ἀλλ᾽. This is the only attestation of χειμάδιον in the classical period. **Θάσωι καὶ Σκιάθωι:** D. specifies Thasos and Sciathos because they are closer to Macedon than are other Athenian allies and possessions. Both were members of the second Athenian League (*IG* II² 43.86, 100 = *GHI* no. 22, 3.28n. οὕς). **ταῖς ἐν τούτωι τῶι τόπωι νήσοις:** i.e., Peparethos (*IG* II² 43.85, D. 18.70) and Scyros ([D.] 7.4, Aesch. 2.72). **σῖτος:** three northern islands – Lemnos, Imbros, and Scyros – had long been held by the Athenians and were major producers of grain. An inscription records their production for the year 329/8 and illustrates the significance of their contribution to the Athenian food supply; the discovery of Agyrrhios' grain-tax law of 374/3 provides further detail regarding taxation and production. See Stroud 1998: 32–7 on *IG* II² 1672 and *SEG* 47.96 = *GHI* no. 26. **τὴν δ᾽ ὥραν τοῦ ἔτους** "during that part of the year"; accusative of duration (Smyth §1582), explained by the ὅτε clause. **πρὸς τῆι γῆι γενέσθαι** "to put ashore." For the idiom cf. Thuc. 2.90.4, Xen. *Hell*. 5.1.9. **τὸ τῶν πνευμάτων ἀσφαλές** "[there is] safety from the winds." **πρὸς αὐτῆι τῆι χώραι ... ῥαιδίως ἔσται** "[our force] will be easily [at the ready] near that very land and the entrances to his markets." The expression is elliptical, and it is not clear what should be supplied for ῥαιδίως to modify, or whether to take it with ἔσται; textual corruption has been suspected. For the vulnerability of Philip's ports, see 2.16n. κεκλειμένων.

### 33–37 The advantage of dedicated funding
By providing the resources for the force, you will oblige them to serve your interests. Furthermore, they will prevent Philip from plundering at sea. We have an established procedure for funding and administering festivals, and we need the same for the military.

**33 ἃ μὲν οὖν χρήσεται καὶ πότε τῆι δυνάμει** "[the commander will determine] how he will use the force, and when." D. uses the relative pronoun in place of πῶς (Smyth §2668) with χρήσεται (cf. 3.6, LSJ χράω (B) c iii 4), to create parallelism between the ἃ μέν and ἃ δέ clauses. **παρὰ τὸν καιρόν** "at the right moment" (LSJ παρά c i 10; cf. D. 20.41, 44), because the commander will be on the scene and able to act without delay. **ὁ τούτων κύριος καταστάς:** this paraphrase for στρατηγός is pointed: it stresses the authority to act decisively without deference to the political process in Athens. Elsewhere D. ascribes Philip's military strength to his being κύριος (1.4n. πάντων; cf. below on αὐτοὶ ταμίαι). **παρ' ὑμῶν:** emphatic after ὑφ' ὑμῶν. D. reiterates his main point (παρ' ὑμῶν, §§27 (3×), 29), that the commanders and the means for war must come from the Athenians. **ἁγὼ γέγραφα** "that I have proposed" (ἁγώ = ἃ ἐγώ; 9.7n. μήποτε). The pronoun distinguishes the roles of the orator and the audience in the Assembly; D. has done his part by presenting his proposal, and he calls upon the audience to do theirs by enacting it. **ἂν ταῦτ'... τὸν λόγον ζητοῦντες:** the protasis of this future less vivid condition is expansive, built around two verbs (πορίσητε and κατακλείσητε). The second of these is modified by three participles (παρασκευάσαντες, γιγνόμενοι, and ζητοῦντες). The first of those participles governs a string of nouns in apposition to τἆλλα (τοὺς στρατιώτας ... τὴν δύναμιν), and the last two present a crafted parallel between τῶν μὲν χρημάτων and τῶν δὲ πράξεων. In contrast to this intricately mannered protasis, the apodosis (framed by the future indicative verbs παύσεσθε and [§34] ἀφαιρήσεσθε) is shorter and less complex, suggesting that the results of D.'s detailed proposal will be clear and simple. **ἐντελῆ πᾶσαν τὴν δύναμιν** "the whole force in full." ἐντελής describes an expedition that is fully formed and intact, with no reductions to the type or number of troops specified in D.'s proposal. Cf. the specific financial usage at §29. **νόμωι κατακλείσητε ἐπὶ τῶι πολέμωι μένειν** "you compel [them] by law to remain committed to the war" (LSJ κατακλείω i 2 and μένω i 6). D. responds to the concern he raised in §24 about mercenary armies with their own agendas. See also 3.17n. μένειν. **τῶν μὲν χρημάτων ... τῶν δὲ πράξεων:** this and the following clause closely connect two of the key concepts in D.'s proposal, money and action. The two clauses are linked by the initial genitives with μέν and δέ, the parallel participles at the end, and isocolon (they differ in length by one syllable). **ταμίαι καὶ πορισταί** "paymasters and providers." D. suggests that the Athenians (like Philip as ταμίας, 1.4) should avoid outsourcing the financial management of their armies to mercenary generals. There were various specific offices in Athens designated as ταμίας, e.g., the treasurer of the military fund (ταμίας στρατιωτικῶν, Arist. *Ath. Pol.* 43.1) and the treasurers of Athena (οἱ ταμίαι τῆς Ἀθηνᾶς, Arist. *Ath. Pol.* 47.1); the noun is used more widely to describe gods or rulers (e.g., Ar. *Clouds* 566 and S. *Ant.* 1154 with Griffith 1999: 322). ποριστής is also the name of a specific office in Athens (Rhodes 1993: 356), about which little is known, and the wider usage here is more uncommon. **τὸν λόγον ζητοῦντες** "requiring an account." Athenian citizens serving as generals would be subject to audits at the end of their term. See 1.28n. αἱ and 2.25n. κρινόντων. **παύσεσθε ἀεὶ περὶ τῶν αὐτῶν βουλευόμενοι** "you will stop debating about the same things over and over"; cf. §1. The future verb marks the start of the apodosis, and its position is mirrored by the verb that ends the sentence. **πλέον οὐδὲν ποιοῦντες** "making no progress"; LSJ πλείων II 1.

**34 καὶ ἔτι πρὸς τούτωι** "and on top of that"; a typical Demosthenic phrase (D. 21.62, 23.26, 24.36; not in other orators). **πρῶτον** anticipates ἔπειτα below. **τὸν μέγιστον τῶν ἐκείνου πόρων ἀφαιρήσεσθε** "you will deprive [him] of the largest of his revenues"; cf. Hyp. *Eux.* 37. **ἔστι δ' οὗτος τίς;** §2n. τί. **ἀπὸ τῶν ὑμετέρων ... συμμάχων:** the preposition describes the origin of Philip's resources: "from the resources of your own allies" (LSJ ἀπό A III 6). The word order, with the placement of ἀπὸ τῶν ὑμετέρων at the start of the clause in juxtaposition with ὑμῖν, and the noun delayed until the end, focuses attention on the phrase. **ἄγων καὶ φέρων** "by robbing and plundering." ἄγειν καὶ φέρειν is a standard phrase to describe the taking of spoils (e.g., H. *Il.* 5.484, Ar. *Clouds* 241 with Dover 1968: 129, D. 9.52, 18.230), and in the fourth century it was used especially to describe piracy at sea (Pritchett 1991: 108 n. 86). The former verb refers to captured people and animals, the latter to their goods. **τοῦ πάσχειν αὐτοὶ κακῶς ἔξω γενήσεσθε** "you yourselves will be out of reach of being mistreated" (LSJ ἔξω I 2 b). Again, the word order stresses the infinitive, and the delayed placement of κακῶς avoids hiatus. This clause quickly answers the preceding rhetorical question, and then in the rest of the sentence D. illustrates the swift action of Philip with a list of three aggressions presented in asyndeton, each beginning with the name of a different locality. Only the last clause receives a connective (ὑμεῖς δέ ...), as D. slows down to point out the Athenians' weakness. See further Wooten 96–7. **οὐχ ὥσπερ τὸν παρελθόντα χρόνον:** the expression with ὥσπερ is elliptical: "[he will] not [act] as [he did] in the past [when] ...." **εἰς Λῆμνον καὶ Ἴμβρον ἐμβαλών** "after launching an attack on Lemnos and Imbros." The islands had been colonized by the Athenians since the fifth century and were important sources of grain for the city (§27n. ἀλλ' and §32n. σῖτος). This and the following incidents probably all took place in 352 (Cawkwell 2011: 372–3, *HM* 311–12). **αἰχμαλώτους πολίτας ὑμετέρους ὤιχετ' ἔχων** "he left with your citizens as captives." The quick movement from Philip's arrival to his departure stresses his speed. These islands were military colonies (cleruchies), with Athenians in residence. An inscription records the terms of their status as

Athenian citizens on Lemnos; see Stroud 1998: 31 on *IG* II² 30. **πρὸς τῶι Γεραιστῶι τὰ πλοῖα συλλαβών** "after appropriating your [grain] ships at Geraistus" on the southern tip of Euboea, en route to Athens; the series of examples shows Philip moving closer to the city. **ἀμύθητα χρήματ' ἐξέλεξε** "he collected payment of untold sums"; the first attested usage of ἀμύθητος (cf. D. 21.17). **εἰς Μαραθῶνα:** in northeast Attica, not even 40 km from Athens, the site of the Athenians' famous victory over the Persians in 490. The name reminds the audience of how differently they acted then; cf. 3.26. **τὴν ἱερὰν ... τριήρη:** the word order places strong stress on τριήρη, as the audience waits after τὴν ἱεράν; see 1.8n. τήν, Devine and Stephens 2000: 132–3. There were two "sacred triremes" (the phrase also at 21.174), the Paralus and the Salaminia, manned by a crew of select citizens and used for religious and military missions; see further E. M. Harris 2008: 147–8 n. 248, Rhodes 1993: 687–8, S. Hornblower 1991: 414. Androtion and Philochorus report that it was the Paralus that Philip captured (Harp. s.v. ἱερὰ τριήρης = *FGrHist* 324 F 24 and 328 F 47). **εἰς τοὺς χρόνους, οὓς ἂν προθῆσθε** "at the times that you determine"; cf. 3.18n. ὅταν. The plural and the relative clause generalize, giving the impression that Athens repeatedly fails to act upon its decisions. The present tense δύνασθε reinforces the current urgency of this failure.

**35 καίτοι τί δή ποτε;** "and so why in the world?" (LSJ δήποτε 3). **τὴν μὲν τῶν Παναθηναίων ἑορτήν:** (sc. ἱερῶν) the Panathenaic festival was the largest and one of the most expensive Athenian festivals. The Greater Panathenaia was celebrated every fourth year in mid-summer and featured competitions, a large procession to the Acropolis culminating in the presentation of a robe to Athena (famously depicted on the Parthenon frieze), and public sacrifices and distribution of meat. In other years the Panathenaia was smaller and less panhellenic, and included fewer elements. See Parker 2005: 253–69. **τὴν τῶν Διονυσίων:** D. refers to the largest of the festivals for Dionysus, the City Dionysia; he singles out these two because they were the most elaborate and expensive of the state-sponsored festivals. The City Dionysia took place each year in spring and featured sacrifices and a procession second in size only to the Panathenaic procession. It ended at the Theater of Dionysus, where there were civic displays (e.g., a parade of war orphans) and performances of tragedy and comedy. See Parker 2005: 317–18, Csapo and Slater 1995: 103–21. **τοῦ καθήκοντος χρόνου** "at the proper time" (Smyth §1444). For the phrase cf. Aesch. 3.126. **ἄν τε δεινοὶ λάχωσιν ἄν τε ἰδιῶται οἱ τούτων ἑκατέρων ἐπιμελούμενοι** "whether professionals or laymen are appointed as the ones in charge of each of these [rites]." 10 Athlothetae were selected by lot (LSJ λαγχάνω I 2, Hansen 1991: 230–3), one from each tribe, to administer the Panathenaic festival for a period of four years (Arist. *Ath. Pol.* 60.1, Shear 2001: 455–63). A state official (the eponymous archon), also chosen by lot, oversaw the festival for Dionysus; he was aided by a board of ἐπιμεληταί, but since they were elected by this date, οἱ … ἐπιμελούμενοι must describe the broad category of various types of magistrates responsible for the festivals (Arist. *Ath. Pol.* 56.4 with Rhodes 1993: 627–8, MacDowell 1990: 238, Wilson 2000: 24–5). For this contrast between δεινός and ἰδιώτης, cf. Isoc. 13.14, Pl. *Phdr.* 228a, *Plt.* 259a, Lycurg. 31. **εἰς ἃ τοσαῦτα ἀναλίσκεται χρήματα**: the Athenians are estimated to have spent 10–15 talents for each Greater Panathenaic festival, and much less for the lesser Panathenaia, an average of more than six talents per year of public money in the early fourth century (Pritchard 2015: 28–40). The cost of the City Dionysia has been calculated to have been about the same (Csapo and Slater 1995: 141). These sums were substantially supplemented by donations from rich citizens that supported major aspects of the festivals; for example, individual chorus leaders (χορηγοί) underwrote the expense of dramatic productions (§36n. τίς; Wilson 2000: 95 estimates that this amounted to a total of eight talents for the annual City Dionysia). The total annual expense for all religious festivals in mid-fourth century Athens may have been some 100 talents (Pritchard 2015: 48–9). **ὅσα οὐδ' εἰς ἕνα τῶν ἀποστόλων**: lit. "as much [as is spent] on not even one of our expeditions"; i.e., the amount spent on the festivals is more than that for any one military expedition. This is an exaggeration: elsewhere D. reports that the total amount of public and private expenditure for a single campaign against Philip in 352 was more than 200 talents (see 3.4n. τάλαντα), and although he stresses the small size of the force proposed here, the cost of 92 talents would probably approximate the annual expenditure for all the festivals (in the year 351; 350 was a more expensive Greater Panathenaic year). D.'s false assertion here has been highly influential on later views of Athenian spending priorities. For example, Plutarch faults the Athenians for excessive spending on theater productions and for neglecting to dedicate resources to the military protection of the state; he takes D.'s statement here at face value and treats it as the explanation for the decline of Athens (Plut. *Mor.* 349a; cf. Hanink 2014: 247–8). This belief has been prevalent until very recently, when new analyses of epigraphic data have shown that D. seriously misrepresents the priorities of Athenian public spending. See Pritchard 2015: 3–5. **τοσοῦτον ὄχλον καὶ παρασκευήν** "so much fuss and equipment" (sc. ἃ [= τὰ ἱερά] ἔχει and see LSJ ὄχλος II). παρασκευή is any object that is prepared as equipment, often for a military expedition (as frequently in this speech, e.g., §§12–13); for the use to describe festival equipment (paid for by a private individual), cf. D. 21.106. **ὅσην οὐκ οἶδ' εἴ τι τῶν ἁπάντων ἔχει**: lit. "that I doubt whether anything else at all has as much"; sc. ὄχλον καὶ παρασκευήν (ὅσην agrees with the latter). For the idioms cf. D. 18.311, 21.6. **τοὺς δ' ἀποστόλους πάντας**: parallel with τὴν μὲν τῶν Παναθηναίων ἑορτήν. The long sentence exemplifies D.'s point about the amount of energy devoted to the festivals as compared to military matters. The long and complex account of the fuss and bother of the former is sharply contrasted with the short summary of the latter that begins here. ὑμῖν: dative of disadvantage (Smyth §1481). ὑστερίζειν τῶν καιρῶν "miss their moments"; cf. D. 18.102. τὸν εἰς Μεθώνην, τὸν εἰς Παγασάς, τὸν εἰς Ποτείδαιαν: Philip took control of these regions in 354, 352, and 356 respectively (1.9n. Μεθώνη, 1.13n. Φεράς, 1.9n. Ποτείδαια). The non-chronological order here probably arises from concern for euphony and rhythm: words with initial π are grouped together, and the longest item is last. As in §34, the cumulative and continued aggression is suggested by the series of three examples in asyndeton.

**36 ὅτι ἐκεῖνα μὲν ἅπαντα νόμωι τέτακται** "[it is] because all those [events] have been prescribed by law" (LSJ τάσσω III 2, cf. D. 22.11). ὅτι answers the rhetorical question (τί ... νομίζετε). Some laws regarding the management of the City Dionysia are attested and paraphrased at D. 21.9–11 (see Pickard-Cambridge 1968: 64, 68; the text itself of the laws preserved in the speech is not authentic: see Harris in Canevaro 2013a: 211–16). **πρόοιδεν ἕκαστος ὑμῶν ἐκ πολλοῦ:** sc. χρόνου: "each of you knows far in advance." Arist. *Ath. Pol.* 56.3 specifies the appointment of χορηγοί for the City Dionysia as one of the first tasks of the eponymous archon upon entering office for the year, almost nine months before the festival (Wilson 2000: 51–2). **τίς χορηγὸς ἢ γυμνασίαρχος τῆς φυλῆς:** sc. ἔσται. The χορηγοί were wealthy Athenians who paid for dramatic productions; the γυμνασίαρχοι underwrote the costs of athletic contests. These were public obligations (liturgies) for the richest group of Athenians (the same group who were eligible to be trierarchs, although in practice trierarchs must have been the most wealthy, because the festival liturgies were more numerous and required less outlay, sometimes less than 1000 drachmas, whereas a trierachy could cost as much as a talent; Hansen 1991: 111 and see 2.30n. τριηραρχεῖν). Like the military leaders (§26n. δέκα), they were appointed by tribe (D. 21.13 with MacDowell 1990: 236–7). See Wilson 2000: 35–6, 50–7. **πότε καὶ παρὰ τοῦ καὶ τί λαβόντα τί δεῖ ποιεῖν** "when and from whom and what he is to receive, [and] what he must do." λαβόντα probably points back to τίς, referring to the chorus leader; alternatively it refers to ἕκαστος, and D. thus highlights the wide involvement of various citizens and officials. The details behind these questions, regarding "the handover of materials, the specifications of times and personnel" (Wilson 2000: 51, 331 n. 2), are elusive, but the overall image created here is that of a well-ordered process with ample lead time and widespread participation. **οὐδὲν ἀνεξέταστον οὐδ' ἀόριστον ἐν τούτοις ἠμέληται** "nothing is left undecided or undetermined in these [matters]." The asyndeton gives the sense of a quick summa-

## 4 FIRST PHILIPPIC 36

tion before the connective (δέ) introducing military matters. The litotes is emphatically positive and prepares the way for the strongly negative contrasting phrase that follows. **ἄτακτα ἀδιόρθωτα ἀόριστα ἄπαντα** "everything is unfixed, unrevised, undetermined." The assonance sums up D.'s key complaint. The emphatic final placement of ἄπαντα marks the contrast with ἄπαντα νόμωι τέτακται at the start of the period. The series of three asyndetic alpha-privative adjectives is portentous; the device appears as early as H. *Il.* 9.63 (ἀφρήτωρ ἀθέμιστος ἀνέστιος), and "the form and content are associated with solemn imprecations" originating in the language of curses (Fraenkel 1950: 217 on A. *Ag.* 412, who collects examples from tragedy and elsewhere; see also Rutherford 2012: index s.v. "alpha-privative adjectives"). Consummate prose stylists borrow the technique to mark emotional passages: e.g., Gorg. fr. 11a §36 (Diels–Kranz) ἄθεον ἄδικον ἄνομον, Pl. *Phdr.* 240a ἄγαμον ἄπαιδα ἄοικον, D. 9.40, *GPS* 101. **τοιγαροῦν** "and that is why." The particle signals a strong logical inference and "confers an air of utter certainty" (Yunis 188 on D. 18.134; *GP* 568). **ἅμα ἀκηκόαμέν τι** "it is only once we have heard some [news] that ..." ἅμα coordinates ἀκηκόαμεν with the four following verbs connected by repetition of καί; then the series of three εἶτα clauses adds to the effect. The polysyndeton and series of short clauses stress the slowness of the process for dispatching military missions. **τριηράρχους ... ἀντιδόσεις ποιούμεθα** "we appoint trierachs and conduct their challenges"; see 2.30n. τριηραρχεῖν and τίς χορηγός above. The στρατηγὸς ἐπὶ τὰς συμμορίας was elected each year and upon entering office was responsible for selecting trierarchs and assigning them to specific ships; he would then oversee any challenges (Arist. *Ath. Pol.* 61.1). A man chosen as trierarch could challenge the appointment through the process of ἀντίδοσις, which required that he identify a wealthier man who could more readily perform the liturgy. That man must either undertake the obligation or else exchange property with the original appointee, in which case the latter would pay for the liturgy from the exchanged property. The person proposed seems to have had the option of requesting a court hearing, presumably with the possibility of having the challenge quashed. We have various references to such hearings, but none to any actual exchange of property. See Todd 2007: 323–4, Hansen 1991: 111–12. Since 358 a system of symmories had added new complexity to the process of dividing up responsibility for payment; see 2.29n. πρότερον. **περὶ χρημάτων πόρου σκοποῦμεν** "we deliberate about a funding source"; cf. 1.19n. περί. **ἐμβαίνειν τοὺς μετοίκους ἔδοξε**: sc. ἡμῖν: "[we] decree that the metics should man the fleet." The aorist must be present in sense, echoing the prescript of actual decrees (§21n. ἐξ). Metics were non-citizen residents of Athens who were obliged to pay taxes and were liable to conscription. As hoplites they probably served in separate units from the citizens, and they are well attested as rowers on ships. See Whitehead 1977: 82–6. **τοὺς χωρὶς οἰκοῦντας**: lit. "those dwelling apart." The unparalleled term perhaps summarizes D.'s criticism of Athenian reliance on mercenaries (Sosin 2015). Alternatively, Harpocration (s.v. τοὺς χωρὶς οἰκοῦντας) thought it referred to freed slaves, whether to a general group (Kamen 2011) or to a specific subgroup liable to conscription (Canevaro and Lewis 2014). **εἶτ᾽ αὐτοὺς πάλιν** "then again that [you] yourselves [should man the fleet]"; for the omission of ὑμᾶς, cf. §16. **ἀντεμβιβάζειν** "put [others] aboard instead [of yourselves]." This must refer to some group not already named, i.e., either mercenaries or slaves (cf. Thuc. 7.13.2 ἀνδράποδα … ἀντεμβιβάσαι ὑπὲρ σφῶν).

**37 ἐν ὅσωι ταῦτα μέλλεται**: sc. χρόνωι: "while these delays occur." For ἐν ὅσωι cf. D. 19.169, 21.108. **προαπόλωλεν τὸ ἐφ᾽ ὃ ἂν ἐκπλέωμεν** "our reason for sailing is lost." The προ- prefix stresses that the campaign is a failure before it even begins; the perfect of ἀπόλλυμι is used emphatically to refer to present circumstances (Smyth §1947b). **τὸν γὰρ τοῦ πράττειν χρόνον εἰς τὸ παρασκευάζεσθαι ἀναλίσκομεν** "we waste on preparation the time for action." In tragedy this metaphorical use of ἀναλίσκω (LSJ 2) commonly refers to useless speech (Finglass 2011: 435 on S. *Aj.* 1049); for its use with reference to time (a dead metaphor, like English "spend time"), cf. D. 18.173, 19.8, 155, 161. **οἱ δὲ τῶν πραγμάτων … καιροὶ τὴν ἡμετέραν βραδυτῆτα καὶ εἰρωνείαν** "opportunities for action do not await our sluggishness and evasion." The word order draws attention to καιροί, and the juxtaposition with τὴν ἡμετέραν … εἰρωνείαν is pointed. See §7n. πᾶσαν and §8n. διά. **ἃς δὲ τὸν μεταξὺ χρόνον δυνάμεις οἰόμεθ᾽ ἡμῖν ὑπάρχειν** "but the interim forces that we suppose are ours." ἅς … δυνάμεις = αἱ δυνάμεις ἅς (Smyth §2537). D. refers to the mercenaries who pursue their own agendas (§24) while the Assembly debates in Athens. **οὐδὲν οἷαί τ᾽ οὖσαι ποιεῖν … ἐξελέγχονται** "are proved to be incapable of action at those very moments." For an outline of D.'s frequent uses of ἐπί with the gen. to describe various sorts of "occasions and circumstances," see MacDowell 1990: 222 (this is "the particular occasion when an event occurs"; cf. 21.72, 204). **ὁ δ᾽ εἰς τοῦθ᾽ ὕβρεως ἐλήλυθεν**: a common formulation in Assembly and court speeches; e.g., Lys. 3.7, Is. 5.11, D. 21.5, [D.] 17.12, 59.72. For the rhetorical device (hypostasis), see 3.1n. τά. Cf. also 1.23n. ὑβριστής. **ΕΠΙΣΤΟΛΗΣ ΑΝΑΓΝΩΣΙΣ**: for the reading of the document, cf. §29n. ΠΟΡΟΥ, 9.27n. οὐ. The content and circumstances of the letter are unknown; possibly it was connected with Philip's recent seizure of the Athenian transports at Geraistus (§34n. πρός). A scholion surmises that Philip threatened the Euboeans and warned them against an alliance with Athens (92 Dilts; see also MacDowell 2009: 217).

## 38–46 Act now

You have been reacting too slowly to Philip's offenses. His provocations must spur us to action. As long as you sit at home the situation will deteriorate.

**38 ἀληθῆ μέν ἐστι τὰ πολλά:** the letter must have suggested that the Euboeans were powerless to resist Philip's threats. **ὡς οὐκ ἔδει:** lit. "as it ought not [to be]"; i.e., "I wish it were not the case." D. uses the parenthesis to comment on the preceding point, to say how unfortunate the situation is; cf. 9.59n. ταῦτ'. For the imperf., cf. §27n. οὐ. For the tone cf. Hyp. *Against Diondas* (Carey et al. 2008) 176r/173v 27 ὡς οὐκ ἂν ἐβουλόμην (the orator expresses dismay that many Thebans are exiled in Athens after Philip has destroyed their city). **οὐ μὴν ἀλλ':** 2.22n. οὐ. **ἡδέα:** cf. D. 3.18. **εἰ μέν ... εἰ δ':** μέν and δέ link two conditions that are parallel in structure but opposed in sense. Each starts with a protasis that is briefly interrupted with a short inserted negative clause (ἵνα μὴ λυπήσηι and ἂν ἦι μὴ προσήκουσα) highlighting the Athenians' reluctance to face the truth of their situation. Then each continues with a short apodosis (δεῖ ... δημηγορεῖν and αἰσχρόν ... ἑαυτούς); the contrasting sense of these paired conclusions reinforces the point that being receptive to demagogues is a form of shameful self-deceit. **ὅσα ἄν τις ὑπερβῆι** "whatever someone leaves out" (LSJ ὑπερβαίνω I 3); the unexpressed antecedent of ὅσα (sc. τοσαῦτα) is the object of ὑπερβήσεται. **τὰ πράγματα** "the reality of the situation" (cf. D. 2.29, 3.1n. τά); the subject of ὑπερβήσεται. **πρὸς ἡδονὴν δημηγορεῖν** "pander to pleasure." For the accusation of demagoguery, cf. 3.3n. ὁρᾶτε. **ἂν ἦι μὴ προσήκουσα** "if it is not appropriate." **ἔργωι** "in actuality"; the contrast between speech and reality is continued from the preceding condition with variation in vocabulary. **φενακίζειν ἑαυτούς** "to deceive ourselves." D. regularly uses the verb to describe Philip's manipulations; see 2.7n. οὐδείς. **καὶ ἅπαντ' ἀναβαλλομένους ἃ ἂν ἦι δυσχερῆ πάντων ὑστερεῖν τῶν ἔργων** "and, by putting off everything that is unpleasant, to miss every moment for action." D. extends the apodosis of this condition with two further infinitives (ὑστερεῖν and [§39] δύνασθαι) parallel to φενακίζειν.

**39 μηδὲ τοῦτο** "not even this." **ὅτι δεῖ ... οὐκ ἀκολουθεῖν τοῖς πράγμασιν** "that those who manage a war correctly should not be guided by the situation." Above D. used ὀρθῶς to describe proper political policy (§28n. ἴσως); now he extends that sense to military leadership in anticipation of the following comparison of orators and generals. **αὐτοὺς ἔμπροσθεν εἶναι τῶν πραγμάτων** "they themselves [should] be ahead of the situation." After the preceding negative, this positive formulation with the repetition of the key term at the end of each clause is strongly

emphatic (see *GPS* 88, cf. D. 19.338). **οὕτω καὶ τῶν πραγμάτων τοὺς βουλευομένους:** sc. ἀξιώσειέ τις ἄν and ἡγεῖσθαι. **ἃ ἂν ἐκείνοις δοκῇ:** the relative clause explains the following ταῦτα. **μὴ τὰ συμβάντα ἀναγκάζωνται διώκειν:** this final summation of the main point again varies vocabulary: τὰ συμβάντα is an alternative for τὰ πράγματα, διώκειν for ἔμπροσθεν εἶναι.
**40 ὑμεῖς δέ:** D. now applies the preceding generalization to the Athenians. **πλείστην δύναμιν ἁπάντων:** Athens was "the largest politically unified territory" in fourth-century Greece (E. E. Cohen 2000: 13; he contrasts Sparta, which controlled more territory but maintained strict political divisions among peoples) and as such had the potential to mobilize more forces and collect more taxes than other cities. On the size of the Athenian navy and cavalry, see §16nn. τριήρεις and τοῖς; on hoplites see 1.28n. τοὺς δ᾽ ἐν ἡλικίαι. **χρημάτων πρόσοδον** "public revenue"; for the phrase cf. [D.] 13.10, Thuc. 2.13.2. In fact Athenian revenues declined markedly in the 350s, when they lost tribute from allies and spent money pursuing the Social War. By the late 350s the state was nearly bankrupt (D. 10.37, 20.24, Isoc. 8.19), though that situation had begun to turn around by the early 340s, probably because of increases in trade and new financial policies in Athens (Pritchard 2015: 15, Cawkwell 2011: 359–60). **εἰς δέον τι** "for any appropriate use." Cf. §14 and see 3.28n. εἰς; D. hints at his earlier point, that the military is more active at home than abroad (§26), and anticipates his complaints about the use of the military fund for domestic purposes in the third *Olynthiac* (3.11, 19). πώποτε drives home the assertion of repeated and constant negligence. **οὐδὲν δ᾽ ἀπολείπετε, ὥσπερ οἱ βάρβαροι πυκτεύουσιν, οὕτω πολεμεῖν:** lit. "in no regard are you short of waging war in the same way that non-Greeks box" (LSJ ἀπολείπω A IV 2); i.e., "you wage war just as ..." On D.'s use of similes, see Introd. §3.4. The Greeks regarded non-Greeks as naturally inferior in athletic competition and ability: cf. Pl. *Sym.* 182b–c τοῖς γὰρ βαρβάροις ... αἰσχρὸν ... ἡ φιλογυμναστία; Eur. *IT* 1368–74, where Orestes uses his boxing skills to rescue his sister from her barbarian captors (see E. Hall 1989: 124). And so panhellenic festivals such as the Olympics excluded non-Greeks and featured athletic contests as a defining aspect of Greek culture (see further Nielsen 2013: 135–6). D.'s image of Athenian sluggishness is thus intended to shame his audience because they are not living up to their own ideal. This point is further developed by the emphasis on the speed and activity of Philip presented elsewhere (2.15n. πράττων; Mader 2007b: 54–5). **ἐκείνων ὁ πληγείς** "when one of them is hit." **ἀεὶ τῆς πληγῆς ἔχεται** "every time he clutches at where he is hit" (LSJ ἔχω C 1). For this sense of ἀεί, see 2.7n. τήν. **ἐκεῖσε εἰσὶν αἱ χεῖρες** "that is where his hands are." ἐκεῖσε + εἰμί *sum* suggests both movement and rest; for this type of *constructio praegnans*, see LSJ δεῦρο and Smyth

§1659b.  **προβάλλεσθαι δ' ἢ βλέπειν ἐναντίον**: προβάλλεσθαι refers to the use of hands or a shield for protection (Harp. s.v. προβαλλομένους· ἀντὶ τοῦ προτείνειν τὰς χεῖρας ὡς εἰς μάχην; LSJ B III). For the idiom (προσ)βλέπειν ἐναντίον, cf. Eur. *Med.* 470, *Heracl.* 943. **οὔτ' οἶδεν οὔτ' ἐθέλει**: unlike the foreign boxer who does not know how to fight for himself, D.'s Athenian audience is here being told what they should do. The concluding point, that the boxer is unwilling to act in his own interest, then serves as a criticism if the Athenians refuse to act on D.'s advice.

**41 καὶ ὑμεῖς** switches the focus from the foreign boxer. Cf. 9.70. **ἂν ἐν Χερρονήσωι πύθησθε Φίλιππον**: sc. ὄντα; ἄν = ἐάν. D. refers to Philip's siege of Heraion Teichos in late 352; see 1.13n. ἠσθένησεν and cf. §17. **ἐκεῖσε βοηθεῖν ψηφίζεσθε**: the repetition of ἐκεῖσε from §40 reinforces the comparison with the boxer. On the abandoned aid decree, see D. 3.4–5. **ἂν ἐν Πύλαις, ἐκεῖσε**: the compression (sc. πύθησθε Φίλιππον and βοηθεῖν ψηφίζεσθε) and repetition suggest that these individual episodes should be regarded as a part of a constant series; the language contributes to the image of the Athenians reeling from one of Philip's aggressions to the next. Here D. leaves out the success of the expedition to block Philip at Thermopylae (see 1.26n. ἐάν) because it would distract from his focus on the reactive nature of Athenian policy. **ἂν ἄλλοθί που**: D. breaks off the list of specific aggressions and concludes with the following striking generalization. **συμπαραθεῖτε ἄνω κάτω** "you run along beside [him] all over the place." The compound verb is not attested elsewhere in the classical period (παραθέω appears occasionally in fourth-century authors); it draws attention to the absurd image. See 2.16n. ἄνω. **στρατηγεῖσθ' ὑπ' ἐκείνου**: the culmination of D.'s complaint in §26, that the Athenian generals are not concerned with war. **βεβούλευσθε**: the close link between military leadership and political policy is reiterated from §39. (συμ)βουλεύω, συμφέρος, and προοράω are key terms that D. uses to describe his ideal role as a politician in the Assembly (cf. 1.1nn. τό and συμβουλεύειν, 18.93). The assertion here is stronger than the cautious phrasing in §1. **πρὶν ἂν ἢ γεγενημένον ἢ γιγνόμενόν τι πύθησθε** "until you learn that something either has happened or is happening." **ἐπ' αὐτὴν ἥκει τὴν ἀκμήν** "[the situation] has reached a critical point." ἀκμή is frequent in contexts that stress "imminent necessity" (Finglass 2007: 101; LSJ ἀκμή III). **οὐκέτ' ἐγχωρεῖ** "there is not any more time" to put off action. Sc. ὁ χρόνος, as often in this idiomatic impersonal use of the verb; see LSJ ἐγχωρέω I 1 and I 2.

**42 θεῶν τις**: the gods take an active role in protecting Athens; see 2.1n. τήν and cf. *GPM* 136–7. **ὑπὲρ τῆς πόλεως αἰσχυνόμενος** "ashamed for the city." The sense of shame correlates with the depiction of Philip as an agent of hybris; see 1.23n. ὑβριστής, 1.24n. εἶτ'. D. very frequently describes Philip's aggressions in these terms; cf. §10, 1.24, 27, 2.2, 3.8, 16. **τὴν φιλοπραγμοσύνην ταύτην ἐμβαλεῖν Φιλίππωι**: 1.14n. καί. The use of ἐμβάλλω to describe the gods' responsibility for mortals' feelings is a common metaphor originating in Homer: e.g., H. *Il*. 3.139, 17.118, *Od* 19.10. **ἃ κατέστραπται καὶ προείληφεν**: §6n. πάντα, §31n. τά. The repetition of earlier points signals that the speech is coming to a conclusion. **ἀποχρῆν ἐνίοις ὑμῶν ἄν μοι δοκεῖ** "I suppose some of you would have been content [with those circumstances]." The omitted material is to be supplied from the following relative clause; for this sort of omission, cf. §8 and see *GPS* 27. **ἐξ ὧν ... ὠφληκότες ἂν ἦμεν δημοσίαι** "[although] we as a people would have incurred shame from them, and would have deserved the charge of cowardice and all that is most shameful." ὀφλισκάνω has two different senses here: with the first object (αἰσχύνην) it describes "anything which one deserves or brings on oneself" (LSJ II 1), and with the latter two objects (ἀνανδρίαν and πάντα τὰ αἴσχιστα) it is "incur a charge" (LSJ II 2). Both usages typically describe the action of individuals; for the ascription of these qualities to the city as a whole, cf. §10n. τοῖς. For the culminating neut. pl. τὰ αἴσχιστα, cf. 3.16. **νῦν δ᾽**: 2.6n. νῦν. **ἐπιχειρῶν ἀεί τινι καὶ τοῦ πλείονος ὀρεγόμενος** "since he is always attacking someone and grasping for more." For the contrast of Philip's tireless activity with the Athenians' lethargy, cf. §9, 2.15, 23. **εἴπερ μὴ παντάπασιν ἀπεγνώκατε** "if indeed you have not completely given up." For this sense of ἀπογιγνώσκω, cf. D. 19.51, 54.

**43 θαυμάζω ... εἰ** "I am amazed that"; cf. D. 2.24. **ἐνθυμεῖται μήτε ὀργίζεται**: D. regularly pairs ἐνθυμέω with λογίζομαι (1.21n. ἐνθυμηθῆναι); the unexpected second element here signals rising vehemence. **τὴν μὲν ἀρχὴν τοῦ πολέμου**: D. refers to the Athenian reaction to Philip's seizure of Amphipolis in 357 (§25n. Φιλίππωι). This and the following clause are parallel in word order and syntax, with the initial contrast between the start and the end of the war marked by μέν and δέ, then a participle in indirect statement (γεγενημένην and οὖσαν), and finally a concluding prepositional phrase with an articular infinitive and the emphatic repetition of Philip's name at the end of the clause. **ὑπὲρ τοῦ μὴ παθεῖν κακῶς**: cf. 3.1n. ὅπως for the same movement from earlier speeches about punishing Philip to current apprehension about mistreatment at his hands. **ἀλλὰ μὴν ... γε**: 1.23n. ἀλλά. The new point in the argument is marked by a switch in style, with a series of short clauses. **ὅτι γε οὐ στήσεται, δῆλον** "[it is] clear that he will not stand still." **εἶτα τοῦτο ἀναμενοῦμεν**; "what then, will we wait for this?" τοῦτο refers to the idea of the preceding clause, that someone will stop Philip. εἶτα introduces a question that expresses indignation by pointing to the consequences that arise from a situation of which the speaker disapproves; e.g., D. 1.24, 9.18, 18.243 with Yunis 244. **τριήρεις κενὰς καὶ τάς**

## 4 FIRST PHILIPPIC 43–45

παρὰ τοῦ δεῖνος ἐλπίδας ἂν ἀποστείλητε "if you send off empty ships and [empty] hopes [arising] from some [orator]." The delayed placement of ἄν (= ἐάν) puts stress on the preceding accusatives. κενάς is to be construed in two different senses with the two nouns (syllepsis): with the first it is a technical term referring to ships to be manned by mercenaries (3.5n. δέκα); with the second it is an idiom to describe unrealistic wishes that are dangerously misleading (for κενὴ ἐλπίς describing debate in the Assembly, cf. Isoc. 8.75, D. *Pr.* 35.4, Aesch. 2.119, 3.91, Din. 4.91; and for the phrase in poetry, see Garvie 2009: 309–10 on A. *Pers.* 804, Finglass 2007: 533 on S. *El.* 1460–1). The phrasing of ἐλπίδας as the object of ἀποστέλλω is difficult, but the jarring expression emphasizes that the Athenians are not dispatching actual forces. **καλῶς:** the final placement is strongly stressed; cf. D. 3.1 (κακῶς) and *GPS* 47.

**44 οὐκ ἐμβησόμεθα;** the series of four brief questions with οὐ and the fut. indic. reiterates the main points of §§16–17, but with increased urgency and exasperation, underscored by asyndeton (Smyth §1918). **οὐκ ἔξιμεν αὐτοί:** 1.6n. αὐτούς. **μέρει γέ τινι στρατιωτῶν οἰκείων** "with some portion of our own soldiers"; i.e., some part of the army should be composed of Athenian citizens. **νῦν, εἰ καὶ μὴ πρότερον:** §7n. νῦν. **ἐπὶ τὴν ἐκείνου:** sc. χώραν. **ἤρετό τις** "someone asked"; 1.14n. τί. The aorist is less speculative than the usual τις ἂν εἴποι and contributes to the sense of urgency. **εὑρήσει τὰ σαθρά** "will find the weaknesses." σαθρός is the opposite of sound physical health (Pl. *Grg.* 493e); for the metaphor see 2.21n. For the phrasing, cf. Pl. *Euthphr.* 5c εὕροιμ' ἄν ... ὅπηι σαθρός ἐστιν. This initial presentation of the verb and object puts emphasis on them. **ἂν ἐπιχειρῶμεν:** ἄν = ἐάν. Cf. §42 ἐπιχειρῶν; the use of the verb to describe both Philip and Athens marks their different levels of engagement. **ἂν μέντοι καθώμεθα οἴκοι** "but if we sit at home idly" (2.23n. καθήμεθα). This protasis is pointedly juxtaposed with the previous one. **λοιδορουμένων ... καὶ αἰτιωμένων:** D. regularly pairs these verbs (or the cognate nouns) to describe slanderous speeches lacking proof (D. 18.15, 22.21–2, 57.17; cf. 2.5n. λοιδορίαν); here the usage implies that other speakers in the Assembly disregard the facts of the matter at hand. **οὐδέποτ' οὐδὲν ἡμῖν μὴ γένηται τῶν δεόντων** "nothing of what must [happen] will ever occur for us." The two οὐ- terms reinforce each other, and the combination with μή and the aor. subj. is a strongly "emphatic denial" (Smyth §1804).

**45 μέρος τι τῆς πόλεως συναποσταλῆι** "some part of the city joins in the expedition." The συν- prefix, repeated in the main clause, stresses the goal of active Athenian participation (D. here avoids the more common verb ἀποστέλλω); cf. 2.9n. ὅταν. **πᾶσα:** sc. ἡ πόλις συναποσταλῆι. **τὸ τῆς τύχης:** a common paraphrase for τύχη (cf. §12n. τά); e.g., Thuc.

**4.18.3**, Thphr. *Char.* 8.9 with Diggle 2004: 287.   ὅποι δ' ἂν στρατηγὸν … ἐκπέμψητε "if you dispatch a general and an ineffective decree and [empty] hopes from the speaker's platform" (LSJ κενός I 2). D. summarizes earlier points and echoes §43. In §24 he asserted that generals who have to recruit and provision their own troops will have their own priorities. In §30 he criticized proposals that are not followed up with action. In §1 he distinguished himself from other orators who give misleading advice; on ἐλπίδας see §43n. τριήρεις. On the βῆμα and topography of the Athenian Assembly, see Hansen 1991: 128–9; D. uses the noun as a symbol for political speaking (cf. 18.66).   οὐδὲν ὑμῖν τῶν δεόντων γίγνεται: the repetition from §43 is emphatic. For the technique cf. 2.25n. ἅπας. By switching to the second-person D. distances himself from Athenian decisions that do not accord with his advice (cf. 1.2n. ἡμεῖς). καταγελῶσιν: the prefix adds a tone of aggression and mockery. This sort of laughter is to be regarded "as an intrinsically aggressive, harmful act," akin to hybris and demanding a response (Halliwell 2008: 25; 1.23n. ὑβριστής).   τεθνᾶσι τῶι δέει τοὺς τοιούτους ἀποστόλους "they are scared to death of such expeditions." D. uses the phrase τεθνᾶσι τῶι δέει as if it were a verb that governs the accusative (cf. 19.81 τεθνάναι τῶι φόβωι Θηβαίους, with MacDowell 2000: 243); the idiom gravely reminds the audience that their allies are victimized while the Athenians stay at home (cf. §24). δέος (like φόβος) is a verbal noun, and the idea of action implicit in it governs the direct object, even though τεθνᾶσι is intransitive; for this type of construction cf. A. *Th.* 290–1 μέριμναι ζωπυροῦσι τάρβος | τὸν ἀμφιτειχῆ λεών ("worries kindle fear of the army around the wall") with Hutchinson 1985: 93 and Finglass 2007: 141.

**46** οὐ γὰρ ἔστιν, οὐκ ἔστιν: 1.19n. ἔστιν.   ἕνα ἄνδρα δυνηθῆναί ποτε "for a single man ever to be able." ἕνα ἄνδρα refers to a mercenary general unsupported by Athenian troops.   πάντα ὅσα βούλεσθε: for similar formulations describing unrealistic expectations of the Assembly, cf. D. 3.18, 18.35.   ὑποσχέσθαι μέντοι καὶ φῆσαι καὶ τὸν δεῖνα αἰτιάσασθαι καὶ τὸν δεῖνα "for this one or that one to make promises and affirmations, and lay blame" (LSJ φημί III). Any single individual mercenary general can say what the Athenians want to hear, or blame someone else for failures. For the critical tone of τὸν δεῖνα … καὶ τὸν δεῖνα, see 2.31n. ὁ. As above, D. does not name specific individuals in order to stress the continued and repeated effect of Athenian military policy. The general Chares (2.25n. κρινόντων) in particular was famous for making extravagant promises of lavish donations to Athens (*Suda* χ 101; Pritchett 1974: 80 n. 122, 3.31n. βοίδια).   τὰ δὲ πράγματα ἐκ τούτων ἀπόλωλεν "as a result of which our opportunities are lost." For the phrasing cf. D. 19.217 ὑπὲρ πραγμάτων αἰσχρῶς καὶ δεινῶς ἀπολωλότων τὴν ὑπάρχουσαν αἰσχύνην ("the shame arising from opportunities shamefully and terribly lost"). ὅταν governs the three verbs ἡγῆται, ὦσιν, ψηφίζησθε. The sequence moves from the general on expedition, to his agents working in Athens, to the Athenians themselves; the movement suggests that the generals and the Athenians are together responsible for failed campaigns and policy. ἀπομίσθων "unpaid" (LSJ 1, Harp. s.v. ἀπόμισθοι). οἱ δ᾽ ... ἐνθάδ᾽ ὦσιν "there are men here who readily lie to you about anything he does." Like ὅταν, ἄν + subj. here and below are indefinite and conditional. For ψευδόμενοι ῥᾳδίως, cf. Is. 11.20, D. *Pr.* 24.2, [D.] 52.17. ὅ τι ἂν τύχητε ψηφίζησθε "you vote in any old way." With ὅ τι ἂν τύχητε sc. ψηφιζόμενοι; for the idiom cf. LSJ τυγχάνω A I 4, Is. 11.20, Isoc. 12.25. τί καὶ χρὴ προσδοκᾶν; "what in the world are we to expect?" καί puts stress on the question (Smyth §2884). After the extended ὅταν clauses, this short outburst expresses D.'s indignation.

### 47–50 Stop being foolish
Go out yourselves and stop him. Take control of the future before it is too late.

**47 ὅταν:** D. answers as if his previous interrogative were "when?" (πότε), not "how?" (πῶς), to give the effect of rushed spontaneity. τοὺς αὐτοὺς ... μάρτυρας τῶν στρατηγουμένων "when you appoint the same men as soldiers and as witnesses of the campaign"; cf. §25n. στρατιώτας. καὶ δικαστὰς οἴκαδ᾽ ἐλθόντας τῶν εὐθυνῶν "and as judges of the accounts upon their return home." Like magistrates, generals had to submit accounts, εὔθυναι, to the δῆμος; see 1.28n. αἱ. μὴ ἀκούειν μόνον ... ἀλλὰ καὶ παρόντας ὁρᾶν: D. underlines his insistence on Athenian participation in the campaign with this commonplace assertion of the superiority of firsthand knowledge. For this type of polarization, see Garvie 2009: 152, Diggle 1994: 81 n. 60. εἰς τοῦθ᾽ ἥκει τὰ πράγματ᾽ αἰσχύνης "the situation has reached such a point of shame." For the construction and rhetorical device (hypostasis), see 3.1n. τά, §37n. ὁ. τῶν στρατηγῶν ἕκαστος δὶς καὶ τρὶς κρίνεται: the procedure of εἰσαγγελία allowed any citizen to denounce another for political crimes; if the Assembly decided to pursue the case, it was heard by either the Assembly or the courts, and guilty parties were often subject to the death penalty (Hansen 1991: 214–18). The orators describe generals as frequent targets of these prosecutions (e.g., D. 8.29, 13.5, 20.79, Hyp. *Eux.* 27), and more of the attested cases from the period 432–355 involve generals than any other type of individual or magistrate, with one (Timotheos, *LGPN* s.v. 32, *PAA* 886180) known to have been tried at least three times (Hansen 1975: 59). D.'s comparison of risk in battle and on trial is not a wild exaggeration: it is estimated that 20% of generals experienced such prosecutions, and in the attested cases more than 75% of the accused were found guilty, and more than 75% of those were given the death penalty; in the fourth century six or eight Athenian generals are known to have been killed by this procedure, as compared with three known to have died in battle (Hansen 1975: 63–4, cf. Low 2011: 70–1). πρὸς δὲ τοὺς ἐχθροὺς ... ἀγωνίσασθαι περὶ θανάτου τολμᾶι "not one of them dares even once to risk death contending against the enemy." οὐδ' ἅπαξ is contrasted with δὶς καὶ τρίς. D. chooses the verb ἀγωνίζομαι because it regularly describes war and also competition in the courts (LSJ I A 2 and II). τὸν τῶν ἀνδραποδιστῶν καὶ λωποδυτῶν θάνατον "the death of kidnappers and thieves." Kidnappers and thieves are paired (cf. Isoc. 15.90 and see Todd 2007: 674) as two of the types of criminals classified as public menaces (κακοῦργοι), for whom there were special judicial procedures resulting in the execution of guilty parties (MacDowell 1978: 148–9; Gagarin 2003). See 9.22n. καθ'. κακούργου μὲν γάρ ἐστι κριθέντ' ἀποθανεῖν "for it is the fate of a common criminal to die after being tried." This and the following clause are parallel in construction: the initial genitive is a predicate describing the person who has the typical characteristic of the subject infinitive; the accusative participle refers to the subject of the infinitive. See Smyth §1304 and cf. 1.1n. τῆς. στρατηγοῦ δὲ μαχόμενον τοῖς πολεμίοις: sc. ἐστι and ἀποθανεῖν.

48 ἡμῶν δ' οἱ μὲν περιιόντες "some of us go around." D. illustrates the range of wild rumors in Athens with four repetitions of substantive articles, all subject of φασί. Each introduces a different indirect statement, until he breaks off the construction and ends with a summary generalization. The περι- prefix at the beginning and end encloses the sentence and reinforces the images of the Athenians going round in circles. D. repeats his point and phrasing from above; see §10n. περιιόντες. μετὰ Λακεδαιμονίων ... τὴν Θηβαίων κατάλυσιν: the supposed collusion of the Spartans and Philip for the destruction of Thebes is otherwise unattested; the rumors that D. reports here are similar to those in §11 and have little basis in reality. It was plausible, however, that Sparta would work for the destruction of Thebes, since they had fought in battle very recently (D. S. 16.39.2, HM 309). τὰς πολιτείας διασπᾶν "tear apart their constitutions." D. refers to the Boeotian cities of Thespiae, Orchomenus, and Plataea, which were dominated by Thebes. In one of his early Assembly speeches, For the Megalopolitans (353/2), D. advises the Athenians to resist Spartan moves to grant independence to these cities in an effort to weaken Thebes (16.4, 25; MacDowell 2009: 208–10). At that time the Athenians did not get involved and Sparta was unable to pursue these plans, but later, after the battle of Chaeronea in 338, Philip did liberate these cities from Thebes (Harris 134). ὡς πρέσβεις πέπομφεν ὡς βασιλέα "that he has sent ambassadors to the [Persian] king." This was a plausible rumor, and communication could have been occasioned by Philip's reception of the fugi-

tive satrap Artabazus (D. S. 16.52.3, *HM* 308–9; §24n. πρός). There is a single late reference to an alliance struck between Philip and the Persian king Artaxerxes, but all the details are vague, and the reliability of the report is doubtful (see Arr. 2.14.2 with Bosworth 1980: 229–30). **ἐν Ἰλλυριοῖς πόλεις τειχίζειν:** 1.13n. ἐπ᾽. **λόγους πλάττοντες ἕκαστος περιερχόμεθα:** the expression λόγους πλάττειν mocks gossip-mongerers. Elsewhere D. uses it to ridicule his opponent in court (18.121), and Plato's Socrates similarly mocks courtroom fictions (*Ap.* 17c). For ἕκαστος with the plural verb, cf. §7n. παύσησθε.

**49 ἐγὼ δὲ οἶμαι μέν ... νὴ τοὺς θεούς** "I really think." The oath with νή stresses a positive statement; for an overview of D.'s use of oaths see MacDowell 2009: 402–4. **μεθύειν:** 2.18n. μέθην. **τῶν πεπραγμένων:** the phrasing of this section repeatedly stresses Philip's activity (πράττω 3×, ποιεῖν) in contrast to the Athenians' mindless gossipmongering (Wooten 117); cf. §42n. ἐπιχειρῶν. **ὀνειροπολεῖν:** the reference to dreaming, like that to drunkenness, is disdainful, suggesting that Philip was deluded and out of touch with reality (on this connotation of dreaming, see W. V. Harris 2009: 139–41). **τήν τ᾽ ἐρημίαν τῶν κωλυσόντων ὁρῶντα** "because he perceives the absence of those who are going to stop him"; 3.27n. ὅσης. For the phrase τῶν κωλυσόντων, cf. D. 20.74, (and in the singular) S. *Ant.* 261, *El.* 1197. **ἐπηιρμένον** "encouraged" (LSJ ἐπαίρω II 1). In the *Against Meidias*, D. twice uses this verb to describe the subject's incitement to commit hybris (21.159, 211), and here the tone is similarly foreboding. **οὐ μέντοι γε μὰ Δί᾽ οὕτω προαιρεῖσθαι πράττειν ὥστε** "but [I do] not really [think] he would choose to act in such a way that." See 1.23n. μά. This oath is often combined with μέντοι, and the tone is conversational; γε adds emphasis, and the whole phrase here responds to μέν and the positive oath in the first half of the sentence (*GP* 401–2, 405). **ἀνοητότατοι γάρ εἰσιν οἱ λογοποιοῦντες:** the repetition of ἀνοητότατος (the word is a favorite of D.'s; cf. 8.58, 21.149) highlights D.'s scorn for those who rely on rumors. As the speech draws a close D. returns to his initial point, that he has a unique perspective (§1) because he sees the reality of the situation. "The verb λογοποιεῖν ... belongs to the polemical vocabulary of the orators" (Diggle 2004: 277 collects examples); it describes those who circulate false tales in order to bolster their own authority (S. Lewis 1996: 4–5, 77–80).

**50 ἀλλ᾽ ἂν ἀφέντες ταῦτ᾽ ἐκεῖνο εἰδῶμεν** "but if we dispense with these [rumors] and recognize this." ἐκεῖνο points to the series of indirect statements that follow. The series comprises three pairs of statements talking about the present (ἐχθρὸς ἄνθρωπος and ἀποστερεῖ), past (ὕβρικε and εὕρηται), and future (τὰ λοιπὰ ... ἐστί and ἀναγκασθησόμεθα).

ἐχθρὸς ἄνθρωπος: 3.16n. ἐχθρός, 1.3n. ἄνθρωπος. τὰ ἡμέτερα ἡμᾶς ἀποστερεῖ "he is robbing us of our possessions." D. sums up his point from §§2–12. ὕβρικε echoes the first reference to Philip in the speech (§3); see 1.23n. ὑβριστής. ἅπανθ' ὅσα πώποτ' ἠλπίσαμέν τινα πράξειν ὑπὲρ ἡμῶν "everything that we ever hoped someone would do for us." The phrasing recalls §7, where D. urges the Athenians to act for themselves and not rely on others. καθ' ἡμῶν εὕρηται "has been found [to have been done] against us." D. highlights the Athenians' disengagement from reality by juxtaposing the prepositional phrases; cf. 3.12n. μή. τὰ λοιπὰ ἐν αὐτοῖς ἡμῖν ἐστί "the future is in our hands" (LSJ ἐν A I 6). ἐθέλωμεν ἐκεῖ ... ἐνθάδ' ἴσως ἀναγκασθησόμεθα: D. draws out the consequences of the Athenians' refusal to recognize the actual situation with contrasting terms in a chiastic sequence: ἐθέλωμεν is opposed to ἀναγκασθησόμεθα and ἐκεῖ to ἐνθάδε (cf. §20n. τά). For the argument cf. 1.25. ἂν ταῦτ' εἰδῶμεν repeats the initial clause of the sentence; ταῦτα points back to the preceding series of indirect statements. τὰ δέοντ' ἐσόμεθα ἐγνωκότες "we shall decide [to do] our duty"; fut. perf. indic. (Smyth §600, cf. 1.14n. εἰ). λόγων ματαίων ἀπηλλαγμένοι "we shall be rid of idle rumors" (LSJ ἀπαλλάσσω B 1). ἅττα ποτ' ἔσται "what will happen"; ἅττα = ἅτινα. φαῦλα: sc. ἔσται and τὰ πράγματα τῆς πόλεως vel sim. (cf. 2.26, §3). εὖ εἰδέναι: parallel to σκοπεῖν; sc. δεῖ.

### 51 I speak for the good of Athens
This advice is for the good of the state, even at the risk of danger to myself.

**51 ἐγὼ μὲν οὖν** draws attention to the speaker's unique perspective; D. often uses this phrase to mark a concluding statement (15.35, 16.32, 34.52, 60.37). οὔτ' ἄλλοτε πώποτε πρὸς χάριν εἱλόμην λέγειν "neither did I ever on another occasion choose to speak in order to win your favor"; on πρὸς χάριν see 3.3n. ὁρᾶτε and Smyth §1695.3c. οὔτ' is paired with τε below (Smyth §2945). ὅ τι ἂν μὴ καὶ συνοίσειν πεπεισμένος ὦ "anything that I am convinced will not be advantageous also." The indefinite conditional relative clause is the object of λέγειν; the subj. mood, instead of the regular optative after a past tense main verb, is emphatic and stresses the continued truth of this statement. The adverbial καί modifies συνοίσειν (fut. of συμφέρω) and succinctly states that when D. has given pleasing speeches, they have also contained sound advice. ἃ γιγνώσκω πάνθ' "all my beliefs"; the object of πεπαρρησίασμαι. For the political sense, cf. §§1, 12 and §1n. ἅ. ἁπλῶς, οὐδὲν ὑποστειλάμενος, πεπαρρησίασμαι "holding back nothing, I have spoken freely"; 1.16n. ὑποστείλασθαι. At the end of the speech, as in the third *Olynthiac*, D. presents himself as an advisor who says what must be said despite the potential risks to himself; see 3.32n. οὐδέ. ἐβουλόμην δ' ἄν "I should have liked"; the imperf. with ἄν denotes an impossibility (Smyth §1789). **συμφέρει**: through repetition of this verb (5× in this final section of the speech) D. stresses this theme as the distinctive point that sets him apart from other speakers in the Assembly (§1). See 1.1n. τό.  **συνοῖσον**: sc. τὸ τὰ βέλτιστα εἰπεῖν.  **πολλῶι γὰρ ἂν ἥδιον εἶχον** "I would be much happier."  **νῦν δέ**: 1.9n. νῦν.  **ἐπ' ἀδήλοις οὖσι τοῖς ἀπὸ τούτων ἐμαυτῶι γενησομένοις** "despite the outcomes for myself from these [proposals] being uncertain." D. obliquely refers to the possibility of being prosecuted for making an illegal or undesirable proposal; see 3.12n. παθεῖν. For this sense of ἐπί, cf. D. 21.30 and see 9.34n. ἐφ'. **ἐπὶ τῶι συνοίσειν ὑμῖν, ἂν πράξητε, ταῦτα πεπεῖσθαι** "in order to persuade [you] that these [proposals] will be beneficial for you, if you take action." The interlocked word order puts emphasis on the key term συνοίσειν; see 2.8n. συμφέρον. For ἐπί denoting purpose, cf. 1.24n. ἐφ'. **νικώιη**: optative of wish (Smyth §1814).  **ὅ τι πᾶσιν μέλλει συνοίσειν**: this optimistic closure is typical of other Assembly speeches and very similar to the end of the third *Olynthiac* (see 3.36n. ὑμεῖς). D.'s final words reiterate the stress on τὸ συμφέρον.

# 9 THIRD PHILIPPIC

### 1–5 Prooemium

Unlike other speakers, D. will speak frankly, without flattering the Athenians. Their interests are threatened, but if they stop neglecting their duty, they can gain control of the situation.

**1 πολλῶν ... λόγων γιγνομένων:** D. distinguishes himself from other politicians, as he often does at the start of Assembly speeches (3.1n. οὐδέν). **ὀλίγου δεῖν καθ' ἑκάστην ἐκκλησίαν** "at almost every Assembly meeting" (LSJ ὀλίγος IV 1 and δεῖ II b). For background see Introd. §2.  **περὶ ὧν** = περὶ τούτων ἅ, a frequent formula at the start of Assembly speeches to describe the subject of debate: cf. D. 1.1, 6.1, 7.1, 8.2, 10.1.  **Φίλιππος**: earlier speeches begin with vague generalities and delay specific references (see 1.4n. τοῦθ', 2.6n. Ὀλυνθίους, 3.2n. τούς, 4.3n. τῆι νῦν). Now D. is more confident that his audience understand the threat Philip poses, and he comes straight to the point.  **τὴν εἰρήνην**: in early 346 Philip and the Athenians agreed to the peace of Philocrates (named after an Athenian ambassador who proposed the decree in the Assembly to initiate negotiations, *LGPN* s.v. 76, *PAA* 937530). The terms were thus: each party kept control of the territories it held at the time of the agreement; each agreed to keep the peace and to aid the other militarily for an indefinite period of time; each would protect shipping lanes from pirates; the allies of each were subject to these provisions (*HM* 338–41, Harris 70–94).

Two of the ambassadors, D. and Aeschines, describe the peace process in a pair of trial speeches from 343, when D. prosecutes Aeschines for corruption during the negotiations (D. or. 19 and Aesch. or. 2; the peace process is revisited in the pair of speeches, Aesch. or. 3 and D. or. 18, from a later trial in 330 in which Aeschines prosecutes D.'s ally Ctesiphon for sponsoring a measure in praise of D.). These speeches preserve an abundance of background information, but most of it is untrustworthy, since each speaker aims to defend his own policies and behavior while vilifying his opponent; however, the amount of detail and the way in which it is presented allows modern readers to evaluate the strengths and weaknesses of D. and Aeschines' cases (for criteria of analysis see Harris 7–16). In the present speech D. repeats his key arguments from the trial of 343 (which are largely tendentious; see the specific notes): that the other ambassadors were bribed (§9n. τῶν), and that they colluded in Philip's destruction of Phocis (§11n. ἤριζον, §19n. ἀφ') and his aggressions in Thrace (§15n. ἄρτι). **τοὺς ἄλλους ἀδικεῖ:** D. presents the cause as that of all the Greeks against Philip. Cf. 2.24n. εἰ. **πάντων οἶδ' ὅτι φησάντων γ' ἄν ... πράττειν** "all would agree, I am sure, even if they do not act accordingly, that [we] must speak and act." For parenthetic οἶδ' ὅτι see LSJ εἴδω B 8, Smyth §2585. γε emphasizes φησάντων and points to the contrast with ποιοῦσι. For ἄν with the participle, cf. 3.8. τοῦτο refers to λέγειν and πράττειν; the pair of verbs sums up the range of activity practiced by citizens who put the best interests of Athens ahead of their own (see 3.15n. τό). The range is reiterated with more specificity below in λέγειν and χειροτονεῖν. **τῆς ὕβρεως:** 1.23n. ὑβριστής. **δίκην δώσει:** D. regularly asserts that the correct and necessary policy would aim to punish Philip, and that the Athenians instead are forced to consider how they may avoid suffering themselves because they neglect to do their duty; cf. 3.11n. ὅπως, 4.15, 43. **εἰς τοῦθ' ὑπηγμένα πάντα τὰ πράγματα καὶ προειμένα** "all our affairs have been strung along to this [point] and mismanaged." D. repeatedly uses ὑπάγω to describe how the Athenians (and others) are led along and deceived by Philip; cf. 5.10, 6.31, 8.62–3. The ὑπο- prefix conveys a sense of trickery (LSJ ὑπάγω A III, Smyth §1698.4). προειμένα (acc. pl. neut. perf. pass. participle of προΐημι), on the other hand, refers to mistakes that the Athenians made on their own; see 1.9n. ἀεί. **ὥστε** makes best sense governing ἡγοῦμαι; D. sees the situation as being so bad that he does not think it can get worse. Alternatively, some editors omit the dashes and put a colon after ᾖ, so that ὥστε governs δέδοικα; but that leaves ἡγοῦμαι without a conjunction. **μὴ βλάσφημον μὲν εἰπεῖν:** sc. ᾖ. "[I am afraid] that [it may be] a slanderous thing to say." Unusually, here the μέν clause carries more weight than the following δέ clause (*GPS* 74). The infinitive is explanatory and to be understood with both βλάσφημον and ἀληθές. βλάσφημος describes verbal insults; D. voices apprehension about directly attacking other politicians in Athens because of the potential legal consequences; see 3.12n. παθεῖν. **οἱ παριόντες**: those who come forward to speak in the Assembly; cf. 2.31, 3.21n. οἱ. **χειροτονεῖν ὑμεῖς**: sc. ἐβούλεσθε. **ἐξ ὧν ὡς φαυλότατα ἔμελλε τὰ πράγμαθ' ἕξειν** "in accordance with what was likely to keep the situation as bad as it can be" (LSJ ἐκ III 7 and ἔχω A II 13). ἐξ ὧν = ἐκ τούτων ἅ, like περὶ ὧν above (§1). D. makes the same point in similar words at the start of the first *Philippic* (cf. 4.2n. πάνυ). **οὐκ ἂν ἡγοῦμαι δύνασθαι**: sc. τὰ πράγματα and διατεθῆναι. ἄν modifies δύνασθαι.

**2** This sentence comprises three pairs of μέν/δέ clauses (πολλὰ μέν/μάλιστα δέ, τινες μέν/ἕτεροι δέ, ἡ μὲν πόλις/Φιλίππωι δέ). The successive pairs are nested; the second pair is subordinate to the first δέ clause, and the third pair to the second δέ clause. Throughout, the δέ clauses carry more weight, because they are longer and they present more detailed and vital information than the corresponding μέν clauses, which are redundant and generalizing here. For a focused discussion of the "spiralling effect" of this sentence, see Wooten 1999 (quotation on 451). **μὲν οὖν**: 2.3n. **οὐ παρ' ἓν οὐδὲ δύο** "not because of one [reason] or two" (LSJ παρά C III 7, cf. D. 4.11). The phrase "not one or two" meaning "too many" is idiomatic as early as Homer; cf. *Od.* 14.94 with Bowie 2013: 180. It is an example of redundancy after πολλά. **εἰς τοῦτο τὰ πράγματ' ἀφῖκται** echoes εἰς τοῦθ' … τὰ πράγματα above. **ἐξετάζητε ὀρθῶς**: this Demosthenic collocation (23.124, *Ep.* 4.5) urges the Athenian δῆμος to hold politicians accountable for bad leadership; cf. 1.28n. αἵ, Phot. *Lexicon* ε 33 εὔθυναι· ἐξετάσαι ὀρθῶς. **εὑρήσετε διὰ τοὺς χαρίζεσθαι … λέγειν προαιρουμένους**: sc. εἰς τοῦτο τὰ πράγματ' ἀφῖχθαι. The phrase with διά is equivalent in sense to a causal clause. Both infinitives depend upon προαιρουμένους. D. constantly characterizes himself as an ideal advisor who gives frank advice for the good of the city, in contrast to others who pander to the pleasure of the δῆμος and harm the city. See 3.3n. ὁρᾶτε, 3.11n. τήν, 3.21n. δικαίου. **ἐν οἷς εὐδοκιμοῦσιν αὐτοὶ καὶ δύνανται, ταῦτα φυλάττοντες** "in an effort to preserve the situation in which they themselves gain distinction and power" (LSJ φυλάσσω B 3). ἐν οἷς describes circumstances (Smyth §1687a; cf. §56), and its antecedent is the following ταῦτα. The pres. participle can express purpose or intent (as the fut. participle regularly does, Smyth §2065). **περὶ τῶν μελλόντων πρόνοιαν** "foresight regarding the future." πρόνοια is a quality that marks the difference between good and bad leaders; see 3.21n. τόν. **οὐκοῦν οὐδ' ὑμᾶς οἴονται δεῖν ἔχειν**: the first of 17 places in which the MSS for the third *Philippic* present a shorter and a longer version of the speech. The difference between these is indicated by smaller type, and is also recorded in the apparatus. All the passages are discussed as a group in Introd. §6.2. **τοὺς ἐπὶ τοῖς πράγμασιν ὄντας αἰτιώμενοι**

## 9 THIRD PHILIPPIC 2–3

καὶ διαβάλλοντες "making accusations and attacks against those engaged with the situation." D. refers generally to prosecutions and denunciations of military leaders (see 2.25n. αἰτιωμένων and cf. 2.12, where ἐπὶ τοῖς πράγμασιν describes military activity); διαβάλλω and its cognates regularly refer to malicious public prosecutions with no basis in fact (E. M. Harris 2013b: 306–7, Rizzo and Vox 1978: 314–21). More specifically, he recalls recent debate about the appointment of the general Diopeithes, who was sent to the Chersonese to protect Athenian interests (see Pritchett 1974: 92–3, §§15–16 below, *LGPN* s.v. 48, *PAA* 363675). Philip sent a letter of complaint to the Athenian Assembly (cf. §27n. οὐ), and D.'s speech *On the Chersonese* (or. 8), delivered a month or two before this speech, defends Diopeithes from others demanding his recall. The allusion is clear; in the previous speech D. describes the critics of Diopeithes with the same pair of verbs: 8.23 τοῖς αἰτιᾶσθαι καὶ διαβάλλειν βουλομένοις.    οὐδὲν ἄλλο ποιοῦσιν ἢ ὅπως "they do nothing other than see to it that." πάντα ποιεῖν regularly takes an object clause with ὅπως + fut. indic. (Smyth §2210); here οὐδὲν ἄλλο ἤ is a variation for the frequent idiom with πάντα. Cf. too Pl. *Ap.* 24d ἄλλο τι ἢ περὶ πλείστου ποιῆι ὅπως ὡς βέλτιστοι οἱ νεώτεροι ἔσονται;    παρ' αὑτῆς δίκην λήψεται "will inflict punishment on itself." δίκην λαμβάνειν is the opposite of δίκην διδόναι (above §1, LSJ δίκη IV 3; cf. D. 21.92 for the construction with παρά). The pointed phrase and the pronouns highlight the absurdity of the situation. D. refers to legal and rhetorical attacks on generals, such as Diopeithes, who conduct campaigns against Philip, and on politicians, such as himself, who advocate those campaigns.    περὶ τοῦτ' ἔσται "will be occupied with this" (LSJ περί C I 3; cf. D. 54.27).    λέγειν καὶ πράττειν: another echo of §1, intended to ridicule Athenian priorities. It is their failure to "speak and act" as they should that empowers Philip.

**3 αἱ δὲ τοιαῦται πολιτεῖαι** "these sorts of political activity," i.e., trials and criticisms of Athenian leaders. πολιτεία can refer broadly to political action, as opposed to particular policies. Cf. 3.21, 18.59 with Yunis 143, Bordes 1982: 116–23, 377.    **συνήθεις μέν εἰσιν ... τῶν κακῶν:** after the ponderous sentences that open the speech, D. now stresses his point succinctly in two contrasting four-word phrases marked by parallel word order and sound: both συνήθεις ... ὑμῖν and αἴτιαι ... κακῶν begin with a (three-syllable) predicate adjective followed by μέν/δέ, and conclude with a (two-syllable) word ending in -ν.    **ἀξιῶ** "I ask." The request is expressed with the accus. + infin. below (μηδεμίαν ... ὀργὴν γενέσθαι). **ἄν τι τῶν ἀληθῶν μετὰ παρρησίας λέγω:** ἄν = ἐάν. D. continues to characterize himself as a selfless and well-informed advisor (cf. §1 δέδοικα, ἀληθές). It is a commonplace at the start of a speech to ask the audience to forgive the speaker's candor and advise them to consider whether what he says is true. See 2.28n. εἰ, 3.3n. μετά.    **μηδεμίαν ... ὀργήν:** orators (and critics of democracy) often complain that the δῆμος blames individual politicians for its bad decisions, and that anger at military failures leads to trials of generals and politicians (cf. §31n. ὅσωι, 1.16n. πολλάκις, 8.57). **ὑμεῖς τὴν παρρησίαν:** the subject and object are put first for emphasis; they are to be construed with all three second-person verbs in the period. The lack of a connecting particle (asyndeton) is typical after an introductory phrase such as σκοπεῖτε γὰρ ὡδί (cf. §56n. ἦσαν, *GPS* 110). **ἐπὶ μὲν τῶν ἄλλων** "in other cases," contrasted with ἐκ δὲ τοῦ συμβουλεύειν. The context suggests that this vague phrase refers broadly to any sort of communication at all, aside from speeches in the Assembly. ἐπί with the genitive refers to "particular instances" (MacDowell 1990: 222); see further 4.37n. οὐδέν. **οὕτω κοινήν** "so available"; κοινός refers to a "public" civic right, and the verb μεταδίδωμι regularly describes the granting of such rights (e.g, Lys. 16.5, Pl. *Rep.* 8.557a, Isoc. 16.17). For the claim, cf. Pl. *Grg.* 461e with Dodds 1959: 222. **τοῖς ξένοις καὶ τοῖς δούλοις:** the residents of Attica could be broadly grouped as citizens, foreigners, or slaves (e.g., Thuc. 6.27.2, Isoc. 8.48; cf. [D.] 59.85); here D. specifies the latter two groups to represent non-citizens as a whole. The term ξένος often refers specifically to metics (Whitehead 1977: 11, 21 n. 34), foreign residents in Athens with a defined legal status that conferred rights and imposed obligations (see Hansen 1991: 116–20). The suggestion here that metics and slaves enjoyed freedom of speech as a political right in Athens is highly exaggerated; D. presents this point as a criticism of the Athenians' reluctance to follow his recommendations. Metics were able to bring charges in Athenian courts, but were otherwise excluded from the city's political institutions; slaves had no political rights. D.'s exaggeration here is akin to that of the "Old Oligarch," who complains that slaves and metics could not be distinguished from citizens on the streets of Athens ([Xen.] *Ath. Pol.* 1.10). **μετὰ πλείονος ἐξουσίας** "with more freedom." **ὅ τι βούλονται** echoes the end of §2. The repetition emphasizes D.'s point that orators lack the freedom available to everyone else. **ἢ πολίτας:** the comparison is elliptical: "than [the freedom with which one would see] citizens [speaking]." In this hyperbolic context the phrase ἐν ἐνίαις τῶν ἄλλων πόλεων is not specific; it simply distinguishes Athens from other places. **τοῦ συμβουλεύειν** "participating in Assembly debates"; see 1.1n. συμβουλεύειν.

**4 εἶθ' ὑμῖν συμβέβηκεν ἐκ τούτου** "and then in consequence of this for you the result has been that" (cf. 1.2n. εἶτα). As in the previous sentence, the important items, ὑμῖν συμβέβηκεν, are placed at the start and are to be taken with the following μέν and δέ clauses; the impersonal construction (LSJ συμβαίνω III 1 b) governs the following three infinitives. ἐκ τούτου is used idiomatically with this construction; the neuter pronoun lacks a specific antecedent; cf. 23.8. **ἐν μὲν ταῖς ἐκκλησίαις:** D. often criticizes the Athenians by contrasting their preference for pleasing speeches in the Assembly with their refusal to acknowledge the reality of their military situation; cf. 3.1n. ὅταν, 3.19, 4.38. **τρυφᾶν** "to be at ease" or "to be comfortable," when the situation does not warrant it. **κολακεύεσθαι πάντα πρὸς ἡδονὴν ἀκούουσιν** "to be spoiled by hearing everything [said] for your pleasure." ἀκούουσιν is pres. act. participle in agreement with ὑμῖν. For D.'s characterization of his political opponents as panderers to the pleasure of the δῆμος, see 2.19n. κόλακας, 4.38n. πρός. **τοῖς πράγμασι καὶ τοῖς γιγνομένοις:** synonymous. **περὶ τῶν ἐσχάτων ἤδη κινδυνεύειν** "already to be in the most extreme dangers." For κινδύνευω + περί cf. 1.15, 15.24. **καὶ νῦν οὕτω διάκεισθε** "even now you are so disposed" as to be reassured by a flattering speech. **οὐκ ἔχω** "I do not know" (LSJ ἔχω A III 2). λέγω is a deliberative subjunctive (Smyth §1805). **ἃ συμφέρει:** D. often begins and ends speeches with this theme; cf. §76, 1.1n. τό, 4.51n. συμφέρει. **ἕτοιμος:** sc. εἰμί. **εἰ πάνυ φαύλως τὰ πράγματ' ἔχει:** the same phrase at the start of the first *Philippic*; see 4.2n. πάνυ and cf. §1. **πολλὰ προεῖται:** cf. §1 and see 1.9n. ἀεί. **τὰ δέοντα ποιεῖν:** 2.3n. προτρέπειν. **ἐπανορθώσασθαι:** unlike the many standard tropes noted above linking this speech introduction with earlier ones, this key theme (also in the conclusion, §76) distinguishes this speech from ones given before Philip had become so powerful. In earlier speeches D. simply warns of the threat that Philip poses, now he goes further by suggesting that the Athenians must "restore" what they have lost.

**5 παράδοξον:** at the beginning of his Assembly speeches D. often uses paradoxes such as this, asserting that what appears to be the worst situation is actually the best. They engage the audience and create a sense of optimism (1.4n. τοῦθ', 4.2n. ὅ). Compared with those earlier instances, D. softens the tone here by adding this prefatory apology. **τὸ χείριστον:** the passage from here down to γενέσθαι βελτίω is repeated almost verbatim from 4.2; only differing phrases are noted here. **τοῖς παρεληλυθόσι** "past events" or just "the past"; for the plural cf. 18.191, 242. **οὔτε μικρὸν οὔτε μέγα οὐδέν:** an idiomatic and emphatic phrase. Cf. D. 19.17, 21.75, and many instances in Plato (e.g., *Ap*. 19c, 21b, 24a, 26b). **νῦν δέ:** 1.9n. **τῆς ῥαθυμίας τῆς ὑμετέρας καὶ τῆς ἀμελίας:** 3.33n. ἔστι. **ἀλλ' οὐδὲ κεκίνησθε** "no, you have not even made a move." For the passive cf. 19.324.

### 6–20 Peace or war?
We must agree that Philip is at war, and take measures to defend ourselves. Philip and his Athenian partisans claim that we are starting a war and that he is at peace. But we must judge him by his actions. He has broken the peace and threatens Athens and Greece.

## 9 THIRD PHILIPPIC 6–7

**6** The structure of this argument follows a common pattern; on the textual issue see Introd. §6.2. D. begins with a present contrary-to-fact condition that points to the problem at hand (εἰ μὲν οὖν ἅπαντες ὡμολογοῦμεν ... παραβαίνειν) and asserts that there is no alternative to his position (οὐδὲν ... ἔδει). He then reiterates the existing problem (ἐπειδὴ δέ ... οἱ ποιοῦντες τὸν πόλεμον) and concludes with a strong reassertion of the necessity of his position (ἀνάγκη ... περὶ τούτου). This pattern and phrasing are repeated from the first words of his earliest speech (27.1 εἰ μέν ... οὐδὲν ἂν ἔδει ... ἐπειδὴ δέ ... ἀνάγκη ἐστίν...), and the same pattern and wording are found at [D.] 44.5–6. This type of argument, however phrased, must have been common in appeals to the Assembly (e.g., Thuc. 2.61.1, D. 4.1). **Φίλιππον τῆι πόλει πολεμεῖν**: D. presented the period from Philip's seizure of Amphipolis (in 357) to the peace of Philocrates (346) as one continuous war (4.25n. Φιλίππωι). Since at least the time of the speech *On the Chersonese* (early 341), he has argued that the war has resumed even though the Athenians pretend otherwise (8.8, 58). **τὴν εἰρήνην παραβαίνειν**: already in 344 D. had accused Philip of violating the peace (6.2). **οὐδὲν ἀλλ᾽ ... συμβουλεύειν ἢ ὅπως** "a speaker would need to say and advise nothing other than how" (cf. §1n. οἱ). ἀμυνούμεθα is fut. indic. in an object clause (Smyth §2211). **ἔνιοι**: although D. often uses this word to describe rival politicians, the context makes it clear that here he refers to members of the audience (cf. 4.42, 6.34, 8.24). **ὥστε**: governs ἀνέχεσθαι. **πόλεις ... ἀδικοῦντος**: the three genitives absolute form a tricolon. Each is marked by an initial π, and the parallelism is maintained by the device of isocolon (the three phrases πόλεις ... ἐκείνου, καὶ πολλὰ ... ἔχοντος and καὶ πάντας ... ἀδικοῦντος differ in length by only one syllable). πολλὰ τῶν ὑμετέρων specifically stresses Philip's violation of the treaty (see §1n. τήν). As often, D. caps the tricolon with an undefined final item (cf. 1.6n. καί); the phrase πάντας ἀνθρώπους characterizes D. as an advocate for all humankind (cf. 8.42, 18.72, §1n. τούς). **ἀνέχεσθαί τινων ... λεγόντων**: the genitive with ἀνέχομαι idiomatically refers to "people whose behaviour is tolerated" (Denyer 2008: 109 on Pl. *Prt.* 323a); see LSJ c ii 4, D. 19.16, 24 with MacDowell 2000: 213, 217. **ὡς ἡμῶν τινές εἰσιν οἱ ποιοῦντες τὸν πόλεμον**: indirect statement depending on λεγόντων. D. refers to accusations directed at the orators in Athens who advocated war; cf. 8.56. **διορθοῦσθαι περὶ τούτου** "to straighten out this [business]." D. refers generally to Athenian policy regarding Philip; cf. §4n. ἐπανορθώσασθαι. The middle voice (φυλάττεσθαι also) stresses that the safety of speaker and audience depends on these actions.

**7 μήποτε ὡς ἀμυνούμεθα γράψας τις καὶ συμβουλεύσας**: μήποτε is a conjunction introducing ἐμπέσηι in a fear clause. ὡς ἀμυνούμεθα should be taken as an indirect statement dependent on γράψας and συμβουλεύσας. Its position before those participles adds emphasis (hyperbaton), and the phrasing is a pointed variation for ὅπως … ἀμυνούμεθα above (§6); this accounts for the unusual syntax (an infinitive is commonly used for indirect statement with these verbs; the fut. indic. is echoed from above). D.'s point is that when the Athenians should be considering *how* (ὅπως) to defend themselves, it is dangerous for a politician even to propose *that* (ὡς) they defend themselves. For γράφω meaning "move a proposal," cf. 1.19, 4.33, Chadwick 1996: 85. **εἰς τὴν αἰτίαν ἐμπέσηι** "may incur the charge" (for the phrase cf. Pl. *Tht.* 150a). The following genitive presents the substance of the charge (Smyth §1375). **ἐγὼ δὴ τοῦτο πρῶτον ἁπάντων λέγω** "I state this as the first of all [my arguments]." τοῦτο points to what follows (Smyth §1247). **διορίζομαι εἰ ἐφ' ἡμῖν ἐστι** "I am determining whether it is in our power" (LSJ ἐπί B I 1 g). διορίζομαι describes the process of drawing a line, or of making a definition or distinction. Here D. uses it to pose the question as a binary one, with no room for doubt between a positive and a negative answer. The alternatives are presented in more detail in the μέν and δέ clauses in §8. For διορίζομαι introducing an indirect question with εἰ, cf. D. 21.114 (and LSJ I 3 for other interrogatives). **περὶ τοῦ πότερον** "about whether." The neuter article makes the following question a noun phrase (Smyth §1153g collects Demosthenic examples); cf. 3.10n. τό.

**8 ἵν' ἐντεῦθεν ἄρξωμαι** "to begin with this point" (LSJ ἐντεῦθεν III). The phrase indicates that there are various arguments that could be taken in any order; cf. 21.43 with MacDowell 1990: 257, Xen. *Lac.* 1.3.1. **φήμ' ἔγωγε** "I agree." The initial (enclitic) verb and the first-person pronoun are strongly emphatic. Cf. 3.19n. The structure of this main clause forms a chiasmus; the two first-person verbs come at beginning and end, with dependent infinitives between them and the accusatives (ἡμᾶς, τὸν … λέγοντα) at the center of the clause. **τὸν ταῦτα λέγοντα γράφειν … ἀξιῶ:** for the construction see §3n. ἀξιῶ. D. implies that his political opponents are unwilling to make proposals in the Assembly and expose themselves to possible prosecutions (cf. §2n. τούς). The verb φενακίζειν goes further, accusing them of the sort of deceit and manipulation that Philip himself practices; see 2.7n. οὐδείς, 4.38n. φενακίζειν. **ἕτερος:** just as D. used διορίζομαι above (§7) to suggest that there can be no middle ground in policy toward Philip, here and elsewhere D. uses this generic term to characterize him (and Alexander) as the opponent of Athenian (and Greek) interests; cf. 5.15, 18.320, 323. **τὰ ὅπλα ἐν ταῖς χερσὶν ἔχων:** D. refers to Philip's maintenance of a standing army. D. uses the same phrase in *On the Crown* in an outline of the key differences between Philip's rule and the democratic system in Athens, where armies were formed as needed by a vote of the people; cf. D. 18.235 and see also 1.4n. πάντων. **δύναμιν πολλὴν περὶ αὑτόν:** for the size of Philip's army, see 4.4n. τό τε. In a recent speech D. similarly described Philip's standing army as a "force always at the ready by his side" (8.11 δύναμιν συνεστηκυῖαν ἀεὶ περὶ αὑτόν). **τοὔνομα μὲν τὸ τῆς εἰρήνης ὑμῖν προβάλλει** "throws before you the pretense of peace." This and the following δέ clause develop a sharp contrast by means of parallel word order and antithetical terminology: ὄνομα μέν/τοῖς δὲ ἔργοις, τῆς εἰρήνης/τοῦ πολέμου, ὑμῖν/αὐτός; see 4.3n. παραδείγμασι for the same technique. D. puts the strongest emphasis on the initial antithesis between words and reality (on ὄνομα/ἔργον see LSJ ὄνομα III 1) by presenting the contrasted nouns alone at the start of the clause and then delaying the modifying genitives (cf. 19.53). προβάλλω is confrontational in tone; in its most literal sense it describes one "throwing forward" offensive weapons or defensive obstacles in war (cf. 4.40n. προβάλλεσθαι). Here the description of Philip using the word "peace" as a weapon is an oxymoron. **τί λοιπὸν ἄλλο;** sc. ἐστί (cf. 3.8n. τί). **φάσκειν** depends on εἰ βούλεσθε and introduces the indirect statement εἰρήνην ἄγειν. Its initial placement means that it is strongly stressed. Cf. §73n. **ὥσπερ ἐκεῖνος:** sc. εἰρήνην ἄγειν φησίν. **οὐ διαφέρομαι** "I have no objections" (LSJ διαφέρω IV).

**9 ταύτην εἰρήνην:** sc. εἶναι. ταύτην = τοῦτο; it has been assimilated to the gender of εἰρήνην (Smyth §1239). **ἐξ ἧς** "as a result of which" (LSJ ἐκ III 6). **ἐφ᾽ ἡμᾶς ἥξει** "he will attack us." **ἐκείνωι παρ᾽ ὑμῶν, οὐχ ὑμῖν παρ᾽ ἐκείνου:** the syntactical parallelism and the chiastic repetition of the pronouns, with the Athenians framing the negative οὐχ at the center of the expression, underscore D.'s complaint that the peace is "from you [and] not for you." Cf. *GPS* 75–6. **τῶν ἀναλισκομένων χρημάτων πάντων:** genitive of price (Smyth §1372). Like the call to restore Athenian losses (§4n. ἐπανορθώσασθαι), this theme distinguishes the present speech from those given prior to the peace of Philocrates (though an early example of this type of charge can be found in D. 15.32–3). When the peace turned almost immediately into an embarrassment to Athens, D. sought to distance himself from the process by accusing other ambassadors, chiefly his enemy Aeschines, of being bribed by Philip (see §1n. τήν; the charge of bribery is central in D.'s speech *On the False Embassy*, e.g., 19.4–8), and he continued to make these accusations in later speeches against Philip (e.g., 8.76, 18.20, 31 and *passim*; Brock 2013: 178 n. 73, Cawkwell 1996: 100–4, Ronnet 154–7). Such accusations were a common tactic in political and personal disagreements in Athens, and politicians who negotiated with Philip were particularly susceptible to them, although it seems very unlikely that Aeschines or other ambassadors actually were working against the interests of Athens; see Taylor 2001: 61–4, 162–3, Harris 116–18, Harvey 1985: 86–7, 106–7. **αὐτός** "[Philip] himself." The subject of the infinitives is the same as the subject of ὠνεῖται, and is not expressed; this adjectival modifier is thus nominative (see Smyth

§1974a, MacDowell 1990: 289–90). πολεμεῖν ὑμῖν, ὑφ' ὑμῶν δὲ μὴ πολεμεῖσθαι: the repetition and chiasmus again point to the absurdity of the Athenian position. For the central juxtaposition, cf. 3.12n. μή. **10 εἰ … περιμενοῦμεν:** εἰ + fut. indic. here refers to current intent, not to future time (Smyth §2301). εὐηθέστατοι: 1.15n. τίς. **ἂν ἐπὶ τὴν Ἀττικὴν αὐτὴν βαδίζηι καὶ τὸν Πειραιᾶ:** ἄν = ἐάν. βαδίζω strictly speaking refers to invasion by land (cf. 1.12); the reference to the Athenian port of Peiraeus gives the verb a wider sense here and reminds the Athenians that Philip's actions, in both central Greece and the Chersonese, could potentially hinder the passage of shipments of grain to the Athenian port. After Philip seized control of Phocis and Thermopylae in the midst of the peace negotiations of 346, the Athenians feared invasion and passed a decree to fortify Attica and the Peiraeus (D. 19.125, Harris 97–8). D.'s argument here is a recapitulation of a point from the earlier debate regarding the appointment of Diopeithes (8.7, §2n. τούς). Later, after the battle of Chaeronea (338), the Athenians again took emergency measures to defend Attica (Lycurg. 37). Despite these fears, Philip never invaded. **τοῦτ' ἐρεῖ:** i.e., that there is a state of open war. **οἷς** = τούτοις ἅ. The dative is instrumental with τεκμαίρεσθαι (Smyth §1512).

**11 τοῦτο μέν:** paired with τοῦτο δέ below. The two phrases are adverbial: "in the first place … and secondly." The usage is very common in certain works (e.g., Herodotus and some speeches of Antiphon), otherwise rather rare. It may be "a primitive manner of making a contrast, since the writer does not have to go to the trouble of picking out contrasted words to put with μέν and δέ" (MacDowell 1962: 139 on Andoc. 1.103); for its use in fourth-century authors, including D. (cf. §24, 20.59, 25.38), see Dover 1997: 95. **Ὀλυνθίοις:** the dative is to be taken with εἶπεν. This initial word presents the topic for the first of four examples from recent history; D. marks out the four items, which are presented in chronological order, by putting this sort of geographical key word at the start of each (εἰς Φωκέας, [§12] Φεράς, τοῖς … Ὠρείταις). **τεττaράκοντ' ἀπέχων τῆς πόλεως στάδια** "when he was 40 stades from the city" (LSJ ἀπέχω III 1 a) during the siege of Olynthus in 348. 40 stades is about five miles. **εἶπεν ὅτι δεῖ δυοῖν θάτερον** "he said that one of two things must [happen]." The two options are detailed in the ἤ … ἤ phrases, which are in apposition to θάτερον (cf. D. 19.102 with MacDowell 2000: 249). This statement is not reported elsewhere, and must have been made at some point during the siege when the Olynthians offered to surrender (Cawkwell 2011: 385). Philip presents his terms with "an almost oracular solemnity"; this is likely to be a direct quotation (*HM* 323). **αὐτὸν ἐν Μακεδονίαι:** sc. μὴ οἰκεῖν. This is an inconceivable possibility, implying that the Olynthians have no options. **πάντα τὸν ἄλλον χρόνον:** this accusative of duration (Smyth §1582; cf. 4.32n. τήν) is ambiguous; ἄλλος can refer to "the rest of time" in the past or in the future (LSJ ἄλλος II 6). Other Demosthenic usages refer to the past (§22, 24.6, 30.4, 61.5, *Pr.* 21.1), and that is probably what is meant here; in that case the phrase is to be taken with the participles that follow. Alternatively, if it refers to the future (cf. Pl. *Alc.* 121c, Lys. 14.4, Lycurg. 79), it modifies οἰκεῖν and provides an ominous conclusion to Philip's threat. **αὐτὸν αἰτιάσαιτό τι τοιοῦτον** "should make such an accusation against him," i.e., suggest that he is an aggressor at war. **ἀγανακτῶν ... πέμπων**: the participles are equivalent to imperfect indicatives in a past general condition ("he would be annoyed ..."; Smyth §§2340, 2350). They modify the subject of εἶπεν and do not need a connective particle or conjunction to join them to that verb. **εἰς Φωκέας ὡς πρὸς συμμάχους ἐπορεύετο** "he marched into Phocis as if [he were marching] to his allies" (LSJ ὡς C II a, Smyth §2996). During the period in 346 when Philip and the Athenians were negotiating the peace of Philocrates, Philip assured the Phocians of his friendship. Later, when the Phocian leader Phalaecus feared punishment from the Phocians and Athenians (for his role during the Phocian seizure of Delphi), he made an agreement with Philip, and that allowed Philip to claim responsibility for settling the third Sacred War. The Phocians were then forced to surrender to Philip when he entered central Greece. In this second example of Philip's duplicity D. alleges that Philip allowed the Athenians to believe he would punish Phalaecus and not interfere with the Phocians, when all the while he was planning a very different series of actions. However, there is no evidence to support D.'s allegation, and it is likely that these developments came about without planning on Philip's part; he took advantage of the opportunity that Phalaecus presented to him. See Harris 88–9, 97–8. **πρέσβεις Φωκέων**: Aeschines reports that when Athenian ambassadors met Philip in Pella (in early summer 346), other ambassadors from Sparta and Thebes were present, and that Phalaecus too was appealing to Philip (Aesch. 2.104, 135–6). Philip and Phalaecus may have been in touch for some time (*HM* 334–5), but we have no other contemporary evidence regarding Phocian ambassadors or where they marched with Philip (who campaigned first in Thrace and then in central Greece in summer 346). **παρ' ἡμῖν**: at Athens (cf. 4.49, §§3, 59). **ἤριζον οἱ πολλοὶ Θηβαίοις οὐ λυσιτελήσειν τὴν ἐκείνου πάροδον** "many contended that Philip's approach would be disadvantageous to the Thebans." There was fierce debate in Athens regarding Philip's intentions in 346, and the accounts that are preserved in D.'s speech *On the False Embassy* and Aeschines' response in *On the Embassy* are difficult to unravel. The verb ἐρίζω reflects that contentious disagreement. While Philip was allowing the Phocians to believe they would be treated fairly at his hands in the settlement of 346, he let some Athenians believe that his involvement in central Greece would limit the power of the Thebans (cf. D. 19.22, 74, Aesch. 2.117–19, D. 18.35–6), who were then the enemies of the Phocians and Athenians (see 1.26n. Θηβαῖοι). When Philip marched on the pass of Thermopylae, the Phocians were defenseless and the Athenians could not come to their aid (see *HM* 343–7). Philip then returned Phocian holdings in Boeotia to the Thebans, thus stabilizing Theban power in central Greece after 346 (see Harris 99–101). For the litotes in οὐ λυσιτελήσειν, see 1.23n. οὐδέν.

**12 Φεράς:** the object of ἔχει and καταλαβών, put first to maintain the structure of the list of examples (§11n. Ὀλυνθίοις). Philip's role in the third Sacred War gave him control over affairs in Pherae and Thessaly (see 1.13n. Φεράς, 2.7n. Θετταλούς). Probably in 344 he established garrisons in the region after failed attempts to solicit voluntary contributions to his campaigns (D. 8.59, 19.320, *HM* 523–5). **ὡς φίλος καὶ σύμμαχος:** §11n. εἰς. **ἔχει καταλαβών:** ἔχω + aor. part. is equivalent to a perfect tense and emphasizes the current situation: "he took [Pherae] and now holds it" (Smyth §1963a). Cf. §6 καταλαμβάνοντος ἐκείνου καὶ ... ἔχοντος. **τὰ τελευταῖα:** adverbial, marking the final item in the series of examples (cf. 2.7). **τοῖς ταλαιπώροις Ὠρείταις τουτοισὶ ἐπισκεψομένους** "[soldiers] who would tend to these people of Oreus in their pain." The demonstrative τουτοισί points out this fourth example as the closest one to the Athenians both in terms of geography and chronology. ταλαίπωρος refers to physical distress, and ἐπισκοπέω has a technical sense of "looking after" someone who is sick (Robertson 1944 collects examples); this cluster of medical vocabulary (also παρεῖναι below) shows that the political metaphor in νοσοῦσι is live and felt (see 2.14n. νοσοῦσι). In 342 Philip took advantage of political unrest in various cities in Euboea, and with his support the tyrant Philistides took control of the state of Oreus (see §§59–62, Sealey 259–64, *HM* 546–7). **ἔφη** introduces three infinitives in indirect statement (πεπομφέναι, πυνθάνεσθαι, εἶναι). Philip is to be understood as the subject of the first two, and the third is impersonal. **πυνθάνεσθαι γὰρ αὐτοὺς ὡς νοσοῦσι** "he heard that they were sick." The infinitive is imperfect in sense (cf. 3.21n. τούτωι), and the pronoun is emphasized by being placed before the subordinate clause (prolepsis, see 1.21n. τὰ πράγματα). **συμμάχων δ᾽ εἶναι καὶ φίλων ἀληθινῶν:** for the predicate genitive see 3.20n. οὗ. The repetition of φίλος and σύμμαχος links this example with the previous one and signals that the list is coming to an end (for the technique, cf. 1.11n. τι). **παρεῖναι:** synonymous with ἐπισκοπέω in the technical medical sense of caring for a patient; cf. LSJ πάρειμι (εἰμί *sum*) I 4 and [D.] 59.56 ἐβάδιζον γὰρ πρὸς αὐτόν, ὡς ἠσθένει καὶ ἔρημος ἦν τοῦ θεραπεύσοντος τὸ νόσημα, ... ἐπισκοπούμεναι· ἴστε δήπου ... ὅσου ἀξία ἐστὶν γυνὴ ἐν ταῖς νόσοις, παροῦσα κάμνοντι ἀνθρώπωι ("they went to him intending to care [for

## 9 THIRD PHILIPPIC 12-14    215

him], because he was weak and lacking a nurse for his illness; you know how valuable a woman is during sickness, tending one who is suffering"). **13 εἶτα** introduces an indignant question; see 4.43n. εἶτα.    **αὐτόν:** accus. subject of αἱρεῖσθαι and πολεμήσειν in indirect statement.    **οἳ ἐποίησαν μὲν οὐδὲν ἂν κακόν:** the relative is put before its antecedent τούτους for emphasis (cf. 2.19n. οὕς). The aor. indic. + ἄν expresses a potentiality in the past (Smyth §1784).    **μὴ παθεῖν δ' ἐφυλάξαντ' ἂν ἴσως** "but might perhaps have avoided suffering [any harm]" (LSJ πάσχω III b 2, φυλάσσω C II 3).    **τούτους μέν:** contrast with ὑμῖν δέ. The two indirect statements have a chiastic structure, with ἐξαπατᾶσθε echoing ἐξαπατᾶν and προλέγοντα βιάζεσθαι corresponding with ἐκ προρρήσεως πολεμήσειν.    **προλέγοντα βιάζεσθαι** "give warning and use force." The present tenses here and in ἐξαπατᾶν αἱρεῖσθαι, combined with the plural τούτους, generalize about all four of the previous examples and describe Philip's customary policy.    **ἐκ προρρήσεως πολεμήσειν** "will go to war after [giving] a warning." The singular πρόρρησις and the fut. tense draw attention to the switch from generalizations about past examples to a specific focus on the impending threat to Athens. **ταῦθ' ἕως ἄν** "[and that he will do] these things when all the while." ἕως ἄν + pres. subj. describes a duration stretching into the future (Smyth §2423a).    **ἑκόντες ἐξαπατᾶσθε:** D. similarly described the Athenians' tendency toward self-deception in the third *Olynthiac* (3.19n. ῥᾷστον). The repetition of ἐξαπατάω, and the placement at the end of the period, underline the accusation (cf. *GPS* 78-9).

**14 οὐκ ἔστι ταῦτα** "Impossible!"; this blunt response to a preceding indignant question is characteristic of D.'s style (e.g., 6.22, 8.26, 19.223). **ἀβελτερώτατος** "the silliest." The term is not primarily opprobrious (see MacDowell 2000: 248), but rather suggests that Philip would be remiss not to take advantage of the Athenians' self-deception.    **τῶν ἀδικουμένων … αἰτιωμένων:** gen. abs.; τῶν ἀδικουμένων ὑμῶν is a substantive noun phrase: "those of you who are wronged." μηδέν is used, rather than οὐδέν, because of the conditional context. ἐγκαλούντων and αἰτιωμένων overlap in sense (cf. D. 18.76); however, the former can refer to Assembly decrees, while the latter describes legal prosecutions (cf. 8.14, §2n. τούς).    **ἐκεῖνος** = Philip, the subject of προείποι and ἀφέλοιτο in the conditional protasis introduced by εἰ.    **ἐκλύσας τὴν πρὸς ἀλλήλους ἔριν ὑμῶν καὶ φιλονικίαν** "putting an end to your disagreement and contention among one another." As with the participles above, the two nouns here are nearly synonymous. Throughout this sentence D. devotes many more words to the Athenians than to Philip, who is the grammatical subject; the repetition of the second-person pronoun adds to the effect (cf. 3.36n. ὑπέρ). This syntax reinforces the content: Philip does not need to do anything while the Athenians are busy causing problems for themselves. ἔρις is a very rare word in the forensic and deliberative speeches of the orators (see Yunis 119 on D. 18.18, the only other attestation); D.'s use of it evokes poetic images of discord and strife. Cf., e.g., H. *Il.* 1.8 and Sol. 4.38 (West), quoted by D. 19.255. **προείποι τρέπεσθαι** "he should warn [you] to direct [your disagreement and contention]." The usage of προλέγω (LSJ II 3) echoes §13. **τῶν παρ' ἑαυτοῦ μισθοφορούντων** "those who have been hired by him." See §9n. τῶν. παρά is used instead of ὑπό because μισθοφορέω is lit. "receive pay from"; see LSJ παρά A II 3. **ἀναβάλλουσιν ὑμᾶς** "they distract you"; cf. 8.52.

**15 πρὸς τοῦ Διός:** the oath with πρός regularly adds emphasis to a rhetorical question (e.g., D. 8.34, 14.12, 21.98; MacDowell 2009: 403). **ὅστις εὖ φρονῶν ... σκέψαιτ' ἄν;** "who in his right mind would judge one who acts peacefully or with hostility toward him according to his words rather than his deeds?" For εὖ φρονῶν cf. 2.20, 1.23n. ἀφορμή. **οὐδεὶς δήπου:** sc. ἔστι; cf. 3.9n. δήπου. **ὁ τοίνυν Φίλιππος:** the particle is transitional, marking the move from a general argument to the specific case at hand (*GP* 576). **ἐξ ἀρχῆς** is explained by the following genitives absolute: Philip has been acting as an enemy from the start of the peace of Philocrates in 346. **ἄρτι τῆς εἰρήνης γεγονυίας:** D. repeats the false allegations he made against Aeschines in *On the False Embassy*, that Philip seized the Thracian towns mentioned below after the Athenians had sworn to the peace, but before their ambassadors received an oath from him (D. 19.155–6; cf. 18.25–7, Harris 79–80). Here it suits his rhetorical purpose to focus blame on Philip; in the court speeches his goal is to fault the policy of his political opponents in Athens. For this reason, he gives a fuller narrative of the peace negotiations in the court speeches that is not consistent with his brief presentation here, as noted below. **οὔπω Διοπείθους στρατηγοῦντος:** the pres. part. is equivalent to an imperfect describing continuous action at the same time as the main verb ἐλάμβανε (Smyth §1872a). Diopeithes (see §2n. τούς) was appointed probably in 343/2 as a military commander in charge of protecting a new settlement of Athenian colonists (cleruchs) in the Chersonese (Pritchett 1974: 92). **οὐδὲ τῶν ὄντων ἐν Χερρονήσωι νῦν ἀπεσταλμένων:** νῦν modifies τῶν ὄντων. The perf. part. is equivalent to a pluperf. describing action antecedent to ἐλάμβανε (see LSJ ἀποστέλλω II for the dispatching of colonies). **Σέρριον καὶ Δορίσκον ἐλάμβανε:** the imperfect stresses that Philip was engaged with these campaigns while the Athenian ambassadors were waiting at Pella for him to swear to the peace in 346. D. and others provide various lists of the Thracian towns and fortifications that Philip seized at this time, and, despite D.'s statement in §16, it is unclear which were allied with Athens at this point (D. 8.64, 18.27, 70, [D.] 7.37; see MacDowell 2000: 8 n. 23, 267–8). Serrium, Doriscus, and Hieron Oros are located along the coast in eastern Thrace (Barrington Atlas 51 G3, 52 A3; Harris 165, *HM* 555; the latter site is so called "because it [the mountain] was regarded as sacred by indigenous inhabitants of the area," Langdon 2000: 465). **τοὺς ἐκ Σερρείου τείχους καὶ Ἱεροῦ ὄρους στρατιώτας ἐξέβαλλεν** "he was expelling the soldiers from the fortification of Serrium and from Hieron Oros" (LSJ ἐκβάλλω I 2). D.'s imprecise chronology serves his larger rhetorical point. Aeschines reports that Philip took Hieron Oros the day before the Athenian Assembly finalized the terms of the peace (Aesch. 2.82–90, MacDowell 2000: 8 n. 22); in any case, the localities named here were not included in the peace, since they were not Athenian allies or territories (Harris 74–6, 165, Cawkwell 1963: 201). **ὁ ὑμέτερος στρατηγός:** the general Chares (2.25n. κρινόντων) represented Athenian interests in the Chersonese in 346 (cf. Aesch. 2.70–3, 90).

**16 καίτοι** introduces a rhetorical question following up on the premise of the previous sentence (*GP* 562–3). D. varies the tone and pace with this short indignant question in place of a positive statement that Philip is at war. **ταῦτα πράττων τί ἐποίει;** "by pursuing these policies what was he doing?" πράττω is "pursue a policy" or "conduct affairs" (LSJ III 5); ποιέω is "achieve a result" or "produce" an object (LSJ A). D. frequently juxtaposes the two verbs; often he carefully maintains these distinct senses (e.g., 2.30, 3.36, §20), while at other times he blurs the distinction (e.g., 4.5, see LSJ ποιέω B 1). **εἰρήνην μὲν γὰρ ὠμωμόκει:** μέν contrasts this statement with the preceding argument that Philip is at war (*GP* 377–8), and γάρ explains why D. posed the preceding question. D. here distorts the chronology: Philip had not yet sworn the peace when he took the Thracian towns listed above (§15n. ἄρτι). For ὄμνυμι + accus. see LSJ II 1. **μηδεὶς εἴπηι:** D.'s tone is more confrontational here than in other instances of this rhetorical device (1.14n. τί), where he entertains imagined objections from the audience. **τί δὲ ταῦτ᾽ ἐστίν;** the sense of the question is clarified by the following rephrasing and D.'s response. δέ here expresses "a note of surprise, impatience, or indignation" (*GP* 173–4). **εἰ μὲν γὰρ μικρὰ ταῦτα:** the alternative indirect questions introduced by εἰ and ἤ (Smyth §2675c) depend upon ἄλλος λόγος, and the combined idea they represent is the antecedent for οὗτος, which is masc. (rather than neut.) to agree with λόγος. D. himself admits elsewhere that these Thracian towns are small and not well known in Athens, and his political opponent Aeschines used precisely this argument against him (D. 10.8, Aesch. 3.82, MacDowell 2000: 268). **τὸ δ᾽ εὐσεβὲς καὶ τὸ δίκαιον:** D. frames the question of Philip's violation of the peace treaty in both religious and legal terms, in order to depict Philip as someone who affronts all Greek values (see further Martin 2009: 225–6, cf. 2.21n. τῶν); this sort of ethical appeal is rare in the Assembly speeches (cf. 1.1n. τό). D. makes frequent allegations that Philip was a perjurer who offended the gods by violating his oaths (e.g., 2.5, 10). This passage is the most specific regarding his alleged offenses, and in it we can see that D. distorts his account to make Philip out to be a perjurer when in fact Philip scrupulously avoided violating the treaty by concluding his campaigns in Thrace before swearing to it (cf. Harris 79–80). The depiction of Philip as a liar contributes to the characterization of him as a tyrant; see 1.3n. τὰ δ' ἀπειλῶν. **ἄν ... παραβαίνηι** "if someone commits an offense, whether in a matter small or great" (ἄν = ἐάν 2×). The verb is used absolutely, without an object; for the use of ἐπί, cf. §3n. ἐπί. For the combination of μικρός and the comparative μείζων (from μέγας), cf. D. 21.14, Pl. *Rep.* 6.485b, *Lg.* 10.893d. **φέρε δή:** 4.10n. εἰπέ. **νῦν** signals the move from Philip's alleged violations of the peace in 346 in Thrace to more recent developments in the Chersonese; D. is following the order (and repeating νῦν as a signpost) of the genitives absolute in §15. **εἰς Χερρόνησον:** the city of Cardia (on the northwest shore of the Chersonese; Barrington Atlas 51 H3) complained to Philip about Diopeithes' activity in the Chersonese in 343/2 (§15n. οὔπω), and Philip sent troops to aid them and wrote in protest to the Athenian Assembly when Diopeithes raided the territory during Philip's campaign in Thrace (Harris 119). **βασιλεύς ... ἐγνώκασιν εἶναι:** Athenian interests in the region date back to the time of Miltiades (late 6th to early 5th cent. BC), and fourth-century orators refer to the region as an Athenian possession (see Moreno 2007: 305). The Persian king may have formally recognized Athenian control of the Chersonese in the 360s, after the battle of Leuctra; see Cawkwell 2005: 294, Jehne 1992: 277–81. Cardia was the most important city on the Chersonese; it paid tribute to Athens as part of the Athenian empire in the fifth century. The city had been in alliance with Philip since 352. (For this background see J. Hornblower 1981: 6–8.) D.'s generalization distorts the reality of the current situation (cf. Cawkwell 1963: 200): for the moment, he avoids naming the city of Cardia and instead refers vaguely to the Chersonese, where Athenians had long maintained a presence. (Cf. §35, 8.64 οὐ νῦν τὴν πόλιν τὴν Καρδιανῶν ἔχει καὶ ὁμολογεῖ.) **ἐπιστέλλει ταῦτα:** the letter is attested at D. 8.16; cf. §27n. οὐ.

**17 ἐγὼ δὲ τοσούτου δέω ... τὴν πρὸς ὑμᾶς εἰρήνην** "I am so far from agreeing that he, in achieving these ends, is acting peacefully toward you" (§19n. πολλοῦ). The repetition of ὁμολογεῖν from §16 highlights the absurdity of the situation; according to D., Philip admits he is at war while the Athenians debate the question. **ὥστε** introduces φημί after the series of five accusative participles (ἁπτόμενον ... ποιοῦντα), modifying the unexpressed subject (sc. ἐκεῖνον = Philip) of the infinitives λύειν and πολεμεῖν in indirect statement introduced by φημί. **Μεγάρων ἁπτόμενον** "by engaging with Megara" (LSJ ἅπτω III 1 a). In late 343 oligarchs attempted to take power in Megara and received support from Philip. It seems probable that this was the occasion when Athens sent troops under Phocion (*LGPN* s.v. 2, *PAA* 967590) to aid the democratic resistance to the coup; the outcome of these events is unknown, but §75 suggests that Megara was prepared to resist Philip still in 341. See D. 19.87, 294–5 with MacDowell 2000: 245–6, Harris 115, *HM* 497–9. **Εὐβοίαι τυραννίδα κατασκευάζοντα:** 2.6n. κατασκευάσαι. Between 343 and 341 tyrants came to power in Eretria and Oreus with the support of Philip (cf. §§27, 57–62, §12n. τοῖς); his attempts to intervene in Chalcis were less successful (*HM* 547–54). It should be noted that they are regularly labeled as tyrants by Athenian sources because Philip supported them; this label may not accurately characterize the nature of their rule. **ἐπὶ Θράικην παριόντα** "by advancing on Thrace" (LSJ πάρειμι [εἶμι *ibo*] III 1). **τὰ ἐν Πελοποννήσωι σκευωρούμενον** "by rigging up affairs in the Peloponnese." The verb literally refers to physical gear or equipment for a campaign or project, and is used often by D. with the sense "contriving" (e.g., 32.11, 36.33, 45.5). Philip apparently sent money and troops to aid Messene and Argos against Sparta in 344 (D. 6.15, *HM* 476–8). In 343 oligarchs in Elis, supported by Philip, violently suppressed an attempted democratic coup (§27, 19.260, 294 with MacDowell 2000: 315, *HM* 499–501). **φημὶ ... πολεμεῖν:** the repetition from the start of the section again highlights D.'s point. **εἰ μὴ ... φήσετε** "unless you are going to say"; see §10n. εἰ. D.'s other uses of the phrase μηχανήματα ἐφιστάναι specifically describe Philip's style of fighting (§50, 18.87); Philip (and later Alexander) owed much of his success to the use of catapults and towers for sieges, devices that had not previously been deployed to such an extent in Greece; for examples, cf. D. 1.9, 3.4, 18.71, and see Garlan 1974: 212–14, 225–6, Cawkwell 1978: 160–3. **ἕως ἂν ... προσαγάγωσιν:** ἕως ἄν + aor. subj. is "until" (Smyth §2426a; cf. §13n. ταῦθ'). **οἷς ἂν ἐγὼ ληφθείην** "the means by which one may be captured" (LSJ λαμβάνω I 1 b). ἐγώ and ἐμοί here refer not to D. personally, but to any hypothetical person (Smyth §1193). The antecedent for the relative is the following ταῦτα. **κἂν μήπω βάλληι μηδὲ τοξεύηι** "even if he is not yet hurling [projectiles] or shooting arrows." For the pairing of these verbs, see LSJ βάλλω A I 1.

**18 τίσιν οὖν ὑμεῖς κινδυνεύσαιτ' ἄν;** "in what regards would you be in danger?" (LSJ κινδυνεύω 2). The dat. pl. τίσιν is explained by the following three articular infinitives in the dat. sing. **εἴ τι γένοιτο:** a euphemism referring to a bad turn of events; cf. D. 37.16, *Prooem.* 22.3, 2.15n. ἄν, 4.11n. καί. **τῶι τὸν Ἑλλήσποντον ἀλλοτριωθῆναι:** Philip's activity in Thrace and the Chersonese (§§15–16) jeopardized Athenian influence in the region. It was vital for the Athenians to maintain control over the Hellespont in order to protect grain shipments from the Black Sea. D.'s fears will be realized in 340, when Athens abandons the peace after Philip lays siege to Byzantium, imposes controls on cargo at the Hellespont, and seizes the Athenian grain fleet (D. 18.72, 87–8, 241, Did. *In D.* 10.40–50 with Harding 2006: 210–13, Harris 124–5, *HM* 573–81). **Μεγάρων καὶ τῆς Εὐβοίας:** the genitives modify κύριον; they are placed immediately after the article to maintain parallelism between the three articular infinitive phrases. See §17nn. Μεγάρων and Εὐβοίαι. D. pairs the two localities here because they are closest to Athens, though in opposite directions. The phrase τὸν πολεμοῦνθ᾽ ὑμῖν reminds the audience that these locations are ideal bases for attacks on Attica. **τῶι Πελοποννησίους τἀκείνου φρονῆσαι** "the Peloponnesians taking his side" (LSJ φρονέω II 2 c); §16n. τά. **εἶτα:** §13n. **τὸ μηχάνημα:** §17n. εἰ. The usage here is metaphorical; Philip's siege engine consists of the territories around Athens that he controls. For a similar metaphor cf. 4.5n. ἔχουσι, Ronnet 158. **φῶ:** deliberative subjunctive (Smyth §1805). **πρὸς ὑμᾶς:** to be taken with εἰρήνην ἄγειν, as in §17.

**19 πολλοῦ γε καὶ δεῖ** "far from it" (LSJ δέω [B] 2; Smyth §1399). **ἀφ᾽ ἧς ἡμέρας ἀνεῖλε Φωκέας** "since that day when he destroyed the Phocians" (LSJ ἀναιρέω II 1). The Phocians surrendered to Philip in summer 346, less than a month after he swore to the peace with Athens; D. exaggerates regarding their treatment by Philip (cf. §26; see §1n. τήν, D. 19.57–9, Harris 95–8, *HM* 343–7). **ὁρίζομαι** "I make a determination" or "I define" (LSJ ὁρίζω IV 2), introducing the accus. + infin. Cf. §7n. διορίζομαι. **ὑμᾶς:** accus. subject of σωφρονήσειν and δυνήσεσθαι. The initial placement of the pronoun makes a sharp turn from Philip to the Athenians and prepares for the contrast between his aggression and their failure to act. **ἤδη:** 4.8n. **σωφρονήσειν:** the word choice stresses that this would be sensible, realistic policy; see 2.22n. σώφρονος. **ἐὰν δὲ ἐάσητε** "but if you neglect [to defend yourselves]." **τοῦτο** = τὸ ἀμύνασθαι, the object of ποιῆσαι. **τοσοῦτόν γε ἀφέστηκα τῶν ἄλλων ... τῶν συμβουλευόντων** "I stand so far apart from the other politicians" (LSJ ἀφίστημι B 1); i.e., "I disagree so much." **οὐδὲ δοκεῖ μοι περὶ Χερρονήσου νῦν σκοπεῖν** "it seems best to me not even to debate now about the Chersonese." οὐδέ modifies σκοπεῖν.

**20 ἀλλ᾽ ἐπαμῦναι μὲν τούτοις:** sc. δοκεῖ μοι. ἀλλά introduces four infinitives that contrast with σκοπεῖν. In the first three of these (ἐπαμῦναι, διατηρῆσαι, ἀποστεῖλαι), D. stresses the need for military action rather than debate. In the fourth item (βουλεύεσθαι), he concedes the need for deliberation, but urges the Athenians to have a wider perspective on the threat that Philip poses. **διατηρῆσαι μή τι πάθωσι** "watch out that they do not come to any harm." The construction with μή is more common with the uncompounded verb (LSJ τηρέω I 2, II 1). For the euphemism see

4.11n. καί.   **βουλεύεσθαι μέντοι περὶ πάντων τῶν Ἑλλήνων** "[it seems best to me] to deliberate, but about all the Greeks." The use of μέντοι, combined with the repetition of περί, stresses that this point responds to οὐδὲ ... σκοπεῖν.   **ὡς ἐν κινδύνωι μεγάλωι καθεστώτων** "on the grounds that they are in great danger" (LSJ καθίστημι II B 5). ὡς modifies the participle, and indicates that the Athenians should assume this to be the case (Smyth §2086).   **βούλομαι δ᾽ εἰπεῖν ... ἐξ ὧν** "I want to tell you [the reasons] why." The antecedent for ὧν is to be understood from the context, and ἐκ is causal (Smyth §1688c).   **εἰ μὲν ὀρθῶς λογίζομαι**: 4.28n. ἴσως. εἰ + pres. indic. (in contrast to ἐάν + pres. subj. below) refers only to the specific debate at hand (Smyth §2298c).   **πρόνοιάν τινα ὑμῶν γ᾽ αὐτῶν**: D.'s switch to the second-person may be deferential in tone (see 1.2n. ἡμεῖς); typically political leaders display πρόνοια (cf. §2, 3.21n. τόν), but here D. acknowledges the authority of the δῆμος.   **εἰ μὴ καὶ τῶν ἄλλων ἄρα βούλεσθε**: sc. πρόνοιάν τινα ποιήσασθαι. εἰ ἄρα is "if, after all," indicating that the speaker has just realized this point (*GP* 37–8).   **ἐὰν δὲ ληρεῖν καὶ τετυφῶσθαι δοκῶ** "if I seem to talk nonsense and to be deluded." ἐάν + pres. subj. refers to a generality extending beyond the current debate (Smyth §2337). ληρέω is often used to insult others (e.g., D. 5.10, 8.31), and D.'s application of it to himself here contributes to the deferential tone (cf. 20.20 with Kremmydas 2012: 223). τυφόω is probably derived from τυφώς, a violent wind that can drive people crazy (Harp. s.v. τετύφωμαι· ἀντὶ τοῦ ἐμβεβρόντημαι; cf. D. 18.243, 19.231). The verb is not attested in the works of other orators, but D. is fond of it and often uses it to mock others (e.g. 21.116, 23.137, 184); when he applies it to himself elsewhere it is negated or sarcastic (18.11, 19.219). The iambic trimeter (ἐὰν ... δοκῶ) must be an "accidental creation" (Dover 1997: 172).   **μήτε νῦν μήτ᾽ αὖθις** "neither now nor in the future." For the pairing cf. Pl. *Ap.* 24b.   **ὡς ὑγιαίνοντί μοι προσέχητε**: sc. τὸν νοῦν; the usage of ὡς is the same as above. ὑγιαίνω refers here to mental soundness (cf. LSJ I 2, D. 23.118, 24.74); it is the opposite of τυφόω.

### 21–31 Philip's hegemony threatens all the Greeks
Previously, when one state dominated Greece, the other states protected one another. Now Philip's aggressions are unchecked. The Greeks are not uniting to protect themselves from a non-Greek aggressor.

**21** D. uses the device of paraleipsis to provide a transition to the next section of the speech (2.4n. ταῦτα). παραλείψω governs the two ὅτι clauses (ὅτι μὲν ... οἱ Ἕλληνες and ὅτι πολλῶι ... ποιήσασθαι) and then takes πάντα as an object.   **μέγας ἐκ μικροῦ καὶ ταπεινοῦ τὸ κατ᾽ ἀρχὰς Φίλιππος ηὔξηται** "from [being] slight and poor at first, Philip grew [to become] great" (LSJ αὐξάνω II 3). See 1.12n. τό, 3.29n. ἐκ and cf. 2.5.

## 9 THIRD PHILIPPIC 21–22

**ἀπίστως καὶ στασιαστικῶς ἔχουσι πρὸς αὐτοὺς οἱ Ἕλληνες:** D. makes the same point in *On the Crown* as he narrates Philip's rise prior to the battle of Chaeronea (338), and he explicitly links it with the previous point by explaining that Philip gained power by taking advantage of instability in Greece (18.61 πρότερον κακῶς τοὺς Ἕλληνας ἔχοντας πρὸς ἑαυτοὺς καὶ στασιαστικῶς ἔτι χεῖρον διέθηκε, "when the Greeks were already ill-disposed and factious toward one another, [Philip] made it still worse"). **τοσοῦτον αὐτὸν ἐξ ἐκείνου γενέσθαι** "that he became so great from that [condition]." ἐξ ἐκείνου refers back to ἐκ μικροῦ καὶ ταπεινοῦ. **ἢ νῦν:** sc. παράδοξόν ἐστι, introducing ποιήσασθαι. **ὅθ' οὕτω πολλὰ προείληφε:** ὅθ' = ὅτε. See 4.31n. τά. **καὶ τὰ λοιπὰ ὑφ' αὑτῶι ποιήσασθαι** "he brings the rest under his control too." Cf. D.'s description of Philip's manipulations of the Greeks in 346: πάντα τὰ πράγματ' ἐκεῖνον ὑφ' ἑαυτῶι ποιήσασθαι (18.40; see Smyth §1698.2b). **πάνθ' ὅσα τοιαῦτ' ἂν ἔχοιμι διεξελθεῖν:** the third item depending on παραλείψω is a generic capping phrase, as often (e.g., 1.24n. πρεσβευομένους). The vague expression implies that D. could add much more (see 3.27n. οἷς).

**22 συγκεχωρηκότας ἅπαντας ἀνθρώπους:** sc. τοῦτο as object of the participle in indirect statement, and as antecedent for ὑπὲρ οὗ. **ἀφ' ὑμῶν ἀρξαμένους** "including you, first and foremost" (LSJ ἄρχω I 2). The phrase is idiomatic, stressing the Athenians' complicity. **ὑπέρ** = περί here (Smyth §1697b). **τὸν ἄλλον ἅπαντα χρόνον** "on every other occasion"; §11n. πάντα. **τί οὖν ἐστι τοῦτο;** 4.2n.; cf. §5. **τὸ ποιεῖν:** the article modifies the four infinitives that follow; after the emphatic rhetorical question, these articular infinitives are in apposition to the omitted object of συγκεχωρηκότας. **καθ' ἕνα οὑτωσὶ περικόπτειν καὶ λωποδυτεῖν τῶν Ἑλλήνων** "destroying and robbing [each] of the Greeks individually in this way." The choice of verbs depicts Philip as a danger to the Greek way of life. περικόπτω is lit. "cut around" and refers to agricultural destruction deliberately caused by invading enemies; this tactic was so widespread that the verb acquired this more generalized sense (see Hanson 1998: 61–2, 193). λωποδυτέω is lit. "slip into [another person's] clothes" and steal them; clothing was expensive, and such thieves were regarded as public menaces subject to summary arrest and the death penalty (see Dunbar 1995: 341–2, 4.47n. τόν). For the phrasing, cf. 2.24n. καθ'. **καταδουλοῦσθαι τὰς πόλεις ἐπιόντα:** ἐπιόντα is "attacking" here (LSJ ἔπειμι [B], [εἶμι *ibo*] I 1 b). For the characterization of Philip as a slave-master, see 1.2n. δεσπότην. D. is not being hyperbolic here (cf. §26n. δουλεύωσιν): in 356 Philip is reported to have enslaved the people of Potidaea (1.9n. Ποτείδαια), he enslaved 10,000 captured Olynthians in 348 (1.5n. ἀνδραποδισμοῦ), and in 344 he punished 10,000 captured Sarnousians by forcibly relocating them from Illyria to Macedonia (Polyaen. 4.2.12, G. M. Cohen 1995: 16–17).

**23 προστάται** has a positive connotation (see 3.27n. χρωμένοις); as a contrast to Philip's power, D. stresses this positive term by repeating it twice with μέν and δέ (cf. *GPS* 85). **ἑβδομήκοντα ἔτη καὶ τρία:** from the formation of the Delian League in 477 to the battle of Aegospotami in 405 (counting inclusively). The number is unusually precise; cf. 3.24n. πέντε, Lys. 2.55, Isoc. 4.106 (both reckon this period to be 70 years), Lycurg. 72 (90 years), Isoc. 12.56 (65 years), Thomas 1989: 202–3 n. 22. **τριάκοντα ἑνὸς δέοντα** "for 29 [years]" (Smyth §350c), perhaps from the battle of Aegospotami in 405 to the formation of the second Athenian League in 378/7 (see 3.28n. οὕς), or from the end of the Peloponnesian War in 404 to the battle of Naxos in 376. It is strange that D. does not here extend the Spartan hegemony to the battle of Leuctra in 371 (cf. 3.27n. Λακεδαιμονίων). **ἴσχυσαν δέ τι καὶ Θηβαῖοι** "the Thebans too acquired some power." The Thebans dominated central Greece in the 360s, and defeated the Spartans at Leuctra in 371 and Mantinea in 362. But D. hesitates to describe the Thebans as being as powerful as the Athenians and Spartans had been. Cf. 3.27–8, where he misleadingly describes the period after Leuctra as one of Athenian domination, and see 1.26n. Θηβαῖοι. **οὔθ' ὑμῖν οὔτε Θηβαίοις οὔτε Λακεδαιμονίοις:** the sequence may be motivated by euphony: items are ordered by length (cf. 4.35n. τόν). The first and last receive more emphasis; the medial placement of the Thebans is consistent with the hesitant praise above. **τοῦθ'** refers to ποιεῖν; the repetition from §22 marks the conclusion of this particular argument (for the technique cf. 1.11n. τι, 3.29n. τάς). **βούλοισθε:** the second-person verb is prompted by the first item in the above list, but it refers to the hegemonies of the Thebans and Spartans too. The optative refers to a generality in the past (Smyth §2568). **οὐδὲ πολλοῦ δεῖ** "Not at all!" This negated version of πολλοῦ γε καὶ δεῖ (§19n.) is frequent in D. (e.g., 8.42, 19.30, 54.40; it is not attested in other classical or earlier authors). The meaning is equivalent to the positive formulation, but the assertion is stronger, lit. "it is not even 'far from it'," i.e., "it is completely untrue." Alternatively, commentators treat οὐδέ as a repetition of a preceding negative, but that interpretation does not account for an instance where a positive statement precedes (20.20). See MacDowell 2000: 220.

**24 τοῦτο μέν:** adverbial (see §11n. τοῦτο), paired with καὶ πάλιν below, linking the two parallel examples in the sentence. Each begins with an extended dative noun phrase (ὑμῖν ... Ἀθηναίοις, Λακεδαιμονίοις ... ὑμῖν), followed by an ἐπειδή clause, followed by a main clause beginning with πάντες. Repetition of key words and phrases reinforces the parallelism. **ὑμῖν:** construed with πολεμεῖν (cf. §9). **μᾶλλον δὲ τοῖς τότ' οὖσιν Ἀθηναίοις:** for the rhetorical technique see 2.2n. μᾶλλον. D. refers to the period of the fifth-century Athenian empire; see 4.3n. ἀνάξιον. **τισιν**

οὐ μετρίως ἐδόκουν προσφέρεσθαι "they seemed to treat some people unreasonably"; on these aggressions see 3.24n. πέντε. For οὐ μετρίως cf. D. 18.18, describing the behavior of the Thebans during the third Sacred War. In *Against Meidias* D. repeatedly uses similar phrasing to describe his opponent's hybris (MacDowell 1990: 256); the paraphrase here avoids distracting provocation and allows D. to reserve the charge of hybris for Philip (e.g., §§1, 32). ᾤοντο δεῖν introduces πολεμεῖν. καὶ οἱ μηδὲν ἐγκαλεῖν ἔχοντες αὐτοῖς "even those with no complaint against them." The infinitive is explanatory with μηδέν. In Assembly speeches ἐγκαλέω (and the cognate noun ἔγκλημα) usually refer to official complaints made by one state against another; cf. §14n. τῶν ἀδικουμένων, 1.7n. ἐκ. μετὰ τῶν ἠδικημένων "on the side of those who had been wronged" (Smyth §1691.1). καὶ πάλιν: D. often uses the phrase to adduce further examples; e.g., 1.9, 19.62, 20.84, 21.33 with MacDowell 1990: 251. παρελθοῦσιν εἰς τὴν αὐτὴν δυναστείαν ὑμῖν: ὑμῖν depends on τὴν αὐτὴν δυναστείαν: "the same power as you [had]" (Smyth §1500). The participle reiterates the notion of succession from §23; D. refers to the period after the Peloponnesian War. Athenian public discourse and political theorists use the term δυναστεία to refer specifically to oligarchic rule, which is contrasted with the democratic rule of law (e.g., Andoc. 2.27, Lys. 2.18, D. 60.25, Pl. *Grg.* 491b with Dodds 1959: 295, Arist. *Pol.* 4.5.1 [1292b]). Here the term may reflect the language of the grievances against Athens and Sparta; in Thucydides the Thebans publicly complain that the Athenian empire is a tyrannical δυναστεία, not a democracy (3.62.3). πλεονάζειν: another term antithetical to democratic ideals; see 2.9n. πλεονεξίας. In the 380s Spartan aggressions against other Greek states culminated in the occupation of the Theban Cadmeia in 382; see Seager in *CAH* 159–61. τὰ καθεστηκότα ἐκίνουν "they were meddling with [other states'] governments" (LSJ καθίστημι A II 2b). After the Peloponnesian War, the Spartans supported oligarchies in Athens and throughout the Peloponnese; see Austin in *CAH* 529–32. εἰς πόλεμον κατέστησαν "went into a state of war" (LSJ καθίστημι B V).

**25 καὶ τί δεῖ τοὺς ἄλλους λέγειν;** such questions are a frequent device to change topics and vary the pace of a speech, while implying that the speaker could multiply examples; e.g., §§59, 22.15, 23.114, Isoc. 5.63, Is. 9.22, Pl. *Phdr.* 241e. Here D. chooses not to remind the Athenians about the Theban hegemony, perhaps because it was more recent (whereas he stresses both above and below that the Athenian aggressions were those of a different generation), and a reminder could have jeopardized his efforts to forge an alliance between Athens and Thebes in the late 340s. οὐδὲν ἂν εἰπεῖν ἔχοντες ἐξ ἀρχῆς "although we could not refer to any matter in the beginning" of the period D. has just outlined, during the Athenian empire and at the beginning of the Peloponnesian War, when

Athens and Sparta took action against each other's allies (e.g., at Corcyra and at Potidaea in the late 430s) prior to the outbreak of direct hostilities between the two states. For the construction see 3.27n. οἷς.   **ὅ τι ἠδικούμεθα** "in which we were wronged" (Smyth §1625).   **ὑπὲρ ὧν** = ὑπὲρ τούτων ἅ.   **Λακεδαιμονίοις ... τοῖς ἡμετέροις προγόνοις:** both dat. of agent with the perf. pass. ἐξημάρτηται. D. rounds the numbers from §23, perhaps because the sum total of the two figures is more important for his point here.   **ὧν** = τούτων ἅ. The relative is one of the objects (the internal object: Smyth §1620) of ἠδίκηκε.   **ἐν τρισὶ καὶ δέκα οὐχ ὅλοις ἔτεσιν:** the period from Philip's capture of Methone in 354 (§26) up to the delivery of this speech in 341. D. seems to minimize the length of Philip's rule here, in contrast with other passages where he lists Philip's conquests prior to Methone (1.5, 9) or describes Philip's role as a king negotiating with Athens between 359 and 357 (2.6n. τῶι).   **οἷς ἐπιπολάζει** "during which he has been rising to the top."   **μᾶλλον δέ:** 2.2n.   **οὐδὲ μέρος τούτων ἐκεῖνα** "those [wrongs committed by the Athenians and Spartans] are not even a fraction of these [committed by Philip]" (LSJ μέρος IV 1).

**26 ῥᾴδιον δεῖξαι:** sc. ἐστί; the infinitive depends on ῥᾴδιον.   **Ὄλυνθον:** first in the list for emphasis. D. stresses Philip's capture of Olynthus in 348 for several reasons: Olynthus was an Athenian ally, and in the *Olynthiacs* D. had strongly advocated Athenian intervention in 349; this example may remind the Athenians of the longstanding consistency of D.'s policy regarding Philip. Furthermore, Philip's treatment of Olynthus was especially harsh; elsewhere, D. depicts the enslavement of the Olynthians and Philip's destruction of their city as a *cause célèbre* (19.263–7). He presents a moving portrayal of their pitiful plight (19.196–8) and is especially proud of his own role providing ransom on their behalf during the peace negotiations in 346 (18.268, 19.166–71).   **Μεθώνην:** 1.9n. Μεθώνη. Philip probably did not destroy Methone, but rather resettled it as a Macedonian city (*HM* 362).   **Ἀπολλωνίαν:** east of the Chalcidice and Amphipolis in Thrace (Barrington Atlas 51 C3, *HM* 194 n. 2). Presumably Philip destroyed the city in the 350s, in connection with the campaigns at Amphipolis (2.2n. πόλεων); we have no further details beyond this passage (*HM* 363; Str. 7 F 33 briefly refers to Philip's razing of the city).   **δύο καὶ τριάκοντα πόλεις ἐπὶ Θράικης:** members of the Chalcidian League attacked by Philip in the course of the campaign against Olynthus in 348 (cf. 2.2n. δύναμιν). D.'s number gives an air of authority, but if it is accurate, many of these must have been tiny places, little-known in Athens. Other contemporary evidence confirms that Philip destroyed one or two other cities near Olynthus, and it is very likely that D. is exaggerating here. See Tsigarida 2011: 152–4, *HM* 371–6.   **ἐῶ** marks an instance of paraleipsis (cf. §21n.), as does σιωπῶ below.   **ἃς ἁπάσας**

οὕτως ὠμῶς ἀνῄρηκεν "all of which he has destroyed so savagely" (LSJ ἀναιρέω II 1). ὠμῶς characterizes Philip's behavior as uncivilized; cf. D. 24.171, where "civic character" (τὸ τῆς πόλεως ἦθος) is contrasted with "savage treatment of the masses" (τοὺς μὲν πολλοὺς ὠμῶς μεταχειρίζεσθαι). εἰ πώποτ' ᾠκήθησαν: the indirect question depends on εἶναι ῥᾴδιον εἰπεῖν. The archaeological record at Olynthus confirms D.'s account. Numerous missiles and arrowheads, some with Philip's name on them, have been recovered, and the presence of valuables that were abandoned in private homes suggests that the occupants left hastily or died in the fighting. See Cahill 2002: 45–8. προσελθόντα: accus. subject of εἰπεῖν, referring to a hypothetical visitor to the sites of these cities. τὸ Φωκέων ἔθνος τοσοῦτον ἀνῃρημένον: §19n. ἀφ'. Sc. ὄν with τοσοῦτον; the quantitative emphasis reinforces the assertion in §25 regarding the number of Philip's crimes. D. 19.123 refers to 22 Phocian cities, and Paus. 10.3.1–3 lists 20 that were razed (κατεσκάφησαν) by Philip in 346 (see MacDowell 2000: 256). ἀλλά: a strong response to the preceding μέν clause. The use of ἀλλά rather than δέ suggests that the two items are out of balance (GP 6); Philip's recent treatment of the Thessalians surpasses his earlier aggressions. οὐχὶ τὰς πολιτείας καὶ τὰς πόλεις αὐτῶν παρῄρηται; "has he not taken away their governments and cities?" This allusive assertion is explained by what follows. Philip had installed garrisons at Pherae, and probably elsewhere in the region, during the third Sacred War (§12n. Φεράς, D. 19.260 with MacDowell 2000: 315). Then, or not long after, he required changes in the governments of Thessalian cities too (see HM 523–8). The former residents of razed cities were resettled in small scattered villages (D. 19.81, D. S. 16.60.1–3, Dmitriev 2011: 78–9). D.'s statement here refers broadly to these restrictions imposed on the Thessalians. τετραρχίας κατέστησεν: Philip created or reinstituted a new system of political districts for Thessaly, presumably based on tribal affiliation (κατ' ἔθνη below); like the prohibitions against urban settlements, this policy was designed to forestall organized opposition to his control of the region after 346. Theopompus also refers to the tetrarchies (FGrHist 115 FF 208, 209), but provides no more details than does D. See Dmitriev 2011: 79–80. (It is unclear how D.'s reference in 344 [6.22] to a different arrangement of decadarchies imposed on the Thessalians by Philip relates to this passage; see HM 528–32.) δουλεύωσιν: for the hyperbole, cf. D. 19.81, §36n. τό.

**27 αἱ δ' ἐν Εὐβοίαι πόλεις:** §17n. Εὐβοίαι. **Θηβῶν καὶ Ἀθηνῶν:** there had long been tension between Thebes and Athens (cf. 1.26n. Θηβαῖοι), but by the late 340s D. is working toward an alliance against Philip as their common enemy (cf. §25n. καί), and here he is clearly turning in that direction. His efforts will come to fruition when Philip invades central Greece in 339, and Thebes and Athens join together and suffer a disastrous defeat at the battle of Chaeronea in 338. **οὐ διαρρήδην εἰς τὰς ἐπιστολὰς γράφει** "does he not write explicitly in a letter." διαρρήδην introduces the direct quotation that follows. In Assembly speeches and court cases D. regularly refers to numerous letters of Philip to the Athenians, and cites this diplomatic correspondence in much the same way as laws and other documents (e.g., 4.37n. ΕΠΙΣΤΟΛΗΣ); see Ceccarelli 2013: 274–80. He sometimes quotes directly, as here (e.g., 19.40), and in other places he paraphrases the content of these letters (e.g., 19.41). However, in addition to the short extracts and specific points that D. discusses in detail, there are extensive versions of some of these letters that are included in some MSS (e.g., 18.77–8, [D.] 12 with MacDowell 2009: 363–6); these are very unlikely to preserve authentic material from Philip, and should be considered additions made by later editors and scribes (cf. Canevaro 2013a: 3–5, 250). **ἐμοὶ ... ἐμοῦ**: the repetition of the pronoun presents Philip as assertive and uncompromising. ἀκούειν is "obey" (LSJ II 2). **καὶ οὐ** "and it is not the case that." οὐ negates the combination of the μέν and δέ clauses (cf. D. 18.179). ἀλλά responds to this negative and introduces four short examples that illustrate the extent of Philip's aggressions and culminate in the summation of the last clause of the period (οὔθ᾽ ἡ Ἑλλάς ... τἀνθρώπου); for the technique, cf. 1.12–13, Wooten 155–6. **ἐφ᾽ Ἑλλήσποντον**: §18n. τῶι. **πρότερον ἧκεν ἐπ᾽ Ἀμβρακίαν**: in 343/2, after campaigning in northwest Greece, Philip advanced with a small force on Ambracia (Barrington Atlas 54 C3), a colony of Corinth well situated for access to the Peloponnese by sea. In response Athens sent an army to the region and ambassadors, including D., to the Peloponnese calling for resistance. These efforts led to Philip's withdrawal from the region. See §§34, 72, 18.244, Sealey 176–7, 308–9 nn. 52–3, *HM* 507–9. **Ἦλιν ἔχει**: §17n. τά. **Μεγάροις ἐπεβούλευσε**: §17n. Μεγάρων. **ἡ Ἑλλάς ... ἡ βάρβαρος**: sc. γῆ. **τὴν πλεονεξίαν χωρεῖ τἀνθρώπου** "can contain that man's greed" (LSJ χωρέω III 1). The echo of πλεονάζειν (§24; cf. 2.9n. πλεονεξίας) concludes D.'s point, that Philip's recent acts of aggression surpass those of the Athenians and Spartans in times past. The final placement of τἀνθρώπου allows the speaker to pause and stress this scornful formulation (1.3n. ἄνθρωπος).

**28–29** After the series of short and syntactically simple examples depicting Philip's actions, D.'s style now becomes more complex and slow, reflecting the inactivity of the Athenians. He presents the new subject with expansive phrasing and tautological participles (ὁρῶντες ... ἀκούοντες) and continues in this repetitive mode by doubling many of the phrases in the long sentence (e.g., πέμπομεν and ἀγανακτοῦμεν, συμφερόντων and δεόντων, πρᾶξαι and συστῆναι, βοηθείας and φιλίας). As the long sentence continues in §29, the repetition continues, and the pace is slowed further by complex subordination that is repeatedly placed before the words on which it depends (introduced by ὄν, ὅπως, ἐπεί, ὅτι), by a parenthetical aside (ὥς ... δοκεῖ), and by a simile (ὥσπερ περίοδος ... προσέρχεται). The sharp contrast in syntax and style from §27 to §§28–9 mirrors D.'s point, that Philip quickly achieves his goals while the Athenians delay and miss opportunities. See further Wooten 156.

**28 ὁρῶντες ... καὶ ἀκούοντες:** for this polarization see 3.3n. ἐξ, 4.47n. μή. **περὶ τούτων πρὸς ἀλλήλους:** the two prepositional phrases are to be construed ἀπὸ κοινοῦ with both verbs. **κἀγανακτοῦμεν** "and we [do not] express complaints" (LSJ ἀγανακτέω II 2). **διορωρύγμεθα κατὰ πόλεις** "we are entrenched in our cities." διορύσσω refers to "digging through" earth to make a canal or mine, and here the passive is used metaphorically to present an image of the Greeks cut off from one another in their individual cities as if by physical obstacles. This vivid usage is not found in contemporary and earlier writers (see LSJ I 2; in contrast, "entrenched" is a dead metaphor in English). κατά is distributive in sense, lit. "city by city" (Smyth §1690.2c). **ἄχρι τῆς τήμερον ἡμέρας:** for the phrasing and argument, cf. 4.40. **οὔτε τῶν συμφερόντων οὔτε τῶν δεόντων:** 4.51n. συμφέρει, 2.3n. προτρέπειν. **συστῆναι** "join together" (LSJ συνίστημι B III 1). The infinitive depends on δυνάμεθα. **κοινωνίαν βοηθείας καὶ φιλίας** "partnership for aid and friendship." The phrasing is not paralleled in literary sources or inscribed Athenian decrees.

**29 περιορῶμεν** "we allow." περιοράω is "watch something [bad] happen and do nothing about it" (Olson 2002: 87). D. uses the term to stress the Athenians' passivity and present them as mere observers who are not taking action; cf. §73n. τά, 18.63 with Yunis 146–7. **τὸν χρόνον κερδᾶναι τοῦτον ὃν ἄλλος ἀπόλλυται ἕκαστος ἐγνωκώς** "each [of us] perceives that he profits from that time while another is ruined"; in other words, the Athenians "buy some time" by allowing others to suffer when attacked by Philip. For the sing. ἕκαστος see 4.7n. παύσησθε. For the idiom cf. Eur. fr. 912b.3–5 (Kannicht) εἰ δέ τις πράσσει καλῶς | κακὸς πεφυκώς, τὸν χρόνον κερδαινέτω· | χρόνωι γὰρ οὗτος ὕστερον δώσει δίκην ("If someone who is bad fares well, let him gain the time as profit. Later he will pay the price"), Lys. 13.84 εἰ δὲ πάλαι δέον τιμωρεῖσθαι ὕστερον ἡμεῖς τιμωρούμεθα, τὸν χρόνον κερδαίνει ὃν ἔζη οὐ προσῆκον αὐτῶι ("If we punish [him] later when he should have been punished long before, he profits from that time during which he was alive when he should not have been"). **ὅπως σωθήσεται τὰ τῶν Ἑλλήνων** depends on σκοπῶν (2.2n. ὅπως). **σκοπῶν οὐδὲ πράττων:** σκοπέω is often paired with a synonymous verb (2.6n. θεωρῶν); here the addition of οὐδὲ πράττων is surprising and emphatic (cf. D. 16.10). **ἐπεί** introduces οὐδείς ἀγνοεῖ. The causal clause does not explain the reasoning of the Athenians, but rather explains why D. argues that the Athenians must take action. **ὥσπερ περίοδος ἢ καταβολὴ πυρετοῦ** "just like a recurrence or attack of fever." D.'s use of medical imagery stresses his own expertise and the Athenians' need for it; see 2.21n., 3.33n. τοῖς. **καὶ τῶι πάνυ πόρρω δοκοῦντι νῦν ἀφεστάναι προσέρχεται** "[Philip] attacks even the one who considers himself now to be very far away"; i.e., Philip's advance is like a spreading sickness that eventually will afflict those who now suppose themselves immune.

**30 καὶ μὴν κἀκεῖνό γε ἴστε** "furthermore, you know this too." καὶ μήν introduces a new argument and γε puts emphasis on the demonstrative that points forward to the ὅτι clause comprising the remainder of the sentence (*GP* 351–2; cf. D. 21.56). **ὅσα ... οἱ Ἕλληνες** refers back to §25. Sc. πάντα as antecedent for ὅσα and subject of ἠδικοῦντο. **ἀλλ' οὖν ὑπὸ γνησίων γ' ὄντων τῆς Ἑλλάδος ἠδικοῦντο** "well then, at least [all those wrongs] were committed by genuine children of Greece." ἀλλ' οὖν ... γε rejects complaints about the harshness of the Athenians and Spartans by introducing this moderating remonstrance (*GP* 442–3; cf. D. 16.31, 19.249). γε stresses γνησίων (sc. παίδων), which refers to legitimate children, as opposed to bastards or adoptees (LSJ I 2; for the expression here, cf. D. 60.4). **τὸν αὐτὸν τρόπον ἄν τις ὑπέλαβεν τοῦτο:** ὑπολαμβάνω is "regard" or "consider" (LSJ III 1). The aor. indic. + ἄν denotes a possibility in the past (see §13n. οἵ). τὸν αὐτὸν τρόπον is adverbial, correlating with ὥσπερ (as at §33, 1.15, 4.21, 39). **ὥσπερ ἄν:** sc. ὑπέλαβε, governing two infinitives (εἶναι, ἐνεῖναι) after the conditional protasis (εἰ ... ὀρθῶς). **διώικει τι** "was managing some [part of his property]" (LSJ διοικέω I 1). **κατ' αὐτὸ μὲν τοῦτο** "for this very reason." **ἄξιον μέμψεως εἶναι καὶ κατηγορίας:** sc. αὐτόν. D. suggests that a wasted inheritance would meet with general disapproval and blame; for the phrasing, cf. 18.65: if Philip had been mild toward the Greeks after his victory at Chaeronea, then a politician who had refused to compromise would deserve μέμψις καὶ κατηγορία. In this generalizing simile κατηγορία does not refer to specific legal prosecutions, though ῥήτορες could be prosecuted and disbarred for squandering their inheritance (Aesch. 1.30, MacDowell 2005). **ὡς δ' οὐ προσήκων ἢ ὡς οὐ κληρονόμος τούτων ὤν** "that he is not family nor the heir of these [inheritances]" (LSJ προσήκω III 3): indirect statement depending on λέγειν. D.'s point is that the Athenians and Spartans are Greeks, whatever they may have done in the past, just as a prodigal son is still a son. **ταῦτα ἐποίει:** i.e., the mismanagement of the estate.

**31 ὑποβολιμαῖος** "a supposititious son," an illegitimate heir who displaces a family member. The ὑπο- prefix suggests deception (cf. §1n. εἰς) and -βολ- refers originally to the surreptitious placement of the child in the family (LSJ ὑποβάλλω II 1). On the phenomenon see Austin and Olson 2004: 163 on Ar. *Thesmo.* 339–41. **τὰ μὴ προσήκοντα:** i.e., the family estate. μή underlines the assertion that the δοῦλος and ὑποβολιμαῖος are not members of the family. **ἀπώλλυε καὶ ἐλυμαίνετο:** the verbs are paired for emphasis (1.14n. ἵνα). They combine to form a single idea (hendiadys): the latter is more specific, describing a state of physical disrepair (LSJ λυμαίνομαι I 3), and the former stresses the resulting loss and waste. D. is fond of such pairings of ἀπόλλυμι with a more specific verb; cf. §39n. ἀπόλωλε, 19.90, 98. **Ἡράκλεις:** vocative exclamation expressing disgust and outrage (cf. D. 19.308, 21.66, Olson 2002: 102–3 on Ar. *Acharn.* 94). **ὅσωι μᾶλλον δεινὸν καὶ ὀργῆς ἄξιον** "so much more outrageous and rightfully infuriating." ὅσωι introduces an exclamation (Smyth §2682). The phrase ὀργῆς ἄξιον and the appeal to the anger of the δῆμος echoes the rhetoric of courtroom prosecutions, especially those concerning public issues (see Rubinstein 2004, Whitehead 2000: 212, 217, Carey 1994: 29–31); for the pairing with δεινός, cf. D. 19.7, 45.53. Below D. similarly urges his audience to hate Philip's advocates in Athens (§53n. μισῆσαι). **εἶναι:** sc. αὐτόν. **ὑπὲρ Φιλίππου καὶ ὦν:** ὑπέρ = περί (§22n.), ὦν = τούτων ἅ. **οὐχ οὕτως ἔχουσιν:** D. refers to the lack of outrage among the Greeks. οὐχ is repeated for emphasis, and then D.'s indignation culminates in the abundant series of negations in the following genitives absolute and dependent clauses that end the paragraph. **προσήκοντος οὐδὲν τοῖς Ἕλλησιν** "related to the Greeks in any way." οὐδέν reinforces the negation in the conjunction οὐδέ. This is D.'s most detailed statement about the ethnicity of the Macedonian kings (see 3.16n. βάρβαρος). Elsewhere he is content to classify them simply as βάρβαροι; here he goes further and puts them at the bottom of a hierarchy of non-Greeks. This "scale of valuation" is consistent with other Athenian categorizations of non-Athenians according to their moral worth (*GPM* 279–83, quotation on 281 on this passage). **οὐδὲ βαρβάρου ἐντεῦθεν ὅθεν καλὸν εἰπεῖν:** lit. "[he is] not even a foreigner from a place that [it is] fine to say [one is from]." The term βάρβαρος gained currency in the fifth century, during the Persian Wars and the Athenian empire. Although it could refer to anyone who did not speak Greek, it was widely used more specifically to describe the Persians and other peoples who were part of the Persian empire; collectively, as βάρβαροι, they represented the antithesis of the emerging Hellenic self-definition (see E. Hall 1989: 3–13). D. here refers to this limited sense of βάρβαρος. **ὀλέθρου Μακεδόνος** "a damned Macedonian." As an adjective (Smyth §986), ὄλεθρος specifically refers to destructive capability, but D. and others employ it as a general term of abuse (LSJ II, MacDowell 1990: 414 on D. 21.202). **ὅθεν οὐδ' ἀνδράποδον σπουδαῖον οὐδὲν ἦν** πρότερον πρίασθαι "[a place] from which it used not to be in any way possible to buy a decent slave." Slaves generally came from other regions: the Balkans, Thrace, the Black Sea, Asia Minor, and the Levant; see D. Lewis 2011. Various Attic inscriptions record the origins of about 100 slaves, two of whom are Macedonian (*IG* I³ 422.79–80 [414 BC], II² 9273 [4th cent. BC]).

**32–46 Macedonian outrages and Greek acquiescence**
Philip has usurped Greek prerogatives and continues to assault the Greeks while we do nothing. Our corruption and complaisance make possible his success. Our forefathers adopted a different attitude toward the Persians.

**32 καίτοι:** §16n.   **τί τῆς ἐσχάτης ὕβρεως ἀπολείπει;** ἀπολείπω, "be wanting" or "lacking," governs the gen. (LSJ A IV 2); τί is adverbial. This general rhetorical question leads to a series of five further queries that provide detailed examples of Philip's hybris (on which see 1.23n. ὑβριστής). For the technique, cf. 3.16–17.   **πρὸς τῶι πόλεις ἀνηιρηκέναι:** the verb echoes §§19, 26 and refers to the capture of the towns listed there: Olynthus, Methone, Apollonia, Phocis.   **τίθησι μὲν τὰ Πύθια:** after capturing Phocis, Philip assumed the Phocians' seat on the Amphictyonic Council at the end of the third Sacred War (3.8n. ἀπειρηκότων), and the Council put him in charge of (LSJ τίθημι A VI) the Pythian festival at Delphi in 346 (D. 5.22, D. S. 16.60.2, Ryder 2000: 70–1). The Athenians regarded this as an act of impiety and refused to participate (D. 19.128–32, Hunt 2010: 88–9).   **κἂν** = καὶ ἐάν. καί joins τίθησι and πέμπει; both verbs are negated by οὐ.   **τοὺς δούλους:** in 342 Philip sent one of his generals (Antipater; see Heckel 2008: s.v. 1) to preside at the Pythian Games. The associates and subordinates of tyrants and kings were regularly labeled as slaves; cf. 1.4n. δεσπότην, Hyp. *Epit.* 21 with Herrman 2009b: 91, Eur. *Hel.* 276 with Allan 2008: 181, Brock 2013: 158, 182 n. 106.   **Πυλῶν καὶ τῶν ἐπὶ τοὺς Ἕλληνας παρόδων** "Thermopylae and the entryway to the Greeks": sc. οὐ here and with the following questions. For the pl. παρόδων see LSJ πάροδος (B) II a and cf. Hyp. *Epit.* 12. Philip took control of the pass at Thermopylae when he entered central Greece to settle the third Sacred War in 346; see §11n. ἥριζον.   **φρουραῖς καὶ ξένοις** "garrisons and mercenaries"; §12n. Φεράς, §26n. οὐχί.   **τὴν προμαντείαν τοῦ θεοῦ:** the privilege of priority in consulting the Delphic oracle. The Delphians held the privilege originally and extended it to the Athenians and Spartans in the fifth century (Bowden 2005: 17). By the time of this speech, that privilege must have been extended to the member states of the Amphictyonic Council, and upon entry to the Council in 346 Philip was given precedence over the other members (cf. D. 19.327 with MacDowell 2000: 348). See further Sánchez 2001: 467–8, Lefèvre 1998: 42–3.   **παρώσας:** παρωθέω, "push aside," colorfully characterizes Philip; cf. 2.18n. παρεῶσθαι.   ἧς οὐδὲ τοῖς Ἕλλησιν ἅπασι μέτεστι "[a privilege] that not even all the Greeks enjoy." The adverbial use of οὐδέ stresses that Philip is not a Greek. **33 γράφει δὲ Θετταλοῖς;** sc. οὐ, as above (§32n. Πυλῶν). On Philip's letters, cf. §27n. οὐ.   ὃν χρὴ τρόπον πολιτεύεσθαι: §26n. τετραρχίας. **τοὺς μὲν εἰς Πορθμόν:** Porthmus was a port of Eretria on the island of Euboea. After a period of civil strife in Eretria Philip intervened in 343, and his mercenaries took control of the port and installed a new political regime; see §§57–8, 19.87 with MacDowell 2000: 245, Harris 115–16, *HM* 502. D. uses coordinated μέν and δέ phrases to link Philip's interventions at Eretria and Oreus and imply that he had a unified plan to gain control of the entire island of Euboea. More likely, Philip took advantage of individual opportunities as they arose; the use of mercenary troops on these missions allowed him to become involved without a substantial commitment on his part.   **τοὺς δ' ἐπ' Ὠρεόν:** §12n. τοῖς.   **ταῦθ' ὁρῶντες οἱ Ἕλληνες ἀνέχονται:** the repetition from §28 (cf. also §6n. ἀνέχεσθαι) underscores D.'s main point.   **τὸν αὐτὸν τρόπον:** §30n.   **ὥσπερ τὴν χάλαζαν:** similes invoking the natural world are not as common in D. as other types of similes; see Introd. §3.4. (Homer, by contrast, abounds in nature similes; for χάλαζα in this context, cf. *Il.* 10.6, 15.170.) In his later political speeches D. presents a series of brief comparisons with the natural world, consisting of ὥσπερ + noun phrase, that stress the dangers threatening the city (18.153, 188, 308, 19.136, Yunis 212, Ronnet 180–1). Here he creates a vivid image of the threat, not in order to depict Philip as an unstoppable force of nature, but rather to present him as a danger to all the Greeks alike, and in order to stress the need for mutual aid among them as an antidote to the isolation observed in §28. The image was memorable; Sallust borrows it for a speech in the Roman Senate (see 3.1n.). **θεωρεῖν:** sc. ταῦτα.   **εὐχόμενοι μὴ καθ' ἑαυτοὺς ἕκαστοι γενέσθαι** "each praying that [he] not come against them." γίγνομαι with κατά + accus. refers to an opposing enemy (LSJ γίγνομαι II 3 c), i.e., Philip (as opposed to the hailstorm). The pl. ἕκαστοι refers to the populations of the various Greek cities individually.   **κωλύειν δ' οὐδεὶς ἐπιχειρῶν:** again, D. focuses clearly on Philip, whose advance the Greeks can stop (unlike that of a hailstorm). The switch to the singular prepares for the following contrast.

**34 οὐ μόνον** coordinates with ἀλλ' οὐδ' (as in §31). The point is the contrast expressed in the two relative clauses, between Greece as a whole and individual persons and places.   **ἐφ' οἷς:** the antecedent is to be supplied from the context: "in those cases in which." ἐπί describes the circumstances or situation (LSJ B I i).   **ἀλλ' οὐδ' ὑπὲρ ὧν** "but also [no one protects himself], not even concerning matters in which." ὑπὲρ ὧν is

# 9 THIRD PHILIPPIC 34–35

equivalent in sense to ἐφ᾽ οἷς here; ὑπέρ + gen. is the more regular construction with ἀμύνομαι (LSJ ἀμύνω B 3). **τοῦτο γὰρ ἤδη τοὔσχατόν ἐστιν** "this is now the worst thing"; i.e., that individual Greek states do not even help themselves. **οὐ Κορινθίων ἐπ᾽ Ἀμβρακίαν ἐλήλυθε;** "has he not attacked Ambracia, which belongs to the Corinthians?" (LSJ ἔρχομαι v 8). See §27n. πρότερον, and on Ambracia and Corinth, Salmon 1984: 270–80. The possessive genitives (sc. a participle of εἰμί with each of the accus. place names) are put first in the following examples to stress that for these individual states it was in their own interest to help others (cf. *GPS* 47). The series of questions is presented as a simple list, without connectives (asyndeton). Each example illustrates D.'s assertion that the Greek states are not helping themselves; the combined effect of the series of examples shows that D.'s point applies to Greece as a whole, that each item is part of a larger pattern. For the technique; cf. 1.9n. Πύδνα, 3.7n. **Λευκάδα:** Leucas was near Ambracia, and also a Corinthian colony; it was threatened along with Ambracia in 343/2 (*HM* 508). **Ναύπακτον:** on the north coast of the gulf of Corinth (Barrington Atlas 55 B4), controlled at this time by the Achaeans. As part of his maneuvers against Ambracia, Philip offered to seize the territory for the Aetolians, but upon his withdrawal from the region (§27n. πρότερον) this promise was postponed, to be fulfilled later, after the battle of Chaeronea in 338 (Sealey 177, 197, *HM* 508–9). **Ἐχῖνον:** on the north coast of the gulf of Malia (Barrington Atlas 55 D3), possibly used by the Thebans as a fortification against Thessaly, until Philip intervened in 341 (Sealey 190, *HM* 543 n. 4). **συμμάχους ὄντας:** sc. Θηβαίοις; D. links this example with that of Echinus to explain why the Thebans should have taken action. Byzantium had recently supported Thebes as an ally during the third Sacred War (*IG* VII 2418.9 [354–352 BC] = *GHI* no. 57). This phrase is widely misunderstood as a reference to an alliance between Philip and Byzantium, mentioned at D. 18.87; but that passage is tendentious (see Yunis 158), and such an interpretation misses D.'s point here.

**35 ἐῶ τἄλλα:** this parenthetical insertion, to which ἀλλά responds, is abrupt and has no connective particle (cf. D. 18.266). The list of Philip's provocations culminates with Athens, and this insertion implies that D. could adduce further examples of hostility toward the allies and territories of Athens. **Καρδίαν:** §16nn. εἰς and βασιλεύς. **μέλλομεν:** 4.9n. κύκλωι. **μαλακιζόμεθα:** in this context, where D. faults the Athenians' failure to engage Philip, the verb refers to cowardice rather than physical illness (LSJ 1, not 3; cf. Thuc. 3.40.7, a similar context). Sallust's imitation (3.1n.) paraphrases it as *mollities animi* ("cowardice," *OLD mollitia* 6). **πρὸς τοὺς πλησίον βλέπομεν** "we look to our neighbors," or rely on them to take action (LSJ βλέπω II 2, Finglass 2007: 398 on S. *El.* 954); the idiom implies weakness or inferiority (Diggle 2004: 183) and shirking of duty (cf. D. 14.15, Isoc. 3.18). **ἀπιστοῦντες ἀλλήλοις** "although we distrust one another"; ἀλλήλοις refers to the Greek states (as at §§25, 28) rather than different Athenians (as at 2.25, 29, 4.21, 44, §§14, 38), since D. here focuses on foreign policy, not domestic politics. **τῶι πάντας ἡμᾶς ἀδικοῦντι:** D. repeats the verb from §34, where it applied to wrongs that affected individual cities. πάντας emphasizes the cumulative effect of those individual aggressions. **τὸν ἅπασιν ἀσελγῶς οὕτω χρώμενον** "one who treats everyone so aggressively" (LSJ χράω c IV 1); accus. subject of ποιήσειν. See 2.19n. ἀσελγεστέρους. **καθ' ἕν** "one by one" (LSJ κατά B II 3). **τί ποιήσειν;** τί is object of ποιήσειν, repeated for clarity in emphatic final position after the intervening temporal clause (cf. D. 18.240, *GPS* 97).

**36 τί οὖν αἴτιον τουτωνί;** cf. 3.30n. τί, a similar question, also leading to a comparison of fifth- and fourth-century Athens. **οὐ γὰρ ἄνευ λόγου καὶ δικαίας αἰτίας** "not without reason and just cause." οὔτε ... οὔτε reinforces the initial οὐ; i.e., there is a reason for the difference between Greeks then and now. **οὕτως εἶχον ἑτοίμως πρὸς ἐλευθερίαν** "they were so zealous for freedom." Public accounts of Athenian history in the state funeral orations focused on the Persian Wars and celebrated Athens for liberating the other Greeks from the Persian invaders (e.g., Thuc. 2.36.1, Lys. 2.33–4, Pl. *Menex.* 240e; cf. D. 18.205). Whereas D.'s earlier speeches against Philip saw him as a threat to the freedom of other Greek states (1.23, 2.8), now it is a question of the freedom of Athens itself. This shift in perspective anticipates a more pronounced change in public speeches after the battle of Chaeronea, which will adapt and mimic traditional descriptions of the Persian Wars to present the fight against Philip and his successors as a fight for the freedom of Athens and the Greeks (e.g., D. 60.23, Lycurg. 50, [D.] 17.9, Hyp. *Epit.* 19, Herrman 2009a: 183). **τὸ δουλεύειν:** D. polarizes the situation with this contrast between servitude and freedom; this simplified presentation was typical in Assembly speeches. Cf. Thuc. 2.63.1, Hunt 2010: 112–13. **ἦν τι τότ':** D. adopts an elevated tone in this sentence, with the abstract indefinite τι as subject, unusual vocabulary, metaphor, and alliteration. The pace is leisurely, with a string of short clauses and repetition of key points in opposite terms (Wooten 1989: 583–4). The overall message is very pessimistic; typically, D. urges his audience to emulate their ancestors, but here he allows for no such possibility (§41n. τῶν, 3.24n., 4.3n. ἀνάξιον, *GPM* 108, 124). **ἦν:** 1.19n. ἔστιν. **ταῖς τῶν πολλῶν διανοίαις:** D.'s focus on the mindset of Athenian predecessors as the key to their success sets this speech apart from earlier Assembly speeches. According to D., διάνοια is the key to success in all human affairs (61.37 τῶν μὲν τοίνυν ἐν ἀνθρώποις διάνοιαν ἁπάντων εὑρήσομεν ἡγεμονεύουσαν; see MacDowell 2009: 27), and in this speech it is the value that distinguishes the generation of the Persian Wars from the present day (cf. §§43, 53). **τοῦ Περσῶν ἐκράτησε πλούτου:** this metaphorical usage (LSJ κρατέω II 3 a) is unusual in D. (cf. 2.27, §5, Ronnet 159–60). In the funeral orations the Athenian ancestors are praised for preferring the freedom of the Greeks to the wealth of the Persians (Lys. 2.33; cf. Pl. *Menex.* 241b). This point introduces the discussion of bribery that follows. **ἐλευθέραν ἦγε τὴν Ἑλλάδα** "kept Greece free." This use of the simplex verb (as opposed to the compound διάγω) with a predicate accus. is unusual (LSJ ἄγω IV 3 cites only this passage). **οὔτε ναυμαχίας οὔτε πεζῆς μάχης οὐδεμιᾶς:** gen. with ἡττᾶτο: "neither in any sea battle…" The expansive phrase can generally refer to any engagement, though Athenian accounts tended to focus on the army's triumph at Marathon and the naval victory at Salamis as the two defining events of the Persian Wars (e.g., Pl. *Menex.* 241b ὑπ' ἀμφοτέρων δὴ συμβαίνει, τῶν τε Μαραθῶνι μαχεσαμένων καὶ τῶν ἐν Σαλαμῖνι ναυμαχησάντων, παιδευθῆναι τοὺς ἄλλους Ἕλληνας, "the other Greeks were educated by both the men in the army at Marathon and those in the navy at Salamis"). **ἀπολωλὸς ἅπαντα λελύμανται** "the loss [of that something] has ruined everything." The verbs are repeated from §31, recalling the imagery of a squandered legacy. λελύμανται is 3rd sing. perf. mid. indic. (Smyth §407, 409d). **ἄνω καὶ κάτω πεποίηκε πάντα τὰ πράγματα** "all our affairs have been turned upside down." D.'s earlier uses of ἄνω (καὶ) κάτω referred to actual marches (2.16n. ἄνω); for this sense of throwing things into confusion, cf. 18.111, 19.261, 21.91. The alliteration calls attention to the expression, and this clause is linked with the former by the repetition of πάντα in the same position.

**37 οὐδὲν ποικίλον οὐδὲ σοφόν, ἀλλ' ὅτι:** sc. ἦν. For this usage of ποικίλος cf. D. 29.1, Pl. *Men.* 75e, *Tim.* 59c. D. regularly answers rhetorical questions with ὅτι (e.g., 2.3n. διά, 4.36n. ὅτι). **τοὺς … λαμβάνοντας:** the extensive noun phrase is the object of ἐμίσουν; ἄρχειν and διαφθείρειν depend on βουλομένων. D. refers to the time of the Persian Wars, and his point is perhaps corroborated by the absence of Persian bribes as a prominent theme in Herodotus' account of the war; cf. Hdt. 9.2.3, in which the Thebans advise Persian generals to distribute bribes to win over the leading men of Greece, but the advice is not followed. Later fifth-century attempts by Persians to bribe Greeks were ineffective; see Flower and Marincola 2002: 104, D. M. Lewis 1997: 372. **χαλεπώτατον ἦν τὸ δωροδοκοῦντα ἐλεγχθῆναι** "being convicted for taking bribes was very serious." δωροδοκοῦντα is masc. accus. pres. act. participle modifying the unexpressed subject of ἐλεγχθῆναι. **τιμωρίαι μεγίστηι:** the penalties for Athenian officials guilty of accepting bribes or gifts ranged from disenfranchisement to a fine of 10 times the amount received, and in extreme cases could include the death penalty (see Harris in Canevaro 2013a: 234–5),

MacDowell 1983. **καὶ παραίτησις οὐδεμία ἦν οὐδὲ συγγνώμη** "and there was no recourse or leniency." This phrase is omitted from some MSS (see Introd. §6.2), and editors have deleted it as an unwanted addition to the preceding tricolon. It makes an important point, however, in that it explains what ἀτιμία meant in the case of the pronouncement against Arthmius (§§42–6). The term had two distinct senses: in the case of Arthmius it describes someone who was excluded from all legal protections, someone whom Athenians are under moral obligation to execute; in its more common fourth-century usage it refers to political disenfranchisement, a citizen's loss of political rights; cf. §39n. συγγνώμη and D.'s own explanation in §44, and see Youni 2001: 124–32. The terms παραίτησις and συγγνώμη apply to this stricter form of ἀτιμία, and thus make D.'s point, that the generation of the Persian Wars had a harsh penalty for corruption.

**38 τὸν οὖν καιρὸν ἑκάστου τῶν πραγμάτων** "the moment for each instance of action"; direct object of πρίασθαι, antecedent of ὄν. For the theme see 1.2n. καιρός.   **ἡ τύχη:** a personified agent responsible for καιρός; see 1.11n. τῆι. For the trope of Athens being saved even when the Athenians do not help themselves, see 2.1n. τήν.   **τοῖς ἀμελοῦσι:** 3.3n. τῆς.   **κατὰ τῶν προσεχόντων:** sc. τὸν νοῦν. κατά is "against" here. This general contrast echoes D.'s frequent distinction between Philip's stern discipline and Athenian negligence; cf. 4.5n. ὑπάρχει.   **ποιεῖν κατὰ τῶν πάντα ἃ προσήκει πραττόντων:** for the alliteration see 3.36n. καὶ … κατέλιπον, and for the sense see §16n. ταῦτα.   **οὐκ ἦν πρίασθαι** "it was not possible to purchase." This key theme distinguishes the Athenians of the Persian Wars from D.'s contemporaries. Cf. §9n. τῶν, §37n. τούς.   **τῶν λεγόντων οὐδὲ τῶν στρατηγούντων:** speakers in the Assembly were regularly paired with military generals; the two groups comprised the leadership of Athens (see Hansen 1991: 143–5, 268–9).   **τὴν πρὸς ἀλλήλους ὁμόνοιαν:** parallel to τὸν καιρόν as an item not up for sale. ὁμόνοια is a political ideal of civic harmony and a lack of factionalism, and the noun refers more specifically to the consensus arising from vigorous debate in the Assembly (Canevaro 2018, 2019). D. presents it as a hallmark of his own political leadership (18.246), and the theme is prominent in political philosophy and oratory, often characterizing the reconciliation in Athens after the civil war at the end of the fifth century (see Christ 2012: 50–61, Yunis 1997: 63, W. C. West 1977: 309–14). A fourth-century manual on siege warfare singles out ὁμόνοια as an essential element for resistance to enemy attacks (Aen. Tact. 14.1 with Whitehead 2001: 137).   **τὴν πρὸς τοὺς τυράννους καὶ τοὺς βαρβάρους ἀπιστίαν:** for the assertion that free citizens protect themselves from tyranny by means of ἀπιστία, cf. 1.5n. ἄπιστον, 6.24. Tyranny was regarded as the polar opposite of democracy and the rule of law, in the same way that the βάρβαροι were distinguished from Greeks, and tyrants and non-Greeks were often associated in this way; cf. Hdt. 8.142.3, E. *Heracl.* 423, Pl. *Sym.* 182b, E. *Hall* 1989: 192–3.   **ὅλως:** 2.7n.

**39 ὥσπερ ἐξ ἀγορᾶς:** a typical simile; see Introd. §3.4.   **ἐκπέπραται ταῦτα, ἀντεισῆκται:** ταῦτα refers back to the items listed as unavailable for sale in §38. The two verbs are virtual antonyms: "sell for export" and "import as a replacement" (LSJ ἐκπιπράσκω and ἀντεισάγω); the unexpressed subject of the latter is to be understood as the antecedent of ὧν.   **ἀπόλωλε καὶ νενόσηκεν** "has become deadly ill." The two verbs express a single thought (hendiadys); the first is more general, referring to the destruction that results from the second (see §31n. ἀπώλλυε). For the metaphorical use of νοσέω for political strife, see §12n. τοῖς, 2.14n. νοσοῦσι.   **ταῦτα δ' ἐστὶ τί;** ταῦτα refers back to the unexpressed subject of ἀντεισῆκται. The sing. τί as predicate with a neut. pl. is common (LSJ τις B I 2, Dodds 1959: 340 on Pl. *Grg.* 508b).   **εἴ τις εἴληφέ τι** "if anyone has gotten some profit" (LSJ λαμβάνω A II h). D. shows how far Athenian values have declined by presenting a series of examples in which the reaction of contemporary Athenians is completely the opposite of what it used to be. The switch from εἰ + indic. to ἄν (= ἐάν) + subj. is a stylistic variation.   **γέλως** "derision"; cf. 4.45n. καταγελῶσιν.   **συγγνώμη τοῖς ἐλεγχομένοις** "leniency for those who are convicted." This item responds to the similar point above, and similarly gives a concrete example of actual change: the current sense of ἀτιμία refers to a more lenient penalty than it used to do (see §37n. καί).   **ἄν τούτοις τις ἐπιτιμᾷ** "if anyone objects to these actions" that result from bribery.   **ὅσα ἐκ τοῦ δωροδοκεῖν ἤρτηται** "whatever is linked with the taking of bribes" (LSJ ἀρτάω II 2).

**40 ἐπεί** "and yet" (Smyth §2380, LSJ B 4). ἐπεί + γε presents a concession to D.'s previous statement that is answered by the following ἀλλά. Cf. 4.25, 24.125.   **τριήρεις ... ἀφθονία:** sc. εἰσί/ἐστί. D. briefly summarizes the Athenians' resources. The abundant phrasing, with the repetition of synonyms (πλῆθος/ἀφθονία, πλείω καὶ μείζω) and the sequence of different materials, illustrates his assertion. For the size of the Athenian navy at this time, see 4.16n. τριήρεις; see 4.40n. χρημάτων on public revenues. σώματα and χρήματα are regularly linked to describe the costs of war (e.g., Thuc. 1.85.1, 6.12.1, D. 16.12, 18.66, 60.18).   **ἐστί:** the sing. verb stresses the collectivity of the preceding nominatives, and is regular after a neut. pl. (τὰ ἄλλα; Smyth §959).   **τῶν τότε** = ἢ τοῖς τότε (genitive of comparison).   **ἄχρηστα ἄπρακτα ἀνόνητα:** 4.36n. ἄτακτα. The three adjectives are virtually synonymous; the last is particularly solemn: D. uses it elsewhere in a prayer, and then characterizes his use of it as being οὑτωσὶ σφοδρῶς, "very serious" in tone (18.142–3).   **ὑπὸ**

τῶν πωλούντων "because of those who sell [our resources]" by accepting bribes from Philip.

**41 ὅτι δ᾽ οὕτω ταῦτ᾽ ἔχει** "[as proof] that these matters are such [as I have said]," a Demosthenic formula introducing proof in the form of evidence or an argument (cf. 18.37, 23.159, 45.27, 46). D. produces two types of proof: τὰ μὲν νῦν and τὰ δ᾽ ἐν τοῖς ἄνωθεν χρόνοις are subcategories of ταῦτα.   **δήπου:** 3.9n.   **ἐν τοῖς ἄνωθεν χρόνοις** "in earlier times" (LSJ ἄνωθεν II 1).   **ὅτι τἀναντία εἶχεν** "that they were the opposite [of our current practice]." τἀναντία = τὰ ἐναντία, adverbial accus. neut. pl.   **γράμματα:** sc. λέγων: "by reciting the inscription" (LSJ γράμμα II d, λέγω [B] III 13; Chadwick 1996: 82). D.'s appeal to the authority of the written inscription is emblematic of changing attitudes in the fourth century, when written contracts, pleas, and testimony became increasingly common in Athenian courts (on the history of written documents in courts, see Faraguna 2008, Pébarthe 2006: 315–43). The complementarity of D.'s own arguments and the written inscription illustrates Aristotle's distinction between "artistic proofs" and "non-artistic proofs" (*Rh.* 1.2.2 [1355b] τῶν δὲ πίστεων αἱ μὲν ἄτεχνοί εἰσιν αἱ δ᾽ ἔντεχνοι); the former are arguments crafted by speakers, while the latter include items such as witness testimony or supporting documents (see Gagarin 2008: 188–90).   **τῶν προγόνων τῶν ὑμετέρων:** D. and other orators frequently invoke the Athenian ancestors, especially those who fought the Persian Wars, either as a model for emulation, or, as here, to draw a contrast between past and present practice and attitudes; e.g., 3.23–4, 6.10–11, 18.203–5. See E. M. Harris 2016: 148, Jost 1935: 190–2; cf. 3.24n.   **εἰς στήλην χαλκῆν γράψαντες:** Athenian inscribed bronze stelae were "large and impressive monuments, built to last, and capable of carrying a text of considerable length and importance"; almost no examples survive, but literary testimonia suggest that decrees of ἀτιμία were often recorded on monumental bronzes (Stroud 1963: 138, quotation on 143). The orators frequently refer to and quote from this decree against Arthmius of Zelea as an accessible and well-known stele (D. 19.271, Aesch. 3.258, Din. 2.25). It is one of a handful of decrees regarding the Persian Wars that appear frequently in fourth-century sources, but the authenticity of them as a group is doubtful, in that their historical accounts are sometimes demonstrably inaccurate, the phrasing is often questionable, and they are not attested before the fourth century (see Habicht 1961: esp. 23–5). In the case of the Arthmius decree further suspicion is raised by conflicting evidence regarding the proposer of the decree (see §42n. τόν).   **εἰς ἀκρόπολιν:** the Arthmius decree was prominently placed to the right of the bronze Athena dedicated to the victory over the Persians, the Athena Promachos, one of the most conspicuous monuments on the Acropolis (D. 19.272).   **οὐχ ἵνα αὐτοῖς ἦι χρήσιμα:** for the emphatic negation followed by ἀλλά, cf. D. 15.35, 16.28. **τὰ δέοντα ἐφρόνουν** "they were mindful of their duties" (LSJ φρονέω II 2 a). **ὑμεῖς ἔχητε ὑπομνήματα καὶ παραδείγματα:** the prominent placement of the Arthmius decree clearly indicates that it was to be viewed as a model for democratic responses to treason. In this regard it is comparable to other famous decrees denouncing treasonous or tyrannical behavior, such as the Attic Stelae cataloguing the confiscated property of Alcibiades and his associates in 414, which were probably displayed at the Eleusinion in the Agora (Meiggs and Lewis 1988: 245 no. 79, Wycherley 1957: 79 no. 207, cf. 3.26n. τῆς); see Teegarden 2013: 105 n. 44. The close correspondence is confirmed by the similar language the orators use to refer to these inscribed decrees; cf. Din. 2.24, who describes this decree against Arthmius as a παράδειγμα, and more generally cf. this passage's correspondence to Lycurg. 127 (ὑπομνήματα δ' ἔχετε καὶ παραδείγματα τῆς ἐκείνων τιμωρίας τὰ ἐν τοῖς περὶ τῶν ἀδικούντων ψηφίσμασιν ὡρισμένα, "you have as reminders and models for the punishment of those [traitors] the decisions in [your ancestors'] decrees concerning criminals"), describing the decree of Demophantus against traitors, and stressing its display in the Athenian Agora (see the discussion of E. M. Harris 2014, who demonstrates that the version of the Demophantus decree presented by Andoc. 1.95–8 is not authentic). **ὡς … προσήκει:** indirect discourse introduced by ὑπομνήματα.

**42 τί οὖν λέγει τὰ γράμματα;** 2.3n. διά. **Ἄρθμιος … Πυθώνακτος Ζελείτης** "Arthmius, son of Pythonax, from Zelea." Individual Greeks are identified by name, father's name, and the name of their home city (or a civic subdivision of their city); the full name here is typical of inscribed decrees (without the definite article – see apparatus; cf. Hansen and Nielsen 2005: 58–9). Other sources provide a few additional details not found in this passage, that Arthmius was a πρόξενος (i.e., an ambassador with established ties) to the Athenians, and that he stopped in Athens (Aesch. 3.258 with Meiggs 1972: 510). Zelea was a Greek πόλις in Phrygia (Barrington Atlas 52 B4), attested on inscribed tribute lists as a member of the Delian League ($IG$ I$^3$ 271.38 [441/0 BC], 71.102 [425/4]). **ἄτιμος καὶ πολέμιος:** sc. τεθνάτω; on ἄτιμος, see §37n. καί; the discussion of the term in §44 guarantees its appearance in the actual decree. πολέμιος must be accurately quoted, since it appears in all the orators' versions of the decree; it adds a distinct injunction: Arthmius is to be treated as an enemy at war, whom the Athenians are obliged to kill, with legal and moral impunity (E. M. Harris 2014: 136–7). **τοῦ δήμου τοῦ Ἀθηναίων καὶ τῶν συμμάχων:** this refers to the Delian League; Aeschines' version explains that the decree barred Arthmius "from Athens and all territory that the Athenians controlled" (Aesch. 3.258 ἐξεκήρυξαν δ' ἐκ τῆς πόλεως καὶ ἐξ ἁπάσης ἧς ἄρχουσιν Ἀθηναῖοι). **αὐτὸς καὶ γένος:**

the provision for the punishment of a criminal's descendants is typical in cases involving the subversion of the state; see Parker 1983: 203–4. This phrasing is consistent with the fourth-century inscribed law against tyranny (*IG* II³ 320.20 [337/6] = *GHI* no. 79), whereas a fifth-century disenfranchisement decree uses the phrase αὐτὸν καὶ παῖδας τὸς ἐχς [ἐκένο] (*IG* I³ 46.27 [c. 445 BC]). **ἡ αἰτία γέγραπται:** Din. 2.25 asserts that this is the only Athenian decree providing a reason for a specific banishment. Surviving inscriptions refer to disenfranchisement as a prospective penalty for failure to abide by the terms of a decree (e.g., *IG* I³ 40.33–4 [446/5 BC], 46.27). In contrast, honorary decrees for individuals do regularly list specific reasons (see Veligianni-Terzi 1997: 165–87). **τὸν χρυσὸν τὸν ἐκ Μήδων εἰς Πελοπόννησον ἤγαγεν:** the precise context for the decree is not clear. It is reported to have been sponsored by Cimon (Crater. *FGrHist* 342 F 14), or alternatively, by Themistocles (Plut. *Them.* 6.4); see Erdas 2002: 179–85. Thucydides reports that the Persians attempted to bribe the Spartans to invade Attica in the 450s, and perhaps Arthmius was involved with this mission (Thuc. 1.109.2–3, D. M. Lewis 1997: 373); another possibility is that the Persians sent Arthmius to support the Spartan regent Pausanias in the 460s (Meiggs 1972: 511–12).

**43 πρὸς θεῶν:** the oath colloquially reinforces an imperative; cf. 8.32, 15.26, 19.147, 21.58. **τίς ἦν ποθ':** 1.14n. εἰς. **ἡ διάνοια:** §36n. ταῖς. **τί τὸ ἀξίωμα** "what their purpose [was]" (LSJ ἀξίωμα II 1). D. similarly appeals to the ἀξιώματα of the ancestors as a guide for the present generation in *On the Crown* (18.210). **δοῦλον βασιλέως:** §32n. τούς; the following γάρ clause explains this assertion. Zelea's location in Asia Minor meant that the Greek city was subject to a provincial administrator (a satrap) for the Persian king. **ἐστι τῆς Ἀσίας** "is in Asia" (Smyth §1303). **τῶι δεσπότηι διακονῶν** "serving his master." D. reiterates the judgment already expressed in δοῦλον; cf. his description of Philip's senior generals: δεσπότηι διακονοῦντες (19.69). See also 1.4n. δεσπότην. **οὐκ Ἀθήναζε:** D.'s own comment, anticipating the argument in §§45–6. **ἐχθρὸν αὐτῶν ἀνέγραψαν** "they registered [him] as their enemy" (LSJ ἀναγράφω I 2: "record" on a stele). ἐχθρόν is a paraphrase for πολέμιον; cf. D. 19.271 Ἄρθμιον ... ἐχθρὸν εἶναι καὶ πολέμιον τοῦ δήμου τοῦ Ἀθηναίων. **ἀτίμους:** pl. after the collective γένος.

**44 τοῦτο:** the neut. refers generally to the preceding sentence (Smyth §2501a), but then in the following relative clause D. focuses on the specific term ἀτιμία. **ἣν οὑτωσί τις ἂν φήσειεν ἀτιμίαν** "what someone would ordinarily speak of as disenfranchisement" (LSJ οὕτως IV). Cf. §37n. καί. **τί γὰρ τῶι Ζελείτηι;** sc. τοῦτ' ἐστί: "what [concern] is this to a man from Zelea?"; explained by what follows. For the colloquialism, cf. §16, 19.82, Austin and Olson 2004: 203 on Ar. *Thesmo.* 498. **τῶν**

Ἀθηναίων κοινῶν ... μεθέξειν "partake in Athenian political rights" (LSJ μετέχω I 1). τὸ Ἀθηναίων κοινόν is a regular paraphrase for the δῆμος (cf. Hdt. 9.117 with Flower and Marincola 2002: 306, Th. 1.89.3 with S. Hornblower 1991: 135–6); the phrase is emphasized here by its placement before the conjunction (*GPS* 49). ἀλλ᾽ οὐ τοῦτο λέγει "but this is not what it means" (LSJ λέγω III 9; cf. §1.27n.). This phrase is omitted in some MSS and in an ancient quotation of this passage (Harp. s.v. ἄτιμος). The repetition of ἀλλά and τοῦτο λέγει below perhaps indicates that D. was considering textual alternatives. ἐν τοῖς φονικοῖς γέγραπται νόμοις: Athenian homicide laws were the oldest element in the classical Athenian law code, instituted, according to tradition, by Draco in the late seventh century and preserved when the laws were reformed by Solon in the early sixth century (see Rhodes 1993: 109–12, MacDowell 1978: 41–3). Orators frequently refer to the homicide laws as a venerable authority (e.g., D. 20.158, 21.43); here D. cites them to illustrate the ancient concept of ἀτιμία. The best sources for the texts of these laws are D.'s speech *Against Aristocrates*, in which he quotes and discusses numerous detailed provisions (23.22–64 with Canevaro 2013a: 37–73, demonstrating that the documents preserving the laws are "mainly reliable" [39]; cf. D. 43.57) and a late fifth-century inscription that preserves a portion of a republished version of the laws (*IG* I³ 104 = Meiggs and Lewis 1988: no. 86). For further bibliography see MacDowell 1990: 258. ὑπὲρ ὧν ἂν μὴ διδῶι φόνου δικάσασθαι "regarding [those] for whose murder [the lawgiver] does not grant that there be a trial" (LSJ δίδωμι III 1). The phrasing probably echoes the law; cf. D. 23.67 δίδωσ᾽ ὁ νόμος καὶ κελεύει τοῦ φόνου δικάζεσθαι [ἐν Ἀρείωι πάγωι] ("the law grants and provides for a case of murder to be tried [in the Areopagus court]"; on this sense of κελεύω, see E. M. Harris 2006: 131). The law permitted homicide in various circumstances, such as when the victim was a convicted murderer violating the terms of exile, or when a death occurred as an accident in an athletic competition or in battle, or when the homicide was in self-defense (D. 23.51–6, 60; E. M. Harris 2013b: 50–3). ἀλλ᾽ εὐαγὲς ἦι τὸ ἀποκτεῖναι: lit. "[regarding those whose] killing is lawful." ἦι is parallel to διδῶι, and ἀλλά responds to μή. εὐαγής is a religious term, "free from pollution." It is D.'s rephrasing for the term καθαρός (see below; Parker 1983: 366–9 on the variation here); it does not appear in inscribed laws or decrees and hence should not be regarded as part of the direct quotation. (Its appearance in the law quoted at Andoc. 1.96, a later forgery, is likely to originate from this passage; see E. M. Harris 2014: 137–8.) "καὶ ἄτιμος" φησὶ "τεθνάτω": "[the lawgiver] states 'let him die unavenged'." The quoted version of the law at D. 23.60 uses the phrase νηποινεὶ τεθνάναι in the same sense (in a different section of the law); for further parallels see Barrett 1964: 412. The perf. imperative stresses the "permanent result" (Smyth §1864c). **καθαρὸν τὸν τούτων τινὰ ἀποκτείναντα εἶναι:** τούτων τινά refers to Ἄρθμιος αὐτὸς καὶ γένος. καθαρός is literally "pure" and in this context means "not guilty" (a synonym for εὐαγής; E. M. Harris 2015: 19–21 shows that a religious sense, "unpolluted" predominates in fifth- and fourth-century Athens, and that the suggestion of Parker 1983: 367, that this sense died out with the development of formal legal institutions, is misleading); the adjective appears regularly in similar contexts regarding justifiable homicide: cf. D. 20.158, 23.55, 37.59, Lycurg. 125.

**45 οὐκοῦν** marks a logical inference (*GP* 438). D. explains how the historical example of Arthmius is relevant to his argument in §§36–40. **αὐτοῖς ἐπιμελητέον εἶναι:** αὐτοῖς is dat. of agent with the verbal adjective (cf. 4.16), which governs the gen. **οὐ γὰρ ἂν αὐτοῖς ἔμελεν ... διαφθείρει** "it would not have mattered to them that someone in the Peloponnese was bribing and corrupting people" (both verbs frequently refer to bribes: LSJ ὠνέομαι I 4, διαφθείρω I 2). For μέλω introducing an εἰ clause, cf. Lys. 21.12. For the use of the imperfect in a past contrary-to-fact condition, see 1.8n. εἰ, 3.17n. εἰ. **μὴ τοῦθ᾽ ὑπολαμβάνουσιν** "if they had not held this opinion." ὑπολαμβάνουσιν is dat. participle, modifying αὐτοῖς, equivalent to an imperf. indic. in a conditional protasis. **ἐκόλαζον ... ἐτιμωροῦντο:** according to Aristotle, the former verb refers to corrective punishment benefiting the one who is punished, while the latter refers to retaliatory action for the restoration of the τιμή of the one who inflicts it (Arist. *Rh.* 1.10.17–18 [1369b]; cf. Plat. *Prt.* 324c with Denyer 2008: 113). The two roots are often used in conjunction as synonyms, e.g., §37, Lys. 14.12, Lycurg. 51, 65; such calls for punishment are frequent in court cases on public matters (γραφαί), where they are linked with appeals to the audience's hatred and anger (Rubinstein 2004: 193, cf. §31n. ὅσωι). These appeals stress that the community itself is a victim, and imply that the δῆμος is obliged to exact τιμωρία on the wrongdoer (cf. Cairns 2015: 657–65). **οὓς αἴσθοιντο** "anyone that they saw [bribing and corrupting people]." For the indefinite conditional relative clause, cf. 4.6n. οὕς. **ὥστε καὶ στηλίτας ποιεῖν:** the echo of §41 (εἰς στήλην χαλκῆν) connects this generalized conclusion with the specific case of Arthmius, and signals that D. is wrapping up this section of the speech. For a list of examples of stelae recording traitors sentenced to ἀτιμία, see Stroud 1963: 138 n. 1. **τὰ τῶν Ἑλλήνων:** in §29 D. used this phrase to describe the Greeks' neglect of their common interests. Here the repetition reinforces his contrast between the current situation and the united action of the Greeks during the Persian Wars. **ὁ βάρβαρος:** sc. βασιλεύς; the substantive adjective is a common paraphrase for "the Persians" (e.g., Hdt. 8.144.5, Thuc. 1.18.2, Ar. *Wasps* 1079). **οὔτε πρὸς τὰ τοιαῦτα οὔτε πρὸς τἆλλα:** τὰ τοιαῦτα refers to Philip's bribes (e.g.,

## 9 THIRD PHILIPPIC 45–47

§§9, 40), τἄλλα to his broader efforts to undermine Athenian interests, such as the establishment of client regimes in Greek states (e.g., §§17–18) or attacks on Athenian allies (e.g., §§15, 18, 26, 34).
**46 ἴστ' αὐτοί:** for the appeal to the audience's knowledge, cf. §§30, 41, 49.     **περὶ πάντων ὑμῶν κατηγορεῖν** "make accusations against you regarding every point."     **παραπλησίως δὲ καὶ οὐδὲν βέλτιον ὑμῶν:** sc. ἔχουσι. βέλτιον is adverbial, coordinate with παραπλησίως.     **σπουδῆς πολλῆς ... προσδεῖσθαι:** as D. moves to the next section of the speech, he prepares for the presentation of his proposals; the phrasing here is close to the beginning of the third *Olynthiac*, where it serves a similar purpose (cf. 3.3 ὁ μὲν οὖν παρὼν καιρός ... πολλῆς φροντίδος καὶ βουλῆς δεῖται).     **τίνος;** sc. βουλῆς.     **εἴπω κελεύετε;** "do you bid me speak?" εἴπω is a deliberative subjunctive, and the collocation of the two verbs is "a fusion of two distinct questions," i.e., "am I to speak" and "are you commanding" (Smyth §1806; cf. D. 22.67, 69, 24.174, 176 βούλεσθε εἴπω).     **ὀργιεῖσθε:** §3n. μηδεμίαν.     **ΕΚ ΤΟΥ ΓΡΑΜΜΑΤΕΙΟΥ ΑΝΑΓΙΓΝΩΣΚΕΙ** "[the secretary] reads from the document." The only other calls for documents to be read aloud in Assembly speeches are the budget statement and Philip's letter in the first *Philippic*; see 4.29n. ΠΟΡΟΥ. Here, the nature of the document is not specified, and it is difficult to imagine a document that would suit the context. As earlier editors have suggested, the heading must be a scribal error arising from confusion caused by the different versions of the text.

### 47–52 Changes in tactics

Philip is less powerful than Sparta was, but he has adopted new modes of waging war. We must adjust our response.

**47 τις εὐήθης λόγος παρὰ τῶν ... βουλομένων:** παρά modifies λόγος: "talk from," i.e., "pronouncements made by," introducing the indirect statement ὡς ... ἀνηρπάσθη. D. uses the same phrasing and construction to present his opponents' views at 16.11 and 21.134. For εὐήθης, cf. §10, 1.15n. τίς.     **Φίλιππός ἐστιν:** sc. τοιοῦτος.     **οἳ θαλάττης μὲν ἦρχον καὶ γῆς ἁπάσης:** D.'s regular designation for the Spartan hegemony after the Peloponnesian War; cf. 15.22, 18.96, 19.264, 4.3n. τῆι τότε.     **βασιλέα δὲ σύμμαχον εἶχον:** the Persian king, Artaxerxes II, played a vital role in the Corinthian War, at first by giving financial aid to the Athenian general Conon (4.24n. ξενικόν), and then, after 391, by supporting Sparta. The King's Peace in 387 ended the war by defining exclusive Persian and Spartan spheres of control. See Seager in *CAH* 106–8.
**ὑφίστατο δ' οὐδὲν αὐτούς** "whom nothing could resist" (LSJ ὑφίστημι B IV 1). αὐτούς replaces an accus. relative pronoun; cf. 3.24n. αὐτούς, Smyth §2517, *GP* 369 n. 1.     **οὐκ ἀνηρπάσθη** "it was not snatched up," as if by a storm; a common metaphor for destruction in war (LSJ ἀναρπάζω

III). ἐγὼ δέ: the emphatic pronoun at the start of the sentence, far ahead of its verb (ἡγοῦμαι), pointedly distinguishes D.'s viewpoint from that of his unnamed opponents. ἁπάντων ὡς ἔπος εἰπεῖν πολλὴν εἰληφότων ἐπίδοσιν "when practically everything has achieved a great advance"; gen. abs. ὡς ἔπος εἰπεῖν often qualifies οὐδείς or πᾶς (LSJ ἔπος II 4, cf. D. 6.1, 18.4, 19.264). ἁπάντων, and τῶν νῦν in the following parallel clause, vaguely refer to everything that is not encompassed in τὰ τοῦ πολέμου; cf. GPS 23 on the accumulated abstract substantives here. λαμβάνειν ἐπίδοσιν perhaps echoes Isocrates (e.g., 4.10, 8.127, 10.68, 15.267; elsewhere only here and D. 61.41, 46). For the interlocked word order, cf. 2.8n. συμφέρον. οὐδὲν ὁμοίων ὄντων τῶν νῦν τοῖς πρότερον: D. may be recalling Isoc. 15.159 ἐνθυμοῦμαι ... ὅσον τὰ τῆς πόλεως μεταπέπτωκεν, καὶ τὰς διανοίας ὡς οὐδὲν ὁμοίας περὶ τῶν πραγμάτων οἱ νῦν τοῖς πρότερον πολιτευομένοις ἔχουσιν ("I notice how much the city's affairs have changed, and that people now have attitudes concerning these matters [i.e., financial service to the city] that are in no way similar to those who served the city before"). Cf. 4.4n. εἰ. κεκινῆσθαι κἀπιδεδωκέναι "has changed and improved." For an overview of fourth-century innovations in Greek warfare, see Hanson 1998: 81–2.

**48 ἀκούω:** 4.24n. καί. τέτταρας μῆνας ἢ πέντε: D. exaggerates the brevity of the fighting season. Prior to the fourth century, military activity was avoided over the winter, when it was difficult for armies to march and for fleets to sail, and when provisions were hard to come by. Military forces were generally made up of non-professionals, and cities were not able to maintain them for distant campaigns over extended periods of time. See Hanson 1998: 38–40, Pritchett 1971: 28 n. 110. τὴν ὡραίαν αὐτήν: sc. ὥραν: "just during the season" (LSJ ὡραῖος I 3), acc. of duration (cf. 4.32n. τήν) referring here to summer campaigns. ἐμβαλόντας ἂν καὶ κακώσαντας τὴν χώραν "after invading and ravaging a region." ἄν modifies ἀναχωρεῖν. Such tactics were repeatedly employed by the Spartans, e.g., at the start of the Peloponnesian War, when they invaded and occupied Attica for the duration of the fighting season almost every year between 431 and 425. ὁπλίταις καὶ πολιτικοῖς στρατεύμασιν: the dative of association explains who took part in the action (Smyth §1523b). The terminology stresses that the soldiers fought in the traditional mode, as hoplites (4.23n. δύναμιν), and that they were citizen–soldiers, not mercenaries. ἀναχωρεῖν: the infin. + ἄν represents an imperf. tense describing repeated action in the past (Smyth §1846a). μᾶλλον δὲ πολιτικῶς "rather, [they were so] civic-minded"; i.e., willing to fight on behalf of their own πόλις. Cf. 2.2n. μᾶλλον. ὥστε οὐδὲ χρημάτων ὠνεῖσθαι παρ' οὐδενὸς οὐδέν: for the genitive, see §9n. τῶν, for the verb, §45n. οὐ, and on παρά, §14n. τῶν. The negation in οὐδέ is emphatically reinforced by οὐδενός and οὐδέν (as in §§31, 36). The use of οὐ, rather than μή, must be occasioned by the indirect statement introduced by ἀκούω (Smyth §2269), as if this result clause depended on an infinitive ἔχειν rather than the indic. εἶχον. **εἶναι νόμιμόν τινα καὶ προφανῆ τὸν πόλεμον** "warfare was something that was customary and clear." Traditional hoplite warfare was waged in accordance with well-known rules. Both sides understood and followed a shared protocol that dictated how, when, and where battle took place; see Connor 1988a.

**49 τὰ πλεῖστα τοὺς προδότας ἀπολωλεκότας** "traitors have caused the most destruction." D. refers to Greeks bribed by Philip; cf. D. 18.19, 61, 19.258, where the identification of treachery as bribe-taking is explicit. **ἐκ παρατάξεως οὐδὲ μάχης** "because of a regular battle." On ἐκ see §20n. βούλομαι. The two nouns denote a single idea (hendiadys), a traditional battle between lines of hoplite soldiers (see 4.23n. δύναμιν). **τῶι φάλαγγα ὁπλιτῶν ἄγειν:** Philip relied on a large infantry force (see 4.4n. τό), as D. well knew; here D. chooses to downplay their role and to assert instead that it was the specialist divisions identified below that were responsible for Philip's success. In fact, Philip's hoplite units were crucial at Chaeronea in 338, and it was from this group that select divisions were chosen, on which Philip relied (cf. 2.17n. πεζέταιροι). See Sekunda 2010: 449–52. **βαδίζονθ' ὅποι βούλεται:** participle in indirect statement. D. repeats the phrase to stress Philip's unrestricted command; cf. 1.12. **τῶι ψιλούς, ἱππέας, τοξότας, ξένους, τοιοῦτον ἐξηρτῆσθαι στρατόπεδον** "by equipping himself with light infantry, cavalry, archers, mercenaries, an army of this type" (LSJ ἐξαρτάω ιι 5). Light troops did not engage on the front lines in hoplite encounters, but rather performed support roles, often as slingers on the flank; archers functioned similarly (Sekunda 2010: 458–9). D. plays to the prejudices of his Athenian audience, who regarded hoplite warfare as a more respectable mode of fighting, since hoplite soldiers came from the wealthy classes and bravely fought their enemy face to face, whereas light-armed troops and archers were disparaged as being non-Greek or lower-class soldiers who took part from a cowardly distance (Trundle 2010: 141–7). The Athenians would have looked down on Philip's cavalry, too, since that division was manned by his ἑταῖροι, an elite group of "Companions," characterized by D. as flatterers (cf. §2.19n. κόλακας) and depicted in a sculpture of 333/2 in decadent Persian garb (the "Alexander Sarcophagus"; see Sekunda 2010: 467–70).

**50 ἐπὶ τούτοις** "in addition to these." The phrase modifies the whole period; D. adds Philip's siege engines to the specialized troops named in §49. **πρὸς νοσοῦντας ἐν αὑτοῖς:** 2.14n. νοσοῦσι, §12n. τοῖς. For the phrase, cf. Pl. *Rep.* 3.407d νόσημα ... ἐν αὑτοῖς. **δι' ἀπιστίαν:** the reference to civil discord (νοσοῦντας) makes it clear that this phrase refers to mutual distrust among the citizenry in the cities attacked by Philip; cf.

§§21, 35. ἐξίηι "comes out" to encounter the enemy (LSJ ἔξειμι [A], [εἶμι *ibo*] 3). **μηχανήματ' ἐπιστήσας:** §17n. εἰ. **σιωπῶ θέρος καὶ χειμῶνα:** for the rhetorical technique, see 3.27n. οἷς. D. emphasizes θέρος καὶ χειμῶνα by pulling them from the ὡς clause (prolepsis); see 1.21n. τὰ πράγματα. **ὡς οὐδὲν διαφέρει:** sc. θέρος καὶ χειμών. D. exaggerates; Philip campaigned all year round, but surely must have faced differences in climate and availability of supplies (4.31n. φυλάξας). **ἐξαίρετος** "excepted" (LSJ II 2). **διαλείπει** "leaves as an interval" (LSJ II 1). Philip does not take a break from campaigning.

**51 εἰδότας καὶ λογιζομένους:** sc. ἡμᾶς. For the emphatic pairing see 1.14n. ἵνα and cf. D. 8.19. **οὐ δεῖ προσέσθαι** "[we] must not invite" (LSJ προσίημι II 1; 1.8n. οὐ). δεῖ governs the following four infinitives. **εἰς τὴν εὐήθειαν ... βλέποντας** "by looking to [our] simple-mindedness during that past war against the Spartans." Cf. 1.15n. τίς, §35n. πρός. During the Peloponnesian War a state of war was determined by an actual attack, and the fighting followed a prescribed pattern in terms of when and how it was fought. D. urges the Athenians to reject this old-fashioned view of war, and to adapt to new circumstances, by recognizing Philip's efforts to bribe men in Athens and to support tyrannies in Greece as an act of war, and by understanding that such a war will not be fought in the same way as earlier wars. Cf. Nouhaud 1982: 90. **ἐκτραχηλισθῆναι** "fall into ruin," lit. "break one's neck" (LSJ ἐκτραχηλίζω I 2), is the everyday colloquial sense of the verb (e.g., Ar. *Clouds* 1501). It can also refer to a horse throwing a rider from its neck (LSJ I 1), but when D. uses a similar metaphor elsewhere there is other language to help the audience see that imagery (see 2.9n. ἅπαντα). Alternatively, some editors have seen a wrestling metaphor, developed below in συμπλακέντας διαγωνίζεσθαι, but there are no parallels for this sense of the verb. **ὡς ἐκ πλείστου φυλάττεσθαι τοῖς πράγμασι καὶ ταῖς παρασκευαῖς** "from as far off as possible, [we must] protect ourselves with our policies and preparations" (LSJ πρᾶγμα III 2); cf. 4.12 ταῖς παρασκευαῖς καὶ ταῖς γνώμαις. ἐκ πλείστου can refer to time (as at D. 21.220, with φυλάττεσθαι as here) or physical distance (as at Xen. *Eq.Mag.* 4.5 and *Lac.* 12.3, the only other fourth-century attestations of the phrase); the following ὅπως clause suggests that D. has the latter sense in mind here. **ὅπως οἴκοθεν μὴ κινήσεται σκοποῦντας** "by seeing to it that he not move from his home [region]" (2.6n. θεωρῶν). The middle of κινέω is equivalent to the passive and is reflexive in sense (Chadwick 1996: 184–5). σκοποῦντας is syntactically parallel to βλέποντας and συμπλακέντας. **οὐχὶ συμπλακέντας διαγωνίζεσθαι** "[and we must] not determine the contest in close engagements"; the infinitive is added without a conjunction (asyndeton). συμπλακέντας presents the image of wrestlers entangled in combat (see 2.21n. συμπλακῇι).

**52 πρὸς μὲν γὰρ πόλεμον** "as far as a war is concerned."   **ἄν περ ... ποιεῖν ἐθέλωμεν:** D. regularly calls for the support of the δῆμος in this way; e.g., 3.33, 4.7, 50. περ puts stress on ἄν (= ἐάν): "if in fact."   **ἡ φύσις:** in apposition to πλεονεκτήματα. The extent of Philip's kingdom made its defense difficult. D. recommends that the Athenians commit to a general war effort to harass Philip's territories, rather than engage him directly in battle.   **ἄγειν καὶ φέρειν:** 4.34n. ἄγων. The phrase is transitive; its object, πολλήν, is assimilated to the gender of χώρας.   **κακῶς ποιεῖν:** 1.17n. τῶι.   **ἄλλα μυρία:** in apposition to πλεονεκτήματα. D. is fond of capping lists with this asyndetic finale (e.g., 10.3, 19.228, 25.23), giving the impression that he could go on and on, while providing no further details (cf. §21n. on paraleipsis).   **εἰς ... ἀγῶνα** "for a battle." For the contrast between ἀγών and πόλεμος, cf. D. 14.9–10. For the description of a battle as an athletic contest, see 3.27nn. ὅσης and τῶν, 4.5n. ἆθλα. That imagery is reinforced by ἤσκηται; cf. 3.28n. ἠσκήκαμεν.

### 53–62 Traitors in Athens and elsewhere

We must beware of Philip's supporters in Athens. Such men were responsible for the destruction of Olynthus and the revolutions in Eretria and Oreus.

**53 οὐδὲ τοῖς ἔργοις ἐκεῖνον ἀμύνεσθαι τοῖς τοῦ πολέμου** "and not [only must we] resist that man with acts of war."   **τῶι λογισμῶι καὶ τῆι διανοίαι:** the former noun describes an analytical process; on the latter see §36n. ταῖς. Plato uses the phrase τῶι τῆς διανοίας λογισμῶι to refer to thought as the mind's activity (*Phd.* 78a).   **τοὺς παρ' ὑμῖν ὑπὲρ αὐτοῦ λέγοντας:** on Philip's partisans in Athens, see 2.4n. τοῖς.   **μισῆσαι:** sc. δεῖ ὑμᾶς. The aorist is ingressive; D. urges the Athenians to begin hating (Smyth §1865b). In earlier speeches D. regularly presented Philip as an object of hatred (e.g., 4.8, 6.18). The extension of that hatred to Philip's supporters in Athens is a new development, beginning in the speeches after the peace of Philocrates (cf. 8.61, 76; Cawkwell 1978: 122–3), and this passage is the most explicit allegation of treasonous behavior by politicians working in the Assembly. This sort of appeal to hatred is typical of the way prosecutors attack their opponents in court (e.g., D. 21.98, 22.64, 24.170; cf. §31n. ὅσωι).   **τῶν τῆς πόλεως ἐχθρῶν:** D.'s appeal to hatred allows him to connect his rival politicians in Athens with the city's enemies; cf. D. 1.7, 3.16n. ἐχθρός, where Philip is so labeled, not other Athenian politicians. This sentence is repeated almost verbatim from 8.61, and reused in 10.63.   **πρὶν ἂν τοὺς ἐν αὐτῆι τῆι πόλει κολάσητε ὑπηρετοῦντας ἐκείνοις:** for the construction, cf. D. 2.27, 4.41. ἐκείνοις refers to τῶν ἐχθρῶν. The repetition of πόλις with the intensifying αὐτός is strongly emphatic, and the delayed placement of ὑπηρετοῦντας draws attention to the entire noun phrase (for the technique cf. 1.8n. τήν, 3.24n.).

πολλά). On the verb, see §45n. ἐκόλαζον. D. began the speech by observing how absurd it is that politicians such as himself face punishment for supporting war against Philip (§2n. παρ'); now he explicitly calls for the same treatment of others in Athens. In the period after the peace, Philip's supporters in Athens were regularly labeled οἱ ὑπηρέται (e.g., D. 18.138, 19.85, 299, Aesch. 2.37, Hyp. *Eux.* 29; cf. §56), and the label is consistent with the image of Philip as a slave-master (§32n. τούς).

**54 ὅ:** the neuter connecting relative refers back to the notion of punishing Philip's supporters in Athens; here it is the object of ποιῆσαι. **μὰ τὸν Δία καὶ τοὺς ἄλλους θεούς:** 1.23n. μά. The addition of τοὺς ἄλλους θεούς is a precaution common in D. (e.g., §65, 8.49, 18.129); the speaker worries that his bluntness may offend and hopes that the additional gods will lend strength to his asseveration (Sommerstein 2007: 130–1, MacDowell 1990: 406 on 21.198). **εἰς τοῦτο ἀφῖχθε μωρίας** "you have reached such a degree of foolishness"; for the rhetorical device (hypostasis), see 3.1n. τά. In §15, D. categorizes those who agree with his view as being εὖ φρονοῦντες; here the charge of μωρία encompasses anyone who does not agree with him; on the opposition of these terms, see Finglass 2011: 357 on S. *Aj.* 745. D. attributes to Philip's supporters in Athens the same madness that he sees in Philip (1.23, 2.20). **παρανοίας:** the accusation is not simple slander; rather, it hints at the possible dangers that may result for the city. In 343 a violent revolution arose in Elis because partisans of Philip filled the city with "derangement and madness" (D. 19.260 παρανοίας καὶ μανίας; cf. §17n. τά); similarly, corruption led to madness causing the fall of Olynthus (19.267). **οὐκ ἔχω:** §4n. D. breaks off the construction and leaves the next noun in the series up to his audience's imagination; for this device (aposiopesis), see 3.27n. οἷς. **ἔμοιγ' ἐπελήλυθε καὶ τοῦτο φοβεῖσθαι** "fear of this too has occurred to me" (LSJ ἐπέρχομαι I 3); φοβεῖσθαι is subject, and τοῦτο refers to the following μή clause. **τι δαιμόνιον τὰ πράγματ' ἐλαύνηι** "some divine power steers our affairs." δαίμονες controlled the various fortunes, good and bad, of individuals and collective groups (see M. L. West 1978: 182 on Hes. *Op.* 122). In τὰ πράγματα D. expresses his specific concern with the potential political results of factionalism in the city. For the phrase δαίμων ἐλαύνει, cf. P. *Nem.* 5.16, S. *Aj.* 504, *OC* 1750. **ὥστε** introduces λέγειν κελεύετε: "you bid hired men speak." D. refers generally to speeches given by Philip's partisans in the Assembly and courts. **λοιδορίας, φθόνου, σκώμματος** "abuse, malice, ridicule." ἕνεκα governs the series of genitives, explaining the motives of the δῆμος by listing the material they want to hear; they are characterized as delighting in rhetorical vituperation rather than sound argumentation (cf. 2.5n. λοιδορίαν and see Spatharas 2006: 379–83). For λοιδορία as a characteristic of Assembly debate, cf. D. 4.44, 6.32. For φθόνος as an inappropriate motivation for court cases, cf. D. 18.13, 121, 279, and for court cases as sources of laughter, cf. D. 18.15, 54.13. **ἧστι-νος ἂν τύχητε ἕνεκ' αἰτίας** "whatever reason you may have" (LSJ τυγχάνω A I 3; cf. 1.3n. ἡνίκα, 2.10n. ἄν). **ἀνθρώπους μισθωτούς:** those bribed by Philip; a standard label, cf. D. 18.38, 52, 19.110. **ὧν οὐδ' ἂν ἀρνηθεῖεν ἔνιοι:** the relative is a partitive genitive modifying ἔνιοι. The common word for bribe-taking, δωροδοκέω (lit. "receive gifts"), illustrates the difficulty of distinguishing hospitality and gifts from bribes and corruption; politicians, soldiers, and ambassadors might freely admit to receiving benefits for their service, while their enemies would accuse them of being bribed. See Taylor 2001: 160–2. **ὡς οὐκ εἰσί:** indirect statement introduced by ἀρνηθεῖεν. οὐκ is redundant after a verb of denial (Smyth §2743). **ἄν τισι λοιδορηθῶσιν** "if they abuse some people" (aor. pass. has active sense: LSJ λοιδορέω II).

**55 καὶ οὐχί πω τοῦτο δεινόν, καίπερ ὂν δεινόν** "and this is not yet what is outrageous, though it *is* outrageous." οὐχί πω explains that worse is to come; cf. D. 19.113 καὶ οὐχὶ τοῦτό πω τηλικοῦτον (MSS interpolate readings from the present passage). The placement of ὂν before δεινόν emphasizes the repetition; cf. the same phrase at D. 21.72, with MacDowell 1990: 290. For the repetition of δεινόν in an oxymoron, cf. D. 8.30 δεινὸν ὂν οὐ δεινόν ἐστιν and see in general *GPS* 83. **μετὰ πλείονος ἀσφαλείας:** D. repeatedly asserts that corrupt politicians enjoy more security in Athens because they pander to the δῆμος, and that they are able to harass advisors such as himself, those who look to the long-term good of the city (e.g., 8.64–6, 18.138). He characterizes himself as putting the interests of Athens before his own safety (e.g., 1.16, 3.12, 18.220). **πολιτεύεσθαι δεδώκατε τούτοις:** δίδωμι here is "allow," governing the dat. and infin. (LSJ III 1). τούτοις refers to Philip's Athenian supporters. **συμφοράς** is euphemistic, "misfortunes" (LSJ II 2). **τὸ τῶν τοιούτων ἐθέλειν ἀκροᾶσθαι:** D.'s preference for this abstract articular infinitive instead of a personal subject is typical of his style (cf. 1.23, 2.1 with *GPS* 37–8). Here the expression softens his blunt criticism. **ἔργα** "facts," in contrast to his opponents' speeches. **εἴσεσθε:** fut. of οἶδα.

**56 ἦσαν ἐν Ὀλύνθωι τῶν ἐν τοῖς πράγμασιν:** D. refers to the period leading up to the fall of Olynthus in 348 (cf. §11). τινὲς μέν and τινὲς δέ are the subjects; τῶν ἐν τοῖς πράγμασιν is partitive, modifying both ("among those in charge of affairs," Smyth §1687.1a). This material preceding the first subject applies to both parts of the period. The asyndeton is typical in the opening of a catalogue of evidence; see §3n. ὑμεῖς. **Φιλίππου:** sc. ὄντες with the possessive genitive. **πάνθ' ὑπηρετοῦντες:** §53n. πρίν; πάντα is adverbial. **τοῦ βελτίστου:** the gen. is parallel to Φιλίππου, but the usage with the abstract substantive is bolder; the phrase is shorthand for τῶν τὰ βέλτιστα λεγόντων, echoing the slogan that D. uses to describe good political advisors (3.11n. τήν). ὅπως μὴ δουλεύσουσιν οἱ πολῖται depends on πράττοντες. A poignant detail; D.'s audience will recall the fate of the Olynthians (§26n. Ὄλυνθον). ἐξώλεσαν: the verb is rare in classical prose (elsewhere only D. 10.11 and 4× in Pl. *Euthd.*); frequently in Euripides and Aristophanes it expresses an oath or a curse, with the gods as an implied or expressed agent of destruction (and the adjective ἐξώλης is used exclusively for similar imprecations in the orators; e.g., D. 19.172 with MacDowell 2000: 274–5). That regular usage elevates the tone here, and stresses the terrible fate of Olynthus. The implication recalls D.'s fear in §54. τοὺς ἱππέας προὔδοσαν "betrayed the cavalry." Two Olynthian commanders, Lasthenes and Euthycrates, were said to have surrendered 500 of the city's cavalry to Philip after being bribed by him, with the hope of preferential treatment when the city was captured. See D. 19.265–7 with MacDowell 2000: 316–7, *HM* 323. ὧν προδοθέντων: gen. abs. The link between betrayal and the destruction of the city is marked by repetition and chiasmus. οἱ τὰ Φιλίππου φρονοῦντες: sc. τὴν πατρίδ' ἐξώλεσαν καὶ τοὺς ἱππέας προὔδοσαν. The article modifies the three nominative participles, which are imperfect in sense. For the expression cf. §18n. τῶι. ὅτ' ἦν ἡ πόλις "when the city existed" (LSJ εἰμί [*sum*] A 1); another reminder of the price of corruption. συκοφαντοῦντες "harassing." D. describes the factionalism in Olynthus in Athenian terms, in order to remind his audience that what happened there could happen in Athens. Athenian politicians characterize their opponents' use of the legal and political system for their own gain (either from funds awarded by the courts, or by extorting payments from their victims) as sycophancy; since public institutions relied on citizen volunteers, it was always possible to assign such motives to any opponent, though in reality there were strict measures to discourage frivolous prosecutions (Harvey 1990, E. M. Harris 2013b: 74–6). In *On the Crown* D. repeatedly attacks his opponents as sycophants who harm the city by harassing civic-minded advisors such as himself with malicious prosecutions (18.138, cf. 189). διαβάλλοντες: D. presents strife in Olynthus in the same terms used to describe Athens above (§2n. τούς). Ἀπολλωνίδην καὶ ἐκβαλεῖν "even to banish Apollonides" (LSJ ἐκβάλλω I 2). Nothing beyond this bare fact is known regarding this event (cf. §66). Most likely it is to be placed during the early period of Philip's attack on Olynthus, when the city had hope of coming to terms (*HM* 298–9). ἐπείσθη: the choice of verb reaffirms the influence of the corrupt politicians in Olynthus.

**57 οὐ τοίνυν** "and it is not the case that." The negative applies to both εἰργάσατο and the following δέ clause. The combination of οὐ and οὐδαμοῦ is strongly positive. Cf. §27n. καί. παρὰ τούτοις μόνον: i.e., at Olynthus and nowhere else. τὸ ἔθος τοῦτο "this [harmful] practice."

## 9 THIRD PHILIPPIC 57–58

The context makes the tone clear; for this sense of ἔθος, cf. D. 3.33, 10.76, 19.2. In a parallel passage describing the harm caused by civil strife, D. refers to it as ἔθος τι φαῦλον (18.138). **πάντα κακὰ εἰργάσατο** "has done [them] every sort of harm" (LSJ ἐργάζομαι II 2); for the same phrase in similar contexts, cf. Lys. 12.57, D. 19.314. **ἄλλοθι δ᾿ οὐδαμοῦ:** i.e., the same thing happens everywhere. **ἐν Ἐρετρίαι:** §17n. Εὐβοίαι. **ἀπαλλαγέντος Πλουτάρχου καὶ τῶν ξένων:** gen. abs. In 349/8 the Athenians sent a force to Eretria under the command of Phocion, to support Plutarch, who had recently come to power in Eretria, against his rivals. Phocion and Plutarch had a falling out, and Phocion was instrumental in his expulsion from Eretria. See Sealey 140–1, Harding 2006: 107, Tritle 1988: 76–89. **ὁ δῆμος εἶχε τὴν πόλιν:** D. focuses on the role of the Eretrian δῆμος, rather than the Athenian intervention, in order to make his point to the Athenian Assembly, that their decisions are vital for the preservation of Athens. Philochorus also attests to the power of the δῆμος in Eretria after the expulsion of Plutarch (Philoch. *FGrHist* 328 F 160 = Did. *in D.* 1.19–25; cf. Sealey 260). **τὸν Πορθμόν:** §33n. τούς. **ἐφ᾿ ὑμᾶς ἦγον τὰ πράγματα** "were directing affairs toward you" (LSJ ἄγω II 1–2; cf. D. 18.151), that is, they were sympathetic to continued Athenian involvement in Eretrian politics. **ἐπὶ Φίλιππον:** sc. ἦγον τὰ πράγματα. **ἀκούοντες δὲ τούτων τὰ πολλὰ μᾶλλον** "listening more to many [points] of those [partisans of Philip]." ἀκούοντες, like ἐπείσθη above and ἐπείσθησαν below, stresses the link between corrupt leadership and the bad decisions of the δῆμος. **οἱ ταλαίπωροι καὶ δυστυχεῖς Ἐρετριεῖς:** the adjectives suggest that the δῆμος required from its advisors the sort of care and attention that sick patients need from doctors; cf. §12n. τοῖς. **τελευτῶντες** "in the end." The word choice plays on the medical sense in the preceding adjectives, suggesting the image of patients who perished as a result of malpractice. **τοὺς ὑπὲρ αὐτῶν λέγοντας** echoes §55, explicitly connecting the situation in Eretria with that in Athens.

**58 καὶ γάρ τοι:** 4.6n. **Ἱππόνικον:** after the expulsion of Plutarch, during the period of popular rule, Clitarchus rose to ascendancy in Eretria. When another faction fled the city and seized the harbor of Porthmus, Philip sent Hipponicus and his troops, in 343, who recovered the port and installed Clitarchus and two others as political leaders. See Harris 115–16, Sealey 260, §17n. Εὐβοίαι, §33n. τοὺς μέν. **ὁ σύμμαχος αὐτοῖς** "their ally" (Smyth §1529). **τὰ τείχη περιεῖλε** "dismantled the walls" (LSJ περιαιρέω 1). **Ἵππαρχον, Αὐτομέδοντα, Κλείταρχον:** Clitarchus is regularly referred to as the sole leader of Eretria at this period (§66, D. 18.71, 81–2, Philoch. *FGrHist* 328 F 160). Clitarchus and Hipparchus are included as the Euboeans in D.'s famous list of traitors who betrayed the Greek states to Philip (D. 18.295 includes with them a third man, otherwise unknown; Hyp. *Against Diondas* 176v/173r 32–175r/174v 1 (Carey et al. 2008) lists just the pair). Automedon is known only from this passage; D. includes him here in order to accumulate details and thus emphasize Philip's involvement in Greece (§59n. Μένιππος). **ἐξελή-λακεν:** perf. of ἐξελαύνω: "[Philip] has exiled [opponents of Clitarchus]." The two episodes here mentioned are not otherwise known, and are probably to be dated to 342 (Sealey 177, 260, *HM* 546). **δὶς ἤδη βουλομένους σώιζεσθαι** "who twice now were wanting to be saved"; i.e., they hoped to be rid of the tyrants, but Philip sent two expeditions to secure Clitarchus' rule. For δὶς ἤδη in this sense with a following participle, cf. Isoc. 8.51, 123. **τότε μὲν πέμψας ... τοὺς μετὰ Παρμενίωνος:** Eurylochus is otherwise known only as one of Philip's ambassadors to negotiate the peace in 346 (hyp. 2 to D. 19 with MacDowell 2000: 237). Parmenio was Philip's most accomplished general; he rose to prominence after a victory over the Illyrians in 356, and his successful career continued under Alexander (Heckel 2008: s.v. Parmenion).

**59 καὶ τί δεῖ τὰ πολλὰ λέγειν;** §25n. καί. **ἐν Ὠρεῶι:** §12n. τοῖς, §17n. Εὐβοίαι. **Φιλιστίδης:** he emerged as tyrant in Oreus at the same time as Clitarchus was installed in Eretria; the two are paired by D. in *On the Crown* (18.71, 81–2). Like Clitarchus, Philistides rose to prominence following a period of civil strife; the passage is the most detailed narrative of this background. Philip's involvement appears to have been financial in 343; the expedition that year to Eretria led by Hipponicus is not reported to have intervened at Oreus (§58n. Ἱππόνικον; cf. Sealey 175, 261, *HM* 546–7). **ἔπραττε Φιλίππωι** "managed affairs to Philip's advantage" (Smyth §1529). **Μένιππος ... Ἀγαπαῖος:** all otherwise unknown. The rapid and detailed list gives D. an air of authority and emphasizes the extent of Philip's influence. For similar lists, cf. 1.12n. τό, 4.4n. Πύδναν, Ronnet 76. **οἵπερ νῦν ἔχουσι τὴν πόλιν:** Philistides and his associates were removed from power by a campaign of Athens in alliance with Callias of Chalcis that took place in the last month of the year 342/1, not long after the delivery of this speech (Philoch. *FGrHist* 328 F 160 = Did. *in D.* 1.15–18). D. moved the proposal for the alliance in the Assembly (Develin 1989: 333). **ταῦτ' ἤιδεσαν ἅπαντες** "everyone knew about these matters" (LSJ εἴδω B 1). The parenthesis is tacked on to stress the notoriety of Philistides' allegiance to Philip. For the technique, cf. 4.38n. ὡς, *GPS* 65. **Εὐφραῖος δέ τις ἄνθρωπος:** sc. ἔπραττε, introducing the ὅπως clause (LSJ πράσσω III 6). Euphraeus is presented sympathetically as the popular rival to Philistides for the leadership of Oreus. He had been a student of Plato in Athens (Harp. s.v. Εὐφραῖος), and from there he went to Macedon, where he spent time in the court of Perdiccas, Philip's predecessor; he is said to have alienated Philip, while also helping him rise to the throne (Athen. 11.506f, 508e; Cawkwell 1978: 51–5). **ἐλεύθεροι**

## 9 THIRD PHILIPPIC 59–60

καὶ μηδενὸς δοῦλοι: the tautology emphasizes the contrasting characterizations of Athens as the defender of freedom (§36n. ἑτοίμως) and Philip as a slave-master (§32n. τούς). Euphraeus had firsthand experience with both. **60 οὗτος:** subject of the ὡς clause, placed first for emphasis (prolepsis). τὰ μὲν ἄλλ': subject of εἴη; the phrase signals the device of paraleipsis (3.27n. οἷς). ὑβρίζετο καὶ προὐπηλακίζετο: a favorite pair of emphatic synonyms in D. (21.7, 22.58, 23.120). D. regularly makes Philip the agent of hybris (1.23n. ὑβριστής), and by assigning that role to the δῆμος of Oreus he reinforces his main point, that the people of Oreus brought destruction upon themselves. The latter verb (lit. "spatter with mud") is widely used in this metaphorical sense of "grossly abuse" (Austin and Olson 2004: 177 on Ar. *Thesmo.* 386). πόλλ' ἂν εἴη λέγειν "would be [too] numerous to describe." The infinitive is explanatory. For the idiom cf. D. 19.180, Lys. 32.11, Pl. *Prt.* 344b, *Phdr.* 274e. ἐνιαυτῶι πρότερον τῆς ἁλώσεως "the year before the [city's] capture" (LSJ πρότερος A IV on neut. adverb + gen.); §59n. οἵπερ. ἐνέδειξεν "filed a complaint." As in his account of Olynthus above (§56nn. συκοφαντοῦντες and διαβάλλοντες), D. uses Athenian terminology throughout this section to make his point that the case of Oreus is parallel to the situation in Athens. The verb is a technical term, rather loosely applied here, for the legal procedure of ἔνδειξις, which describes a written declaration that could be filed by any citizen against public debtors or κακοῦργοι (4.47n. τόν) who had been punished with disenfranchisement (ἀτιμία, see §37n. καί) and were barred from various public institutions, such as the courts and Assembly. See MacDowell 1978: 75, Hansen 1976a: 9–17. ὡς προδότην τὸν Φιλιστίδην: sc. ὄντα: "[declaring] that Philistides was a traitor." ὡς indicates that this was Euphraeus' belief as he lodged the complaint (Smyth §2086b). συστραφέντες "conspiring together" (LSJ συστρέφω III). χορηγὸν ἔχοντες Φίλιππον "with Philip as their provider." D. again applies Athenian terminology to Oreus. An Athenian χορηγός performed his liturgy obligation (see 2.30n. τριηραρχεῖν) by paying for the costs involved in a choral production, such as tragedy. This more general usage of the term arises from that specific Athenian context (see Wilson 2000: 71, 337 n. 94), and here it implies that Philip paid for and orchestrated the public policy of Philistides. Cf. D. 19.216. πρυτανευόμενοι "subject to the leadership" of Philip. Another Athenian term. The Athenian Council was made up of 500 men, 50 from each of the Athenian tribes (a civic division; every Athenian citizen was a member of a tribe, a φυλή). These 10 groups took turns managing the day-to-day affairs of the Council; the group in charge during any given period were the πρυτάνεις (see Rhodes 1972: 16–21). The verb here derives from that institution and is passive; lit. "those being presided over by the πρυτάνεις."

ἀπάγουσι τὸν Εὐφραῖον εἰς τὸ δεσμωτήριον "they arrested Euphraeus and imprisoned him." The present tense adds vividness to the narrative. The phrase εἰς τὸ δεσμωτήριον ἀπάγειν is a formula for the Athenian process of ἀπαγωγή, or summary arrest (LSJ ἀπάγω IV 3). Men against whom a complaint (ἔνδειξις) had been lodged were subject to this type of arrest, and they would be imprisoned until a trial was held; men accused of homicide, and those caught stealing, were also liable to this procedure (MacDowell 1978: 120–2, Hansen 1976a: 21–4). The loose applicability of all the specific Athenian terminology is evident here: Euphraeus lodged the complaint (ἔνδειξις), but was himself arrested. ὡς συνταράττοντα τὴν πόλιν "because he was causing disorder in the city." The phrase regularly describes revolutions that subvert the establishment: cf. Andoc. 1.68, Xen. *Hell.* 3.4.7, D. 25.19. The usage of ὡς is the same as in ὡς προδότην above.

**61 ὁρῶν δὲ ταῦθ᾽ ὁ δῆμος:** D. focuses on the perception of the δῆμος, as he did for Eretria; cf. ἀκούοντες δὲ τούτων τὰ πολλά (§57). **ἀντὶ τοῦ τῶι μὲν βοηθεῖν, τοὺς δ᾽ ἀποτυμπανίσαι** "instead of helping that man and executing those others." Here and below the substantive ὁ μέν is Euphraeus, and οἱ δέ are Philistides and the other tyrants. The order of the noun phrases here and in the main clause is chiastic; cf. D. 23.103 with *GPS* 77. ἀποτυμπανισμός was a method of state execution in Athens, in which the condemned man was attached to a plank and exposed until he died. This method of capital punishment probably made a public spectacle of the victim in order to emphasize his inferior status and exclusion from society (Todd 2000). D. repeatedly asserts that Greeks who betrayed their cities to Philip deserved such treatment (8.61, 10.63, 19.137). **τὸν δ᾽ ἐπιτήδειον ταῦτα παθεῖν:** sc. ὄντα: "that he is deserving of this punishment" (for the construction cf. D. 20.83, 22.57). The adjective has a technical sense, referring to the applicability of a law (cf. Canevaro 2016a: 329, Kremmydas 2012: 48–9). **ἐπέχαιρεν:** the compound regularly describes pleasure at seeing someone receive deserved punishment (MacDowell 1990: 353–4 on D. 21.134). **ἐπ᾽ ἐξουσίας ὁπόσης ἐβούλοντ᾽:** here ἐπί + gen. refers to "the circumstances which make an action possible" (MacDowell 1990: 355 on D. 21.138 τὸ γὰρ ἐπ᾽ ἐξουσίας καὶ πλούτου πονηρὸν εἶναι καὶ ὑβριστήν, "being wicked and arrogant on the basis of power and wealth"). **ἔπραττον ὅπως:** §59n. Εὐφραῖος. **κατεσκευάζοντο τὴν πρᾶξιν:** for the pejorative sense of the verb, see 2.6n. κατασκευάσαι. D. used the same verb to denigrate Philip's actions on Euboea (§17n. Εὐβοίαι), and now its repetition stresses the complicity of the traitors in Oreus. **τῶν δὲ πολλῶν:** partitive gen. modifying τις, put first for emphasis and to signal the switch in subjects. **ἐσίγα καὶ κατεπέπληκτο** "he was scared speechless"; the two verbs form a single idea (*GPS* 63). **τὸν Εὐφραῖον οἷ᾽ ἔπαθεν:** Euphraeus is emphasized by being pulled out of the subordinate clause (prolepsis); see §12n. πυνθάνεσθαι. **μεμνημένοι**: the plural arises from the collective generalization in τις; cf. 2.18n. τούτους, 4.7n. παύσησθε. **οὐ πρότερον** anticipates πρίν, and the negative is reiterated in οὐδείς: "no one dared ... until." **τοιούτου κακοῦ προσιόντος**: gen. abs., referring to the Macedonian advance toward Oreus. The historical context remains vague until §62. **ῥῆξαι φωνήν** "utter a sound." The phrase follows on ἐσίγα, describing the breaking of silence (LSJ ῥήγνυμι A 4). **πρὶν διασκευασάμενοι πρὸς τὰ τείχη προσῆισαν οἱ πολέμιοι** "until the enemy reached the walls in full battle array." The imperf. is unusual with πρίν; it designates simultaneous action (Smyth §2441a). **τηνικαῦτα** "only then"; the adverb stresses that it was too late for any resistance. **οἱ μὲν ἡμύνοντο, οἱ δὲ προὐδίδοσαν**: the brief parallel clauses summarize the conflict between rival factions in Oreus. The absolute use of the two transitive verbs without objects suggests that the battle was inconsequential and neither side achieved anything new (cf. 2.23n. ἡμῶν), because the city had already been betrayed to Philip. The imperfects are conative, describing each side's intent (Smyth §1895).

**62 τῆς πόλεως ... κακῶς**: gen. abs.; ἁλούσης is aor. pass. participle of ἁλίσκομαι. **οἱ μὲν ἄρχουσι καὶ τυραννοῦσι**: as in §61, the two verbs form a single idea: "they [the traitors] rule as tyrants." The subject is modified by the two nominative participles (ἐκβαλόντες and ἀποκτείναντες), which take the preceding accusatives as their objects. **τοὺς τότε σώιζοντας ἑαυτοὺς καὶ ... ὄντας** "and as for those who wanted to save them [the tyrants] and were prepared to do anything whatever to Euphraeus." The participles are imperf. in sense, and ἑαυτούς refers to οἱ μέν. The expansive noun phrase refers broadly to the entire group of supporters of the tyrants; it is subdivided into two groups (τοὺς μέν and τοὺς δέ) in the following participial clauses. **ἐκβαλόντες**: for the sense of the verb, see §56n. Ἀπολλωνίδην. For the same pattern of events in Eretria, cf. §58n. ἐξελήλακεν. **ὁ δ' Εὐφραῖος ἐκεῖνος**: contrasted with οἱ μέν. ἐκεῖνος marks the final scene in this account of Euphraeus; for the usage cf. 2.19n. Καλλίαν, 3.21n. τὸν Ἀριστείδην. **ἀπέσφαξεν ἑαυτόν** "cut his own throat." The verb is very graphic, usually referring to executions or assassinations of enemies in war (e.g., D. 23.169, Lycurg. 112). The historian Carystius of Pergamum (2nd cent. BC) reports that Euphraeus was captured by Parmenio and killed (Athen. 11.508e); these two accounts can be reconciled if it is inferred that Euphraeus took his own life while in custody (*HM* 546–7 n. 3, Sealey 261). This piece of information suggests that these events at Oreus happened in 342, if Parmenio's intervention occurred in conjunction with his mission to Eretria (§58). **ἔργωι μαρτυρήσας** "proving by this action," in contrast to the speeches used by the tyrants in Eretria and Oreus to corrupt the δῆμος. **καθαρῶς**:

καθαρός describes someone who is "pure" in the sense that he has not committed the crime of murder (§44n. καθαρόν); the point here is to contrast the innocence of Euphraeus with the guilt of the murderous traitors. **ὑπὲρ τῶν πολιτῶν:** at the close of this digressive narrative D. circles back to the point with which it was introduced, when he told his Athenian audience that they paid too little attention to τοῖς ὑπὲρ ὑμῶν λέγουσιν (§55; cf. §63).

### 63–69 The appeal and danger of Philip's faction
Eretria and Oreus have been ruined because the people were misled by leaders who represented Philip's interests, not their own.

**63 τί οὖν ποτ' αἴτιον;** §36n. τί.   **θαυμάζετε ἴσως:** parenthetical. **τὸ** ... **ἔχειν** "[the reason that] the Olynthians ... were more favorable toward those speaking on behalf of Philip" (LSJ ἡδύς III 1). The accus. articular infinitive phrase explains αἴτιον (cf. D. 8.56), and the infinitive is imperfect in sense. D.'s account in §§63–4 provides a generalized overview of the rise of demagoguery in the other cities, using the phrasing and terminology that he frequently applied to Athens.   **ὅπερ καὶ παρ' ὑμῖν:** sc. αἴτιόν ἐστι: "[the reason is] something which [exists] among you too." **ὅτι** answers the rhetorical question (2.3n. διά).   **τοῖς μὲν ὑπὲρ τοῦ βελτίστου λέγουσιν:** dat. with ἔνεστιν. See §56n. τοῦ; these advisors are contrasted with οἱ δέ below.   **οὐδὲ βουλομένοις ἔνεστιν:** οὐδέ is adverbial, emphatic for οὐ (cf. 4.2), negating ἔνεστιν. βουλομένοις is concessive ("even if they want to").   **πρὸς χάριν** ... **εἰπεῖν:** i.e., to act like demagogues; see §2n. εὑρήσετε, 3.3n. ὁρᾶτε.   **τὰ γὰρ πράγματα ἀνάγκη σκοπεῖν ὅπως σωθήσεται** "[they] must consider how the situation will be kept safe." D. stresses τὰ πράγματα, because that is what the demagogues ignore, by putting it first, outside the ὅπως clause. Above he observed explicitly that selfish leaders do not consider the safety of the Greeks (§29 οὐχ ὅπως σωθήσεται τὰ τῶν Ἑλλήνων σκοπῶν).   **ἐν αὐτοῖς οἷς χαρίζονται:** sc. τῶι δήμωι; οἷς = τούτοις ἅ: "in those very matters in which they indulge [the people]."   **συμπράττουσιν:** cf. 19.202, where οἱ συμπράττοντες are "the collaborators" in Athens who took bribes from Philip.

**64 εἰσφέρειν ἐκέλευον:** sc. οἱ μέν; for the omission see *GP* 166. D. refers to calls for taxes to fund the military made by politicians with an outlook similar to his own; see, e.g., 1.6n. χρήματα, 2.13, 3.4, 4.7.   **οἱ δ':** Philip's supporters.   **οὐδὲν δεῖν** "that it was not necessary [to contribute] anything."   **πολεμεῖν καὶ μὴ πιστεύειν:** sc. οἱ μέν, again referring to men like D. See §38n. τὴν πρὸς τούς.   **ἄγειν εἰρήνην:** sc. δεῖν ἔφασαν. See §1n. τήν.   **ἕως ἐγκατελήφθησαν** "until they [the people] were caught up in [war]." The verb refers to capture in a trap or net, and is generally found in battle narratives; for this metaphorical sense cf. Aesch.

3.239 οὗτος ... ἐγκαταληφθεὶς ὑπὸ τῶν νυνὶ παρόντων αὐτῶι κινδύνων ("that man caught up in the dangers now present to him"). **τἄλλα τὸν αὐτὸν τρόπον οἶμαι πάντα:** sc. ἔλεγον. οἶμαι is parenthetical. See 1.15n. τόν. **ἵνα μὴ καθ' ἕκαστα λέγω:** D. explains that the preceding summary statement was offered "in order that I not go through each point individually." This is an idiomatic formula marking paraleipsis and implying that D. could go on and on; e.g., D. 1.9, 18.313, 19.100. **οἱ μέν:** D. now switches the μέν/δέ groups, but the repetition of key terms prevents confusion. He stresses the patriots' noble intentions by putting them at the end of the period. **ἐφ' οἷς χαριοῦνται** "for which they would gain approval." **οἱ δ':** sc. ταῦτ' ἔλεγον. **ἐξ ὧν ἔμελλον σωθήσεσθαι:** sc. τὰ πράγματα: "as a result of which [the situation] would be likely to be kept safe." For the phrasing cf. §1n. ἐξ. **πολλὰ δὲ καὶ τὰ τελευταῖα** "the most recent [items advocated by demagogues], for the most part"; object of προσίεντο. D. summarizes and explains τἄλλα. **οὐχ οὕτως οὔτε πρὸς χάριν** "not so much with a view to pleasure." οὔτε reiterates the negation in οὐχ and coordinates the two prepositional phrases. οὐχ οὕτως is answered by ἀλλά below. See also 4.51n. οὔτ'. **προσίεντο** "submitted to" (LSJ προσίημι II 2 b; cf. §51n. οὐ). **ὑποκατακλινόμενοι** "because they had given up." The verb is literally "lie down underneath," and is used by later authors to describe a wrestler who gives up a fight, or one who yields a place of honor to others at a symposium. In the two other attested instances from the classical period, it is used as here, to refer to people accepting the pronouncements of others without questioning or independent thought (Pl. *Rep.* 1.336c, e). The use of ἡττᾶσθαι below may suggest that D. has the athletic sense in mind here. **τοῖς ὅλοις ἡττᾶσθαι:** sc. πράγμασιν: "were defeated by their overall circumstances"; cf. 2.31n. βέλτιον.

**65 ὅ:** the connecting relative refers to the general notion of the preceding sentence (cf. §54n. ὅ) and is the object of πάθητε. **νὴ τὸν Δία καὶ τὸν Ἀπόλλω:** νή + accus. emphasizes a positive statement (MacDowell 2009: 402–3); cf. §1.23n. μά, §54n. μά. **πάθηθ' ὑμεῖς:** the emphatic pronoun marks the move from the past experience of other cities to future prospects for Athens. **εἰδῆτ' ἐκλογιζόμενοι:** for the emphatic pairing, cf. §51n. εἰδότας. This point responds to ἐνόμιζον in §64. **μηδὲν ὑμῖν ἐνόν** "that nothing is possible for you" (LSJ ἔνειμι [εἰμί *sum*] II 3) because of the momentum of the situation created by bad policy decisions. The point of comparison is τοῖς ὅλοις ἡττᾶσθαι in §64. **εἰς τοῦθ' ὑπάγοντας:** §1n. εἰς. **οὐκ ὀρρωδῶ, ἀλλὰ δυσωποῦμαι** "I do not feel dread so much as shame." D. qualifies δέδοικα. **ἐξεπίτηδες ἢ δι' ἄγνοιαν:** adv.: "because of an ulterior motive or out of ignorance." For ἐξεπίτηδες, see MacDowell 1990: 278 on D. 21.56. The repetition of δι' ἄγνοιαν from §64 underscores D.'s harsher assessment of the orators, as compared to their audience.   χαλεπὸν πρᾶγμα "a difficult situation."   μὴ γένοιτο μέν ... τὰ πράγματα ἐν τούτωι "[I pray that] such a situation may not arise [now] at this point."   τεθνάναι δὲ μυριάκις κρεῖττον: sc. ἦν (for the imperf., see 4.27n. οὐ, Ar. *Wasps* 210 with Biles and Olson 2015: 153). In his prosecutions D. often says the accused deserve multiple deaths (see MacDowell 1990: 341 on D. 21.118); the implication here may be that failure to follow good advice is tantamount to criminal corruption. κολακείαι: §4n. κολακεύεσθαι.   καλήν γ' modifies χάριν; the emphatic placement (hyperbaton) draws attention to the word as D. commences a series of exclamations summing up the examples of Oreus, Eretria, and Olynthus. The three units in the series are linked by asyndeton and by the initial repetition in καλήν ... [§66] καλήν ... καλῶς; in the first two items γε underscores the repetition and adds a note of ironic disgust. See *GPS* 107, 115, *GP* 129–30.   ἀπειλήφασιν "received in return." The verb can refer to receipt of payment, and thus recalls the allegations of bribery (see §60n. χορηγόν).   Ὠρειτῶν: partitive gen. modifying οἱ πολλοί. τοῖς Φιλίππου φίλοις: i.e., Philistides and the others (§59). The term φίλος echoes Φιλίππου and stresses their personal ties to Philip as the basis of their power; such terminology frequently characterizes monarchs and their subordinates (Konstan 1997: 95–8).   τὸν δ' Εὐφραῖον ἐώθουν: the verb must here have the sense of ἀπωθέω, "reject," rather than its usual reference to political exile (LSJ ὠθέω I 3), since Euphraeus was arrested and jailed (§60n. ἀπάγουσι). D.'s narration develops the parallelism between Euphraeus and Apollonides below (§67).

**66 καλήν γ':** sc. χάριν ἀπειλήφασιν.   τοὺς ὑμετέρους πρέσβεις ἀπήλασεν: the details of this incident are not known. It is likely to refer to diplomatic efforts, possibly undertaken by D. himself, during the period of volatility in Eretria prior to the arrival of Parmenio in 342 (§58n. τότε); cf. D. 18.79, Sealey 264.   Κλειτάρχωι: §58n. Ἵππαρχον.   δουλεύουσί γε μαστιγούμενοι καὶ σφαττόμενοι: as above (§65n. καλήν), asyndeton and γε express an exclamation. The participles describe the condition of the enslaved; σφαττόμενοι graphically presents the possible extreme to which their situation may extend (cf. §62n. ἀπέσφαξεν). The variant reading στρεβλούμενοι, "tortured," would add more explanatory detail.   ἐφείσατο "[Philip] spared," governing the gen. The tone is sarcastic.   τὸν μὲν Λασθένην: §56n. τούς. Not long before this speech, D. said that Lasthenes (and his colleague Euthycrates) "have been most vilely destroyed" (D. 8.40 πάντων κάκιστ' ἀπολώλασιν; see *HM* 374–5 n. 2). τὸν δ' Ἀπολλωνίδην: §56n. Ἀπολλωνίδην.

**67 μωρία καὶ κακία:** above D. leveled the charges of folly and cowardice at the Athenians (§54n. εἰς and §35n. μαλακιζόμεθα); here those terms sum up the situation in Oreus, Eretria, and Olynthus, and thus link past situations there with the present circumstances in Athens. **τὰ τοιαῦτα ἐλπίζειν:** i.e., that the people in those cities hoped to fare well while following the advice of leaders who had been corrupted by Philip. The infinitive is explanatory with μωρία καὶ κακία. **καὶ κακῶς βουλευομένους:** καί connects ἐλπίζειν and ἡγεῖσθαι; the unexpressed subject of the latter infin. is modified by the three accus. participles (βουλευομένους, ἐθέλοντας, ἀκροωμένους). D. deliberately avoids a finite verb construction and omits the accus. pronoun with the infin. in order to create ambiguity. His summary of these historical examples is presented in terms that apply fully to the current situation in Athens; as a referent for the participles the audience may understand τούτους (the people of the other cities) or ἡμᾶς (themselves). **μηδὲν ὧν προσήκει ποιεῖν ἐθέλοντας:** a regular formula in D.'s criticism of Athens; cf. 2.22, 4.13, 50. **ὑπὲρ τῶν ἐχθρῶν:** the vague plural contributes to the general applicability and ambiguity. Above D. referred to those who spoke ὑπὲρ αὐτοῦ/Φιλίππου (§§53, 63). **τηλικαύτην ἡγεῖσθαι πόλιν οἰκεῖν τὸ μέγεθος** "to suppose that [they/you] live in a city so great in stature." **ὥστε μηδ' ἂν ὁτιοῦν ᾖ δεινὸν πείσεσθαι** "that whatever may happen, it will not experience terror." For idiomatic μηδ' ἂν ὁτιοῦν ᾖ negating the following verb, cf. D. 19.6, 324.

**68 καὶ μὴν ἐκεῖνό γε:** §30n.; ἐκεῖνο points to εἰπεῖν. **τίς γὰρ ἂν ᾠήθη ταῦτα γενέσθαι;** "who would have expected these things to happen?"; a remonstrance from an imagined citizen of Oreus, Eretria, or Olynthus (see 3.22n. τί). γάρ explains why these cities acted as they did: they had no idea how events would turn out (*GP* 76–7). **νὴ τὸν Δία:** a typical marker of an imaginary exchange; see §4.10n. νή. **τὸ καὶ τό** "this or that" (LSJ ὁ A VII 2). Then τό (μὴ ποιῆσαι) is "something else." Cf. D. 18.243, where the same idiom similarly characterizes an excuse offered by an imaginary speaker. **πόλλ' ἂν εἰπεῖν ἔχοιεν:** for the construction, see §3.27n. οἷς. ἅ = ταῦτα; it is a connecting relative and the object of προείδοντο. **πόλλ' ἂν Ὠρεῖται:** sc. εἰπεῖν ἔχοιεν. The list of Philip's aggressions is set out in short clauses with asyndeton and initial repetition of πολλά (the device of anaphora; cf. §65n. καλήν). This type of emphatic repetition is more developed in D.'s later Assembly speeches, and this example with four instances is especially noteworthy (see Ronnet 65–9); cf. 2.31n. εἰσφέρειν. **Φωκεῖς ... τῶν ἀπολωλότων ἕκαστοι:** §11n. εἰς. After his extended treatments of Oreus, Eretria, and Olynthus, D. now stresses the extent of Philip's aggressions by reminding the audience of other places he might have discussed too, and then by ending his list with a poignant generalization.

**69 τούτων:** i.e., the many things they all might say. **ἕως ἂν σῴζηται τὸ σκάφος** "as long as the ship is safe." τὸ σκάφος is a ship's hull; the usage of it as the ship itself (the device of synecdoche) is typical of the elevated language of tragedy (cf. Mastronarde 2002: 161 on E. *Med.* 1, Olson 2002: 214 on Ar. *Acharn.* 541). D.'s audience would not have been confused by this abrupt introduction of naval imagery, which is pervasive in Athenian literature and reflects the broader Athenian experience. Audiences in the theater encountered comparably abrupt transitions (e.g., A. *Th.* 208–10 with Hutchinson 1985: 80, S. *Ant.* 715–17 with Griffith 1999: 159), and the "ship of state" is a traditional image prominent in early poetry (e.g., Archil. 4 [West]), tragedy (D. himself quotes S. *Ant.* 189–90 at 19.247), and prose (e.g., Pl. *Rep.* 6.487e–9a); see Brock 2013: 53–67, Rutherford 2012: 128–30. **ἄν τε μεῖζον ἄν τ' ἔλαττον ἧι** "whether it is large or small"; ἄν = ἐάν 2×. The expression stresses the universality of the proposition; cf. Andoc. 1.29, D. 18.139, §16. **ναύτην καὶ κυβερνήτην καὶ πάντα ἄνδρα ἑξῆς:** the first two terms correspond to the members of the δῆμος and the politicians who steer the state; the third item again emphasizes the universal applicability of the comparison. πάντα ἄνδρα ἑξῆς echoes language used to describe participation in the Athenian democracy; cf. [Xen.] *Ath.* 1.6, where a critic complains: ὡς ἐχρῆν αὐτοὺς μὴ ἐᾶν λέγειν πάντας ἑξῆς μηδὲ βουλεύειν ("that they should not all be allowed to speak or participate in turn"). **προθύμους:** D. regularly includes the term in his appeals to the Athenians, and here transfers it to the sailors. Cf. 1.4, 2.27, 3.8. **μήθ' ἑκὼν μήτ' ἄκων:** the comparison implies generous acknowledgment of a range of complicity on the part of the δῆμος and the politicians in the cities defeated or controlled by Philip. **ἀνατρέψει** "overturns"; frequently applied both to ships and states (LSJ ἀνατρέπω I 1, 2). **ὑπέρσχηι** "rises up" to sink the boat (LSJ ὑπερέχω II 1). **μάταιος:** 1.17n.

### 70–75 Plan for resistance
We must protect ourselves and appeal to the others to join in the fight. We must prepare supplies and lead the alliance. We cannot sit idle.

**70 καὶ ἡμεῖς:** 4.41n. καί. **ἕως ἐσμὲν σῶιοι:** cf. §69 ἕως ἂν σώιζηται τὸ σκάφος. As D. turns explicitly to the situation in Athens, his phrasing stresses the connection between the examples of the other cities and the naval comparison that preceded. **πόλιν μεγίστην** echoes §67 τηλικαύτην πόλιν τὸ μέγεθος. **ἀφορμάς:** 2.22n. **ἀξίωμα κάλλιστον** "an excellent reputation" (LSJ ἀξίωμα I 2; cf. §43n. τί, a different sense). Cf. D. 18.149, 20.142 with Canevaro 2016a: 405, Kremmydas 2012: 418. **πάλαι τις ἡδέως ἂν ἴσως ἐρωτήσας κάθηται** "perhaps someone has been sitting here for a while, wishing he could ask [that]." ἡδέως ἄν modifies ἐρωτήσας; the idiom is regularly used in the first-person to introduce a question (ἡδέως ἂν ἐροίμην: "I should like to ask"; LSJ ἡδύς III 1, D. 18.64, 217, 20.2, 129). Here the unparalleled use of the idiom in

## 9 THIRD PHILIPPIC 70–71          261

the third-person to describe an audience member highlights the "reverse apostrophe" (see 1.14n. τί) in the preceding question. **νὴ Δί'**: §65n. **νή. καὶ γράψω δέ** "and I will make a proposal, too"; *GP* 201, §7n. μήποτε. **χειροτονήσετε**: the repetition from §1, and the reference to a specific proposal, signal that the speech is moving to a conclusion. See also 4.30n. ἐπειδάν. **αὐτοὶ πρῶτον ἀμυνόμενοι**: the construction with these nominatives is abandoned, and then resumed below in [§71] αὐτοὶ παρεσκευασμένοι. αὐτοί emphasizes that the Athenians must take an active role, and not rely on others; cf. 1.6n. αὐτούς. At the start of the speech D. was hesitant to make such a proposal for defense, because the Athenians did not realize that they were at war (§§6–7); now he takes that point as proven by the arguments expressed in the body of the speech. **παρασκευαζόμενοι**: 4.6n. παρεσκευασμένους. **τριήρεσι καὶ χρήμασι καὶ στρατιώταις λέγω**: D. adds these details as a clarification and an afterthought, as λέγω indicates (cf. 1.27n. λέγω). D.'s earlier Assembly speeches frequently urge the Athenians to pay for military missions and to volunteer to serve themselves (e.g., 1.6, 2.13, 3.4, 4.7); because D.'s goal is to engage Philip in the north, the expedition will necessarily be naval (cf. 4.16–22 for a more detailed call to man a fleet). **καὶ γὰρ ἄν**: ἄν = ἐάν; for the expression, cf. 4.11n. **δήπου**: cf. 3.9n. The particle's placement underscores ἅπαντες and δουλεύειν; the confident tone then extends to the characterization of the Athenians as defenders of freedom. **δουλεύειν συγχωρήσωσιν** "consent to being enslaved" (LSJ συγχωρέω II 2); cf. §22n. καταδουλοῦσθαι, §26n. δουλεύωσιν. **ἡμῖν γ' ὑπὲρ τῆς ἐλευθερίας ἀγωνιστέον** "but we must fight for freedom." The Athenian role is stressed by γε; cf. §36n. ἑτοίμως. For the expression, cf. D. 18.177.

**71 παρεσκευασμένοι καὶ ποιήσαντες**: the perf. participle resumes from παρασκευαζόμενοι above, and combined with the aor. participle presents a sequence of actions. **τοὺς ἄλλους ἤδη παρακαλῶμεν** "let us then summon the other [Greeks to join the war]" (LSJ παρακαλέω II 1); for the context and sense, cf. D. 18.24. **τοὺς ταῦτα διδάξοντας**: 2.11n. ἤ; here too ταῦτα refers to the preparations to which the Athenians are committed. For the functions of these ambassadors, cf. D. 8.76 πρέσβεις ἐκπέμπειν πανταχοῖ τοὺς διδάξοντας, νουθετήσοντας, πράξοντας ("[I propose that we] send out ambassadors everywhere who will give instructions and warnings and take action"). **εἰς Πελοπόννησον, εἰς Ῥόδον, εἰς Χίον, ὡς βασιλέα λέγω**: λέγω is used as above (§70n. τριήρεσι). A series of embassies was dispatched in 341/0; for details see Develin 1989: 334–5. D. went to the Peloponnese as a diplomat twice prior to this speech, in 344/3 (Develin 1989: 327) and in 343/2 (§72n. οὐδ'). The testimonia are not precise, and it is not possible to disentangle the reports for D.'s efforts in the Peloponnese; but it is likely that there was a third trip after this speech, in 341/0. In that year, Hyperides (*LGPN* s.v. 3, *PAA*

902110) went as a diplomat to Rhodes ([Plut.] *Mor.* 850a with Roisman et al. 2015: 260) and probably to Chios too (Engels 1993: 86–8). The politician Ephialtes (*LGPN* s.v. 4, *PAA* 452925) is reported to have visited the Persian king at this time (there were malicious and probably exaggerated allegations that whatever funds he received were appropriated by Demosthenes and Hyperides; [Plut.] *Mor.* 847f, 848e with Roisman et al. 2015: 243). **τῶν ἐκείνωι συμφερόντων ἀφέστηκε** "[it] is not disconnected with his own interests" (§19n. τοσοῦτον). ἐκείνωι = the Persian king. The subject is τὸ μὴ … ἐᾶσαι. For a more detailed account of the advantage common to the Athenians and the Persian king in opposing Philip, see D. 10.32. **τὸ μὴ τοῦτον ἐᾶσαι πάντα καταστρέψασθαι:** τοῦτον = Philip. Cf. 4.6n. πάντα. **ἐὰν μὲν πείσητε:** sc. τοὺς ἐν Πελοποννήσωι κτλ. **κοινωνοὺς … τῶν ἀναλωμάτων:** D. almost anticipates later complaints against himself. D. will be instrumental in the creation of the Greek alliance that faced Philip at Chaeronea in 338, and one of the charges against him after the defeat there is that the Athenians bore a disproportionate share of the expenses; see D. 18.237–8, Aesch. 3.106, 143, Hyp. *Against Diondas* 145v/144r 10–12 (Carey et al. 2008). **ἄν τι δέηι:** ἄν = ἐάν; for the euphemism for war, cf. D. 4.16, 14.23. **εἰ δὲ μή:** sc. πείσετε; for the tone cf. 1.12n. εἰ. **χρόνους γ' ἐμποιῆτε** "at least you may cause some delay" for Philip's diplomatic overtures among the Greeks. For the phrasing cf. Thuc. 3.38.1, D. 23.93, 36.2, *Pr.* 21.4.

**72 πρὸς ἄνδρα καὶ οὐχὶ συνεστώσης πόλεως ἰσχύν:** D.'s encouragement depends on Greek prejudices against monarchy. Cf. D. 2.9–10, where he similarly stresses the fragility of a monarch's life and power, which he contrasts explicitly with the collective power of shared governance within Athens and among an allied league. The sense of συνεστώσης ("united") is repeated from that passage (2.9n. ὅταν). **τοῦτ' =** χρόνους ἐμποιεῖν. Philip may die or be overthrown. **οὐδ' αἱ πέρυσιν πρεσβεῖαι** "nor [were] last year's embassies [pointless]"; D. refers to events in 343/2 (testimonia at Develin 1989: 329; see also §27n. πρότερον). πέρυσιν is frequent in D., and colloquial in tone (e.g., 22.40, 23.31; see Biles and Olson 2015: 390 on Ar. *Wasps* 1038). **κατηγορίαι** "complaints" expressed on those diplomatic missions, presumably protesting against any sympathy for Philip; for this usage, cf. §28n. κἀγανακτοῦμεν, D. 8.37, 16.1. **ἄς:** the antecedent is πρεσβεῖαι. **Πολύευκτος ὁ βέλτιστος ἐκεινοσί** "Polyeuctus here, an excellent [Athenian]." The deictic ἐκεινοσί points to him in the Assembly. βέλτιστος is commonly used in the orators with specifically civic and political connotations (see Todd 2007: 311 on Lys. 3.4); cf. D. 21.17, where it distinguishes D.'s political ally from his enemies. Polyeuctus (*LGPN* s.v. 49, *PAA* 778285) shared a similar outlook with D., as a staunch opponent of Philip (Plut. *Phoc.* 19.5). His surrender was demanded in 335 by Alexander along with that of other Athenian enemies of Macedon (Plut. *Dem.* 23.4). **Ἡγήσιππος:** Hegesippus (*LGPN* s.v. 17, *PAA* 481555) was, like Polyeuctus and D., famous for his opposition to Philip (for this group see Sealey 163), a position evinced in his surviving Assembly speech, or. 7 in the Demosthenic corpus (accepting the attribution in Lib. *Arg.D.* or. 7, with MacDowell 2009: 344). A contemporary inscription attests to his involvement in Athenian policy regarding Eretria (*IG* II² 125 [343?] = *GHI* no. 69). On his career and the speech, see Davies 2011, Fisher 2001: 204–5. **οἱ ἄλλοι πρέσβεις:** these included the orator Lycurgus (*LGPN* s.v. 2, *PAA* 611335; Plut. *Mor.* 841e). **περιήλθομεν:** the ambassadors "went around" the Peloponnese; they made alliances with Achaea, Arcadia, Argos, and Megalopolis; see Harris 119–20, 205 n. 30. **καὶ ἐποιήσαμεν ἐπισχεῖν ἐκεῖνον** "and we caused that man to halt" (LSJ ποιέω II 1 b, ἐπέχω IV 2). The clause is syntactically parallel to ἅς … περιήλθομεν, but the relative construction is abandoned; it should be taken as a new main clause. ἐποιήσαμεν governs ἐλθεῖν and ὁρμῆσαι. **εἰς Πελοπόννησον:** if Philip's advance on Ambracia and Naupactus (§34n.) had been successful, he would have been well positioned to enter the Peloponnese.

**73 οὐ μέντοι λέγω** "I am not proposing, however"; cf. 2.31n. λέγω, 4.21n. **αὐτοὺς ὑπὲρ αὐτῶν:** both pronouns refer to the Athenians; the juxtaposition is emphatic, and strongly contrasted with τοὺς ἄλλους. Cf. §70n. αὐτοί. **ἐθέλοντας ποιεῖν:** a conditional participle: "if [we] are willing to do." ἀναγκαῖον is a variant for D.'s typical phrasing with προσήκω (§67n. μηδέν) or δεῖ (1.6n. τοῦ). **παρακαλεῖν:** §71n. τούς. Indirect statement introduced by λέγω. **εὔηθες:** sc. ἐστί; see 1.15n. τίς. **τὰ οἰκεῖα αὐτοὺς προϊεμένους** "for those who themselves neglect their own [affairs]" (§1n. εἰς). The use of αὐτούς and the juxtaposition with τὰ οἰκεῖα is continued from the last sentence, as is the contrast between the Athenians' concerns and those of the other Greeks (τῶν ἀλλοτρίων). The accus. is subject of φάσκειν. **φάσκειν:** the infinitive is explanatory, depending on εὔηθες. The verb has a connotation of duplicity or self-deception; cf. D. 2.6, §8. **τὰ παρόντα περιορῶντας:** §29n. περιορῶμεν; parallel to προϊεμένους. D. adds a contrast between present and future to that between Athenians and other Greeks. **ὑπὲρ τῶν μελλόντων:** cf. §2n. περί. **τοῖς μὲν ἐν Χερρονήσωι:** the troops commanded by Diopeithes; see §15n. οὐδέ. **φημὶ δεῖν:** a formal proposal; cf. 1.17n. φημί, 2.27. **τἄλλ'… ποιεῖν:** parallel to χρήματ' ἀποστέλλειν. D. refers to the dispatch of additional ships and soldiers, along with money for food and supplies; cf. §70n. τριήρεσι. **συγκαλεῖν, συνάγειν, διδάσκειν, νουθετεῖν:** the four infinitives in asyndeton constitute a resounding final summary of D.'s proposal (cf. *GPS* 102, 113). The συν- prefixes stress cooperative unity in Athens and among the Greeks (2.9n.

ὅταν) and bind the first two infinitives as a pair. These two verbs are chosen for this sound effect; they are redundant in sense and otherwise very rare in the Assembly speeches (συγκαλέω: only here and D. 14.38; συνάγω only here). The ending in -ειν (for the homoioarchon and homoioteleuton, cf. 1.1n. προθύμως) and the trisyllabic units link the entire sequence. The latter two verbs are repeated from the similar ending to the speech *On the Chersonese*; see §71n. τούς. **ταῦτ' ἐστὶν πόλεως:** ταῦτ' refers to the preceding infinitives. πόλεως is a predicative genitive (1.1n. τῆς). **ἀξίωμα ἐχούσης ἡλίκον ὑμῖν ὑπάρχει** "that has as great a reputation as you do." Cf. §70n. ἀξίωμα. The second-person plural pronoun is repeated below to drive home D.'s point; cf. 3.36n. ὑπέρ, also at speech-end.

**74 εἰ δ' οἴεσθε:** D. maintains the emphasis on the second-person plural; usually this expression with the conditional protasis and οὐκ ὀρθῶς is more deferential, with τις ὑμῶν in the third-person singular (e.g., D. 2.9, 4.29, 21.70). **Χαλκιδέας ... Μεγαρέας:** Chalcis remained independent of Philip and was shortly to ally itself with Athens; §17n. Εὐβοίαι, §59n. οἵπερ. On Megara see §17n. Μεγάρων. **ὑμεῖς δ' ἀποδράσεσθαι τὰ πράγματα** "[if] you suppose that you will escape your circumstances." ἀποδιδράσκω regularly refers to individuals shirking military service or taxes (e.g., D. 21.165, 22.17, Aesch. 3.253); for the reference to Athens as a whole, cf. D. 8.3. **ἀγαπητὸν ... ἑκάστοις** "each of these [cities] is happy if they themselves remain safe." For the construction, cf. 3.30n. ἀγαπητόν. ἐὰν αὐτοὶ σώιζωνται stands in place of the infinitive there. **ὑμῖν:** dat. of agent. The parallel placement of the pronoun at the start of this and the next clause reiterates the emphasis. **οἱ πρόγονοι ... κινδύνων:** the sentence is closely modeled on 3.36. Here D. adds τὸ γέρας, an epic word referring to the royal prerogative to distribute meat at a sacrifice, or prizes for success in battle or games (see Carlier 1984: 151–4). D. uses that royal vocabulary to characterize the Athenians' rank among the Greeks: they have the privilege of presiding over the protection of the entire group. The other vocabulary here is typical of idealized accounts of Athenian history in the state funeral orations (see 3.36n. ἦν); γέρας does not appear in the surviving speeches, but cf. Hdt. 9.27.5, from a speech in which the Athenians defend their right to command the other Greeks at Plataea, which shares many elements with the funeral orations: ἀπὸ τοῦ ἐν Μαραθῶνι ἔργου ἄξιοί εἰμεν τοῦτο τὸ γέρας ἔχειν ("because of our achievement at Marathon we deserve to have this privilege").

**75 ὃ βούλεται ζητῶν ἕκαστος καθεδεῖται:** cf. 8.77, also at speech-end, where D. characterizes the audience in the Assembly as eager to achieve their goals while sitting idly without serving. καθέζομαι is used here like κάθημαι elsewhere (2.23n. καθήμεθα). **ὅπως μηδὲν αὐτὸς ποιήσει σκοπῶν:** the participle is parallel to ζητῶν. For the complaint, cf. 4.7.

πρῶτον μέν introduces the first main clause, followed by ἔπειτα with the second (*GP* 377).    **οὐδὲ μήποθ' εὕρηι** "he will never find." οὐδέ is used as an emphatic alternative for οὐ (cf. 4.2n.), and the combination with μή + subj. presents a strong denial for the future (see 4.44n. οὐδέποτ').    **ὅπως μή** introduces fut. indic., equivalent to μή + subj. in a fear clause (Smyth §2231).    **ὅσα οὐ βουλόμεθα** explains πάντα and contrasts with ὃ βούλεται; the switch from the singular to the plural stresses the need for support from the whole city.

### 76 Conclusion
Whatever we decide, it is not too late to improve our situation.

**76 ἐγὼ μὲν δή:** for this final first-person statement, see 4.51n. ἐγώ. The repetition of ταῦτα signals the end of the speech.    **ἔτι ἐπανορθωθῆναι:** repeated from the speech's introduction (§4n. ἐπανορθώσασθαι). **τούτων γιγνομένων** "if these measures are taken"; τούτων refers to D.'s proposals in §73.    **τι βέλτιον:** the conclusion to the second *Olynthiac* similarly focuses on other speakers and the audience's choice of what is best for the city (2.31n. βέλτιον).    **ὅ τι δ' ὑμῖν δόξει:** the fut. indic. refers to the time of the Assembly's decision. For the verb usage, see 4.21n. ἐξ.    **ὦ πάντες θεοί:** this vocative phrase is rare and powerful. D. uses it to close three of his later speeches (also 6.37, 18.324 with Wankel 1976: 1353, cf. too 19.16; elsewhere in classical and archaic authors only at Ar. *Lysistrata* 778, Xen. *Cyr.* 2.2.10, 8.7.3). Other speeches end on an optimistic note, but without the solemn prayer.    **συνενέγκοι:** 4.51n. ὅ.

# WORKS CITED

Adams, C. D. (1927) *Demosthenes and his influence*. New York.
Allan, W. (2008) *Euripides. Helen*. Cambridge.
Anson, E. M. (2009) "Philip II and the creation of the Macedonian pezhetairoi," in P. Wheatley and R. Hannah (eds.), *Alexander and his successors: essays from the Antipodes*. Claremont, CA. 88–98.
Austin, C. and S. D. Olson (2004) *Aristophanes. Thesmophoriazusae*. Oxford.
Badian, E. (1992) "Jaeger's Demosthenes: an essay in anti-history," in W. M. Calder III (ed.), *Werner Jaeger reconsidered*. Atlanta. 289–315.
(2000) "The road to prominence," in I. Worthington (ed.), *Demosthenes: statesman and orator*. London. 9–44.
Balot, R. K. (2001) *Greed and injustice in classical Athens*. Princeton.
(2004) "Free speech, courage, and democratic deliberation," in I. Sluiter and R. Rosen (eds.), *Free speech in classical antiquity*. Leiden. 233–59.
Barrett, W. S. (1964) *Euripides. Hippolytos*. Oxford.
Beresford, J. (2013) *The ancient sailing season*. Leiden.
Bers, V. (1985) "Dikastic thorubos," in P. A. Cartledge and F. D. Harvey (eds.), *Crux: essays presented to G. E. M. de Ste. Croix on his 75th birthday*. Exeter. 1–15.
(2009) *Genos dikanikon. Amateur and professional speech in the courtrooms of classical Athens*. Washington, DC.
(2013) "Performing the speech in Athenian courts and Assembly: adjusting the act to fit the *bema*," in C. Kremmydas, J. Powell, and L. Rubinstein (eds.), *Profession and performance: aspects of oratory in the Greco-Roman world*. London. 27–40.
Biles, Z. and S. D. Olson (2015) *Aristophanes. Wasps*. Oxford.
Bishop, C. (2015) "Roman Plato or Roman Demosthenes? The bifurcation of Cicero in ancient scholarship," in W. H. F. Altman (ed.), *Brill's companion to the reception of Cicero*. Leiden. 293–306.
(2016) "How to make a Roman Demosthenes: self-fashioning in Cicero's *Brutus* and *Orator*," *Classical Journal* 111: 167–92.
Blanshard, A. J. L. and T. A. Sowerby (2005) "Thomas Wilson's Demosthenes and the politics of Tudor translation," *International Journal of the Classical Tradition* 12: 46–80.
Blass, F. (1893) *Demosthenes*. 2nd ed. Vol. 3.1 of *Die attische Beredsamkeit von Alexander bis auf Augustus*. Leipzig.
Bollansée, J. (1999) *Hermippos of Smyrna and his biographical writings. A reappraisal*. Leuven.
Bordes, J. (1982) *Politeia dans la pensée grecque jusqu'à Aristote*. Paris.
Bosworth, A. B. (1980) *A historical commentary on Arrian's History of*

*Alexander*. Vol. 1. Oxford.
Bowden, H. (2005) *Classical Athens and the Delphic oracle: divination and democracy*. Cambridge.
Bowie, A. M. (2007) *Herodotus. Histories book VIII*. Cambridge.
(2013) *Homer. Odyssey books XIII and XIV*. Cambridge.
Bowra, M. (1944) *Sophoclean tragedy*. Oxford.
Braswell, B. K. (1988) *A commentary on the fourth Pythian ode of Pindar*. Berlin.
Briant, P. (2017) *The first European. A history of Alexander in the age of empire*. Translated by N. Elliott. Cambridge, MA.
Brock, R. (2013) *Greek political imagery from Homer to Aristotle*. London.
Brun, P. (1983) *Eisphora–Syntaxis–Stratiotika. Recherches sur les finances militaires d' Athènes au IVe siècle av. J.-C*. Paris.
(2015) *Démosthène: rhétorique, pouvoir et corruption à Athènes. Nouvelles biographies historiques*. Paris.
Buckler, J. (1989) *Philip II and the Sacred War*. Leiden.
(2003) *Aegean Greece in the fourth century BC*. Leiden.
Buckler, J., M. Chambers, and J. Vaio (1996) "'Of the Athenian government.' Introduction and text," in W. M. Calder III and S. Trzaskoma (eds.), *George Grote reconsidered: a 200th birthday celebration with a first edition of his essay 'Of the Athenian Government'*. Hildesheim. 75–94.
Bugh, G. R. (1982) "Introduction of the Katalogeis of the Athenian cavalry," *Transactions of the American Philological Association* 112: 23–32.
(1988) *The horsemen of Athens*. Princeton.
Bühler, W. (1978) "Tendenzen nachdemosthenischer Bearbeitung der 3. Philippischen Rede des Demosthenes," in H. Beck, A. Kambylis, and P. Moraux (eds.), *Kuklos. Griechisches und Byzantinisches: Rudolf Keydell zum neunzigsten Geburtstag*. Berlin and New York. 59–77.
Burr, D. (1933) "The terracotta figurines," *Hesperia* 2: 184–94.
Butcher, S. H. (1903) *Demosthenis orationes*. Vol. 1. Oxford.
Cahill, N. (2002) *Household and city organization at Olynthus*. New Haven.
Cairns, D. L. (1993) *Aidōs: the psychology and ethics of honour and shame in ancient Greek literature*. Oxford.
(1996) "Hybris, dishonour, and thinking big," *Journal of Hellenic Studies* 116: 1–32.
(2015) "Revenge, punishment, and justice in Athenian homicide law," *Journal of Value Enquiry* 49: 645–65.
Cairns, D. L. and L. Fulkerson (2013) "Introduction," in D. L. Cairns and L. Fulkerson (eds.), *Emotions between Greece and Rome*. London. 1–22.
Canevaro, M. (2013a) *The documents in the Attic orators. Laws and decrees in the public speeches of the Demosthenic corpus*. Chapter 5 by E. M. Harris. Oxford.
(2013b) "*Nomothesia* in classical Athens: what sources should we

believe?," *Classical Quarterly* 63: 139–60.
(2015) Review of Worthington 2013, *Klio* 97: 323–9.
(2016a) *Demostene, Contro Leptine: introduzione, traduzione e commento storico*. Berlin.
(2016b) "The procedure of Demosthenes' *Against Leptines*: how to repeal (and replace) an existing law," *Journal of Hellenic Studies* 136: 39–58.
(2018) "Majority rule vs. consensus: the practice of democratic deliberation in the Greek poleis," in M. Canevaro, A. Erskine, B. Gray, and J. Ober (eds.), *Ancient Greek history and the contemporary social sciences*. Edinburgh. 101–56.
(2019) "Democratic deliberation in the Athenian Assembly: procedures and behaviours towards legitimacy," *Annales. Histoire, Sciences Sociales* 73.
Canevaro, M. and D. Lewis (2014) "*Khoris oikountes* and the obligations of freedmen," *Incidenza dell' Antico* 12: 91–121.
Canfora, L. (1968) *Inventario dei manoscritti greci di Demosthene*. Padua.
(2009) "Ideologies of Hellenism," in G. Boys-Stones, B. Graziosi, and P. Vasunia (eds.), *The Oxford handbook of Hellenic studies*. Oxford. 173–9.
Carey, C. (1992) *Apollodorus. Against Neaira [Demosthenes] 59*. Warminster.
(1994) "Rhetorical means of persuasion," in I. Worthington (ed.), *Persuasion: Greek rhetoric in action*. London. 26–45.
(2012) *Trials from classical Athens*. 2nd ed. London.
(2015) "Solon in the orators," *Trends in Classics* 7: 110–28.
Carey, C., M. Edwards, Z. Farkas, J. Herrman, L. Horváth, G. Mayer, T. Mészáros, P. J. Rhodes, and N. Tchernetska (2008) "Fragments of Hyperides' *Against Diondas* from the Archimedes Palimpsest," *Zeitschrift für Papyrologie und Epigraphik* 165: 1–19.
Carey, C. and R. A. Reid (1985) *Demosthenes. Selected private speeches*. Cambridge.
Cargill, J. (1981) *The Second Athenian League: empire or free alliance?* Berkeley and Los Angeles.
Carlier, P. (1984) *La Royauté en Grèce avant Alexandre*. Strasbourg.
(1990) *Démosthène*. Paris.
Carney, E. (2007) "Symposia and the Macedonian elite: the unmixed life," *Syllecta Classica* 18: 129–80.
Cawkwell, G. L. (1963) "Demosthenes' policy after the peace of Philocrates II," *Classical Quarterly* 13: 200–13.
(1978) *Philip of Macedon*. London.
(1984) "Athenian naval power in the fourth century," *Classical Quarterly* 34: 334–45.
(1996) "The end of Greek liberty," in E. M. Harris and R. W. Wallace

(eds.), *Transitions to empire: essays in Greco-Roman history, 360–146 BC in honor of E. Badian.* Norman. 98–121.
(2005) *The Greek wars. The failure of Persia.* Oxford.
(2011) *Cyrene to Chaeronea. Selected essays on ancient Greek history.* Oxford.
Ceccarelli, P. (2013) *Ancient Greek letter writing. A cultural history (600 BC–150 BC).* Oxford.
Chadwick, J. (1996) *Lexicographica Graeca. Contributions to the lexicography of ancient Greek.* Oxford.
Christ, M. (2001) "Conscription of hoplites in classical Athens," *Classical Quarterly* 51: 398–422.
— (2006) *The bad citizen in classical Athens.* Cambridge.
— (2007) "The evolution of the eisphora in classical Athens," *Classical Quarterly* 57: 53–69.
— (2012) *The limits of altruism in democratic Athens.* Cambridge.
Clemenceau, G. (1926) *Demosthenes.* Translated by C. M. Thompson. Boston.
Cohen, E. E. (2000) *The Athenian nation.* Princeton.
Cohen, G. M. (1995) *The Hellenistic settlements in Europe, the islands, and Asia Minor.* Berkeley and Los Angeles.
Colvin, S. (2007) *Historical Greek reader: Mycenaean to the Koine.* Oxford.
Connor, W. R. (1971) *The new politicians of fifth-century Athens.* Princeton.
— (1984) *Thucydides.* Princeton.
— (1988a) "Early Greek land warfare as symbolic expression," *Past and Present* 119: 3–29.
— (1988b) "'Sacred' and 'secular.' ἱερὰ καὶ ὅσια and the classical Athenian concept of the state," *Ancient Society* 19: 161–88.
Cooper, C. (2000) "Philosophers, politics, academics. Demosthenes' rhetorical reputation in antiquity," in I. Worthington (ed.), *Demosthenes: statesman and orator.* London. 224–45.
— (2009) "(Re)making Demosthenes: Demochares and Demetrius of Phalerum on Demosthenes," in P. Wheatley and R. Hannah (eds.), *Alexander and his successors: essays from the Antipodes.* Claremont, CA. 310–22.
Cribiore, R. (2013) *Libanius the sophist. Rhetoric, reality, and religion in the fourth century.* Ithaca.
Csapo, E. and W. J. Slater (1995) *The context of ancient drama.* Ann Arbor.
Csapo, E. and P. Wilson (2014) "The financial organisation of the Athenian theatre in the time of Eubulus and Lycurgus," in E. Csapo, H. R. Goette, J. R. Green, and P. Wilson (eds.), *Greek theatre in the fourth century BC.* Berlin. 393–424.
Cunningham, I. C. (1971) *Herodas. Mimiambi.* Oxford.
Damon, C. (1997) *The mask of the parasite: a pathology of Roman patronage.* Ann Arbor.

Davies, J. K. (2011) "Hegesippos of Sounion: an underrated politician," in S. D. Lambert (ed.), *Sociable man. Essays on ancient Greek social behaviour in honour of Nick Fisher*. Swansea. 11–23.
de Souza, P. (1999) *Piracy in the Graeco-Roman world*. Cambridge.
Denyer, N. (2008) *Plato. Protagoras*. Cambridge.
Develin, R. (1989) *Athenian officials 684–321 BC*. Cambridge.
Devine, A. M. and L. D. Stephens (2000) *Discontinuous syntax: hyperbaton in Greek*. Oxford.
Dickey, E. (1996) *Greek forms of address from Herodotus to Lucian*. Oxford.
Dickie, M. W. (2001) "Mimes, thaumaturgy, and the theatre," *Classical Quarterly* 51: 599–603.
Diggle, J. (1994) *Euripidea. Collected essays*. Oxford.
   (2004) *Theophrastus. Characters*. Cambridge.
Dilts, M. R. (2002) *Demosthenis orationes*. Vol. 1. Oxford.
Dmitriev, S. (2011) *The Greek slogan of freedom and early Roman politics in Greece*. Oxford.
Dodds, E. R. (1959) *Plato. Gorgias*. Oxford.
Dover, K. J. (1968) *Aristophanes. Clouds*. Oxford.
   (1993) *Aristophanes. Frogs*. Oxford.
   (1997) *The evolution of Greek prose style*. Oxford.
Drerup, E. (1916) *Aus einer alten Advokatenrepublik. Demosthenes und seine Zeit*. Paderborn.
Ducrey, P. (1999) *Le Traitement des prisonniers de guerre dans la Grèce antique: des origines à la conquête romaine*. Paris.
Dunbar, N. (1995) *Aristophanes. Birds*. Oxford.
Dyck, A. R. (2013) *Cicero. Pro Marco Caelio*. Cambridge.
Efstathiou, A. (2007) "Euthyna procedure in 4th c. Athens and the case On the False Embassy," *Dike* 10: 113–35.
Engels, J. (1989) *Studien zur politischen Biographie des Hypereides: Athen in der Epoche der lykurgischen Reformen und des makedonischen Universalreiches*. 2nd ed. Munich.
Erdas, D. (2002) *Cratero, il Macedone: testimonianze e frammenti*. Rome.
Erskine, A. (1989) "The ΠΕΖΕΤΑΙΡΟΙ of Philip II and Alexander III," *Historia* 38: 385–94.
Faraguna, M. (1998) "Aspetti amministrativi e finanziari della monarchia macedone fra IV e III sec. a.C.," *Athenaeum* 86: 349–95.
   (2008) "Oralità e scrittura nella prassi giudiziaria ateniese tra V e IV sec. a.C.," in E. M. Harris and G. Thür (eds.), *Symposion 2007*. Vienna. 63–82.
Finglass, P. J. (2007) *Sophocles. Electra*. Cambridge.
   (2011) *Sophocles. Ajax*. Cambridge.
Fisher, N. R. E. (1992) *Hybris. A study in the values of honour and shame in ancient Greece*. Warminster.

(2001) *Aeschines. Against Timarchos*. Oxford.
Flower, M. A. (1994) *Theopompus of Chios. History and rhetoric in the fourth century BC*. Oxford.
Flower, M. A. and J. Marincola (2002) *Herodotus. Histories book IX*. Cambridge.
Fraenkel, E. (1950) *Agamemnon. Edited with a commentary*. 3 vols. Oxford.
— (1965) *Noch einmal Kolon und Satz*. Bayerische Akademie der Wissenschaften, philosophisch-historische Klasse: Sitzungsberichte, 2. Munich.
Fröhlich, P. (2008) "Les Magistrats militaires des cités grecques au IVe siècle a.c.," *Revue des études anciennes* 110: 39–55 and 423–41.
Frost, F. J. (1969) "Themistocles' place in Athenian politics," *Classical Antiquity* 1: 105–24.
Fuhr, C. (1914) *Demosthenis orationes*. Vol. 1. Leipzig.
Gabrielsen, V. (1994) *Financing the Athenian fleet*. Baltimore.
Gagarin, M. (1996) "The orality of Greek oratory," in E. A. Mackay (ed.), *Signs of orality: the oral tradition and its influence in the Greek and Roman world*. Leiden. 163–80.
— (1997) *Antiphon. The speeches*. Cambridge.
— (2003) "Who were the *kakourgoi*?," in G. Thür and F. J. Fernández Nieto (eds.), *Symposion 1999*. Vienna. 183–91.
— (2008) *Writing Greek law*. Cambridge.
Garlan, Y. (1974) *Recherches de poliorcétique grecque*. Athens and Paris.
Garvie, A. F. (1994) *Homer. Odyssey books VI–VIII*. Cambridge.
— (2009) *Aeschylus. Persae*. Oxford.
Gibson, C. A. (2002) *Interpreting a classic: Demosthenes and his ancient commentators*. Berkeley and Los Angeles.
Goldstein, J. A. (1968) *The letters of Demosthenes*. New York.
Goodwin, W. W. (1901) *Demosthenes. On the crown*. Cambridge.
Gray, V. (1989) *The character of Xenophon's Hellenica*. London.
Grethlein, J. (2010) *The Greeks and their past. Poetry, oratory and history in the fifth century BCE*. Cambridge.
Griffith, M. (1999) *Sophocles. Antigone*. Cambridge.
Grusková, J. (2009) "Neue Vorschläge zu einigen Demosthenes-Papyri," *Archiv für Papyrusforschung* 55: 40–53.
Habicht, C. (1961) "Falsche Urkunden zur Geschichte Athens im Zeitalter der Perserkriege," *Hermes* 89: 1–35.
— (1997) *Athens from Alexander to Antony*. Translated by D. L. Schneider. Cambridge, MA.
Hall, E. (1989) *Inventing the barbarian. Greek self-definition through tragedy*. Oxford.
Hall, J. M. (2001) "Contested ethnicities: perceptions of Macedonia within evolving definitions of Greek identity," in I. Malkin (ed.),

*Ancient perceptions of Greek ethnicity*. Cambridge, MA. 159–86.
Halliwell, S. (2008) *Greek laughter: a study of cultural psychology from Homer to early Christianity*. Cambridge.
Hamel, D. (1998) *Athenian generals: military authority in the classical period*. Leiden.
Hammond, N. G. L. (1994) *Philip of Macedon*. London.
Hanink, J. (2014) *Lycurgan Athens and the making of classical tragedy*. Cambridge.
Hansen, M. H. (1974) *The sovereignty of the People's Court in Athens in the fourth century BC and the public action against unconstitutional proposals*. Odense.
 (1975) *Eisangelia: the sovereignty of the People's Court in Athens in the fourth century BC and the impeachment of generals and politicians*. Odense.
 (1976a) *Apagoge, endeixis and ephegesis against kakourgoi, atimoi and pheugontes. A study in the Athenian administration of justice in the fourth century BC*. Odense.
 (1976b) "The Theoric fund and the graphe paranomon against Apollodorus," *Greek, Roman and Byzantine Studies* 17: 235–46.
 (1983) *The Athenian Ecclesia. A collection of articles 1976–83*. Copenhagen.
 (1987) *The Athenian Assembly in the age of Demosthenes*. Oxford.
 (1989) *The Athenian Ecclesia II. A collection of articles 1983–89*. Copenhagen.
 (1991) *The Athenian democracy in the age of Demosthenes*. Oxford.
 (1995) "The 'autonomous city-state'. Ancient fact or modern fiction?," in M. H. Hansen and K. Raaflaub (eds.), *Studies in the ancient Greek polis*. Stuttgart. 21–43.
 (2007) "The Attic orators," in M. H. Hansen (ed.), *The return of the polis: the use and meanings of the word* polis *in archaic and classical sources*. Stuttgart. 192–203.
 (2014) "Political parties in democratic Athens?," *Greek, Roman and Byzantine Studies* 54: 379–403.
Hansen, M. H. and T. H. Nielsen (2005) *An inventory of archaic and classical poleis*. Oxford.
Hanson, V. D. (1998) *Warfare and agriculture in classical Greece*. Revised ed. Berkeley and Los Angeles.
Harding, P. (1979) "'Orations … most nedeful to be rede in these daungerous Dayes'," *Echos du monde classique/Classical Views* 23: 51–63.
 (1994) "Comedy and rhetoric," in I. Worthington (ed.), *Persuasion: Greek rhetoric in action*. London. 196–221.
 (2000) "Demosthenes on the underworld: a chapter in the *Nachleben* of a *rhētōr*," in I. Worthington (ed.), *Demosthenes: statesman and orator*. London. 246–71.

(2006) *Didymos: on Demosthenes*. Oxford.

Harris, E. M. (1989) "Iphicrates at the court of Cotys," *American Journal of Philology* 110: 264–71.

(2000) "The authenticity of Andocides' *De Pace*. A subversive essay," in P. Flensted-Jensen, T. H. Nielsen, and L. Rubinstein (eds.), *Polis and politics: studies in ancient Greek history*. Copenhagen. 479–506.

(2006) *Democracy and the rule of law in classical Athens*. Cambridge.

(2008) *Demosthenes. Speeches 20–22*. Austin.

(2010) "The rule of law and military organisation in the Greek polis," in G. Thür (ed.), *Symposion 2009*. Vienna. 405–17.

(2013a) "The plaint in Athenian law and legal procedure," in M. Faraguna (ed.), *Archives and archival documents in ancient societies*. Trieste. 143–62.

(2013b) *The rule of law in action in democratic Athens*. New York and Oxford.

(2014) "The authenticity of the document at Andocides *On the Mysteries* 95–98," *Tekmeria* 12: 121–53.

(2015) "The family, the community and murder: the role of pollution in Athenian homicide law," in C. Ando and J. Rüpke (eds.), *Public and private in ancient Mediterranean law and religion*. Berlin. 11–35.

(2016) "Alcibiades, the ancestors, liturgies, and the etiquette of addressing the Athenian assembly," in V. Liotsakis and S. Farrington (eds.), *The art of history. Literary perspectives on Greek and Roman historiography*. Berlin. 145–56.

(2018) "The stereotype of tyranny and the tyranny of stereotypes. Demosthenes on Philip II of Macedon," in M. Kalaitzi, P. Paschidis, C. Antonetti, and A.-M. Guimier-Sorbets (eds.), Βορειοελλαδικά: *tales from the lands of the ethne. Essays in honour of Miltiades B. Hatzopoulos*. Athens. 167–78.

Harris, W. V. (2009) *Dreams and experience in classical antiquity*. Cambridge, MA.

Harvey, F. D. (1985) "Dona ferentes: some aspects of bribery in Greek politics," in P. A. Cartledge and F. D. Harvey (eds.), *Crux: essays presented to G. E. M. de Ste. Croix on his 75th birthday*. Exeter. 76–117.

(1990) "The sykophant and sykophancy: vexatious redefinition?," in P. A. Cartledge, P. Millett, and S. C. Todd (eds.), *Nomos. Essays in Athenian law, politics and society*. Cambridge. 103–21.

Hatzopoulos, M. (2011) "Macedonians and other Greeks," in R. Lane Fox (ed.), *Brill's companion to ancient Macedon: studies in the archaeology and history of Macedon, 650 BC–300 AD*. Leiden. 51–78.

Headlam, W. (1922) *Herodas. The Mimes and fragments*. Cambridge.

Heath, M. (1990) "Justice in Thucydides' Athenian speeches," *Historia* 39: 385–400.

Heckel, W. (2008) *Who's who in the age of Alexander the Great: prosopography of Alexander's empire*. Malden.
Henderson, J. (2003) "Demos, demagogue, tyrant in Attic old comedy," in K. A. Morgan (ed.), *Popular tyranny*. Austin. 155–79.
Henry, A. S. (1983) *Honours and privileges in Athenian decrees: the principal formulae of Athenian honorary decrees*. Hildesheim.
Hernández Muñoz, F. G. (2007) "Los papiros y las arengas demosténicas (Or. I–XVII)," *Zeitschrift für Papyrologie und Epigraphik* 162: 43–50.
  (2012) "Demosthenes, *First Philippic*: critical edition," in F. G. Hernández Muñoz (ed.), *La tradición y la transmisión de los oradores y rétores griegos*. Berlin. 129–46.
  (2014) "La *Tercera Filípica* demosténica: nueva edición crítica," *Cuadernos de Filología Clásica. Estudios griegos e indoeuropeos* 24: 369–92.
Herrman, J. (2004) *Athenian funeral orations*. Newburyport.
  (2008) "The authenticity of the Demosthenic *Funeral Oration*," *Acta antiqua Academiae Scientiarum Hungaricae* 48: 171–8.
  (2009a) "Hyperides' *Against Diondas* and the rhetoric of revolt," *Bulletin of the Institute of Classical Studies* 52: 175–85.
  (2009b) *Hyperides. Funeral Oration*. New York and Oxford.
Hesk, J. (2001) *Deception and democracy in classical Athens*. Cambridge.
Heskel, J. (1996) "Philip II and Argaios," in E. M. Harris and R. W. Wallace (eds.), *Transitions to empire: essays in Greco-Roman history, 360–146 BC in honor of E. Badian*. Norman. 37–56.
Heslin, P. (2016) "The dream of a universal variorum: digitizing the commentary tradition," in C. S. Kraus and C. Stray (eds.), *Classical commentaries. Explorations in a scholarly genre*. Oxford. 494–511.
Hornblower, J. (1981) *Hieronymus of Cardia*. Oxford.
Hornblower, S. (1987) *Thucydides*. Baltimore.
  (1991) *A commentary on Thucydides. Volume I: books I–III*. Oxford.
  (1996) *A commentary on Thucydides. Volume II: books IV–V.24*. Oxford.
  (2011) *The Greek world 479–323 BC*. 4th ed. London.
Hunt, P. (2010) *War, peace, and alliance in Demosthenes' Athens*. Cambridge.
Hunter, R. (2003) "Reflecting on writing and culture: Theocritus and the style of cultural change," in H. Yunis (ed.), *Written texts and the rise of literate culture in ancient Greece*. Cambridge. 213–34.
Hunter, R. and D. A. Russell (2011) *Plutarch. How to study poetry*. Cambridge.
Hutchinson, G. O. (1985) *Aeschylus. Septem contra Thebas*. Oxford.
Jaeger, W. (1938) *Demosthenes. The origin and growth of his policy*. Berkeley.
Jameson, M. (1990) "Private space and the Greek city," in O. Murray and S. R. F. Price (eds.), *The Greek city: from Homer to Alexander*. Oxford. 171–95.
Jebb, R. C. (1883) *Sophocles. The plays and fragments. Part I: The Oedipus*

*Tyrannus*. Cambridge.
Jehne, M. (1992) "Die Anerkennung der athenischen Besitzansprüche auf Amphipolis und die Chersones: zu den Implikationen der Territorialklausel ἔχειν τὴν ἑαυτῶν (χώραν) in Verträgen des 4. Jahrhunderts v. Chr.," *Historia* 41: 272–82.
Jenkyns, R. (1980) *The Victorians and ancient Greece*. Cambridge, MA.
Johnson, W. A. (2004) *Bookrolls and scribes in Oxyrhynchus*. Toronto.
de Jong, I. J. F. (1987) "The voice of anonymity: *tis*-speeches in the *Iliad*," *Eranos* 85: 69–84.
  (2012) *Homer. Iliad book XXII*. Cambridge.
Jost, K. (1935) *Das Beispiel und Vorbild der Vorfahren bei den attischen Rednern und Geschichtsschreibern bis Demosthenes*. Regensburg.
Kallet, L. (2003) "Demos tyrannos: wealth, power, and economic patronage," in K. A. Morgan (ed.), *Popular tyranny*. Austin. 117–53.
Kamen, D. (2011) "Reconsidering the status of *khoris oikountes*," *Dike* 14: 43–53.
Keaney, J. J. (1991) *Harpocration. Lexeis of the ten orators*. Amsterdam.
Kemmer, E. (1903) *Die polare Ausdrucksweise in der griechischen Literatur*. Würzburg.
Kennedy, G. A. (1963) *The art of persuasion in Greece*. Princeton.
Konstan, D. (1997) *Friendship in the classical world*. Cambridge.
Kremmydas, C. (2012) *Commentary on Demosthenes* Against Leptines. Oxford.
Krentz, P. (2002) "Fighting by the rules: the invention of the hoplite agōn," *Hesperia* 71: 23–39.
  (2013) "Hoplite hell: how hoplites fought," in D. Kagan and G. F. Viggiano (eds.), *Men of bronze: hoplite warfare in ancient Greece*. Princeton. 134–56.
Lambert, S. (1994) *Inscribed Athenian laws and decrees 352/1–322/1 BC*. Leiden.
  (2010) "Inscribed treaties ca. 350–321: an epigraphical perspective on Athenian foreign policy," in G. Reger, F. X. Ryan, and T. F. Winter (eds.), *Studies in Greek epigraphy and history in honor of Stephen V. Tracy*. Pessac. 153–60.
Langdon, M. K. (2000) "Mountains in Greek religion," *Classical World* 93: 461–70.
Lausberg, H. (1998) *Handbook of literary rhetoric*. 2nd ed. Translated by M. T. Bliss, A. Jansen, and D. E. Orton; edited by D. E. Orton and R. D. Anderson. Leiden.
Lawler, L. B. (1964) *The dance of the ancient Greek theatre*. Iowa City.
  (1965) *The dance in ancient Greece*. Middletown.
Lefèvre, F. (1998) *L'Amphictionie pyléo-delphique: histoire et institutions*. Athens.

Lefort, M. (2016) "Les Connotations d'ἀνήρ et ἄνθρωπος chez les orateurs attiques du IVe siècle," *Hermes* 144: 157–70.
Lehmann, G. A. (2004) *Demosthenes von Athen: ein Leben für die Freiheit. Biographie*. Munich.
Lendon, J. E. (2000) "Homeric vengeance and the outbreak of Greek wars," in H. van Wees (ed.), *War and violence in ancient Greece*. London. 1–30.
Leopold, J. W. (1981) "Demosthenes on distrust of tyrants," *Greek, Roman and Byzantine Studies* 22: 227–46.
Lewis, D. (2011) "Near Eastern slaves in classical Attica and the slave trade with Persian territories," *Classical Quarterly* 61: 91–113.
Lewis, D. M. (1997) *Selected papers in Greek and Near Eastern history*. Edited by P. J. Rhodes. Cambridge.
Lewis, S. (1996) *News and society in the Greek polis*. London.
Liddel, P. (2007) *Civic obligation and individual liberty in ancient Athens*. Oxford.
  (2014) "The comparative approach in Grote's *History of Greece*," in K. N. Demetriou (ed.), *Brill's companion to George Grote and the classical tradition*. Leiden. 211–54.
Lintott, A. (2013) *Plutarch: Demosthenes and Cicero*. Oxford.
Loomis, W. T. (1990) "Pausanias, Byzantion and the formation of the Delian League: a chronological note," *Historia* 39: 487–92.
  (1998) *Wages, welfare costs, and inflation in classical Athens*. Ann Arbor.
Low, P. (2007) *Interstate relations in classical Greece*. Cambridge.
  (2011) "Athenian foreign policy and the quest for stability," in G. Herman (ed.), *Stability and crisis in the Athenian democracy*. Stuttgart. 67–86.
Maas, P. (1928) "Zitate aus Demosthenes' Epitaphios bei Lykurgos," *Hermes* 63: 258–60.
MacDowell, D. M. (1962) *Andokides. On the Mysteries*. Oxford.
  (1978) *The law in classical Athens*. London.
  (1983) "Athenian laws about bribery," *Revue internationale des Droits de l'Antiquité* 30: 57–78.
  (1990) *Demosthenes. Against Meidias (Oration 21)*. Oxford.
  (2000) *Demosthenes. On the False Embassy (Oration 19)*. Oxford.
  (2005) "The Athenian procedure of *dokimasia* of orators," in R. W. Wallace and M. Gagarin (eds.), *Symposion 2001*. Vienna. 79–87.
  (2008) *Demosthenes. Speeches 27–38*. Austin.
  (2009) *Demosthenes the orator*. Oxford.
Mader, G. (2003) "Quantum mutati ab illis…: satire and displaced identity in Demosthenes' first Philippic," *Philologus* 147: 56–69.
  (2006) "Fighting Philip with decrees: Demosthenes and the syndrome of symbolic action," *American Journal of Philology* 127: 367–86.
  (2007) "Foresight, hindsight, and the rhetoric of self-fashioning in

Demosthenes' Philippic cycle," *Rhetorica* 25: 339–60.
Marincola, J. (2007) "Speeches in classical historiography," in J. Marincola (ed.), *A companion to Greek and Roman historiography*. Malden. 118–32.
Martin, G. (2009) *Divine talk: religious argumentation in Demosthenes*. Oxford.
Mastronarde, D. J. (2002) *Euripides. Medea*. Cambridge.
McCabe, D. F. (1981) *The prose-rhythm of Demosthenes*. New York.
McQueen, E. I. (1986) *Demosthenes. Olynthiacs*. London.
Meiggs, R. (1972) *The Athenian empire*. Oxford.
Meiggs, R. and D. M. Lewis (1988) *A selection of Greek historical inscriptions to the end of the fifth century BC*. Revised ed. Oxford.
Mikalson, J. D. (1983) *Athenian popular religion*. Chapel Hill.
Millett, P. (1989) "Patronage and its avoidance in classical Athens," in A. Wallace-Hadrill (ed.), *Patronage in ancient society*. London. 15–47.
Montana, F. (2015) "Hellenistic scholarship," in F. Montanari, S. Matthaios, and A. Rengakos (eds.), *Brill's companion to ancient Greek scholarship*. Leiden. 60–183.
Moreno, A. (2007) *Feeding the democracy. The Athenian grain supply in the fifth and fourth centuries BC*. Oxford.
Morrison, J. S. and J. F. Coates (1986) *The Athenian trireme. The history and reconstruction of an ancient Greek warship*. Cambridge.
Morrison, J. S. and R. T. Williams (1968) *Greek oared ships 900–322 BC*. Cambridge.
Munn, M. H. (1993) *The defense of Attica*. Berkeley and Los Angeles.
Muñoz Flórez, J. (2012) "Los papiros de Demóstenes," in F. G. Hernández Muñoz (ed.), *La tradición y la transmisión de los oradores y rétores griegos*. Berlin. 195–204.
Naiden, F. S. (2013) *Smoke signals for the gods. Ancient Greek sacrifice from the archaic through Roman periods*. Oxford.
Nesselrath, H.-G. (1990) *Die attische Mittlere Komödie: Ihre Stellung in der antiken Literaturkritik und Literaturgeschichte*. Berlin and New York.
Nevett, L. C. (1999) *House and society in the ancient Greek world*. Cambridge.
Nielsen, T. H. (2013) "Panhellenic athletics at Olympia," in P. Christesen and D. G. Kyle (eds.), *A companion to sport and spectacle in Greek and Roman antiquity*. Malden. 133–45.
Nippel, W. (2015) *Ancient and modern democracy: two concepts of liberty?* Translated by K. Tribe. Cambridge.
Nouhaud, M. (1982) *L'Utilisation de l'histoire par les orateurs attiques*. Paris.
Obbink, D. (1996) *Philodemus. On Piety*. Oxford.
Ober, J. (1985) *Fortress Attica. Defense of the Athenian land frontier 404–322 BC*. Leiden.
  (1989) *Mass and elite in democratic Athens*. Princeton.
Olson, S. D. (1998) *Aristophanes. Peace*. Oxford.

(2002) *Aristophanes. Acharnians*. Oxford.
(2007) *Broken laughter: select fragments of Greek comedy*. Oxford.
Osborne, M. J. and S. G. Byrne (1996) *The foreign residents of Athens. An annex to the* Lexicon of Greek personal names: Attica. Leuven.
Parke, H. W. (1977) *Festivals of the Athenians*. London.
Parker, R. (1983) *Miasma. Pollution and purification in early Greek religion*. Oxford.
(1996) *Athenian religion. A history*. Oxford.
(2005) *Polytheism and society at Athens*. Oxford.
Pasquali, G. (1962) *Storia della tradizione e critica del testo*. 2nd ed. Florence.
Pearson, L. (1981) *The art of Demosthenes*. Atlanta.
Pébarthe, C. (2006) *Cité, démocratie et écriture. Histoire de l'alphabétisation d'Athènes à l'époque classique*. Paris.
Pernot, L. (2006) *L'Ombre du tigre. Recherches sur la réception de Démosthène*. Naples.
Pickard-Cambridge, A. W. (1914) *Demosthenes and the last days of Greek freedom, 384–322 BC*. London.
(1968) *The dramatic festivals of Athens*. 2nd ed. Revised by J. Gould and D. M. Lewis. Oxford.
Pownall, F. (2003) *Lessons from the past: the moral use of history in fourth-century prose*. Ann Arbor.
Pritchard, D. M. (2013) *Sport, democracy and war in classical Athens*. Cambridge.
(2015) *Public spending and democracy in classical Athens*. Austin.
Pritchett, W. K. (1956) "The Attic Stelai. Part II," *Hesperia* 25: 178–328.
(1971) *The Greek state at war*. Vol. 1. Berkeley and Los Angeles.
(1974) *The Greek state at war*. Vol. 2. Berkeley and Los Angeles.
(1991) *The Greek state at war*. Vol. 5. Berkeley and Los Angeles.
Prudhommeau, G. (1965) *La Danse grecque antique*. Paris.
Psoma, S. (2001) *Olynthe et les Chalcidiens de Thrace: études de numismatique et d'histoire*. Stuttgart.
Raaflaub, K. (2004) *The discovery of freedom in ancient Greece*. Chicago.
Race, W. H. (1981) "The word καιρός in Greek drama," *Transactions of the American Philological Association* 111: 197–213.
(1982) *The classical priamel from Homer to Boethius*. Leiden.
(1987) "Pindaric encomium and Isokrates' *Evagoras*," *Transactions of the American Philological Association* 117: 131–55.
Ramsey, J. T. (2003) *Cicero: Philippics I–II*. Cambridge.
Rauchenstein, R. (1908) *Ausgewählte Reden des Isokrates: Panegyrikos und Areopagitikos*. Revised by K. Münscher. Berlin.
Renehan, R. (1969) *Greek textual criticism: a reader*. Cambridge, MA.
Reynolds, L. D. and N. G. Wilson (2013) *Scribes and scholars. A guide to the transmission of Greek and Latin literature*. 4th ed. Oxford.

Rhodes, P. J. (1972) *The Athenian boule*. Oxford.
(1993) *A commentary on the Aristotelian Athenaion Politeia*. Revised ed. Oxford.
Rizzo, R. and O. Vox (1978) "Διαβολή," *Quaderni di storia* 8: 307–21.
Roberts, J. T. (1994) *Athens on trial. The antidemocratic tradition in western thought*. Princeton.
Robertson, D. S. (1944) "Four notes on Aeschylus," *Classical Review* 58: 34–5.
Roisman, J., I. Worthington, and R. Waterfield (2015) *Lives of the Attic orators. Texts from pseudo-Plutarch, Photius, and the Suda*. Oxford.
de Romilly, J. (1958) "Eunoia in Isocrates or the political importance of creating good will," *Journal of Hellenic Studies* 78: 92–101.
Rosivach, V. J. (1988) "The tyrant in Athenian democracy," *Quaderni urbinati di cultura classica* 30: 43–57.
(2001) "Manpower and the Athenian navy in 362 BC," in R. W. Love, L. Bogle, and B. Vandemark (eds.), *New interpretations of naval history*. Annapolis. 12–26.
Rubincam, C. R. (1979) "Qualification of numerals in Thucydides," *American Journal of Ancient History* 4: 77–95.
Rubinstein, L. (2004) "Stirring up dicastic anger," in D. L. Cairns and R. A. Knox (eds.), *Law, rhetoric, and comedy in classical Athens. Essays in honour of Douglas M. MacDowell*. London. 187–203.
Russell, D. A. (1983) *Greek declamation*. Oxford.
Russell, F. S. (1999) *Information gathering in classical Greece*. Ann Arbor.
Rusten, J. S. (1986) "Structure, style, and sense in interpreting Thucydides: the soldier's choice (Thuc. 2.42.4)," *Harvard Studies in Classical Philology* 90: 49–76.
(1989) *Thucydides. The Peloponnesian War: book II*. Cambridge.
Rutherford, R. B. (1992) *Homer. Odyssey books XIX and XX*. Cambridge.
(2012) *Greek tragic style. Form, language and interpretation*. Cambridge.
Ryder, T. T. B. (2000) "Demosthenes and Philip II," in I. Worthington (ed.), *Demosthenes: statesman and orator*. London. 45–89.
de Ste. Croix, G. E. M. (1963) "The alleged secret pact between Athens and Philip II concerning Amphipolis and Pydna," *Classical Quarterly* 13: 110–19.
Salmon, J. B. (1984) *Wealthy Corinth. A history of the city to 338 BC*. Oxford.
Sánchez, P. (2001) *L'Amphictionie des Pyles et de Delphes. Recherches sur son rôle historique, des origines au IIe siècle de notre ère*. Stuttgart.
Sanders, E. (2016) "Generating goodwill and friendliness in Attic forensic oratory," in R. R. Caston and R. A. Kaster (eds.), *Hope, joy, and affection in the classical world*. New York and Oxford. 163–81.
Sandys, J. E. (1897) *The first Philippic and the Olynthiacs of Demosthenes*. London.

(1913) *On the peace, second Philippic, on the Chersonesus, and third Philippic*. London.
Sansone, D. (1984) "On hendiadys in Greek," *Glotta* 62: 16–25.
Schaefer, A. (1885–7) *Demosthenes und seine Zeit*. 2nd ed. 3 vols. Leipzig.
Schein, S. (2013) *Sophocles. Philoctetes*. Cambridge.
Schindel, U. (1963) *Demosthenes im 18. Jahrhundert. Zehn Kapitel zum Nachleben des Demothenes in Deutschland, Frankreich, England*. Munich.
Seager, R. (2001) "Xenophon and Athenian democratic ideology," *Classical Quarterly* 51: 385–97.
Sealey, R. (1955) "Dionysius of Halicarnassus and some Demosthenic dates," *Revue des études grecques* 68: 77–120.
Sekunda, N. V. (2010) "The Macedonian army," in J. Roisman and I. Worthington (eds.), *A companion to ancient Macedonia*. Malden. 446–71.
Shear, J. L. (2001) *Polis and Panathenaea: the history and development of Athena's festival*. Ph.D. thesis. University of Pennsylvania. UMI no. 3015371.
Silk, M. S. (1974) *Interaction in poetic imagery, with special reference to early Greek poetry*. Cambridge.
Sing, R. (2017) "The authenticity of Demosthenes 13, again," *Classical Quarterly* 67: 106–17.
Sommerstein, A. H. (2007) "Cloudy swearing: when (if ever) is an oath not an oath?," in A. H. Sommerstein and J. Fletcher (eds.), *Horkos. The oath in Greek society*. Bristol. 125–37.
Sosin, J. (2015) "'Those who live apart' were mercenaries," *Historia* 64: 413–18.
Spatharas, D. (2006) "Persuasive ΓΕΛΩΣ: public speaking and the use of laughter," *Mnemosyne* 59: 374–87.
Steinbock, B. (2013) *Social memory in Athenian public discourse: uses and meanings of the past*. Ann Arbor.
Steiner, D. (2010) *Homer. Odyssey books XVII and XVIII*. Cambridge.
Strömberg, R. (1954) *Greek proverbs*. Göteborg.
Stroud, R. S. (1963) "A fragment of an inscribed bronze stele from Athens," *Hesperia* 32: 138–43.
(1998) *The Athenian grain-tax law of 374/3 BC*. Princeton.
Tacon, J. (2001) "Ecclesiastic 'thorubos': interventions, interruptions, and popular involvement in the Athenian Assembly," *Greece & Rome* 48: 173–92.
Taylor, C. (2001) "Bribery in Athenian politics," *Greece & Rome* 48: 53–66 and 154–72.
Teegarden, D. (2013) *Death to tyrants! Ancient Greek democracy and the struggle against tyranny*. Princeton.
Thomas, R. (1989) *Oral tradition and written record in classical Athens*. Cambridge.

(1994) "Law and the lawgiver in the Athenian democracy," in R. Osborne and S. Hornblower (eds.), *Ritual, finance, politics: Athenian democratic accounts presented to David Lewis*. Oxford. 119–33.
  (2003) "Prose performance texts: epideixis and written publication in the late fifth and early fourth centuries," in H. Yunis (ed.), *Written texts and the rise of literate culture in ancient Greece*. Cambridge. 162–88.
Todd, S. C. (1990) "The use and abuse of the Attic orators," *Greece & Rome* 37: 159–78.
  (2000) "How to execute people in fourth-century Athens," in V. Hunter and J. Edmondson (eds.), *Law and social status in classical Athens*. Oxford. 53–74.
  (2007) *A commentary on Lysias speeches 1–11*. Oxford.
Tompkins, D. P. (1972) "Stylistic characterization in Thucydides: Nicias and Alcibiades," *Yale Classical Studies* 22: 181–214.
  (1993) "Archidamus and the question of characterization in Thucydides," in R. M. Rosen and J. Farrell (eds.), *Nomodeiktes. Greek studies in honor of Martin Ostwald*. Ann Arbor. 99–111.
  (2013) "The language of Pericles," in A. Tsakmakis and M. Tamiolaki (eds.), *Thucydides between history and literature*. Berlin. 447–64.
Torrance, I. C. (2014) "Swearing oaths in the authorial person," in A. H. Sommerstein and I. C. Torrance (eds.), *Oaths and swearing in ancient Greece*. Berlin and Boston. 348–71.
Trédé-Boulmer, M. (2015) *Kairos: L'À-propos et l'occasion. Le mot et la notion, d'Homère à la fin du IVe siècle avant J.-C.* Revised ed. Paris.
Trevett, J. (1996) "Aristotle's knowledge of Athenian oratory," *Classical Quarterly* 46: 371–9.
  (1999) "Demosthenes and Thebes," *Historia* 48: 184–202.
  (2011) *Demosthenes. Speeches 1–17*. Austin.
Tritle, L. A. (1988) *Phocion the good*. New York and Sydney.
Trundle, M. (2010) "Light troops in classical Athens," in D. M. Pritchard (ed.), *War, democracy and culture in classical Athens*. Cambridge. 139–60.
Tsigarida, B. (2011) "Chalcidice," in R. Lane Fox (ed.), *Brill's companion to ancient Macedon: studies in the archaeology and history of Macedon, 650 BC–300 AD*. Leiden. 137–58.
Tuplin, C. (1998) "Demosthenes' 'Olynthiacs' and the character of the demegoric corpus," *Historia* 47: 276–320.
Usher, S. (1974) *Dionysius of Halicarnassus. Critical essays I*. Cambridge, MA.
  (1993) *Demosthenes. On the crown*. Warminster.
  (1999) *Greek oratory. Tradition and originality*. Oxford.
  (2004) "*Kairos* in fourth-century Greek oratory," in M. Edwards and C. Reid (eds.), *Oratory in action*. Manchester. 52–61.
  (2007) "Symbouleutic oratory," in I. Worthington (ed.), *A companion to*

*Greek rhetoric*. Malden. 220–35.

(2008) "Possibility: a neglected topos," *Bulletin of the Institute of Classical Studies* 50: 1–18.

Veligianni-Terzi, C. (1997) *Wertbegriffe in den attischen Ehrendekreten der Klassischen Zeit*. Stuttgart.

Vickers, B. (1988) *In defence of rhetoric*. Oxford.

Wallace, R. W. (1989) "The Athenian proeispherontes," *Hesperia* 58: 473–90.

(2004) "The power to speak – and not to listen – in ancient Athens," in I. Sluiter and R. Rosen (eds.), *Free speech in classical antiquity*. Leiden. 221–32.

Walters, K. R. (1981) "'We fought alone at Marathon': historical falsification in the Attic funeral oration," *Rheinisches Museum* 124: 204–11.

Wankel, H. (1976) *Demosthenes, Rede für Ktesiphon über den Kranz*. 2 vols. Heidelberg.

Waterfield, R. (2014) *Demosthenes. Selected speeches*. Oxford.

Watkins, C. (1967) "An Indo-European construction in Greek and Latin," *Harvard Studies in Classical Philology* 71: 115–19.

West, M. L. (1978) *Hesiod. Works & Days. Edited with prolegomena and commentary*. Oxford.

West, W. C. (1973) "The speeches in Thucydides: a description and listing," in P. A. Stadter (ed.), *The speeches in Thucydides*. Chapel Hill. 3–15.

(1977) "Hellenic homonoia and the new decree from Plataea," *Greek, Roman and Byzantine Studies* 18: 307–19.

Westwood, G. (2017a) "The orator and the ghosts: performing the past in fourth-century Athens," in S. Papaioannou, A. Serafim, and B. da Vela (eds.), *The theatre of justice: aspects of performance in Greco-Roman oratory and rhetoric*. Leiden. 57–74.

(2017b) "Plutarch's Aesion. A note on Plutarch *Demosthenes* 11.4," *Mnemosyne* 70: 316–24.

Whitehead, D. (1977) *The ideology of the Athenian metic*. Cambridge.

(1983) "Competitive outlay and community profit: φιλοτιμία in democratic Athens," *Classica et Mediaevalia* 34: 55–74.

(1993) "Cardinal virtues: the language of public approbation in democratic Athens," *Classica et Mediaevalia* 44: 37–75.

(2000) *Hypereides. The forensic speeches*. Oxford.

(2001) *Aineas the Tactician. How to survive under siege*. 2nd ed. Oxford.

Will, W. (2013) *Demosthenes*. Darmstadt.

Wilson, N. G. (1996) *Scholars of Byzantium*. London.

(2016) *Aldus Manutius. The Greek classics*. Cambridge, MA.

(2017) *From Byzantium to Italy. Greek studies in the Italian Renaissance*. 2nd ed. London.

Wilson, P. (2000) *The Athenian institution of the khoregia.* Cambridge.
Wolpert, A. O. (2003) "Addresses to the jury in the Attic orators," *American Journal of Philology* 124: 537–55.
Wooten, C. (1977) "A few observations on form and content in Demosthenes," *Phoenix* 31: 258–61.
— (1979) "Unnoticed medical language in Demosthenes," *Hermes* 107: 157–60.
— (1983) *Cicero's* Philippics *and their Demosthenic model. The rhetoric of crisis.* Chapel Hill.
— (1989) "Dionysius of Halicarnassus and Hermogenes on the style of Demosthenes," *American Journal of Philology* 110: 576–88.
— (1999) "A triple division in Demosthenes," *Classical Philology* 94: 450–4.
Worthington, I. (1992) *A historical commentary on Dinarchus. Rhetoric and conspiracy in later fourth-century Athens.* Ann Arbor.
— (2013) *Demosthenes of Athens and the fall of classical Greece.* New York and Oxford.
Wycherley, R. E. (1957) *Athenian Agora 3: literary and epigraphical testimonia.* Princeton.
Wyse, W. (1904) *The speeches of Isaeus.* Cambridge.
Youni, M. (2001) "The different categories of unpunished killing and the term ΑΤΙΜΟΣ in ancient Greek law," in E. Cantarella and G. Thür (eds.), *Symposion 1997.* Vienna. 117–37.
Yunis, H. (1996) *Taming democracy: models of political rhetoric in classical Athens.* Ithaca and London.
— (1997) "Thrasymachus B1: discord, not diplomacy," *Classical Philology* 92: 58–66.
— (2000) "Politics as literature: Demosthenes and the burden of the Athenian past," *Arion* 8: 97–118.

# INDEXES

## GREEK

ἀβέλτερος 215
ἀγαθός 157
ἄγαν 173
ἀγανακτέω 228
ἀγαπάω 89, 156
ἀγαπητός 155, 264
ἄγειν καὶ φέρειν 187, 247
ἄγω 235, 251
ἀγών 115
ἀγωνίζομαι 200
ἀεί 85, 107, 114, 194
ἀθροίζω 144
αἰσθάνομαι 89
αἰσχύνη 97, 99, 103, 136, 169, 196, 199
αἰτιάομαι 123, 197, 206, 213, 215
ἀκέραιος 99
ἀκμή 195
ἀκούω 131, 227
ἀκρασία 116
ἀκριβῶς 118
ἀλλά 98, 144, 157, 226, 227;
  ἀλλὰ μήν 136; ἀλλὰ μήν ... γε
  95, 196; ἀλλ᾽ οὖν ... γε 229
ἄλλος 213
ἄλλως 116, 146; ἄλλως τε κἄν 82
ἀμέλεια 86, 173
ἀμελέω 236
ἀμύθητος 188
ἀμύνω 233
ἀναγιγνώσκω 22
ἀναγράφω 240
ἀναιρέω 220, 226
ἀναλίσκω 182, 192
ἀνάξιος 163
ἀναρπάζω 243
ἀνατρέπω 260
ἀναχαιτίζω 109

ἀνέχομαι 209
ἄνθρωπος 79, 96, 202, 227
ἀνοητότατος 201
ἄνπερ 170
ἀντεισάγω 237
ἀντίδοσις 191
ἀντιλαμβάνω 78
ἀντίρροπος 86
ἀνυπέρβλητος 115
ἄνωθεν 238
ἄνω καὶ κάτω 114, 195, 235
ἀξίωμα 240, 260
ἀπάγω 254
ἀπαλλάσσω 84, 202
ἀπαρτάω 170
ἀπεῖπον 136
ἀπέχω 212
ἀπιστέω 111, 234
ἀπιστία 236, 245
ἄπιστος 82, 95, 222
ἀπο- 93, 170
ἀπό 187
ἀπογιγνώσκω 196
ἀποδιδράσκω 264
ἀπολείπω 194, 231
ἀπόλλυμι 139, 192, 230
ἀπομίσθων 199
ἀποστέλλω 216
ἀποστροφή 168
ἀποσφάζω 255
ἀποτρίβω 87
ἀποτυμπανισμός 254
ἅπτω 218
ἄρα 151
ἆρά γε 152
ἀρρώστημα 119
ἀρτάω 237
ἀρχαῖος 90

ἀρχή 110, 131, 155
ἄρχω 222
ἀσέλγεια 168
ἀσελγής 117
ἀσθενής 112
ἀσκέω 154
ἄσμενος 108
ἀστρατεία 128
ἀσφαλής 131, 139
ἀτακτέω 138
ἀτάκτως 159
ἀτιμία 236-8, 240-2, 253
αὐξάνω 221
αὐτοκράτωρ 81
αὐτόματος 85
αὐτόνομος 96, 165
ἀφίστημι 220
ἀφορμή 96, 120, 183, 260

βαδίζω 212, 245
βάλλω 219
βάρβαρος 142, 230, 237, 242
βασιλεύς 85
βέλτιστος 262
βλάσφημος 204
βλέπω 233
βραδυτής 168
βωμολοχία 118

γάρ 80, 86, 87, 169, 217, 240, 259
γε 79, 99, 125, 142, 158, 171, 179, 201, 204, 229, 258, 261
γελάω 118
γέλοιος 118
γέλως 179, 237
γενναῖος 145
γίγνομαι 127, 232
γνήσιος 229
γνώμη 166, 170, 184
γράμμα 238
γραφὴ παρανόμων 1, 138, 139, 157

γράφω 93, 147, 186, 210, 261
γυμνασίαρχοι 190

δαίμων 102, 248
δέ 80, 91, 115, 217
δεῖ 93, 203; τὰ δέοντα 78, 83, 94, 103, 125, 128, 131, 132, 137, 141, 144, 162, 163, 208, 228, 239
δείκνυμι 118
δεῖνα 129
δεινός 118, 137, 189, 230
δέος 198
δεσπότης 81, 240
δεῦρο 194
δέω 220
δή 79, 92, 114, 121, 154, 265; δὴ καί 182
δῆμος 155
δήποτε 188
δήπου 137, 143, 216, 238, 261
διά 205
διαβάλλω 206, 250
διαλείπω 246
διαλύω 109
διάνοια 234, 240
διαφέρω 211
διαφθείρω 242
δίδωμι 241, 249
δίκαιος 12, 116, 153
δίκη 206
διοικέω 229
διορίζομαι 210
διορύσσω 228
δοκέω 174
δύναμις 141
δυναστεία 224
δυνατός 26
δωροδοκέω 235, 237, 249

ἐγκαλέω 224
ἔγκλημα 83
ἐγχωρέω 195

# INDEXES

ἐγώ 91, 93, 106, 117, 131, 142, 202, 244, 265; ἔγωγε 86, 120, 144, 210
ἔθος 251
εἰ ἄρα 221
εἴδω 204, 252
εἰέν 177
εἰκότως 85
εἰμί 125, 250
εἴπερ 78, 131, 144
εἰρωνεία 166
εἰς 182
εἷς 85
εἰσαγγελία 199
εἰσφορά 1, 82, 126, 127, 133
εἶτα 95, 196, 215
ἐκ- 83, 120
ἐκ 154, 162, 205, 211, 221, 245; ἐκ διαδοχῆς 176
ἕκαστος 166, 201, 228
ἐκβάλλω 217, 250
ἐκεῖνος 121
ἐκκλησία 9, 208
ἐκνευρίζω 155
ἐκπιπράσκω 237
ἐκπλήσσω 105
ἐκτραχηλίζω 246
ἐκφέρω 95
ἔλεγχος 105, 172
ἐλεύθερος 96, 165, 169, 235, 253
ἐμβάλλω 196
ἐμποδών 136, 174
ἐν 137, 150, 202
ἔνδειξις 253
ἔνειμι 257
ἕνεκα 141
ἐνθένδε 103, 106
ἐνθυμέω 196
ἐντελής 186
ἐντεῦθεν 210
ἐξαίρετος 246
ἐξαπατάω 215
ἐξαρτάω 245

ἔξειμι 82, 246
ἐξελέγχω 111
ἐξεπίτηδες 257
ἐξετάζω 205
ἐξετασταί 125
ἔξω 187
ἐπαίρω 201
ἐπανορθόω 208
ἐπεί 237
ἔπειμι 95, 222
ἐπέρχομαι 78, 248
ἐπέχω 161, 263
ἐπί 90, 150, 166, 168, 192, 203, 207, 210, 232, 254
ἐπιμεληταί 189
ἐπισκοπέω 214
ἐπιστέλλω 175
ἐπισφαλής 113
ἐπιτήδειος 254
ἐπιχειροτονέω 184
ἐπόπτης 179
ἔπος 244
ἐργάζομαι 251
ἔργον 114, 193, 249
ἐρημία 153
ἐρίζω 213
ἔρις 216
ἔρχομαι 233
ἐρῶ 141, 162
ἑταῖροι 245
εὐαγής 241, 242
εὐεργεσία 102
εὐήθεια 90, 106, 246
εὐήθης 243, 263
εὔθυναι 100, 123, 199
εὔνοια 86, 100, 102, 109
εὐτρεπής 95, 174
εὐτρεπίζω 88, 173
ἐφίστημι 125
ἐφορμέω 135
ἐχθρός 142, 171
ἔχω 170, 194, 205, 208

ἡγεμόνες 127
ἤδη 124
ἡδύς 256, 260
ἥκω 83

θαυμάζω 137, 196
θαύματα 117, 118
θαυματοποιός 117
θεαροδόκος 84
θεός 102
θόρυβος 133
θρυλέω 83, 106, 136

ἴδιος 114
ἰδιώτης 189
ἱεροποιός 180
ἰσηγορία 132
ἰσονομία 159
ἴσος 152, 159

καθαρός 241, 242, 256
καθείργνυμι 156
κάθημαι 121
καθίστημι 221, 224
καὶ γάρ τοι 165, 251; καί ... γε 109; καί ... δέ 141; καὶ δή 111, 171; καὶ μήν 108, 229, 259
καιρός 13, 26, 78, 84, 85, 94, 97, 102, 108, 128, 131, 135, 141, 170, 174, 186, 190, 192, 236
καίτοι 148, 217, 231; καίτοι καί 170
κακοῦργος 200, 253
κατα- 167, 198
κατά 228, 234, 236
καταγελάω 198
κατακλείω 114, 186
καταπτήσσω 167
καταρραθυμέω 167
κατασκευάζω 106, 142
καταστρέφομαι 166, 168, 196, 262
κατηγορία 229, 262

κείμενα ἐν μέσωι 165
κελεύω 241
κενὴ ἐλπίς 197
κενός 198
κινδυνεύω 81, 91, 113, 208, 219
κίνδυνος 125, 161
κινέω 246
κοινός 95, 207; τὸ Ἀθηναίων κοινόν 241
κολακεία 258
κόλαξ 116
κομιδῆι 95
κόπτω 114
κορδακισμός 116
κοροπλάσται 180
κρατέω 235
κρίνω 123, 124, 126, 171, 199
κύκλος 165, 168
κύριος 81
κωλύω 87, 95, 98, 171, 201, 232

λαγχάνω 188
λαμβάνω 93, 219, 237
λανθάνω 86
λέγω 99, 238, 241
ληιστεύω 177
ληιστής 116
λῆμμα 125, 157
ληρέω 221
λογίζομαι 196
λογισταί 100
λογογράφος 1
λογοποιέω 201
λόγος 126
λοιδορέω 249
λοιδορία 105, 248
λυμαίνομαι 230
λύω 138
λωποδυτέω 222

μαλακίζομαι 233
μέθη 116
μέλω 242

μέν 115, 122, 217; μέν ... δέ 79, 108, 109, 119, 126, 130, 140, 144, 160, 177, 186, 193, 205, 212, 232; μὲν δή 108; μὲν οὖν 78, 91, 103, 104, 131, 162, 172, 202, 205
μέντοι 98, 201, 221, 263
μένω 109, 143, 164, 186
μέρος 116, 156, 225
μετα- 155
μεταδίδωμι 207
μετέχω 109, 241
μήν 91, 133
μισέω 247
μισθός 145, 182, 183
μισθοφορέω 216
μόνος 78, 150
μοχθηρία 132
μωρία 248, 258

νέμω 158
νή 169, 201, 257, 259, 261
νομοθέται 137, 140
νοσέω 112, 214, 237, 245
νῦν 85, 106, 124, 162, 169, 196, 203, 208, 218

ξένος 114, 174–6, 207, 231

ὁ 259
οἷ 168
οἴομαι 121
οἷον 112
ὄλεθρος 230
ὀλίγος 203
ὅλως 107
ὄμνυμι 217
ὁμόνοια 236
ὅμορος 120
ὀνειροπολέω 201
ὄνομα 211
ὅπου 160
ὀργή 91, 206, 230, 243

ὁρίζω 220
οὐ 83, 227, 244; οὐ μετρίως 224; οὐ μὴν ἀλλά 80, 120, 193; οὐ μὴν οὐδέ 141
οὐδέ 163; οὐδὲ πολλοῦ δεῖ 223
οὐδὲν ἄλλο ἤ 206
οὐκοῦν 158, 242
οὖν 136, 169
οὗτος 83, 123; οὕτως 86, 240
ὀφλισκάνω 98, 196
ὄχλος 189

πάλιν 167
πανοῦργος 79
παρα- 83
παρά 170, 186, 205, 206, 216
παράδειγμα 148, 164, 239
παράδοξος 137, 162, 208
παρακαλέω 261
παρακρούω 105
παρακύπτω 179
παραλείπω 88
παράνοια 248
παραπίπτω 83
παρασκευάζω 166
παρασκευή 189, 246
παρατάσσω 177
πάρειμι 84, 146, 214, 219
παρίστημι 92, 130, 173
πάροδος 231
παροράω 174
παρρησία 132, 157, 206
παρωθέω 116, 231
πᾶς 128, 176
πάσχω 215
πεζέταιροι 114
πέμπω 180
περ 247
περαίνω 111, 182
περι- 168, 200
περί 206
περιαιρέω 251
περιβάλλω 168

περιίστημι 100, 136
περικόπτω 222
περιοράω 228, 263
περιστοιχίζω 169
πέρυσιν 262
πήγνυμι 167
πικρός 98
πλείων 187
πλεονεξία 109, 113, 224, 227
πλοῖον 173
ποιέω 217, 263
ποικίλος 235
πολέμιος 239
πόλις 165
πολιτεία 82, 206
πολιτεύω 104
ποριστής 187
πόρος 92
πότε 154
πρᾶγμα 86, 94, 101, 111, 130, 145, 162, 168, 172, 193, 204, 246, 258
πράσσω 217, 252
προ- 192
προβάλλω 195, 211
πρόγονος 148, 225, 238
προεισφορά 126
προΐημι 85, 102, 204
προλαμβάνω 131, 142
προλέγω 216
πρόνοια 205, 221
πρόξενος 239
προοράω 195
προπίνω 148
προσ- 156, 168
πρός 83, 156, 182, 216
προσηκόντως 163
προσήκω 229
προσίημι 246, 257
πρόσοδος 194
προστάτης 152, 223
πρότερος 131, 178, 253
προτίθημι 144, 161

προτρέπω 103
προὖπτος 140
πρυτάνεις 253
πταῖσμα 109
πώποτε 194

ῥαθυμέω 90
ῥαθυμία 158, 168, 208
ῥᾴδιος 85
ῥῆγμα 119
ῥήγνυμι 255
ῥήτορες 127
ῥοπή 120

σαθρός 197
σθένος 135
σκάφος 259
σκευωρέομαι 219
σκοπέω 102, 228
σοφός 120
στενός 95
στοῖχος 168
στρέμμα 120
συγκροτέω 115
συγχωρέω 261
συζῶ 89
συκοφαντέω 250
συμβαίνω 113, 207
σύμβουλος 77, 91, 131, 195, 207
συμμορία 126
συμπαραθέω 195
συμπλέκω 120, 246
συμπονέω 128
συμπράσσω 256
συμφέρος 12, 77, 195, 203, 208, 265
συμφορά 249
συν- 108, 142, 155, 178, 197, 263
συναιρέω 166
συναίρω 97
συνεστώσης 262
συνεχῶς 114
συνίστημι 228

συνοικέω 89
σύνταξις 93
συστρέφω 253
σφάζω 258
σχεδόν 161
σῶς 99
σώφρων 99, 120, 145, 151, 220

ταλαιπωρέω 112
ταλαίπωρος 214, 251
ταμίας 81, 186
τάξις 159
τάσσω 190
τε ... καί 91, 130
τηρέω 220
τιθασεύω 156
τίθημι 86, 137, 231
τιμή 242
τιμωρέω 130, 131, 167, 242
τιμωρία 235, 242
τις 103, 112, 131, 167, 237
τοι 145, 163, 174
τοιγαροῦν 191
τοίνυν 77, 96, 102, 133, 216, 250
τόπος 102, 184
τότε 142
τοῦτό γε 123
τρόπος 88; τὸν αὐτὸν τρόπον ... ὥσπερ 90, 176, 229
τροφή 145, 175, 178, 182
τυγχάνω 79, 109, 199, 249
τυραννίς 82
τυφόω 221
τύχῃ 86, 102, 120, 143, 170, 197, 236

ὕβρις 96, 97, 99, 164, 168, 192, 198, 202, 204, 231, 253
ὑγιαίνω 221
ὑπάγω 204
ὑπάρχω 85, 135, 145
ὑπερ- 105

ὑπερβαίνω 193
ὑπερβολή 151
ὑπερέχω 260
ὑπερηφανία 168
ὑπηρέται 248
ὑπο- 204, 229
ὑποβάλλω 230
ὑποβολιμαῖος 230
ὑπόθεσις 110
ὑποκατακλίνω 257
ὑπολαμβάνω 229
ὑποστέλλω 91
ὑπόσχεσις 172
ὑφίστημι 243

φενακίζω 105, 107, 193
φημί 82, 91, 110, 124, 144, 168, 172, 198, 210, 219, 263
φθόνος 150, 248
φίλος 258
φιλοτιμία 113, 114
φρονέω 118, 216, 220, 239, 250
φυλάσσω 184, 205, 215
φύσις 165, 247
φωράω 110

χάλαζα 232
χάρις 140, 146, 149, 202, 256
χειμάδιον 185
χειροήθης 156
χειροτονέω 180
χορηγός 189, 190, 253
χράω 89, 107, 186, 234
χωρέω 227

ὦ ἄνδ. Ἀθην. 89, 104, 118, 161
ὦ τᾶν 98
ὠθέω 258
ὠμῶς 226
ὠνέομαι 242
ὡραῖος 244
ὥσπερ 155, 179, 187, 232

## ENGLISH

Achaea 233, 263
Aeschines 7, 22, 29, 30, 84, 133, 145, 153, 155, 204, 211, 213, 216, 217, 239
Aesion 21, 22
Agyrrhios 93, 185
Alcibiades 147, 151, 152, 239
Alcidamas 22
Aldus Manutius 30
Alexander II 3
Alexander III 10, 32, 96, 134, 168, 210, 219, 252, 263
Alexander of Molossus 88
Alexandria 23, 27, 33
Amadocus 165
Ambracia 8, 227, 233, 263
Amphictyonic League 7, 107, 136, 231
Amphipolis 4, 5, 78, 81, 82, 84, 99, 102, 106, 131, 146, 153, 164, 170, 180, 196, 209, 225
Amyntas 3, 149
Anaximenes 11–13, 108, 115
Androtion 188
anger *see* ὀργή (Greek)
Antiphon 24–6, 212
Apollonia 231
Apollonides 250, 258
Argaeus 3, 4
Argos 7, 219, 263
Aristides 34, 146, 147, 151
Aristophanes 151, 155, 156, 162, 250
Aristotle 9, 11–13, 113, 116, 117, 238, 242
Artabazus 126, 179, 180, 201
Artaxerxes 179, 201, 243
Arthmius of Zelea 236, 238–40, 242
Arybbas 88
Assembly speeches 2, 10–14, 18, 20–5, 27–30, 32, 33, 77, 85, 91, 101–3, 132, 141, 143, 147, 151, 162, 163, 184, 200, 203, 208, 217, 224, 227, 234, 243, 259, 263, 264
Athens: Acropolis 9, 149, 150, 180, 188, 238; Agora 9, 26, 178, 180, 239; Dionysia 188–90; Panathenaia 180, 188, 189; Peiraeus 150, 212; Pnyx 9; sacred triremes 188; Stoa Poecile 150
Automedon 252

Beloch, Karl Julius 32
Bessarion 30
Blass, Friedrich 31, 33, 37
Boeotia 122, 163, 173, 200, 214
bribery 204, 211, 235, 237, 238, 240, 242, 245, 246, 249, 250, 256, 258
Byzantium 29, 153, 220, 233

Callias of Athens 117, 118
Callias of Chalcis 8, 252
Callimachus 33
Cardia 218
Carr, Nicholas 30
Cetriporis 165
Chabrias 178
Chaeronea 8, 11, 114, 175, 200, 212, 222, 227, 229, 233, 234, 245, 262
Chalcidice 3–6, 92, 101, 106, 112, 135, 142, 225
Chalcis 8, 219, 252, 264
Chares 123, 125, 126, 153, 156, 179, 180, 198, 217
Charidemus 5, 115, 134
Charles VIII of France 31
Cheke, John 30

INDEXES 293

Chersonese 8, 206, 216–19
Chrysoloras, Manuel 29
Cicero 17, 24, 25, 28, 29
Clemenceau, Georges 32
Cleon 12, 147
Clitarchus 251, 252
compounds 20, 80, 87, 93, 105, 108, 112, 113, 120, 155, 167, 168, 170, 195, 235, 254
Conon 178, 243
Corcyra 113, 178, 225
Corinth 146, 178, 227, 233
Corinthian War 173, 178, 243
Cos 153
Critias 26
Crocus Field 4, 5, 87

Delian League 149, 151, 223, 239
Delphi 7, 136, 213, 231
demagogues 32, 132, 146, 147, 151, 156, 193, 256, 257
Demetrius of Phalerum 22, 26, 27
Demochares 26
Demosthenic speeches: early court (or. 38–40, 43, 48) 1; early deliberative (or. 14–16) 2, 200; public prosecutions (or. 20–1, 23–4) 1, 3, 134, 241; 1 first *Olynthiac* 26, 30, 31, 161, 164; 2 second *Olynthiac* 130, 132, 161; 3 third *Olynthiac* 93, 161, 194, 202, 203; 4 first *Philippic* 2, 5, 11, 13, 31, 36, 157, 205, 208, 243; 5 *On the Peace* 6; 6 second *Philippic* 7, 10, 30, 31; 7 *On Halonnesus* 10, 23, 24, 263; 8 *On the Chersonese* 8, 25, 206, 209, 264; 9 third *Philippic* 8, 10, 20, 25, 34, 36; 10 fourth *Philippic* 10, 25; 17 *On the Treaty with Alexander* 10; 18 *On the Crown* 8, 29, 81, 103, 139, 145, 204, 210, 222, 240, 250, 252; 19 *On the False Embassy* 147, 204, 211, 213, 216; 21 *Against Meidias* 201, 224; 60 *Funeral Oration* 8; 61 *Eroticus* 26; *Prooemia* 23, 25, 26, 77, 129, 132, 133, 135, 161, 162
Didymus 27, 150
Dionysius of Halicarnassus 21, 22, 25, 27, 148, 152, 157, 184
Diopeithes 8, 206, 212, 216, 218, 263
Doriscus 216
Drerup, Engelbert 32

Eleusinian Mysteries 134
Elis 8, 219, 248
Elizabeth I of England 30
Ephialtes 262
Epirus 8, 88
Eretria 219, 232, 247, 251, 252, 254–6, 258, 259, 263
Etesian winds 184
Euboea 8, 78, 84, 122, 165, 173, 188, 192, 193, 214, 232, 251, 254
Euphraeus 252–6, 258
Eupolis 151
Euripides 26, 132, 250
Eurylochus 252
Euthycrates 250, 258

funds, Athenian: military 2, 91, 93, 94, 138–40, 144, 145, 157, 159, 186, 194; Theoric 93, 94, 138, 140, 144, 154, 156, 157
funeral orations 8, 9, 103, 122, 142, 143, 149, 150, 160, 234, 235, 264

Geraistus 188, 192
Gorgias 25
Grote, George 31

Haliartus 173
Halonnesus 114
Harpocration 29, 35, 192
Hegesippus 263
Hellespont 5, 6, 8, 126, 153, 178, 219, 220
Heraion Teichos 5, 88, 132, 195
Hermippus 21, 22
Hermogenes 28, 34, 155
Herodotus 212, 235
hiatus 16, 37, 77, 107, 108, 187
Hierax 84
Hieron Oros 216, 217
Hipparchus 251
Hipponicus 147, 251, 252
historical examples 12, 112, 149, 151, 153, 163, 178, 214, 238, 242, 259
Homer 3, 11, 18, 20, 26, 29, 30, 120, 167, 196, 205, 232
Hyperides 8, 261, 262

Illyria 3, 88, 95, 96, 165, 222, 252
Imbros 5, 185, 187
infinitives: antithetical 15; appositive 15, 108, 139, 222; articular 15, 80, 85, 91, 101, 104, 105, 107, 141, 152, 196, 219, 222, 249; explanatory 118, 120, 135, 204, 224, 225, 253, 256, 259, 263; imperfect 146, 214, 256; indirect command 128; tricolon 93, 124, 126, 144, 207, 214, 220; with ἄν 77, 100, 171
Iphicrates 178
Isocrates 9, 16, 22, 148, 156, 172, 183, 244

Jaeger, Werner 32

Lampsacus 125, 126
Lasthenes 250, 258
Lechaeum 178
Lemnos 5, 181, 185, 187, 188
Leucas 233
Leuctra 153, 164, 218, 223
Libanius 29, 30, 93, 118, 138
liturgies 82, 128, 138, 189–91, 253
ps.-Longinus 28, 169
Lucian 77, 130
Lycurgus 263
Lysias 26, 27

Macedon(ia) 3, 4, 8, 10, 28, 82, 88, 112, 114, 116, 142, 149, 181, 185, 222, 230, 231, 252, 255, 263
Magnesia 107, 108, 110
Mantinea 153, 223
Marathon 5, 111, 122, 151, 235, 264
Megalopolis 2, 3, 200, 263
Megara 8, 146, 218, 219, 264
Menelaus 181
mercenaries *see* ξένος (Greek)
Messene 7, 219
metaphor 18, 19, 91, 109, 110, 112, 124, 127, 132, 135, 139, 148, 155, 160, 165, 167, 168, 192, 196, 197, 214, 220, 228, 234, 235, 237, 243, 246, 253, 256
Methone 4, 164, 225, 231
Miltiades 151, 181, 218
Mytilene 12

Napoleon I of France 31
Naupactus 263
Naxos 223
Nicias 147
Niebuhr, Barthold Georg 31

oaths 20, 96, 109, 156, 169, 201, 216, 218, 240, 250
Olympias 88
Olynthus 5, 6, 29, 78, 80–3, 86, 88, 92, 97, 100–3, 106, 107, 109, 111, 112, 123, 130, 134–6, 142, 146, 149, 212, 222, 225, 226, 231, 247–50, 253, 256, 258, 259
Onomarchus 4, 5, 87, 107
Orchomenus 200
Oreus 134, 214, 219, 232, 247, 252–6, 258, 259

Paeonia 3, 88, 95, 96, 165
Pagasae 4, 87, 95, 108, 110
parallelism 14, 85, 90, 92, 103, 112, 119, 123, 124, 126, 139, 140, 152, 164, 165, 168, 171, 177, 182, 186, 193, 196, 200, 206, 209, 211, 220, 223, 255, 264
parenthesis 18, 36, 79, 80, 99, 115, 173–5, 193, 204, 228, 233, 252, 256, 257
Parmenio 252, 255, 258
participles: imperfect 161, 213, 250, 255; tricolon 83, 97, 111, 121, 186, 259; with ἄν 153, 204; with ὡς 105, 221
Pausanias 240
Pella 213, 216
Peloponnese 2, 3, 7, 219, 224, 227, 242, 261, 263
Peloponnesian War 11, 122, 147, 149, 153, 163, 164, 172, 182, 223, 224, 243, 244, 246
Peparethos 185
Perdiccas 3, 252
Pericles 12, 146, 147, 150, 151, 156
Persia 2, 142, 164, 179, 218, 240, 243, 262

Persian Wars 12, 115, 122, 147, 149, 150, 230, 234–6, 238
personification 18, 25, 78, 86, 130, 131, 155, 170, 236
Phalaecus 6, 213
Pherae 4, 5, 87, 107, 110, 112, 214, 226
Philip II: activeness 79, 84, 89, 90, 92, 113, 114, 121, 122, 165, 166, 185, 187, 196; and Greeks 4–8, 88, 136, 137, 169, 212, 214, 219, 226, 227, 231, 233, 251, 263; as slave-master 146, 222, 248, 253; as tyrant 3, 80, 82, 96, 105, 116, 117, 120, 167, 231; duplicity 82, 107, 109, 111, 204, 218; hybris *see* ὕβρις (Greek); northern campaigns 4–8, 81, 82, 84, 87, 88, 99, 101, 102, 107, 146, 164, 165, 180, 190, 216, 219, 225; peace with Athens 6, 7, 90, 107, 203, 209, 213, 217; resources and power 81, 101, 154, 164, 187, 210, 245, 246; weakness 94, 104, 112, 119, 247
Philistides 214, 252–4, 258
Philochorus 188, 251
Philocrates 6, 7, 90, 107, 180, 203, 209, 211, 213, 216, 247
Phocion 219, 251
Phocis 4–7, 98, 107, 110, 112, 136, 204, 212–14, 220, 226, 231
Pickard-Cambridge, A. W. 32
Plataea 86, 147, 200, 264
Plato 22, 26, 78, 89, 98, 113, 154–6, 160, 176, 201, 208, 247, 252
Plutarch 1, 21, 22, 28–30, 117, 189
Plutarch of Eretria 251

Polybius 184
Polyeuctus 262, 263
Polystratos 178
Porthmus 232, 251
Potidaea 4, 5, 84, 101, 102, 107–9, 112, 131, 164, 222, 225
psilosis 144
Pydna 4, 82, 106, 146, 164
Pythonax 239

Quintilian 22, 28

Reuchlin, Johannes 31
rhetorical devices: alliteration 16, 99, 121, 139, 161, 167, 234–6; anacolouthon 18, 97, 182; anaphora 17, 259; antithesis 15, 17, 19, 85, 108, 116, 118, 137, 140, 145, 150, 164, 211, 224, 230; aposiopesis 18, 152, 248; apostrophe 18, 25, 89, 161, 261; asyndeton 15, 17, 84, 111, 123–5, 129, 134–6, 143, 147, 155, 156, 158, 161, 171, 183, 187, 190, 191, 197, 207, 233, 246, 247, 249, 258, 259, 263; chiasmus 16, 107, 112, 122, 123, 130, 162, 176, 179, 202, 210–12, 215, 250, 254; epanadiplosis 17, 92; epidiorthosis 18, 93, 102, 108, 141, 223, 225, 244; figura etymologica 180; hendiadys 118, 146, 230, 237, 245, 254, 255; homoioarchon 16, 77, 111, 165, 264; homoioteleuton 16, 77, 97, 111, 152, 165, 264; hyperbaton 16, 17, 25, 84, 88, 102, 150, 210, 258; hypophora 18, 98, 142; hypostasis 17, 130, 192, 199, 248; isocolon 16, 17, 126, 165, 186, 209; juxtaposition 16, 21, 37, 78, 91, 106, 109, 123, 139, 143, 154, 165, 169, 176, 187, 192, 197, 202, 212, 217, 263; litotes 17, 96, 99, 112, 136, 191, 214; oxymoron 18, 106, 211, 249; paradox 18, 80, 162, 208; paraleipsis 18, 88, 103, 152, 175, 221, 225, 247, 253, 257; polyptoton 92; polysyndeton 15, 165, 167, 173, 191; priamel 101; prolepsis 16, 94, 142, 171, 214, 246, 253, 255; questions 15, 25, 88, 98, 103, 123, 136, 141, 142, 147, 152, 154, 161, 163, 169, 175, 177, 187, 190, 196, 197, 199, 215–17, 222, 224, 231, 233–5, 256; ring composition 17, 92, 100, 152, 154, 174, 176, 181, 196, 214, 223, 227, 242, 256; syllepsis 170, 197; synchysis 16, 108, 131, 141, 160, 203, 244; synecdoche 260; tricolon 14, 83, 90, 93, 100, 104, 111, 136, 182, 209, 236
Rhodes 2, 153, 262
rhythm 14, 16, 17, 27, 31, 35, 37, 103, 111, 120, 190, 221

Sacred War (third) 4–7, 98, 107, 136, 140, 153, 169, 213, 214, 224, 226, 231, 233
Salamis 122, 147, 235
Sallust 129, 130, 232, 233
Schaefer, Arnold 31
Sciathos 185
Scyros 185
Serrium 216, 217
shame *see* αἰσχύνη (Greek)
Sigeum 125, 126
simile 18, 19, 86, 90, 110, 119, 120, 158, 194, 228, 229, 232, 237

Social War 4, 5, 106, 153, 166, 178, 179, 194
Solon 151, 241
Sparta 2, 4, 7, 10, 122, 153, 163, 164, 173, 178, 179, 194, 200, 213, 219, 223–5, 227, 229, 231, 240, 243, 244, 246
stichometry 23, 35
Stratocles 84
synonymous pairs 20, 87, 89, 92, 94, 106, 110, 111, 123, 131, 164, 171, 177, 196, 197, 208, 215, 219, 228, 230, 246, 253, 257

Tacitus 28
taxes *see* εἰσφορά (Greek)
Thasos 185
Thebes 6–8, 83, 84, 98, 122, 136, 137, 140, 153, 173, 193, 200, 213, 214, 223–6, 233, 235

Themistius 29
Themistocles 147, 151, 240
Theophrastus 116
Theopompus 106, 111, 116, 226
Thermopylae 5, 7, 88, 98, 133, 173, 195, 212, 214, 231
Thespiae 200
Thessaly 3–7, 88, 94, 95, 107, 109–12, 135, 214, 226, 233
Thrace 3, 5–8, 88, 165, 178, 204, 213, 216–19, 225, 231
Thrasymachus 26
Thucydides 11–13, 24, 25, 27, 113, 134, 146, 147, 149, 177, 183, 224, 240
Timotheus 84, 112, 183
Treves, Piero 32

Wilson, Thomas 30

Xenophon 11, 13, 118, 178